Books by Robert Jay Lifton

THE BROKEN CONNECTION

HOME FROM THE WAR

EXPLORATIONS IN PSYCHOHISTORY *(editor, with Eric Olson)*

LIVING AND DYING *(with Eric Olson)*

HISTORY AND HUMAN SURVIVAL

BOUNDARIES: PSYCHOLOGICAL MAN IN REVOLUTION

DEATH IN LIFE: SURVIVORS OF HIROSHIMA

REVOLUTIONARY IMMORTALITY: MAO TSE-TUNG AND THE
     CHINESE CULTURAL REVOLUTION

THOUGHT REFORM AND THE PSYCHOLOGY OF TOTALISM

BIRDS

CRIMES OF WAR *(editor, with Richard Falk and Gabriel Kolko)*

AMERICA AND THE ASIAN REVOLUTIONS *(editor)*

THE WOMAN IN AMERICA *(editor)*

THE LIFE OF THE SELF: TOWARD A NEW PSYCHOLOGY

SIX LIVES/SIX DEATHS: PORTRAITS FROM MODERN JAPAN
(with Shuichi Kato and Michael Reich)

PSYCHOBIRDS

THE BROKEN CONNECTION

On Death and the Continuity of Life

Robert Jay Lifton

A Touchstone Book
PUBLISHED BY SIMON AND SCHUSTER
NEW YORK

Copyright © 1979 by Robert Jay Lifton

First Touchstone Edition, 1980

Published by Simon and Schuster
A Division of Gulf & Western Corporation
Simon & Schuster Building
Rockefeller Center
1230 Avenue of the Americas
New York, New York 10020
TOUCHSTONE and colophon are trademarks of Simon & Schuster

Manufactured in the United States of America

1 2 3 4 5 6 7 8 9 10
1 2 3 4 5 6 7 8 9 10 Pbk.

Library of Congress Cataloging in Publication Data

Lifton, Robert Jay, date.
  The broken connection.

  (A Touchstone book)
  Includes bibliographical references and index.
  1. Death—Psychological aspects.   I. Title.
[BF789.D4L52   1980]   155.9'37   80-16496
ISBN 0-671-22561-8
ISBN 0-671-41386-4 Pbk.

The author is grateful to the following authors and publishers for permission to quote
from their works:

Sylvia Anthony, *The Discovery of Death in Childhood and After*. N.Y.: Basic Books,
1972. Copyright © 1971 by Sylvia Anthony.

Ernst Becker, *The Denial of Death*, N.Y.: The Free Press, 1973. Copyright © 1973 by
Maria Becker.

John Bowlby, *Attachment and Loss*, N.Y.: Basic Books, 1969. Vol. 1, Copyright © 1969
by Tavistock Institute of Human Relations.

Norman Oliver Brown, *Love's Body*, N.Y.: Random House, 1976. Copyright © 1966 by
Norman O. Brown.

Joseph Campbell, *The Masks of God*, N.Y.: The Viking Press, 1959–68. Copyright © 1959 by Joseph Campbell.

Kurt Robert Eissler, *The Psychiatrist and the Dying Patient*, N.Y.: International Universities Press, 1955. Copyright © 1955 by International Universities Press., Inc.

Leslie H. Farber, *The Ways of the Will: Essays Toward a Psychological and Psychopathology of Will*, N.Y.: Basic Books, 1966. Copyright © 1966 by Leslie H. Farber.

Sigmund Freud, "Thoughts for the Times on War and Death," Standard Ed. vol. XIV, ed. James Strachey. *The Complete Psychological Works of Sigmund Freud*. London: The Hogarth Press, 1953.

———, "Civilization and Its Discontents," Standard Ed. vol. XXI, ed. by James Strachey. *The Complete Psychological Works of Sigmund Freud*. London: The Hogarth Press, 1953.

———, "Instinct and Its Vicissitudes," Standard Ed., vol. XIV, ed. by James Strachey. *The Complete Psychological Works of Sigmund Freud*. London: The Hogarth Press, 1953.

———, "The Unconscious," Standard Ed., vol. XIV, ed. by James Strachey. *The Complete Psychological Works of Sigmund Freud*. London: The Hogarth Press, 1953.

———, "Inhibitions, Symptoms and Anxiety," Standard Ed., vol. XX, ed. by James Strachey. *The Complete Psychological Works of Sigmund Freud*. London: The Hogarth Press, 1953.

———, "The Ego and the Id," Standard Ed., vol. XIX, ed. by James Strachey. *The Complete Psychological Works of Sigmund Freud*. London: The Hogarth Press, 1953.

———, "Beyond the Pleasure Principle," Standard Ed., vol. XVIII, ed. by James Strachey. *The Complete Psychological Works of Sigmund Freud*. London: The Hogarth Press, 1953.

———, "Character and Anal Eroticism," Standard Ed., vol. IX, ed. by James Strachey. *The Complete Psychological Works of Sigmund Freud*. London: The Hogarth Press, 1953.

———, "Mourning and Melancholia," Standard Ed., vol. XIV, ed. by James Strachey. *The Complete Psychological Works of Sigmund Freud*. London: The Hogarth Press, 1953.

———, "On the Psychical Mechanism of Hysterical Phenomena: Preliminary Communication," Standard Ed., vol. II, ed. by James Strachey. *The Complete Psychological Works of Sigmund Freud*. London: The Hogarth Press, 1953.

———, "Fragment of an Analysis of a Case of Hysteria," Standard Ed., vol. VII, ed. by James Strachey. *The Complete Psychological Works of Sigmund Freud*. London: The Hogarth Press, 1953.

———, "Moses and Monotheism," Standard Ed., vol. XXIII, ed. by James Strachey. *The Complete Psychological Works of Sigmund Freud*. London: The Hogarth Press, 1953.

———, "Criminals from a Sense of Guilt," Standard Ed., vol. XIV, ed. by James Strachey. *The Complete Psychological Works of Sigmund Freud*. London: The Hogarth Press, 1953.

Helen Louise Gardner (ed.), *The New Oxford Book of English Verse*, 1250–1950. New York & Oxford: Oxford University Press, 1972. Copyright © 1972 by Oxford University Press. Poem on pages 31–32 is "The Ecstasy" by John Donne.

Leslie R. Groves, *Now It Can Be Told; The Story of the Manhattan Project*, N.Y.: Harper & Bros., 1962; Copyright © 1962 by Leslie R. Groves.

Carl Gustav Jung, *Memories, Dreams, Reflections*, recorded and ed. by Aniela Jaffe, trans. by Richard and Clara Winston. N.Y.: Pantheon, 1963. Copyright © 1961, 1962, 1963 by Random House.

Herman Kahn, *On Thermonuclear War*. Princeton, N.J.: Princeton University Press, 1960. Copyright © 1960 by Princeton University Press.

Suzanne K. Langer, *Philosophy in a New Key*. Cambridge, Mass.: Harvard University Press, 1960. Copyright © 1942, 1951, 1957 by President and Fellows of Harvard College.

William Leonard Laurence, *Men and Atoms*, N.Y.: Simon & Schuster, 1959. Copyright © 1946, 1959 by William L. Laurence.

Konrad Z. Lorenz, *On Aggression*, trans. by Marjorie Kerr Wilson, N.Y.: Harcourt, Brace & World, 1966. Copyright © 1966, by Konrad Lorenz.

Norman Mailer, *Advertisements for Myself*, N.Y.: Signet Books, 1960. Copyright © 1959 by Norman Mailer.

Rollo May, *et. al.* (eds.), *Existence: A New Dimension in Psychiatry*, N.Y.: Basic Books, 1958. Copyright © 1958 by Basic Books.

Elting Elmore Morison, *Turmoil and Tradition: A Study of the Life and Times of Henry L. Stimson*, Boston: Houghton Mifflin, 1960. Copyright © 1960 by Elting E. Morison.

Martin J. Sherwin, *A World Destroyed: The Atomic Bomb and the Grand Alliance*. 1st ed. N.Y.: Knopf, 1975. Copyright © 1973, 1975 by Martin J. Sherwin.

Edward Albert Shils, *The Torment of Secrecy: The Background and Consequences of American Security Policies*, Glencoe, Ill: The Free Press, 1956. Copyright © 1956 by The Free Press, a corporation.

Baldwin Spencer, and F.J. Gillen, *The Nature Tribes of Central Australia*, London: MacMillan & Co., 1899, 1938. Copyright 1st ed. 1899, reprinted in 1938.

Edward Teller and Allen Brown, *The Legacy of Hiroshima*, Garden City, N.Y.: Doubleday, 1962. Copyright © 1962 by Edward Teller and Allen Brown.

U.S. Atomic Energy Commission. *In the Matter of J. Robert Oppenheimer: Transcript of Hearings Before Personal Security Board and Texts of Principle Documents and Letters*. Forward by Philip M. Stern, Cambridge, Mass., MIT Press, 1971.

Acknowledgments

I associate this book with many years of conversations with friends—with Erik Erikson, David Riesman, and Kenneth Keniston—from its very beginnings. In summer meetings on psychohistory, at Wellfleet, Massachusetts, many of its ideas have been shared with Norman Birnbaum, Margaret Brenman-Gibson, Peter Brooks, Robert Holt, Richard Sennett, Kai Erikson, Charles Fisher, and Gerald Holton; and, at a small conversation group at Yale, with Colin Williams, Hillel Levine, Arnold Wolf, Louis Dupre, John Dunne, and Henri Nouwen. In recent years conversations with Eric Olson have been especially important for clarifying and extending ideas of all kinds. And talks with Kurt Eissler have, in other ways, done the same. In the Department of Psychiatry at Yale, Fritz Redlich, Theodore Lidz, Morton Reiser, Stephen Fleck, Marshall Edelson, and Myrna Weissman (who made available to me the facilities of the Depression Research Unit), have done much to further the work, as have many younger psychiatrists who participated in my seminars and taught me a great deal.

Alice Mayhew, friend and editor of long standing, has made a particularly great contribution to this book. Susannah Rubenstein and Esther Cohen provided important editorial suggestions. Lily B. Finn, my assistant at Yale since 1962, typed and coordinated many drafts, and helped in more ways than I can name. Betty Jean Lifton lived through all of it with me, articulately and lovingly; and our children, Kenneth and Karen, made their inimitable contributions as well.

I am indebted to the Harry Frank Guggenheim Foundation for enabling me to take a year's leave from Yale to complete the book, and to Lionel Tiger and Robin Fox, research directors of that foundation, for valuable discussions of its ideas. For additional support at various times I am grateful to the Rockefeller Foundation, and particularly to Michael Novak, Joel Colton, and the late John Knowles; to the Hazen Foundation, especially to Paul Braisted and William Bradley; and to the Foundation's Fund for Research in Psychiatry.

Contents

But I suppose even God was born
too late to trust the old religion . . .

—ROBERT LOWELL

Last night I dreamt of a jauntier principle of order;
Today I eat my usual diet of shadows.

—THEODORE ROETHKE

For B. J.—continuing the journey

The Lost Theme

WE LIVE ON IMAGES. As human beings we know our bodies and our minds only through what we can imagine. To grasp our humanity we need to structure these images into metaphors and models. Writers, artists, and visionaries have always known this—as have philosophers and scientists in other ways. Depth psychologists, however, take on the special and perhaps impossible task of bringing order to this dazzling array of images and the equally impressive range of feelings associated with them.

To create this order, psychologists and social theorists make their own choices of models or paradigms. We, too, require prior structures that seem relatively reliable as guides and maps to the terrain of imagery and feeling. In other words, psychologists do not simply interpret or analyze; we also construct; we engage in our own struggles around form. We are much concerned with narrative, and we inevitably contribute to the narrative of whatever life we examine.

But something has gone seriously wrong with everyone's images and models. When we invoke God and the devil, dialectical materialism and the perfectibility of man, or libido and death instinct, we perceive something familiar and perhaps explanatory or even moving—but these images rarely lead to an exhilarating sense of illumination or truth. We have difficulty seeing ourselves and our experienced work in the models handed down to us. At the same time we feel nagged if not threatened by a new wave of millennial imagery—of killing, dying, and destroying on a scale so great as to end the human narrative. We sense that our models should address that threat, but we do not know just how.

In recent work I have suggested a sequence in psychological thought from Freud's model of instinct and defense, to Erikson's of identity and the life cycle, to an emerging paradigm of death and life-continuity taking shape in the work of a number of people including myself. The general contours of this "new" paradigm were an attempt to move toward a new psychology. It is time to examine more closely the theme of death and continuity at the heart of the paradigm and to begin to fill in a few of the details of that "new psychology."

The "lost theme" to be addressed is not quite death itself. These days, in fact, one has the impression, at least in America, that death has been all too much found. Much more elusive is the psychological relationship between the phenomenon of death and the flow of life. Psychological theory has tended either to neglect death or render it a kind of foreign body, to separate death from the general motivations of life. Or else a previous deathless cosmology is replaced by one so dominated by death as to be virtually lifeless. As theorists, we seem to be all too susceptible both to the enormous cultural denial of (or numbness toward) death and to rebound reactions against that denial and numbness. The necessary dialectical focus on death and continuity poses formidable intellectual difficulties and imaginative requirements. And once that focus is taken seriously, the question is no longer how to incorporate death into psychological theory but how to transform the theory.

That transformation is best approached carefully. Though deviating from various Freudian positions, this book is itself a child of the Freudian revolution. In reexamining many of Freud's ideas, I have been surprised at their relevance for important directions he failed to take or even explicitly rejected. Freud is more present than I had intended him to be, and many of my views emerge in respectful, critical dialogue with him.

Books also begin with models and metaphors. This one emerged from compelling questions about death and holocaust that I originally encountered in my Hiroshima study. I was struck then by how little psychological literature seemed to speak to what I had observed. This deficiency was partly a matter of historical lag: there could be no adequate principles for the unprecedented. It also had to do with the limitations of the psychoanalytic paradigm, with Freud's own brilliant conceptual imbalance. Twentieth-century holocaust exposed rather than created that imbalance, and made urgent demands on psychology in general. Contained within those demands, I felt, were possibilities for new directions, significant insight, and even fundamental advance, for I was convinced that the extreme experiences described to me had considerable relevance for everyday existence.

With that in mind, at the end of my Hiroshima study I suggested relationships between survivor patterns and various forms of psychological disorder we encounter in our clinics and among ourselves. More generally, I spoke of a historical shift from Victorian struggles concerning sexuality and moralism to our present preoccupation with absurd death (and by implication, absurd life) and unlimited technological violence. But the elaboration of that shift has been no easy matter. Though I still think of this book as an outcome of my Hiroshima work, I seem to have required a decade or so to further test its ideas, to examine their application to other cataclysms as well as to clinical syndromes, before attempting a comprehensive synthesis. Now I am ready to risk that effort.

The broken connection exists in the tissues of our mental life. It has to do with a very new historical—one could also say evolutionary—relationship to death. We are haunted by the image of exterminating ourselves as a species by means of our own technology. Contemplating that image as students of human nature, we become acutely aware that we have never come to terms with our "ordinary"—that is, prenuclear—relationship to death and life-continuity. We seem to require this ill-begotten imagery of extinction to prod us toward examining what we have so steadfastly avoided. So this book has a double task. It first seeks general principles concerning death imagery and struggles for continuity, and applies these principles to explorations of the individual life cycle, the varieties of psychiatric disorder, and aspects of the historical process. It then goes on to consider some of the consequences of our imagery of extinction or what I call the "nuclear image." My conviction is that neither of these two tasks is properly undertaken separately from the other. You need to know about the mind's general possibilities and most extreme pitfalls around death imagery if you are to begin to understand radical new influences; and by the same token, can no longer look at "ordinary" relationships to death and life-continuity outside a context of ultimate threat. There is a logic, then, to the seemingly outrageous scope of this book. But invoking so broad a spectrum has its special vulnerabilities. One repeatedly introduces large questions that cannot be independently pursued. I have had to restrain myself from more detailed probing of many fascinating questions—whether about adolescence, schizophrenia, violence, or awareness—in order to hold to the general narrative, within which each of these large questions is no more than a fundamental example. My effort throughout is to press toward integrating principles that can have meaning for psychological work and general living in our time.

More specifically, the plan of the book is this. Part I describes a basic set of propositions that make up an open system in the sense of the Greek idea of *sustēma* or composite whole, one that enables its components to stand together. I stress the mutuality of ultimate and proximate levels of the paradigm. The ultimate level has to do with symbolizing our connection to our history and our biology; the proximate level includes more immediate feelings and images; and the two levels combine in the human struggle not merely to remain alive but to *feel* alive. I discuss man's evolutionary leap as including his knowledge that he dies, his capacity to symbolize, and his creation of culture. All these are of an imaginative piece: man does not create culture out of his need to deny death (the view put forward by both Freud and Rank and many of their modern disciples), but rather as his way of living out his unique awareness that he both dies and continues.

I examine ways in which these proximate and ultimate involvements are expressed over the course of the life cycle. A key principle is that of the formative process: the continuous creation of psychic images and forms, so that every encounter with the environment is newly constructed according to prior and anticipated experience—according to what one "knows" and expects. Here I extend the classical psychoanalytic idea of a symbol as a relatively primitive, conscious substitution of one thing for another (say, sea for mother or pencil for penis) to a more contemporary view of symbolization: the specifically human need to *construct* all experience as the only means of perceiving, knowing, and feeling. My extensive use of Japanese examples, especially when discussing cultural constructs, may strike some readers as a bit odd in a general study written by an American. To be sure, those examples come to mind because of past work and life experience. But it is also true that Japanese culture is particularly vivid and concrete in its attitudes toward death and life-continuity. The examples I choose reflect my conviction that seemingly alien and exotic cultural patterns teach us as much about universals as about the particular characteristics of that culture.*

Part II applies this open system to concepts of the fundamental emotions (attachment and love, anxiety and tension, conscience and guilt, anger and violence); to the classical neuroses and to schizophrenia; and to the phenomenon of suicide. I explore the relationship of all these to death imagery, perceived threat, and struggles toward vitality and meaning. I give special emphasis to traumatic disorder (the experience of death-related stress or extreme situations) and to the more general issue of depression as central to all mental suffering and the life process in general. I view schizophrenia as embodying the most extreme death-like maneuvers to avoid feeling; and suicide as always containing a vision, however desperate, of revitalization.

Part III examines broader historical phenomena around the theme of death and continuity. I consider collective versions of the "broken connection," of the loss of a sense of continuity (or symbolization of immortality) and the sequence that can potentially result—from dislocation to totalism to victimization and violence. I particularly stress victimizers' struggles with death imagery and

---

*As I have emphasized in earlier work, all collective behavior can be understood within a trinity of what is common to all people in all eras (psychobiological universals), what is given stress by a particular culture (cultural emphases), and recent historical directions (especially ways in which they support and conflict with cultural emphases). From this standpoint no shared experience is merely "cultural," "universal," or "historical"—every experience is simultaneously all three. But in the present study I am most concerned with universals, especially in the early sections; and then with the impact of widely shared recent history upon these universals. Inevitably, therefore, I neglect cultural differences. I believe I can be justified in doing so to the extent that the more general point is validly made.

aberrant quests for renewal. Then I apply that model to the influences of the nuclear age and its imagery of extinction. Here I examine threats to our sense of historical continuity posed by the mere existence of the weaponry, and some of the resulting patterns of psychic numbing on the one hand and of worship of the nuclear deity (the phenomenon of "nuclearism") on the other. Finally I say something about the principle of awareness—perhaps the touchstone of the entire study—as a source of more genuine directions of renewal.

My effort throughout is to explore the place of death in the human imagination, and its bearing on our sense of endings, changes, and beginnings. The spirit of the work is captured in a parable of the Jewish reinterpretation of the Adam and Eve story told by Nahum Glatzer. According to Glatzer, that description of man and woman being extruded from the Garden of Eden was not a "fall" but a "rise." It meant "becoming human," that is, "giving up immortality for knowledge." For becoming human meant surrendering both ignorance of death (the state of other animals) and the expectation of living forever (a prerogative only of God). "Knowledge," in our sense, is the capacity of the symbolizing imagination to explore the idea of death and relate it to a principle of life-continuity—that is, the capacity for culture. The parable thus depicts an *exchange of literal for symbolic immortality*. It suggests an ideal of a mortal being who need not remain numbed toward (ignorant of) the fact of death, who can know death and yet transcend it.

That perspective in turn connects us with recent anthropological views of man as the "cultural animal." For, as Robin Fox goes on to claim, "Culture is part of the biology of man . . . a characteristic of our species, as much a characteristic as the long neck of the giraffe." The metaphor of the "long neck" can be carried further: Culture, our means of symbolizing death and continuity, takes us to a higher place, permits us to see and imagine more, but also becomes a source of vulnerability in that very extension (if not overextension) of the brain-body axis.

The goal here is theory with an evolutionary spirit but without narrow biological determinism. For instance, Edward O. Wilson's synthesis of "sociobiology" relates to our paradigm in distinguishing the "proximate causation" of functional biology (the characteristics of a particular organ system—say, the digestive or nervous system of wolves or bees) with his own stress on the "ultimate causation" of evolutionary biology: the influence on species and individuals of the "prime movers of evolution," those environmental influences (weather, predators, stressors, living space, food sources, and accessible mates) that maintain continuous procreation and species' survival. Wilson's argument is that from the vast gene pool available in any species, those genes with the greatest survival value are perpetuated via mating arrangements, even when they propel the individual animal toward a sacrificial or "altruistic" death on behalf of group survival. With human beings, however, this argument runs into difficulty precisely around Wilson's neglect of the crucial symbolizing function.

He thus speaks of "a genetic predisposition to enter certain classes and to play certain roles," of "upwardly-mobile genes," "conformer genes," and "genes favoring spite" and the like. What I call symbolization of immortality (the ultimate level in our paradigm) could be understood as equivalent to Wilson's prime movers of evolution (his ultimate level). For in human experience, one must give primacy to the internal environment of the symbolizing mind and its capacity to envision human connection on a variety of levels. That is why we can speak of the evolutionary principle of staying psychologically as well as physically alive. There is room in this view for principles of genetic legacy around the capacity for symbolizing skills of different kinds. But that legacy must be recast into specifically human constructions around living and dying.

As we explore the nuances of our imaginative relationship to death we must question one particular philosophical claim now so widespread as to have become conventional wisdom: the principle that we are incapable of imagining our own deaths. This observation was made by many existential philosophers, as well as by such luminaries as Goethe and Freud. The truth in the claim is apparent enough: we are unable to imagine—that is, experience through imagery—our own nonexistence. But the fallacy lies in letting the matter end there. For while I cannot imagine my nonexistence, I can very well imagine a world in which "I" do not exist. That imaginative capacity is the basis for our theory of symbolic immortality. For as Paul Edwards has put it, "even existential philosophers . . . appoint literary executors."[1]

There is also the crucial question of the literality of the "I" involved. While "I" will cease to exist (which is why I cannot imagine my own death), elements of my "self"—of its (my) impact on others (children, students, friends, and, one may hope, readers)—will continue. These will exist not as a cohesive entity (the self as such) but as a part of a human flow that absorbs and recreates the components of that impact to the point of altering their shape and obscuring their origin. I can well imagine *that* process, and doing so contributes importantly to my acceptance of the idea of my own death.

We have been much too quick to posit imaginative limitations around death and continuity. We have much more to learn, once we make the critical distinction between literal perpetuation of the intact self—an illusion and frequently a dangerous one—and imagined (symbolized) perpetuation of elements of the self through connection with larger forms of human culture. We can then open our imaginations to a post-death (postself) future—and at the same time to the idea of the termination and disintegration of the self, of the individual mind and body.

Heinrich Böll's observation that "The artist carries death within him like a good priest his breviary" has never been more important than in our death-haunted time. And not only for the artist. For the attempt to exclude from the psychological imagination death and its symbolizations tends to freeze one in death terror, in a stance of numbing that can itself be a form of psychological death. Much of this study is devoted to exposing that process as it operates individually and collectively.

In all this the investigator can hardly be neutral. He resides *in* a particular history, and he badly misleads when he assumes a vantage point outside that history. His own advocacies and their relationship to his time and place are very much part of his narrative. Buber's equilibrium of "distance and relation" is the model here. The author's every exploration of death and continuity must both include and extend beyond himself.

PART I

Death and Immortality

ONE

Approaches and Modes

UNTIL RECENTLY, psychiatrists have mostly looked upon explorations of death and immortality either as forms of religious superstition or as matters of private belief separate from professional concern. While the denial of death is universal, the inner life-experience of a sense of immortality, rather than reflecting such denial, may well be the most authentic psychological alternative to that denial.

Conceptually speaking, psychoanalytic psychiatry's problems and possibilities in this area, as in so many others, begin with Freud.

Consider his celebrated statement about death and immortality:

> It is indeed impossible to imagine our own death: and whenever we attempt to do so we can perceive that we are in fact still present as spectators. Hence the psychoanalytic school could venture on the assertion that at bottom no one believes in his own death, or, to put the same thing in another way, that in the unconscious every one of us is convinced of his own immortality.[1]

For Freud death is unimaginable, psychically unavailable. And belief in immortality is compensatory and illusory. Elsewhere, Freud speaks of the inner pretense that one will not die as a "cultural and conventional attitude" fostered by the defense mechanism of "denial of death." Freud traces that denial to what he believes to be its prehistoric origins. Primeval man, he tells us, had two opposing unconscious attitudes toward death: "the one which acknowledges it as the annihilation of life and the other which denies it as unreal." Modern man, he goes on to say, has embraced only the denial, and at severe psychological cost. But Freud's implication is that the denial itself is rooted in instinct, which, in turn, derives from primeval sources and is the basis for fundamental unconscious attitudes ("in the unconscious everyone of us is convinced of his own immortality").

In the face of this overwhelming pattern of denial, Freud characteristically calls for a rallying of reason to combat unreason. Writing under the impetus of the general death immersion of World War I, he makes an eloquent plea for greater honesty and psychological integrity in relationship to living and dying:

> Should we not confess that in our civilized attitude towards death we are once again living psychologically beyond our means, and should we not rather turn back and recognize the truth? Would it not be better to give death a place in reality and in our thoughts which is its due, and to give a little more prominence to the unconscious attitude towards death which we have hitherto so carefully suppressed? . . .
>
> We recall the old saying: Si vis pacem, para bellum. If you want to preserve peace, arm for war.
>
> It would be in keeping with the times, to alter it: Si vis vitam, para mortem. If you want to endure life, prepare yourself for death.[2]

For Freud giving death its due meant surrendering all doctrines that deny the "significance of annihilation"—all images of an afterlife or of "immortality of the human soul." These images, he insists, are nothing but the denial of that annihilation, and therefore denial of death itself. We may characterize Freud's position as rationalist-iconoclastic.

Carl Jung takes the opposite position. He looks to the mythologies of the world, and stresses that all of them contain beliefs about life after death. These mythologies, he insists, hold hidden maps of our own psychic terrain— important "hints sent to us from the unconscious." He also refers to dreams, his own and others', and to experiments in extrasensory perception, from which he concludes that "at least a part of our psychic existence is characterized by a relativity of space and time . . . [which] seems to increase, in proportion to the distance from consciousness, to an absolute condition of timelessness and spacelessness."[3] What he seems to be saying is that we cannot quite know whether there is some form of life beyond what we call death—there are mysteries about the nature and scope of the mind's perceptions—but that in the absence of certainty either way, he is favorably inclined toward such a belief. When near the end of his own life, he reasserted that inclination toward such a "personal myth," because it was psychically hopeful and enriching, and because it kept one in touch with the most fundamental kind of instinctual image-structure or "archetype."

Yet death is an important interest, especially to an aging person. A categorical question is being put to him, and he is under an obligation to answer it. To this end he ought to have a myth about death, for reason shows him nothing but the dark pit into which he is descending. Myth, however, can conjure up other images for him, helpful and enriching pictures of life in the land of the dead. If he believes in them, or greets them with some measure of credence, he is being just as right or just as wrong as someone who does not believe in them. But while the man who despairs marches toward nothingness, the one who has placed his faith in the archetype follows the tracks of life and lives right into his death. Both, to be sure, remain in uncertainty. But the one lives against his instincts, the other with them. Mythological and religious imagery of life beyond death, that is, constitutes an "archetype," a primordial, inherited, instinctual structure that is worthy of one's "faith."[3]

In defending the idea of life beyond death, Jung moved back and forth throughout his work between a "hygienic" principle—

As a physician I am convinced that it is hygienic to discover in death a goal toward which one can strive; and that shrinking away from it is something unhealthy and abnormal which robs the second half of life of its purpose. I therefore consider the religious teaching of a life hereafter consonant with the standpoint of psychic hygiene. When I live in a house that I know will fall about my head within the next two weeks, all my vital functions will be impaired by this thought; but if, on the contrary, I feel myself to be safe, I can dwell there in a normal comfortable way.[4]

and a more powerful insistence upon the psychic truth of ancient, archetypical images:

. . . beyond [the intellect] there is a thinking in primordial images—in symbols that are older than historical man; which have been ingrained in him from earliest times, and, eternally living, outlasting all generations, still make up the groundwork of the human psyche. It is possible to live the fullest life only when we are in harmony with these symbols; wisdom is a return to them. It is a question neither of belief nor knowledge, but of the agreement of our thinking with the primordial images of the unconscious. They are the source of all our conscious thoughts, and one of these primordial images is the idea of life after death.

Death's annihilation, in Jung's view, is less significant than the enriching (hygienic) value and awesome primordial (mythical) persistence of symbolism of life after death. We may therefore characterize Jung's position as *mythic-hygienic*.

The differences and similarities between these two great stubborn figures are nowhere more evident. Freud, the patriarchal, secular Jew, carries the torch for the Enlightenment and for an assumption upon which modern, post-theocratic reason must rest: that of death as absolute annihilation of the human organism. He links that insistence with his revolutionary psychology in his plea for greater awareness of death and with his focus on the cost of continuing denial. Above all, he brings to bear his fierce rationalism on what he considers antiscientific self-deception around the idea of immortality. In this way he affirms nobly what his life and work stand for, and also (but not incidentally) lays to rest (or almost to rest) the troubling personal questions of the wilder, less science-bound, more magical and mystical borders of his own psyche. We can hardly blame him for ignoring, in the process, not only the *symbolic* significance of universal imagery of immortality but also the *prospective* importance of individual imagery concerning death and continuity.

For whether or not we imagine our own death as a specific event, we do anticipate the end of the self—its annihilation, cessation (stasis), and total separation (from the world). And Freud was by no means immune from the crucial, prospective question concerning the extent to which that anticipated end of the self is viewed as the end of *everything*. I have written elsewhere of his transformation of an early fear of death to impressive mastery of that fear over sixteen years of extremely painful and humiliating symptoms of, and treatment for, mouth cancer. As his work developed, what concerned him much more than death was the prospective issue of the fate of his theories. Of one disciple and patient he asked anxiously, "What will they do with my theory after my death? Will it still resemble my basic thoughts?"[5] And as early as 1894, at the age of thirty-eight, when ill with what may or may not have been a genuine cardiac episode and fearful of the outcome, he wrote:

> Among the gloomy thoughts of the past few months there is one that is in second place, right after wife and children—namely, that I shall not be able to prove the sexual thesis anymore. After all one does not want to die either immediately or completely. . . .
> . . . They look upon me as pretty much of a monomaniac, while I have the distinct feeling that I have touched upon one of the great secrets of nature.[6]

Freud was, in other words, less a postdeath spectator than a deeply involved predeath participant in the endless symbolizations of his own magnificent mental products—with as much concern with this kind of symbolic immortality as anyone else, and indeed more reason than most for such concern.

Jung, the Protestant visionary, brings his tough-minded, obscurantist, medieval imagination and distrust of secular pieties to a reassertion of immortality that combines a modern therapeutic ethos with premodern Christian hope. Listening to his insistence that we hearken to the message of a "beyond," we recall Jung's very early conflict with Freud over a similar issue of symbolization—Jung's stress on "the spiritual significance of incest as a symbol" as opposed to Freud's clinging "to the literal interpretation of it" as "a personal complication."

So Jung does take us toward a symbolizing perspective. But he hedges and mystifies when he advocates that one "place . . . his faith in the archetype." The archetype itself, as an inherited-instinctual image, becomes a suprahistorical truth, which we are unquestioningly to pursue. We are asked specifically to recover and reexperience the archetype of immortality. But in all this Jung fails to distinguish—or at least distinguishes inadequately—between the symbolic truth of the imagery and the literal idea of an "afterlife" or "immortal soul." This combination of premodern "mythicism" and modern "therapism" takes us outside the realm of natural history—and negates, rather than broadens, psychology's relationship to the scientific tradition.

The similarity we also feel in the two men has to do not only with their stubbornness and stature but their nineteenth-century instinctualism (which we will return to when we talk about Freud's death instinct). Within that instinctualism and what we would now consider its explanatory limitations, the two men shared a heroic sensibility to death and immortality as an ultimate matter for psychological man.

There is a third position, a *formative-symbolizing* perspective. We may accept both Freud's insistence on confronting death as the annihilation of the self, and Jung's insistence on the psychological importance of mythic imagery of immortality. But I would focus more specifically on the symbolizing process around death and immortality as the individual's experience of participation in some form of collective life-continuity. To be sure our knowledge that we die pervades all such larger perceptions of life's endings and beginnings. And our resistance to that knowledge, our denial of death, is indeed formidable, as Freud and the others have emphasized. But that denial can never be total; we are never fully ignorant of the fact that we die. Rather we go about life with a kind of "middle knowledge" of death,* a partial awareness of it side by side with expressions and actions that belie that awareness. Our resistance to the fact that we die—the numbed side of our middle knowledge—interferes considerably with our symbolizing process. We, in fact, require symbolization of continuity—imaginative forms of transcending death—in order to confront genuinely the fact that we die.

A *sense* of immortality, then, is by no means mere denial of death, though denial and numbing are rarely absent. Rather it is a corollary of the knowledge of death itself, and reflects a compelling and universal inner quest for continuous symbolic relationship to what has gone before and what will continue after our finite individual lives. That quest is central to the human project, to man as cultural animal and to his creation of culture and history. The struggle toward, or experience of, a sense of immortality is in itself neither compensatory nor "irrational," but an appropriate symbolization of our biological and historical connectedness.

---

* The term "middle knowledge" was first used in connection with patients who were actually dying,[7] but it applies equally to the rest of us, who differ from dying patients mainly in relationship to the timing of our deaths.

This view is influenced by Rank's concept of man's perpetual struggle for "an assurance of eternal survival for himself," and his further assertion that "man creates culture by changing natural conditions in order to maintain his spiritual self."[8] But in seeing the whole process as part of man's fundamental "irrationality," Rank placed the whole matter in a realm of religious aspirations that are "beyond psychology." We may instead place a version of this principle at the center of a psychology, and view the struggle for symbolic immortality as neither rational nor irrational but as a psychic expression of man's existential and organismic state. We need not then trace it back to an unchanging "archetype," but can view it instead as a core area of the self—one in which central motivating issues around life-continuity and threats to it are experienced.

In terms of biological connectedness, August Weismann spoke nearly a century ago of the principle of literal cellular immortality— "the immortality of unicellular beings and of the reproductive cells of multicellular organisms." But that literal cellular immortality is just one aspect of our general biological (species) continuity. The psychological power of that biological continuity is expressed by such terms as "ties of blood" and "my people," and by the limitless images of origin and life-source, including that of "my mother's womb." We must wonder at the neglect of these primal emotions in depth-psychological theory, as at the neglect of equally powerful historical feelings—based not so much on specific knowledge of national or cultural past as on a more inchoate involvement in the transmission, over many generations, of images, ideas, and practices that inform or bedevil our lives. We require a psychological language—our own system of professional symbolization—to express a sense of endless biohistorical continuity.

Death does indeed bring about biological and psychic annihilation. But life includes symbolic perceptions of connections that precede and outlast that annihilation.

The sense of immortality may be expressed in five general modes: the biological, theological, creative (through "works"), natural, and the special mode of experiential transcendence. Awareness of our involvement in these modes can vary enormously, and cannot necessarily be equated with the power a particular mode, or combination of modes, holds for us.

The biological mode of immortality is epitomized by family continuity, living on through—psychologically speaking, in—one's sons and daughters and their sons and daughters, with imagery of an endless chain of biological attachment. This has been the most fundamental and universal of all modes. A classical expression was in premodern East Asian cultures, especially in the traditional Chinese family system, and in somewhat lesser and modified form in the Japanese family system as well. It was philosophically elaborated in Confucianism, particularly in the mystique (near-religion) of filial piety. Thus

Mencius, Confucius's great disciple, could say: "There are three unfilial acts, and of these, lack of posterity is the greatest."

In Japan, even today, very many homes retain the mortuary tablets *(ihhai)* for deceased family members kept in the Buddhist household shrine *(butsudan)*. The practice is a remnant of the longstanding Japanese combination of original Shinto reverence toward nature and ancestors and later Buddhist influence. This ritual has never been associated with the structured belief system characteristic of Western religion, and has undoubtedly lost much of its psychological force in modern and postmodern Japan. Yet it remains important to Japanese cultural experience, and can be especially reawakened in crises. Many Hiroshima survivors, for instance, told me of the special solace they felt when literally talking to family members killed in the bomb and enshrined in their household altars. What they conveyed was much less a sense of religiosity than of ritualized effort to hold onto at least some part of those relationships and to maintain an unbroken sense of family continuity.

These sentiments are in no way unique, and one encounters related practices in Western cultures. The early Roman "paterfamilias" was both family monarch and priest of the family ancestor cult, and his authority and property were legally transmitted down the male family line. Much of the Roman system was maintained in the secular and canon law of Western Europe until the nineteenth century, and its influences are still present in contemporary life.

Because man is the "cultural animal," the biological mode can never remain purely biological. The family itself is always symbolized at least partly in social terms. An example is the Japanese family practice, still active, of "adopting" adult male heirs where none (or in some cases, merely none with adequate talent) are available in that biological generation.* The biosocial mode of immortality can be extended outward from family to tribe, organization, subculture, people, nation, or even species. That extension can be associated with varying ethical principles.†

---

* Another example is the stress on "family honor." In Japan, the principle of "clearing one's name"—wiping out stains on one's reputation, repaying social and economic debts, avenging insults—has never been a purely individual matter but has always been subsumed to the "family name" that has defined so much of the individual's moral as well as biological existence.

† In premodern Japan, the biosocial mode extended from family to feudal lord, and then in varying ways at different times to the larger clan, clan groups, *shogunate* (the system of military government under which Japan was ruled from the late twelfth to late nineteenth centuries), and the emperor (in whose name the shogun ruled). Then the Meiji restoration of 1868 was followed by a revitalization of the emperor system that combined its mythology (of unbroken descent from the sun goddess) with more modern expressions of nationalism, so that World War II could be fought around a sacred constellation of family, feudal past, emperor, and nation. While the Japanese case has unique features, some such constellation always characterizes modern nationalism. The individual is energized by merging with what can be called an "immortal biocultural substance" for which he may willingly give his life, and even more willingly take the lives of others.

It is precisely because of the psychic force of the biosocial mode that there is such a fine line between love of country and people on the one hand, and hate-filled, violent nationalism on the other. Nor have we made more than the smallest beginnings toward extending the mode beyond that immortal bio-cultural substance usually associated with nations. That kind of extension has been advocated by evolutionary theorists such as Julian Huxley and Pierre Teilhard de Chardin, the latter movingly but precariously combining evolutionary theory with elements of Christian mysticism. Our restless search for life on other planets could also be viewed as a struggle toward extension of the mode still further. An encompassing vision of biosocial immortality—and we have at least glimmerings of such a vision—would provide each individual anticipating death with the image: "I live on in humankind."

A second expression of symbolic immortality—the one that comes most readily to mind when the word is used—is the theological or religious mode. It may include a specific concept of a life after death, not only as a form of "survival" but even as a release from the profane burdens of life into a higher plane of existence. A related concept is that of the "immortal soul," which Freud saw as man's characteristic expression of denial of death.

But the theological mode need not rely on a literal vision of immortal soul or afterlife. No such vision occurs in most Jewish and Buddhist belief. And even in the case of Christianity it is probably less fundamental than the quality of spiritual achievement symbolized in the Christ story.* The common thread in all great religions is the spiritual quest and realization of the hero-founder that enables him to confront and transcend death and to provide a model for generations of believers to do the same. Thus the lives of Buddha, Moses, Christ, and Mohammed came to encompass various combinations of spirituality, revelation, and ultimate ethical principles that could, for themselves and their followers, divest death of its "sting" of annihilation. The basic spiritual principle, with or without a concept of afterlife or immortal soul, is the ancient mythological theme of death and rebirth. One is offered the opportunity to be reborn into a timeless realm of ultimate, death-transcending truths. In that realm one can share the immortality of the deity, obtain membership in a sacred community or a "covenant with God." Or that ultimate realm might take on the more concrete imagery of a "heaven," or of the negative immortality (unending suffering) of hell.

Whatever the imagery, there is at the heart of religion a sense of spiritual power.[9] That power may be understood in a number of ways—dedication, capacity to love, moral energy—but its final meaning is life-power and

---

* Paul Tillich, in personal conversation, once contrasted what he called the "vulgar theology" of afterlife imagery, usually for the "common people," with more symbolized and sensitive "higher theologies" around spiritual attainment. But the Christ story does differ from those of other spiritual heroes in its more specific focus upon individual death and resurrection.

power over death. There are specific words to suggest that power. In Japan, for instance, the word *kami*, while often translated as "god," "gods," or "spirit," has the more general meaning of "a thing or person . . . felt to possess some superior quality or power." The word, in fact, resembles the Polynesian term *mana* and the Roman idea of *numen*[10]—to which one could add the Eskimo concept of *tungnic*, the Greek idea of *areté*, and the Christian image of grace. All of these convey a quality of spiritual power derived from a more-than-natural source. The state of possessing (or of living under the protection of) this power, rather than the concrete idea of afterlife, is the more universal to religious experience.

Claims by priests to possess this power, and their political institutionalization of it, converts theology to theocracy. Monarchies in particular, both western and eastern, tend to derive from these theocratic routes.*

The third mode of symbolic immortality is the creative—whether through great works of art, literature, or science, or through more humble influences on people around us. The artist has long been recognized as participating in this mode of immortality—either in his prophetic function or, as Malraux believed, through "the continuity of artistic creation" by means of which "not the individual, but man, human continuity, reveals itself," so that "more than any other activity, art escapes death."[11]

Similarly each scientific investigator becomes part of an enterprise larger than himself, limitless in its past and future continuity. Whatever his additional motivations—the need to know and the quest for personal glory and reward—he operates within a framework of larger connectedness. Hence the concern of the individual scientist for the lasting quality of the tradition within which he works—all the more so when he himself is the originator of a tradition whose future must be considered uncertain (as mentioned above in Freud's case).†

---

* The Japanese emperor system has been particularly striking as a modern theocratic phenomenon. In stressing the absolute divinity of the emperor—his descent from the sun goddess—Meiji reformers (late nineteenth century) managed to build around the emperor not only the imagery of biosocial immortality already mentioned but a compelling theological mode as well. Those governing in his name could take on quite readily the totalist claim to the dispensation of truth and of existence itself. To serve and revere the emperor-centered state could then permit one to share in an especially vivid sense of immortality derived from experiencing the entire nation as a "sacred community" with unlimited spiritual power.

† Gerald Holton has gone further in demonstrating how themes addressed by physical science reflect specific struggles of a particular century with ultimate questions. The Greek idea of the atom, for instance, expressed a powerful impulse to "keep back the void," an impulse by no means absent today in physicists' use of ever more extensive technology to demonstrate ever more minuscule particles, even as their very physicality comes into doubt.[12]

The great historical transition from religion to science refers to a major shift in the imagery through which large numbers of people in general (not just scientists or theologians) experience the continuity of human existence. Our psychological relationship to each of these world views lies not so much in the virtues of the one or the other as in the extent to which the vitality of either gives way to a dogmatic literalism that limits feeling and suppresses imagination. Everyone in this age participates in a sense of immortality derived from the interlocking human projects we call science and technology.

At more concrete levels of individual encounter, any kind of service or care can enter into this mode of continuity. Physicians and psychotherapists, for instance, associate their therapeutic efforts with beneficent influences that carry forward indefinitely in the lives of patients and clients and *their* children or posterity. Consequently, any sense on the part of care-givers that those efforts are ineffective can set off in them deep anxieties about ultimate personal questions. *

These issues are germane to more humble everyday offerings of nurturing or even kindness—in relationships of love, friendship, and at times even anonymous encounter. Indeed, any form of acting upon others contains important perceptions of timeless consequences.

The fourth mode of symbolic immortality is that associated with nature itself: the perception that the natural environment around us, limitless in space and time, will remain. This mode has been especially vivid in traditional Japanese culture, steeped as it was in a great variety of nature symbolism.† In early Shinto belief, as in much animistic religion, supernatural gods emerge from, and eventually retire to, the trees, mountains, and rivers, where they are joined by immortal human souls. No wonder that survivors of Hiroshima, struggling to absorb their holocaust and to reestablish their own sense of continuity, so often quoted the ancient Japanese (originally Chinese) saying: "The state may collapse but the mountains and rivers remain."

---

* Leslie Farber has described the experience of "therapeutic despair"[13] as an occupational hazard of those psychiatrists who devote major energies over long periods of time to treating severely withdrawn schizophrenic patients. Farber attributes that state to the unacceptable perception that nothing of significance is really happening in the therapy. What might really be at stake, however (and this is perfectly compatible with Farber's views), is the therapist's larger relationship to the creative or professional—in this case, therapeutic—mode of immortality in which he has invested so much of his life energies. Hence, he engages in the little games of self-deceit Farber so vividly describes, illusions that exchanges between the patient and himself, understood by no one else, signify progress in the therapy and, by implication, confirmation of his own sense of meaningful work.

† Sansom thus locates the earliest and most persistent object of Japanese religious feelings in "the forces of nature in their divine embodiments as gods of mountain and valley, field and stream, fire and water, rain and wind."[14]

Indeed, immediately after the bomb fell, the most terrifying rumor among the many that swept the city was that trees, grass, and flowers would never again grow in Hiroshima. The image contained in that rumor was of nature drying up altogether, life being extinguished at its source, an ultimate form of desolation that not only encompassed human death but went beyond it. The persistence and continuing growth of wild "railroad grass" (which, in fact, had to serve as food for many during immediate postbomb days) was perceived·as a source of strength. And the subsequent appearance of early spring buds, especially those of the March cherry blossoms, symbolized the detoxification of the city and (in the words of its then mayor) "a new feeling of relief and hope." *

The assaults on the natural mode by advanced industrial society both threaten our relationship to it and awaken image-hungers within us (as expressed in widespread American return-to-nature impulses, organized and informal, during the 1960s and 1970s). However our perceptions of nature change—to include outer space, the moon, other planets—we continue to seek in those perceptions an ultimate aspect of our existence.

---

* Consider such expressions of the natural mode of immortality as the ideology of nineteenth-century European romanticism, carried over into twentieth-century "return-to-nature" expressions of German youth movements (some of which were all too readily absorbed by the murderous romanticism of Hitlerism); the American cult of the "great outdoors," with its roots both in Europe and in transcendent perceptions of the natural dimensions of the New World and of the American frontier; and the longstanding Anglo-Saxon preoccupation with vigorously confronting the infinite dimensions of nature and with "cultivating one's garden." In that last image, the idea of nurturing and communing with one's own small plot of land becomes a metaphor for tending to one's own realm, whether of domestic national policy or the individual psyche.

TWO

The Experience of Transcendence

THE FIFTH MODE of symbolized immortality, that of experiential transcendence, is of a different order from the others. It depends entirely on a psychic state—one so intense and all-encompassing that time and death disappear. This state is the classical mode of the mystic. But it turns out to have significance far beyond that, to be, in fact, the indicator of the other four modes as well.

Ruth Benedict suggested that whole cultures could be classified according to the Nietzschean duality of Apollonian stress upon measure, control and moderation; and the Dionysian embrace of excess, of "annihilation of ordinary bonds and limits of existence" in the struggle to "break through into another order of experience."[1]* In a more recent study of ecstasy, Marghanita Laski speaks similarly of a psychic breakthrough and of a quality of experience "extraordinary to the point of seeming as if derived from a praeternatural source." She identifies this state in places we would expect to find it—in mysticism, religious and secular, and in various premodern cultural rites where it may be brought about with the aid of drugs, starvation, sleep deprivation, or some other form of imposed ordeal. But she also locates it in less obvious places, in more familiar activities, such as song, dance, battle, sexual love,

---

* Nietzsche's distinction was actually much more subtle. He viewed the Apollonian as itself dream and illusion, a "deep and happy sense of the necessity of dream experiences expressed by the Greeks in the image of Apollo," and spoke of the "fair [Apollonian] illusion of the dream sphere . . . [as] a precondition not only of all plastic art, but even . . . of a wide range of poetry." In this Apollonian mode, he went on, "we enjoy an immediate apprehension of form, all shapes speak to us directly, nothing seems indifferent or redundant."[2]

childbirth, athletic effort, mechanical flight, contemplation of the past, and artistic or intellectual creation.[3]

Characteristic of the ecstatic state in all of these activities is a sense of extraordinary psychic unity, and perceptual intensity, and of ineffable illumination and insight.

The list suggests a continuum from extraordinary Dionysian "excess" (sexual orgy or absolute union with God) to relatively "ordinary excess" (sexual intercourse, athletics) to much quieter, indeed, Apollonian moments (contemplation of the past or any kind of beauty). The crucial requirement for feeling ecstatic—"outside of oneself"—would seem to be not so much excess per se as the breakout from prosaic psychic complexities into a state of pure focus, of inner unity and harmony. What excess or Dionysian drama does provide is a vivid psychological model which helps us to understand more muted expressions of that model at the quieter, softer end of the continuum.

From that standpoint we may reconsider the widespread contemporary form of ecstasy accompanying the use of LSD, a synthetic drug variously described as "psychedelic" (mind-manifesting), "consciousness-expanding," "mysticomimetic," or "psychotomimetic." As these names suggest, the psychic state produced can take the form of expanded mental capacities on the one hand, or of psychotic dissociation on the other. Psychic explorers have emphasized the former possibility; psychiatrists have tended to stress the latter danger. All have come to recognize that much depends on the setting in which the drug is used, on what is expected by the person taking it, and by those around him who administer the drug or in one way or another set the tone of the experience. Even while granting the dangers, some psychiatrists have emphasized the drug's usefulness to the therapeutic process—its stimulation of a "transcendental reaction . . . a temporary loss of differentiation of the self and the outer world . . . (which) may lead to a lessening of alienation, to a rediscovery of the self, to a new set of values, to the finding of new potential for growth and development, and to a new beginning."[4]

These descriptions—by sober research scientists no less than radical young seekers—suggest an inner experience of "uncentering" or breaking down of existing psychic forms followed immediately by a vivid sense of reintegration and recentering. The specific psychic experience has to do with what Freud called the "'Oceanic feeling,' or the 'sensation of eternity,' . . . of something limitless, unbounded." Freud attributed this sense of "oneness with the universe" to a return to the unity characteristic of early childhood prior to the separation of ego from outer world. He called this a "restoration of limitless narcissism."[5] He would undoubtedly have said the same of Sir Thomas Browne's characterization of the Christian mystical experience:

> And if any have been so happy as truly to understand Christian annihilation, ecstasies, exhaltation, liquification, transformation, the kiss of the spouse,

gustation of God, and ingression into the Divine shadow, they have already had a handsome anticipation of heaven; the glory of the world is surely over, and the earth in ashes unto them.

Freud is certainly right to insist that such experiences be examined *as psychic states*. But we must reject his characterization of them as merely regressive phenomena, as no more than residua from early childhood. Let's assume that the ecstatic experience, like all experience, takes place only in the present, and is indeed characterized by extraordinary immediacy and "presentness." We can speak of psychic models of inner unity as being established in early childhood, prior to life's differentiations and ambiguities, and prior to the adult loss of much of the capacity to harmonize passion and idea. But in this psychic state there is a rediscovery of that harmony in a specifically *adult* experience, a sense of strong inner coherence within the originally symbolized adult psychic universe.

The self feels uniquely alive—connected, in movement, integrated—which is why we can say that this state provides at least a temporary sense of eliminating time and death. What it eliminates is the destructive side of the death symbol—proximate imagery of separation, stasis, and disintegration, as well as ultimate imagery of meaninglessness and impaired symbolic immortality. This kind of psychic experience can (as Laski suggests) lead to significant inner change:

> It is generally agreed that ecstatic experiences are to be valued not only for the delight they give—which is great—but for their beneficial results. These results may be generally expressed as improved mental organization, whether this takes the form of replacing uneasiness and dissatisfaction with ease and satisfaction, or of appearing to confirm a sought belief, or of inspiring to moral action or of enabling the expression of a new mental creation.[6]

One never "returns" to exactly the same inner structure of the self. Having once broken old forms, one senses that they can be broken again, or at least extended beyond earlier limitations. In addition an important memory remains, a still active image-feeling of intense inner unity. A personal model is thus constructed for the symbolic reordering necessary to psychological change. The process is reminiscent of William James's classical descriptions of religious conversion. But whether taking the form of that high drama, or of a quieter ecstasy, what is crucial is the moment of perfect centering—of ideal blending of immediate and ultimate involvements. *

* By centering I mean ordering of the experience of the self along the various dimensions that must be dealt with at any given moment—temporal, spatial, and emotional. On the temporal plain centering consists of bringing to bear on any immediate encounter older images and forms in ways that can anticipate future encounters. On the spatial plane, centering involves unifying immediate (proximate) exposure of the body and mind with ultimate ("immortalizing," "abstract," or "distant")

That whole sequence can be regularized in cultural ritual, as in the use of peyote (a natural, mescaline substance whose action resembles that of LSD) by certain groups of American Indians in the past:

> Peyote gave them faith in a new power and a new road that they might follow from the path that was still in their hearts and minds to a feared and little understood future. The meeting of compelling forces, conscious and unconscious, of racial memories, the loss of tribal security and religious beliefs, added to the . . . creative urge to make live, in form and color, the spirit of the Indian.[7]*

Ecstatic transcendence here overcomes the confusions associated with the passage of time, and blends all in transtemporal harmony. This form of symbolic reordering is central to various kinds of individual and collective revitalization. But it requires a reservoir of shared cultural imagery—usually religious or at least cosmological, almost always touching upon issues of life and death—imagery that can be communally evoked under structured ritual conditions. Even if a person seeks the experience alone, he must call forth symbolizations of immortality available to his people, symbolizations that provide not only energy for the ecstatic experience but order and form within which it can be immediately understood and later absorbed. Through such traditional symbolizations of life-continuity and ultimate meaning, the moment of ecstasy is given a firm context within which it can connect with prior and subsequent experience of a more prosaic kind.

Precisely these conditions have been lacking for contemporary non-Indian

---

meanings. A third aspect of centering has to do with discriminations in emotional valence between our most impassioned images and those less important to the structure and function of the self.

The self can maintain this centering only to the degree it has the capacity for decentering, for sufficient detachment from involvements to permit it to make judgments upon events and principles beyond itself. The absence of decentering renders the self static, devoid of new content, while absence of centering is associated with inability to connect new experience with viable inner forms.

Both centering and decentering depend in turn upon grounding, which is the relationship of the self to its own history, individual and collective, as well as to its biology. Where grounding is precarious, decentering is likely to be replaced by *uncentering*, the breakdown of the ordering or centering process. The significance of grounding can be seen in the contrast between the imaginative qualities of the schizophrenic person and those of the genuine innovator. The former can have many original ideas and images, but they are "ungrounded" (insufficiently anchored in experience).

The latter's capacity to innovate stems from a more grounded imagination, imagery includes contradictions and paradox—and may even be quite "wild"—but nonetheless has roots in developed psychic forms.[8]

* Thus the experiences Carlos Castaneda brought back to us had old and broad cultural roots—though Castaneda's mentor, Don Juan, apparently initiated him into an esoteric version of such tradition.[9]

seekers of similar goals and visions via LSD. With rare exceptions, the seekers have had no specific cultural reservoir of imagery, and have had to improvise—sometimes sensitively but often chaotically—missing communal and ritual elements. This improvised ecstasy undoubtedly has a lot to do with the "bad trips" and drug-induced psychoses observed in relation to the use of LSD. No doubt American Indians, too, had bad trips in the past, but it is quite likely that they occur much more frequently in the absence of cultural symbolization of immortality. Present-day drug users expose themselves to the "death dimension" of the ecstatic experience—the further disruption of immediate and ultimate ties—in the absence of reliable cultural symbolization for supporting, guiding, and sustaining the experience of "rebirth."

Japanese culture has emphasized quiet forms of experiential transcendence in spiritual and physical disciplines. In both Zen itself, as well as in jūdō, karate, kendō (fencing), and archery, all of which call upon Zen-related principles, there is a stress upon freeing the mind of extraneous thoughts to reach a "pure state." That state permits one to achieve a quality of effortless concentration—what has been called "alert passivity."* This can then be applied to a particular skill. So stressed is the element of consciousness that we may view these disciplines as motor forms of meditation.

In Zen itself, the enlightenment (satori) is said to be sudden and absolute, but the feelings experienced may be either those of ecstatic breakthrough or calm awareness. In either case spiritual achievement is associated with an exquisite moment of centering: the harmonious merging of immediate and ultimate experience (self and world), past and prospective imagery, and of the varying emotional shadings that ordinarily complicate psychic life.

In contrast to the disciplined exclusions of the Zen experience is the same culture's feeling-tone of "sad beauty" or "suchness" of existence (mono no aware). The feeling is often used to express one's involvement in and, in a sense, passive acceptance of the slow, sad truths of life and nature. The feeling borders on what we would call the sentimental, and is often expressed in popular culture in the shallowest forms. Yet it has profound Buddhist associations, and has been called forth over decades and centuries in Japanese art, literature, film, and psychological and cultural life in general. The acceptance of and even pleasure in sadness—the sadness of change, loss, and death—has to do with one's sense of being part of the cosmic and the eternal. Death-tinged sadness—lovers parting, life ending, cherry blossoms falling—is inseparable from and an evocation of the larger life process as manifested by beauty. Beauty and loss become a single constellation which, in unending

---

* Significantly, the term "alert passivity" applies equally to these adult spiritual-physical disciplines and to the stance of the infant (as Peter Wolff tells us) anticipating its next interaction. This does not mean that the state is a form of "regression," but it does suggest that the capacity for inner harmony and near-perfect centering does have very early experiential roots.

cycles and variations, provides a means of psychologically realizing death while affirming an aesthetically dominated culture's imagery of continuing life.

Contemporary American meditators and seekers tend to enter these realms as cultural outsiders. They are fully capable of intense psychic experience, but lack the connecting imagery of transcendence that cultures can provide. So they seek that imagery (along with techniques of meditation) elsewhere, often from Japanese or Indian tradition. They can then make use of fragments of alien traditions for their own struggles around awareness and centering, around beauty, death, and continuity. By conducting these struggles as they do, outside of any framework provided in their own culture, many experience the process as a continuing Protean search. Even the "high" is likely to have an ad hoc quality, however intense the inner harmony experienced. One "comes down" to old confusions, or, at best, partially reordered disharmonies. That absence of content—of images of symbolic immortality—is the key to the fallacy of spiritual cure via experiential transcendence alone. Dedicated meditators and seekers construct, over time, the beginnings of new versions of immortalizing imagery, attempting to combine image-fragments into more enduring constellations. But the more pervasive tendency is a very American form of technicizing the spiritual—of converting quest into technique, transcendence into "feeling good." The ecstatic or meditative experience then takes on the near-absolute irony of furthering the very focus on the technical and prosaic it was originally called forth to transcend.

Yet there are still places where relatively intact rituals of transcendence can be found within a cultural matrix of shared imagery and belief. I have in mind a modern version of the ancient phenomenon of the "festival," deriving from early fertility rites in agricultural societies, here represented by Octavio Paz's evocation of some of the meanings in the orgiastic features of the Mexican fiesta.*

The plunge into chaos (disintegration, death) includes wildness and spontaneity but is culturally stylized. The "experiment in disorder" is controlled—in the sense that it takes place within ordered ritual and imagery, within an ordered cosmos. Each participant, even when in the midst of "drowning," anticipates personal and communal revitalization—that anticipation based on generations

---

*The fiesta is not only an excess, a ritual squandering of the goods painfully accumulated during the rest of the year; it is also a revolt, a sudden immersion in the formless, in pure being. . . . In the confusion that it generates, society is dissolved, is drowned insofar as it is an organism ruled according to certain laws and principles. But it drowns in itself, in its own original chaos or liberty. Everything is united: good and evil, day and night, the sacred and the profane. Everything merges, loses shape and individuality, and returns to the primordial mass. The fiesta is a cosmic experiment, an experiment in disorder, reiniting contradictory elements in order to bring about a renaissance of life. Ritual death promotes a rebirth; vomiting increases the appetite; the orgy, sterile in itself, renews the fertility of the mother or of the earth . . . we shrug our shoulders at death, as at life, confronting it in silence or with a contemptuous smile.[10]

of transmission of the appropriate imagery of renewal. The sense of play pervading the ritual drama, though childlike in its quality of make-believe, is at the same time very adult precisely because of this mature cosmological commitment to the sacred and profane cultural principles that lie behind the mock-demonic plunge into formlessness.

The festival is thus a very old game that makes one new, a means of transcending prosaic existence in order to be able to live in it most of the time, a shared ecstasy that subverts in order to integrate, unites the sacred and profane. *

But to explore the human hunger for the ecstatic we need not limit ourselves to the exotic. We can turn to the more immediate and constant adult quest for sexual pleasure and experience of sexual union. Here we have much to learn about the mysterious blending of sex and death that has so long haunted our literary and psychological imaginations.

Freud viewed sex and death as "the great instinctual adversaries." Within his ingenious dualism, these adversaries do battle at all levels. They contend for control of each individual psyche and for the fate of the human species. Yet in Freud's view of everyday (or proximate) experience, death has no place. To be sure, aggression and destructiveness and even guilt derive from the "death instinct." But that instinct is as vague as it is cosmic. Only the other of the adversaries, sexuality, provides the image-content and texture of individual psychological development. Even in Freud's later work, with its greater emphasis upon aggression, death remains, psychologically or at least *conceptually* speaking, absent from ordinary life. Sexuality, from the beginning, provides the imagery and energy that keeps life going.

Ernest Becker, in contrast, provides a death-centered view, within which sexuality seems much less important. Becker stresses man's inexorable conflict between the body and the self—the body a perpetual reminder that we die, the self always striving toward "cosmic specialness" or a form of "heroism" that is "first and foremost a reflection of the terror of death." Life itself becomes an existential entrapment. And sexuality, through its association with death, epitomizes that entrapment: "[Sex] reminds [man] that he is nothing himself but a link in the chain of being, exchangeable with any other and completely expendable in himself." And, "From the very beginning . . . the sexual act represents a double negation: by physical death and of distinctive personal gifts." [12] The sexual energies Freud associated with life-power now become little

---

* In Eliade's terms one moves out of "historical [linear] time" into a realm of sacred or "mythic" timelessness. Eliade sees these festivals as reactualizing a sacred event of the mythical past, one that took place "in the beginning," and which "can be homologized to eternity." What he calls the "continuous present," then, is a kind of absolute temporal harmony. [11] That form of exquisite centering in relationship to time—with imagery reaching back to earliest beginnings and extending indefinitely forward toward the eternal—probably enters into all forms of experiential transcendence.

more than provokers of death-terror. That terror subsumes all else and provides most of the content and texture of existence.

This view reverses Freud's experiential precedence of sex over death, but it seems to me to retain both the dualism (self versus body instead of eros versus death) and the monolithic causation within that dualism (death-terror instead of sexuality) that have so bedeviled Freudian theory.

We need a different perspective. And to that purpose the sex act can prod the mind no less than the body toward a view that is dialectic rather than dualistic, formative rather than monocausal, and centered on direct experience. The sex act is unique in its combination of intense physical pleasure with total psychic immersion and boundlessness. The ideal of the sex act, then, is a double merging—of the physical and psychological into a unique blend of feeling, and of two individuals into something like a single, transcendent entity. That ideal—let us call it the heterosexual vision—haunts and stirs the adult psyche throughout its small triumphs, failures, and absurdities. When the ideal is approached, the self is both nonexistent and most alive.

Consider the expressions of that vision in two literary men separated by three hundred and fifty years (and by just about everything else), John Donne and Norman Mailer. In Donne's poem, "The Ecstasy," sexual union is the ultimate source of wisdom no less than pleasure. Two souls that "spake the same," Donne tells us, "a new concoction take" that enables the lover to "part far purer than he came." Donne connects this special "knowledge" with both immediate encounters and ultimate human images:

> This ecstasy doth unperplex
>   (We said) and tell us what we love,
> We see by this, it was not sex,
>   We see, we saw not what did move. . . .

> A single violet transplant,
>   The strength, the colour, and the size,
> (All which before was poor and scant)
>   Redoubles still, and multiplies. . . .

> We then, who are this new soul, know
>   Of what we are composed, and made. . . .

> So soul into the soul may flow,
>   Though it to body first repair. . . .

> Because such fingers need to knit
>   That subtle knot, which makes us man. . . .

> To our bodies turn we then, that so
>   Weak men on love revealed may look;
> Love's mysteries in souls do grow,
>   But yet the body is his book.
>
> And if some lover, such as we,
>   Have heard this dialogue of one,
> Let him still mark us, he shall see
>   Small change, when we're two bodies gone.[13]

As a metaphysical poet, Donne's ultimate concept is that of the soul. But he also gives the body its due, as "book" or text of the soul's ecstasy. Ecstatic knowledge emerges from being "moved" and from recognizing what most moves us, what enables us to feel most alive. The answer for Donne lies beyond sex itself in the special *experience* of the expanded and exquisitely connected soul or self. One leaves the ecstatic encounter renewed, infused by its indelible image. The self has been purified and vitalized, is now closer to wholeness and integrity. The loving sexual union, that is, is man's ultimate source of awareness and form.

Norman Mailer's voice seems at first to come from a different planet, but is what he says (taking off from the work of Henry Miller) much different?

> He [Miller] has slipped the clue across . . . a clue to the lust that drives a man to scour his balls and his back until he is ready to die from the cannonading he has given his organs, the deaths through which he has dragged some features of his soul, it is a clue which all but says that somewhere in the insane passions of all men is a huge desire to drive forward into that seat of creation, grab some part of that creation in the hands, sink the cock to the hilt, sink it into as many hilts as will hold it; for man is alienated from the nature which brought him forth, he is not like woman in possession of an inner space which gives her link to the future, so he must drive to possess it, he must if necessary come close to blowing his head off that he may possess it. [In Miller's words] "Perhaps a cunt, smelly though it may be, is one of the prime symbols for the connection between all things."[14]

Mailer's heterosexual vision is no less lyrical—no less romantic—than Donne's. There is a direct echo of Donne in the Mailer-Miller principle of the "cunt [as] one of the prime symbols for the connection between all things," the contrast in language rendering the similarity all the more impressive. *

Mailer goes on to become more explicit about the male quest for immortality via the encounter with the female and her "seat of creation." He speaks of

---

* The main difference may be in the Mailer-Miller location of the ultimate "connection" in a specific bodily place as opposed to Donne's in the total experience of sexual union. But even that difference seems minimal, since either "place" is important only as a kind of metaphor or symbol of transcendence.

"man's sense of awe before woman, his dread of her position one step closer to eternity," as the cause of his tendency to "detest women, defile them, humiliate them, defecate symbolically upon them, do everything to reduce them so that one might dare to enter them and take pleasure of them." Hence, men "go through the years of their sex with women in some compound detachment of lust which will enable them to be as fierce as any female awash in the great ocean of fuck, for as it can appear to the man, great forces beyond his measure seem to be calling to the woman then." Man's envy of woman, Mailer is telling us, is the ultimate kind—a life-creating envy, an immortality envy. And out of that envy he degrades her. Now a number of psychological writers, from Horney to Bettelheim, have discussed male envy of woman's capacity to become pregnant and give birth. But more fundamental is the image of woman as source, possessor, and guardian of the life process itself; and of sexual union as an absolute expression of centering in which the immediate blends with the ultimate and the present with a sense of timelessness.

The experience of awe and dread, then, extends beyond male imagery of women—or woman's imagery of herself, or for that matter female imagery of men.* Awe and dread on the part of both sexes has to do with the special psychic investment that we human beings, death-aware creatures that we are, make in the sex act. That act seems to have to do more for us than for other creatures. We depend upon it for reproducing and maintaining the life of our species (here we are no different from other animals). But we also rely upon it—pursue it quietly or flamboyantly, calmly or desperately—as our most primal and consistent source of immediate and ultimate connectedness, vitality, and (for many) integrity. Much of our terror of the sex act has to do with the gap between what we demand and what we can receive from it. Sexual ecstasy is real but tantalizingly transient; its "pure" and centered pleasure contrasts painfully with our more enduring mind-body confusions and pervasive death equivalents. Yet the sex act seems not only to evoke these death-centered contrasts but to require them. We can experience the transcendent only because we know too well the prosaic. Our capacity for symbolizing and *feeling* in the sex act dimensions beyond our finiteness is inseparable from our fearful awareness of death, separation, disintegration. I do not mean that this experience of intense vitality is merely compensatory, or that sexual transcendence in itself is no more than a denial of death. Rather, sexual transcendence and death awareness are part of the dialectic bequeathed in human evolution, a dialectic that, perpetually unresolved, lives at the heart of human energies.

---

* "Penis envy" may well be related to female envy of immortalizing male power. Girls perceive very early that the organ seems to be associated with a variety of adult attitudes encouraging its possessor to be assertive and to share various skills and forms of authority that can later be equated with the kinds of ultimate symbolization of life-continuity (around work and works, for instance) that we have discussed under the concept of symbolic immortality.

Our sense of the gap between demand and actuality is painfully heightened when the experience itself grants us no more than a glimmer of routinized or ambivalent pleasure, or when we judge our "performance" to be a failure. Unrealized transcendence, in the face of our hunger for it, renders us newly vulnerable to waves of our own death imagery. We cannot understand this dialectic of sex and death as merely the one representing a vital force and the other lifelessness—for death can be vitalizing and sex deadening. What the dialectic contains most fundamentally is the human struggle to combine awareness of death, loss, and terror with the capacity to feel, love, transcend, and become whole.

We are now in a better position to understand that the special state of experiential transcendence is the indicator of the other four modes of symbolic immortality—that, wildly or gently, one must psychologically travel outside oneself in order to feel one's participation in the larger human process. The claim assumes that a quality of *experience* (that of transcendence) must connect with significant *content* (grounded relationship to any of the other four modes) to vitalize that sense of participation. There seem to be various translations between experience and content, involving all five modes. Profound awareness of loving connection to the continuing human nexus through one's children and theirs can evoke moments of felt transcendence; and ecstatic experience of sexual love—or of intense beauty—can evoke the sense of those endless biological ties. Our feelings move in and out of the various modes, and the ecstatic message may be no more than a momentary sense of pleasure or wholeness. But even then our principle (and I refer to a strictly psychological principle) prevails: ecstasy when grounded and full is our source of awareness of larger connection.

The psychological key to the principle is the state of near-perfect centering. With inner forms in harmony, psychic action is intense and focused, and there is a free flow of psychic and bodily energy—all in the "continuous present." Whether the initiating event seems primarily psychic (as in contemplation or meditation) or physical (as in the sex act), or is some combination of these, the resulting awareness and energy flow are in the truest sense psychosomatic.

Would it not be better to speak of a "sense of continuity" rather than a "sense of immortality" to convey these ideas? One cannot deny the extensive baggage—philosophical, emotional, religious—carried by the word immortality.

The feelings described here include a sense of continuity, but they also extend to the order of experience Kenneth Rexroth has called "the ecology of infinity." Infinity means unbounded—whether in space, time, or (as the dictionary adds) "quality." An aspect of the quality of infinity, then, is the idea of eternity, which means everlastingness. Immortality as "endless life" can also be placed within this ecology. Finally there is transcendence, a state beyond the self's immediate involvements. These words describe specific experiences that can be examined within the broad realm of natural history. Psychological science should enter the domain it has tended either to ignore, further mystify, or else misrepresent by nervously and reductively invoking its own clinical terms instead of examining the phenomenology of man's experience of his larger connectedness. Depth psychology is capable of returning to an area it has mostly abandoned to the theologians. The formative, life-continuity paradigm provides a framework for addressing this domain of "ultimate concern" and charting some of the ecology of infinity.

None of this is meant to imply that the sense of immortality is inevitably constructive or healthy. The ecstatic component of that sense can be pursued all too easily by means of murder and terror, no less than by love and creative works. While this study is devoted to making psychological distinctions between the two, it rests on the assumption that, whatever the consequences, the quest for symbolic immortality is an aspect of being human.

THREE

The Inchoate Image

WITHIN THE FRAME of the ultimate involvements we have been discussing are *immediate* feelings about death and continuity. But how do such immediate feelings originate, and then evolve over the life cycle? Are they present at birth as part of immutable instinct? Or do we acquire them through learning? Neither instinct nor learning can account for the beginnings of our feelings about death. We require a bridging concept that allows for both innate tendencies and considerable mutability. For that purpose we may speak of an *inchoate image*.

Although the term "image" suggests the visual it has been regularly used to include almost any form of psychic representation. In early Freudian and Jungian usage, image was closely related to instinct, and was thought to be biologically inherited. Classical psychoanalysis, for instance, referred to "imago" (image-representations) of parents and parent-substitutes, derived from a combination of instinct and infantile experience, preserved in the individual unconscious over the course of the life cycle, and genetically transmitted from generation to generation. Jungian psychology has carried the concept of inherited "primordial images" still further by viewing them as elements of "archetypes" (unconscious representations of the most fundamental human themes) of the "collective unconscious" that are derived from the whole of human historical and evolutionary experience. Jung always made clear that he considered the archetypes and their primordial images to be the visual or representational components of instinct. The instinctualism of Freud and Jung in many ways obscured their concepts of the image, and a contemporary image-theorist understandably feels the need to break out of that instinctualism. But instinctualization of the image was an effort on the part of these two giants to convey their sense of the primal quality of the image, which, within the prevailing intellectual currents, meant calling forth the instinctual idiom. If we can rescue the image for a formative-symbolizing age without losing a sense of its primal qualities, we can perhaps begin to recognize more clearly *the central significance of the image for all of human motivation.*

Recent work in psychology has been moving in this direction, but considerable controversy remains about the nature of the image and how inclusive it is.[1] Few question characterizing it as "psychic representation" or "thought representation." And most are willing to extend that principle beyond the visual to include all sensory perception, so that we may speak of auditory, tactile, olfactory, or taste images as well. But there is a still more radical view that strains at the very limits of the psychic-representation concept to suggest the idea of the image as a "plan" for the organism, whatever the level of awareness of that plan. Important expressions of this view come from biological and social theorists who bring a sense of larger patterning to immediate observations on human behavior. This sense of the image as plan—let us say interpretive plan—provides a useful way to understand the sequence of feeling about death and life from the beginning to the end of individual existence.

The Swiss biologist Adolf Portmann speaks of a "realm of images" or "inner world" that is present in lower as well as higher animal forms, which constitutes a kind of "self" and "involves the body as a whole." That primitive "self," for instance, can guide the regeneration of each part of a planaria (a form of flatworm) that has been cut in half. Portmann sees a parallel in the "self"(or realm of images) contained in the human gene, a guiding self that "builds a brain with all the sense organs, and lays the basis for the emergence of a conscious ego." Portmann gropes toward a concept of guiding imagery that combines the innate with the basic features of a species' psychobiological life plan.[2]

Norman Cameron expresses a similar spirit in a specifically psychological approach. He speaks of the early internal imagery that "keeps the infant 'on course'" in its feeding activities. And he goes on to define imagery more generally as "active central [nervous system] representation" that "marks the beginning of an internal functioning . . . now generally called mental or psychic functioning."[3] Thus Portmann's innate biological guide becomes, with Cameron, the basis for the distinctly human forms of mental activity.

Kenneth Boulding, economist by trade and brilliant gadfly of social and ethical thought, goes still further in using a concept of the image to incorporate what he considers to be common principles of communication and information at every level of biological and social behavior. For Boulding even the lowliest of creatures, the one-celled amoeba, "has something like an image of its universe," which enables it to divide that universe "into food and non-food, [so that] the messages which it receives from the particles with which it comes into contact are interpreted and classified according to this abstract system." Like

Portmann, though in a communications idiom, Boulding speaks of an image operating genetically as "a teaching-learning operation" stressing "the organization of matter into pattern structures through the transfer of information." He then, at a more general level, lays stress on the important motivational principle that "behavior depends on the image," and the historical (and formative) principle that the image is "built up as a result of all past experience of the possessor of the image" so that "part of the image is the history of the image itself."[4]

Susanne Langer equates this Gestalt quality with an interpretive or conceptual dimension: "Only an image can hold us to a conception of a total phenomenon, against which we can measure the adequacy of the scientific terms wherewith we describe it." For her the image is both "a genuine conception" and a carrier of a "whole cargo of feeling," central as it is to the overall symbolizing process.[5] Thus, Langer, while retaining some of Boulding's "image radicalism," shifts its focus from information to feeling and to the specifically human attributes of symbolization and meaning.

In earlier work I spoke of "modes of imagery" and "images of time" to suggest emotionally charged conceptions of self and world (ideology), and their relationship to ongoing personal development (self-process). At an interface between psychology and history this approach adhered to Boulding's principle that "behavior depends on the image." Furthering that principle I defined the individual image as a *structured anticipation of interaction with the environment.* * It is necessary to distinguish between the image as an immediate link of the nervous system and the environment, and the psychic constellation as a more enduring and complex symbolization containing many images. Here the distinction is one of degree. No adult image is a simple recording of the external environment—one receives no perceptions nakedly. The image comes into being only through central nervous system involvement—through inner recreation of whatever is encountered from the outside. That is the basic law of symbolization, which both images and constellations, as varieties of psychic forms, must obey.[6]

The self is the most inclusive of all individual forms, one's symbolization of one's own organism. Within our paradigm, maintaining the life of the self—an overall sense of organismic vitality—becomes the central motivating principle for psychic action, for the creation and recreation of images and constellations. That principle of organismic vitality applies to image formation from the beginning of life (long before one can speak of a sense of self) in relationship to the earliest psychic precursors of the self.

The image, then, is integral to human life. Its absence or breakdown

---

*While working with me on this perspective, Eric Olson came to a more succinct characterization of the image as "a schema for enactment."

threatens life. Indeed human existence itself can be understood as a quest for vitalizing images and image-constellations.

There is evidence that by the time of birth the quest is well under way. To reject instinct theory is by no means to understand the newborn as a *tabula rasa* or blank screen. We have, in fact, overwhelming evidence of the infant's inborn inclination toward enhancing its own life process. It "expects" to be fed, and "knows" something about how to make use of the breast or its substitute. The vital image here is the newborn's inchoate organismic inclination toward receiving the nurturing it requires.

Given the combination of the innateness of these patterns and the absence in the newborn of anything we could speak of as an "inner life," one can readily understand the temptation, on the part of Freud and many others, to consider this behavior "instinctual." But there are difficulties in doing so, which become evident when we take a closer look at what Freud meant by "instinctual drive." Freud viewed that concept as "on the frontier between the mental and the somatic . . . the . . . physical representative of the stimuli originating from within the organism and reaching the mind, as a measure of the demand made upon the mind of work in consequence of its connection with the body."[7] The strength of the concept lies precisely in its blending of biological and psychic elements to explain behavior. Its weakness, however, is its dichotomy between the two dimensions, and particularly its nineteenth-century assumptions of primary physicalistic forces creating secondary psychological effects. These assumptions, in turn, lead all too readily to (perhaps require) Freud's grand dualistic vision of "instinctual antagonists"—and of course away from a unitary framework.

Freud actually vacillated on the issue of "psychic representation" of instinctual drives (reflecting both the basic problem in his instinctual-physicalistic perspective as well as his achievement in transcending that perspective). As James Strachey, his leading translator, points out, Freud sometimes regarded instinct itself as the psychic representative of somatic or bodily forces, and at other times he drew a sharp distinction between the two, describing instinct as a *non*psychic part of a somatic impulse.[8] Thus in his first two instinctual formulations—the sexual and self-preservative drives, and then the erotic and destructive drives—Freud understood these instincts to have specific psychic representation (for instance, sexual fantasies and feelings). But psychic representation was considerably less clear in relationship to his last formulation of instinctual dualism—the life and death instincts. Freud, in fact, stressed the absence of psychic representation of the death instinct in particular. And as early as 1915 (in his paper, "The Unconscious"), he definitively separated the somatic instinct and its psychic representation.

An instinct can never become an object of consciousness—only the idea that represents the instinct can. Even in the unconscious, moreover, an instinct cannot be represented otherwise than by an idea. If the instinct did not attach itself to an idea or manifest itself as an affective state, we could know nothing about it.[9]

Freud needed to call upon something like this "idea" to move from the somatic to the psychological. Then, in juxtaposing "idea" and "affective state," Freud suggested a level of organismic logic or direction that subsumes them both. But rather than pursue that level of understanding around integrative concepts of image and symbolization, Freud's instinctual paradigm required him to understand both idea and affective state as secondary to physico-mechanical energic forces, whether sexual energy (libido) or aggressive or destructive energy (derived from the death instinct). That energy, the driving force of the organism, was produced much in the way a generator produces steam or electricity; and when blocked or dammed up, had harmful consequences for the organism.

Instead we may speak of a vital or controlling image, which determines the direction of the organism's activity and calls forth the energy for that activity. This image is an inborn psychobiological plan or scenario which, if realized, allows for increasing malleability. The image is inchoate because it is essentially a vector or direction of the organism, prior to the image-awareness it presages. The inchoate image is a product of human evolution, and, in fact, serves as a connecting point between evolution and the beginning individual life cycle. (We recall Boulding's observation that the image is "built up as a result of all past experience of the possessor [so that] . . . part of the image is the history of the image itself.") With early psychological development the inchoate image gradually takes on psychic flesh in the form of sensory impressions and increasingly symbolized constellations of feeling, including ideation. This formative sequence is no less somatic than psychological; a sharp distinction between the two no longer serves us.

Man's symbol-making tendencies distinguish him from lower animals, but his dependence upon the image suggests his evolutionary continuity with all animal species.* In the human life cycle there is a progression from the physiological to the symbolic—or, more accurately, the exclusively physiological to the physiological-symbolic (in the sense that the symbolic function is an expression of, and subsumes, physiological function). That progression, like much of individual development, retraces the phylogenetic (or evolutionary) history of our species. These various levels are integrated in the image—that is, the imagery that evolves over the course of the life cycle.

* No wonder this mode of thought has been pioneered by biologists (Portmann, von Bertalanffy and John Tyler Bonner) and by philosophers of science and culture with a bent for integrative visions that transcend individual disciplines (Susanne Langer, Ernst Cassirer, Lancelot Law Whyte, and Kenneth Boulding). Especially pertinent is Langer's description of the symbol-making function as "one of man's primary activities, like eating, looking, or moving about . . . the fundamental process of his mind . . . *essential to thought*, and prior to it."[10]

Recent work in two important areas, ethology and studies of sleep and dreaming, are relevant here. Both areas combine increasingly established findings with highly controversial implications. But each, while awaiting its grand consolidation, provides highly suggestive data for a concept of the inchoate image.

Ethology has been characterized by its systematic observations on animals either in their natural environments or in environments that either closely resemble or are modified for contrast with the natural one. As ethologists came to document consistent behavior patterns in animals with clear resemblance to human counterparts, there has been a tendency to celebrate a reassertion of instinctual determinism.[11] But careful evaluation of ethological findings has suggested something else: the profound complexity of behavior patterns, their reliance on innate tendencies and environmental responses, even in the "lowest" animal species. These complexities have made numerous ethologists humble before the word "instinct," so that many no longer use it in relationship to man and some have abandoned it altogether.

Whatever their view of instinct, ethologists have emphasized a "reaction chain" that parallels the controlling function for the inchoate image of the human newborn. Ethologists, for instance, speak of "reaction-specific energy" to describe the dependence of the organism upon particular kinds of environmental experience (such as feeding opportunities provided by the mother) for its life energies to be maintained. The young animal is said to demonstrate "appetitive behavior," which propels it toward such desirable environmental "stimuli," so that its built-in physiological mediator ("innate releasing mechanism") can interact with environmental "sign stimuli" to produce the "consummatory act" or "end-response"—whether that of feeding, fighting, display, or whatever. Prior to these observations, the final link in the chain had been too simply understood as the entire "instinct."[12] *

In nonhuman species the overall pattern tends to be relatively fixed and limited in variation, and in that sense can be called instinctual. Human newborns *seem* to start out that way too, but from the beginning their inchoate imagery contains the potential for the more elaborate and varied environmental encounters they are to have. And over the course of the human life cycle every "act" or "response" becomes infused with symbolized function. If the term

* Susanne Langer, without necessarily disagreeing with many of the ethologists' observations, has criticized what she calls their "highly simplified mechanical model" reflected by such terms as "stimulus," "releasers," and "triggers." She suggests an alternative "conception of animal life as an advancing stream of activity," and a view of animal acts as "all made out of elements in the agent's native repertoire and steered by the current advance of the motivating situation . . . from move to move."[13] In this way she brings ethological observations nearer to a prehuman version of an innate, inchoate image that anticipates and propels the animal toward specific environmental interactions.

"reaction chain" can be used at all, it is open, attuned to a self-generating human imagination with its endless flow of prospective inner forms. The human brain requires that we do no less. As in the case of other animals there are biological limits to the process. These are most clear during early infancy, but the extraordinary human symbolic repertoire makes sharp definition of any such limits extremely difficult.

The inchoate image, then, is man's innate plan as a cultural animal.[14] Directing the newborn toward what his environment can offer, that image may be viewed as a crucial link between the organism and culture. Culture infuses the plan contained in the image, so that from the standpoint of life history as well as from evolution, "cultural resources are ingredient, not accessory, to human thought."[15]

The inchoate image both parallels and initiates the individual into inchoate culture:

> The crux of the matter is this: Even if a species sheds its dependence on instincts, it still has to do the same things that instincts were designed to do . . . to get culture to do the same jobs as instinct had been doing, one had to make cultural behavior in many ways like instinctive behavior. It had to be "automatic" so that certain stimuli would automatically produce it, and it had to be common to all members of the population. . . . [Mind] got there—as did every other natural and biological feature—by natural selection. The tool-making animal needed mind to survive; that is, he needed language and culture and the reorganization of experience that goes with these. And having got the rudiments and become dependent on them, there was no turning back, there was no retreat to the perilous certainty of instinct. It was mind or nothing.[16]

The inchoate image exemplifies the human shift from instinct to culture. As such it anticipates cultural complexity in its function as a built-in psycho-biological guide.

Studies of sleep and dreaming raise questions about imagery in a different way. Conducted mostly on humans but also on other mammals, they have uncovered what some investigators call a "third state," physiologically distinct from both sleep and wakefulness. The most dramatic feature of this state, and the basis for its discovery, is that of rapid eyeball movements (REM state). Other features are increased muscle movements (often including sucking activity), disappearance of postural tone, various forms of irregularity of the cardiac and respiratory systems, and increased brain activity as recorded by the electroen-cephalogram. Early reports closely correlated dream activity with the REM state, and although subsequent work has demonstrated dreaming to occur outside of the REM state as well, the general correlation seems to hold. Some observers have interpreted the eye movements to be the dreamer's visual response to his own dream content, as the following of objects and events in the dream. But since the eye and muscle movements occur in the human newborn, as well as in many other animal species (including guinea pigs in utero), this explanation is dubious.

More generally, does the newborn infant actually dream? Or does it undergo some form of hallucinatory experience that is a precursor to dreaming and resembles dreaming? Considering those questions, and extending them to the guinea pig in utero, one is reminded of Beckett's question: "Who knows what the ostrich sees in the sand?" One psychoanalytic researcher gives a classical Freudian interpretation to the effect that the REM state reveals in the newborn the "pressure of instinctual drives toward discharge," and thereby serves the same function as the dream itself later does.* In all this, confusions remain around "instinct" and "psychic representation," and the obscurities surrounding the relationship between the two.

But there is a way out. A number of observers have begun to view the REM phenomenon as a more general central nervous system process, having to do not only with vision but with the development and maintenance of brain function around learning, focal attention, and memory.[18] Of special interest to us is the suggestion of one research group that this marked REM activity in very young human organisms may represent neurophysiological preparation for later image function.†

In other words, REM states may be understood as still another, primarily neurophysiological, manifestation of inchoate imagery. And "'dreaming' as physiological process" may be understood as the organism's direct preparation for the later dreaming function.‡ We may say that in most mammals the later image formation is associated either with instinct or with learning that is closely related to instinct, while in humans it extends to the near-infinite reaches of

---

* Another investigator, without entirely disagreeing, puts the matter more searchingly: "If anyone should insist upon the notion that the four-hour-old infant is hallucinating a breast which it has never seen, I would object; but what we now know of the REMS is certainly not incompatible with Freud's premise that dreaming begins as the hallucinatory gratification of elementary needs, primarily oral in nature."[17]

† In their own more technical words, a "neurophysiological setting for hallucinatory repetition of accumulated experience."[19] Assuming that "the REM state must originate from inborn neurophysiological processes, as opposed to being engendered by experience," they further suggest: "Prior to the infant's acquisition of visual perception and visual memory, rudimentary hallucinations might be expressed in sensory modalities in which intrauterine experience has occurred. Speculations aside, however, whether or not "dreaming" understood as subjective sensation exists in the newborn, "'dreaming' understood as physiological process certainly does."

‡ Or it may be, as Susanne Langer claims, in her discussion of the REM state, "an independent process with its own dynamic pattern, probably an elementary cerebral function." She has in mind a more general preparation of the central nervous system for complex behavior of various kinds that may not even be primarily visual. In response to her own question about what the eyeball movements have to do with dreaming, she answers: "Probably, nothing and everything. Nothing direct, such as recording dream events or starting the hallucinatory process; but everything, in that the periodic

symbolization. In that sense we can speak of the REM state as the kind of evolutionary meeting-ground we mentioned earlier in our discussion of the inchoate image. Whether or not primarily visual in its prospective function, it clearly involves the entire organism. And it equally clearly prefigures crucial forms of further development—which is why it is most intense in young organisms. The REM state, as an observable manifestation of the inchoate image, suggests to us in an evolutionary as well as an ontological sense, the beginnings of the human capacity for dreaming, for holding visions, for prospective imagination.

---

reinforcement of forebrain activity is essential for hallucinations [dream images] to occur."[20] That more general relationship to brain development is consistent with the inchoate image as a Gestalt guide for the organism rather than as a prefiguring of later visual imagery. But given the close relationship between early brain development and the capacity for imagery, the difference in the two views may be negligible.

FOUR

The Natural Unity of Death

THE SEQUENCE FROM INSTINCT to image has special importance for our approach to death and continuity. While recognizing the significance of Freud's discoveries, we must question his rendering of instinct as the ultimate and transcendent human quality. That is, we need to replace this "biomysticism" with something closer to a natural history of the self in both its immediate and ultimate connections. We seek a psychology that is evolutionary in spirit, genuinely biological in its focus on image-making.

This image-centered view, together with the stress on symbolic immortality, enables us to cast a critical eye on certain forms of conventional wisdom concerning death. Consider, for instance, Merleau-Ponty's contention that

> Neither my birth nor my death can appear to me as *my* experiences . . . I can only grasp myself as "already born" and "still living"—grasping my birth and death only as pre-personal horizons.[1]

Merleau-Ponty here echoes Freud's assertion that it is "indeed impossible to imagine our own death." He is, in fact, more explicit than Freud in his assertion of the absence of psychological access to either of our two transitions between "this side" and "the other side," between life and nonlife. But as a proper theorist of the subjective, his statement is more qualified than Freud's in its focus on the self or the "I" ("I can only grasp myself as 'already born' and 'still living' . . .").

Yet the matter is not nearly so absolute as both Merleau-Ponty and Freud would have it. The child's preoccupation with origins and the adult's anticipation of death are in one sense efforts to grasp birth and death as aspects or experiences of the self. Depending entirely upon my capacity for constructing images, for symbolic imagination, I can at least approach a point where these fundamental events "appear to me as my experiences"—at least in the sense of images I call forth of "the beginning" and "the end" of my own self.

The basic issue is the capacity to imagine not so much the event or the moment (of being born, of dying) as some form of relationship to the existential fact that one was born, that one will die. In terms of death specifically the prospective (postdeath) distinction between "*my* world" and "*the* world" has been mentioned earlier. One needs that distinction in order to have the capacity and courage to relinquish the self; and only in that capacity can death be anticipated as a destiny that is inherent in the very existence of the self, of the "I." The opposite, absolute equation between "my world" and "the world" reflects a fundamental impairment in self-concept, an inability to recognize the self's boundaries, or the fact that the self *has* boundaries, in the general human dialectic of separateness and larger connection.

There are two meanings to the word death—the act of dying and the state of nonlife. The first is associated with suffering and loss, the second with the nonexistence of the self. Yet, to consider these two meanings as unrelated is misleading: they are part of a basic unity.

For example, one psychoanalytic writer insists that "death as such is not feared," and anxiety about death is actually "anxiety of ugly dying" or "dread of the process of dying, fears of violent, helpless, painful, protracted and useless dying."[2] There is something too schematic, too absolute in this distinction. What is required instead is a dialectical view that retains distinctions between our images of death as a state and dying as an event, and at the same time enables us to perceive them together in a unitary anticipation, a single constellation. The fact that the word death serves as a noun for both process (of dying) and state (of nonbeing) is a hint in that direction. When I think of my death, my fears include images of debility and helplessness (from old age or illness); of an end to and absence of "me" and my relationships and projects; and a further image of that end coming when these projects and relationships are at a flawed, incomplete state. This, in turn, results in anxious dissatisfaction at my way of living them.

Whatever our criteria for death ("brain death" as opposed to the cessation of breathing), and whether we give emphasis to the event or the state, we understand death as involving the entire organism. As symbolized images reflect that totality, so should our conceptualizations. This can be accomplished by holding to a unitary principle even as we seek precision in distinctions.

From this unitary perspective there are a number of ways of symbolizing death.[3]

The first and most fundamental is the perception of death as the end of life, as a form of organic and psychological destiny, part of the "natural history" of each of us. However that basic perception is resisted, denied, distanced by means of psychic numbing, it continues to underlie whatever additional constructs or gaps we call forth in our symbolizing activity.

A second perception of death is mimetic, that of life imitating death: the idea of "death in life," or loss of vitality, or being frozen in some form of death terror as mentioned earlier.* The reversal is perceived as "unnatural"—life becomes deathlike precisely because of the numbed negation of death, and *only* the dead possess "vitality." But this seemingly unnatural reversal is, in fact, a continuous (and therefore "natural") potential of the organism, both necessary and highly dangerous.

A third meaning of death, that of challenge and even muse, equates (with Böll) the artist's relationship to death with the priest's to his breviary. That symbolization depends upon a heightened awareness of the natural function of death as a counterpoint to life, and as an ever-present limitation that gives shape to existence and grounding to wisdom.

Death is rendered formative by its very naturalness. In real psychological ways one must "know death" in order to live with free imagination.

A fourth meaning is that of death as inseparable from disaster, holocaust, absurdity. One's individual death cannot be separated from the sense that (as Hiroshima survivors put it) "the whole world is dying." This perception is truly unnatural. It is partly a product of our holocaust-dominated age, discussed later in connection with imagery of extinction that haunts contemporary man. It is also connected with early exposure to specific forms of the kind of imagery (school children subjected to drills as preparation for nuclear war) that brings about the equation of death and holocaust. But even in the absence of holocaust, people can equate the end of the self with the end of everything. Where this latter tendency is present, one's own death is anticipated, irrespective of age and circumstances, as premature, absurd, unacceptable. Much of this book will concern this relationship between holocaust and individual-psychological struggles.

All four meanings, and others as well, are probably present in much of our death imagery. The relative importance of each of these meanings varies greatly, of course, especially around the issue of death as natural or unnatural. But death, for the human imagination, never ceases to be a many-sided, seemingly contradictory yet ultimately unitary psychological form.

That perspective helps place death both in our life and in our theory. There is, however, a specifically psychoanalytic obstacle to overcome: the tendency to subsume fear of death to fear of castration. Freud initiated this tendency with his insistence that "the fear of death should be regarded as analogous to the fear

---

*Heinrich Böll, who has sensitive antennae for such things, sums up this sense of reversal in the sentence, "The living are dead and the dead live."⁺

of castration,"[5] and that of the two only the fear of castration can have genuine psychic representation—can be genuinely experienced.* While Freud recognized that the fear of death "dominates us oftener than we know,"[6] he viewed it as "something secondary . . . usually the outcome of a sense of guilt."[7] He could finally "regard the fear of death, like the fear of conscience, as a development of the fear of castration."[8] As a result much subsequent Freudian thought has, almost automatically, turned away from the idea of death anxiety, turned away from death itself, and looked instead for the psychosexual conflict—that of castration anxiety—assumed to lie "underneath." †

The issue for us, at least for the moment, is the claim of primacy for castration anxiety as opposed to the secondary, compensatory quality assigned death anxiety. That false claim to primacy is maintained by two confusions. One has to do with the assumption that if (again in Freud's words) "death is an abstract concept with a negative content for which no unconscious correlative can be found,"[10] then it cannot be viewed as a fundamental or primary experience or motivation for behavior. Death is indeed essentially a negation— the epitome of all negations—but that does not mean that the mind has no way of "representing" death, of constructing its versions of death. Nor does it mean that such a representation or construction must be secondary to a more partial but also more concrete "negation," that of castration, the "cutting off" of the male organ—or of a counterpart in the female, the nature of which is never quite agreed upon. ‡ The second misunderstanding has to do with an ever-present human willingness (as observed by Eissler) to risk or court death on

---

* ". . . the unconscious seems to contain nothing that could give any content to our concept of the annihilation of life. Castration can be pictured on the basis of the daily experience of the feces being separated from the body or on the basis of losing the mother's breast at weaning. But nothing resembling death can ever be experienced; or if it has, as in fainting, has left no observable traces behind."

† Kurt Eissler, in a valuable exploration of many issues around death, defends Freud's conceptual position. Eissler goes on to emphasize that the fear of castration is so great that for many death seems preferable: "Man's reaction seems to be, with surprising frequency: rather dead than castrated."[9] But that little aphorism is more complicated than it seems. On one level Eissler mocks the notorious "Better dead than red!" slogan of the time, and suggests (with Freud) that castration, not death, is what men *really* fear. But the aphorism also suggests something else—namely that a transcendent principle (whether or not associated with despotic slogans) can take precedence over death itself. Outwardly that principle may be political (combating communism in the name of freedom) or psychological (avoiding castration and asserting manhood), but in either case becomes associated with some form of ultimate commitment, with a principle that extends in some way beyond the self. In a certain sense Freud made "instinct," and especially sexual instinct, into such an immortalizing principle.

‡ Sometimes Freud emphasized actual castration imagery in females, usually in the form of feeling "seriously wronged" from the beginning, so to speak, because of the absence of a penis.[11] At other times he stressed the fear of loss of love as being particularly strong in women and playing a role in them equivalent to that of castration

behalf of a life principle, either a vision one wishes to affirm (such as a revolution) or a fear or doubt one wishes to combat (concerning, say, one's masculinity). Even when this fear is literalized in an image of castration, overcoming it is associated with a larger vision, in this case that of male power (all too often the warrior ethos) that one seeks to affirm in oneself. Conscious fears about maleness are probably much more frequently experienced than fear of death. And everyone seems to agree that psychologically the two fears are closely related. Little is gained by arguing about which is more important, or even by assuming that one is completely secondary. Rather, both should be placed within a framework that is inclusive, applies to the entire life cycle, and suggests basic sources of experience and motivation. According to those criteria castration anxiety and fears about masculinity should be subsumed to a larger symbolic structure of death and continuity, and not the reverse.

It is important to understand Freud's conceptual neglect of death in terms of the innovator's inevitable one-sidedness—his characteristic need to neglect alternative possibilities as he presses his central discovery to, or even beyond, its limits. That one-sidedness, however, can be transmitted over generations of disciples, until eventually contested (perhaps by other innovators who are in turn subject to the same principle). In this sense there is evidence that depth psychology has been moving toward redressing the balance, so that castration anxiety is increasingly seen as a manifestation of death anxiety, the more inclusive phenomenon, instead of the reverse. But that redress is at best partial and intermittent, with inconsistencies and gaps surrounding impressions, therapeutic policies, and conceptual principles.

Freud's position in all this is not merely one-sided, but ·complex and enigmatic. On the one hand, he more or less dismissed death in a conceptual sense. On the other, he was profoundly aware of his own death anxiety, and wrote with great insight about the psychological costs of the denial of death in human life in general. Moreover, in the one area in which he gave death a prominent conceptual place—his theory of the death instinct—he provided the beginnings of a unitary view of life and death, even if hidden beneath his insistent instinctual dualism. That dualism is obvious enough: life versus death, Eros versus Thanatos. Or as Freud wrote in *Beyond the Pleasure Principle*:

> Our views have from the very first been *dualistic*, and today they are even more definitely dualistic than before—now that we describe the opposition as being, not between ego instincts and sexual instincts but between life instincts and death instincts.[12]

---

fear in men. The latter form of anxiety is associated with separation and loss, and is what we have been calling a death equivalent. Here we may say that Freud touches upon a very central matter but at the same time takes two dubious steps: he subsumes separation and loss to libido theory, and women's experience to a male model.

Yet there is an accompanying unitary vision, a quest for what L. L. Whyte called "one general form." One encounters that vision in statements of Freud as *"The aim of all life is death,"* and the dominating principle of mental life (even subsuming instinct itself) is *"a need to restore an earlier* [inorganic] *state of things."* [13] Freud's vision had a majestic quality that approached "one general form," even if vision and form were obscured by the instinctual mechanics of the specific theory.

And those mechanics are considerable. The "death instincts" become the ultimate source of all self-destructiveness, aggression, and violence (the last two seen as self-destructiveness turned outward)—in direct opposition to the sexual energy and love generated by the "life instincts." One result is a reductionist entrapment, within which real exploration of important questions—for instance, those of psychic representation and psychic energy—is virtually impossible. One can well understand the inclination on the part of Freudians, neo-Freudians, and post-Freudians alike to jettison the death instinct altogether. Yet doing that creates two other sizable pitfalls. One ignores the unitary vision Freud bootlegged into the death instinct, leaving one in most cases devoid of a unitary vision altogether. And one is also likely to lose the idea of death in general as important to human motivation. As a result, depth psychologists are inclined to ignore questions of death imagery, or at best to address them in seemingly more precise, but actually more fragmented, ways than did Freud.

There have been some interesting exceptions. Perhaps the least of these has been the attempt not only to retain the death instinct but to instill it with an energic counterpart of libido: concepts of "mortido" and "destrudo" occasionally proposed by psychoanalysts to suggest quantitative emanations of destructive psychic energy from the death instinct. Much more useful and provocative have been the occasional glimmers of Freud's unitary spirit. We need to implement that unitary principle in a psychology that integrates death with the life-processes.*

---

*Consider Eissler's statement that "one could . . . view the panorama of instinctual processes as a secret cooperation between the two, as Freud has done at one point." But Eissler's wisdom—he makes many other valuable observations—is at least partly vitiated by an ultimate commitment to a more mechanistic instinctualism than Freud's.

> Without the instincts of life, the death instincts would reach their goal in a short-circuit-like manner. Life would cease as suddenly as a clock whose spring had broken. The instincts of death would not—if that image is accepted—find their proper resistance in the instincts of life which would thus enable the instincts of death to take their full and unbending course. [14]

Norman O. Brown at first appears to do much better. He is critical of Freud's "preference for dualism rather than dialectics," and insists that "What our argument is reaching for is not death rather than life but a reconciliation of life and death." And in the electrifying images of his classic *Life Against Death,* [15] he explores man's struggle with

This book, then, is not a thanatology per se. While a thanatology can be liberating in its insistent exposure of death-linked dimensions, so long ignored and denied in psychological theory among other places, it runs the risk of

---

death as the fundamental source of human anxiety. Brown's achievements render all the more troubling his simplistic resolution of the matter in a vision of instinctual restoration: the lifting of repression and return to the unbounded, "polymorphous perverse" instincts of infancy and childhood. Even where Brown seeks a unitary vision, he must find it in a harmonious joining of the two great instinctual antagonists to achieve "the primal unity Eros seeks to reinstate in its unity with its opposite, the death instinct." Brown, in fact, goes further than either Eissler or Freud in projecting an instinctual utopia beyond history itself: "After man's unconscious search for his proper mode of being has ended—after history has ended—particular members of the human species can lead a life which, like the lives of lower organisms, individually embodies the nature of the species. . . . The attainment of individuality by the human species would therefore mean the return of the restless pleasure-principle to the peace of the Nirvana-principle."[16]

Brown's visionary brilliance can take hold of the reader and render *Life Against Death* an extraordinary, transcendent experience. But when one comes down from that experience and probes that vision more carefully and more deeply, one realizes that it depends upon a misperception of human mental life, and of its symbolizing nature. Brown can thus say that "the *animal symbolicum* (Cassirer's definition of man) is *animal sublimans*, committed to substitute symbolical gratification of instincts for real gratification, the desexualized animal."[17]

But then Brown, without exactly telling anyone, in his next book, *Love's Body*, dramatically reverses his position: "When the problem in psychoanalysis becomes not repression, but symbolism; when we discover that even if there were no dream-censor we should still have symbolism, then personality (soul, ego) becomes not substance, but fiction, representation; and the primal form of politics becomes not domination (repression), but representation."[18]

Here Brown moves from his literalized (in a way post-Reichian) instinctual utopia toward a formative-symbolizing perspective. But the aphoristic quality of *Love's Body*— the book consists of a series of separate, exquisite, dazzling, metaphysically slippery, and ephemeral paragraphs—does not lend itself to clarification of matters instinctual, imagistic, and symbolic.

Ernest Becker takes us beyond Brown on these death-centered matters. Toward Freud's death instinct, he is unambiguously critical and yet sympathetic, seeing it as a "device that enabled [Freud] to keep intact the earlier instinct theory, now by attributing human evil to a deeper organic substratum than merely ego conflict with sexuality." And he is in accord with our argument when he points out that this instinctual model "allowed Freud to keep the terror of death outside his formulations [and avoid seeing that terror] as a primary human problem of ego mastery." Becker then takes us on a magnificent journey centered always on precisely that terror of annihilation.

In the process, however, he builds a *compensatory* psychology and in so doing falls into a reductionism different from but parallel to Freud's. Like Brown (and also Rank) Becker substitutes consciousness of death for sexuality and declares that "*This* is what is creaturely about man, *this* is the repression on which culture is built."[19] Terrified by this awareness, all man can do is to call forth illusions—the "irrational" immortality ideologies and "the lie of character"—to enable him to keep going. By retaining the kind of compensatory ethos that has so long plagued depth psychology, Becker all too readily falls into a series of dualisms of his own: that of the "truth" of death terror versus the "lie"

replacing a dogma of sex with a dogma of death. For the one animal capable of consciously recognizing it, death lurks everywhere. We must open ourselves to the full impact of death in order to rediscover and reinterpret the movement and sequence of life.

of character, culture, and immortality ideologies; that of the doomed body versus the eternal reach of the mind; and that of the "rational" fact of death versus the "irrational" quest for immortal life. Absent in Becker is a sense of the full significance of symbolization, and especially of the symbolization of the life process. Without that he can offer a brilliant thanatology but little in the way of a theory of vitality or life. In his work a unitary life-death paradigm is not realized.

FIVE

Infant and Child

IF WE ACCEPT the natural unity of death and life, then we must assume that death does not suddenly appear out of nowhere but is "present" for us in some way at all times. If that is so, how does the experience of death begin for the individual? And how does it, over the course of life, relate to life?

Images of death begin to form at birth and continue to exist throughout the life cycle. Much of that imagery consists of "death equivalents"—image-feelings of separation, disintegration, and stasis. These death equivalents evolve from the first moment of life, and serve as psychic precursors and models for later feelings about actual death. Images of separation, disintegration, and stasis both anticipate actual death imagery and continue to blend and interact with that imagery after its appearance.

Each of these death equivalents has a counterpart associated with vitality and affirmation: connection is the counterpart of separation, integrity of disintegration, and movement of stasis. The predominance of a vital image (for instance, that of connection) or of a death equivalent (that of separation) is relative, a matter of degree, though there are some situations that dramatically evoke the one or the other. These three parameters relate to specific feelings and multiple observations already made by psychological observers. At the same time they are sufficiently general to apply to the various levels of human experience, from their primarily physiological character at birth to their increasingly elaborate psychic and ethical flowering over the course of life. The parameters operate at both proximate and ultimate levels of experience, and in so doing help us to understand the inseparability of the two levels.

Connection-separation is the most fundamental of the three in human life.

This and the other two parameters have great early significance for the development of the infant's early imagery—for the origins of the "inner life." Attachment behavior, while quite active at birth in most primates, seems to take four to six months to evolve in the human infant.[1] * And by that time—from about four months or so—he has also learned to recognize his mother. We conclude then that something of a discriminating image precedes or at least accompanies active initiation of attachment by the young organism. Impulses toward attachment are inseparable from the beginnings of that specifically human trait of imagination. To be sure, "mediators" of attachment behavior—particularly the infant's crying, but also his calling, babbling and smiling, clinging, nonnutritional sucking, and various forms of locomotion—begin to have their effects on the mother from birth onward. But all of these seem to be subsumed to a "plan"[2] of special human complexity—a plan that is itself an image and a sequence of further image formation.

John Bowlby and a number of ethologists focus upon a shared model of primate behavior while others (including Langer and myself) emphasize a fundamental psychobiological shift from nonhuman primate to man. The shared primitive model tends to be associated with human instinct theory, and has the advantage of becoming the basis for rather precise behavioral observations. But only the stress on shift engages the phenomenon of human imagination, its evolution over the life cycle, and its relationship both to knowledge of death and the evolutionary principle of continuity of life. †

* John Bowlby has explored many dimensions of connection around his concept of "attachment behaviour," by which he means a variety of patterns (or "behavioural systems") that serve to bring about or maintain the infant's proximity to the mother or mother figure. Bowlby points out, concerning infant and mother, that "only after he has become mobile does he seek her company" in preference to others.

Bowlby holds to what he calls "a new type of instinct theory" that allows for man's "two main characteristics" in comparison with other primates, "his versatility and his capacity for innovation." He cites evidence for the primacy of attachment behavior, in humans as well as other primates: its occurrence even when the infant is not responded to with food or affection. At the same time, as a student of contemporary ethology and systems theory, he is well aware of the considerable importance of the infant's social environment for realization of inborn capacities. Bowlby can thus say that "instinct behaviour is not inherited: what is inherited is a potential to develop certain sorts of . . . behavioural systems, both the nature and forms of which differ in some measure according to the particular environment in which development takes place."[3] Bowlby may be quite right about the primacy of attachment behavior as an innate tendency of the young organism, included in its inchoate image. Here we come to a meeting-ground between Bowlby's behavioral systems, the Miller *et al* concept of "plan," the Boulding view of directional "image," and the Langer sense of the "biological function . . . in image-making" as fundamental to the specifically human cultivation of symbolized images.

† Langer puts the matter well when she speaks of "The veritable gulf that divides human from animal mentality, in a perfectly continuous course of development of life

The parameter of connection-separation is especially illustrative of that distinction, partly because it is crucial to survival in both primates and man. For instance, Bowlby stresses the principle of "proximity." But there is a relative scaling down in the human of literal nearness in favor of interior representation, or symbolization, of that proximity or "closeness." That interiorization is as "biological" as other primates' more narrow, "instinctual" repertoire. Langer in fact speaks of the "dialectic of separation and connection" as familiar to biology and "typical of organic structure." For humans, symbolization must do the things that instinct does for animals—and *more as well*. Thus the more gradual human sequence of attachment, associated with the psychological symbolization of dependency, is part of an extended opportunity for the early shaping of images, for the development of interiority. Many, beginning with Freud, have associated that prolonged dependency with human susceptibility to every kind of emotional disturbance and to unquestioning compliance with dubious forms of authority. But this valid observation should be placed within the framework of two other specifically human traits—knowledge of death, and pan-*symbolization*.

The capacity for image-making in early human life seems to require at least a minimum of protective connection with others. Only then can separation, the experiential precursor of the knowledge of death, contribute in a different way to richness and variation in that evolving imagery.

What Bowlby describes as "the use of Mother as a base from which to explore" can be understood as the dialectic of connection and separation in action: the eight-month-old's acquisition of an *image*-base for subsequent expansion and deepening of inner forms around both vitality and death.*

---

on earth that has no brakes. For animals have mental functions, but only man has a mind, and a mental life. Some animals are intelligent, but only man can be intellectual . . . his departure from the normal pattern of animal mentality is a vast and special evolution of feeling in the hominid stock. This deviation from the general balance of functions usually maintained in the complex advances of life is so rich and so intricately detailed that it affects every aspect of our existence, and adds up to the total qualitative difference which sets human nature apart from the rest of the animal kingdom as a mode of being that is typified by language, culture, morality, and the consciousness of life and death."[4]

* Bowlby's contrasting emphasis upon separation may be said to lack this dialectical spirit but has its own richness. Bowlby urges a return to the "simple view" that "separation from loved figures, or the threat of separation" is "a principle source of anxiety and distress," and that such separation anxiety has a primal quality that is "not reducible to other terms."[5] We shall see that there is much to be said for this view. But it neglects an alternative emphasis, found notably in the work of Margaret Mahler, that relates separation to individuation and the capacity to explore and grow. These two different emphases around separation are partly a matter of language and convention— Bowlby means essentially the infant's losing the mother when he needs her, and Mahler the infant's capacity to move beyond symbiosis to "the sense of being a separate individual."[6] And both lay great, carefully documented stress on the importance of the

An intriguing, perhaps unanswerable question remains: Does the early human organism's inchoate imagery include negative anticipation, the expectation of limited, insufficient, or failed nurturing? In other words, is there innate anticipation of separation as well as of connection? Bowlby suggests that possibility, while leaving the matter open. Perhaps the most we are entitled to say is that the newborn's combination of inchoate image and enactment includes *provision for* imperfect fulfillment. That kind of provision is at least suggested by the newborn's immediate capacity to cry—to express hunger or any kind of discomfort, as well as to "signal" mother and bring her closer. *

Otto Rank turned to the trauma of birth itself to explain this kind of early negative experience. His emphasis may well have wisdom beyond its exaggerations. Rather than Rank's idea that the *event* of birth creates specific lifelong effects,[8] we can at least view birth as the beginning of a chain of events, important to the infant's imagery. The birth experience could well provide an initial imprint or image-model for separation. The total bodily involvement of the infant in the birth process might well lend particular intensity to this early image. † Rank probably had something similar in mind when he later associated the idea of "birth fear" with "trauma of separation" and "loss of the mother." He could then move toward a unitary position, including all of these elements, as he spoke of a "primal fear . . . [which] manifests itself now as fear of life, another time as fear of death."[10]

Rank went on to associate that primal fear with "loss of connection with a greater whole, in the last analysis with the 'all'," as opposed to castration fear which "is symbolic of the loss of an important part of the ego, which however is less than the whole, that is, is partial." Rank is uncertain about the ultimate origin of this primal fear, telling us that the child may first experience it in the birth process or "perhaps even brings it with him" to the birth process. But Rank stresses that from the beginning this fear "has in it already both elements, fear of life and fear of death, since birth on the one hand means the end of life (former life) and on the other carries on the fear of a new life."

Beyond raising the virtually insoluble question of innateness, Rank makes a

---

maternal tie. Yet Bowlby and Mahler are not talking about two entirely different issues. Rather, their contrasting emphases express the subtle, seemingly paradoxical nature of human imagery of separation, and of death as well.

* Peter Wolff, in his valuable observations on the "natural history" of crying in infants, stresses the extent to which crying is built into the organism's physiology, its relationship to breathing no less than to a mood or behavioral state.[7]

† Thus Mahler approvingly quotes Phyllis Greenacre: "I have the idea that the process of birth itself is the first great agent in *preparing for awareness of separation*; that this occurs through the considerable pressure impact on and stimulation of the infant's body surface during birth and especially by the marked changes in pressure and thermal conditions surrounding the infant in his transfer from intramural to extramural life."[9] (italics mine)

direct association between early separation and death imagery, and he places castration fear within a larger life-death frame. Imagery of separation, present from the beginning of life, is the basic precursor for the idea of death. At the same time such separation imagery, like the death imagery it prefigures, is necessary to life and to the experience of vitality. At issue is not so much the polar distinction between separation and connection but rather the degree to which separation and connection can be integrated, as opposed to various forms of inner "splitting," and other forms of dysfunction. In the latter case imagery of separation and death becomes especially fearful and threatening. But in all cases separation imagery has a certain negativity which, reactivated and expanded over the many "small deaths" of parting and loss, interweaves with life's expanding imagery of connection through deepening involvements with people, groups, and ideas.

The second parameter, that of integrity-disintegration, overlaps the first. The inner sense of "disintegrating"—of falling apart—is often associated with separation and isolation, beginning very early in life with what Margaret Mahler called "the fear of annihilation through abandonment."[11] (Indeed it is quite likely that the birth experience itself [however one stands on Rank's ideas] leaves an imprint of threat to bodily integrity as much as one of traumatic separation.)

More than any other writer, Melanie Klein has focused on very early "fear of annihilation," which she understood to be "revived and repeated" in connection with a variety of later anxieties.[12] Klein, moreover, explored the relationship between imagery of annihilation and of death. But she rather reversed the two. Carrying the idea of a death instinct further than Freud ever did, she could say: "Anxiety is aroused by the danger which threatens the organism from the death instinct." Instead of imagery of separation and annihilation prefiguring that of death, it is "the inner working of the death instinct" that causes the "fear of annihilation of life" and is "the first cause of anxiety." She understands the infant to experience the death instinct, from the beginning of life, "as an overwhelming attack, as persecution," so that subsequent fear of annihilation and death is generally experienced as fear of persecution. Despite the tortuousness of her instinctual explanation, Klein made the important connection between earliest imagery of bodily threat and later death fears. She could then suggest that all anxiety relates to death. Apart from her instinctual framework, she describes the early fear of annihilation as a beginning manifestation of imagery of disintegration in the organism's struggle to hold together, toward integrity. As a sense of self evolves, imagery of integrity extends beyond the physiological to various forms of psychological and moral self-judgment. The negative side of the parameter can then take the form of what is spoken of as "fear of extinction of the ego"[13] or of the "self-image"[14]—fears that carry the death equivalent of disintegration very close to actual death imagery.

Movement-stasis, the last of these parameters, has been the most neglected of the three in psychological theory. That neglect has been partially redressed, at least for the beginning of life, by Mahler's sensitive observations. She points out that the observer of infants must go beyond "general modes of psychoanalytically derived observations" and take advantage of "a special observational opportunity: the opportunity to observe the body in movement." She emphasizes the centrality of the infant's "motor, kinesthetic [pertaining to bodily reaction], and gestural . . . phenomena"—because they enable us to 'read' the infant's "inner state,"[15] prior to the acquisition of language or the symbolic function.*

Thrashing arms and legs are the infant's first self-induced expressions of vitality. Body movement never ceases to retain some of that significance. Correspondingly, infants and young children respond with considerable discomfort and protest to physical restraint or any form of restriction of bodily movements. And even without restraint or restriction, maximum *in*activity—specifically, the state of sleep—becomes one of the earliest models children can call upon for their beginning understanding of death. Overall, the idea of death or nonlife is associated with imagery of total stasis, cessation of all activity, absence of movement or energy toward movement.

As in the case of the other parameters, the sequence over the life cycle is from the physiological to the more visual imagery to symbolized forms; from physical motion to images of movement to the sense of development, growth, and change. Yet even from the beginning, developing imagery is not based merely on literal motion. Consider, for instance, the cultural custom of swaddling—wrapping infants almost from birth in strips of material that hold their legs straight and their arms down at their side, as has been the tradition in Russia and other parts of Europe. We cannot say that swaddled babies manifest, on that score, an overwhelming sense of stasis. The close contact swaddling affords with the mother may, for instance, present opportunities for especially active participation in nursing, and may permit the infant to experience rather directly his mother's bodily rhythms and activities in ways that contribute to his own imagery of movement. Of the greatest importance is the extent to which such patterns are part of a larger cultural configuration that "feeds" attitudes and images into immediate physical behavior.

Again there is a dialectical principle dictating the necessity of the negative dimension for the organism. Just as animals when threatened may freeze or act as if dead to enhance survival, so does the human organism require imagery of stasis and deathlike inactivity under certain forms of duress, and more generally

---

* Mahler explains that: ". . . the motor and kinesthetic pathways are the principle expressive, defensive, and discharge pathways available to the infant (long before verbal communication takes their place). We make inferences from them to inner states because they are the end products of inner states. One cannot be certain of the inner state, but, in the effort to infer it, multiple, repeated, and consensually validated observations and inferences offer some safeguard against total error. This state is expressed in what Piaget calls the "sensorimotor phase"—a state whose imagery, in our terms, is bound up with direct sensory and motor perceptions and activities."

as a counterpoint to its physical expressions of vitality. Thus the sense of movement and growth is never free of contrasting, sometimes threatening, imagery of static lifelessness. But the human trait of interiority—of substituting inner for outer activity—infuses the movement-stasis parameter with complexity and nuance.

The birth experience activates the infant's innate potential for both life and death imagery and even more, provides the first model for combining these two. Extrauterine life begins with an extrusion. There is the physical separation, rather sudden and certainly absolute, from the mother's body. And there is the equally sudden emergence into a radically different kind of environment, which immediately confronts the infant with a flood of new stimuli to contend with. No wonder that so many authors have understood the birth process as "the model for all later anxiety."[16] But birth is also an emergence. In that separation and encounter with the new environment, the infant might also experience an opening out—a rush of vitality and movement, the beginnings of bodily autonomy. Extrusion and emergence, death equivalents and vitality, the prefiguring of death and renewal—the dialectic is there from the beginning.

To understand this process, we must concern ourselves not with isolated behavioral fragments but rather with larger units of the human organism's "advancing stream of activity,"[17] with pattern, "plan," "schemata," or imagery. From that standpoint the first two years of life are the time in which inchoate experience gradually becomes "mentalized." "Felt" imagery becomes increasingly structured, pictorial, associated with enactment and competence, and with verbal articulation. The sequence is from a primarily bodily "sensorimotor" phase, in Piaget's term, to a "transition from sensorimotor intelligence to early symbolic activity as a substitute for motor action." This beginning interiority, which is to develop into the imagination that characterizes man, is itself prefigured in our earliest bodily experiences. Everything counts; nothing is lost. For "life is a continuous creation of increasingly complex forms and a progressive balancing of these forms with the environment."[18] And by eighteen months or so—some would say well before that—the symbolizing mind has begun to take hold of these "forms."

What Erikson calls "basic trust" can be understood as the infant's earliest "feeling" that the life process is reliable: that which one's inchoate image propels one toward (the nurturing mother) provides responses (propelled by her own imagery) that satisfy and vitalize. But there are always impediments, flaws in the "fit" between what the infant anticipates and what he experiences.* The resulting "basic mistrust," the absence of "an essential trustfulness of others as

* Similarly, Winnicott states that "the mother's love, displayed as human reliability, does in fact give the baby a sense of trust . . . of confidence in the environmental factor."[19] The "fit" we speak of between baby and mother, then, depends upon the healthy functioning of both the infant's inchoate image and (again in Winnicott's terms) the "good-enough mother."

well as a fundamental sense of one's own trustworthiness,"[20] is associated with nonspecific imagery of negation that includes separation, disintegration, and stasis. The impediments may be severe where there is either radically deficient nurturing or genetically impaired infantile image-structure. Even under favorable circumstances the "fit" is always less than perfect; the special human sensibility always includes mistrust, as well as trust, in one's own life process. That sense of the world as unreliable and threatening is initially no more than a diffusely "felt" image. But over the course of the first and then the second year it is increasingly associated with more specific imagery of separation and abandonment, which, in turn, presses toward conscious awareness.

The relatively slow development of attachment behavior in the human infant, along with his priming for increasing responsibility in the "attachment partnership," enables him to build up elaborate imagery around connection and separation. That imagery in turn provides him with a variety of imaginative possibilities, but also renders him uniquely vulnerable not only to separation from specific nurturing figures but to more indirect suggestions of separation as well.

The beginning expressions of this vulnerability in very young children have been demonstrated by a number of observers, and described in detail by John Bowlby. Reluctant to speculate about the psychological experience of infants during the first six months or so of life, Bowlby has concentrated upon observable patterns of infantile mourning in fifteen to thirty-month-old children separated from their mothers. He delineated a three-stage process: of "protest," "despair," and "detachment." * Though Bowlby says relatively little about the psychology of death per se, his work is invaluable for exploring the psychological interplay of separation and death. This unitary spirit is consistent with our own formative theory when he points out that "the phase of *protest* is found to raise the problem of separation anxiety; *despair* that of grief and mourning; *detachment* that of defence."[22] From the standpoint of our paradigm we note the importance of the three stages in providing a bridge between death equivalents and the emerging idea (late in the second or early in the third year) of death itself. That resemblance makes all the more important observations summarized by Bowlby that children as young as six or seven months tend to undergo essentially the same mourning sequence when separated from their mothers. The older children in Bowlby's groups (age two to three) may experience imagery of their mother as dead. They confuse imagery of death with that of immediate separation, whereas younger children (six to twelve months) experience only rudimentary imagery of separation. †

Mahler provides a dimension missing in Bowlby's work: Early forms of

* "Protest ('at first with tears and anger he demands his mother back and seems hopeful he will succeed in getting her'); despair ('[Several] days later he becomes quieter, but to the discerning eye it is clear that as much as ever he remains preoccupied with his absent mother and still yearns for her return . . . but his hopes have faded'); and detachment ('Eventually . . . he seems to forget his mother so that when she comes for him he

separation on behalf of individuation, and the subtle interplay of such separation with "separation anxiety."

For Mahler separation is part of normal "hatching," the "second" or "psychological birth" that takes place at about three months. In describing this sequence her concern is with "an intrapsychic rather than a behavioral condition," with the "inner sensations [that] form the *core* of the self."[24] She must therefore infer much that cannot be reported or directly observed. Such inference clearly has its pitfalls when overinfluenced by classical psychoanalytic assumptions about instinctual drive. But it also has the advantage of taking us beyond the limits of naked empiricism and including the idea of the evolving human mind—what the infant is moving toward—in judgment about what the infant is doing and experiencing. She is concerned with what has been called "the unrememberable and the unforgettable,"[25] which in our terms means the earliest imagery of the infant. What she describes as its "dual unity" with the mother "within one common boundary" as mediated by "perceptual experiences of the total body" (the symbiotic phase, from about the third to the sixth month) is the "inner experience" of what Bowlby calls early attachment. Then with "separation-individuation" or hatching, "the baby begins to differentiate his own from the mother's body and there is "a steady increase in awareness of the separateness of the self and the 'other' which coincides with the origins of a sense of self, of true object relationship [with another person], and of awareness of a reality in the outside world."[26] Mahler adds, in a pithy footnote, "We now know that the drive is not toward separation per se, but the innate given is the drive toward individuation, which cannot be achieved without autonomous separation." Separation cannot be achieved without anxiety. That anxiety, in response to ordinary, transient separation from the mother (as opposed to Bowlby's more extreme forms) is expressed not through protest but rather through "toned-down" responses, diminished activity and interest in surroundings, a special, highly subdued "state of self" which Mahler calls "low-keyedness."[27] * This is a total psychobiological response that, as Mahler points out, resembles the "conservation withdrawal" that can be observed in monkeys separated from their mothers. The point for us here is the elaborate early human psychic structuring of the separation experience

---

remains curiously uninterested in her, and may seem even not to recognize her'). All three phases are likely to be accompanied by anger and aggression ('. . . the child is prone to tantrums and episodes of destructive behaviour, often of a disquietingly violent kind')."[21] In subsequent books Bowlby has held to this schema, and has increasingly elaborated on principle-of-separation anxiety as central to a good deal of human distress. In so doing he was following one strand of Freud's work. But he was also making use of empirical evidence around the mother-child relationship as a whole to raise questions about other Freudian and post-Freudian assumptions, especially the more mechanistic aspects of libido theory.

† Mahler calls this "a dawning awareness that the symbiotic mothering half of the self was missed."[23]

* Mahler believes that these infants "appeared to be preoccupied with inwardly

The dialectical relationship between connection and separation is directly expressed during the second year of life by the toddler's combined patterns of "shadowing" and "darting away." The first means incessant watching and close following of the mother, and the second sudden forays "away from her, with the expectation of being chased and swept into her arms." The child needs the mother for his "home base" as he simultaneously experiments and struggles with three related psychological aspirations: independence from mother via separation; reunion with mother; and fear of "reengulfment" by mother. A baby becomes something like a miniature Camus rebel— "autonomy is defended by the 'No'"—and what appears to be negativistic behavior can be a 'warding-off' pattern directed against impingement upon his recently achieved autonomy."[28] All of these struggles have some form of psychic representation, and evolving imagery becomes increasingly structured and available to conscious ideation. In that process, as Mahler points out, separation and individuation are closely intertwined but on distinct "developmental tracks." Individuation is the fundamental impulse—the "innate given, which reveals itself with particular force in the beginning of life and which seems to continue during the entire life cycle."[29]

Early experience of separation, then, is in the service of a controlling image (originally inchoate but increasingly formed and conscious) of individuation. Little is gained by calling either individuation or separation an "instinct"; rather, both are integral to the human life "plan" contained in the genes and expressed in imagery of various kinds from birth onward.* In sum, the dialectical principle in the infant's early connection-separation experience finds its source in evolutionary legacy and its later expression in the interwoven imagery of life and death. The emergence of a sense of self stems precisely from that dialectical sequence.

This emergence of the rudiments of the self is very much bound up with early body imagery. Struggles around intactness (or integrity-disintegration) are not only simultaneous with those around connection-separation but may in fact

---

concentrated attention" or with what has been called "imaging." That "imaging" can only be inferred, but if it does occur it probably consists of intensified internal pictures of the absent mother. Certainly by this time the infant has learned to distinguish his mother and (late in the first year and early in the second) is beginning to store and symbolize images.

* Relevant here are Winnicott's ideas about the "transitional object," the blanket, piece of blanket, or cuddly toy the infant clings to— "the first not-me possession," and the means by which the child "symbolizes the union of two now separate things, baby and mother, at the point of the initiation of their state of separateness. . . ." Here the combination of the transitional object and the mother's continuing nurturing "the mental representation [of the mother] in the inner world [of the infant] is kept significant . . . the imago in the inner world is kept alive." He can then speak of "a separation that is not a separation but a form of union."[30]

provide the more "internal" of these beginning psychic experiences. Imagery of separation and bodily threat probably merge: Mahler describes a toddler, at first "impervious to knocks and falls," becoming "visibly bewildered when he hurt himself and noticed that his mother was not automatically close by."[31] There comes a moment when threat to bodily intactness is insufficiently counter-balanced by the sustaining power of maternal nurturing. We can never be fully certain of the internal sequence, depending as we must on supposition and reconstruction. But it is probable that the earliest image of annihilation is directly associated with separation (during the symbiotic phase of the first few months of life), and is the source of the "persecutory anxiety" Melanie Klein attributed to the death instinct.

Gradually the young child sharpens his imagery of annihilation, so that by the second and third years he fears what he perceives as forces from without that (in Klein's words) "devour, tear up, poison, flood."[32] Klein and other psychoanalytic observers have emphasized related aggressive impulses, also bodily, and especially associated with bodily orifices—with biting, urinating, defecating, and with early sexual behavior. Within our paradigm we would understand these impulses to be part of the struggle for bodily intactness, and also related to fears of loss of bodily substances as well as harm from outside materials entering bodily openings or unprotected areas.

While the entire body seems to be vulnerable, intensified vulnerabilities are increasingly associated with specific bodily parts. One experiences cuts, wounds, falls, accompanied by fear, pain, the idea of being "hurt" or injured. Always there is a double level, part and whole, and from that combination evolves what Paul Schilder called the "body image." That "image" is really a constellation of images, having many components related to size (small to big), shape (thin to fat), and capacity for movement and action. The body image represents one's symbolization of the physical self, notably the sense of where the body begins and ends. The struggle to keep the body intact, increasingly to symbolize its integrity and coordination, depends on a series of physical affirmations—the taste of food when hungry, the touch and warmth of loving parents, the sensual pleasures of one's own body. Yet it is quite possible that the emergence of an inclusive body image depends as much on the three-year-old's experience of blood oozing from a slightly cut finger as, say, his pleasurable discovery of his sex organs. Both are integral to the bodily dialectic of vitality and vulnerability. Injury and threat, however, are specific to the bodily lesson of finitude, limitation, and boundary. Again, the prefiguring of mortality is inseparable from individuation.

Imagery of stasis is also primarily bodily, as shown by Sylvia Anthony in a very young child's typical answer to the question of what it means to be dead: "Can't move, can't see, can't hear, can't breathe." Absolute stillness suggests the negation of vitality. The importance of the model of sleep for death, mentioned earlier, is revealed further in a description by Sylvia Anthony of the behavior of a little girl (three years and three months) whose mother died suddenly of a heart attack while making a bed. The father returned to find the child asleep on the floor beside the mother's body. Four months later the child gave her explanation: "Mother lay down on the floor and went to sleep, so I went to sleep too." [33]

Her struggle around the relationship between sleep and death seems to include several image-possibilities—her mother is asleep and will therefore wake up normally, her mother is "dead" but will wake up anyway, or her mother is dead and will never wake up. Lying down and falling asleep next to her mother is, of course, a form of strong identification with her, a shared immersion in that confusing in-between domain of sleep-dying. Probably the child hoped that she could thereby influence the outcome—that both would wake up together. But all through the experience the little girl also moves a little closer to assimilating the idea of death's finality—probably the most difficult and consistently resisted idea in human life.

Early experience with bodily wastes involves all three parameters. Our life-continuity paradigm shares with classical psychoanalytic theory a sense of the importance of such experience. But rather than stressing "anal eroticism" and "anality" in terms of sexual instinct or libido, we would emphasize the many-sided image-feelings involved. There are undoubtedly pleasurable feelings in defecating and urinating, and these activities also provide an expanding sense of the body's possibilities and, eventually, capacity for control. But there is also an early sense of material coming from one's own body, a material that is inert, static, devoid of the self-generating capacity the baby gradually comes to associate with life itself. Fecal elements especially could also be associated with a threat to intactness, with imagery of bodily disintegration. One is, in the process, separated from what appears to be a portion of oneself, and subsequent tendencies toward valuing and holding onto one's feces can be understood, at least in part, as a fending off of that kind of separation experience. It would seem that every kind of wisdom concerning life's finitude has important origins in feces. No wonder that the same substance, degraded but also elevated into "shit," comes to represent just about every powerful human emotion from disgust to precious accumulation to magical power. [34]

Beginning knowledge of death itself occurs at the same time as the early capacity to symbolize, that is, during the middle of the second year of life. There is also the development of language which, like the idea of death, is a manifestation of the symbolizing function. From now on all encounters must be given psychic form by the interposing mind. Everything must be constructed and recreated. Death is constructed from its already existing equivalents. Expanding encounters with the environment contribute importantly to that process, but as psychologists and as parents we probably overestimate the specificity of environmental death encounters. The human being is constructed to come to knowledge of death—that knowledge is part of a psychic system built into the organism. Death is prefigured from the beginning.

Consider one description of the "death-exposure response" of an eighteen-month-old boy who encountered a dead bird. The child's initial sense of excited discovery quickly changed to that of "puzzlement" and then to "a frozen ritualized expression resembling nothing so much as the stylized Greek dramatic mask for tragedy . . . a grief mask." The little boy would not touch the bird, but returned to the same spot each of the next few mornings to seek out the dead creature, still refraining from touching it. A few weeks later he encountered a second dead bird, and this time picked it up and "gestured with it"—held the bird above his head while reaching up toward a tree, making it clear (with the help of rudimentary language) that he was commanding his father to put the bird back into the tree. At the same time he made additional gestures resembling a bird flying. The little boy, undeterred by his father's insistence that putting the bird back up there would not bring it back to life, demanded that this be demonstrated (it is not clear whether the bird remained limp on a branch or fell to the ground). The whole process had to be repeated several times before he finally lost interest. And a few weeks later, when walking in the woods with his father, the little boy focused on a single fallen leaf, tried unsuccessfully to put it back on its tree, and insisted that his father do the same.* The authors suggest the possibility that "the problem of death is the first vital intellectual challenge to engage the child's mind and, as such, is a prime stimulus to his continued mental development." Whether or not the *first* statement is accurate, the idea of death is indeed an intellectual challenge and one tied up with vitality. This early symbolization conveys the futility of drawing a sharp distinction between cognitive and emotional function. It calls upon the entire scope of the young mind, including still earlier death images, however fragmentary. Thus the little boy's approaches to dead birds and leaves, his attempts to reconnect and revivify them, were informed by his prior flow of attachments and separations from parents, and by his experience with "dead" wastes from his own body. Death for the eighteen-month-old child, in other words, already has a considerable history. The new issues are finality and irreversibility—the deadness of death. †

* "When daddy started to try again, David shook his head 'no.' He looked both sober and convinced. Although leaves were repeatedly seen to fall and dead animals were encountered every now and then, little David made no further attempts to reverse their fortunes."[35] The authors stress that "death is already providing an intellectual challenge . . . the young child *tries* to understand . . . is able to recognize that a problem has risen before his eyes."

† Adah Maurer points to very early games and exercises the infant engages in as experiments with nonbeing. Peek-a-boo and various related disappearance-and-return games, for Maurer, enable the infant, from as early as three months, to develop a sense of contrast between being and nonbeing, and thereby move toward a grasp of death.[36] The general principle here would seem to be the infant's impulse, in accordance with his

That is the salient issue when we observe children around the ages of two to four chatting freely about death. In their verbal experiments with a less-than-comprehensible concept they are accumulating imagery (of such things as people dying and then awakening or not awakening) as appropriate to their stage of the struggle with death's irreversibility as is adult imagery (of say friends' deaths or awareness of one's own advancing age) to later stages.* They are struggling to combine what they already "know" with what they are now finding out. Yet in coming to terms with this new imagery of a mysteriously threatening thing that happens to people, called "death" or "dying," young children have more resources—and more of a need to know—than most adults (busy struggling with and against their own "knowledge" of the same) tend to realize. These image-experiments are flexible and ingenious, as Sylvia Anthony suggests:

> . . . as though it were one aspect only of an ambiguous design, death in fantasy continually reverses its appearance, so that the murderer becomes the murdered, and the dead the newly born.[37]

This may well be "magical thinking," an expression of the "primary process" without boundaries and in defiance of logic and sequence. But that traditional psychoanalytic characterization obscures the child's fundamental struggle around symbolizing the relationship of death to his own existence.

Earlier that principle had been realized in the sense of "oneness" emphasized by Rank (which includes the "symbiotic phase" described by Mahler but extends well into early individuation). Now the idea of death shatters that oneness, as does the accompanying idea of birth. For both birth and death suggest nonexistence—as opposed to the sense that immediate, total nurturing arrangements have always prevailed and will continue forever. The young child quite naturally calls forth his death equivalents for the necessary image experimentation: the totally separated being regains connection as the dead becomes the newly born, and the annihilated victim is not only restored but becomes himself the arbiter of life and death as the murdered person becomes the murderer. In that reversal is an early image of violence in response to what the child perceives

---

developing imagery, to experiment in *play* with death equivalents in preparation for integrating the idea of death.

* Death can be made relatively more acceptable by certain cultures, where there is less denial and numbing around it from the beginning to the end of life. But one should not be too quick with these judgments, as anxieties around death can take a great variety of forms, hidden and manifest. The psychological struggle around death's irreversibility would seem to be universal, an aspect of the evolutionary emergence of the human mind. This model of universal struggle around irreversibility along with variation in manner and degree of numbing and denial, could be the basis for useful cultural comparisons beginning with very young children.

(the idea of death) as a threat to his own vitality.* This seemingly illogical interchangeability between death and death equivalent, and dead person and killing force, is by no means limited to the young child. It is found throughout adult life, the difference being that the older child and adult combine these image-associations with an increasing commitment to making distinctions.

Those distinctions depend upon the emerging capacity for decentering,† for making judgments that reach beyond the immediate struggles of one's organism. That capacity gives rise to cognitive skills, but (as our paradigm would insist) involves the full scope of the developing mind. Decentering is itself a manifestation of the symbolizing function. For by now (from the middle of the second year onward) the child has become an active symbolizer, a creature who can know or experience only by inwardly recreating, and then "representing," each encounter. To symbolize in that way is both to abstract and to achieve a special kind of mental focus. For decentering and symbolization do not mean detachment; they mean storing and combining images in a more complex relationship to time and space. Images become more flexible as they expand and contribute to psychic structures that can be simultaneously inclusive and discriminating, always on behalf of psychic survival and vitality.

With decentering, the child must replace at least partially his earlier image of oneness, of undifferentiated totality, with more mature parallels to that image. Now the emerging self must locate itself in both inner and outer connectedness. Oneness is replaced by centering.‡ The self struggles to combine imagery of distinctness and finitude with the sense of being part of a much larger life principle, perceived at first as coming mainly from parents and nurturers but eventually extended to symbolize the different modes of immortality described earlier. From the second to fourth years of life, the beginnings of the

---

* Joseph Campbell points to the equation of death and murder in primitive mythology, which demonstrates "the coming of death into the world, and the particular point . . . that death comes by way of a murder." Campbell goes on to explain that such mythology conveys the principle that "the plants on which man lives derive from this death. The world lives on death."[38] Such mythology recognized murderous feelings and actions as part of man's death-associated struggles. The child must learn this association from the very beginning, from the time of his discovery of death itself.

† Piaget states: "The child's initial universe is entirely centered on his own body and action in an egocentrism as total as it is unconscious (for a lack of consciousness of the self). In the course of the first eighteen months, however, there occurs a kind of Copernican revolution, or, more simply, a kind of general decentering process whereby the child eventually comes to regard himself as an object among others in a universe that is made up of permanent objects (that is, structured in a spatio-temporal manner) and in which there is at work a causality that is both localized in space and objectified in things."[39]

‡ The image of oneness is never entirely relinquished (as we observed in connection with adult experiences of ecstasy and transcendence). So we may speak of a continuing movement of the self between "oneness" (as included in particularly intense experiences of centering) and "multiplicity" (as included in the interpretive divisions of decentering).

delineation of proximate and ultimate levels of involvement take place. This *spatial centering* depends upon *temporal centering* (the use of memory to form images that anticipate the immediate and distant future) and an *energic centering* (the development and distribution of varied and nuanced feeling accompanying different images and forms).* In all this the organism is neither denying nor affirming the fact that it must ultimately die, but rather struggling with its increasingly articulated relationship to death and continuing life. Centering and decentering, then, are launched by the discovery of death.

Still extremely dependent upon those who nurture him, the child continues for some time to equate death with separation. He thinks of the dead as having "gone away," an image that allows for the possibility of their return. He doesn't just model death on death equivalents, he also begins to model death equivalents on what he comes to understand about death. The three-year-old child who equates separation from his mother with her death now constructs frightening images of irreversibility—his mother permanently asleep, buried underground, forcibly carried off and murdered. This "double modeling" is probably most terrifying during the early years, but it is a lifelong process. We continue to construct our sense of death from our separations; to react to death with feelings of being annihilated or wiped out; to move back and forth in our minds between death and death equivalents.

In sum, the beginning of life-death imagery is mainly an extension of the inchoate image-vector and then of the death equivalents that evolve from it. Separation is the paramount threat from the beginning of life and can give rise, very early, to the rudiments of anxiety and mourning. If the separation is sufficiently extreme, as in situations where mechanical feeding is the only form of human contact, the infant responds with his own severe stasis, with limited reactivity and impaired development even to the point of death.[40] From the age of six months, connection and separation become more specifically associated with a particular person, usually the mother, as do manifestations of separation anxiety and infantile mourning. Actual death imagery, the beginning awareness that living creatures die, occurs during the last half of the second year of life; it is anticipated by imagery around death equivalents, including sleep (stasis), cuts, pain, and bruises (disintegration), feelings about feces (stasis, disintegration, and separation), and of course separations of any kind; and can also be evoked or intensified by exposure to the death of animals, human beings, or even plants. Then begins a process of mutual interaction, or double modeling, between death equivalents and actual death imagery; and a dialectic of centering and decentering, from which the image of a delineated and connected self takes shape.

* We shall later discuss a concept of energy within our paradigm that seeks to recover the organic-spiritual sense of that term that prevailed prior to its being usurped (beginning from the early eighteenth century) by modern physics to become a measurable, mechanical force.

With further development of symbolization, especially in speech (third or fourth through seventh years of life), actual death imagery becomes much more autonomous. The child shapes an increasingly formed notion of being or becoming dead. Death equivalents continue to provide feeling-tone and modeling, but in the service of the specific constellation, or complex symbol, of death. The child now ruminates in endless detail about people who have "gone away *for good*"; undergone violent disintegration through shooting, stabbing, bombing, burning, biting, an air or automobile crash; being flushed down the toilet or sewer, or having the heart or another bodily organ break open so that "all the blood comes out"; or who have become permanently still, "asleep *for good*" because their "heart stopped" or because "they can't breathe any-more."[41] *

Now questions become more insistent and more concrete. The child wants to know exactly what happens when people die, where they go, what becomes of their bodies, whether they can still feel anything. At the same time questions about origins become more insistent—not only, "Where did I come from?" "How are children born?" "How did you and daddy (or mommy) make me?" but also, "Who was the first man?" and "How was he born?" There is a single, fundamental theme behind the fear, aggressiveness, and confusion contained in the first set of questions, and the strong sexual curiosity in the second. That theme is the quest for images at a border of life and nonlife—for a way of imagining both the fact of death and the beginnings of life. At issue are the boundaries of the self as a symbolized entity, and for that issue the end and the beginning are of a piece.† There is a clear sense of the relationship between awareness of death and a delineated self. The second is impossible without the first. Even prior to the disturbing syllogism, "If death exists, then I will die," is an earlier one: "Since 'I' was born and will die, 'I' must exist."

This self-delineation depends greatly upon the cognitive advances of these years, upon what Piaget calls the "growing conceptualization" based upon the increasing ability to coordinate "representative relations" or elements of imagery.[43] Now the child is asking what may well be the central human question, something like: "Why should there be—and how did there come to be—an 'I' which must come to an end?" (Ionesco puts the question more

---

* These images are by no means mere products of mass-media violence. Mass media indeed spread them, quickly and luridly, but they are fundamentally reflections of early struggles around vulnerability to death. Television violence in particular exploits and concretizes these struggles but it does not create them. By the same token, that concretization may have a much more malignant impact than we have realized: the question is the degree to which the literalized models provided by television replace or block or otherwise interfere with experimental imagery of dying and killing.

† The significance of the quest for knowledge of origins is greatly underestimated in most psychological work. Without viable imagery around origins, the sense of self is likely to remain tenuous and identity problems at adolescence become severe. Precisely these difficulties have been demonstrated in adoptees denied such knowledge.[42]

succinctly: "Why was I born if it wasn't forever?") What counts here is the question, not the answer. For the very dilemma signifies the movement of self toward confluence—of awareness of death as well as of origins, of existence and of something resembling history.

Sylvia Anthony speaks of the eighth year of life as "critical in the development of the concept of death" because it is then that for the first time the child really seems to grasp cause-and-effect relationships having to do with living and dying. That observation is consistent with Piaget's delineation of the emergence of "logico-arithmetical and spatio-temporal operations" at that time. That capacity, of course, can vary in timing with individual children and with different cultures. Further, one could claim that *every* year prior to the eighth has also been "critical" in paving the way for what clearly is a mental leap, the appearance of logic or rational thinking, which can be understood as "a highly specialized phase of that constant symbolization and symbol concatenation which seems to be a spontaneous activity of the human brain."[44] Certainly, around the eighth year death imagery begins to approximate that of the adult— to be extended, modified, and activated in many directions, especially during major transitions and crises (including actual death encounters). It will never again undergo the fundamental structural alterations of earlier years. "Latency period" is the psychoanalytic term for the long, important sequence between five or six and adolescence. But the "latency" is dubious from the standpoint of either sex or death. Rather, what seems to take place is an intricate process of testing, consolidating, and extending all kinds of experience in a mind now able to imagine and construct almost anything.

Children now ask questions both with more informed concreteness and increasing concern with cause-and-effect logic. In terms of our paradigm, there is a probing concern with process and transition, and particularly the transition from life to death. Consider the following telephone conversation between a father away from home on a short trip and his ten-year-old daughter. They are discussing the death of their pet dog, his cremation, and the spreading of his ashes on the sand dunes near the family's summer home, all of which occurred while the little girl and her older brother were away at camp.

> Daughter: Daddy, Ken [her brother] and I were talking—why did you and Mommy spread Jumblie's ashes without us?
> Father: Well, you and Ken were at camp, so Mommy and I thought we should go ahead and do it.
> Daughter: What were the ashes in?
> Father: They were in a jar.
> Daughter: All of them?
> Father: Yes, all of them.
> Daughter: Well, how big was the jar?
> Father: It was round like a bottle and about six or eight inches high.
> Daughter: But where was *Jumblie*?

Father: The ashes were all that was left of Jumblie after he was cremated.

Daughter: But what about his bones?

Father: They were all burned down to ashes.

Daughter: But what about the rest of him? What about his ears?

Father: Everything was burned to ashes.

Daughter: Daddy, are you and Mommy going to have your ashes spread out on the dunes when you die?

Father: I think so—that's our plan now. What do you think of that plan?

Daughter: I don't know. Who will spread them?

Father: Well, it depends on who dies first—whoever dies first, the other will spread them, and maybe you and Ken.

Daughter: But what if you die together?

Father: Then I guess you and Ken will spread them. But that isn't very likely. Anyhow, we don't plan to die for a while.

Daughter: Daddy, do you believe that when you die you are reborn again?

Father: No, dear, I don't. I believe that when you die, that's the end.

Daughter: I don't think Mommy believes that.

Father: Well, maybe not. But that's what I believe.

Daughter: Then how could it be the *end*? You must feel *something*.

Father: No, not after you're dead.

Daughter: But what happens to *you*?

Father: Well, when you die, there is only your body left—not really you—and you can't feel anything at all anymore.

Daughter: Does it hurt?

Father: Not after you're dead.

Daughter: But you can still *dream*, can't you?

Father: No, not after you're dead. You can't dream either. You just don't have any feeling at all. That must be pretty hard to understand, isn't it?

Daughter: Yeah, it is.

Father: Well, even adults like us have a hard time understanding it.

(Daughter then changes the topic of conversation and begins to discuss Christmas, explaining that she wants only "big presents"—no little ones this year—even though she knows that means fewer presents—and even trying to extract [unsuccessfully] from her father a dollar figure for these big presents.)

An important theme of the dialogue is the little girl's struggle to grasp and participate in family symbolization and ritual around death and continuity. In cagily testing her parents' beliefs about death, she partly looks for an out but more basically seeks a way to assimilate the difficult truth of death as termination. She brings the concrete concerns of a sensitive ten-year-old to her struggle to construct workable imagery around the troubling absoluteness of death; to absorb the frightening shift from vital being to inanimate nonbeing, which involves first her dog and then (in her associations) her parents and (by implication) herself. The details she explores in her inquiry would seem to be those that for her most impressively characterize the living. For a physical characteristic she chooses the ears, so important in evaluating dogs, and so convoluted and protruding in humans. For mental function, she chooses the fundamental capacities to feel and to dream. Through that choice of detail she gives force to her ultimate question: What happens to the *existence*—or self—of the animal or person? How can such a vital entity cease, so absolutely, to exist?

The image of death as termination is by no means new for her, but the dog's death activates it in her with great force. While she experiences considerable pain, she also senses an opportunity, which she grasps, for further exploration and understanding. When she feels she has done enough exploring, at least for the time being, she changes the subject. She is to bring it up again in the future, and for that matter had discussed aspects of it with her brother and her parents in the past. Whether her talk about Christmas is an association with the death imagery on which that holiday is based is hard to say—she certainly knew the Christ story, but had not been exposed to much talk about the origins and meanings of Christmas. In any case, her focus on Christmas presents, more than merely changing the subject, seems to express her wish to be reimbursed, so to speak, for her difficult psychic work; to be given ever larger "gifts"—in the sense that, both in primitive cultures and our own, material goods can symbolize what Becker calls "more life."

Another aspect of the struggle with death at this stage is the need to bring to bear on one death the technology of the culture. The child must try to understand in concrete terms the options her culture offers for handling or "treating" a dead body. She intuitively equates mechanical techniques with general attitudes, and for a long time must struggle with the ways in which a culture tries to distinguish between the two, and the further principles, rationalizations, and hypocrisies that enter into the distinctions made. But this early equation of "death technology" with her culture's general technological ethos never quite leaves her. Of great importance are the ways in which parents mediate between culture and child, whether about technology and death or anything else. But at this point, when the child is undergoing a surge of awareness of technological matters, she is especially sensitive to any message of technological numbing or avoidance her culture or her parents may convey to her. She is asking such questions as: What is done to bodies with machines? And what does it mean about life, and about death as "the end," to subject bodies to machinery—or machine-like processes—in this way? She needs all the potentially useful imagery she can get. For now, in a sense for the first time, everything—death itself as well as the continuing struggle to reconcile death and death equivalents—everything is "for real."

SIX

Adolescent and Adult

ADOLESCENCE IS AN INTENSE testing time for both life and death imagery, and is therefore of special importance for our theory and paradigm. A focus on this life-death imagery can illuminate the extravagant psychic processes involved.

A number of writers have observed that adolescence is in itself a social discovery of the last two centuries or so. Only for modern Western (or Western-influenced) man or woman, the argument goes, can we speak of what William James called "the ordinary storm and stress and moulting-time of adolescence." For most societies the transition from the child to the adult has been a more standard, less experimental sequence in which there has been a clear set of expectations all around. The *Oxford English Dictionary* still defines the word adolescence in neutral terms as "The process or condition of growing up; the growing age of human beings; the period which extends from childhood to manhood or womanhood; youth; ordinarily considered as extending from 14 to 25 in males and from 12 to 21 in females." (In actual current usage, at least in the United States, the word means more, something closer to a time of youthful troubles along with the growth. When I recently spoke critically to my fifteen-year-old son about what I took to be the deceitful behavior of a friend of his, his reply was: "Dad, he's an *adolescent*." There is evidence that in premodern usage (the word has old French and Latin origins) the simpler, more descriptive idea of the in-between "growing age" prevailed.

Taken too strictly this perspective may obscure some of the most important issues around adolescence. These issues are apparent in puberty, puberty rites, and initiation procedures. Puberty is the time of appearance of adult sexual characteristics and the capacity to procreate. In our culture, puberty begins somewhere between eleven and thirteen and marks the onset of adolescence. It is more difficult to say exactly when puberty ends. Most definitions would have it somewhere between eighteen to twenty-five, but the end of puberty is much more determined by cultural attitudes than is the beginning. Puberty rites in primitive cultures were traditional, highly structured, and communally regulated, and yet they were by no means free of the "ordinary storm and stress and moulting-time" of modern adolescence.

Those ritual ceremonies of initiation into the adult community could be characterized as carefully staged death immersions culminating in honorable survival and earned rebirth. The details of the death immersion varied greatly from culture to culture, but in all cases there are vivid combinations of death equivalents and actual death imagery.*

Joseph Campbell summarized the characteristic sequence of the initiation ceremony as "separation from the community, transformation (usually physical as well as psychological), and return to the community in the new role."[2] For boys that means "separation from the world of women and children"[3] and then subjection to a terrifying ordeal—mutilation, confrontation with sacred objects, or exposure to what appear to be monsters, ghosts, or grotesque corpses. All this the boy not only endures but actively accepts, invites, conquers. For girls the stress is on extreme seclusion following the first menses, including a great variety of taboos—about eating, exposure to the sun, touching the earth, being seen, and sometimes physical restraint to the extent of living in tiny rooms or cages for weeks, months, or even years. In surviving her ordeal, the girl is acted upon (rather than active) and made ready for roles having to do with service and nurture (rather than conquest).

In terms of death equivalents, separation for both sexes is stark and absolute—separation from parental nurturers, and, more generally, from the childhood state of dependent privilege and protection. The initiate must psychically experience a new dimension of separation imagery that not only lends intensity to his subsequent reintegration but deepens his knowledge of isolation, abandonment, and death.

But disintegration may be the essence of the matter. Mutilation in males can take forms we would judge to be extremely brutal—not only circumcision but subincision (the slitting of the length of the urethra from below, via the underside of the penis), the knocking out of teeth, scarifications, removal of a

---

*Van Gennep speaks of "social puberty" to stress the loose relationship in most primitive cultures between the appearance of adult sexual characteristics and the staging of initiation rites (he therefore objects to their being called "puberty rites").[1] His point is that these rites symbolize a psychological and social transition, especially the transition from nonsexual to sexual existence, as prescribed by a particular culture. Van Gennep probably overstated this idea of independence of initiation rites from puberty, given the extremely widespread occurrence of these rites somewhere around the time of puberty, adolescence, or young adulthood. But his approach has the advantage of emphasizing the symbolic death and rebirth involved.

testicle, bitings, burnings, and the cutting off of a portion of a finger. There are analogous female mutilations—deformation of the labia minora, excision of portions of the clitoris, perforation of the hymen, and section of the perineum, though they tend to be a little less extreme and perhaps less central to the ceremonies.

These societies seem to view menstruation, which signifies the beginning of puberty, as a natural female form of "mutilation" or bodily disintegration. More than that, the mutilating process is considered dangerous to others. Hence the terror of menstruating women that pervades primitive societies. That terror is evident in attitudes around female seclusion not only at the time of the first menses but (in the practice of many societies) with each ensuing menses as well. At the very glance of a menstruating woman, it is believed, "men become fixed in whatever position they happen to occupy . . . and are changed into trees that talk"; if such a woman were to touch any possessions of a man he would fall ill; and should she handle any of his weapons, he would be killed in the next battle.[4] Similarly, Pliny's *Natural History* records beliefs in early European cultures to the effect that menstruating women "turned wine to vinegar, blighted crops, killed seedlings, blasted gardens, brought down the fruit from the trees, dimmed mirrors, blunted razors, rusted iron and brass . . ., killed bees . . ., caused mares to miscarry, etc."[5] The mutilating taint, in other words, is plague-like and supernatural in its capacity to destroy life, nutrient, metals, anything.

This imagery of ritual uncleanliness around menstruation resembles that held by many societies toward corpses, especially the newly dead. For no other natural function in either sex is characterized by bleeding and exfoliation of bodily tissue. The imagery of mutilation we have mentioned in association with the passing of feces and urine is neither comparable in degree nor accompanied by blood. And the terror associated with menstrual "mutilation" may in fact be the source of more general male terror and awe toward women. That is, there seems to be a psychological equation of the experience of "natural mutilation" with the capacity to mutilate. And that form of destructive power becomes equated with the equally exclusive female bodily power to give rise to biological life. In the male mind these special expressions of female power are extended to the sexual realm, and become intermixed with every kind of fearful image of female sexual capacity and threat. But the larger, most fundamental context of such imagery is that of the life-death parameter.

Perhaps within the initiation ritual itself, the more radical mutilation of the male, at least in part, serves the psychological purpose of helping him to share in the mutilation-linked female power over life and death. This association is most directly symbolized by subincision, which creates a virtual male vagina. One cannot say that the male is made into a female, but rather that he is enabled to become symbolically androgynous. The androgynous state can be felt to include the vital force of both male and female, and is in many traditions mythic and mystical, associated with special power. * That special power, along with the actual experience of mutilation, becomes specifically associated with the male warrior function and related male rituals. In contrast, the female, seen as already mutilated and dangerously mutilating, has her power curtailed by the radical isolation she is generally subjected to during initiation rites.

A quality of stasis also pervades the ceremonies, at least at certain moments. In male initiations the frenzied activities are frequently interrupted by a "long night of silence," often in the forest or wilderness, usually in the presence of sacred objects before whom elders perform gentle rites—the boys' motionless rest compared by Campbell to the "deep sleep that fell upon Adam when Eve was taken from his side." In the female ceremonies stasis is more marked and prolonged, and, in fact, tends to characterize the predominant theme of seclusion. A sense of cessation of all life-power is suggested by the taboos on contact with earth and sun, which are respectively the source of and energy for that power. Air and light may be absent from the hut or cage in which the girl is confined, and where she may remain for a year or so "without fire, exercise, or associates." She may even be sewn into a hammock for two or three days with only a small opening for breathing, "wrapt up and shrouded like a corpse."[9] While in these rites all three death equivalents are closely associated with death itself, patterns of stasis provide the most literal rendition of lifelessness.

The overall ceremony is itself a death equivalent: "The novice is considered dead, and he remains dead for the duration of his novitiate."[10] Or, as Frazer puts it, there is "a pretense of killing a lad and bringing him to life again."[11] This process may vary greatly in length (from days to years), in numbers of ceremonies conducted, and in extent of systematic instruction in tribal or societal law and ceremony. But it inevitably culminates in what Van Gennep

---

* Campbell, for instance, demonstrates a common mythological theme of androgyny in Hebrew ("Before the separation of Eve, Adam was both male and female"), Greek (Plato's version of the earliest human creatures who expressed "our original nature"), Chinese ("The Holy Woman, the Great Original, T'ai Yuan, who combined in her person the active-masculine and the passive-feminine powers of nature, the yang and the yin"), and Indian (the Vedic original "Self" who "divided himself in two parts" to produce man and woman) traditions. Androgyny is associated with ultimate power, that of original Creation.[6] Norman O. Brown speaks similarly of "the androgynous nature of God and of human perfection before the fall"; and in his early work he holds out the ideal of restoring that state and overcoming all such dualisms as man's only salvation. Though that advocacy confuses the symbolic and the literal, Brown brilliantly evokes the psychological power of the myth of androgyny and related visions of dialectical unity, as opposed to disruptive dualisms.[7] When, in his subsequent work, Brown overcame that confusion, he could speak eloquently of the politics and biology of being "all members of one body [in which] . . . there is neither male nor female; or rather there is both: it is an androgynous or hermaphroditic body, containing both sexes"—and hold out the ideal of "one sea of energy or instinct; embracing all mankind, without distinction of race, language, or culture; and embracing all the generations of Adam, past, present, and future, in one phylogenetic heritage; in one mystical or symbolical body."[8]

calls "the final act," in "a religious ceremony . . . which makes the novice forever identical with the adult members."[12] Images of death equivalents, that is, are transmuted into their vital components on behalf of reunion with the group: the initiate is reconnected, reintegrated, and reactivated as an adult in a sacred community.

Sexuality is central to all initiation-rite imagery, the vital force that provides much of the content for the drama of death and rebirth. The call of adult sexual life sets the process in motion, as exemplified by the Indian society in British Columbia in which ceremonies began for the male adolescent between his twelfth and sixteenth year, "when for the first time he dreamed of an arrow, a canoe, or a woman." Then the mutilation of genital organs of either sex and the various taboos upon female menses and sexual activity in general signify the loss of that vital force, the absence of life, followed by the lifting of taboos in the celebration of reunion, including, in the case of girls, joyous, provocative dancing, and of boys, various forms of orgiastic license.

Sexuality is the essence of the new adult power held out before the initiate, a form of vitality that must be earned. Sexual power (heralded in dream images of a woman) is inseparable from warrior strength, courage, and skill (dream images of an arrow or a canoe). Just as one must understand death and be willing to face it in order to become a warrior, *so must one* (in the broader significance of the ritual message) *"know death" in order to become a powerful and responsible sexual adult.*

Since the whole process is part of a sacred cosmology, proximate and ultimate dimensions merge. Immediate sexual pleasure is appreciated and sought after, but in the service of organismic transcendence—one "loses oneself" in order to merge with some form of ultimate life-power. However free or restricted sexuality may be, it is always part of something larger than itself.

More generally, with the completion of the initiation ordeal, "the concept of the ego has been expanded . . . beyond the biography of the physical individual." The adolescent-adult feels himself or herself linked to "a time-transcending order."[13] This transcendent dimension links the emerging adult to history, which in premodern societies and for many in our own society means sacred history. From the standpoint of our psychological paradigm, we may speak of an inner linkage of proximate and ultimate levels and a confirmation of the individual as one who has achieved that linkage.

Ritual does not in itself create the basic psychic imagery involved. *Rather, the initiation process expresses, embellishes, and orders universal psychobiological struggles specific to puberty and adolescence around life and death imagery.* The rituals themselves provide structure and drama through which this universal imagery can be channeled into the immortalizing institutions and belief systems of a particular society or culture. Whatever their excesses (in our eyes), the people we call primitives knew, as we do not know, how to accept, call forth, and orchestrate the life-death struggles that are part of this crucial moment of human growth.

To illustrate most of these principles, consider the following sequence of initiation rites in a primitive, nonliterate, Central Australian people who hunt the kangaroos, the Aranda:[14]

> When a youngster is between ten and twelve years old . . . he and the other members of his age group are taken by the men of the village and tossed several times into the air, while the women, dancing around to the company, wave their arms and shout. Each boy then is painted on his chest and back with simple designs by a man related to the social group from which his wife must come, and as they paint the patterns the men sing: "May he reach to the stomach of the sky, may he grow up to the stomach of the sky, may he go right into the stomach of the sky." The boy is told that he now has upon him the mark of the particular mythological ancestor of whom he is the living counterpart; for it is thought that the children born to women are the reappearances of beings who lived in the mythological age, in the so-called "dreamtime," or *altjeringa*. The boys are told that from now on they will not play or camp with the women and girls, but with the men; they will not go with the women to grub for roots and to hunt for such small game as rats and lizards, but will join the men and hunt the kangeroo. . . .
>
> The real trials of the growing youngster, and the second stage of his initiation . . . commence one evening, suddenly, in the men's camp, when he is pounced upon by three strong young fellows, loudly shouting, who bear him off, frightened and struggling, to a ceremonial ground that has been prepared for his circumcision. The whole community is there to greet him, women as well as men, and when he finds himself among them his struggles cease.
>
> He is placed among the men, and the women at once begin to dance, flourishing shields. They are now the women of the age of dream, the *altjeringa* age, who danced this way when the young men of the age of the ancestors were to be initiated; and the men sing while they perform. When the boy has watched and listened for some time—never having seen such things before—strands of fur string are wound around his head to make a tightly fitting cap, and there is tied about his waist a girdle of twisted hair, such as he has seen the men wear. Three men then lead him through the dancing women to a brake of bushes behind which he is now to remain for a number of days. They paint on him a design and warn him that he is now entered upon a higher stage of young manhood. He must never disclose to any woman or boy any of the secret things that he is about to see and learn. Throughout the coming ceremony he is not to utter a word unless addressed, and then only to answer as briefly as possible. And he is to remain crouching behind his brake until called. Should he attempt to see what he is forbidden to see, the great spirit whose voice he has heard in the sound of the bull-roarers would carry him away. And so he sits alone and silently all night, behind the brake, while the men dance on the ceremonial ground.
>
> The next day the boy's mother arrives, accompanied by the sisters of his father and by the woman whose daughter has been assigned to become his wife. All night the boy's mother has kept a fire burning in her camp, and she now brings in her hands two long sticks lighted from this fire. The men sing a fire-song while the mother hands one stick to the woman who is to become the boy's mother-in-law, and the latter, approaching the boy, ties some bands of fur string around his neck,

hands him the fire-stick, and tells him to hold fast to his own fire; that is to say, never to interfere with women assigned to other men. This rite concluded, the boy returns to his brake with the fire-stick, and the women go back with the second fire-stick to their camp.

The boy is now taken into the forest, where he sits quietly for three days and is given little to eat. The great solemnity of the rites that he is about to behold is thus impressed upon his whole mind and he is prepared to receive the impact of their imagery. On the fourth day he is returned to his brake, and that night the men's performances begin. They are to continue for about a week. . . .

At midnight the boy undergoing the ordeal was blindfolded, led from his brake, and placed face downward at the edge of the dance ground, then, after a time, was told to sit up and look; whereupon he saw lying before him a decorated man who represented, as he was told, a wild dog. A second decorated man was standing with legs apart at the other end of the dance ground, holding up twigs of eucalyptus in each hand, and having on his head a sacred ornament emblematic of the kangeroo. The kangeroo moved its head from side to side, as though watching for something, and every now and then uttered the call of the kangeroo. The dog looked up, saw the other, began barking, and suddenly, running on all fours, passed between the other's legs and lay down behind him, the kangeroo watching the dog over his shoulder. The wild dog then ran between the kangeroo's legs once again, but this time was caught and thoroughly shaken. A pretense was made of dashing his head against the ground, whereupon he howled, as if in pain, until, finally, he was supposed to have been killed. He lay still for a while, but then, on all fours, came running to the boy candidate and lay on top of him. The kangeroo hopped over and lay on top of the two, and the boy had to bear their weight for about two minutes; when they got up, he was told that their mime represented an event of the *altjeringa* age, when a wild-dog man attacked a kangeroo man and was killed. He was sent back to his brake, and the men continued singing throughout the night.

This sort of thing went on for the boy's instruction for six days and nights. Kangeroo men, rat men, dog men, little night hawks and big performed their legends, lay on top of him, and went away. But then, on the seventh day, behind his brake, the boy was solemnly rubbed all over with grease and three men carefully painted his back with a design of white pipe-clay, while on the dance ground a number of performances were enacted in which the women had a role. Suddenly the sound was heard of approaching bull-roarers, and the women fled. The lad was lying on his back. The men piled poles on top of him, banging them up and down on his body, beating time, while they sang, over and over, the following verse:

> Night, twilight, a great clear light:
> A cluster of trees, sky-like, rising red as the sun.

All was now excitement. The fire was giving a brilliant light and the two men who were to perform the circumcision took their position at the western end of the ceremonial ground. With their beards thrust into their mouths, their legs widely extended and their arms stretched forward. the two men stood perfectly still, the actual operator in front and his assistant pressing close up behind him, so that their bodies were in contact with each other. The front man held in his extended right hand the small flint knife with which the operation was to be conducted, and, as soon as they were in position, the boy's future father-in-law, who was to act as shield bearer, came down the lines, carrying the shield on his head and at the same time snapping the thumb and first finger of each hand. Then, facing the fire, he knelt down on one knee just a little in front of the operator, holding his shield above his head. During the whole time the bull-roarers were sounding everywhere so loudly that they could easily be heard by the women and children in their camp, and by them is supposed that the roaring is the voice of the great spirit *Twanyirika*, who has come to take the boy away.[15] . . . .

Still believing in Twanyirika, the boy is lying on his back beneath the rising and falling poles. The deep, loud tones of the circumcision song are being thundered out by all the men, when, suddenly, the poles are removed and the boy lifted by two strong fellows, is carried feet foremost to his shield, upon which he is placed. Quickly the assistant circumciser grasps the foreskin, pulls it out as far as possible, and the operator cuts it off. Immediately, all the men who have acted in any official capacity in the rite disappear, and the boy, in a more or less dazed condition, is told by those who carried him, "You have done well, you have not cried out." He is conducted back to the place where the brake had stood but now is gone, and receives the congratulations of the men. The blood from his wound is allowed to flow into a shield and while he is still bleeding some of the bull-roarers are brought up and pressed against the wound. He is told that it was these, and not Twanyirika, that made the sound—and thus he is forced past the last bogey of childhood. He learns at the same time that the bull-roarers are *tjurunga*, sacred objects deriving from the mythological age and realm. He is introduced to all the functionaries by their ceremonial names and given a packet of *tjurungas* by the eldest.

"Here is Twanyirika, of whom you have heard so much," the old man tells him. "These are *tjurunga*. They will help to heal you quickly. Guard them well and do not lose them, or you and your blood and tribal mothers and sisters will be killed. Do not let them out of your sight. Do not let your blood and tribal mothers see you . . . do not eat forbidden food."

The boy, meanwhile, is standing over a fire whose smoke is supposed to heal his wound; but there is a second meaning to this action of the smoke, for in Australia a child is smoked at birth, to purify it: the lad has just undergone at this moment his second birth. . . .

When the boys have died their death of childhood and survived their painful metamorphosis into incarnations of the original androgynous being, they are told that they have no further operations to fear. There is one more extremely interesting event in store, however, when, following a season of some four full months of continuous dancing and viewing of the world-establishing mythological age of the cosmic "dream time," they will be shown—in a very mysterious way—a particularly important double *tjurunga*, after which they will be roasted on a hot, though smothered fire, and finally sent back to the women's camp to be received by their waiting brides as fully tested and warranted Aranda males.

[This is] known as the Engwura ceremony . . . conducted by a number of tribal groups, which have come together with some eighteen or twenty young men to be initiated . . . the festal spirit, growing greater and greater from week to week, keeps the whole company, by some miracle of the gods, from collapsing in sheer fatigue. The daytime temperature at times reaches a broiling 156° F; nevertheless, the rites go on unabated, and if anyone dies of sunstroke the blame is placed on the black magic of some alien tribe.

A supernatural being called Numbakulla, "Eternal," is supposed to have fashioned the original *tjurungas*, and then, by splitting these, to have made pairs. The pairs were then tied together, one having a man's spirit and one a woman's, the two being mates. And the name of these double *tjurungas* is *ambilyerikirra*.

. . . . The leader of the Engwura remained in camp preparing, with the aid of the men of his locality, a special sacred object which consisted of two large wooden *tjurunga*, each three feet in length. They were bound together with human hair string so as to be completely concealed from view, and then the upper three-quarters were surrounded with rings of white down, put on with great care, and so closely side by side, that when complete the appearance of rings was quite lost. The top was ornamented with a tuft of owl feathers. When it was made it was carefully hidden in the dry bed of a creek.[16]

The men's camp had been divided from the women's throughout the four months of the ceremony by this dry bed of a stream in which the *tjurunga* now lay buried. There it remained until the candidates for initiation, who had been away from the camp all day on a number of assigned adventures, returned and were made to lie in a row on their backs, while an old man, delegated to watch them, walked back and forth along the line. Perfect silence now fell over the camp. Night had descended; the young men were lying still; their guard was slowly pacing; it was perfectly dark; and the leader of the festival, who had spent the day fashioning the double *tjurunga*, was now squatting with the sacred object in his two hands, having dug it up from its place of hiding in the stream bed. He was holding it upright before his face by the undecorated end, holding it like a bat; and kneeling beside him, at either elbow, was an assistant. These two were supporting his arms, and the man was lifting and lowering the sacred object slowly before his face.

When the boys, returning to camp, had been made to lie down, the solemn trio had been screened from view by a phalanx of old men. Throughout the night, therefore, lying on their backs in the silence, the boys were unaware of what was taking place. The old man with his two assistants, however, was continually lifting and lowering the sacred symbol, without any cessation, save for a few seconds at a time, during the whole night.

At a certain moment of the night the older men began chanting, but the boys remained as they were. The guardian still paced before them. And it was not until dawn, when the boys were aroused, that the old leader and the two men supporting him ceased from lifting and lowering the *ambilyerikirra*. There was little wonder that they looked tired and haggard, but even yet their work was not quite done.

Getting up, they moved to the north end of the ceremonial area, the two sidesmen still retaining hold of the leader's arms. The young candidates proceeded to a line of sacred bushes, and having taken boughs, arranged themselves so as to form a solid square behind the leaders. Most of the older men remained on the Engwura ground, from which one of them, the watcher over the candidates, shouted instructions across to the women. The main party, headed by the three men bearing the *ambilyerikirra*, and accompanied by a few of the older men, moved in the form of a solid square out from the Engwura ground, over the river and up the opposite bank to where the women stood grouped together. . . . Each woman, with her arms bent at the elbow, moved her open hand, with the palm uppermost, up and down on the wrist as if inviting the men to come on while she called out "*Kutta, Kutta, Kutta,*" keeping all the while one leg stiff, while she bent the other and gently swayed her body. . . . The party approached slowly and in perfect silence, and when within five yards of the front rank of the women, the men who carried the *ambilyerikirra* threw themselves headlong on the ground, hiding the sacred object from view. No sooner had they done this than the young initiates threw themselves on the top, so that only the heads of the three men could be seen projecting from the pile of bodies. Then, after remaining thus for two minutes, the young men got up and formed into a square facing away from the women, after which the three leaders rapidly jumped up, turned their backs on the women, and were hustled through the square which they then led back to the Engwura ground, and with this the *ambilyerikirra* ceremony came to an end. . . . .

. . . . the way of the young initiate now should be to recognize the wisdom of "*Kutta, Kutta, Kutta*" as well as that of the bull-roarers' thrilling hum, and to let even the subincised penis be a bridge to the toils of life in the world as well as to the garden of the gods.[17]

The absence of formal cultural ritual renders the American adolescent more vulnerable to confusions around his images, but also freer to construct from them idiosyncratic combinations and attitudes.* Adolescence takes on something of an ad hoc quality. Although often structured enough, even rigid, in its group life and its sexual and athletic games, these informal rituals lack the depth of tradition or sacred connection to give firm and reliable shape to its compelling imagery.

That applies especially to the newly developing imagery of power and powerlessness, an issue for adolescents in all cultures and especially unresolved in our own. While power is usually understood as control over others, it is most basically life-power, the experience of vitality, competence, *and* control, as opposed to the powerlessness of feeling inundated by death imagery and reduced to "deadness." Here, as in so many ways, the American adolescent hovers between absolutes.

He or she is likely to be caught up in notoriously unsteady relationships to the death equivalents, gravitating from feelings of absolute separateness and

---

* There are of course various expressions of Christian confirmation ceremonies, and of the Jewish Bar Mitzvah and Bas Mitzvah, but these only rarely achieve the kind of symbolic power of primitive (or earlier religious) rites; they tend more to be social occasions, and may themselves be in various ways modified and improvised.

isolation from everyone and everything to a sense of merging totally with a group of peers—or with a single chum—in something approaching total connection. Similarly, the American adolescent may fluctuate from disintegrative feelings of being "wiped out," reduced to "absolutely nothing," and euphoric feelings of "having everything together," of things being "just right." In terms of stasis, the feeling of being "stuck" or "dead inside" can alternate with a sense of brimming over with energy and vitality. However unstable his relationship to life-death imagery, the contemporary adolescent must nonetheless call forth this imagery in connection with new dimensions of bodily experience, involvements beyond the self, and relationship to knowledge.

Concerning the crucial issue of sexual awakening, our society lacks not only formal ritual but any structure or pattern suggesting that the issue is being recognized and addressed. Experiencing strong bodily impulses, and faced with conflicting social messages of prohibition and encouragement, adolescent individuals and groups must continually improvise around their sexuality. The results vary from a new sense of vitality and liberated growth to mixtures of fear and guilt, despondency over failed performance, and deep confusion. Whether suppressing or numbing themselves to their sexuality (the "old-fashioned" social prescription, still very much present) or openly expressing it (the increasing legitimation of earlier erotic experience, encouraged by improved, available contraception and by imagery of sexual enlightenment), the problem for the adolescent remains: How does this powerful bodily impulse, newly experienced in a fullness that encompasses the entire self, relate to the rest of life and death imagery confronting one in immediate and ultimate ways?

For sexual awakening is virtually simultaneous with historical awakening, a leap in awareness concerning cultural forces (whether political movements, athletic traditions, or schools of art) extending beyond the individual life span. Not that the adolescent has been free of various forms of indoctrination from earliest childhood about such things as religion, the American way of life, private property, or the like. But only now can he begin to grasp the extent to which such issues have given rise to enduring (if now fragile) belief systems, organizations, and institutions. Rather than the single comprehensive cosmology of primitive societies, the American adolescent encounters an endless variety of fragmented images (political, religious, ethical) held vaguely or fiercely by his elders and in confusing relationship to one another. Less bound to a thought system than his counterparts in primitive societies, he is also less able to find coherent expression for his pressing image-feelings.

The fragmentation process reflects the more general symbolic breakdown of institutions and belief systems that has been taking place in the West since the late eighteenth century. Recent adolescent disillusionment in America, centered on Vietnam and Watergate, is an accentuation of a much older and larger process.

The relatively unstructured, *ad hoc* adolescence has in fact been with us long enough to have become something of a tradition of its own—and to have contributed to the many-sided sense of self characteristic of creative Americans. But the discomforts of our adolescent structures (or nonstructures) remain considerable. These discomforts were in one sense apparent during the various upheavals of the young during the late 1960s*—and even more so in the vulnerability of many in late adolescence to the coercive psychological manipulations of the totalistic religious cults during the 1970s. These cults reveal a great deal about the state of society in our time, but one way to understand them, and especially their considerable impact, is in terms of their role in providing "puberty rites" unavailable elsewhere in our society.

In a broader sense, the adolescent seeks knowledge. His relationship to whatever he can learn now takes on special significance for his struggles around a sense of self. For the self must make use of knowledge, whether of automobile engines (the adolescent tinkerer) or of esoteric religion (the adolescent spiritual enthusiast), in its continuing struggles with death imagery. The adolescent self gropes toward adult integration of proximate (largely bodily) and ultimate (largely mental or spiritual) feelings that is, toward adult centering. Adolescent tinkering and spirituality are frequently viewed as the reverse—as means of further separating body from mind via a transformation or sublimation of bodily (erotic) impulses. This view holds some truth, but it misses the central point: whatever the valence of one kind of feeling versus another, the adolescent is moving toward an adult style of symbolization and constructing psychic forms for adult use. Even where the tinkering or spirituality seems to be self-enclosed, rote, and technicized in the extreme, the knowledge-activity now reaches far beyond itself. "Playing with engines" involves images of mastering mechanism and one's physical environment in general, of a form of competence associated with life-power that touches upon all other aspects of existence. The quest for even the most mechanical forms of knowledge as with the most vividly spiritual (or religious) makes manifest the principle that knowledge is *mana*, and *mana* is desperately required by the beleaguered adolescent self. Knowledge is not only cognitive and emotional but also (as the Bible makes clear) erotic, and in all spheres it includes competence in performance. To be sure, knowledge from birth is equated with life-power. And also, from the beginning of life, the acquisition of knowledge can be inhibited by anxiety around death equivalents. But for the adolescent, knowledge attainment becomes especially crucial as he

---

* At the same time those upheavals were much more than mere adolescent or young-adult turmoil. They included confrontation of real political and historical issues, within a framework of confused and dishonored symbolizations—for instance, the various symbolizations of American virtue in the face of Vietnam, victimization of blacks, and extreme economic discrepancies. The young engaged in a wide variety of experiments with the self, and at moments sought to create something close to a "new history"—a new set of symbolic structures that were not only egalitarian but focused upon communal rites and ritual.[18]

senses its new importance for his adult life-power. This accounts for the desperation with which the adolescent can seek knowledge (or, when it is threatening, resist it). He may alternate between claiming absolute knowledge and confessing total ignorance. The same is true for the extremes of group conformity, friendships, and retreat from both into some kind of lonely quest. What is sought is a collective or individual source of the kind of knowledge that might enable him to feel unified—to cope with death and its equivalents and to experience affirmations of life.

In recent years we have heard much of the phenomenon of prolonged adolescence, of extended identity search,[19] of the emergence of a "stage of youth" between adolescence and adulthood,[20] and of variations on a "Protean style" of experimentation that is especially vivid in late adolescence and young adulthood. What these terms suggest in our paradigm is a historically induced extension of struggles with life-death image-feelings during the period between childhood and adulthood. Our contemporary dislocations can greatly intensify the adolescent's imagery of separation, stasis, and disintegration, and make it difficult for him to construct adult images and forms that he himself can believe in. The Protean style involves a wariness toward committing oneself to any particular form, an anxiety around premature closure, and a sense that available images publicly promising vitality are actually harbingers of inner deadness. For accompanying this process is at least a dim awareness that the choices made during the transition from adolescence to adulthood reverberate throughout the remainder of life. While it is true that everything from birth goes into the transition, it is now that one develops or fails to develop adult styles of connection (in love relationships, friendships, ties to groups and to ideas), of integrity (forms of inner harmony and of ethical behavior) and movement (combinations of growth, stability, and change). No wonder that suicide and schizophrenia tend to have their highest incidence at this time, for they represent extremes in unmanageable death anxiety occurring at a time of heightened susceptibility to such anxiety. It is the time, after all, of explosive discovery of the range of human possibility for pleasure and vitality—and the discovery of despair growing out of the beginning recognition of the gap between those possibilities and one's own inner experience.

During the ensuing period of young adulthood (from the early twenties through the late thirties) there tends to be less manifest turmoil and a sustained attempt at consolidation of imagery and life actions. For many there is progressively less concern with great causes or large historical questions and greater preoccupation with day-to-day involvements and with sustained human relationships—sexual ties, parenthood, and other forms of intimacy[21]—and with the development of specialized knowledge and skills around work. Once having entered history and initiated new connections beyond the self, there is no turning back. No matter how routine and narrow a life one may seem to lead, no matter how little one addresses larger questions, no matter how much a culture suppresses a sense of history and of ultimate human ties, adult life is nonetheless lived within the cosmic frame of the historical-immortal quest. *

The issue of death awareness in adulthood is handled differently from culture to culture. My own view is that active consciousness of death is in itself no barrier to "maintaining the world." The reverse may, in fact, be true. From the standpoint of our paradigm, a harmonious form of adulthood, with a balance of immediate fulfillment and ultimate connectedness, goes hand in hand with a capacity for death awareness. One can hardly deny the difficulty of achieving that kind of harmony in this culture in this era. But one can at least hold out as an ideal a style of adulthood, which permits death awareness without creating incapacitating death anxiety. To paraphrase the principle stated earlier, death awareness could well be necessary for deepened adult sexuality and intimacy— and there is evidence throughout this study that such is indeed the case.

Yet we must also acknowledge the possibility of the abrupt intrusion into the most ideal form of adulthood of the image of death as nothingness—the experience of what Erikson calls an "ego-chill" or "shudder which comes from the sudden awareness that our non-existence—and thus our utter dependence on a creator who may choose to be impolite—is entirely possible."[23] Erikson's reference to a creator, however jocular, again suggests that imagery of nonexistence, being "wiped out," has to do with ultimate matters. The process works both ways—the acute death anxiety of the ego-chill both contributes to and is partly created by a sense of radical disruption of all connection and equally radical impairment of the sense of immortality. At this stage (late twenties or so) one has fashioned "an initial life structure"[24] † specific to adulthood but has not yet laid confident claim to one's modes of immortality, especially those of family line and works. The young adult can therefore be stalked by a double image—that of unlived life and premature death—an image expressing one of the greatest of all human terrors. Hence the intensity of the

---

* Erik Erikson conveys this principle in different language: "To be adult means among other things to see one's own life in continuous perspective, both in retrospect and in prospect. By accepting some definition as to who he is, usually on the basis of a function in an economy, a place in the sequence of generations, and a status in the structure of society, the adult is able to selectively reconstruct his past in such a way that, step by step, it seems to have planned him, or better, he seems to have planned *it*. In this sense, psychologically we *do* choose our parents, our family history, and the history of our kings, heroes, and gods."[22]

Erikson believes that the tendency so apparent in young adulthood toward blocking out consciousness of death is an inbuilt more or less biological device that protects one from disturbing emotions that might interfere with the crucial functions of this stage, the creating and nurturing of new lives—with what in Hindu tradition is called "maintaining the world."

† Levinson et al describe their concept of life structure as follows: "In its external aspects it refers to the individual's overall pattern of roles, memberships, interests, condition, and style of living, long-term goals, and the like—the particular ways in

urge to have and rear children, to achieve something important in one's work, to live out a vision of the future that involves in some significant way "leaving a trace." Failing to be in one's own eyes a good mother, good father, good provider can be readily equated with various forms of death imagery— separation from the great chain of being, disintegration in the sense of ethical failure, stasis in the sense of impeding or inadequately contributing to the flow of generations. These ultimate feelings frame and give force to immediate feelings of humiliation and worthlessness. Similarly, the capacity of the young man or woman to love and nurture in an immediate way—for what Erikson calls intimacy and generativity—reverberates through all layers of the self and infuses its ultimate involvements.

For young adults in our society there is a special paradox. They tend to be aware of struggles around death equivalents (separation, disintegration, and stasis) and to a degree, insofar as life is examined at all, around modes of immortality (involvements with family, work, or high principles of any sort). But there is little if any examination—conscious imagery—of actual death. There seems, in fact, to be a retreat from the prior (adolescent) level of death awareness, a retreat which lends an inchoate quality to the important struggles around ultimate commitments characterizing this stage. In brief, the paradox lies in attempting to live the examined life without examining death. This particular sequence of diminished death awareness, from adolescence to young adulthood, probably extends to other cultures—we need much more study of such matters everywhere—but there is good reason to believe that the American suppression of death imagery in young adulthood is uniquely intense and constitutes a cultural suppression of life's possibilities.

There comes a point in adult life—sometime during the late thirties or early forties—when consciousness of one's own death becomes more insistent. Much of that awareness comes directly from perceptions of bodily change—diminution of strength and endurance, graying of hair, loss of muscle tone and changes in the skin and (for men) relative decline in sexual capacity. Just when one is likely to have consolidated one's major life tasks, carrying them out can begin to take on the quality of a struggle against time. That struggle intensifies doubts about the validity of immortalizing projects and at the same time leaves one with the feeling that, whatever one's difficulties and doubts, it is now or never.

The "mid-life crisis," then, is in essence a crisis in ultimate life projects. The crisis may involve dramatic decisions and actions that seem to be inconsistent with what had appeared to be an orderly life pattern. Men and women break away from marriage and families, seeking to take advantage of a "last chance"

---

which he is plugged into society. In its internal aspects, life structure includes the personal meanings these have for the individual, as well as the inner identities, core values, fantasies, and psychodynamic qualities that shape and infuse one's engagement in the world and are to some degree fulfilled and changed by it."

for loving and caring relationships previously denied them. Or they change jobs or even careers for a similar last chance to live out earlier visions and move closer to an equation of work and works. Or else they make no outward changes but inwardly reexamine and recast their images and forms around both love and work.

The process can take the form of low-key self-questioning, or it can be filled with pain and suffering. But it now seems that some period of conflict is a regular aspect of the adult phase of the life cycle, at least in our society. One can speak of an endless wave of death imagery that, building in intensity, causes endless anxiety. Having been so long suppressed, this imagery can break out and overwhelm consciousness. Anxious anticipation of the end of existence throws new doubt and anxiety on to the death equivalents—one wonders whether one has confused rote dependency with genuine connection, unexamined adjustment (or social integration) with authentic integrity, improved operative skill with personal growth and vitality. In sum, the deepened psychobiological awareness of actual death activates all forms of imagery having to do with the balance of vital and nonvital existence in all of our lives.

The questions raised place one at risk. But suppressing those issues can involve risks of a different kind—of remaining in a workable, even manifestly successful mode of being that is fundamentally static, devoid of realization of basic aspects of the self, and infused with numbing. Creative men and women take special pains to permit the inner questions to be raised and to respond to them—even at the cost of personal stability, secure life arrangements, and public acclaim. Such people must, as Erikson has pointed out, reject premature success, which can express a collusion between competent but deadened elements of the self and various forms of social consensus. That conclusion, with or without external success, can result in a more or less permanent despair, a mixture of numbing and various expressions of unmanageable death imagery. The increased capacity to imagine the end of the self can release powerful, revitalizing energies—if one can relate that image to the questioning of ultimate choices and of the quality of immediate experience.

Following upon this crisis (or transition, as Levinson calls it) a later consolidation of life projects takes place. If that consolidation is inwardly perceived to be inauthentic, despair can deepen to a degree previously unknown in the life cycle. Inexorable images of separation from others and from the life process in general, of an unbreakable habit of violated integrity, and of the mind caught in static closure in relationship to whatever external events are taking place around it are prominent features of this despair. Not only are life projects negated but one has lost hope of ever rendering them or oneself vital.

But there is another side to this later consolidation too often neglected by psychological theory. There is a special quality of life-power available only to those seasoned by struggles of four or more decades. That seasoning includes extensive cultivation of images and forms having to do with love and caring, with experienced parenthood, with teaching and mentorship, with work combinations and professional creativity, with responses to intellectual and artistic images around one, and above all with humor and a sense of the absurd. These seasoned psychic forms are by no means devoid of death imagery. Rather they are characterized by ingenious combinations of death equivalents and immediate affirmations, of melancholic recognition of the fragmentation and threat surrounding all ultimate involvements, along with dogged insistence upon one's own connections beyond the self—one's own relationship to collective modes of symbolic immortality. Like the despair, the life-power of this stage can be especially profound. It can include the mature, formative experience of the entire organism and the capacity to call forth in measured ways considerable strength of mind and body, along with a special level of image mastery. For those in their forties and fifties with a minimum of this life-power, important immediate and ultimate ties can still, of course, be questioned but not easily negated or destroyed.

The transition from the consolidations of late middle age to "old age" tends to be gradual, at times obscure. The psychobiological basis for the process lies in significantly diminished physical capacity—it is no longer a question of measured strength but of a marked curtailment of what the body can do—and the accompanying awareness of the nearness of death. The average age of the transition is about the mid-sixties, but it is probably the most varied transition of all—and the one least marked by models or even informal rituals. Immediate involvements of the individual person diminish while his ultimate (social and cultural) reverberations expand. As Campbell has put it, "the shift is from a local to a generally human system of references."[25] In primitive society, old age (which might actually occur in these societies as early as the forties) is mythologized as a border of life and death—a state containing a "threshold image, uniting pairs-of-opposites in such a way as to facilitate a passage of the mind beyond anxiety."[26] In the premodern past, the old person had an image of himself as an exemplary and important repository of the past, one whose life could be summed up and extracted to provide a model for the young, and whose knowledge (especially of sacred ritual) could be directly transmitted in ceremonies over which he presided. We should not romanticize premodern old age. It seems to have had its aspects of terror and taint—much like death itself, for which the old person is always the designated representative. But it also conveyed a sense of special power, derived from having traversed so much of life and moved beyond its immediate struggles, and from now being closer to (in a sense already in) death and therefore more knowledgeable about it than others. The old person, while still alive, moved toward legend, had come closest to the secrets of life and death. The old, as Jung said, reflected the sequence of involvements over the course of the life cycle from nature to culture.

We can turn to traditional China for an ideal model of the old as exemplars and arbiters in a highly literate, premodern culture. One might consider the readiness for death of an elderly patriarch who has lived fully and seen his children and grandchildren prosper; his sons maintain the strength, filial piety, and ritual requirements of his family line as defined by the Confucianist doctrine he has done so much to perpetuate and which his life now illustrates and expresses; his daughters likewise, as wives and mothers in families allied to his own through their marriages; the old man confident that the proper rites will be meticulously carried out when his time comes. Granting that no such ideally realized patriarch ever existed in China or elsewhere, the picture at least conveys something barely imaginable to us—a sense of old age as an acceptable and meaningful stage that provides for everyone the crucial imagery of the oneness of life and death.

No wonder, then, that in many societies the very old and the very young are allies and playmates, free of the work of culture and exemplars of ultimate thresholds, at the beginning and the end of existence.*

One can observe only the barest glimmerings of these functions of old age in our own culture. The alliance with the very young may still be found at times. Here and there the old are still seen (and see themselves) as exemplars of a life trajectory and mediators of ultimate cultural principles that are ancient and perhaps even sacred. More often, however, the old carry only the image of the tainted death mask. They are caught in the middle of a vicious circle in which we reject and seclude them because they remind us of death and undermine our fantasies of perpetual youth, leaving them deprived of a life function and flooded with negative imagery of death and death equivalents. They then manifest little of the benign wisdom of old age and much of its potential for bitter accusation and death-linked curse, resulting in further withdrawal and abuse on the part of the rest of society.

The speed of cultural change, the requirements of technology, the mobility of family life, and the overall flux in symbol systems and ideologies are factors in the decline of old age as a respectable and respected stage of life. But operating behind, between, and within all of these is the fear of death. That fear in turn reflects and contributes to the unique unsteadiness and fragility of our experience as Americans with the various modes of symbolic immortality.

Perhaps in all societies there have been old people, especially men, who have sought to maintain something close to full productive work up to their deaths. Perhaps the question is not so much the extent to which one continues with productive work as the extent to which one inwardly acknowledges a new and

---

* . . . the old in many societies spend a considerable part of their time playing with and taking care of the youngsters, while the parents delve and spin; so that the old are returned to the sphere of eternal things not only within but without. And we may take it also, I should think, that the considerable mutual attraction of the very young and the very old may derive something from their common, secret knowledge that it is they and not the busy generation between, who are concerned with a poetic play that is eternal and truly wise.[27]

final stage of life; a context for that work in which one is less directly involved in personal encounters, and more in a completion of self *and* work as a legacy to both immediate survivors and larger culture. Within that context, one can both work hard into death and grow old gracefully. Without it, the work is driven and compensatory; the denial of old age is denial of death and both reflect despair over the vitality and authenticity of projects and involvements over a lifetime. Both patterns of work into death are widespread in our society, perhaps the second especially so. Yet we also know that there can be equal despair, and for the same reasons, in retirement—with its frequently pathetic substitution of a shallow image of the "good life" for the deeper meanings and connections that have never quite existed.

In general the old in our culture must forage for their means of consolidation. They must struggle with their diminished physical and mental capacities, their generally limited access to family and cultural forms, and with their aura of death in terms of both the fear it instills in them and its aversive effect on others. There is a special importance in our society of what some who work with the elderly call a "life review."[28] This is a slightly formalized therapeutic expression of the tendency of old people to reminisce and endlessly reexamine events, impressions, and sequences in their past. That tendency is a kind of final reckoning around all of the life-death issues we have been discussing, immediate and ultimate. To die well one must feel a measure of self-completion—imagery of a life with connection, integrity, and movement, and of dying as part of some immortalizing current in the vast human flow. These can be momentous issues for the dying. They wish specifically to reassert elements of their individual lives that can connect with the lives of all others. A number of thanatologists have made thoughtful observations concerning the dramatic shifts of the dying, when attended by a sensitive, caring person, from denial, rage, and overwhelming anxiety to relative calm and acceptance of death.[29] What has been less appreciated has been the need of the dying for final assertion of their ties to imagery of continuing life.

SEVEN

Culture and Connection

To UNDERSTAND MORE about an individual person's anticipation of death, we must explore ways in which cultures shape that anticipation to incorporate imagery of both termination and continuity, of endings and beginnings. Indeed the idea of death itself is no more than a human construct, which is what Yeats meant when he said that "man created death." Man created both death and continuity. Death equivalents (and life parameters) have biological origins in the inchoate imagery we have described. But they are embedded in cultural symbolization. Each of them—connection-separation, integrity-disintegration, movement-stasis—is associated with a particular threat, and thereby with a particular standard for evaluating life.

For the individual in any culture, death is anticipated to some important degree as a severance of the self's connections, that is, a loss of the psychic network of family, friends, work, and ideas. Whenever one contemplates death both proximate and ultimate involvements are at issue. They are questioned and reasserted against the real terror: the threat of *total severance*. That threat is reflected in attitudes toward the dead, especially the newly dead.

In Hiroshima I encountered a deep and painful ambivalence of survivors toward the dead. These feelings were related to a universal dilemma around ties to the dead: on the one hand the survivor's need to embrace them, pay homage to them, and join in various rituals to perpetuate his relationship to them; on the other his tendency to push them away, to consider them tainted and unclean, dangerous and threatening. In Hiroshima this sense of taint was intensified by early, grotesque symptoms including severe diarrhea, bleeding into the skin and then from all bodily orifices, and loss of hair. All these were thought at first to be manifestations of a strange epidemic and were only later recognized as radiation effects. There was cruel irony in that the contamination was by no means limited to cultural imagery *about* corpses; they were actually dangerous to handle for a period of time, and those involved in their disposal became vulnerable to radiation effects even if they had been well outside the city when the bomb fell.[1]

Virtually all cultures make a distinction between the *dying body* and the *surviving spirit*, the contaminated (death-ridden) corpse and the pure (immortal) soul. In ancient Japan, long before the arrival of Buddhism, death was profoundly feared, and the dead were looked upon as "unclean and ominous." Between the fourth and sixth centuries a belief developed in a version of eternal soul *(tama)*. After Buddhism, elaborate imagery was created of the soul's journey to paradise or to (as one major sect teaches) the Pure Land, the "realm of compassion" in which *bodhisattvas* (those who have attained perfect wisdom and are candidates for Buddhahood) dwell. On the whole, Japanese imagery of an afterlife has been very limited and subsumed to rather concrete stress upon this-worldly concerns with separation and connection. There has been great stress on the dying person's relationship to his own death, and the survivor's relationship to the dead.[2]

The early Japanese, like many primitive peoples, lacked a clear sense of distinction between life and death. A body was thought to become a corpse at the moment its soul (really, life-principle) separated from it. There were certain steps one could take to prevent the soul from departing, or to call it back when it had just left.* One was to offer water to the person apparently near death; and in Hiroshima the severe guilt experienced by survivors of the bomb over not having given water to the dying could well have been related to that ancient belief. Other steps to retain the apparently departing soul were the serving of rice at the bedside of the dying or dead person (known as *makuramashi* or "pillow rice"); and the calling out of the person's name *(tamayobi*, literally "soul-calling").

But once the soul was thought to have departed, the dead body became something very close to a phobic object, defiled and defiling. Special measures were taken to overcome that defilement: the path along which the dead body was carried from the house had to be swept out; rice bowls that had been used by the dead person were broken; and those who attended the dead person in his final hours remained in isolation for a period of time "so that the foulness of death would not affect other members of the community." In early practice, the corpses themselves were simply taken some distance from the village and thrown into ditches, or else to mountain areas where they were abandoned to beasts and birds of prey. In certain areas of Japan, old people would head for the

* We are still quite uncertain, medically and legally, about where to draw the line between life and death. And our energetic efforts at resuscitating the "dead" person have a certain parallel to primitives' struggles to prevent the soul from departing.

mountains while still alive in order to die there alone. All these practices reflect primitive peoples' characteristic dread of corpses, and enable the living to have the most minimal contact with them.

Those of noble or royal birth were apparently buried more carefully, together with some of their belongings and, on some occasions, the bodies of retainers who had ritually immolated themselves in order to accompany their masters to the grave. And there have been some Japanese mummifications of important religious figures. But even mummification—more widespread in China, and much more so, of course, in ancient Egypt—follows the principle of the inert body and the living soul: what appears to be immortalization of the body can be understood as an attempt to preserve it sufficiently for the soul to return to it.[3] And the same principle applies in the imagined later use of old belongings buried with the corpse.

Even when primitive artistic figures of humans and animals (haniwa, literally, clay rings) were buried together with corpses or placed at the banks or crests of tomb mounds, their purpose was not to honor the corpse but to mark a "sacred enclosure" or "sacred fence" between the living and the dead, barring trespassing in either direction. Later Japanese resorted to widespread cremation, largely through Buddhist influence, reflecting similar attitudes of "little respect for dead bodies or desire to preserve them, but rather . . . the hidden idea of dead bodies as filthy and fearful."[4] The pressing need was to get rid of the death-tainted corpse and to liberate the life-principle, the soul. This done, the remains or ashes could be treated with reverence.

A slightly later Japanese manifestation of the connection-separation dilemma was the "double grave system," which according to some scholars evolved as a compromise in response to Buddhist attempts to inculcate greater reverence for dead bodies.[5] The system included a "burial grave" for the actual corpse and a second "visiting" or "memorial grave" which contained no more than the hair or fingernails of the deceased, and sometimes not even that, but it was the place for family members to pay their respects and conduct their rituals. In some cases the corpse would be dug up, after a safe period of time, and reburied in the memorial grave. The custom literalizes the psychological dichotomy between the "place of enshrinement" for the symbolized life-principle on the one hand, and the "dumping-ground for corpses" on the other. And even where (in Japan and elsewhere) the corpse is treated with greater reverence, the dichotomy of death-taint and immortal life-principle prevails.

What of the soul, the life-principle so determinedly "released"? Early Shinto writings relate the Japanese term for soul, tama, to the idea of "breath" or "wind."[*] The same association is made in a great variety of cultures, as in the

---

[*] Hiroshima survivors thought they saw blue or purple phosphorescent flames rising from dead bodies, and associated these with the fireballs [tama-shi] that, in Japanese folklore, are thought to emerge from the body at the time of death.[6]

biblical image of the "breath of life." Indeed the Western concept of soul has been consistently associated with this vitalizing image—as suggested by the synonyms for soul, *pneuma* and *animus [anima]*, the former Greek, and the latter Latin, for breath, wind, or vital spirit.

Most primitive cultures have subdivisions of souls, as in the early Shinto distinction between soul elements that are "mild, refined, and happy" and those that are "rough, brutal, and raging."[7] Later Buddhist developments extended Shinto influences to formulate three types of souls: the "living soul" *(ikimitama)* residing in the living person; the "new soul" or "year soul" *(aramitama)* that emerges from the recently dead; and the "ancestor souls" *(mitama)* that have found a permanent and peaceful dwelling-place. In terms of our own psychological model the "living soul" symbolizes ongoing biological life, the "new soul" the encounter with death and severance, and the "ancestor soul" a sense of immortality that transcends death. The first and third varieties present no threat. They protect and in fact *are* the life-principle, so long as they are given proper symbolic recognition through prescribed ritual. But the souls of the recent dead belong to a dangerous group of "restless" or "homeless souls," so designated in most primitive cultures. That same group also includes the souls of those who died in precipitous or premature ways: through violence or disaster, in childbirth, after betrothal but prior to marriage, or when far from one's native place. "Homeless souls" are believed to threaten the well-being, even the lives, of the surviving community.[8] For they suggest impairment in the rhythm of life and death, a state of undue vulnerability to death, of severed connection from both the living and the acceptably dead.

The great problem for survivors in all cultures is to convert "homeless souls," particularly those of the recent dead, into comfortably enshrined or immortalizing souls. Funeral ceremonies are rites of passage precisely for this purpose. *What is involved is the symbolic transformation of a threatening, inert image (of the corpse) into a vital image of eternal continuity (the soul)—or of death as absolute severance to death as an aspect of continuous life.*

To accomplish this transformation, Japanese funeral customs, and many others, stress "the rapid separation of spirits from dead bodies."[9] That principle of rapid separation would seem to conflict with desperate efforts (described above) to call back the fleeing soul—and in fact it does. The conflict itself is the essence of the separation-connection dilemma. Continuing connection with the dead person is constantly stressed, but for that connection to be comfortable or even manageable it must be established, as quickly as possible, on a new basis independent of the dead body. Even the rituals to call back the fleeing soul may be perfunctory expressions of courtesy to the dying person, while primary survivor energies are aimed at speeding its journey into a place and state of immortality.*

* To facilitate that journey, the body is washed of its impurities, placed in the special

Survivors' psychological needs include *both* connection and separation. Thus there is burning of incense before the casket and the bidding of farewell; yet family members are the ones who initiate the nailing of the coffin and convey the corpse from the house. Similarly, after cremation, family members in ritual fashion take bones from among the remains with chopsticklike instruments; and the chief mourner places these bones in a wooden box which is wrapped in red cloth and either then or soon afterward buried in the grave. In all this one feels the tension between the need to remain close to the dead person and to stay in contact with evidences of him; the equal need to be rid of his body and of these same evidences; and in the process to absorb the fact of personal separation, the fact of death and image of loss. This is the survivor's "work of mourning," his struggle to reconstitute his psychic life in a way that can enable him to separate from the dead person while retaining a sense of connection with him, free himself from the deadness of that person and reestablish within himself, sometimes in altered form, whatever modes of immortality have been threatened by the death.

Western death practices reflect precisely the same struggle. Writing about a Protestant cemetery in a mid-twentieth-century American city, W. Lloyd Warner tells us that

> The fundamental *sacred* problem of the graveyard is to provide suitable symbols to refer to and express man's hope of immortality through the sacred belief and ritual of Christianity and to reduce his anxiety and fear about death as marking the obliteration of his personality—the end of life for himself and for those he loves . . . the fundamental *secular* problem the graveyard solves is to rid the living of the decaying corpse, thus freeing them from the nauseous smells of corruption and from the horror of seeing the natural decomposition of a human body, thereby helping to maintain the satisfying images of themselves as persistent and immortal beings. . . . [11]

But the American emphasis on cosmetic embalming can confuse the matter

---

position (head facing north) in which Buddha was believed to lie as he entered Nirvana, dressed in "traveling clothes for the dead" (special half-gloves, leggings, stockings, and straw sandals [sometimes an extra pair]), provided with equipment for prayer and even at times money to pay for crossing the river *Sanzu*, the Japanese equivalent of the river Styx. [10] A contemporary Buddhist funeral may still include many of these bodily preparations, even though the body is to be cremated. For it is the soul alone that makes the journey, and the residual customs symbolize survivors' psychological insistence that the journey be made. There also may be an all-night vigil kept by family members—the *otsuia* (literally, "entire night")—during which the priest chants a sutra for the purpose of initiating the soul's journey and enhancing the dead person's entry into Buddhahood. In the traditional past a sword was sometimes placed next to the head of the corpse in order to protect it from "wild beasts or evil spirits," but perhaps both vigil and sword have had the equal purpose of protecting the living from the "evil spirits" that might emanate from the corpse.

considerably, as a number of writers have pointed out. They "play down the death of the person and . . . create the illusion of a living being . . . [who] will receive his friends one last time, in a flower-ladened room and to the sound of sweet or serious—never gloomy—music."[12] The psychological confusion here is the reliance on the dead body for the symbolization of continuity and immortality. It is the confusion of the literal and the symbolic. Simpler Christian burial practices avoid this confusion by openly acknowledging the body's end, its decomposition. And the traditional Jewish stress upon quick burial, with extensive ritual arrangements for both mourning and reassertion of life, does the same.

Significantly, the survivor-mourner is himself generally considered to be in a state of impurity.* The object of the soul's journey is a place of ultimate purity, whether the sacred mountains or other sanctuaries of nature which have always had such hold on the Japanese imagination, or the Pure Land of Buddhist paradise. Once the dead have been purified (and rendered into "ancestral souls") they can have comfortable (though regulated) contact with the living during yearly or twice-yearly "visits" at festivals held for that purpose, as well as in the universal mythological idea of certain animals, particularly birds, as mediating agents between the dead and the living. The imagery is universal: pollution suggests death-taint and total severance; purity equals life-continuity and unbroken connection; and the process of purification, the transformation of the former to the latter.

The purifying-immortalizing process, significantly, involves loss of individual boundaries.†

This communalization of the soul and absence of any sharp concept of the immortal individual soul contrasts with the Judeo-Christian tradition. But one should by no means see that contrast as absolute. For one thing there are roughly analogous kinds of fusion in Judeo-Christian practice, especially in mystical traditions. Partly the fusion stands for transcending *all* boundaries—

---

* In Japanese practice he is not permitted to pass through the *tōri* or sacred gate of the Shinto shrine prior to completing his culturally designated mourning rituals. Until then we may say that he is considered to be tainted by unassimilated death. More than two thousand years ago, Chinese travelers to Japan reported that after a funeral all members of the dead person's family would cleanse themselves in a purifying bath. No culture has placed greater stress on death-associated pollution and purification. But there are related emphases on purification in orthodox Judaism, Christianity, Mohammedanism, and Hinduism.

† One definition of the Japanese word *kami* (or god) is "a soul which has been cleansed from impurity and has thereby lost its individual character."[13] That process, according to most Japanese commentators, requires a thirty-three-year purification sequence, after which the individual soul has become part of a larger entity. Eliade similarly speaks of the general cultural principle of the "transformation of the dead person into an 'ancestor'," and states that this "corresponds to the fusion of the individual into an archetypal category."[14]

spatial, temporal, and organic. But it also suggests a symbolization of the life-principle *in* the individual rather than of the individual himself—and in that sense underscores the symbolic as opposed to literal quality of the immortality.

Some of this kind of imagery may be contained in "liebestod fantasies" in which one's death is seen as an opportunity for reunion with lovers or family members who have already died. The most celebrated artistic expression of liebestod imagery is the Wagnerian opera, *Tristan und Isolde*, based on the Gottfried von Strassburg version of the Irish legend. In that legend Tristan, mortally wounded in battle, dies of despair when convinced that Isolde will not come to him, and she dies of grief upon finding him dead. But each welcomes death as a means of reunion, as a way of eternalizing their love. Such fantasies are generally looked upon as illusion, denial, or indications of various forms of psychopathology, as well they might be, especially when they become associated with suicidal ideas or actions. But liebestod imagery may also express various forms of continuing connection and identification, the sense that whatever one shared with a dead person or persons has ramifications that outlive any individual. Liebestod imagery, whether or not related to psychological disturbance, can thus serve as another form of symbolizing the idea of eventual merging of individual elements of the life-principle, the idea of one's feelings and actions continuing, beyond one's finite life, to blend with those of others.*

Another manifestation of this principle of connection by fusion is the Japanese concept (again mirrored in other cultures) of the "guardian gods." Each "guardian god represents the merging of large numbers of ancestral souls within a particular region, and thus comes to represent a pooling at this spiritual level of "immortal racial and cultural substance."[15] Similarly, guardian gods of different villages fuse in turn to create an expanding supernatural community, which ultimately became fused with the imperial family itself in a national constellation of both organic and ghostly immortal cultural substance. Guardian gods, as their name suggests, are believed to protect and nurture the living. And the whole arrangement is flexible—individual ancestor souls, for instance, may move in and out of the larger fusion in order to make their visits to the living on specific occasions, such as the Japanese New Year and summer festivals for the dead *(obon)*.

A sense of connection with the dead is thus felt to protect and nurture the living. It also serves the principle of what Eliade calls "the regeneration of time": the reenactment of crisis and chaos giving way to resolution (as in the Mexican festival described earlier); a recovery of an ultimate sense of beginnings (origins) and endings; and a return to a sense of "mythical time" within which there can be periodic death-and-rebirth rituals rather than the mere winding

---

* As in the case of symbolic immortality in general, liebestod imagery probably veers toward the pathological when it is literalized—when one believes in a reunion with a specific person that will permit them to continue together exactly as before.

down of life. Without some such ritualized connection with the dead, man becomes rootless, severed from the great chain of being, vulnerable to the vast variety of human and animal ghosts that populate his imagination and symbolize his dread of total severance from fellow human beings.

Japanese culture is unusually intense in its stress both on immediate separation from, and longstanding connection with, the dead. But that equilibrium of ambivalence pervades every culture. In the face of actual death, a survivor requires continuing connection to achieve his necessary separation, and separation to permit himself a new basis for connection. More generally, one can anticipate this equilibrium of ambivalence over the course of life, and associate it with one's eventual death. But in ordinary living the stress is on connection, which is why death is anticipated as both threat and test. Where evolving death imagery is open and blended with the vitality of immediate and ultimate involvements, anticipation of death can itself become more dialectical; severance is still feared but within a sustaining matrix of connection; and separations during life can also be absorbed within this larger matrix in ways parallel to the cultural rituals we have discussed.

EIGHT

Culture, Integrity, and Movement

THE ANTICIPATION OF DEATH as a test of the integrity of life is a familiar idea in literature and philosophy, and has more recently appeared in psychiatric writing.* "Tell me how you die and I will tell you who you are" is the way Paz sums up the matter.

Kurt Eissler distills the cause-and-effect aspect of this view and converts it into what he himself terms an "extreme position of psychic determinism":

> I wish to postulate tentatively the assumption that death—in whatever shape or form it may appear—is always a psychological event, growing out of the individual's total life history . . . that is to say, what appears to the naked eye as the accident, the physical effect of which ends life, is only the proximate cause, which is embedded as a precipitating factor, in the broad stream of the vicissitudes of the death instinct.[2]

The truth in what Paz and Eissler tell us lies not only in the fundamental unity of life and death but in the consequences of that unity: the universal

---

* Again Octavio Paz: Death defines life; a death depicts a life in immutable forms; we do not change except to disappear. Our deaths illuminate our lives. If our deaths lack meaning, our lives also lacked it. Therefore we are apt to say, when somebody has died a violent death, "He got what he was looking for." Each of us dies the death he is looking for, the death he has made for himself. A Christian death or dog's death are ways of dying that reflect ways of living. If death betrays us and we die badly, everyone laments the fact, because we should die as we have lived. Death, like life, is not transferable. If we do not die as we lived, it is because the life we lived was not really ours; it did not belong to us, just as the bad death that kills us does not belong to us.[1]

human fear of a death without integrity—of a death that is disintegrative in its humiliation, incoherence, absurdity, or prematurity. To imagine such a death is to see one's life in the same terms. *

The integrity-disintegration axis is not only a blend of the physiological, psychological, and ethical. It is also an important meeting ground of individual experience with cultural-historical and universal influences. One seeks imagery of integrity wherever one can find it, and that imagery is forever threatened by the anticipation of death.

Psychiatric theory has sometimes hinted at this anticipatory principle.[3] But even where free of causative assumptions around the death instinct, that theory

---

* The difficulty with Eissler's statement is that it literalizes the life-death relationship and reduces it to absolutized causative principles around the interplay of death instinct and life history. How would Eissler explain the death of a five-year-old child in Hiroshima, or of a Texas University student killed by a bullet from a mad sniper who knew nothing of anyone he caught in his rifle sights? All deaths are psychic as well as physical events, but not as expressions of an internal demon known as the death instinct, or even of a specific individual life history. Looking at the death of the Hiroshima child, for instance, we would have to consider Japanese and American historical themes around World War II (which created the American bombing and perhaps influenced the child's being in the center of the city, say working in a factory, rather than at a school farther from the hypocenter) and the new atomic weapon (the radius within which it kills or renders one vulnerable to fatal radiation effects, as well as the American programs and decisions in making and using it); along with such individual-cultural matters as family patterns (which might have dictated proximity of mother and child, and therefore determined where the child was when the bomb fell); and seemingly random factors determining why the child was near the center of the city at 8:15 that morning (mixtures of wartime policy and conscientiousness on the part of officials, parents, or the child, etc.). Similarly the death of the Texas student would have as much to do with the schizophrenic state of the sniper (his mixture of extreme early trauma, genetic susceptibility, and other unknown factors) and American and Texan patterns of violence and policies about guns (including frontier experience, collective themes around masculinity, and commercially powerful gun lobbies) as with the victim's own family and cultural relationships (determining his decision to attend that university, his habits of study and leisure, etc.). Even where there is a clear individual-psychological relationship to dying, as in the lung-cancer death of a man whose psychological needs were such that he could not alter his twenty-five-year pattern of smoking four packs of cigarettes a day, one would have to explore the relationship of his individual psychology to historical and cultural factors around price, availability, nicotine content, and advertising policies on cigarettes; smoking habits of his groups (adolescent, spouse, and other family members) and working unit (fellow laborers, professionals, or members of a firm)—all in the context of his own general imagery around death and vitality as evolved through personal, environmental, and cultural influences, and his genetic-organic susceptibilities (rendering him vulnerable to lung cancer) and strengths (perhaps postponing the onset of lung cancer). (Eissler disarmingly acknowledges that his absolute position "seems preposterous" but asks that we suspend common sense and look into the matter further— and I would hope that the above explanation is in the spirit of what he advocates.) In these examples our formative-symbolic approach resembles what is sometimes called "general systems theory."

has been hampered by another form of literality that sees human beings as existing psychologically only in here-and-now relationships and underestimates the scope of the temporal imagination. When psychiatric commentators speak of the middle-aged man's fear that he will be prevented "from making the mark he considers necessary to satisfy his own standards," or of the psychological strength experienced at the end of life by the person "sustained by his knowledge that something of meaning will continue after his death,"[4] they are groping toward broader temporal assumptions. But without the theoretical framework that posits the anticipatory importance of enduring continuity beyond the self, the psychiatric theorist is apt to fall back on ad hoc impressions, moralistic sentiments or such psychoanalytic platitudes as "a primarily narcissistic orientation." The integrity-disintegration axis is especially helpful here because of its direct bearing on the issue of meaning. It also has bearing on the question of *way of dying*.

The *Hagakure* expresses longstanding Japanese cultural emphases, as in the ringing phrase: "The essence of *Bushidō* lies in the act of dying."* More than this, it counsels continuous image-rehearsal, or imagination, of that act:

> Every morning make up thy mind how to die. Every evening freshen thy mind in the thought of death. And let this be done without end.
>
> Thus will thy mind be prepared. When thy mind is always set on death, thy way through life will always be straight and simple.[6]

Preoccupation with death, then, becomes the means of transcending it. One's dying must serve the immortalizing code of behavior that keeps one's name lastingly "immaculate" or pure:

> If one lives a day let him perform a day's duty and die; if he lives a month let him perform a month's duty and die; if he lives a year let him perform a year's duty and die.[7]

Individual readiness to die was to become so intense as to attain "a state which transcends the distinction between life and death." One was to become,

---

* No culture has given more attention to this matter than the Japanese. Indeed, the idea of a perfect—even transcendent—death is one of the organizing principles of traditional Japanese culture.[5] In the Japanese samurai code the ultimate meaning of life is expressed in a heroic death in battle on behalf of one's lord, a death embodying courage, purpose, and loyalty. When centuries of relative peace interfered with that warrior realization, loyalty and duty were even more absolutized in the classical eighteenth-century compilation of the principles of *Bushidō* (The Way of the Samurai), known as the *Hagakure*. That compilation went so far in its thanatology that some contemporary Japanese historians view it as the unbalanced, politically motivated advocacy of a death cult around absolute loyalty.

as a nineteenth-century philosopher-activist put it, "like a madman." The *Hagakure* declares:

> *Bushidō* means to die insane. Great deeds of *Bushidō* cannot be done if one is sound in mind. Just go mad, and die mad.[8]

In the absence of a religious principle of an afterlife—and samurai often expressed disdain for Buddhist supernatural approximations—immortality was specifically contingent upon the way one died.[9]*

We learn more about death as a test of integrity by reassessing Tolstoy's classic fictional statement on the subject, "The Death of Ivan Ilyich," and then comparing that story to a parallel Japanese statement, a film made in 1952 by the brilliant writer-director, Akira Kurosawa.

When Ivan Ilyich becomes aware that his illness is incurable, he begins to review his past. He is tormented by the thought that "the whole arrangement of his life and of his family, and all his social and official interest, might have been false." He feels that the only authentic expressions he can look back on have been "those scarcely noticeable impulses which he had immediately sup-pressed." Approaching death, he laments his wasted opportunity ("I have lost all that was given me and it is impossible to rectify"). These feelings are accompanied by a guilty awareness of the enormous gap between what he has been and what he might have been. As he struggles painfully toward insight, he dismisses medical preoccupations as meaningless distractions: "'Vermiform appendix! Kidney!' he said to himself. 'It's not a question of appendix or kidney, but of life and . . . death.'" The death he anticipates is abstract, insubstantial, terrifying, and intrusive, an "it" rather than a "thou.":

> . . . suddenly *It* would flash through the screen and he would see it . . . He would go to his study, lie down, and be alone with *It*: face to face with *It*. And nothing could be done with *It* except to look at it and shudder.[10]

Only when he experiences a sudden spiritual revelation, a profound wave of Christian love and pity, especially for his wife and son, does his terror, and in fact death itself, disappear. So that when, in his dying moment, he hears someone mutter, "It is finished," he takes that to mean: "Death is finished . . . it is no more." Death had signified total emptiness and annihilation, based upon a lifelong psychic model of disintegration and an ethical model of inauthenticity. That image of death is overcome only through the vivification of a sense of immortality in his revelation. His intense experiential transcendence

---

* See Appendix A for a more detailed description of Japanese cultural principles around integrity in dying, including additional features of samurai practice, ritual suicide, Buddhist visions of ideal death, and more recent historical behavior (such as that of kamikaze pilots) related to the principle of the "splendid death."

rendered him aware of both a theological mode (contact with eternal Christian image-feelings of pity and love) and a biological one (via his wife and son) as well. Even that brief recognition of the authentic enabled him to overcome this image of death as a terrifying intruder about to terminate a life that had never been lived. A major impediment to that spiritual achievement had been the collusion between his own self-deceptions and the hypocrisies of others— "this falsity around him and within him [which] did more than anything else to poison his last days." Members of his family felt guilty for remaining alive while he was dying, and relieved that the situation was not reversed. They also experienced their own death anxiety. It was the same with colleagues and ostensible friends, so that at the moment of his death, "Each one thought or felt, 'Well, he's dead but I'm alive!'" He would have been totally isolated were it not for the one voice of integrity around him. His peasant servant, rather than offer false reassurances like the rest, encouraged Ivan Ilyich to accept his fate as universal ("We shall all of us die . . ."), which enabled Ivan Ilyich to connect his death with larger rhythms of human existence.

Very similar in theme (and undoubtedly influenced by the Tolstoy story) is Kurosawa's film, *Ikiru* (To Live). The dying man is a petty bureaucrat, a city official whose personal and professional life has been characterized by evasion and numbed withdrawal from others' pain, and from his own. When presented with a death sentence by doctors who discover his advanced cancer, he begins to confront his own despair, his terrible emptiness and inhumanity—the total absence of integrity—characterizing his life. He finds his awakening in building a park for children. He had in the past blocked the project with his characteristic bureaucratic evasions, and now he must overcome the bureaucratic resistances of others. He does overcome them, with dedication and energy that seems superhuman, even demonic. He is determined to complete his task so that this modest expression of works will outlive him and bring more life to others.

There is a final irony in the brilliantly rendered funeral service: precisely those fellow bureaucrats who had tried to block his park now claim the credit. But the park is there—the protagonist's creative legacy and his survivors' bureaucratic hypocrisy are equally enduring. The entire arena of concern, including the immortalizing legacy, is with the human matrix that so characteristically dominates Japanese cultural experience, as opposed to the Christian-Western mode of spiritual revelation expressed in the Tolstoy story.

Kurosawa exquisitely depicts qualities of movement and stasis in the bureaucrat's behavior on discovering that he is dying: first his withdrawal into petulant inactivity, then his desperate flailing out in quest of meaning, and finally his wild swing between movement (from office to office) and stasis (refusal to leave, to "move from the spot," until granted what he needs for the project). Contemporary Japanese often deal with despair by alternating between purposeless inertia and exaggerated activity. While the pattern can be found anywhere, its intensity in Japan seems to be a counterpart of the more characteristic Western pattern (expressed by Ivan Ilyich) of the self-lacerating inner struggle around guilt in association with despair. But concerning the elemental theme of death as a test of integrity and of symbolized immortality, *Ikiru* and "The Death of Ivan Ilyich" are of a piece.

Integrity is tested by death on a number of levels: one's judgment of one's past, one's capacity to anticipate an honorable "trace" one will leave for the future, and the quality of immediate experience in the process of dying. All three levels are concerned with important but elusive questions about "good," "bad," and "appropriate" deaths. Freud was interested in that kind of question, even through the haze of the death instinct. Though he emphasized that "the aim of all life is death," he added the qualification that "the organism wishes to die only in its own fashion." When he said further, by way of clarification, that tendencies toward death were "imminent in the organism itself,"[11] he seemed to be straining against the confines of the death instinct.

From a formative perspective, man's "own fashion" has to do with symbolizations around meaning and continuity. Man's ideal death within his "own fashion"—and with tendencies "imminent in the [human] organism itself"—is associated with a realized life and a symbolized sense of immortality. To the extent that these are absent or less than vivid, death is approached not only with anxiety but deep dread. It is probably fair to say that most of us die somewhere along that continuum.*

Kurt Eissler speaks of the act of dying as "the process of terminal, maximum individualization." As an expression of this quest he quoted Rilke's moving plea, "Oh Lord give everyone his own death." Eissler also spoke of "the final process of structurization"[13] as a rendering of meaning to one's past which otherwise would not have been felt.

A recent poem by J. A. Valente, entitled "The Dying Man" evokes beautifully that ideal of self-completion:

> The dying man saw
> mysterious gestures, forgotten faces
> pass before his eyes,
> birds of another country once his own

---

*Elisabeth Kübler-Ross describes a sequence of feeling in the dying patient—from denial-isolation to anger to "bargaining" and depression—finally culminating, at least ideally, in a stage of acceptance. That last stage can include, for both the dying person and a close companion (perhaps the doctor), a special deepening of sensibility, a "silence that goes beyond words" and an awareness of mortality and of "the uniqueness of each individual in this vast sea of humanity."[12] Kübler-Ross has been criticized by some for creating overly-schematized stages and for a tendency to idealize dying, and, more recently, for hinting at a supernatural process permitting continuing communication with her patients after their deaths. More importantly, however, Kübler-Ross has been restating an ancient theme of self-completion from within her compassionate contemporary experience.

(but in a foreign sky).

Through the open window came the earthy
colour of the storm.
He heard the rustling of the olives
far-off, in his distant childhood, wind-tossed now.

The air crackled with sharp reports.

He saw the fields, the sun,
the south, the years, the distance.

An opaque sky stretched
over a foreign land.

    In a slow voice
he assembled all that was scattered,
the heat of all those hands
and shining days,
into a single sigh,
huge and powerful
as life.

Finally rain broke over the dark siege.
Memory expanded.

    May song
bear witness for him
that in his struggle he won self-completion.[14]

Valente's aesthetic ideal is a far cry from the more usual pained encounters with dying patients. But they too describe moments of inner harmony and communing with others in dying that approach self-completion. It is easier to recognize a "bad death" than a "good death," which is one reason we require ideal images of the latter.[15] Valente's vision of self-completion includes the recreation of the past ("far-off, in his distant childhood") into a realm of natural, spatial, and temporal infinity ("the fields, the sun, the south, the years, the distance"). Within that realm all elements of the self and its connections, proximate and ultimate, retrospective and prospective ("all that was scattered") can be unified, "assembled," integrated. This again is the individuating principle described by Rilke and Eissler, along with Kübler-Ross's "silence that goes beyond words." As a Spaniard, Valente draws upon a culture in which death is always present in evoking the universal quest for inner order and self-completion in dying. Of course nobody dies quite that way and very few even approach such a death. Rather, pervasive human anxiety around death is related to the absence of precisely such self-completion, to the inability to "assemble" inner and outer worlds and associate one's individual existence, at its end, with significance and continuity.

Japanese express dread of premature death through spirits known as the "homeless dead." An equivalent terror in the West is associated with witches, werewolves, and vampires. The vampire probably dates back to ancient Egypt, but has been most prominent in the lore of eastern Europe, specifically, Transylvania. Vampires can be male or female: among actual historical figures, the fifteenth-century Rumanian prince, Count Dracula, and the sixteenth-century Hungarian countess, Elizabeth Bathory, both qualify. The vampire is an "animated corpse," or as the Rumanians say, an "undead" whose main activity is sucking the blood of the living. Like the "homeless dead" or "hungry ghosts," vampires tend to emerge from among those with unfulfilled lives and improperly symbolized deaths—in Transylvania from "criminals, bastards, witches, magicians, excommunicated people, those born with teeth or a caul, and unbaptized children" or from people who died through violence or (especially in the case of women) prior to sexual or biological fulfillment.[16] Classical psychoanalysis tends to interpret vampirism as expressing "unresolved conflicts at the oral sadistic level" and related oedipal and castration fears, emphasizing the vampire's sexual pleasure in the drinking of blood. More fundamental is the vampire's focus on blood as the fluid that distinguishes life from death.*

The dead seek, through blood, the life of the living. The vampire is a product of premature, absurd, unacceptable death—of the terror of these that stalks us all. Rather than death itself, perhaps the aim of life lies in man's elaborate symbolic possibilities for self-completion. Freud is right in sensing that death in general and the experience of dying in particular are integral to that aim.

Some of the difficulties around self-completion and integrity have been evoked by recent psychiatric work. In an already classic paper published in 1961, Weisman and Hackett describe patients with "predilection to death," who "without open conflict, suicidal intention, profound depression, or extreme panic" correctly predicted their own deaths.[17] These patients were interviewed prior to undergoing serious surgery, as were the much larger number of patients who survived that surgery. For the predilection patients, "death held more appeal . . . than did life because it promised either reunion with lost love, resolution of long conflict, or respite from anguish." Since their organic

---

* As McNally and Florescu tell us: "The notion behind vampirism traces way back in time—to man the hunter, who discovered that when blood flowed out of the wounded beast or fellow human, life, too, drained away. Blood was the source of vitality! Thus men sometimes smeared themselves with blood and sometimes drank it. The idea of drinking blood to renew vitality became transferred from the living to the dead, and thereupon the vampire entered history. To the vampire, indeed, 'the blood is the life'—as Dracula, quoting from Deuteronomy 12:33, tells us in Stoker's novel."

pathology was no greater than that of the group that survived, their psychic state must have contributed significantly to their deaths, or at least to the timing of their deaths. From the authors' descriptions of these patients, two different processes emerge: in some, a sense of realized life and confident involvement with human continuity permitted them to accept death with minimal protest; in others, a quiet despair with virtual absence of feelings of integrity or of symbolic immortality. All seemed to be more or less ready to die, but for very different, even opposite, kinds of reasons.

Weisman and Hackett evolve a concept of "appropriate death" which, at least in this first paper, seems to encompass both groups. In later work, however, Weisman clearly distinguishes between "purposeful death," which includes *all* predilection patients, those dominated by imagery of despair and disintegration and those with a sense of self-fulfillment and integrity; and "appropriate death," by which Weisman now means more or less the second group, or at least the most integrated kind of dying possible or feasible for a particular person. Thus he suggests that "at the very end of life, people can undergo changes in outlook, so that the meaning of having existed acquires a special significance," and emphasizes dying itself as a decisive *event* (or kairos) which a person can experience with "a pungency that draws upon every level and period of his existence . . . [so that] it is a unit of reality that may encompass a lifetime." [18] In its admirable clinical lyricism, this description harkens directly back to Valente's poetic evocation of the dying man's self-completion.*

There is limitation in the capacity for self-completion, a border area between despair and self-completion in which the dying person subjectively feels that it is "right to die at that moment." Some writers have stressed more unequivocal forms of angry despair, the tendency of people to "die with the gall of bitter hatred in their mouths." [20] Here there is no sense of integrity, no symbolized immortality, no possibility for self-completion. Others, beginning with Freud, have emphasized the gradual emotional withdrawal of the dying, a phenomenon more discussed than understood. Weisman speaks of a tendency in the dying to "accede to the thrust of extinction." Whatever the combination of self-completion and despair, we can postulate a psychobiological mechanism— not an instinct but a general organic process—in which the mind's own gradual extinction, expressed via progressive psychic numbing, parallels that of the body on the way to death. Many experience no such withdrawal. There is, at least in the West, another way of struggling against death, as in Dylan Thomas's

---

* In a still later study, Weisman responds to a colleague's mild complaint that the concept of appropriate death "is still very elusive" with the suggestion of three criteria: "awareness, acceptability, resolution and relief." But he adds a qualification and a warning: "Don't confuse the pigeon with our pigeonholes. What is appropriate for me may not be appropriate for you. Operational criteria for an appropriate death are all right, but what can they tell us about how to measure the meaning of death for any individual? The final judge is the patient—whether it feels right to die at that moment." [19]

celebrated lines: "Do not go gentle into that good night / Rage, rage against the dying of the light!" Here again there may be various combinations of numbing and denial on the one hand, and on the other a sense of integrity and continuity so intense that very little psychic numbing is required. Clearly there is much more to learn about psychic patterns in dying, and much to overcome in the rationalistic neglect of the psychological significance of a sense of transcendence and self-completion.

A gradual maturing on some of these issues is reflected in changing medical and psychiatric approaches to the dying patient. The recent trend toward death awareness gave rise to an initial rush toward a spirit of absolute candor, an understandable, even healthy reaction to long-standing policies of lying and deceit. At present this movement is more subtle, and more consonant with the principle of "getting in touch with the flow." To do this requires gentle honesty, not unlike that of the peasant servant in *The Death of Ivan Ilyich*. One must expect and respond to the patient's "middle knowledge," a state hovering between complete acceptance and repudiation of the imminence of death. Death tests everyone's integrity; the dying person, immediate survivors, and attending healers contribute to a collective psychic constellation within which issues of continuity and discontinuity, self-completion and disintegration, are addressed.

Death is anticipated as an abrupt termination of the process and motion of life. As a test of the sense of movement one's life has possessed, death raises questions about development, sequence, and change in the continuous human dialectic between "holding firm" and "moving on," between steady sameness and risky individuation. More subtly called into question is the extent to which seemingly quiet phases of living—periods of manifest stasis—enhance receptivity and growth. Or were they instead mere expressions of stagnation and inner deadness? Of the three axes, movement-stasis is the most neglected. But a sense of movement, of continuous psychic action, has overriding importance for individual and collective feelings of vitality.

Beginning with Freud, the countervailing urge toward stillness, constancy, and reduction of tension has been emphasized. Freud (after Barbara Low) called this the "Nirvana principle," and saw it as the essence of life's instinctual movement toward death:

> The dominating tendency of mental life, and perhaps of nervous life in general, is the effort to reduce, to keep constant or to remove internal tension due to stimuli . . .—a tendency which finds expression in the pleasure principle; and our recognition of that fact is one of our strongest reasons for believing in the existence of death instincts.[21]

Freud does suggest something close to a sense of movement when he speaks of the "life instincts" as "breakers of the peace . . . constantly producing tensions." But this idea is ultimately subsumed by his view of instincts per se as having their origin in "a need to restore an earlier state of things." Here Freud expresses a world view of "instinctual restorationism": one in which life either lacks an elemental movement forward, or else can make this movement only in a secondary fashion as a means of overcoming the more fundamental impulse toward biological return. Freud's theory was an ingenious attempt to retain this instinctual world view while acknowledging the psychological importance of death and the relationship between death and stasis or cessation. Once more instinct theory is inadequate to the burden of life-death experience. And once more, in attempting to suggest a formative-symbolizing view of life's forward movement, we do well to take heed of the bold dimensions Freud sought to address.

The term "self-process" (rather than simply "self") expresses this human necessity for a sense of vitality and movement. A "Protean style" of self-process is one of continuous inner experimentation with images and possibilities.[22] It is especially characteristic of contemporary historical dislocations and media inundations. Within the dialectic of movement and stillness mentioned earlier, the Protean style emphasizes experiment and change.

There is a related point to be made here about the holding of ideas, and especially about ideologies. Within our paradigm an ideology is a comprehensive idea-system that connects with important ultimate involvements of the self. Ideologies provide a unique sense of illumination and vitality. The great social and political ideologies of the nineteenth century, notably Marxism, contain organized imagery of wider historical movement as well as of individual participation in constant social flux. Yet ideologies, especially when they become totalistic, also hold out an ultimate vision of utopian perfection in which movement (in the sense of development) is no longer necessary because one is, so to speak, *there*. A fundamental source of ideological appeal may well lie in this embodiment of both ends of the psychic polarity—the continuous movement of agitation and upheaval, and the perfect stillness of truth. Through this polarity ideologies transcend linear time, transcend death itself. There is the promise of a continuing relationship to the "Movement" or "Revolution."

Ideologies are likely to appear and gather momentum during periods of cultural breakdown and historical dislocation, periods characterized by a widespread sense of stagnation and unmanageable death imagery. Central to their function is their invocation of the classical mythological theme of death and rebirth—their exposure and analysis of existing historical "deadness" together with their revitalizing promise of a "new life." *

---

* The vision in Marxist ideology of "permanent revolution" (originally Trotskyist but more recently expressed and evolved as a Maoist principle) attempts to eliminate the "static" pole of the dialectic in favor of continuous revitalizing movement. In practical political terms, as Mao made clear especially in connection with the Chinese cultural revolution of the late 1960s, the goal was to overcome various forms of institutional

Embracing an ideology, then, can create forms of experiential transcendence that extend into much of existence. One lives in an exquisite blend of movement and stillness containing elements of secular grace. Ideology becomes inseparable from imagery of vitality; *all* experience is activated and 'moved' by it; yet the self exists in a still, unchanging realm of ennoblement and invulnerability, that state of grace resulting from the merger of ultimate power and ultimate virtue.

This intensity resembles a religious aura: in a Japanese student-activist who is almost beatific as he envisions "the society which will be created in the future—well, I do not think that we ourselves will be able to see it in its magnificence"; in young Chinese describing moments of collective enthusiasm during an experience of "thought reform"; and still younger Chinese, former members of the Red Guard, describing their teenage rampage against revolutionary impurities under the spiritual inspiration of the thought of Mao Tse-tung; and in middle-aged Nazis recalling the magnificent beauty and purity of their days in the Hitler youth movement.*

Imagery of movement and stasis has enormous importance, mostly hidden, for our judgments of political systems. Consider American images of China during the early and mid-1970s. Many of those visiting the Chinese mainland, after decades of noncommunication between the two countries, have been struck by a sense of vitality and movement, especially impressive when contrasted with the stagnation and relative 'deadness' they associated with their own society. Yet others, whether from direct observation or from afar, have stressed the control over individual thought and action, in effect the imposition of forms of individual and collective stasis within that same Chinese society. Clearly the axis of movement and stasis depends greatly on external perceptions, in conjunction with inner images culturally and psychologically determined. We have much to explore about the extraordinarily neglected psychic components of this axis.

Investigations of intellectual and professional ideologies are also needed. Within psychology, for instance, immersion in either psychoanalysis or Skinnerian behaviorism can provide imagery of movement and stillness parallel

---

"deadness" to which revolutions themselves (with special reference here to the Soviet experience) are prone. China's experience suggests that continuous revitalization as an absolute is simply not possible—revolutionary movements need pockets of stability and claims of realization. Mao has demonstrated that it is possible to maintain a predominant theme of movement in the form of revolutionary activism that includes a certain amount of assault of one's own revolutionary institutions; one does not eliminate the static pole—the revolutionary pauses, consolidating forms, or claim to lasting truth.[23]

*These four examples are drawn from various research studies I have conducted: the first from a study of Japanese youth,[24] the second and fourth from a study of Chinese Communist thought reform,[25] and the third from a study of Mao and the Chinese cultural revolution.[26]

to that experienced with political ideologies. Again, much experience can be subsumed to and energized by the belief system, which in turn confers upon the self a quality of "confirmation" as a member of the "elect"—a secular grace associated with ultimate truth, ultimate psychic power.*

The psychic response to a threat of death, literal or symbolic, is likely to be either that of extreme stillness and cessation of movement, or else of frenetic, compensatory activity. This polarity was shown by the protagonist of the Kurosawa film, *Ikiru*. It was also true among the survivors of Hiroshima. In them, stillness and cessation of movement were by far more prominent, as evident not only in their physical behavior but in their widespread psychic numbing.[27] The early phase of that numbing was a temporary form of symbolic death called forth as a protective device against more absolute psychic death (the psychosis that might result if one were to experience feelings appropriate to the grotesqueness of the environment). In many, however, the numbing itself persisted, even became permanent. It was as if the protective device had turned into a "devil's bargain": an inner agreement to restrain vitality in return for the dubious right to be alive at all. But there was also heightened activity at the time of the bomb, usually of an unfocused, desperate kind. Some of that pattern went into the "frontier atmosphere" of the postbomb years, and the frenetic rebuilding of the city. While much of that energy came from the outside, part of it was a rebound phenomenon, a delayed intensification of movement after sustained cessation.

Of course cessation and stagnation are inseparable from issues of meaning and connection. A World War I poem by Isaac Rosenberg, appropriately entitled "Dead Man's Dump," eloquently conveys the importance of the parameter of movement and stasis for all of human existence:

> They left this dead with the older dead,
> Stretched at the crossroads.
>
> Burnt black by strange decay
> Their sinister faces lie,
> The lid over each eye;
> The grass and colored clay
> More emotion have than they,
> Joined to the great sunk silences.

---

* While it is easy to condemn this process in its extreme form, the probability is that all belief systems, all significant bodies of knowledge, call forth some such intensification and equilibration of movement and stillness. I feel that to be true of myself in my explorations of the formative paradigm around life-continuity put forward in my work. Much of what I observe in others and in myself seems quickened by associating it with this paradigm, and that sense of vitality and movement in turn connects with quiet convictions I am developing around durable ordering principles. Needless to say all this becomes important to me in both immediate, nitty-gritty experience and around ultimate questions and involvements. My point, very simply, is that struggles around movement and stillness and their relationship to ideological structure are universal.

PART II

Death and Emotion
Psychiatric Boundaries

NINE

Love and Energy

THROUGHOUT THE STRUGGLES with death imagery, the individual maintains a life force experienced as a sense of vitality. In psychoanalytic psychiatry that vitality is understood as psychic energy, derived in turn from libido. Love and energy are inseparable. The sexual instinct is active from birth in the experience of bodily pleasure, not only oral, anal, and genital, but involving the entire sensory organism. The individual mind forms around these sexual strivings. That is, the mind takes its shape from sexual imagery and the two antagonists to that imagery: the defense mechanisms (especially repression and sublimation) and the death instincts. For Freud it was libido—or in mental terms, psychic energy—that made the organism go.

Not surprisingly, the Freudian model of psychic energy has been widely questioned. Some particularly trenchant criticisms have come from within psychoanalysis.[1] Critics see the concept as a mechanistic nineteenth-century legacy that became part of Freudian metaphysics or metapsychology, without any real foundation in clinical observation. They see no evidence for assuming there is in all of us a quantified, electricity-like psychic force, seeking discharge but frequently dammed up instead. They suggest that already-existing concepts around motivation and desire, intentionality, and meaning, be used in its place; that psychic energy be abandoned as a concept, and "energy" restricted to descriptions of physiochemical activities of the body. Schafer sees the concept as part of a tendency "to think, with Freud, of energies, forces, structures, and so forth as *acting on the person* rather than as metaphoric approaches to *actions of a person.*"² *

John Bowlby has made the most systematic critique of the psychic energy model, and gives three good reasons for rejecting it. First, its inadequate explanation of the fact that "action not only starts but stops," which the psychic energy model can explain only when quantities of energy are exhausted. This explanation does not work very well, Bowlby points out, in the case of a baby who stops crying when he sees his mother and starts again when she disappears from sight. The second shortcoming is its "limited degree of testability," and the third its violation of current biological thinking about "the living organism as an open and not a closed system." ⁴ But Bowlby's choice of a substitute for the psychic energy model suggests some of the problems faced by those who wish to reject it. He suggests a "new instinct theory" influenced not only by ethological and evolutionary theory but also by "control systems theory":

> In the place of *psychical* energy and its discharge, the central concepts are those of behavioural systems and their control, of information, negative feedback, and a behavioural form of homeostasis. The more complex forms of instinctive behaviour are regarded as resulting from the execution of plans that, depending on the species, are more or less flexible. Execution of a plan, it is supposed, is initiated on the receipt of certain information (derived by the sense organs either from external sources or from internal sources, or from a combination of the two) and guided, and ultimately terminated, by the continuous reception of further sets of information that have their origin in the *results of the action taken* (and are derived, in the same way, by sense organs for external, internal, or combined sources). In the determination of the plans themselves and of the signals that control their execution, both learned and unlearned components are assumed to enter. As regards the energy necessary to make the whole work, none is postulated, except, of course, the energy of physics: that is what differentiates the model from the traditional theory.

There is a logic to this model, just as there was a logic to Freud's psychic energy model in his time. But its own mechanistic emphasis (even if the type of mechanism proposed is more sophisticated and flexible than Freud's) will

---

* Schafer poses a shift to what he calls "action language, the first rule of which is that: "We shall regard each psychological process, event, experience, or behavior as some kind of activity, henceforth to be called action, and shall designate each action by an active verb stating its nature and by an adverb . . . when applicable, stating the mode of this action . . . insofar as it is possible . . . we shall not use nouns and adjectives to refer to psychological processes, events, etc." And extending that principle even more radically: "I would say that mind is something we do; it is neither something we have nor something we are or are not related to or in possession of." ³

neglect certain dimensions that are specifically human and have to do with inner experience in relationship to behavior.*

Is there something to be said for the concept of psychic energy after all? Current and past meanings of the word energy are associated with vigor, power, action, vitality, and life. The original Greek form, *energeia*, is thought to have been coined by Aristotle from *energēs* and *energos*, meaning active or at work (*en-* at plus *ergon*-work). These roots have etymological connections with such terms as liturgy, dramaturge, synergism, surgery, adrenergic, and cholinergic; and also, via the related Greek word *organon* (that with which one works, tool, instrument, bodily faculty or organ), with *orgia* (Greek, secret rites, worship), orgy, orgasm, and organic. From its beginnings, then, the word energy has been related to activity of the mind and body; and even its early instrumental meaning has strong associations with vital function. Indeed, the *Oxford English Dictionary*'s first meaning of energy is a specifically mental one: "With reference to speech or writing: Force or vigour of expression." [5] That meaning, the OED claims, derived from "an imperfect understanding" of Aristotle's original use of energy "for the species of metaphor which calls up a mental picture of something 'acting' or moving." But one wonders why this usage violates that kind of metaphor. Certainly not from the standpoint of our formative theory. The dictionary goes on to give a series of relatively early English examples of this usage: 1581, Sidney, "That same forcibleness or Energia, (as the Greeks call it) or the writer; 1599, Thynne . . . not vnderstandinge the true energye of our tongue"; and 1696, Holder, "When animated by elocution (speech) acquires a greater life and energy." Two later examples have the additional value of suggesting the kind of argument developing here: 1845, Whatley, "The transposition of words which the ancient languages admit of, conduces not merely to variety, but to Energy"; and 1847, Emerson, "The Liturgy, admired for its energy and pathos."

The original Aristotelian use led naturally to the concept of energy in relationship to philosophical (then including psychological) assumptions, where it meant the actual working or operation of things, or the exercise of power. Here too there tended to be human physical and mental reference, as, for example: 1642, H. More, "*Energie* . . . is the operation, efflux or activity of any being: as the light of the Sunne is the energie of the Sunne, and every phantasm of the soul is the energie of the soul"; 1744, Harris, "Call every production, the parts of which exist successfully . . . a motion or an energy: thus a tune and a

---

* Holt and Klein do not postulate an alternative instinctual concept but they too revert to information theory. Schafer does not revert to instinct or to information theory but his program of "action language" tends to deemphasize, if not circumvent entirely, the all-important mental processes of image-making—that is, imagination—on which human action depends.

dance are energies"; and 1833, I. Taylor, "The transition of the passions from momentary energies to settled dispositions." The last is again close to our argument.

Where the usage focused on physical connotations—those of "vigour or intensity of action, utterance, etc.," which seemed to occur a bit later—the stress on the person remained: "Hence as a personal quality: the capacity and habit of strenuous exertion." (OED, p. 864) For example: 1809–10, Coleridge, "To lose the general and lasting consequences of rare and virtuous energy"; 1841–44, Emerson, "The poet admires the man of energy and tactics"; 1855, Macaulay, "He took his measures with his usual energy and dexterity"; and 1856, Cane, "When the hatches were opened, the flame burst out with energy." The meaning that perhaps prefigured the concept of energy in modern science was that of "power actively and efficiently displayed or inserted" or power that was latent. Thus: 1665, Glanvill, "If this mode of Energie . . . must be called Heat . . . I contend not"; 1677, Hale, "We find in so small a particle of a created Being this admirable energy"; and 1742, Bentley, "How can concussion of atoms beget . . . powers and energies that we feel in our minds?" But although the idea of energy as the capacity or equivalent for doing work had been commonplace from the time of its origins in Greek usage, it was not until the early nineteenth century that energy became a generalizing concept in physical science. Thus in 1807 Young wrote: "The term energy may be applied, with great propriety, to the product of the mass or weight of a body, into the square of the number expressing its velocity." In later terminology, actual, kinetic, or motive energy became defined as the power of doing work possessed by a moving body by virtue of its motion. In contrast to the energy of motion is potential, static, or latent energy, which is the capacity for doing work that a body possesses because of its position. (An example given in the *Columbia Encyclopedia* is that of a stone weighing five pounds, and resting on the edge of a cliff forty feet high, which is then said to have two hundred foot-pounds of potential energy, since in falling it could do two hundred foot-pounds of work [the product of its weight and the distance it falls].) [6] From this standpoint energy is always measurable—whether mechanical, chemical or molecular, atomic, solar, or electrical, whether having to do with heat, light, sound, or mass. Energy is readily converted from one form to another, but according to the law of conservation of energy it can be neither created nor destroyed.

This tradition of physicalistic quantification reached a kind of apogee among Freud's teachers during the mid and latter portions of the nineteenth century, extending from physics and the natural sciences to medicine, physiology, and psychology. A key figure in it was Hermann Helmholtz in Berlin, whose name was usually given to the overall school. Helmholtz formulated the law of conservation of energy mathematically and contributed importantly to thermodynamics, electrodynamics, and physiological optics. Another leading member of that school was the physiologist E. Brucke, in whose laboratory

Freud worked for six years. For Freud, Brucke was "the greatest authority who affected me more than any other in my whole life," and Helmholtz "one of my idols." [7] A third significant intellectual influence was Gustav Fechner, a philosopher and physicist considered the founder of psychophysics. When Freud began to construct his fundamental paradigm of instinct and defense he did so around a concept of quantified energy, "the concept that in mental functions something is to be distinguished—a quota of affect or some of excitation—which possesses all the characteristics of a quantity (though we have no means of measuring it), which is capable of increase, diminution, displacement and discharge, and which is spread over the memory-traces of ideas somewhat as an electric charge is spread over the surface of a body." [8] And he went on to say that this hypothesis "can be applied in the same sense as physicists apply the hypothesis of a flow of electric fluid." Freud, of course, brilliantly extended and transcended this narrowly physicalistic model. But he never abandoned it. Thus in one of his last works, *An Outline of Psychoanalysis*, he declared: "We assume, as other natural sciences have led us to expect, that in mental life some kind of energy is at work." [9] Although he recognized the difficulties of making analogies with other forms of energy, he added: "We seem to recognize that nervous or psychical energy occurs in two forms, one freely mobile and another, by comparison, bound"; and he referred to "a synthesis in the course of which free energy is transformed into bound energy."

When Freud wanted to convey the force and drivenness of human passions, then, he quite naturally did so in the prevailing scientific idiom of physicalistic, quantitative energy. By connecting that idiom with an equally prevalent counterpart of biological instinctualism, he came to the idea of instinctual energy as inseparable from psychic energy.*

It is equally natural for serious contemporary theorists, living in a post-Newtonian scientific age, to question fundamentally the mechanistic-mathematical assumptions behind Freud's theory, and to reject the concept of psychic energy out of hand.

But through the mystifications of scientific idiom of his day, Freud seemed to be reaching back toward some of the earlier meanings of energy, notably those concerned with vitality and love. As we know, Freud's paradigm of instinctual energy addressed both. And although we may differ with its way of addressing

---

* That physicalistic-quantitative energic idiom was not only a scientific paradigm but a matter of faith. Hence the "solemn oath" taken by Brucke and Emil DuBois-Reymond, "To put into effect this truth: 'no other forces than the common physical-chemical ones are active within the organism. In those cases which cannot at the time be explained by these forces one has either to find the specific way or form of their action by means of a physical-mathematical method or to assume new forces equal in dignity to the chemical-physical forces inherent in matter, reducible to the force of attraction and repulsion." [10]

them, it did at least take into account the incomparable intensity of these passions (for Freud, fundamentally sexual) around vitality and love and their antagonistic counterparts having to do with death and hate. Much is lost when these passions are no longer addressed—when the *idea* of psychic energy is dismissed along with its baggage of mathematical materialism. We seem to require, no less in our psychological theories than in our lives, a component of energy. Rather than dismissing that component we do better to rescue it from its relatively brief and recent usurpation by Newtonian science. Our paradigm suggests a way to begin to do that.

When we follow our shift from instinct to image, from analysis to formation, we move immediately toward the earlier meanings of the word energy— meanings around psychic intensity, vigor, or expression, the idea of movement (of the body or mind). Artistic experience provides a very important key. As one young artist-critic has written about the abstract expressionist Willem de Kooning: "The conjuring of the image (and destruction) is more about energy than object." About abstract expressionism in general, he said, "Artists have sought new sources of energy and new uses of medium to express that energy." [11] To be sure, abstract expressionism was more specifically focused on transformations of energy than any other artistic school—it is often referred to, in Harold Rosenberg's term, as "Action Painting." There is a sense, though, in which all painting is action painting. Grant Wood, van Gogh, and Rembrandt have been involved with psychic action around transformation of images no less than de Kooning or any other abstract expressionist.

Two additional quotations involving Mark Tobey, a Seattle artist with ties to abstract expressionism, follow. The first is from Tobey himself:

> When I play the piano for several hours, everything is clarified in my visual imagination afterwards. Everything that exists, every human being, is a vibration. If I paint that state of affairs, you may say, "Too bad. No images." But if I were to paint oil on skin and hair, then where would we be? Back to Rubens. But if I can get my feelings into *either* state, it will exist. Picasso and Klee are the greatest artists of our time because they're the freest. There's more variety, more scope in their work. They never stop inventing. They don't make art that seals itself in one invention or one symbol like the walls of a tomb. . . . I can never be sure what Klee or Picasso will do next. [12]

And the second is about Tobey from a fellow Seattle artist, Morris Graves:

> The astonishing thing is that at *no* point does the energy ebb or fail him. If your absorption in the act is kept at this pitch throughout, it's pure yoga; and the same can be said of dancing, truck driving or plumbing. The only possible result is an expanded consciousness. [13]

Tobey's artistic energy consists of reverberations, vividness, vitality, which is the feeling he speaks of as more important than any particular content or style.

He can achieve that energy only when there are no representational images. The free flow of imagination he speaks of (and so admires in Picasso and Klee) seems to require a balance of the kind of disciplined centerings and parallel creative transformations he can experience when playing the piano. And when Graves comments on Tobey's continuous flow of energy, he depicts it very much in terms of experiential transcendence—total absorption (available in almost any kind of activity) and great psychic intensity, resulting in the illumination of extended symbolization (expanded consciousness).

Psychic energy, then, is formative energy. Aristotle is at one with Tobey, Graves, and the young art critic above in viewing energy as the equivalent of, or capacity for, psychic action, for transformation of images. The subjective sense is one of vitality. And the combination of grounding and centering that is involved requires, in turn, a highly functional equilibrium between immediate and ultimate psychological dimensions. As vitality, energy includes various combinations of well-being, possibility, competence, and transcendence. This experience of energy or vitality also involves struggles with, or against, separation, disintegration, and stasis. Freud was right to associate energy with the life force, even if he saw life force as instinct rather than image-making. Etymological associations in the early use of the word energy—liturgy, synergism, orgia—are all experiences of intense psychic activity and transformation. Psychic or formative energy is, in this sense, the passion toward vitality.

Of course that passion is often related to love and Freud was quite right in equating psychic energy with love, though not with libido. Before suggesting alternatives to Freud's equation of love and libido, however, it is well to acknowledge the pathetic limitations of *any* psychological explanation of love. Love is a flow of feeling and images—of image-feeling—toward or about the other (person, group, project, creative entity, set of principles). The work of Mahler and Bowlby surely confirm Freud's idea that the earliest models for love evolve during infancy. But at the same time that work calls into question the "libido vision"—the idea that sexuality (beginning with its infantile manifestations) is the essence of love, and all else an extension or transformation of that sexuality. For Mahler's principle of early symbiosis and Bowlby's of somewhat later attachment suggest a quality of proximity or "holding on" to be the essence of things, at least in the beginning. Just as death is the more fundamental category, to which castration is subsumed, so love is the more fundamental category, to which sexuality is subsumed. The flow of feeling in connection with love has at least three important characteristics. It is directed toward a *relationship*, usually with another person. The image-feeling is *formed and sustained*. (While one can speak of moving quickly in and out of love, these briefer experiences are better termed infatuations.) And finally the feeling has a special quality of intensity—it is not easily altered, controlled, or turned on and off by an act of will. We thus speak of the feeling, when primarily sexual, as passionate, and more generally as a sustained *emotion*.

Emotion is not the opposite of reason or cognition. Langer emphasizes a continuum in which one can view "the entire psychological field—including human conception, responsible action, rationality, knowledge—[as] a vast branching development of feeling."[14] Emotion, moreover, not only can be formed but *informed*—as in works of art as well as profound human relationships. For as Langer also says, "Human emotion is phylogenetically a high development from simpler processes." Nonetheless, emotion means intensity. Its Latin derivative, ēmovēre, means "to move out, stir up, excite," and emotion is associated with such ideas as being "moved," moving others, seeking to *re*move them, or the opposite but related idea of "holding on" to a relationship or "holding to" a principle.

The symbolizations around emotion in general, then, are associated with intense expressions of psychic energy. How intense is a matter not so much of will but of centering. Centering importantly involves the portioning of what Langer calls "emotive values"—of the relative intensity of the mind's involvement in a particular set of images. Robert C. Solomon rightly emphasizes that emotions, or images and constellations associated with emotions, have enormous importance for all of our judgments, and, in fact, are at the center of what we consider meaningful:

> Emotions are self-involved and relatively *intense* evaluative judgments. They are always, whether implicitly or explicitly, judgments involving oneself as well as whatever else—disputes, cantaloupes, movies, other people or situations. The judgments and objects that constitute our emotions are those which are especially important to us, meaningful to us, concerning matters in which we have invested our Selves. Not surprisingly, most of our emotions involve other people, not only as their objects but also intersubjectively, in our concerns for our relationships, trust and intimacy, suspicion and betrayal, what others think of us as well as, insofar as we identify with them, what we think of them.[15]

Emotion is the means by which the human mind articulates, gives form to, and energizes the organism on behalf of that which is perceived as most important. In our paradigm this is likely to concern the following core areas: love, sexuality, and personal bonds; learning, working, and making; death, play, and transcendence; home and place; relationship to society and environment; and nurturance and growth.[16] These are so designated because we sense them to be at the core of our existence, of our struggles and images around life and death.

Nowhere is this more true than in the emotion of love. For to love is to invest that core of the self—in a sense, one's own existence—in a relationship with another. It would seem a rather extreme investment, and it is. Yet the human being is so designed that each of us must make it. Love begins with mother-child symbiosis and attachment, upon which life literally depends. That equation of a human bond with survival and vitality becomes the prototype for love. Later, the experience of vitality becomes symbolized and associated with more elaborate psychic forms. But a love relationship never loses—in fact is defined by—that quality of emotional investment. When one loves another there is always the sense that, should the relationship be destroyed, one's life would end. At stake is not only the immediate connection, but *all* human connection; not only the integrity of the relationship, but *all* integrity; not only the movement and growth in the bond, but *all* movement and growth; and not only the sense of biological immortality inherent in the tie, but all symbolized immortality.

Precisely that absolute quality is what causes such radical turnabouts in loving relationships, from sustenance to threat. If all depends upon a relationship, then all can be shattered by its loss. The possibility of withdrawing love can be perceived by the other as total separation and disintegration, as death itself. In fact imagery of some such threat is probably present in all loving ties. And since we are all imperfect lovers, with our parents and children no less than with our sexual partners, love always includes elements of coercion, of demand for the kind of submission and compliance that promotes stasis and undermines vitality. Not surprisingly, that threat to vitality in a love relationship is greater than in any other kind. The emotion of love, then, is a flow of feeling toward another in which one's sense of vitality is considerably at stake.

That relationship to vitality is epitomized in sexual love. Ideally, as we have suggested (in Chapter 2), sexual experience combines immediate pleasure with feelings of transcendence. That experience may be focused only on itself, or it may be associated with a bond with another whose mixture of lust, need, and affection may or may not add up to love. Sexuality is, in adult life, profoundly involved with centering. It is a form of action in which feelings derive equally from direct bodily experience, imagery of immediate and ultimate pleasure, and the relationship of both to the self and its general vitality. Sex is often characterized as a mixture of "friction and fantasy," but its essence is the locating or centering of those feelings and images within one's life-death struggles and one's capacity to love.

For in that capacity is the specific achievement of the human organism, its transformation of the merely animal experience into the complex, magnificent, and dangerous image-feelings that shape our psychological cosmos, individual and shared. Sexuality itself, in humans, is transformed into the act of exquisite centering we have described. It can be further transformed into a genuine "act of love."

There is a similar human transformation of attachment. Rather than mere proximity, there is an elaboration of particular bonds, including the possibility of a high degree of mutuality. To experience the emotion of loving another may include a strong impulse toward proximity or attachment, or sexual satisfaction, but it must have something more: a quality of perceiving the other's image-feelings so intensely as to approach sharing. The quality of that access to another's experience, physical and mental, is also specifically human. It is what makes possible the intense level of caring that can develop with love. That is why human beings can express and experience love in letters, on long-distance telephone, during and after prolonged physical separations, while being mostly indifferent to others immediately around them. So fundamental is this transformation that, in its absence, attachment or proximity becomes the enemy of vitality, and is deadening. One may feel an overwhelming sense of separation in the midst of apparent connection, along with equally invisible disintegration and stasis. Or one may seek the missing psychic energy in aberrant or destructive ways discussed later. It would seem that, as human beings, we seek always to transform attachment into a tie with greater life-death consequences, that is, a tie of love.

We also avoid such transformations, sensing the responsibility and threat they entail. Either way we are in trouble. We cannot live as vital human beings without that transformation, without love. Yet which of us, in family relationships and in friendships, is capable of transforming attachment into love in ways that maintain and mutually enhance vitality? And which of us can go further and transform both sexuality and attachment into that kind of loving source of aliveness? Once more the ideal is unattainable, but necessary to our bodily and psychic sense of ourselves.

TEN

Anxiety and Numbing

BUT WHAT IS the actual significance of anxiety? What about its subjective experience? What is the relationship between "feeling too much" and "feeling nothing"? And is there a level of anxiety or tension that is necessary to vitality? Our focus on the death equivalents enables us to connect with several directions of thought about anxiety.

Freud, not surprisingly, first thought of anxiety as something close to a substance, emerging from libido that had been neither adequately "discharged" nor contained. As late as 1920, he wrote: "One of the most important results of psycho-analytic research is this discovery that neurotic anxiety arises out of libido, that it is the product of a transformation of it, and that it is thus related to it in the same kind of way as vinegar to wine." [1] But well before that he had come to focus on repression as the cause of the accumulation of sexual energy (libido), and therefore the cause of the anxiety. In his final and most extensive formulation of anxiety, however, he abandoned this general view in favor of a concept of anxiety as "a signal of unpleasure" experienced by the ego, which he now understood to be the coordinating center of the individual, mediating between the outside world ("reality") and the inner demands of instinct (id) and moral aspiration (super-ego). He could then say: "[The ego] makes use of the sensations of anxiety as a signal to give a warning of dangers that threaten its integrity." [2] And ultimately: "The conclusion we have come to, then, is this. Anxiety is a reaction to a situation of danger." [3]

That recasting of anxiety theory, in itself, would seem quite consistent with our death and life-continuity paradigm. Moreover, it represents a recognition on the part of Freud that literalistic libido theory cannot really account for anxiety. One might even say that in those statements Freud was moving toward a more formative, death-related view of anxiety. But his means of pulling back and holding fast to his instinctual paradigm lay in his identification of the nature of the dangers that threaten the integrity of the ego or the organism. These dangers turn out to be instinctual, mostly libidinal, and have to do with unacceptable sexual ideas and impulses. To be sure, these libidinal forces can in various ways combine with external dangers—with memories of early helplessness, separations, and threatened loss of love. And that anxiety, which "the ego alone can produce and feel," [4] can relate to the ego's mediation with the outside world and with the super-ego, no less than with the id or instincts. Mainly internal, instinctual pressures threaten integrity; so anxiety becomes a function of libido once more. And, inevitably, castration anxiety becomes the essence of things—not by any means the *only* kind of anxiety, but the kind at the heart of most neurosis (along with what Freud considered the female counterpart of castration anxiety, " fear of loss of love"). [5]

As always Freud needed the safe ground of his instinctual paradigm for the important advances he made—in this case, a number of observations on the nature of the *experience* of anxiety: anxiety involves anticipation—"has an unmistakable relation to *expectation:* it is anxiety *about* [in the sense of before, or toward] something." [6] At the same time anxiety has a nonspecific quality—"a quality of *indefiniteness and lack of object.*" *

Anxiety involves repetition of an earlier painful experience: "The signal announces: . . . 'the present situation reminds me of one of the traumatic experiences I have had before. Therefore I will anticipate the trauma and behave as though it had already come, while there is yet time to turn aside.'" [7] And finally, anxiety involves helplessness—"The subject's estimation of his own strength compared to the magnitude of the danger and . . . his admission of helplessness in the face of it—physical helplessness if the danger is real and psychical helplessness if it is instinctual." [8] Sensitive Freudians could later connect with those observations in asserting concepts of anxiety that gave greater importance to death and implied equivalents. †

---

* Freud tended to distinguish between anxiety and fear, the latter involving an actual external threat, as opposed to the absence of such a threat (or "object") in the former. But that distinction has been questioned by a number of later writers, including Bowlby and Farber, because in practice it is often impossible to make.

† Robert Waelder summarized a detailed discussion of anxiety with the conclusion that "the various types of danger discussed . . . can . . . be reduced to these apparently elementary ones: loss of object [person], desertion, emasculation, and ego disintegration." Erik Erikson could later connect the experience of anxiety with the predominance of stage-specific vulnerabilities: the predominance at the beginning of life of mistrust over basic trust, and then of shame and doubt over autonomy; during subsequent childhood experience of guilt over initiative and inferiority over industry; during adolescence and early adulthood of role confusion over identity; and during subsequent adulthood of isolation over intimacy, stagnation over generativity, and despair over integrity. And in a

Freud's later stress on threat and anticipation makes contact with what are, broadly speaking, existential descriptions of anxiety. The latter, though, are distinctive in their focus on anxiety (or "dread," another translation from the same German term, *"angst,"* which with Freud is usually translated as "anxiety") as a function of human life in the face of knowledge of death. Ernest Becker points out that Kierkegaard understands dread as a specifically human entity (". . . man himself produces dread") born of man's peculiar combination of animality and spirit. Only by confronting that dread—the "terror, perdition [and] annihilation [that] dwell next door to every man" is true growth possible.[12] For Heidegger too anxiety is inseparable from existence, and concerns especially *"the being in the world as being toward death."* [13] Rollo May extends that kind of definition into the realm of value when he defines anxiety as "the apprehension cued off by a threat to some value which the individual holds

---

similar spirit D. W. Winnicott (a leading figure in the British "object-relations" school) could speak of the "snapping of the thread of continuity of the self." [9]

A few Freudians could even parallel Rank in giving stress to the fear of actual death. Thus Gregory Zilboorg described what he called "the psychology of the fear of death" as active throughout virtually all of childhood and adult life.[10] But he placed his discussion of that fear into a classical Freudian model of repression and "return of the repressed." He could then postulate the sequence of ordinary comfort (relative freedom from anxiety) during periods when the death fear was repressed; a tendency for this repressed anxiety to "return . . . in small doses and in modified form"; so that states of considerable anxiety are likely to occur when various forms of internal and external stress weaken repression of that death fear, which then erupts into consciousness. The value of this formulation lies in its granting a place to actual death anxiety more or less parallel to that of sexual conflict (subject to repression and then causing symptoms in relationship to the "return of the repressed"). But the model, derived essentially from Freud's instinctual paradigm, retains an implication of quantities of anxious energy, much on the model of libido, but now death-related instead of sexual. Similarly, Charles Wahl has more recently castigated his psychoanalytic colleagues for preoccupation with "castration fear" rather than death, suggesting that "these formulations . . . subserve a defensive need on the part of psychiatrists themselves." He emphasizes the child's early and active concern with death, including profound curiosity over "a second half to the riddle of the sphinx," the question, "Whither go I?" or, in essence, "What is it to be dead?" Yet he attributes man's inability to come to grips with the fact of death to the persistence of "narcissistic omnipotence," which "lends . . . a comforting illusion of credence to our wishes for invincibility and immortality." That narcissistic tendency also is reflected in "our magic feelings of omnipotence," which, in turn, add to death anxiety by making the child (and the man) feel that his most malevolent wishes will be fulfilled—that is, wishing others dead will kill them—and that through the law of talion, he, the ill-wisher, will be punished in kind. But by this basic emphasis upon magical thinking and "narcissistic omnipotence" in relationship to death, Wahl retains the libido model (narcissism, in Freudian theory, is sexual energy directed at the self) as well as the Freudian-Cartesian dualism between the "irrational" and the "rational." [11] In so doing there is little possibility for approaching the 'logic' of the death equivalents over the life cycle, their bearing on actual death anxiety, and the relationship of both to the experience of anxiety.

essential to his existence as a personality." [14] May draws upon earlier work by Kurt Goldstein, who employs a related "holistic" (or essentially gestalt) approach in equating anxiety with "the experience of danger, of peril for one's self"; with "a breaking down or dissolution of the world"; and with "the subjective experience of [the] danger to existence" in a "catastrophic condition" (one of disordered behavior and breakdown of "normal constancy"). [15]

Any rapid account of a few anxiety concepts does injustice to them. My purpose here is only to suggest the consistency of threat to the life or integrity of the organism or some inclusive representation (self, ego) of it. One could say that the universality and the nature of anxiety cries out for a psychology with a central place for death and disintegration. No wonder, then, that Ernest Becker responds with a psychology *totally* centered on "death terror." That focus does tell the truth about anxiety. But it does not encompass the subtle human symbolizations and representations around anxiety, around the death equivalents. Anxiety as nothing but death terror is reductionistic, and does not make psychological contact with the flow of life in the face of threat and death.

Leslie Farber makes a thoughtful suggestion about the nature of anxiety as subjective experience. He tells us that an element always present is intention that cannot be realized. "Anxiety is that range of distress which attends willing what cannot be willed." [16] What Farber calls "will," others might speak of as "wish" or simply "impulse." Anxiety involves not just threat or breakdown but struggle toward something. Anxiety involves motivation, or at least frustrated intent.

That intent has to do with aspirations toward, and inner imagery of, vitality. Indeed one definition of anxiety could be, simply, *threatened vitality*. But that threat is experienced in terms of the tension around integrity that is a continuous aspect of human existence. More inclusively defined, then, anxiety is a sense of foreboding stemming from threatened vitality and anticipated breakdown of the integrity of the self. Only when the resources of the self are perceived as inadequate to the threat does tension become anxiety. The motivational element that is countered or even overwhelmed by the threat is the self's impulse toward integrity and vitality and the formative energy behind that impulse.

In this way we can understand anxiety in relationship to death equivalents—separation and stasis as well as disintegration. Just as separation and stasis may have primary bearing on death imagery, disintegration, and its subjective equivalent ("falling apart") is the essence of anxiety. John Bowlby is right to stress separation anxiety, and to emphasize its evolutionary roots in the dangers besetting a young organism when separated from and denied the protection of older, stronger ones. And separation can certainly involve a painful subjective sense of being isolated, unconnected with others. Connection, moreover, can have its own discomfort, around threatened autonomy or in an adult equivalent of Mahler's term, "reengulfment." Similarly, stasis involves such discomforts as feeling immobilized, unable to move or act—or its opposite, feeling oneself (as is frequently true today in connection with the "Protean style") caught up in uncontrolled and uncontrollable motion (which is the very opposite of "movement" in the sense of growth or development). But these various discomforts—feeling cut off or engulfed, immobilized or in purposeless motion—need not necessarily be associated with anxiety. One may feel lonely or unable to act without feeling anxious. For anxiety to be felt it seems necessary that the discomfort (let us say loneliness) be perceived in terms of a threat to the structure of the self ("The world is frightening to me without my mother" or "I cannot survive without her"), which in turn requires an impulse toward resisting or countering the threat ("I *want* my mother" or "I insist on returning to her" or [closer to Farber's concept] "I *will* make my own way without her"). Where the threat is perceived to be stronger than the determination to reunite or cope, anxiety prevails. Where the perception is that coping is possible, one experiences tension (struggle, difficulty, pain, even doubt) rather than anxiety (foreboding, disintegration, falling apart).

Tension becomes anxiety when one feels helpless in the face of the threat despite the impulse to counter it. Freud distinguishes between the original "traumatic situation" of the very young organism in which it felt helpless to bring about satisfaction of an urgent "instinctual demand" (as in the case of separation from a nurturing person), leaving the infant with "growing tension due to need"; and a "danger-situation," or later experience, which reactivates that early feeling, so that "the signal of anxiety . . . announces: 'I am expecting a situation of helplessness to set in', or: 'The present situation reminds me of one of the traumatic experiences I have had before. Therefore I will anticipate the trauma and behave as though it had already come, while there is yet time to turn it aside.'" Freud could thus conclude: "A danger-situation is a recognized, remembered, expected situation of helplessness. Anxiety is the original reaction to helplessness in the trauma and is reproduced later on in the danger-situation as a signal for help." [17]

Freud is right to stress early experience of helplessness as a model for later anxiety, but that experience need not derive from a particular "traumatic situation" or even from a number of them. Rather it stems from a variety of experiences in which earliest inchoate imagery directing the organism toward connection, movement, and integrity is imperfectly realized so that, in one way or another, there is an early image-feeling of threat to life or to physiological or psychic integrity. Now that sense of helplessness is *always* both "psychical" (experienced in the mind, however immature) *and* "real" (in the sense of being actual). One can distinguish between a direct threat to life and various forms of perceived threats to psychic integrity, but the first is no less psychical than the second, and the second no less real than the first. We will also understand that early model of anxiety somewhat differently from Freud. Rather than reactivating something from long ago, it consists of a continuous elaboration of imagery of death equivalents right up to the adult anxiety. All early experience contributes to the adult's immediate "anxious interpretation" of the environment, in that prior imagery is always the means by which such interpretation is made. But the helplessness, the entire anxiety experience, belongs to the adult. It is influenced by one's entire history around both anxiety and realization, but it is nonetheless an immediate function of the complex adult self. Indeed, the extent of elaboration of forms within the adult self—around relationships, beliefs, self-judgments, achievements—renders it in many ways more vulnerable to potential anxiety based on relatively indirect threats, if at the same time more seasoned and ingenious in its capacity to ward off a sense of helplessness. That is, the integrity of the self is more highly symbolized; the assaults upon that integrity can be more various; but the basis for that integrity is older and potentially more stable. And since images constantly accrue and are transformed, the basis for threats to integrity—for the experience of anxiety and helplessness—does not remain static but is altered over time.

Past experience contributes to the anticipatory nature of anxiety, as Freud emphasized. One has learned what to fear. But this anticipatory quality, rather than being limited to anxiety, characterizes all psychic life. Psychic activity, and the images formed, are all (as we have discussed earlier) anticipatory, efforts at maintaining vitality in the face of the flow of environmental influences as interpretively perceived. One is never merely reacting, always constructing and anticipating. Anxiety, then, is a signal of impending danger, and of helplessness in the face of that danger, but not so much a "signal for help" as an anticipation of defeat and decompensation in one's continual struggle for vitality.

Anxiety is morally neutral. In response to feelings of foreboding and helplessness, one may act well or badly. Or as Leslie Farber puts it:

> Anxiety may be an ache which cries for relief, but whether or what relief will occur cannot be a result of anxiety's decision. Unlike the will, anxiety must be considered morally (or psychologically) *inert*, which is to say that, whether good or evil follows anxiety, will depend on forces other than anxiety.[18]

But there is another sense in which anxiety is related to moral and psychological inertia. Anxiety, or the possibility of anxiety, can bring on that inertia, can readily lead to psychic numbing. Rather than experience anxiety, the mind constricts. The symbolizing process, or at least elements of it, shut down. Psychic energy and action, as they relate to those symbolic elements, are curtailed. Where that process is intense and sustained, we are in the realm of neurosis, or even psychosis.

We know also, of course, that anxiety can be associated with the most intense forms of action and emotion. So we may say that anxiety produces a disorder of feeling and action: one either feels and does too much or too little. Images either abound in unmanageable excess or are closed down to the point of virtual disappearance. When tension gives way to anxiety, something fundamental is lost.

What is lost, what ordinary tension helps to maintain, is an equilibrium of feeling, imagery, and action. Tension is crucial, since equilibrium, as we know, is active and involves constant transformation. We can understand the disorder and feeling that develops (even if minimal) when tension gives way to anxiety in terms of grounding and centering. Grounding is impaired in the sense that one's "roots" are part of the disintegration. The self cannot seem to counter the threat with strength derived either from its history or its biological ties. Part of the helplessness and foreboding has to do with the feeling of having been put adrift from ordinary manageable existence and thrust into an alien realm dominated by the threat. For nothing in the experience of the self enables it to counter the threat. The threat is both familiar and alien. In Piaget's term, it cannot be assimilated. Something in it cannot be formulated or felt—and in that sense numbing exists even where the mind seems to be overactive. The numbing is bound up with death equivalents, and we shall see it to be a key to psychiatric disturbance in general. What is involved is not so much the failure of vinegar to be converted into wine as a shutting down in the production of both.

ELEVEN

Guilt

ONE KIND OF ANXIETY is a sense of guilt, and the tension that can spill over into "guilt anxiety" [1] concerns what we ordinarily call conscience. Guilt feelings, like other forms of anxiety, are associated with psychological pain and many kinds of psychopathology. By the same token, guilt can also serve as a signal that the integrity of the organism, or moral integrity, is threatened. It follows that the capacity for guilt is necessary and useful on the one hand, and a potential source of severe psychological harm on the other.

Defining guilt is somewhat problematic. Part of the difficulty lies in a confusion about the relationship between psychological and moral components of the guilt feelings. One starts by making distinctions: moral guilt involves a judgment of wrongdoing, based upon ethical principles and made by an individual (whether or not the transgressor himself), group, or community. (And when such judgments and transgressions are codified in a system of laws, we can speak of legal guilt.) Psychological guilt is an individual sense of badness or evil, with a fear or expectation of punishment. But the distinction, though necessary, hardly solves the problem. Clearly the two meanings overlap. And psychological thought has tended to ignore that relationship or to dichotomize it.

A good deal of existentialist thought, for instance, has distinguished between "true guilt," arising from actual wrongdoing, and "neurotic guilt," or inappropriate self-condemnation having to do with vulnerabilities derived from parental admonitions during childhood. Freud, on the other hand (though his views were complex and sometimes contradictory, as we shall see), essentially took the position that the sense of guilt was a mechanism of the mind, and had to be approached independently from moral considerations. More precisely, moral origins had become so obscured in psychological experience that "the price we pay for our advance in civilization is a loss of happiness through the heightening of the sense of guilt, and that, moreover, the sense of guilt has become "the most important problem in the development of civilization." [2]

Freud's views center around three issues: the moral dimension of guilt as opposed to its function as a psychic mechanism; the neurotic versus the constructive aspects of guilt; and, finally, the relationship of guilt to death and destructive aggression. In each of these areas we find Freud raising crucial questions, all the more so when one's answers differ somewhat from his.

Freud always assumed that the psychological experience of guilt was grounded in moral concerns. But one of his central, early emphases was that the transgression for which one felt guilty need not have been an act but merely a thought. In *Totem and Taboo* (1912–13), where he made his first general conceptualization of guilt and conscience, Freud referred to "the finding arrived at by psycho-analysis from the dreams of normal people, to the effect that we ourselves are subject, more strongly and more often than we suspect, to a temptation to kill someone and that that temptation produces psychical effects even though it remains out of sight of our consciousness." [3] At least in the obsessional neurotic, the "sense of guilt has a justification: it is founded on the intense and frequent death-wishes against his fellows which are unconsciously at work in him." [4] The focus on imagery of murder and death is not, for Freud, incidental. It is consistent with his central theme in *Totem and Taboo*: the origin of human conscience and the sense of guilt in the prehistoric murder of the patriarch of a "primal horde" by a band of brothers previously driven away by a father intent upon maintaining exclusive sexual rights to the females in the horde. The murder and devouring of the father resulted in severe remorse, the subsequent prohibition of murder, and the simultaneous beginnings of human conscience, religion, and society. Another important result was a permanent legacy of guilt, transmitted via biological evolution. Freud could thus suggest that "the sense of guilt for an action has persisted for many thousands of years and has remained operative in generations which can have had no knowledge of that action." [5]

By the time Freud made his later elaboration of theoretical ideas about guilt in *Civilization and Its Discontents* (1929–30) he had developed more complicated views about the superego as the observing, judging, and guilt-stimulating division of the psyche, but retained his insistence that "man's sense of guilt springs from the Oedipus complex [the son's sexual rivalry with the father for the mother] and was acquired by the killing of the father by the brothers banded together." [6] Both the complex and the guilt are inherited in each generation, and then lived out again on a psychological plane in each individual life. In that way Freud could combine his ultimate source of guilt with his ultimate—or "nuclear"—principle of neurosis, the Oedipus complex. He could then claim that "in the course of our analytic work we have discovered to our surprise that perhaps every neurosis conceals a quota of unconscious sense of guilt, which in its turn fortifies the symptoms by making use of them as a punishment." He goes on to say that "we are very often obliged, for therapeutic purposes, to oppose the super-ego, and we endeavor to lower its demands." [7]

In all this, Freud tried to bridge the gap between the moral-cultural influence on guilt and the psychological mechanisms by which the sense of guilt comes to reach neurotic dimensions.

However strongly Freud emphasized the harmful consequences of a sense of guilt, he retained a dialectical approach to that emotion. Thus toward the end of *Totem and Taboo*, when discussing the prohibition of murder that evolved out of the remorse felt by the band of brothers after they had killed their father, Freud comments: "this creative sense of guilt still persists among us." [8] In other words, however distorted by neurosis, our legacy of guilt has been necessary and "creative" because without it we would not have been able to construct our prohibitions of murder—or for that matter, our civilization in general. But Freud's dialectical sense wavered in his later attempt (at the end of *Civilization and Its Discontents*) to make a more or less absolute distinction between *remorse*, "a sense of guilt after having committed a misdeed, and because of it"; and what he calls "the sense of guilt in general," which he increasingly connected with the harmful, neurotic tendency to invoke an appropriately "harsh super-ego" in response to aggressive or destructive *thoughts*.

In much post-Freudian thought and practice, especially in the United States, this dialectical sense is lost altogether. Guilt becomes simply a painful and harmful emotion, which must be analyzed and overcome. That one-sidedness stems in part from a good deal of clinical experience: people do suffer from extremely painful guilt feelings, and if these can be relieved by psychoanalysis or psychotherapy, a great burden is lifted. But beyond psychoanalytic psychiatry, that view fits in readily with a general revulsion within secularized modern and postmodern society toward the excessive stimulation and manipulation of guilt in much premodern religion. (One could, without too much stretch of the imagination, include in the latter category the contemporary practices of various fundamentalist religious cults, certainly premodern in spirit, but embraced by many of the young in a quest to restore lost spiritual intensity and moral certainty.) The pragmatic-secular-optimistic constellation characteristic of much of American life makes the experience of guilt virtually a sin. And this, in turn, contributes to the susceptibility of young Americans to movements demanding that they wallow in guilt. In any case, guilt has acquired a not entirely undeserved bad name. While that one-sided position was by no means Freud's, he contributed to it in another way—by incorporating guilt into his instinct theory.

Freud's sensitive inclination to connect guilt and death had to be articulated within his instinctual cosmology. He emphasized "the similarity between the process of civilization and the libidinal development of the individual" (in fact the development of civilization was predicated upon "renunciation of instinct"). That meant not only sublimating sexuality into various activities contributing to culture, but also doing something with emotions emanating from the aggressive or death instinct. There Freud postulated that aggressiveness is internalized and taken over by the superego so that one's conscience can become harsh, tyrannical, even vicious. The fierceness of conscience is then explained by the pervasive influence of the death instinct. Man is then caught in a vicious circle: the civilizing process requires renunciation of sexual instincts, which in itself leads to anger and exacerbation of the already pervasive influence of the death instinct. He must also renounce elements of his aggressive instinct, and this is achieved via the underground (that is, mostly unconscious) channeling of aggression into conscience, which, in turn (via the agency of the super-ego), stands guard over continuing instinctual renunciation; and the "higher" the civilization, the greater the demand for renunciation of instinct, strengthening of conscience, and increasing the burden of guilt. The result is a boiling cauldron of suppressed revolt: "civilization . . . obtains mastery over the individual's dangerous desire for aggression by weakening and disarming it and by setting up an agency within him to watch over it, like a garrison in a conquered city." For "what we call our civilization is largely responsible for our misery, and . . . we should be much happier if we gave it up and returned to primitive conditions."

Freud did not ignore the importance of childhood experience in the development of guilt: he stressed the evolving equation of "what is bad" (as mostly defined by parents) with "whatever causes one to be threatened with loss of love." Parental authority, representing cultural authority, is then internalized in the formation of conscience and the continuing experience of a sense of guilt. But internalized parental authority is itself drawn into the instinctual cauldron. First of all, that authority used on behalf of suppressing sexual (mostly masturbatory) and aggressive instincts of the child; and then, with its internalization, it becomes attached to the aggressive emanations of the death instinct that dominates the super-ego. Indeed, at bottom, the whole problem is instinctually-determined ambivalence: the child, like the original band of brothers of the parricidal crime, both loves and hates his parents; and that ambivalence, even when fed by experiences both of being taken care of and frustrated, is fundamentally a manifestation of the instinctual adversaries.

The economics of guilt are stacked against man: his instinctual wishes keep recurring "and cannot be concealed from the super-ego," so that even "instinctual renunciation is not enough" and he keeps on feeling guilty—that whole conscience-dominated process encouraged by the forces of community and civilization. Pervasive human unhappiness, whether taking the form of actual guilt feelings or an "unconscious sense of guilt," is expressed indirectly in self-destructive behavior and the need for punishment or in a more general sense of discontent or malaise.[10]

Freud's discoveries about psychological guilt are among his most important.

They are at the center of a vision of human culture that is heroic and profound, whatever our reservations about that vision now. Freud was, in fact, much more sensitive to the relationship between death and guilt than others who sought to revise his views in a more rational and orderly direction. By emphasizing that relationship, Freud can avoid abandoning his dialectical position about guilt, even while emphasizing the destructive energy that may be associated with guilt feelings.

In the end, Freud's insights are undermined by his instinctualism. The "creative" side of guilt is essentially limited to cultural evolution, while only the everyday destructive side has importance for psychoanalysis. And Freud's concept of guilt in cultural history is, at best, severely strained. His insistence that the memory of the "primal crime" was biologically transmitted was even in Freud's day an objectionable Lamarckian idea (an assumption that acquired characteristics can be inherited), and his closest followers pleaded with him to give it up. More important is the contemporary evolutionary principle we have already discussed: namely, that culture is so integral to the beginnings of human adaptation that it was the matrix, and to a considerable degree the stimulus, for the large human brain. That principle casts great doubt upon the kind of instinctual assumptions Freud and others of his day made concerning culture as a deflection or sublimation of human instincts. The older view assumes—and, in fact, Freud came right out and said it—that the "natural," happier human state was the primitive one—either prior to culture or very early in cultural development. This view not only misreads the extreme conflict and pain evident in the most primitive cultures, but also reduces creative, intellectual, and broadly cognitive achievement to instinctual residue.

Freud had to be a creature of his times, had to make use of the available instinctual idiom. But that idiom, when elaborated around Freud's mechanistic-economic views of psychic function, runs the risk of losing much of the feel and complexity of our continuing struggle with guilt. Thus the idea of remorse, which is a key to the constructive or animating possibilities of guilt, is relegated to prehistory (the feelings of the band of brothers after killing their father prior to but on the way toward the creation of human conscience and the sense of guilt), or to regret over having committed a misdeed which is itself overcome by an instinctual mechanism. That is, the "instinctual need" one had expressed in committing the transgression "acquires the strength to achieve satisfaction in spite of the conscience, which is, after all, limited in its strength; and with the natural weakening of the need owing to its having been satisfied, the former balance of power is restored." And Freud could conclude that one need not psychologically pursue this kind of remorse, which can "never help us to discover the origin of conscience and of the sense of guilt in general." [11] Instead, Freud sees an inexorable instinctual push toward guilt that keeps man unhappy and threatens to do him in altogether.

When we consider ways to retain Freud's insights while recasting guilt in a formative way, a natural beginning is to place guilt within the context of its relationship to the death equivalents. Quite simply, the sense of guilt is experienced when one feels responsible, through action or inaction, for separation, stasis, or disintegration. As in the case of other forms of anxiety, the disintegration-integrity parameter is the most fundamental. And guilt in relationship to actual death is prefigured with those death equivalents. From that standpoint parent or child can experience a sense of guilt insofar as he or she feels implicated in negative aspects of the death equivalents. And the child's images and constellations can become dominated by a guilt, or potential guilt, according to patterns of parental influence, as Freud rightly suggested. But we need make no assumptions about instinctual sources of guilt. Rather, our view of guilt would emphasize not only its importance for restraining the impulse to kill but also for contributing to vitality—to connection, movement, and integrity—to feeling alive.

From this view we would not speak of a "super-ego" for three important reasons. First, basic emotions cannot be relegated to a separate agency of the mind, but pervade the mind itself, even if most active around certain issues— nor is the further subdivision into id (essentially instinctual) and ego (essentially mediating and executive) useful to us. Second, we reject the instinctual and Lamarckian elements around guilt so essential to Freud's super-ego. And third, we can hardly find in our present cultural flux the orderly cultural transmission, via parents, of ideas right and wrong, which Freud also connected with the super-ego. The very dislocations of our cultural situation require more subtle assumptions about guilt—or more accurately, reveal, in their very disorder, that more general need. For the absence of the classical super-ego (which in a certain sense never was) in no way means the absence of guilt. There is a relationship of guilt to dislocation, to historical change, to various forms of alienation (inability to feel loyal to anyone or anything). These patterns, in adulthood, can readily connect with imagery of death equivalents evolving from the beginning of life. Since everyone has such imagery, there is bound to be widespread, low-key experiences of this "free-floating guilt"—of the kind of malaise Freud spoke about in connection with "unconscious guilt." And yet for some that very experience of guilt can provide much of the imagery for change—for the process of confrontation—reordering and renewal.[12]

Martin Buber took the right direction when he spoke of guilt as existing when "the human order of being is injured," and the guilty person as "he who inflicted the wound."[13] Buber's imagery of injury and wound suggests the idea of threat to the integrity of the individual or social organism. And indeed, Buber relates death and guilt still more specifically by suggesting that certain forms of action or inaction cause one to be "again and again visited by the memory of . . . guilt," and to be possessed by pain that "has nothing to do with any parental or social reprimand" or with any social or religious "punishing power."

Here rules the one penetrating insight—the insight capable of penetrating into the impossibility of recovering the original point of departure and the irreparability of what has been done, and that means the real insight into the irreversibility of lived time, a fact that shows itself unmistakably in the starkest of all human perspectives, that concerning one's own death.[14]

The pain of this "existential guilt," Buber tells us, stems directly from a specific act, which can neither be undone, attributed to prior experience, nor erased by social or religious confession. That irreparability has a temporal dimension, is in fact bound up with time's irreversibility, so that recognizing the one means recognizing the other along with its ultimate individual consequence, one's own inevitable death. Guilt acquaints us with death imagery, then, in two ways: by making us aware of the injury and disintegration associated with the guilty act; and by holding us to the moment the act was committed, in that sense stopping time long enough to demonstrate that time is irreversible and that its irreversibility has consequences. Very likely these are two aspects of the same process. We learn the principle of time from interruptions in our unquestioned relationship to it, from early experiences that seem to interrupt the flow of life, that is, from the early death equivalents. And the prefiguring of our mortality in those death equivalents always includes imagery of stopped time—whatever the extent to which one takes on inner blame for the experiences and thereby the origins of guilt.

This last point differs somewhat from Buber. For in so sharply delineating existential guilt, as distinguished from neurotic "guilt feelings," Buber gives the former a quality of psychological autonomy that doesn't exist. Buber says that "there exists real guilt, fundamentally different from all the anxiety-induced bugbears that are generated in the cavern of the unconscious."[15] He admits that the two forms of guilt can become "inextricably mingled" but insists throughout the essay upon categorically separating authentic, existential guilt from the inauthentic, neurotic, and "groundless" variety.

That dichotomy blocks out any explanation of how the higher capacity for guilt develops over the course of the life cycle. The adult who seeks to confront a guilty act can only do so by calling forth prior images and feelings, prior standards of self-judgment. That imagery may be such that we judge him oversensitive to guilt—all too ready to feel guilty about almost any kind of action or inaction. Or it may render him relatively insensitive to guilt—able to avoid self-condemnation despite behavior others judge to be wrong or evil. In either case guilt is a form of anxiety, *only* rendered conscious by anxiety. This is precisely the problematic dialectic of guilt: depending upon biological predisposition, early life experience, and social and historical exposure, we evolve from the very same emotion the most ennobling and destructive feelings and actions. Buber is surely right to stress "true guilt" which the psychotherapist should not seek to dissolve via technical-psychotherapeutic means, and in that sense there is a certain autonomy to the guilty action, to the wound inflicted, which cannot be subsumed to something else. Yet the inner experience of guilt for that action has no such autonomy but depends upon a capacity evolved from the very beginning of individual existence.

We can therefore define guilt in general as an image-feeling of responsibility or blame for bringing about injury or disintegration, or other psychological equivalents of death. Our model of guilt includes existing internalized capacity and tendency on the one hand and new self-judgment in response to a specific social encounter on the other. These two components always interact in an ongoing series of images and forms around which the self organizes its struggles with decency and responsibility and with right and wrong behavior.

Freud dealt mostly with hypertrophied and pathological susceptibility to guilt—with "neurotic guilt"—derived from early life. The term *static guilt* is used here for these patterns to emphasize the deadening immobilization of the self. It is central to our concept of neurosis (see the following chapter). Here we need only suggest its two forms. The first is self-lacerating guilt, a sustained *mea culpa* of self-condemnation in which unchanging imagery of unmitigated evil prevents actual "knowledge" of guilt and results instead in what resembles a continuous killing of the self. The second is *numbed guilt*, which may include a series of maneuvers designed to avoid the experience of guilt feelings, among them a "freezing" of the self so that one can be anaesthetized from experience in general—a pattern very close to what Freud meant by an unconscious sense of guilt. But Freud had no provision for the energizing and transforming aspects of guilt, here called *animating guilt*.

An animating relationship to guilt exists when one can derive from imagery of self-condemnation energy toward renewal and change. That revitalizing capacity must draw upon past experience for sensitivity (the capacity for self-condemnation or at least "uneasiness" in the face of wrong) without the immobilization (static forms of guilt). This kind of guilt is the anxiety of responsibility, as it is characterized by a continuous transformation of self-condemnation into the feeling that one must, should, and can act against the wrong and toward an alternative. For certain Vietnam veterans, an animating relationship to guilt meant transforming mere self-condemnation over what one did in Vietnam into (still self-critical) explorations of why one acted that way (including not only one's past psychological tendencies but the nature of the society that created these tendencies and pursued the war itself). This also resulted in various kinds of action against the war and toward social change. An animating relationship to guilt thus requires imagery of possibility beyond the guilt itself, imagery that is no less social than individual. Where that was possible, this kind of confrontation of the various components of guilt could lead to profound individual and social insight. Buber is right, therefore, when he says that "man is the being who is capable of becoming guilty and is capable of illuminating his guilt." [16] That insight or illumination is essentially adult in quality, but the capacity for it is a summation of one's entire formative life. That is why an animating relationship to guilt can be so precarious, and is always in tension with static inclinations.

The capacity for an animating relationship to guilt means, in effect, a well-functioning conscience. But this dialectical view suggests that there is a precarious quality to the most humane conscience, and that the capacity to be sensitive to wrong contains within it potential vulnerability to immobilizing condemnation of oneself or others.

Consider the dialectical relationship to guilt in two survivors of extreme situations: a Vietnam veteran who had been at My Lai, and a "zealot saint" of Hiroshima.

The first, a My Lai survivor, distinguished himself not only by being among the handful of men at My Lai who did not fire, but also by being perhaps the only one who, in addition, did not even pretend to fire (the others who did not fire went through the motions of firing, as they did not want to be identified as stepping out of line in terms of the actions and attitudes of the unit). In the middle of the firing he was, in fact, heard by others to be muttering: "It's wrong! It's wrong!" In my interviews with him I sought to understand the source of his restraint, of what was, under those conditions, an extraordinary act of conscience. Three inner constellations emerged as having the greatest relevance to his behavior. The first had to do with a "Catholic conscience." Raised in a rather devout Catholic atmosphere, he remembered being instilled by his parents, his teachers in Catholic schools, and by priests with rigorous ideas about right and wrong. And although he later rebelled against many of these teachings and more or less left the church, he retained important moral imagery that had to do with transgression and punishment. The second factor was his having grown up as more or less a "loner," as a self-sufficient, somewhat isolated boy who spent a great deal of time by himself near the ocean, in boats, doing things he could do alone. This pattern rendered him relatively autonomous from various kinds of group pressures and attitudes, including those at My Lai.

The third source of conscience, however, was the most surprising. He had enlisted in the army partly because of his personal confusion, poor record at college, and general dissatisfaction with himself. He immediately took to the military, thrived and excelled in all training exercises and programs, felt happy and fulfilled, and decided to make the military his career. But his evolving imagery of military pride and honor, so important to him now, was rudely thrown into question by the continuous abuse of civilians he witnessed in Vietnam. He experienced My Lai as the ultimate violation of that somewhat romanticized military idealism. He had both a military conscience, then, and a Catholic conscience.

His relative autonomy from groups protected him from an alternative set of images around conscience and guilt. The night before My Lai, the company had been put through a very intense emotional experience on an occasion that had elements of funeral ceremony, combat briefing, and intense pep talk. Already distraught at the grotesque deaths of a number of men in the company from exploding mines, their mixture of death guilt (over having survived while their buddies died) and rage was channeled into a passionate need to retaliate, get back at the enemy, a need so intense that it was not too difficult to create enemies where none could be found; and even to experience the illusion that in gunning down women, babies, and old people they had finally engaged the elusive enemy and made him stand up and fight. The My Lai survivor himself experienced this set of emotions, but could keep another portion of himself somewhat separate from them. He was therefore able to extricate himself from the group "survivor mission" of overcoming guilt and rage via slaughter, and to fend off secondary guilt related to violating the ethos and behavior of a cohesive combat group.

After My Lai, by mutual consent, he kept his distance from most of the others in his unit. He was very uneasy about what he had done in not firing as well as what the group had done in firing, until he met up with a former buddy from the same unit who had not been at My Lai but was convinced it was an atrocity and was gathering evidence about it to make it known to the American people. His animating relationship to guilt, then, was enhanced by two images beyond the guilt: first, his military idealism (requiring that one maintain certain standards on the battlefield and fire only as combatants) and later, an ethical position around My Lai and the Vietnam War in general (as reinforced by his friend). He could then embark on a more coherent survivor mission of resigning from the military and doing his share to tell the truth about My Lai to the American people.

But his conflicts about guilt were by no means resolved. He continued to feel somewhat guilty toward his combat buddies, who he knew had to suffer from his revelations. And he also condemned himself for not having done something to *stop* the massacre at My Lai, and for having shared at the time the impulse, however he succeeded in resisting it, to fire at the civilians as the others did. A significant indication of his continuing struggle with guilt was his refusal of an award that a public society concerned with ethics wished to bestow upon him, because, as he put it, he did not want to be considered "either a communist subversive or a saint."

The difficulty here is a conflict between integration and integrity— integration into an immediate group and integrity involving inner commitment (longstanding individual imagery) to ultimate values. Whatever the outcome, however, one's response must connect with earlier image-feelings around guilt—around self-blame for threatened, actual, or wished-for sequences of disintegration (including anger and imagined violence), separation, and stasis. The capacity of the My Lai survivor to transcend integration and act on the basis of integrity emerged from an unusually sensitive conscience, from a lifelong relationship to guilt that rendered him both more vulnerable than others to its harmful personal effects and more open to its animating possibilities. His capacity to act on the basis of the latter had to do with his association of prior image-feelings around guilt to larger principles, as well as his relatively limited susceptibility to group pressures antagonistic to that combination. We see clearly in his experience the dialectical nature of guilt—the simultaneous presence and continuous interaction of the vulnerable-destructive and illuminating-constructive possibilities of that emotion.[17]

That dialectic appears in more extreme operation in a Hiroshima survivor known as "the zealot saint." A small, gaunt man who worked as a laborer and janitor, in his mid-thirties when I first met him, he had, more than anyone else in Hiroshima, dedicated himself totally toward countering what he called the "devilish" influences of the atomic bomb. Sometimes through a children's group he had helped to organize, sometimes on his own, he devoted himself fanatically to visiting sick or destitute bomb survivors in hospitals or in their homes, helping with peace meetings, greeting distinguished visitors to Hiroshima and writing to statesmen throughout the world, collecting and supplying to anyone interested endless documents and pictures having to do with the bomb, even making some of his own tape recordings of victims' stories; and, perhaps his most visible achievement, responding to the death of a thirteen-year-old girl from irradiation-related leukemia by initiating and seeing through a campaign that resulted in the erection of a memorial statue to her and all children killed by the bomb. Wherever he lived—during various stays in Hiroshima I visited him in three different places—his tiny apartment would gradually fill up with atomic-bomb memorabilia, to the point of crowding out everything else, including human inhabitants. His wife, long a partner in his personal antibomb crusade, eventually left him, unable to maintain his level of commitment or live with a man who did. "Intense" is too mild a word to describe him. Rather he was a driven man, propelled into perpetual action by retained images of the atomic-bomb dead, and especially by one of a three or four-year-old boy, being desperately fed some moistened biscuit by a policeman pointing to a dead woman nearby covered with blood and explaining, "This little boy was clinging to his mother and crying, 'I'm hungry! I'm hungry, Mother! Mother, wake up!'"—until the boy became still in the policeman's arms.

I came to call this kind of memory an *image of ultimate horror*, one involving the dead or dying in a way that evokes the survivor's strongest identification and feelings of pity and self-condemnation. Such imagery tended to involve either people who had been very close to the survivor, or else those (such as children or sometimes women or older people) who are looked upon as most vulnerable and helpless. The image of ultimate horror can symbolize the entire death-saturated event, its horror and pity as well as the survivor's sense of debt and responsibility to the dead. That debt to the dead contains the survivor's unanswerable inner question, "Why did I survive while he, she, they died?" and is the essence of death guilt.

Again the source of this sensitivity to the dead, to death guilt, lies in the life story. In this case actual death and death equivalents merged early, and always in a context of guilt as well as imagery of possibility (here in the form of serving and nurturing others) beyond the guilt. Thus his father died when he was two, leaving him on the one hand with the feeling "I was born and he died" but on the other with an image of his father (who had done religious work) as one who "gave his life" in serving others and "spent his last penny on the poor." His developing pattern of excessive and premature responsibility included, later in childhood, nursing his sick mother while trying to keep the small family store going, feeling a deep sense of "failure" when she died, after which, over the course of World War II in Japan, he became more or less a homeless waif at the mercy of unsympathetic relatives. His special history both enabled and required him to make the pain of all bomb victims his own, not only that of orphan children or people rendered homeless, whose fate so closely connected with his own, but the pain and mutilation—the disintegrative process—of victimization itself. More than any survivor I have known, he felt compelled to take inner responsibility for every form of death—biological, psychological, social— around him: his frequent expressions of sympathy ("How pitiful! "How unbearable!") were accompanied by renewed dedication—to nurturing victims, protesting bomb tests, mediating between contending survivor or peace groups (which he was often asked to do because he was known to be without self-interest). These actions were his way of combining early image-feelings of the animating possibilities of guilt, the overwhelming death immersion of the atomic bomb experience itself, and religious formulations (originally Buddhist and Catholic, later Protestant) of all that he had witnessed over the course of his life.[18]

All this does not mean that knowledge of his psychological past would have enabled one to predict his extraordinary response to the bomb—human behavior is too complex for that—there are, in our terms, too many possible combinations of images and forms, too many ways for the self to bring to bear its existing psychological structures on a new and unprecedented encounter. But we can say that his emergence as a "zealot-saint," along with the special relationship to guilt energizing that response, would not be possible without some such personal history. The other important point concerning guilt, perhaps already apparent, is that his relationship to it remained continuously precarious. There were a number of occasions when the total (including sexual) asceticism and drivenness of his equilibrium would nearly break down, and he would become depressed and think of suicide. He could always revitalize himself through action on behalf of others, but his life was a painful illustration of the precariousness that can characterize anyone's balance between an animating and a static relationship to guilt.

The experiences of these two survivors, in their special intensity, take us to the heart of the dialectic of guilt. Their sense of debt to the dead and their profound inclination to bear witness to those deaths are characteristic of survivors in general (even if in more subdued fashion than described here). But objections have been raised to the use of the word guilt to describe these feelings. These objections center on the moral and psychological baggage of the word guilt, its association with wrongdoing as well as psychiatric disturbance. Critics point also to the ethical and political perils of focusing on the alleged guilt of victims as opposed to the actual guilt of victimizers. Some have suggested that we need a new word, perhaps related to guilt but different, to describe survivor reactions. These views must be taken into account in our reexamination of general questions of guilt.

The image of a debt to the dead conveys the idea of something one owes, a duty, an obligation, a matter in which there is some form of accountability. The etymological derivation of the word guilt is apparently uncertain but it is thought to have some relationship to the idea of "debt" and the associated idea of obligation (from old English *scyld* and German *schuld* or "should".) There are similar meanings in the different etymological derivation of the word responsibility (from the Latin *respondēre*, to respond), and the ideas of answering to something and accountability loom large in the history of the word's usage *(Oxford English Dictionary)*.

Once more we are in the realm of the anxiety of responsibility. In the survivor's case, this has to do with responsibility rendered awesome and terrifying not only by the fact of death but also by its prematurity and grotesqueness. Various cultures have parallel patterns of responsibility in human relationships, which are considerably less extreme and of a more everyday variety, though they can include responsibility to the dead. Thus the Japanese speak of *giri*, which means "obligation" or "social obligation," and refers to feelings of accountability toward others in one's human web, especially those in authority such as parents, teacher, or employer. Should one, at least in traditional Japan, fail to live up to *giri*, he was not only severely criticized by others but felt badly and experienced self-condemnation as well. The feeling has as much to do with guilt as with shame—the two are really part of the same basic constellation and constantly overlap, especially in extreme duress. The Japanese evolved an elaborate set of principles around *giri*, but clearly there are related feelings of obligation in Western cultures as well, which are constructed around the anxiety of responsibility, and a ready sense of guilt should such obligations be violated. Those obligations can, of course, include rituals to the dead, as elaborately prescribed in Japanese society. And in that sense the guilt-centered obligations of survivors of family members, especially parents, extend beyond life relationships. In this way guilt serves as a balancing principle, directly related to patterns of mutual dependency [19] and to what we have called centering (harmonizing immediate and ultimate obligations) and grounding (accountability to those most integral to one's historical and biological roots). (See pp. 26–27 fn.) Guilt is experienced as expression of, and responsibility for, the breakdown of the social balance, and an indication of threat to individual centering and grounding. In that sense guilt, as James Hillman states, "belongs to the experiences of deviation, to the sense of being off, failing, 'missing the mark'—to what the Greeks called *hamartia*." [20]

The survivor of disaster, and especially holocaust, faces several formidable problems concerning guilt. He has been witness not to death in appropriate sequence but random, absurd, grotesque, and in many cases man-made death; which, in turn, threatens his most basic commitments and images concerning life's reliability and significance; that is, radically threatens his centering and grounding. He is susceptible to the sense that it could or even should have been he, instead of the other, who died, to guilt over survival priority. His debt to the dead can become permanent and unpayable. All of this can be complicated and intensified by relief, pleasure, even joy at being alive, an emotion central to human experience, but often at the same time unacceptable to the survivor. His struggles about guilt are attempts to reconcile these difficulties; to enable the survivor to "recenter" and recover grounding, to enable him to maintain accountability to the dead and thereby to accept in some degree his own vitality; and, above all, to be able to connect his anxiety and responsibility to larger principles and meanings.

Rather than eliminate the term guilt from this process, or replace it with another term, we do better to recognize the irreducible significance of guilt in the evolutionary function of rendering us accountable for the physical and psychological lives of others. Yet we can certainly use the term "paradoxical guilt" for the psychological experience of victimized survivors, especially when the anxiety of responsibility, if not outright self-condemnation, is notably stronger than that of victimizers. Guilt becomes paradoxical because extreme situations—especially those involving mass murder—strain at our evolutionary mechanisms. Large-scale absurd death in itself creates a debt to the dead so awesome and a pattern of uncentering and loss of grounding so extreme that victims are overwhelmed by the social "deviation" from ordinary standards of harmony or limited disharmony. These issues are central to our later discussion of nuclear weapons and "nuclearism." And where mass death is caused by human beings, the technological and bureaucratic distancing of the victimizer can protect him all too well from guilt—perhaps not totally, but sufficiently for him to call forth alternative psychic patterns, including the ultimate injustice of "blaming the victim."

Yet in another sense the survivor experience, ordinary or extreme, provides a model for understanding guilt in general. From the standpoint of our death equivalents, life consists of a series of survivals, beginning with birth itself. Human culture requires accountability for these "death immersions" and survivals—and the older, stronger person (parent or nurturer) cannot bear *all* of that responsibility. Individuation itself demands that the young organism share that accountability—indeed develop a capacity for a debt to the dead in the specific manner available to the child, through taking on some responsibility for the death equivalents. In that sense, early guilt susceptibility is by no means merely a matter of socialization. It has to do with development of the highest order of guilt and conscience, with the capacity to participate in the functions of guilt both in terms of immediate social balance and ultimate evolutionary responsibility. Guilt threatens either when it predominates in its disintegrating potential or when its absence permits inwardly unchallenged destructiveness. In its relationship to vitality no less than to death imagery, the experience of guilt is central to our paradigm and to the balancing functions of the human mind.

TWELVE

Anger, Rage, and Violence

ANGER IN MANY WAYS parallels guilt. As another form of anxiety it, too, can be a signal, and has its own dialectic. Just as guilt in its most harmful expressions can lead to different degrees of *self*-destruction, so anger can give way to rage and violence toward targets outside the self, toward people and things in one's environment. And there can be an animating or life-enhancing relationship to anger no less than to guilt. Generally speaking, within our paradigm of death and continuity, anger has to do with a struggle to assert vitality by attacking the other rather than the self.

As a way of developing our conceptual structure, it will be helpful to consider two sets of observations—one related to veterans of the Vietnam War and the other to a schizophrenic patient.

For about three years during the early 1970s, I worked intensively with Vietnam veterans, mostly with those who had turned against the war. Over many hours of "rap groups" and individual interviews, we were constantly concerned with issues involving anger, rage, and violence. As feeling-states, each of these combined anxiety with imagery of attack, and the three formed a continuum in which that attack imagery increasingly (moving from anger to rage to a state close to the act of violence) dominated the psyche. An angry veteran's antagonistic image of someone or something was just part of his overall psychic experience, strong enough in itself but fluctuating and alternating with other kinds of image-feelings. An enraged veteran had awareness of very little but images of harm done him by, and harm he would inflict in turn on, his hated adversary. And a veteran close to actual violence felt inwardly driven to act on those attack images. Often sources and targets were obscure—a veteran felt angry or enraged without knowing exactly why, or inclined, for little apparent reason, to take a punch at someone he barely knew.

Veterans' struggles with anger-rage-violence fell into three patterns. They retained a habit of violence; they felt betrayed; and they felt thwarted by others in attempts at integration.

The habit of violence emerged not only from military combat but from fighting a guerrilla war in which one develops the sense that danger lies everywhere and everyone is or could be the enemy. Violence developed into a style or pattern of individual and group behavior in both its numbed and passionate expressions. In that setting, numbed violence meant a businesslike use of technology on targets one did not experience as people. Passionate violence meant killing while enraged, the rage often a product of acute grief reactions to the deaths of close friends. Rage occurs frequently in various kinds of acute grief and the feeling is often diffuse. Rage is associated with imagery of attacking whatever forces one can identify and hold responsible for the death and for one's own survivor pain. For the veteran, violence subsumed different feeling-states—being numbed and feeling nothing, feeling angry periodically, or feeling literally consumed by rage. These feeling-states were a way of acting on their environment (as opposed to being totally inactivated by it), and doing so in a way that gave meaning and purpose to their existence.

We generally think of violence in war as simply what one is trained to do under special conditions, but military violence, and especially its extension into various forms of slaughter, can become important in itself as a way of ordering one's immediate psychological universe: in the act of killing one defines the evil of "the enemy" (even when the victim is a civilian, an old man, an infant), which in turn evokes the necessity of one's actions and one's own relationship to virtue. All these components of the habit of violence might readily spill over into new situations, struggles, or crusades. Vietnam, of course, was the perfect environment for instilling the habit of violence, but that habit, or aspects of it, can also develop during "ordinary" childhood and adolescent experiences in certain kinds of families, peer groups, and subcultures. Those experiences resemble the Vietnam environment in that one injures or kills in response to what one perceives as a threat to life or honor (integrity). The pattern takes hold to the point at which one must kill or maim in order to experience a sense of purpose, in order to feel alive. As in the case of guilt, however extreme the immediate violence-producing (or what in relationship to Vietnam I called "atrocity-producing") situation, one must call upon earlier imagery of attack (around anger or rage, or perhaps numbed states as well) in order to express or act upon these emotions as an adult. Vietnam and other extreme environments, then, can epitomize and illuminate more ordinary ones.

The second pattern involved the theme of betrayal, the veterans' images of themselves as victims: of a filthy war, a corrupted military, and a confused and callous society. Betrayal is possible only by those one has loved or trusted, and the imagery of attack associated with anger or rage has a special intimacy, as well as an intensity derived partly from the struggle to keep one's rage directed at external targets and to avoid its turning dangerously inward as one attacks oneself for one's collusion in that betrayal. The imagery that accompanies this sense of being victimized is likely to involve one's own disintegration in the form of breakdown of moral and psychological integrity. Angry imagery or even violence is expressed in an attempt to reestablish autonomy, pride, integrity. Again, the pattern is a familiar one, encouraged in many subcultures, and sometimes systematically concretized in street gangs and various forms of adolescent warfare and criminality. One feels badly used by the powers that be; the experience of anger and rage become necessary for self-definition. Violence may seem to be the only form of action that can fend off imagery of victimization and disintegration.

When veterans met with resistance and ridicule while attempting to convey the force and complexity of the atrocity-producing situation in Vietnam, their rage had to do with feeling thwarted in their efforts at personal integration. In one such experience an older veteran (of World War II) acknowledged the probable truth of a Vietnam veteran's account of the random slaughter of Vietnamese, but then expressed total unconcern with what happens to "blacks and gooks." The younger veteran became enraged, screamed something at his tormentor about the revolution and "how they would get him," and remembered feeling "for the first time . . . I could really imagine myself resorting to bombs—placing a bomb right there in that . . . building." His strongest inner sense was that "I was destroyed!" That kind of experience, he explained, "threatens everything . . . everything I had initiated myself." The fragile structure of integrity he was struggling to build was directly expressed in his presentation (or self-presentation); and the pointed rejection of it and him negated that structure, made contact with his own inner doubts, and left him with the sense that the entire constellation—literally, his immediate sense of self—was collapsing, being annihilated. He was left with painful image-feelings of inner chaos, confusion, and guilt.[1]

This reaction of rage to thwarted efforts at integration and self-definition need in no way be associated with the assimilation of a death immersion on the order of Vietnam. The "extreme experience" can be internal, an expression of a self that feels itself painfully vulnerable to annihilation. In this overall pattern we are struck by the immediate relationship between threatened inner death and violent impulse.

That relationship, in fact, is central to all experience of anger-rage-violence. One perceives a threat to individual or group integrity. One may respond with anger, to express one's sense (according to the word's derivation) of pain and constriction, of angst or anguish. Where the threat is perceived as greater, one may become enraged, that is, rabid, raving (Latin *rabere*), "mad" in both senses of that word. The self is subsumed and, by implication, altered, by the fury it calls forth to act upon others and thereby hold together. In the case of violence, the sense of being threatened or *violated* is such that one feels impelled to act in kind toward the source of the threat. In its derivation, violence includes the idea of a "vital force" (the Latin *vis*, and the English vim) and the idea of applying force to injure (Latin *violentus*, vehement, violate, violent).

This point of view parallels a suggested hypothesis by Peter Wolff that "the major source of social violence is violence itself," and the broader principle that "the motive for action is action itself." [2] Within our paradigm anger, rage, and violence are progressive stages of symbolized or formed feelings, arising out of inner perception of threat to specific forms of integrity and to vitality in general, and aimed at external targets as a means of asserting or reasserting the threatened integrity and vitality.

The veterans I worked with focused a great deal on the difference between violent imagery and violent action. Violent imagery, as we have seen, may accompany and help initiate not only extreme and sustained forms of rage, but even more limited and volatile forms of anger. That imagery serves, as least in part, to define and "explain" one's troubled existential situation. If one could respect such imagery sufficiently to explore its origins and meaning, it could serve as an alternative to actual violence. The imagery, that is, could represent, and therefore reveal, profound personal struggles having to do as much with one's efforts to reconstitute oneself in the present as with one's wartime death encounter. We could observe many gradations from image to inclination to strong impulse toward violence to sudden violent outburst to repeated or sustained violent behavior. A man could function at one particular gradation, or move from one to another, sometimes back and forth. All depended upon each individual's balance between the inner meaning of violent imagery or actions and his lifelong relationship to them (the extent of an ingrained "habit of violence"). The general assumption in the veterans' rap groups was that anger and rage, along with their violent imagery, were painful and often problematic but also at times useful and even, within limits, appropriate. Violent actions, however, were harmful and to be avoided. Within that framework, the group process, and especially the sharing of violent images among men who wished to maintain self-control, contributed considerably to restraint. Indeed, a number of men sought out the rap groups for the specific purpose of achieving self-restraint over their violence. Quite often, a veteran preoccupied with violent imagery and impulses could find the source of these in a form of fear or anxiety so severe as to resemble perpetual terror. As one such man acknowledged: "Yes, sometimes I think I'm still back with those thirteen guys [in my squad]. . . . It's like going out on a mission and waiting for the first shot." That example suggests, in quite literal terms, the relationship between threatened violation and violent impulse. It also suggests the phenomenon of the "flashback," in which a veteran would suddenly feel himself to be back in Vietnam, would be dominated by that earlier reality to the extent of acting on its images and thereby committing, or coming close to committing, a violent act.

Similar issues of meaning emerged in the crucial transition from mere violent imagery to violent behavior. Prior to My Lai, for instance, rage directed at the South Vietnamese (for being responsible for Americans' having to fight the war, for their corruption, for fighting badly and endangering American lives, for being backward and nonwhite, and for want of a more accessible target) was frequently accompanied by imagery of "wiping them all out" or "gunning down every damn one of them from one end of the country to the other"—with these images expressed in a manner resembling the exchange of "tall stories." Then, with one or two devastating events (first the deaths of a third or so of the company when it stumbled into a hidden minefield, and then the death of a much-admired, father-figure sergeant a few days after that), with the need for enemies and targets, and with the help of pressure from above for a large "body count" of kills, the men were readily propelled into a psychic state in which they could act upon that outrageous tall-story imagery. Or rather that imagery took hold as a way of structuring and coping with an unbearable situation, so that what was at first wishful and even partly whimsical became deadly real as a guide to behavior.

This transition process can occur under many kinds of traditions, and can be enhanced by the perception of acute escalation of threat (including threat to pride or manhood) and the dissolving of restraints of conscience by the sanctioning of violence either by higher authorities or one's peer group, or by the kind of combination of guilt and rage we have observed in association with acute grief. The latter situation can create a "false mission"—acting on imagery that radically distorts the environment and justifies violence as the continuation of the "noble enterprise" that had been thwarted (in the case of My Lai creating a "combat scene" while gunning down helpless civilians as a way of living out the illusion that one had found "the enemy" and made him "stand up and fight" and could now carry out the "noble work" the sergeant would have continued to perform had he not been killed). The transition from anger and rage to actual violence, then, entails a shift in one's perception of what one must do to assert immediate and ultimate forms of vitality.

We encounter strikingly parallel patterns of violent imagery in a very different situation, that of the internal extremity of a schizophrenic struggle. The kind of image-feelings involved are found frequently in schizophrenic experience, but their parallel to what we have just observed in Vietnam veterans who carry no psychiatric diagnosis suggests more general relevance.

Jean D., a woman in her mid-thirties, was introduced to me by the psychiatrist in charge of her hospital ward, in connection with my concerns with anger, rage, and violence. For several years she had been disturbed by the thought that her husband was evil, that he was the devil, and that he would kill her. Her mind was divided about these thoughts so that "part of me knew that he was good, and part of me thought he was going to kill me." At the same time she had the idea that she herself was God, a "reincarnation of Jesus." Later she came to fear that their daughter was "the devil's child." The thought then took hold in her that she had to kill them both. For "without their even knowing it, they're creating all the evil in the world and so it would be my duty to get rid of them and then the world would be at peace." She felt totally entrapped by guilt. These thoughts themselves made her guilty "because I really love them." But on the other hand, "if I were God, and they were evil and I didn't kill them, then all the guilt for the world's suffering would be on my head . . . would be my responsibility." Yet, following that imagery further, "if I killed them, then I'd feel guilty about that."

Like the Vietnam veterans, the motivational imagery around her false mission had to do with overcoming what is perceived as deadly evil, an effort at purification that would help to overcome one's own evil or guilt. Also parallel was her imagery of extreme threat—her husband and, as an extension of him, their daughter would kill her, if she did not kill them first.

Her violent imagery had originated much earlier, however, in connection with a different kind of threat. When she was about twenty and dining with her husband's family just prior to their marriage, she looked around and suddenly all the other people at the table "seemed to recede." That image-feeling extended indefinitely so that "I thought I was real, and that the rest of the world was a dream." That left her with the disturbing sense of being ". . . alone in the whole world." Not long after that she began to wonder about her husband's possible violence, thinking that her husband might really be Richard Speck (notorious at the time for his murder of eight nurses), that he might sneak out and commit murders during the night, or that he might have been replaced by a double who "is really evil." For she herself could recognize that "being left totally alone . . . that's the source of the real fear . . . the scariest feeling that I've ever had." She could relate those images to the fears she experienced at leaving her mother and getting married, fears that were exacerbated by her husband's demanding working schedule, which caused him to be away from her a great deal. At the time we talked, she was partly aware of the delusional nature of many of her ideas, which she could attribute to "a sense of being left alone," and could further suggest that "they [the disturbing feelings] must represent anger that I have toward my husband and child . . . my husband more, because my child . . . is just an extension of my husband." These reverse feelings of unreality and depersonalization (it was the other people who were neither real nor human) expressed her profound sense of being unrelated to them, and, of course, reflected her own sense of being not quite alive. Our main point here, however, is the direct association between these death equivalents—extreme separation, stasis, and disintegration—and her violent imagery (of violence by her husband and daughter toward her or her violence toward them).

And reflecting on that sense of total separation from others, she added: "That's when I first thought I was God, because who else would be all alone . . . in the universe." That idea frightened her also: "I . . . didn't want to be God. I wanted to be me, Jean, a human being." What especially troubled her was "the thought of not being able to be loved as a human being can be loved." (We shall discuss some of these themes in the schizophrenic experience in more detail later.) Her "delusion of grandeur" arose directly from her sense of not being alive, real, connected as a human being. And her imagery of violence within that delusion—God's duty to stamp out evil—reflected her struggle to find some path to humanity and vitality.

That delusion, moreover, in part reverted back to a disturbing experience she had at the age of twelve. Brought up as an Orthodox Jew with great stress on religious practice, and unusually compliant ("a little goodie-goodie type of person") in this and other areas, she was praying in the synagogue on the Jewish New Year when "I suddenly thought, 'Fuck God' . . . and this idea stayed in my head [so that] . . . whenever I tried to pray, it would come back." At the time she was beginning to study science and experiencing her first religious doubts—which for her meant something close to the breakdown of her entire cosmology, at both immediate and ultimate levels: "I felt panicky about thinking maybe there was no God, because here were my parents and my grandparents and all of my relatives really being Orthodox Jews and, you know, all the reassurance of having faith that there is a God, and here I was losing the faith . . . if I didn't believe in God, then I was committing a big sin." Her "violent" imagery toward God reflected her internal perception of extreme threat to her symbolic existence. And that first obsessive thought ("Fuck God") soon gave way to another—"that I would kill somebody . . . I'd heard on the radio about a fifteen-year-old boy who had killed someone just to see what it felt like to kill." The sequence then was: threatened breakdown of vital cosmology; eruption of violent and taboo thoughts; extreme guilt, terror, and fear of retaliation for her sin; and imagery of violence toward other human beings.

There is evidence of earlier precursors of that kind of image sequence: a memory from age five of having tried to push her mother down the stairs because of being angry at her, presumably for coming back from the hospital late but also for having just given birth to a second child whom she had brought back with her. At that time her mother "yelled out that she could have killed me." She brought up the memory to emphasize her fear of her violence: "I'm afraid of the violent impulses inside me—like, that I really would hurt Jim and Margaret (her husband and daughter) . . . here in the hospital I can't hurt anyone, so I feel a lot more peaceful." In that sense not only the hospital but her discussion of violent imagery served, as it did for veterans, as a form of restraint against its being transformed into actual violence. The memory, though only of a single incident, suggests at least the possibility of a habit of violent imagery (or at least of mutually violent feelings) in her relationship with her mother. It was a relationship between a woman who was herself apparently schizoid, was also subject to obsessive ruminations of various kinds, and exerted close and more or less exclusive control over her daughter's every movement ("My father was never really in the picture")—and a little girl who was quiet, obedient, always sought to please, and tended as she grew older not to be very sociable.

In that relationship, and then throughout the rest of her life, Jean seems to have swung between total submission and violent image-feelings. One way of understanding the core of her affective problem is the absence of an in-between capacity for anger and rage.* Whereas the veterans could express themselves constantly in precisely that in-between area, and in fact did so in a way that enhanced their new integration and sense of vitality, she could only struggle with a combination of personal inactivation and overwhelmingly violent image-feelings.

Freud struggled with, and in a sense against, his inevitably instinctual view of violence. Significantly, his way of responding to the extraordinary mass murder of World War I was to focus on what he considered the related hypocrisies of claims to general virtue on the one hand and the denial of death on the other. Thus, well before he had formulated the death instinct as such, he was preoccupied with the attitude toward death as a factor in mass violence. In that essay, written six months after the outbreak of the war, Freud concludes that man's instinctual life is such that "war cannot be abolished," but that we would "do better" were we to "recognize the truth" that "in our civilized attitude toward death we are once again living psychologically beyond our means" and to "give death the place in reality and in our thoughts which is its due."[3] † That at least would help overcome some of the anxiety and confusion over the war's having shattered much of the ordinary denial of death, and could thereby "mak[e] . . . life more tolerable for us once again." The tone of this essay was undoubtedly influenced by Freud's having himself experienced only weeks before, as a fifty-eight-year-old man, the kind of emotional excitement that can accompany war, a "youthful enthusiasm [that was] apparently a re-awakening of the military ardors of his boyhood."[4] Freud spoke of the "splendid news" of an Austro-German victory, and he declared: "All my libido is given to Austro-Hungary." For the first time in thirty years he said he felt himself to be an Austrian. He refused to help neurotic patients avoid conscription because (in

---

* One should not take this absence of an in-between capacity for anger and rage to be the hallmark of schizophrenia. Other schizophrenics are perfectly capable of anger and rage. The more general factor may be the inability to ground or center that anger and rage in a functional way within the experience of the self.

† Here Freud is close to the theme of this book, and seems to confirm my stress on the significance for him of death-related imagery. But as we have repeatedly seen, his view differs from ours on exactly what "death's place in reality . . . which is its due" should be.

Jones's words) "He was of the opinion that they should all try to help in the common interest and that it would do them good to do so." He referred somewhat disdainfully to Otto Rank, then his secretary-assistant, for attempting to avoid conscription, for "fighting like a lion against his Fatherland." [5] All that dampened this enthusiasm, at least at the beginning, was the incompetence of the Austro-Hungarian military.

Before long Freud did become more sensitive to what the war really meant, and wrote in December, 1914, that although "mankind will surmount even this war, . . . I know for certain that I and my contemporaries will never again see a joyous world. It is all too hideous," adding that "the saddest thing about it is that it has come out just as from our psychoanalytical expectations we should have imagined man and his behavior." [6] How much better to be aware of illusion and denial—in this case the denial of death that could permit one illusions of military glory and of accompanying human achievement—than to have so actively participated in them. His plea for confronting the truth about death, and the sadness of his literary voice in making that plea, had to do not only with pessimistic convictions about human violence, but also with his struggles against his own embrace of violence, at least in the sense of having uncritically applauded so violent an enterprise. Freud was on his way to creating the procrustean bed of the death instinct, which, paradoxically, was to enable him to discuss death itself still more freely and to make further inferences concerning relationships between death and violence.

Even later, in his most detailed statement of instinctual dualism *(Civilization and Its Discontents)*, he was preoccupied with the relationship between violence and guilt. The difficulty was that his three-way sensitivity (involving death, violence, and guilt) had, finally, to be pressed into the instinctual mold. Thus Freud had to claim "that a portion of the [death] instinct is diverted towards the external world and comes to light as an instinct of aggressiveness and destructiveness." [7] What Freud is really saying is that the basis for the anger-rage-violence constellation lies in a built-in energy of self-destruction. The energy of the death instinct is also, in the end, the basis for the psychological experience of guilt. Human beings may appear to become violent toward one another because of negative currents between them, or of certain features of one group that are perceived as intolerable by the other, but all that is primarily an externalization of nature's implant of a kind of internal violence working on the organism. Again, one is amazed at what Freud was able to do with what would seem on the face of it to be a highly unpromising set of assumptions.

But that instinctualism has had a harmful influence on explorations of anger, rage, and violence. In moral and political terms, it has been used to justify not only violence but every form of oppression and evil, under the claim that these are inevitable, instinctual. And it has been associated with consistently simplistic and misleading conceptualizations about human violence. Obviously, Freud cannot be held responsible for all this. Nor was he by any means the first to think of violence in instinctual terms. What he did do, however, was to elevate an instinctual theory of violence to new psychological heights by making it part of his revolutionary breakthrough in human thought.

Freud became the pivotal figure in a sequence of instinctual thought not often commented upon: use by post-Darwinian biologists of animal models to develop instinctual theories of aggression; extension of those biological models to make them cornerstones of human psychology (notably by Freud); and more recent embrace of these (mainly Freudian) instinctual assumptions about human violence by certain contemporary biologists. The representative figure here, of course, is Konrad Lorenz, an influential ethologist and Nobel Prize winner. His book, *On Aggression*, contains many valuable observations and interpretations of animal behavior.[8] But when discussing man, he quotes an earlier paper he wrote to express his fundamental principle: present-day civilized man suffers from insufficient discharge of his aggressive drive. Lorenz extracts the concept of aggressive instincts from Freud and the post-Freudians in a quantitative fashion and comes to an "animalistic" image of man that is consistent with Freud. "These deepest strata of the human personality [instinctive behavior mechanisms] are, in their dynamics, not essentially different from the instincts of animals, but on their basis human culture has erected all the enormous superstructure of social norms and rites whose function is so closely analogous to that of phylogenetic ritualization."[9] Within this "superstructure" he focuses upon the problem of "militant enthusiasm." While rightly recognizing it as the source of much violence, his moral-psychological view of militant enthusiasm is much more dubious: militant enthusiasm is an instinct that closely parallels those of other animals, and the only way to deal with it is to contain it by aiming it at ethically acceptable targets.* This argument is considerably more simplistic than Freud's, but the two share an "instinct for instinct" when approaching mass behavior. In "Thoughts for the Times on War and Death," Freud expressed ignorance about such mass behavior: "It is, to be sure, a mystery why the collective individuals should in fact despise, hate and detest one another—every nation against every other—and even in times of peace. I cannot tell why that is so . . . all individual moral acquisitions are obliterated, and only the most primitive, the oldest, the crudest mental attitudes are left."[11] Six years later, when he addressed himself to collective behavior (in *Group Psychology* and *The Analysis of the Ego*), his focus was on various "libidinous ties" among group members

* "There is reasonable hope that our moral responsibility may gain control over the primeval drive, but our only hope of its ever doing so rests on the humble recognition of the fact that militant enthusiasm is an instinctive response with a phylogenetically determined releasing mechanism and that the only point at which intelligent and responsible supervision can get control is in the conditioning of the response to an object which proves to be of genuine value under the scrutiny of the categorical question."[10]

and especially with leaders, which create for the individual "conditions which allow him to throw off the repressions of his unconscious instinctual impulses." Freud goes on to equate "the group mind with the mind of primitive people," and group behavior in general with "the unconscious" and with instinct. He sees the group as "a revival of the primal horde," the murderous band of brothers on whom Freud based his theory of the "primal crime," the killing of the father, in *Totem and Taboo* and subsequent work. Although Lorenz's human psychology is a vulgarization of Freud, it seizes upon Freud's psychological instinctualism and, like Freud, neglects issues having to do with ideology, shared imagery, ultimate concerns, and the need for transcendence. *

---

* Much more than Freud, Lorenz is prescriptive. He suggests four directions of solution for human violence: first, more ethological research on "all the possibilities of discharging aggression in its primal form on substitute objects"; second, further psychoanalytic study of sublimation to seek knowledge of how "this specifically human form of catharsis" can provide "the relief of undischarged aggressive drives"; third, avoiding aggression through personal acquaintance and "if possible, friendship between individual members of different ideologies or nations"; and fourth, and most important, "the intelligent and responsible channeling of militant enthusiasm." [12] These suggestions revolve essentially around the concept of instinctual quanta of aggression that must be in some way "drained off" or converted into something useful. Thus, Lorenz focuses upon sports, and especially Olympic games, as ideal "outlets" for the "discharge" of aggression. Many critics, notably Erich Fromm in *The Anatomy of Human Destructiveness*, have pointed out the contradictions in this instinctivist approach. Fromm, for instance, points out that large sporting events frequently mobilize violence, that recently "the deep feeling aroused by an international soccer match led to a small war in Latin America," [13] and we have seen smaller-scale but nonetheless dangerous forms of violence, in spectators and sometimes in players, during sporting events in the United States. But for understanding what is wrong with Lorenz's view, nothing is more instructive than the events of the Olympic games in Munich in 1972.

In the middle of the games, a group of Palestinian terrorists surreptitiously made their way into the Olympic village, captured a number of Israeli athletes and held them in custody for several days before the television cameras of the world, while negotiating with West German authorities for release of various members of their own and other guerrilla groups. The attack itself by the terrorist group and the German police ambush a few days later killed a total of eleven Israelis, five Palestinian terrorists, and one policeman. The terrorist group responsible called themselves Black September. They took that name from the events in Jordan in September, 1970: the attack on and virtual destruction of Palestinian guerrilla forces by the Jordanian military. That fighting not only eliminated the guerrilla bases in Jordan but brought about the death of about four thousand guerrillas, and included shelling of Palestinian refugee camps. The Black September organization apparently was formed by survivors of that event along with militant members of already existing guerrilla groups. Those 'parent groups' sometimes condoned, and other times condemned, the more violent Black September methods, within a complex structure of rivalry and cooperation. In that sense Black September violence emerged from two survivals: the defeat by the Jordanians in 1970 and the more general Palestinian survival of what is perceived as incursion by outsiders (Israelis) resulting in the loss of their homeland. (Contributing to the excruciating antagonisms in the Middle East are contending forms of survivor imagery: the Jews' sense of creating Israel out of the

Violence of a terrorist group is perceived as a product of others'; and is understood to be in response to overwhelming danger to the life of their own people. Among such groups there is a profound sense of having themselves been violated, of having been thwarted in their aspirations toward vitality and meaning. There is important structuring of the habit of violence: the use of a violent style is by no means merely a matter of gradual accommodation, although there are elements of that, too. Perhaps more importantly, violence among terrorist groups can take on a form of transcendence, even of ecstasy, of its own.

Consider, for instance, the violent act by which Black September made itself known to the world. On November 28, 1971, a group of six young people, five men and one woman, assassinated Wasfi Tell, the prime minister of Jordan, at the entrance to the Sheraton Hotel in Cairo. They had identified their victim as having been responsible for the killing of their compatriots in Jordan. One of the group, just before they all fled, leaned down and drank some of the blood pouring out of the dying man. The process would seem to be a kind of vampirism, with two modifications: the drinker of the blood is not a ghost but a living assassin; and the source of the blood is not one who is intact and alive but at the point of death. But the drinking of the blood of dying enemies was a widespread practice in primitive societies, and certainly has close bearing on patterns we described in relationship to vampirism. We spoke there of how the dead seek, through blood, the life of the living. Here we may say that those who perceive themselves to be psychically and politically dead, drink the blood of their victim as if to symbolize a radical reversal around life and death—the former victimizer made victim, the formerly "dead" assassins now revitalized and able to be arbiters of life and death. *

European holocaust, and the Arab sense of having survived Western colonialism, along with the more specific Palestinian survivor ethos.) From all available evidence, the Black Septembrists, like most terrorists, placed their violence within a vision of justice and, above all, of revitalization and renewal of their group, their people.

On a later occasion, after having killed three diplomats (two American and one Belgian) in Khartoum, the Black Septembrists chastized "those who ostensibly weep today over execution of three enemies of the Arab nation," and demanded instead that all realize "that thousands of the sons of this people have been atrociously slaughtered and that thousands of others are suffering all kinds of torture in Jordanian and Israeli jails."

* The word assassin is Arabic for user of hashish, and is the European name for an Ismaili sect of Islam whose members were distinguished by their blind obedience to their spiritual leader and the use of murder to eliminate foes. They thrived from the early twelfth to the mid-thirteenth centuries. Devotees who achieved the highest degree of initiation into the secrets of the order became the instruments of assassination and in the process sought martyrdom. It is thought they were given hashish and exposed to luxuriant sensual pleasures as a foretaste of the pleasures of paradise they were promised should they achieve their martyrdom. [14]

One can imagine the intensity, the sense of transcendence, at the moment the individual Black Septembrist drank that blood. *

Of importance to our argument is Lorenz's claim that the Olympic games are, reductively speaking, perfectly transmuted aggression, "Virtually the only occasion when the anthem of one nation can be played without arousing any hostility against another . . . [because] the sportsman's dedication to the international social norms of his sport, to the ideals of chivalry and fair play, is equal to any national enthusiasm." [15] While there can exist in sports some of the ennobling forms of experience he describes, the fact is that the modern Olympic games [which began in 1896] began in the mind of an aristocratic Frenchman, troubled by France's defeats by Germany on the battlefield and the absence of physical exercise and games in French education; and then equally troubled by the fact that the ancient site of Olympia was uncovered by a German expedition. As Coubertin, the father of the modern Olympics, put it, "Germany has brought to life the remains of Olympia; why should France not succeed in reviving its ancient glory?" The point is that fierce political rivalries and other impure concerns have had a dominant influence on the Olympics, modern and ancient, and these have infected the events with passions far removed from chivalry and fair play. † Associated with fierce political rivalries are absolute demands for victory that can hardly be mentioned in the same breath with the idea of fair play—whether in the form of blatant hypocrisy concerning amateurism or by cheating (the example of the Russian fencers who used special electrical devices to falsify scoring procedures). Moreover, these patterns were by no means absent from the original Greek version of the games. As a fascinating and authoritative recent study points out, the Olympic games have religious origins within a very flexible polytheism in which "there was no inconsistency between worship and fiercely competitive games as parts of a single religious celebration" and "The gods . . . were patrons of success rather than its creators." Indeed there would seem to have been, from the beginning, something close to a "Vince Lombardi complex": ‡ "Victory alone brought

---

* Concerning the Olympics episode, there could also have been an element of transcendence in the sharing of the Olympic stage—in the sense of its imagery of international communion in *agon* or a competitive struggle, and even more in the extraordinary worldwide visibility (estimated at 500,000,000 viewers) the terrorist drama could immediately achieve.

† One need only mention Adolf Hitler's attempts at manipulating the 1936 Berlin Olympics for the glory of the Third Reich, and questions raised recently (1976) over permitting, or joining in with, the participation of countries that practice overt forms of racism.

‡ Vince Lombardi (1913–70) was a celebrated coach in American professional football, who achieved extraordinary success and was known equally for his fanatical dedication to winning. His motto is said to have been, "Winning is not everything but it is the *only* thing."

glory: participation, games-playing for its own sake, was no virtue; defeat brought undying shame." Thus the great poet Pindar could speak of losers as men who "when they meet their mothers, / Have no sweet laughter around them moving delight./In backstreets out of their enemies' way/They cower; disaster has bitten them." [16] And although Finley and Pleket make clear that it is impossible to assess the amount of early Olympic corruption, there was a very real problem of bribery—including one notable case more significant for the response of a city-state than for the original dishonest act, after an Athenian pentathlete had been exposed as having won by bribing his opponents. "The city of Athens sent its leading orator and politician, Hypereides to . . . plead for suspension of the fine." When the orator failed, the city itself paid the money, "but only after Apollo at Delphi threatened not to provide any more oracles for Athens until this was done." None of that is surprising—nor does it invalidate certain qualities and achievements that the Olympics have embodied. What it does invalidate is the vision of an aggression-discharging process or program existing outside of the shared imagery of a particular group, that is, outside of idea-systems, ideology, history itself. The terrorists' intrusion into the 1972 Olympics, among other things, was a way of mockingly challenging, in the most extreme form, the Olympics' claim to controlled, chivalric competition as a substitute for violence.

Among recent writers on violence, Erich Fromm and Ernest Becker have been notable for their dualistic focus on death and death imagery. Fromm makes a shift from Freud's instinctual dualism to one that is death-centered and characterological.* His view leaves little room for the dialectical nature of violence, and particularly for understanding its embrace in the service of life. That principle holds even, perhaps especially, for the most extreme perpetrators of violence. Adolf Hitler, whom Fromm describes at length as an exemplar of necrophilia, was preoccupied throughout much of his life with imagery of revitalization. It was his group, the German nation, that had been victimized: by the other European countries at Versailles, and by the Jews in their ostensible economic control and nefarious influence. As J. P. Stern has pointed out, one of Hitler's talents "was to create and perpetuate emergency situations in which mental and moral reactions of the kind observed . . . on the threshhold of death would become not just tolerated but indeed 'natural'." [19] And as Uriel Tal has vividly described, Hitler initiated a pattern of Nazi ideology in which

---

*He suggests two basic character types, the necrophylic or death-loving and therefore violent-prone, and the biophylic or life-loving and therefore life-enhancing. The necrophylic individual is seen to be possessed by a *"passion to transform that which is alive into something unalive; to destroy for the sake of destruction."* [17] The two character types, moreover, are polarized: *"Destructiveness is not parallel to, but the alternative to biophile. Love of life or love of the dead is the fundamental alternative that confronts every human being."* [18] Fromm does recognize that there is overlap, and that most people are neither completely the one nor the other but insists that it is "quite possible" to determine which predominates.

the Jew became the embodiment of moral decay, physical perversion, aesthetic degeneration, and spiritual petrifaction, that is, the embodiment of threatening death, while the "counter-Jew" or anti-Jew, the Aryan, possessed directly opposite virtues, a special life-power and immortal destiny. (Later we shall take a more systematic look at historical forms of death imagery, and the collective sequence from historical dislocation to totalism, victimization, and violence.)

Violence cannot be properly understood without including its close relationship to symbolization of immediate or ultimate vitality. This is not to deny Hitler's specific forms of individual psychopathology, which lent radically perverse dimensions to his struggles with death imagery and aspirations toward vitality. But there are at least two limitations in the use of that psychopathology as an explanatory principle. First, there is the collective response of Germans to his movement—the extent to which ordinary men and women, whom we may assume to have no special pathology, could experience new energy, a sense of purpose and meaning in life, a form of personal revitalization through participating in the movement.[20] It is by no means merely Hitler's pathology that created this phenomenon—it was also his genius, the intensity of his vision of revitalization, and the collective historical hunger for this imagery on the part of the German people. Nazi violence, although fundamentally influenced by the extremity of Hitler's personal embrace, was a collective historical phenomenon. More generally, although violence can often be associated with psychopathology, it is a general human proclivity. Invoking psychopathology or aberrant character structure to explain violence may be misleading or even falsifying. The world becomes divided into the bad killers and the good life-lovers. But explorations of death imagery and the quest for vitality teach us that decent men can kill and life-loving men, even if they eschew violence, can bring very bad tidings to others.

Becker's dualism is more subtle and powerful. For Becker, man is psycho-biologically locked into the dichotomy of body and death on the one hand and the self's reach beyond the body's limitations into a boundless, immortal realm on the other. Becker seems right when he says that man kills and dies in quest of "more life." But Becker's theory of violence—what he calls a theory of evil—rests in the end on the inherent logic, the inevitability, of the mind-body dualism. Man must continue to be dangerously aggressive and violent, Becker tells us, because, being organically and existentially incapable of accepting the death of his body, he must conjure up illusions, or what Rank called "irrational immortality ideologies." Becker admits within his dualism much that is illuminating, from the struggle against death in primitive societies, to money as the modern immortality ideology, to the constraints on contemporary quests for heroic transcendence. But in the end he has no place for the normative symbolization (and experience) of transcendence, and therefore cannot make distinctions among symbolizations of immortality and their proclivities for violence. And at the individual level, since selfhood or character is a "lie," a compensatory device built around denial of death, becoming violent or not is simply a matter of one illusion versus another. There is little room either for gradations of anger and violence, or for violent imagery as a necessary aspect of the self's mediation between its own past experience and its immediate, threatening encounters. In this absolute dualism, the body is artificially excluded from the symbolizing process, and therefore can never be part of the self's larger connections or ultimate concerns. We are condemned to a vicious circle of death terror over bodily disintegration and violence to avoid that death terror. Not its pessimism but its oversimplification of human nature makes us question this view.

We must take seriously the operation of anger-rage-violence as part of the tenuous equilibrium around death imagery and guilt. While conscience and guilt provide a specifically human capacity to connect death imagery with internal responsibility and self-blame, the anger-rage-violence constellation provides a means of assigning responsibility and blaming others for that same death imagery. That is part of what Freud meant when he said, within his instinctual idiom, that "a portion of the [death] instinct is diverted towards the external world and comes to light as an instinct of aggressiveness and destructiveness." [21] He sensed that the human psyche must mobilize energy for external judgments no less than internal ones. What Freud spoke of as the "energy of the death instinct" giving rise to a "derivative aggressive instinct," we understand as the energy of the struggle to combine death imagery with vitality and integrity. This conceptual absence of an instinct of violence or evil carries no inherent optimism. Rather, it places man's capacity to destroy and kill within a human dialectic that is as fundamental as it is precarious—one involving the capacity to judge and blame (and therefore hold a concept of justice) on the one hand and the impulse to kill on the other. No wonder we so often waver between virtue and violence, and in the process sometimes become ill.*

---

*The approach in the clinical literature that comes closest to my own is that of Tess Forrest.[22] She states: "To the various theories of self and identity formation . . . I would like to add the thesis that the infant is born with a vital self, which is his drive to preserve the unconditional value of his life and of his self-experience. This psychic energy will ultimately find its outlet in vitality or be transformed to violence." [23]

Dr. Forrest is not always clear about whether or not she views "psychic energy" in a quantitative way when she speaks of its being "transformed" to violence. Nor does she allow for what I have called the habit of violence, a psychological style in which violence takes on an autonomy of its own because it is associated with a constellation of imagery that confers meaning (maintaining life or vitality, defending against being "killed") on that violence. But her stress on the interrelationship of violence and vitality is much in the spirit of my own.

THIRTEEN

Survivor Experience and

Traumatic Syndrome

ANY CLAIM TO PSYCHOLOGICAL insight must be tested against disorder. I believe that principles around death and continuity can contribute to understanding the major psychiatric syndromes. Yet at the clinical and conceptual heart of psychiatry, death-related issues have been most neglected, and here, too, overall symbolizing principles are most required.

There are certain advantages in beginning this section with a consideration of the traumatic syndrome. I confess that I am influenced by the fact that so much of my research has had close bearing on this syndrome, focusing as it has on survivor experiences. That was true not only for my studies of Hiroshima, Vietnam, and the Buffalo Creek disaster, but also of my work on Chinese thought reform and, in a historical sense, of my work with Japanese youth and even young American professionals. Over time I have developed several strong convictions about this general psychological area: direct, intense psychological trauma—perhaps even adult trauma in general—is a kind of stepchild in psychiatry. An exploration of the psychology of the survivor is crucial to understanding such trauma. The study of adult trauma and survival has direct bearing on issues around death and death imagery in ways that shed a great deal of light on both psychiatric disturbance and on our contemporary historical condition.

We have learned to find models in early childhood experience for later adult behavior. But there is a beginning sense in psychiatry that a reverse process may be just as useful. Intense adult trauma can provide a model, at least in terms of understanding, for the more obscure and less articulated traumas of early childhood. This reversal was not unknown to Freud. And it is the basis for the image-model of the human being as a perpetual survivor—first of birth itself, and then of 'holocausts' large and small, personal and collective, that define much of existence—a survivor capable of growth and change, especially when able to confront and transcend those 'holocausts' or their imprints.[1]

The adult traumatic experience, in the form of war neuroses, played a very special part for Freud in his conceptual development in general and in his ideas about death in particular. Freud gives special attention to war neurosis and the concept of trauma in connection with his elaboration of the death instinct in *Beyond the Pleasure Principle*. That book is a crucial one in Freud's opus. James Strachey, for instance, tells us (in his Editor's Note for the Standard Edition) that "In the series of Freud's metapsychological writings, *Beyond the Pleasure Principle* may be regarded as introducing the final phase of his views." Robert Waelder, a distinguished second-generation Viennese disciple of Freud, has noted: "It is probably not accidental that this short work was written soon after World War I . . . [when] Europe was full of shell-shocked soldiers; one could see them shaking in the streets."[2]*

Yet the impact of the traumas of World War I on Freud and his movement has hardly been recorded. World War I (as well as his personal affliction with cancer) had considerable bearing on Freud's elaboration of the death instinct and his preoccupation with it in his later speculative books, and Europe's grotesque death immersion had an equally significant impact on Freud's attitudes toward his own life and toward his struggling psychoanalytic movement. He cared more about the movement than he did about his individual existence. The war's traumas to the movement (personal and professional deprivations, various forms of separation and isolation, as well as deaths of friends and family members) must have been perceived as a struggle for survival. And while Freud had relatively (for him) unproductive periods during the war, he also had bouts of extraordinary creativity. There can be little doubt that he and many of his followers were energized in some degree by their survival, though it is difficult to say at what cost. It is quite likely that the war's many levels of destruction accelerated the spread of psychoanalytic influence throughout the world. Few other groups could offer as compelling an explanation for both the mass killing and the psychological consequences of war. More fundamentally, massive trauma subverts existing systems of symbol-

---

*Waelder goes on to explain: "Some of them had merely been exposed to the 'ordinary' experience of trench warfare; others had been subjected to more particular experiences of concentrated shock, such as, for example, being suddenly covered by a load of earth in an explosion—they had barely escaped being buried alive."[3]

By then a number of psychoanalysts had worked professionally with such people. The Fifth International Psycho-Analytical Congress, held in Budapest in late September, 1918, had in fact included a symposium on "The Psycho-Analysis of War Neuroses," from which a small book eventually emerged.[4]

ization and tends to bring about in its victims a hunger for explanation or formulation, though it also stimulates (perhaps more frequently) an opposite tendency toward a covering over that requires static closure. Freud's movement undoubtedly encountered both kinds of war-linked responses, but it was the receptivity that was new and especially important. There is also the possibility that this psychoanalytic survival of World War I reactivated earlier death anxieties within the movement and contributed to its fearful sectarianism and antagonism to heretics. (We can take it to be more than coincidence that, in an important letter written by Freud to Ernest Jones in February, 1919, an interesting discussion of the nature of traumatic neurosis was followed directly by the sentence: "Your intention to purge the London Society of the Jungish members is excellent.") [5]

Clearly, the war experience raised important theoretical questions for sensitive theorists like Freud. These had to do not only with the nature of homicidal destruction but also with the trauma and neuroses that could be observed in its wake. The problem for Freud was to assimilate these experiences into his already well-developed theoretical system, which meant assimilating them to instinct in general and to the libido concept and the sexual origin of the neuroses in particular.

To be sure, Freud could point out with some pride that earlier psychoanalytic emphases on psychogenic origins of the symptoms of any neurosis, the importance of unconscious impulses, and the part played by psychic gain through or "flight into" illness had been vindicated by widespread observations on the war neuroses. But at the same time he was clearly troubled by the fact that those observations had done nothing to confirm psychoanalytic theory to the effect that "the motive forces which are expressed in the formation of symptoms are sexual and that neuroses arise from a conflict between the ego and the sexual instincts which it repudiates." [6] Freud's response to the challenge was ingenious if a bit convoluted, and characteristically illuminating beyond its conceptual claim. In two of his writings devoted to the question of war neuroses [7] and in a few letters written at the end of World War I, one to Jones in particular, [8] Freud acknowledged the importance of the external trauma but at the same time associated war neurosis with "internal narcissistic conflict." By invoking his newly evolved theory of narcissism, of libido directed not at another person but at one's own self, Freud could at least place this form of traumatic neurosis within the general realm of libido theory. Although Freud was not always entirely clear on the subject the essence of his argument was that traumatic neuroses of peacetime (railway accidents and other injuries in which there remains considerably neurotic overlay) can be explained by means of sexual energy or libido becoming fastened to the particular organ or to the body or ego in general, while traumatic neuroses of war included that narcissistic process along with an added dimension of "the conflict . . . between the soldier's old peaceful ego and his new warlike one, . . . [which] becomes acute as soon as the peace-ego realizes what danger it runs of losing its life owing to the rashness of its newly formed, parasitic double." [9]

That argument carries Freud beyond mere libido theory toward a concept of meaning. The conflict within the self has to do with what one is willing or not willing to die for, and one's "fixation to the trauma" includes a "compulsion to repeat" elements associated with it as a form of mastery or integration. It was, in fact, precisely this compulsion to repeat that Freud described as violating the "pleasure principle" (according to which the quest for pleasure is always a central motivation) and carrying the organism "beyond the pleasure principle."

Moreover, it was in discussing these questions that Freud emphasized a principle of a "protective shield," by which he meant a kind of psychic skin necessary for the important, everyday function of keeping out external stimuli which might otherwise overwhelm the self or ego. Hence *protection against stimuli is an almost more important function for the living organism than reception of stimuli."* [10] He could then define "as 'traumatic' any excitations from outside which are powerful enough to break through the protective shield." And traumatic neurosis became "a consequence of an extensive breach being made in the protective shield against stimuli." Freud could then see in traumatic neurosis something close to a retrospective model for neurosis in general, and even for individual acts of repression that may or may not contribute to neurosis.

Not only did Freud make traumatic neurosis a retrospective model for neurosis in general, but he did so around a concept of blockage of stimuli or what could be called diminished feeling or psychic numbing. The "protective shield" carried out that function toward outside stimuli, but for stimuli arising from within (instinctual impulses or primary process) there had to be an analogous pattern (what Freud called the "binding" of "excitations"). And "a failure to effect this binding would provoke a disturbance analogous to a traumatic neurosis." That failure, incidentally, makes necessary the compulsion to repeat and the operation of the psyche outside or beyond the pleasure principle. Freud is saying the same thing when he concludes his essay on war neuroses with the observation that "we have a perfect right to describe repression, which lies at the basis of every neurosis, as a reaction to a trauma— as an elementary traumatic neurosis." Here Freud associates neurosis with a feeling disorder arising out of the organism's attempt to block excitations caused or released by trauma. This stress on the struggle against feeling reverberates throughout his work. Although Freud did not speak of what we have been calling death imagery, he did associate this struggle around excitation and feeling (as encountered in traumatic neurosis) with his argument for a death instinct. Traumatic neurosis became a cornerstone for neurosis on the one hand, and Freud's death-related conceptualizations on the other. In this juxtaposition, Freud came closest to creating a death-oriented psychology.

But at that point Freud called forth his own protective shield in order to place the traumatic neuroses within libido theory. To do so he had to ward off the potentially transforming influence of death on *theory*, on our understanding of human experience. Freud's conceptual shield was his invocation of the concept of narcissism. That concept approaches conflicts within the self in terms of libido or sexual energy "lodged in the ego." Freud could claim that such "ego-libido" was released by trauma and could no longer be adequately "bound" or constructively contained. Similarly he invoked the concept of narcissism to explain psychological patterns in schizophrenia, and to a lesser extent those in severe depression or melancholia. In all three conditions, Freud used the idea of narcissism or intense, unmanageable self-directed sexual energies to explain actual processes of disintegration and related death equivalents. In that way, Freud could not only reaffirm libido theory but collapse his own observations on meaning (in traumatic neurosis, conflicts over what one will die for) and impaired feeling (the protective shield and related internal blockage or "binding") into a mechanistic-quantifiable energic principle. Yet, the beginnings he made in sorting out these death-related struggles around meaning and feeling have by no means been lost.

Abram Kardiner, for instance, who has distilled much of psychiatric thought on the traumatic syndrome emerging from World War II, began with Freud's explorations of trauma. But by emphasizing his own and Rado's view of "neurosis as a form of adaptation," [11] he was able to stress the need "to unravel the sense behind the symptomatology" as well as issues around feeling and numbing. Concerning the latter, he spoke of a "shrinking" of the ego, of the organism's "shrunken inner resources," and above all of "ego contraction" that interferes with virtually all areas of behavior. Kardiner combined this stress on "ego contraction" with the equally important emphasis on "disorganization rather than regression." Contraction and disorganization—what we would call numbing and disintegration—lead readily to the symptom complex, acute or chronic, that just about everyone has observed: fatigue and listlessness, depression, startle reactions, recurrent nightmares, phobias and fears involving situations associated with the trauma (what Rado calls "traumatophobia"), mixtures of impulsive behavior and unsteadiness in human relationships and projects of all kind (including work or study) that may take the form of distrust, suspiciousness, and outbursts of violence.* A convergence of observations suggests that severe threats to the organism produce patterns of stricture that have relevance for a wide variety of psychiatric impairment.

* Like Freud, Kardiner is struck by resemblances between extreme forms of the traumatic syndrome and schizophrenia, but in terms of these principles of contraction and disorganization rather than narcissism and libido theory. Kardiner's thinking closely approximates our own: "Traumatic neurosis is a disease very closely related to schizophrenia, both from the point of view of central psychodynamics and from the ultimate withdrawal from the world which it set in motion. The deteriorations undergone in both conditions have a striking resemblance to each other. In a manner of speaking, the traumatic neurosis is a kind of persecutory delusion. The persecutor is,

What Kardiner neglected, however, is the place of death and death anxiety in the traumatic syndrome. His advances depended upon bypassing instinctualism. But as in the case of much revisionist work, rejecting the death instinct became associated with neglect of death. The neglect is striking in traumatic neuroses, where death is so close. An evolving view puts the death back into traumatic neurosis. As early as 1953, Joseph D. Teicher entitled a paper on the subject "'Combat Fatigue' or 'Death Anxiety Neurosis,'" [14] advocating the latter. Teicher associates his advocacy of "death anxiety neurosis" with classical emphasis upon the importance of guilt toward the dead, as intensified by prior guilt from "fantasied murder" (feelings toward one's father, for instance, in association with the Oedipus complex). But when he goes on to say that "in the neurotic form of fear of death, the sufferers are afraid to die and afraid to kill; in their illness they avoid death and murder," we find ourselves at first nodding in agreement, but quickly sensing that there is something wrong in the way he is putting things. What is right about the approach is its direct stress on dying and killing, its relationship, that is, to death. What is dubious about the statement is its equation of fear of dying and killing as a *neurotic* state. What Teicher means, of course, is that these fears become incapacitating, and therefore associated with "death anxiety neurosis." But the reader's impulse is to say, "Well, if that is the case, the world could use a good bit more of such a neurosis, or a modicum of its symptoms: if not fear, at least reluctance, to die or kill in military combat." The problem here is the reference point of disturbance or neurosis, a matter that turns out to have considerable importance. Both Kardiner and Teicher wrote from the vantage point of World War II, sometimes referred to as "America's last good war." It was, of course, a dreadful war: its "goodness" lay in the American combination of decisive success and equally decisive moral clarity. So evil was the enemy—at least the Nazi enemy—that to annihilate him could only be perceived as virtuous. Consequently, those soldiers who broke down, who were "afraid to die and afraid to kill" on behalf of this crusade, could be quite comfortably viewed as neurotic.

Not so in the case of the Vietnam War two or three decades later. That war, for American participants, was ambiguous in the extreme. Its combination of doubtful justification, absence of structure (as a counterinsurgency action in which the enemy was nowhere and everywhere), and consequent frequency of killing or even massacre of civilians all contributed to various forms of confusion and reluctance to fight. Under those conditions moral revulsion and psychological conflict became virtually inseparable, sometimes in the form of delayed reactions.

---

however, the outer world. *The entire syndrome is produced by what now appears to be a prominent device in the establishment of schizophrenia, namely, ego curtailment."* [12] (italics added)

This "ego curtailment" or contraction is associated with what other observers have called "a chronic state of over-vigilance . . . which seriously affects . . . [many combat veterans'] lives." [13] We shall return to these elements in our discussion of schizophrenia.

Months or even years after their return to this country, many Vietnam veterans combined features of the traumatic syndrome with preoccupation with questions of meaning—concerning the war and, ultimately, all other areas of living.* Most of these men were not incapacitated by their symptoms and could not be called "neurotic." Indeed, their anxiety, guilt, and anger could serve animating functions in terms of both introspective and "extrospective" (outward-looking or social) exploration. They seemed to need those emotions for their assimilation of the pain and confusion they had experienced. The traumatic experience, or at least elements of it, had a constructive function for them. And in many of these cases, both the syndrome (or some of its components) and the doubts about the war began with a confrontation which broke through existing patterns of numbing and evoked images of dying or killing in Vietnam.

An approach to traumatic syndrome should focus on death and related questions of meaning, rather than requiring us to invoke the idea of "neurosis." This death-centered approach suggests a moral dimension in all conflict and neurosis.

The psychology of the survivor helps us greatly here. The survivor is one who has come into contact with death in some bodily or psychic fashion and has remained alive. There are five characteristic themes in the survivor: the death imprint, death guilt, psychic numbing, conflicts around nurturing and contagion, and struggles with meaning or formulation.[16] Each of these has special relevance for traumatic syndrome, and in combination they affect survivors at both proximate and ultimate levels of experience.

The death imprint consists of the radical intrusion of an image-feeling of threat or end to life. That intrusion may be sudden, as in war experience and various forms of accidents, or it may take shape more gradually over time. Of great importance is the degree of unacceptability of death contained in the image—of prematurity, grotesqueness, and absurdity. To be experienced, the death imprint must call forth prior imagery either of actual death or of death equivalents. In that sense every death encounter is itself a reactivation of earlier "survivals." The degree of anxiety associated with the death imprint has to do with the impossibility of assimilating the death imprint—because of its suddenness, its extreme or protracted nature, or its association with the terror of premature, unacceptable dying. Also of considerable importance is one's vulnerability to death imagery—not only to direct life threat but also to separation, stasis, and disintegration—on the basis of prior conflictual experience. But predisposition is only a matter of degree: if the threat or trauma is sufficiently great, it can produce a traumatic syndrome in everyone, as was

---

* The official incidence of traumatic neuroses has been observed to be lower in Vietnam than in World War II. But, as a number of observers have pointed out, these statistics are misleading because they neglect the delayed reactions and nonclinical manifestations of pain and resistance.[15]

largely the case in the man-made flood disaster at Buffalo Creek, West Virginia, in 1972.*

The survivor retains an indelible image, a tendency to cling to the death imprint—not because of release of narcissistic libido as Freud claimed, but because of continuing struggles to master and assimilate the threat (as Freud also observed), and around larger questions of personal meaning. The death encounter reopens questions about prior experiences of separation, breakdown, and stasis as well as countervailing struggles toward vitality; reopens questions, in fact, around all of life's beginnings and endings. So bound to the image can the survivor be that one can speak of a thralldom to death or a "death spell."

The death imprint is likely to be associated not only with pain but also with value—with a special form of knowledge and potential inner growth associated with the sense of having "been there and returned." The death encounter undermines our magical sense of invulnerability by means of its terrible inner lesson that death is real, that one will oneself die—and this vies with our relief at no longer having to maintain that illusion. The result can be something resembling illumination.

Affecting the outcome and the degree of anxiety is the extent of the sense of grief and loss. Grief and mourning are discussed in the next chapter; what we may say here is that, in severe traumatic experience, grief and loss tend to be too overwhelming in their suddenness and relationship to unacceptable death and death equivalents for them to be resolved. And many of the symptoms in the traumatic syndrome have to do precisely with impaired mourning, or what Mitscherlich has called "the inability to mourn." What is involved in our terms is the inability to reconstruct shattered personal forms in ways that reassert vitality and integrity.

Thus the death imprint in traumatic syndrome simultaneously includes actual death anxiety (the fear of dying) and anxiety associated with death equivalents (especially having to do with disintegration of the self.) This powerful coming together of these two levels of threat may well be the most characteristic feature of image-response in the traumatic syndrome.

The extraordinary power of this imagery—its indelible quality—has to do not only with death but with guilt. What is extremely important, in addition to ultimate threat, is the limited capacity to respond to the threat and the self-blame for that inadequate response. (Some of these principles were mentioned in Chapter 11.)

We have stressed the importance of the image for motivation, its anticipatory

---

* The flood resulted from corporate negligence in the form of dumping coal waste in a mountain stream in a manner that created an artificial dam, which eventually gave way, killing 125 people and leaving 5000 homeless. I consulted with two law firms concerning questions of psychic damage (or "psychic impairment") and, together with Eric Olson, conducted extensive interviews with Buffalo Creek survivors and found that virtually all of those we examined showed significant traumatic effects.[17]

quality in the sense of providing a "plan" or "schema" for enactment. But in the face of severe trauma, precisely that process is radically interrupted. The soldier whose buddy is suddenly killed or blown up right next to him, for instance, experiences an image that contains feelings not only of horror and pity but an immediate inner plan for action—for helping his comrade, keeping him alive, relieving his pain, perhaps getting back at the enemy—or at least a psychic equivalent of any of those forms of action. But under the circumstances—and all the more so in a massive immersion in death (as in Hiroshima and the Nazi death camps)—both physical and psychic action are virtually eliminated. One can neither physically help victims nor resist victimizers; one cannot even psychically afford experiencing equivalent feelings of compassion or rage. Freud raised this kind of issue in trauma when he drew an example from children's play in which he emphasized that "children repeat unpleasurable experiences . . . [so] that they can master a powerful impression far more thoroughly by being active than they could by merely experiencing it passively." And Erikson has similarly stressed the severe psychic consequences of inactivation as opposed to the capacity for activity in any threatening situation. The inactivation of which we speak is within the image itself, and therefore a violation of the kind of psychic flow one can ordinarily depend upon. One feels responsible for what one has not done, for what one has not felt, and above all for the gap between that physical and psychic inactivation and what one felt called upon (by the beginning image-formation) to do and feel.

The image keeps recurring, in dreams and waking life, precisely because it has never been adequately enacted. And there is likely to be, in that repetition, an attempt to replay the situation, to rewrite the scenario retrospectively in a way that permits more acceptable enactment of the image—whether by preventing others from dying, taking bolder action of any kind, experiencing strong compassion and pity, or perhaps suffering or dying in place of the other or others. In that way the hope is to be relieved of the burden of self-blame. But whatever actual recovery and relief from guilt one achieves depends much more on the capacity to grasp and accept the nature of one's inactivation under such circumstances.

From this standpoint we can take another look at survivor or death guilt. We have mentioned the survivor's fundamental inner question: "Why did I survive while he, she, or they died?" The image-centered version of that question is: "Why did I survive while letting him, her, or them die?" It is a relatively simple step to feel that by having so failed in one's image-actions at the time, "I killed him." Or that "if I had died *instead*, he, she, or they would have lived." This last feeling may in part reflect the psychic death one did actually undergo—the extreme stasis or numbing accompanying one's inactivation in the face of death and threat—and the related sense that subsequent resumption of vitality in the absence of true enactment (mostly in the form of preventing the dead from dying) is wrong. Death guilt ultimately stems from a sense that until some such enactment is achieved, one has no right to be alive.

One could define the traumatic syndrome as the state of being haunted by images that can neither be enacted nor cast aside. Suffering is associated with being "stuck." Hence the indelible image is always associated with guilt, and in its most intense form takes the shape of an image of ultimate horror: a single image (often containing brutalized children or dying people whom the survivor loved) that condenses the totality of the destruction and trauma and evokes particularly intense feelings of pity and self-condemnation in the survivor. To the extent that one remains stuck in such images, guilt is static, there is a degree of continuing psychological incapacity, and traumatic syndrome can turn into traumatic neurosis. But there is also the possibility of finding something like alternative enactment for the image that haunts one, of undergoing personal transformation around that image. In that sense the very association of guilt with the traumatic syndrome makes possible a transforming relationship to its indelible imagery. And here are the beginnings of a psychological explanation for religious visions of realization and moral growth through suffering.

Only part of oneself feels discomfort at having survived—the experience is also associated with relief, even joy or exhilaration. These feelings can, in turn, contribute to additional guilt. The joy at having survived remains tainted by its relationship to that gap between image and enactment, between the excruciating, demanding picture one had constructed and the muted, devitalized, limited actions and feelings one could muster.

In all this, self-condemnation strikes us as quite unfair. The traumatized person seems to have to endure the additional internal trauma of self-blame. This is why there is a "paradoxical guilt" experienced by victimized survivors. This guilt seems to subsume the individual victim-survivor rather harshly to the evolutionary function of guilt (p. 145) in rendering us accountable for our relationship to others' physical and psychological existence. This experience of guilt around one's own trauma suggests the moral dimension inherent in all conflict and suffering. We have no choice but to make judgments about trauma and our relationship to it. Just as there is an inseparability between psychological and moral dimensions of guilt, we may say the same about all psychological disturbance. Psychological pain always includes a moral judgment; moral judgments express psychological conflict and realization.

In that sense there is no such thing as a value-free mechanism in either traumatic syndrome or any form of neurosis or psychosis. If we can speak of evolutionary purpose, we may say that the capacity for guilt was given us so that we might imbue all behavior, perhaps especially pain, with an ethical dimension. There is no denying the enormity of the cost, of the secondary pain via the guilt itself. That cost is starkly visible in the "paradoxical guilt" of the traumatic syndrome, which in turn has bearing on equally "unfair" forms of guilt in many different neurotic and psychotic conditions. In such states we observe the destructive manifestations of an emotion necessary to humanity, of the emotion concerned with critical self-judgment. And we come to suspect that beyond guilt itself, neurotic and psychotic versions of it are also integral to the human condition.

At the heart of the traumatic syndrome—and of the overall human struggle with pain—is the diminished capacity to feel, or psychic numbing. There is a close relationship between psychic numbing (including its acute form, "psychic closing-off") and death-linked images of denial ("If I feel nothing, then death is not taking place") and interruption of identification ("I see you dying, but I am not related to you or to your death"). The survivor undergoes a radical but temporary diminution in his sense of actuality in order to avoid losing this sense completely and permanently; he undergoes a reversible form of symbolic death in order to avoid a permanent physical or psychic death. From the standpoint of formative process those patterns can be understood as expressions of an internal decision of the organism concerning investment and, therefore, experience of feeling. When made under conditions of acute trauma, that "decision" is neither voluntary nor conscious.

Freud was acutely aware of such issues. This awareness is reflected in a passage from *Civilization and Its Discontents*:

> No matter how much we may shrink with horror from certain situations—of a galley slave in antiquity, of a peasant during the Thirty Years' War, of a victim of the Holy Inquisition, of a Jew awaiting a pogrom—it is nevertheless impossible for us to feel our way into such people, to divine the changes which original obtuseness of mind, a gradual stupefying process, the cessation of expectations and cruder or more refined methods of narcotization have produced upon their receptivity to sensations of pleasure and unpleasure. Moreover, in the case of the most extreme possibility of suffering, special mental protective devices are brought into operation.[18]

Freud is referring to acute and chronic forms of psychic numbing, in response to the most extreme kinds of trauma. Since he abruptly terminates these observations ("It seems to me unprofitable to pursue this aspect of the problem any further"), I had previously thought that Freud was making a special case of these extraordinary situations of what have been subsequently called "massive psychic trauma" and contrasting them with ordinary existence. But more careful study of the context suggests that Freud is actually making a relativistic statement. The preceding sentence, in fact, reads, "Happiness . . . is something essentially subjective," and Freud was cautioning against making too many assumptions concerning the effects of what we would consider the most extreme forms of trauma on people whose situations were quite removed from our own. He was suggesting that a process of "narcotization" or numbing might well prevent these people from experiencing anything like the degree of pain we might think we would experience. This reading suggests that Freud had a sensitive awareness of the adaptive nature of psychic numbing, and of its importance for the whole gamut of human experience. There is perhaps implicit here also an important distinction between this kind of "gradual stupefying process" and more sudden kinds of trauma for which the organism is totally unprepared.

The passage was surely consistent with Freud's earlier observations about the "protective shield" and the extent to which the sense organs not only receive stimuli but "include special arrangements for further protection against excessive amounts of stimulation and for excluding unsuitable kinds of stimuli." To place all this within his instinctual cosmology, however, Freud (in a passage with which we are already familiar) subsumed this narcotization or numbing to the operation of the death instinct in maintaining the "Nirvana principle": "The dominating tendency of mental life, and perhaps of nervous life in general, is the effort to reduce, to keep constant or to remove internal tension due to stimuli." [19] Freud went on to say that "our recognition of that fact is one of our strongest reasons for believing in the existence of death instincts." And he saw this as an alliance between the pleasure principle, operating to reduce the internal tension caused by stimuli of various kinds, and the death instinct. Where this reduction of stimuli could not be considered exactly pleasurable, it was the latter, the death instinct, that took precedence in guiding the organism toward its own demise, in being "concerned with the most universal endeavor of all living substance—mainly to return to the quiescence of the inorganic world." Via instinctual theory, Freud is doing something interesting here. He is suggesting that a struggle with, or primarily against, feeling is the most fundamental characteristic of the human mind. In one place he suggests that in traumatic neurosis the compulsion to repeat derives from earlier inability to experience feeling appropriate to the trauma—so that repetitive dreams about the traumatic experience "are endeavoring to master the stimulus retrospectively, *by developing the anxiety whose omission was the cause of the traumatic neurosis.*" [20] (italics added) This is close to what we called failed enactment, here a matter of feelings that should have been but were not experienced. But where Freud goes on to see this compulsion to repeat as itself instinctual (part of the organism's urge to restore an earlier state of things), we would emphasize the struggle to assimilate the destructive or annihilating force into prior, or else altered, mental structures.

For the numbing in severe versions of the traumatic syndrome consists of *the mind being severed from its own psychic forms.* To explain this process let us consider two quotations:

> The whole situation around me was very special . . . and my mental condition was very special too. . . . About life and death . . . I just couldn't have any reaction. . . . I don't think I felt either joy or sadness. . . . My feelings about human death weren't really normal. . . . You might say I became insensitive to . . . death.

We were all too exhausted to react, and almost nothing stirred our emotions. We had all seen too much. In my sick and aching brain, life had lost its importance and meaning, and seemed of no more consequence than the power of motion one lends to a marionette, so that it can agitate for a few seconds. Of course, there was friendship . . . but immediately behind them [two close friends] there was that hole full of guts, red, yellow, and foul smelling; piles of guts, almost as large as the earth itself. Life could be snuffed like that, in an instant, but the guts remained for a long time, stamped on the memory.

The first quotation is from a Hiroshima survivor,[21] the second from a former soldier in the German infantry during World War II.[22] In the case of the Hiroshima survivor the overwhelming trauma was the experience of the bomb and its immediate aftermath of grotesque death immersion. The German soldier had experienced years of perpetual death-linked trauma. Their tone is strikingly similar in its combined suggestion of desensitization toward death and the annihilation of physical and psychic life. In order to dissociate itself from grotesque death, the mind must itself cease to live, become itself deadened. The dissociation becomes intrapsychic in the sense that feeling is severed from knowledge or awareness of what is happening. To say that emotion is lost while cognition is retained is more or less true, but does not really capture what the mind is experiencing. What is more basic is the self's being severed from its own history, from its grounding in such psychic forms as compassion for others, communal involvement, and other ultimate values. That is what is meant by the mind's being severed from its own forms. And that severance, in turn, results in the failed enactment and guilt we spoke of above. This kind of process was described even before Freud by Janet under the concept of dissociation. It includes not only stasis in the sense of inactivation, but also disintegration in the sense of a coming apart of crucial components of the self. To be sure, that disintegration, like the stasis, is partial and to a considerable degree temporary— in fact, is in the service of preventing more total and lasting forms of disintegration. But we can say that this dissociative disintegration characterizes the psychic numbing of the traumatic syndrome, and is at the heart of that experience.

There is a close relationship between the phrase used by a Hiroshima survivor, "A feeling of paralysis of my mind," and a Buffalo Creek survivor's sense, in explaining his isolation from people around him, "Now . . . it's like everything is destroyed." Those two comments refer respectively to patterns of stasis and disintegration, and suggest important elements of separation as well. For all three death equivalents are important in the dissociative disintegration of the traumatic syndrome. As a consequence, psychic action, the essence of the formative-symbolizing process, is virtually suspended, and the organism is in a state of severe desymbolization. In that sense psychic numbing undermines the most fundamental psychic processes. That is why we can speak of it as the essential mechanism of mental disorder.

These manifestations of psychic numbing are directly responsible for the two additional survivor struggles we have not yet discussed, those around suspicion of the counterfeit and quest for meaning. The survivor struggles toward—and in a way, against—reexperiencing himself as a vital human being. Conflicts over nurturing and contagion have to do with the human relationships he requires for that revitalization, and with their impaired state. The survivor experiences feelings of weakness and special need, along with resentment of help offered as a reminder of weakness. Any such help is likely to be perceived as counterfeit. This is so not only because of its association with weakness, but because prior forms of dependency in human relationships have proven themselves unreliable; one's human web has been all too readily shattered, and in rearranging one's image-feelings, one is on guard against false promises of protection, vitality, or even modest assistance. One fends off not only new threats of annihilation but gestures of love or help. Part of this resistance to human relationships has to do with a sense of being tainted by death, of carrying what might be called the psychic stigma of the annihilated. This stigma, which victims have always experienced, is usually explained around the idea of self-concept: if one is treated so cruelly, one tends to internalize that sense of being worthless. To modify and add to that principle, we could say: having been annihilated and "killed," one feels oneself to have become part of the entire constellation of annihilation and destruction, to be identified with—live in the realm of—death and breakdown. The whole process, of course, is intensified by others' fear of the survivor's death taint. He becomes associated in their minds with a constellation of killing and dying which, should one let him get too close, endanger "ordinary healthy people." That is, associations to his experience can activate latent anxieties in others concerning death and death equivalents.

The struggles around nurturing and contagion are directly related to an insufficiently appreciated survivor emotion, that of perpetual anger and frequent rage. We discussed in Chapter 12 various kinds of survivor anger, rage, and violence, as directly related to a sense of inner death and a desperate effort at vitality. The survivor seems, in fact, to require his anger and rage—and all too often, his violence—as an alternative to living in the realm of the annihilated. Many have noted that anger is relatively more comfortable than guilt or other forms of severe anxiety; it can also be a way of holding onto a psychic lifeline when surrounded by images of death.

Maybe that is something of the way we live all the time, but in the case of severe trauma we can say that there has been an important break in the lifeline that can leave one permanently engaged in either repair or the acquisition of new twine. And here we come to the survivor's overall task, that of formulation, evolving new inner forms that include the traumatic event, which in turn requires that one find meaning or significance in it so that the rest of one's life need not be devoid of meaning and significance. Formulation means establishing the lifeline on a new basis. That basis includes proximate and ultimate involvements. The survivor seeks vitality both in immediate relationships and ultimate meaning, the one impossible without the other. Some Hiroshima survivors, for instance, could reanimate their lives around peace-movement activities, which offered a sense of immediate activity in like-minded groups and ultimate significance within which their otherwise unassimilable experience could be understood. If the world could receive a valuable message from Hiroshima, that is, and they could be the agents and disseminators of that message, then what happened to them could be said to have a larger purpose. The same principle applied to Nazi death-camp survivors in their struggle to establish and participate in the State of Israel. More typical is the quest for vitality around direct biological continuity—the tendency of many survivors to reassert family ties and reproduce, and thereby assert biological and biosocial modes of symbolic immortality. In any case, the ultimate dimension, the struggle for resurgent modes of symbolic immortality, is crucial to the survivor, though rarely recognized as such.

Without this kind of formulation the survivor remains plagued by unresolved conflicts in the other areas mentioned—by death anxiety, death guilt, psychic numbing, and immobilizing anger and suspicion of the counterfeit. Numbing in particular, the desymbolizing center of the traumatic syndrome, is likely to persist. For to overcome that numbing, new psychic formations that assert vitality and one's right to it must evolve.

A close student of people with grief reactions around survival once spoke of their need for "emancipation from bondage to the deceased." [23] Even where deaths have not occurred, the survivor of a traumatic situation requires parallel emancipation from the bondage of his own inner deadness. In neither case does emancipation mean total severance, but rather the creation of imagery that maintains fidelity to the end or to one's experience of inner deadness, fidelity in the sense of remembering what the experience entailed and including its excruciating truths in the self that is being recreated. What one does with feelings of self-condemnation or guilt is crucial to the outcome. There is a three-stage process available to the survivor of actual or symbolic death encounter, consisting of confrontation, reordering, and renewal. [24] The second of these stages, reordering, is likely to be dominated by struggles with guilt, and especially with converting static to animating forms of guilt. Confrontation, in the sense of recognizing the threat to existing forms and allowing for a certain amount of necessary dissolution of them, must precede those struggles. And for them to bear fruit they must be followed by renewal at both proximate and ultimate levels, and, equally important, in centering arrangements that integrate these levels. But without guilt-associated struggles around fidelity to the dead and the experience of deadness, and to oneself as a witness, no such renewal or formulation is feasible.

A major difficulty here is the literalism the survivor imposes upon himself in viewing his death encounter. So terrifying and awesome does he find it, so demanding are his requirements of fidelity to it, that he may bind himself to what he takes to be its absolutely unaltered reality and permit himself no psychic movement from that perceived reality. But where that is the case the "reality" he locks himself into is a false one, since perception of any experience is achieved only by inner recreation of it. And the literalism he imposes upon himself turns out to be a form of numbing in the area of image-formation, a suppression of psychic action. To be literally bound to a traumatic experience is to permit oneself no psychic vitality in relationship to the experience itself, and to limit vitality in other areas of life as well. This near-sanctification of the literal details of the death immersion was a considerable barrier to writers and artists attempting to give form to Hiroshima. The same issue affects every survivor within the confines of his own psyche. Here we may speak of a vicious circle in which death guilt and death anxiety reinforce numbing, which, in turn, holds one to suspicion of the counterfeit and to a relationship to the death immersion that is literalized and unformulated, which, again in turn, leaves one naked to death anxiety and death guilt.

To break out of this vicious circle in the direction of formulation, the survivor must find a balance between appropriate blaming (which may indeed include considerable anger toward those who bear some responsibility for the traumatic events) and scapegoating (total concentration on the target for anger in a way that continues to literalize and inhibits assimilation of the experience). He must look backward as well as forward in time. His tendency to claim a personal "golden age" prior to the death encounter can, it is true, distort, but may also serve as a source of life-sustaining imagery now so desperately required. To be forward-looking, to be receptive to experience that propels one toward the future, one must assemble those image-feelings available to one that can assert, however tenuously, the continuity of life.

FOURTEEN

Depression—Static Protest

In CONTRAST TO the more immediate involvement of other animals, human beings experience their world by symbolizing. Crucial to this psychic function are images and feelings of vitality, and psychiatric disorder occurs when those images and feelings are impaired.

As with all mental activity, this impairment exists simultaneously on proximate and ultimate levels. On the proximate level, impairments have to do with separation, disintegration, and stasis; on the ultimate level, with larger discontinuities and the absence of significant images and feelings extending beyond the self. When Winnicott aptly referred to traumatic neurosis as a "break in the lifeline," he came close to articulating not only the spirit of our paradigm but our reason for using the traumatic syndrome to epitomize all psychiatric disorder. For what is "broken"—shattered—is the *experience* of life, the *construction of vitality*. In one way or another that break occurs in all psychiatric disturbance. The definition of the traumatic experience as one in which the individual is "threatened with his . . . death or the destruction of a part of his body" has reverberations for *every* expression of mental *disturbance*. The form taken by the impairment must reflect the complexities of human mentation—of image, idea, and, above all, metaphor and symbol, which make up what we call language. And we shall see that the specificity of various neurotic and psychotic syndromes depends upon their characteristic combinations of metaphor and "compromise formations" in regard to impaired vitality.

Each of the two elements—constriction or numbing, and relationship to death or death equivalents—has a considerable tradition, in the literature on neurosis especially. (Today we call some of these psychosis.) Pierre Janet, the gifted French psychiatric student of Charcot and a contemporary of Freud, built an elaborate theory of the neuroses which laid special emphasis upon patterns of constriction, dissociation, and diminished psychic tension. In hysteria he spoke of the narrowing of the field of consciousness, of the tendency of the hysterical personality to "sacrifice" or "abandon" certain phenomena. These "abandoned phenomena" became "dissociated" from the rest of the mind, and especially from conscious function, and could then become "automatisms" or split-off symptom complexes.* Janet spoke of psychic weaknesses, dissociations, and constrictions, but could not trace these to a dynamic source, a larger motivational process. Freud provided that motor with his instinct theory, though he may well have owed much more to Janet than many have realized. And Freud's very advance—his focus on dynamic, causative principles—may have somewhat obscured a central principle in Janet worth maintaining: namely, that of the fundamental relationship between mental constriction or impaired feeling and all psychiatric syndromes. Yet, Freud kept returning to that principle as central to mental life in general, as in his concept of the "protective shield."

The other of our emphases, that of death-relatedness, was expressed as early as 1908 by Wilhelm Stekel, an early follower of Freud, in his description of neurotics as people who "die every day" and who "play the game of dying." It was Otto Rank, however, who combined both emphases in his description of the neurotic's "constant restriction of life" because "he refuses the loan (life) in order thus to escape the payment of the debt (death)." † This Rankian position suggests at least a possibility of viewing all mental disturbance from the paradigm of death and continuity, and thereby suggesting a beginning basis or a comprehensive theory of mental disturbance that connects equally with evolutionary-biological and social-historical dimensions.

Our attempt at a unitary approach to psychiatric disorder emphasizes three principles. The first has to do with threat—to the organism itself or its symbolic world—that is, with inner perceptions of death and death equivalents. The second principle has to do with feeling and resistance to feeling: to the sense that "if I feel nothing, then death and its equivalents do not exist for me, or can at

---

* For the remaining neuroses, Janet coined the term "psychasthenia," which simply means "psychological weakness" (a parallel to the older term, "neurasthenia," in which the "weakness" is juxtaposed to the organic neurological system). Janet was concerned with loss of the sense or the "function of the real" (Fonction du Réel), and with impairments to "psychological force" (by which he meant available psychic energy) and "psychological tension" (by which he meant the capacity to utilize psychic energy in active mental syntheses).¹ Janet's careful documentation of neurosis as impaired feeling has been insufficiently appreciated by contemporary theorists. This is partly because Janet's system lacked what Henri Ey (a contemporary French theorist who *does* appreciate Janet) spoke of as "a motor, the instinct." ²

† Paul Tillich later similarly characterized neurosis as "the way of avoiding non-being by avoiding being" and "the inability to take one's existential anxiety upon oneself."

least be fended off"; that is, with psychic numbing. The third principle has to do with impaired meaning and deformation; with the sense that "if death and its equivalents exist, then life is counterfeit."

These patterns occur in the major psychiatric syndromes: depression, the classical neuroses, and the schizophrenic process. In this chapter our subject is depression.

I remember a discussion with a close friend in which we agreed that there was no one we felt close to who did not have a touch of melancholy about him or her. We meant that the capacity to feel sadness and loss affirmed something in the human condition, but made one vulnerable to depression.

Depression is increasingly recognized as the most common form of psychiatric disorder and of everyday psychological debilitation. There is some question whether depression, at least in the United States, is increasing in incidence. Many think so. This would be consistent with my own views on the various forms of symbolic breakdown accompanying our contemporary psycho-historical dislocations.* Clinicians understand the concept "as a normal mood, as a symptom, and as a group of symptoms."[4] Something about this all-inclusive concept becomes a little clearer, perhaps, if we view depression as the fundamental human response to death and loss, and therefore the core condition for psychiatric disorder. It is closely related to the traumatic syndrome, and can be understood as a structuring of certain key elements of the threat and loss that characterizes that syndrome.†

Numbing and overall constriction in depression are so predominant that, among psychic disorders, it comes closest to organismic imitation of death, to what we might call a *mimetic death*. The pattern resembles the extreme form of numbing in the Hiroshima survivor who "undergoes a reversible form of symbolic death in order to avoid a permanent physical or psychic death."[6] Even more so, perhaps, the Musselmänner, the "walking corpses" of the Nazi death camps, the "non-men who march and labor in silence, the divine spark dead within them, already too empty to really suffer. One hesitates to call them living: one hesitates to call their death death, in the face of which they have no fear, as they are too tired to understand."[7] Depression, then, is inseparable from many forms of numbing in massive psychic trauma.‡

But depression probably has more to do with death equivalents than with actual death. This is apparent in the static apprehension and negation that

---

* And when a distinguished student of the subject speaks of our "age of melancholia,"[3] I hear echoes of my own frequent claim that ours is an "age of numbing." Any such characterization at best provides brief and hazy illumination.

† One recent summary of its most prominent symptoms includes "diminished activity, lowered self-assurance, apprehension, constricted interests (including the sexual one), and a general loss of initiative."[5]

‡ Becker, following Rank, thus spoke of the depressed individual who "ends up *as though dead* in trying to avoid life and death."[8]

characterize depression as a clinical syndrome, and in many descriptions of depression emphasizing feelings of separation and disintegration as well. The principle applies both to depressions described as "reactive," occurring in response to a specific environmental stress, usually in the form of loss; and those considered "endogenous," occurring in the absence of such environmental stress, that is almost exclusively from internal causes, and more likely to be psychotic. The latter kind is also more likely to be "bipolar," that is, to include manic as well as depressive phases. But recent work has questioned these categorical distinctions, viewing depression as an overall entity along the continuum (suggested earlier) from normal inclination to mild or moderate disturbance to severe incapacity, sometimes psychotic and sometimes life-endangering. At the more malignant end of the continuum, there is greater evidence for genetic predisposition, but some such inherited predisposition probably exists throughout the depressive continuum.*

In order to explore some of the images and feelings involved, I conducted a series of interviews in 1973 with patients experiencing varying degrees of depression. The work enabled me to reconsider the phenomenon of depression in the light of this book's paradigm. I found, first, that the static negation (one could equally call it, negativistic stasis) of depression represented a particularly intense coming together of death and death equivalents.

A typical example was that of a twenty-year-old woman, a college student, who felt herself to be "stuck," especially so during depressive episodes, but to some degree all the time. She described herself as "always . . . tired and lazy . . . sort of still." And "very heavy, sort of like an elephant trying to do a tap dance or something." Her first depressive episode, during which she became especially aware of this debilitating sense of stasis, occurred directly after seeing the film *Catch-22*. She felt "disgusted" by the bloodshed in the film, especially by "one part where a plane ripped a man right in half," and equally disgusted by the way others, including those in her group, seemed to react to the film: ". . . people were laughing at some of the most disgusting parts of the movie and . . . the absurdity of that really got to me." This response included diffuse terror around death and violence, fear of her own mortality and her own rage or violence, and a sense of both life and death as dislocated, out of joint, absurd. She, like other depressed patients, seemed almost committed to her stasis, repeatedly affirming her negations. That "commitment"—what one writer has called the "practice of depression" [10]—may be necessary because stasis, psychic and physical, comes to represent the entire depressive constellation of impaired image-feeling around death and the death equivalents. Imagery of disintegration, for instance, was apparent in the same patient not only in her response to

---

* Thus Gerald Klerman can speak of the "depressive affect" as "clearly a part of human adaptation, if not all mammalian adaptation . . . a final common pathway, a heterogeneous group of symptoms, with multiple causations." [9]

Catch-22, but in "a sick feeling in my stomach [that] sort of reached out into my whole being [so that] I began to shake a little bit inside . . . [and] felt like I was on the edge, just on the edge of breaking down. . . . It was the feeling of nonreality. I didn't feel I was a person anymore." Closely related was her feeling of being unconnected with others: "I wasn't joining in at all. I just felt very alone . . . just sort of sitting there. I have been isolating myself all year." At that time she was in the process of undergoing two painful separations: from the Catholic Church, which had ceased to have meaning for her but which was very hard for her to leave, and from her parents, her mother especially, in preparing to go off to college.

One word—zombie—which she used repeatedly, seemed to embody her impaired image feelings about herself. In her usage, "zombie" or "zombielike" referred to being unresponsive, unrelated, and without vitality. Despite the easy, informal usage of the word in our culture, perhaps especially among the young, its literal meaning, that of a living or reanimated corpse, seemed to be of considerable importance for her either consciously or unconsciously. Death and death equivalents were combined in an inclusive image of inner deadness.

In another patient, a thirty-one-year-old housewife whose depressive episodes had psychotic features, death and death imagery were much more prominent, indeed, overwhelming. She told me that death and suicide were always on her mind, that during a recent depression she had become convinced she was terminally ill: "I knew I was dying of cancer." The main events of her life history, as she told it, were deaths and separations. She was, so to speak, born into a survival: that is, her father's sister had died shortly before, and although her impression was that she was an unwanted child, she was named after the dead sister, more or less as a psychological replacement. But during her early life, the father remained so grief-stricken about the dead sister that "he couldn't stand any mention of the name," so that the patient had to be called by a nickname instead. Her father also had a series of heart attacks, which provided the ostensible reason for the patient being turned over to a housekeeper.

Her mother's constant rage and threats of violence terrified her. She remembered that when she and her older brother were very little, her mother held the boy upside down outside of a window several stories above the ground and threatened to drop him if he did not behave. (Whether or not the memory is accurate, it suggests a perception of her mother as one who might kill.) Her marriage also followed a death, that of her husband's former girl friend. And her pregnancy resulted in still another death, that of her premature child. It was after that last death that her most severe depression occurred.

She felt she was both death-tainted and deadly. But she was unable to express—or perhaps experience—genuine grief. Instead, she would become severely depressed and would manifest the most extreme form of static negativism. She would also, at times, mutilate herself with a knife, or else set fires. She described herself as empty, less than human, "like an animal." She spoke of her husband as dictatorial, and compared herself to Eva Braun, Hitler's mistress. Death and violence, she became convinced, followed upon anything she touched or sought.

One can find a parallel combination of impaired death imagery and death equivalents in a case described by Gary R. Davis:

> Emily is 50 years old and was recently hospitalized for depression. Two husbands' had died, and the third had left her. In recent years, she had undergone a mastectomy for breast cancer, and had a tibial fracture that left her with a limp. She described her response to these losses: "I went to pieces. Things kept piling up on me. I wasn't accomplishing anything. I couldn't take care of my children or myself. I wanted to die. I got so mad I started to break things." [11]

The passage suggests (though Davis gives it a different emphasis) a sense of being a death-tainted perpetual survivor who is at the same time stalked by death and by loss, and who feels herself disintegrating and immobilized. Her anger seems to be a form of protest against her state, an aspiration toward something better.

No wonder, then, that Freud, in discussing melancholia, could speak of something close to "a pure culture of the death instinct, . . . [which] in fact . . . often enough succeeds in driving the ego into death, if the latter does not fend off its tyrant [the super-ego] in time by the change round into mania." [12] As elsewhere, Freud's death-related sensibility was keen, but too quickly submerged by instinctual metaphysics, and in subsequent psychoanalytic disentanglement from those metaphysics some of that original sensibility was lost.

Indeed, the theme of death and death equivalents was emphasized by Karl Abraham in his classic paper written prior to most of Freud's work on depression, one of the few examples in Freudian psychoanalysis in which fundamental insights predated those of the master.[13] Early in the paper Abraham makes a general statement that more or less anticipates our own paradigm: "Every neurotic state of depression, just like every anxiety-state, to which it is closely related, contains a tendency to deny life." [14] He goes on to emphasize the sense of inner death and death taint in a representative depressed patient he treated: "He was inhibited, had to force himself to do the simplest things, and spoke slowly and softly. He wished he was dead, and entertained thoughts of suicide. . . . He would often say to himself, 'I am an outcast,' 'I am accursed,' 'I am branded,' 'I do not belong to the world.' . . . He felt nonexistent and would often imagine himself disappearing from the world without leaving a trace." [15] Abraham became even more specific in speaking of "the tendency towards a 'negation of life,'" of the "symbolic dying" contained in the depressed patient's "higher degrees of inhibition," and in his observation that the depressed patient, in his nonreactivity, behaves "just as though he were no longer alive." [16] In rereading this early study by Abraham, I am struck both by the strength of its emphasis on death-related imagery and by the failure of subsequent psychoanalytic writers on depression (virtually all of whom refer to the paper) to mention this emphasis. (The problem once more seems to lie in the absence of usable, death-related theory, within which such observations could be lodged. Thus, thirty-three years later, Otto Fenichel could write that people become depressed following disappointments in love because "with their love, they lose their very existence," but then invoke the concept of "narcissistic gratification" rather than explore further any ramifications of the sense of losing one's "very existence."[17]

The association of depression with narcissism stems directly from Freud's own classical study, "Mourning and Melancholia."[18] That paper was described by Freud's major editor as "an extension of the one on narcissism which Freud had written a year earlier." (The paper on narcissism was written and published in 1914, while that on "Mourning and Melancholia" was written in 1915 and published in 1917.)[19] As with (but prior to) his treatment of traumatic neurosis, Freud invoked the concept of narcissism to explain a process of internal collapse. That is, he attributes the patterns of the melancholic he so sensitively observed—his unremitting "inhibition and loss of interest . . . extraordinary diminution in his self-regard, [and] impoverishment of his ego on a grand scale"—to his having "incorporated" the "lost object" (the person who died) so that "an object-loss was transformed into an ego-loss."[20] One must then, Freud argues, presuppose a "narcissistic basis" or "object-choice" in the original relationship, an actual tendency to direct libido toward oneself that is ostensibly expressed toward another. Freud could thus claim depression for libido theory. But prior to doing that, earlier in the same paper, Freud made a remarkable statement that others were to build upon much later: "In mourning it is the world which has become poor and empty; in melancholia it is the ego itself."

Much subsequent psychoanalytic writing on depression has taken its cue from this experiential self or ego-oriented side of Freud and Abraham. That emphasis has amounted to a focus on death equivalents. And while all of these are represented, most observers come to emphasize something resembling stasis.* Again all roads lead to numbing. And painful as the feelings around depression can be, recent observers have viewed the state as one of blocking out still more painful feelings. One acts depressed partly in order to avoid "the feelings of helplessness or hopelessness" and "the conscious idea of giving up and . . . feelings of loss and being immobilized."[23] That is, stasis and numbing as behavior and symptoms are intensified in order to avoid the image-feelings of stasis and numbing. One behaves statically to avoid experiencing the full

---

* For instance, many point to the precariousness of self-esteem—the devaluing of the self and the feeling of worthlessness. That impairment to self-esteem tends to be so radical as to suggest breakdown or death-haunted disintegration or "a feeling of being

actuality of one's stasis. This numbing toward one's numbing again closely resembles patterns in survivors of holocaust. *

It is often said that the depressed person is devoid of energy. But that is not quite so. Rather, his psychic energy is "locked in." Indeed that psychic energy, as a motor of insistent negativism, becomes a major element in his sense of entrapment. The energy conflict in depression is succinctly conveyed by a single sentence of E. C. Reid, written in 1910: "I have the impulse to act, but it seems as if something shuts down and prohibits action." [25]

We can speak of a vicious circle around energy impairment: diminished psychic energy toward the outside; a negativistic assertion of the unavailability of vital energy; a struggle against that negativistic stance and a sense that one should or must call forth energy to "do something"; and a retreat back into static negativism. Though painful, this static negativism is more comfortable than either facing another loss or failure or continuing with the frustrating struggle to redirect energy toward the outside world. In this sense the depressed person derives a certain amount of comfort from imagery around death and its equivalents—even from his own "inner death."

From the earliest papers of Abraham and Freud, psychoanalytic studies have focused on "the lost love object." And the recent work of John Bowlby has revitalized that emphasis by stressing the interrelationship of separation, loss, and yearning for the "lost object" (dead person or lost beliefs of values) in ordinary grief and mourning as well as depression. [26] †

---

doomed." [21] Moreover there is something else underneath that impairment—what Bibring calls "a state of helplessness and powerlessness of the ego." There is a sense of threat but "the ego is paralyzed because it finds itself incapable to meet the 'danger'." Or the emphasis may be on emptiness, as in Gary R. Davis's recent view that "a feeling of psychic emptiness analogous to somatic hunger or starvation . . . is at the core of depression." But the depressed person, according to the same author, feels not only empty, but "void of energy." [22] And he stresses the depressed patient's sense of absence of activity, of "air" to breathe and sense of shrinkage, so that "if 'expansive' describes mania, 'contractive' may describe depression."

* This is part of a psychobiological pattern described by Schmale and Engel as "conservation-withdrawal," the state of "relative immobility, quiescence, and unresponsiveness to external environment input" called forth in depression. The pattern is adaptive for the organism, protecting it from an environment that is "either overstimulating or nonstimulating," and offering an opportunity for some form of internal repair or renewal. [24] Their claim, moreover, is that the feeling or affect of depression (the conservation-withdrawal response) is as fundamental a human adaptation and maladaptation as that of anxiety. That view is close to our own sense of feeling and numbing as a fundamental continuum in human experience, including psychiatric disorder.

† Bowlby's work, moreover, along with that of Lindemann, [27] Engel, [28] and Parkes [29] has helped place the processes of grief and mourning in purposeful evolutionary perspective. By the same token, these three writers stress the relationship of grief reactions to psychic imbalance and disease. In particular, Bowlby and Parkes stress—and here we move

Our paradigm enables us to discuss meanings associated with loss and with yearning. Loss implies a certain prior psychological attainment: one can only lose that which one believes one has previously possessed. At issue is not so much the loss of an object but the loss of a state or mode of existence. In the case of the young child separated from his mother, for instance, what is lost is twofold: he loses an overall pattern of relating to the world that is comfortable, pleasurable, and enhances vitality in its various forms; and he loses a particular person, the mother, who embodied all of these good things and had become his first loving "other." With her the child loses what could be called the natural flow of existence. No longer can he depend on the environment to support and enhance his psychic and physiological forays into further reaches of the human life process. We know that there had always been impediments to that flow, experiences of frustration and incomplete nurturing, which is why Melanie Klein speaks of the infant's internalization of both "good mother" and "bad mother," and the "depressive position" emerging from the fear of losing or destroying the former. Her work (whatever its convolutions around instinct and literalized views of "incorporation") has the virtue of suggesting early meanings around the infant-mother relationship, along with a stance or "position" around those meanings. And when she goes on to say that "both in children and adults suffering from depression, I have discovered the dread of harboring dying or dead objects (especially the parents) inside one and an identification of the ego with objects in this condition," she associates those meanings specifically with death and vitality.[30] In our own language the mimetic deadness of the depressive stance is a response not only to the loss of connection with the sources of vitality but to the *loss of expectation of vitalizing experience*. The stance and the loss are experienced totally in the present, but are inseparable from one's experiential past and anticipated future.

There is much discussion in psychoanalytic literature concerning the extent to which very young children are capable of grief and mourning. What we can say is that they are surely capable of protest, as Bowlby has so well documented, and that such protest is integral to the development of adult grief and adult depression. What distinguishes adult grief and depression is symbolization around loss that is, compared to childhood counterparts, much more elaborate and more intensely focused. The adult survivor can inwardly construct around the dead person a vast set of meanings pertaining to everything from the rhythms of daily life to memories of shared experience and an empty future. And this entire constellation can be so specifically associated with the one dead

---

further toward formative significance or meaning—the relationship of such grief symptoms as weeping, anxiety, anger, and pining to the "urge to recover the lost object." Parkes elaborates the phenomenon of "searching" in mammalian species as well as humans. Similarly, we recall Bowlby's emphasis upon "protest" during the initial (grief) phase of mourning.

person—a husband, wife, lover, child, parent, special friend—that his or her death is totalized to mean the death of everything, the loss of all life. Identification is extremely important in all this, although in ways different from those described by Freud and Abraham. The survivor identifies both with the dead person and with death itself. I do not mean that he "introjects" or "orally incorporates" the dead person, but he does embrace psychic elements associated with that person, thereby seeking inner continuity around the loss as well as necessary separation from the dead person. Identifying with death itself means losing a prior state of relative innocence in which one felt safer if not invulnerable, more protected against and removed from the idea of death. Again, compared to the child, the adult is also more accustomed to losses and more capable of absorbing them and even building upon them in ways that deepen and enhance subsequent life experience. Comparisons between childhood and adult grief, therefore, defy simple generalities: the child is less equipped to deal with loss or (if the loss is a crucial one) to recover from it, while the adult has greater symbolic investment in the loss along with the capacity to experience both suffering and renewal. The last depends not just on acceptance of a new "reality," as early students of depression have emphasized, but also on the inner construction of psychic forms, altered or new, that help one through the changed self-world relationships.

Hence the strong force of protest in adult as well as infantile depression. That protest is directed at the loss itself, at the altered inner circumstances brought about by the loss (therefore to some degree at oneself), at the powers that be for bringing the whole thing about, and often at those who seek to help the mourner accept the new reality. The protest, then, is directed at everything associated with the loss. During acute grief, the protest in adults may be as painfully visible as in children. But even when less evident compared to the mood of sadness and pattern of constriction, or when seemingly muted over time, protest remains an important dimension of adult depression. It may, in fact, be more sustained in adults and therefore more important than in children. Indeed much of the power of adult depression has to do with its combination of constricted sadness and suppressed rage, and a "depressive position" around the rage that can come to characterize an entire community, as it did at Buffalo Creek. One representative situation there involved a young married couple:

> Both remember their relationship prior to the flood as "calm" and "loving," but afterward the wife found her husband to be "touchy about everything . . . something . . . always bothering him." He in turn said his wife was "hateful and doesn't want to turn toward me." They ceased having sexual relations and had little to do with one another. What little improvement began to occur in their relationship had to do with their gradual recognition that their grief was behind their behavior. As the wife said of her husband, "He's still grieving—he cries out

in his sleep . . . he still says he'd like to kill Jim V. [the former manager of the Pittston mining operation at Buffalo Creek] because Jim said the dam wouldn't break." And she could add: "I still grieve too. It hurts me awful bad that you can't walk down the road and see them [dead relatives]. . . . A big part of my touchiness does seem to be related to my grieving." [31]

This grief constellation of sadness and protest has been so pervasive and consuming at Buffalo Creek that for years (at least three) following the flood, outsiders coming into the community were deeply affected by it and experienced considerable difficulty remaining there and carrying out their work among survivors. What the protest seems to be saying is: We are defeated, inwardly dead, helpless, but we do not accept this state of things. We in fact cry out in pain, and perhaps in silence, against our fate. We know of something better because we have lived it in the past, and although we can hardly imagine a return to that privileged state prior to the loss, neither can we surrender it nor accept the new actuality imposed upon us. What eats away at everyone in depression is not so much ambivalence toward the dead person, as Freud thought, as this terrible duality of simultaneous immersion in the deep sadness of irreplaceable loss and the perpetual, ineffectual protest against that loss.

Acknowledging the importance of protest in depression helps put in perspective the role played by rage. Freud and Abraham understood much of depression to be a result of anger turned inward on the self—in Freud's formulation, the anger felt originally toward the "lost object" which is internalized along with that "object." But that assumption was tied to the instinctual energy-hydraulics of early Freudian theory. Moreover, the assumption in the theory is that essentially one becomes depressed instead of angry, or angry instead of depressed. A number of recent observers, however, have rejected the concept, emphasizing the frequency with which anger accompanies depression and the many forms of interaction of the two.* Bowlby speaks of the biological value of anger, for instance, the infant's protest reducing the likelihood of the mother's "deserting" him again. Similarly in adults anger can be directed "against those believed to have been responsible for the loss, and . . . against those who seem to impede reunion," as well as against the actual "lost love object." From the standpoint of our paradigm, a protest could also include a more general struggle against inner deadness, and toward a form of vitality. Again, in Buffalo Creek, I observed a great deal of free-floating anger and rage, for which people could not find adequate targets. Rage is an emotional burden and can be static, but it can also be an agitated scanning of

---

* Klerman, for instance, points out that findings from virtually all recent studies "have confirmed the independence of depression from hostility. The conclusions are consistent with the desirability of rejecting the 'hostility turned against self' mechanism as universally necessary and primary in the pathogenesis of depression." [32]

the environment for ways to reassert vitality—for a principle of cause and effect that permits one to place blame and restore meaning.

To be sure, certain forms of protest and anger can also be associated with denial and avoidance, with the static negativism of the depressive stance. But without at least a minimum of anger and protest, depression slides either into schizoid withdrawal or hopeless despair.

I have said little so far about feelings of guilt in depression. Here the psychiatric literature is especially contradictory, in part because not enough attention has been paid to questions of meaning around guilt in depression.

When I began my work in psychiatry in the early 1950s, everyone assumed that guilt had great importance in depression. That was the view expressed in both classical studies and the writings of the time, and seemed to me consistent with the strikingly self-deprecating patterns I could observe in depressed patients. Looking back about a quarter of a century later, that initial impression seems overly simple, but still basically true. But, at the very least, it calls for a bit more refinement of claims and concepts.

The Freud-Abraham studies not only emphasized guilt, but also deemphasized it. Very early in his work (1897) Freud connected mourning for dead parents with melancholia, and spoke of the tendency "to reproach oneself for their death (what is known as melancholia) or to punish oneself in a hysterical fashion (through the medium of the idea of retribution) with the same states [of illness] that they have had."[33] And two decades later, in his classic essay on the subject, he described the "self-reproaches and self-revilings in melancholia that "culminate . . . in a delusional expectation of punishment."[34]* But at the same time—and this is what I mean by Freud's deemphasis of guilt—his concept of identification with and internalization of the "lost object" led him to claim that one of the reasons that melancholic patients are so insistent in their self-exposure is that "everything derogatory that they say about themselves is at bottom said about someone else."[36]† What Freud seems to be saying is that guilt, even while vividly present, is a secondary consequence of anger turned inward or what has been called "retroflexed rage."[38]

Yet there is also a psychoanalytic view, most forcefully expressed by Sandor Rado, that views guilt as *fundamental* to depression.‡ It is difficult to say how

---

* Freud was not always clear about the question of self-condemnation in ordinary mourning, but was convinced that "In the clinical picture of melancholia, dissatisfaction with the ego on moral grounds is the most outstanding feature."[35] And he related those findings to his evolving concepts of guilt and of conscience "that . . . become diseased on its own account," that is, with what he was later to call the "self-punitive super-ego."

† Or as Gaylin explains: "In Freudian theory the self-punishment is only an accidental and incidental result of the attack on the internalized mother [or other lost love object]."[37]

‡ Rado, in 1928, focused on the sequence of "guilt, atonement, and forgiveness," and viewed much of melancholia as an attempt at expiation.[39] The Freud-Abraham principle of retroflexed rage remained important for Rado, and he understood the guilt-expiation

and why guilt was subsequently deemphasized in depression. Part of the reason lies in the kind of paradox with which we have become familiar: advances in detailed knowledge and rejection of early psychoanalytic formulae accompanied by neglect or rejection of a fundamental psychological element. *

Yet I have the distinct impression that most psychiatrists continue to believe that guilt is central to depression, and that the conceptual conflict with this belief has to do with the failure to take into account the various dimensions of guilt. In a condition so characterized by stasis, basic emotions are themselves likely to be static, that is, nonformative. We know that static guilt can take two forms. One of these is the self-lacerating kind, precisely the static litany of self-condemnation described so frequently in classical forms of psychotic depression or "melancholia," but by no means limited to them. The other form of static

---

stance to be a kind of last resort after the failure of rebellious behavior or "embittered vehemence" to prevent the loss or bring about a reunion. But once established, guilt takes hold so that condemnation is clearly aimed at the self rather than another and blame for the loss is clearly *self*-blame. Moreover, in claiming that the guilt-atonement-forgiveness sequence emerges from very early nursing patterns, Rado, while adhering to libido theory, at the same time reasserts the fundamental importance of guilt mechanisms not only for melancholia but for all human behavior.

And in a later (1950) paper, Rado deemphasizes libido theory in favor of a principle of adaptation, and understands the entire constellation of depression, whether mild or psychotic, as "miscarried repair."[40] He defines what he calls "the depressive spell" as "a desperate drive for love, precipitated by an actual or imagined loss which the patient feels endangers his emotional (and material) security." This "endangered security" amounts to what we would call a threat to one's image-feelings of vitality, and the "cry for love" is equally a "cry for life."

* But the deemphasis of guilt takes many forms, and may be part of the larger cultural tendency discussed in Chapter 11. Bowlby and Parkes deemphasize guilt in favor of overall evolutionary principles around anger and search for the dead person or lost object. And a number of post-Freudian and neo-Freudian psychoanalytic writers deemphasize guilt in favor of observations on self-esteem, helplessness, and hopelessness. Others call forth the Freud-Abraham stress on guilt as a secondary consequence of internalized anger. Another factor involved is the shift in psychotic forms of depression or "melancholia" (now not nearly as commonly diagnosed) to less severe, neurotic forms, which lack the former's florid expressions of self-deprecation and remorse. And some researchers, in the contemporary spirit of pragmatic observation, claim that they frequently encounter depressions in which there is little or no evidence of guilt as being of much importance. I have in mind here especially the work of Martin Harrow and Millard J. Amdur.[41] Perhaps the main point in their studies is the absence of dramatic displays of guilt and self-condemnation described in hospitalized depressive patients in the past. They are judicious in presenting their findings, and in their speculations about possible causes for this change. And they also raise interesting questions concerning apparent disparities—limited guilt but severe expressions of conscience in depressed patients. My own impression is that the trend they suggest is part of a more general tendency toward relatively less flamboyant or "classical" symptomatology throughout psychiatric disorders. That tendency in turn could be part of a still larger historical process involving diminished capacity for creating and sustaining symbolic structures (to

guilt, what we have called numbed guilt, is more obscure and more difficult to identify. I have mentioned its relationship to the freezing of the self, to the avoidance of experiencing the self-condemnation with which one is threatened. The historical shift involved in depression may well be one from self-lacerating to numbed forms of guilt. Numbed guilt is one of the keys to understanding depression, and it plays a major part in all psychiatric disorders. In Freud's discussion of his concept of unconscious guilt, he spoke of its existence in people who "cannot endure any praise or appreciation" and "refuse . . . to give up the punishment of suffering."[42] In others, he said, "This unconscious sense of guilt can turn people into criminals," meaning that one commits a crime in order to be punished. He in fact later suggested that the term "need for punishment" replace "unconscious sense of guilt" because the latter was incorrect in that feelings as such cannot be described as unconscious. At one point Freud used a term very close to numbed guilt:

> But as far as the patient is concerned this [unconscious] sense of guilt is dumb; it does not tell him he is guilty; he does not feel guilty, he feels ill.[43]

Freud was struggling with the fact that people behaved in accordance with a sense of badness, wrong-doing, or evil, in that they expected or invited—in some cases, required—punishment and suffering.

From the standpoint of formative theory, this "dumb" or numbed guilt consists of a motivating image without corresponding feeling. The image is an ordering principle, which is why Freud spoke of the need for punishment. From our standpoint we can better speak of a need to behave as if dead (or deadened); death or killing, moreover, is perceived (or "imaged") as deserving and necessary, and brought on by the self.* Freud contrasted the awareness of guilt in melancholia with the unconscious sense of guilt in visions as hysteria and obsessive-compulsive neurosis. But many contemporary forms of depression are characterized by exactly this kind of unfelt guilt, by images of badness and self-blame that evoke further numbing in order to avoid potentially painful *feelings* precisely around that imagery.

---

be discussed in Part III). Guilt is likely to be less structured, less visible, and less detectable. Harrow and Amdur do find that depressed patients have notably diminished self-concepts, and that "negative self-concepts are a more consistent feature of depressive (as opposed to nondepressive) patients than is guilt." Although they made use of psychiatrists' observations as well as patient self-assessment questionnaires, it is still quite possible that these methods are insufficiently sensitive to "unconscious" or numbed forms of guilt.

* This form of guilt is probably never totally numbed (or unconscious), in that the image of badness or blame tends not to be totally unfelt, but rather felt only slightly, vaguely, indirectly. Those feelings are resisted, however, and the very sense of self-blame instigates maneuvers toward nonfeeling.

The problem of depression is not merely one of static guilt so much as the imbalance of static and animating forms of guilt. Whether self-lacerating or numbed, the guilt in depression is notably self-perpetuating. There is a characteristic inability to achieve animating relationships to guilt, to connect self-blame with imagery of change and possibility, with imagery beyond guilt. The depressive's struggle against inner death, then, is not so much toward eliminating guilt as toward achieving an animating relationship to it.

The same principles hold for anger. The intense anger in depression is not merely guilt turned inward, as originally described by Abraham and Freud, but a separate system, also discordant. Anger, too, can either be static or animating, as we know from our previous discussion. But in depression we can say that both guilt and anger—the two blaming systems—are impaired.

One could, in fact, characterize depression as a disorder of blame. There can be fluctuation between self-blame (guilt) and blaming others (anger), but more important is the tendency of both forms of blaming to be enmeshed in static structures.* When systems of blaming are impaired, so is one's overall moral and cause-and-effect cosmology. Something has gone wrong—one feels deprived of someone or something—and therefore someone or something must be blamed, or at least understood to be the cause. Part of the early predisposition to depression, then, probably includes disorders of blame early in childhood around losses in life-support, the loss or absence of someone or something one needs, or any form of failed or conflicted dependency. Everyone requires early imagery of guilt and anger, ways to blame oneself as well as others for imperfect vitality or inevitable experiences of separation, disintegration, and stasis. One becomes prone to depression not because of tendencies toward guilt or anger per se, but toward guilt and anger that, because static, cannot do their job in helping one to cope with loss.

The low self-esteem or "depreciated self-concept" emphasized by so many writers on depression is a function of guilt or self-blame,[45] as are feelings of worthlessness and uselessness. Again the problem of depression is to confront the guilt underneath such feelings, to respond to rather than cover over what has been called "signal guilt" that is likely to accompany descent into depression.[46] That guilt may signal "the unconscious perception of the decrease in psychic energy," which is the onset of the numbed, static depressive state.

The implication of all this is that guilt, like anger, either may contribute to the deadening process in depression, or may vitalize alternatives to depression in coping with loss. Indeed precisely these alternatives, deadness versus vitality, are at the heart of the deep ambivalence of the depressed person. The issue is not so much internalized ambivalence toward a lost love object, as Freud thought, as

---

* Schmale makes a related distinction between "need to prove neglect" and "need to prove self-neglect." His association of the latter mainly with endogenous, more severe forms of depression seems to me somewhat dubious, but the approach does focus on the question of blame.[44]

an unresolvable inner struggle around deadness and vitality, around numbness and feeling, around the mind's (and sometimes the body's) dying or living.

Another important issue of meaning in depression has to do with the kind of self-absorption frequently referred to as narcissism. We are aware of Freud's focus on narcissism in conditions that seem to us characterized by disintegration or anticipated annihilation. Hence Freud's use of the concept of narcissism (regression to the early stage of libido development characterized by self-love) in melancholia, as opposed to the absence of that kind of pattern in ordinary mourning. Here, as in traumatic neurosis and (as we shall see) schizophrenia, invocation of this concept of primary narcissism enabled Freud to keep libido theory at the conceptual center of these conditions.* But there remains a problematic tendency to use the word "narcissistic" as a more or less descriptive term for extreme preoccupation with the self, self-absorption, and apparent self-love, all of which are prominent in depression. Similarly, threats to self-esteem or self-concept are referred to as "narcissistic injuries." But from the standpoint of our paradigm, those "narcissistic injuries" are actually a sense of being annihilated, disintegrating, falling apart. And what looks like "self-love" is a sense of nonlove, of being separate, immobilized, static.

No one seems to have commented on the inherent contradiction, in descriptions of depression, between manifest self-condemnation and self-hate on the one hand and ostensible "narcissism" or "self-love" on the other. The simple point is that extreme self-absorption is a way of struggling with what are perceived as extreme threats to the self.

Recently, writers on depression have begun to stress a "cognitive approach," a view of depression as an impairment in the way one thinks about oneself. Silvano Arieti, for instance,[48] states that "There is always a preceding ideology, or a way of seeing oneself in life in general, or in relation with another particular person, that prepares the ground for the depression." And the "cognitive construct" which, in his view, is especially impaired is the interpersonal one around "the dominant other," who, until lost, "provided . . . the evidence, real or illusory, or at least the hope that acceptance, love, respect, and recognition of . . . human worth were acknowledged by at least another person."[49] Aaron T. Beck concludes that the theme of loss "revolves around a *cognitive problem*"—the "cognitive triad" of "negative view of [his] future, of his environment, and of himself." The emphasis gets at something important in depression, but in my view also perpetuates the false Cartesian dichotomy between the cognitive and the emotional. Arieti and Beck are talking about questions of meaning, and by implication are addressing what we speak of as the ultimate dimension of experience. In doing that we do better to speak of a

---

*The conceptual approach becomes much less strained when analysts begin to view narcissism in depression as itself secondary to loss or threatened loss of love. Thus Michael Balint speaks of "the secondary nature of all narcissistic features . . . if I am not loved by the world (in the way I want it), I must love myself."[47]

formative or symbolizing approach because that terminology need not exclude (or overemphasize) passionate sentiments in their contribution to meaning.

Schmale and Engel's stress on "helplessness and hopelessness" * may be better understood in terms of depression versus despair. From this standpoint, depression would have to do with immediate imagery of loss, and with severe inner conflict between a sense of helplessness (being locked in stasis) and a struggle against that sense in the direction of vitality. Despair, however, has to do with ultimate involvements, with impaired symbolization of elements of life-continuity around what we have called symbolic immortality. Some despair, of course, accompanies all depression—there is bound to be a significant element of impairment in symbolization of ultimate involvements. But considerable despair—the inability to experience a sense of immortalizing principles or human involvements—can occur in the absence of any significant degree of depression. The sense of hopelessness becomes part of a persistent, even workable psychological style, which places limits on one's enthusiasm and vitality, but need not in any sense immobilize one or cause one to feel extremely sad or depressed. In that sense despair is a more or less permanent but partial inner death; a sense of hopelessness and continuous constriction without necessarily being accompanied by more acute, incapacitating psychological disturbance. † Depression could then be understood as a more acute disorder around loss and blame, characterized by a significant degree of stasis and general immobility. In both conditions, one balances varying degrees of stasis, separation, and inner disintegration. Generally speaking, either depression or despair alone is more or less manageable; it is the combination that devastates.

*"Helplessness," according to Schmale and Engel,[50] derives from early (first year of life) trauma of separation, and includes "an awareness of discomfort that can be overcome only by a change in the external environment while at the same time the individual feels unable to do anything to bring about this needed change," and can be "reexperienced at various times in life" in relationship to various kinds of stress and denied gratification. This kind of helplessness is associated with "need to prove neglect," that is, to blame external factors for one's plight. "Hopelessness," on the other hand, is not experienced until somewhere between the third and sixth years, and includes a sense of goals that are unachievable and the individual's feeling that "he cannot have . . . what he desires because of his own inadequacies." Associated with this kind of hopelessness is the "need to prove self-neglect." Schmale and Engel admit that these categories are far from exclusive, and that they frequently overlap. They are understood as different emphases within the general category of depression.

†Observations by Harrow et al tend to confirm this distinction.[51] They found that people hospitalized for depression reported that they were discouraged and felt hopeless, but that they nonetheless expected to get well and did not "despair of the future." Here there is some confusion concerning the word "hopeless," which these authors now think meant something in the nature of "temporarily hopeless." In any case their findings make the important suggestion that even (and perhaps especially) in depression people retain a distinction between *immediate* immobilization and sadness and *ultimate* possibility.

Despair predisposes to depression, prevents or delays recovery from it, and leads to recurrence. And when severe depression combines with despair, suicide is likely to become an urgent question.

This interplay between depression and despair takes us back to the model of the survivor experience. The person inclined toward depression is a repeated survivor who struggles perpetually to find significance in his survivals, to achieve survivor "formulation." To the extent that he fails in this struggle, he becomes locked in despair (whether or not clearly depressed), and all the more vulnerable to the depressive constellation of numbed inner death and static negativism as maneuvers to avoid the full pain of lifeless, separated, and disintegrated existence. In that experience, and in the accompanying traumatic syndrome, the key elements are threat and loss. Where depression persists, loss seems to be primary. And we may suspect the early predominance of death equivalents around separation and loss, along with a pattern of stasis and numbing that limits the psychological pain of loss. There is also likely to be considerable self-blame around both the original losses and the subsequent pattern of numbed withdrawal. That self-blame can resemble the survivor's sense of having been responsible for another's death, of having killed both that person and one's own self. The depressed person may feel poisonous, threatening to the life potential, if not the existence, of all he touches. At the same time he struggles against these image-feelings—toward anger (and its psychological vicissitudes) and toward the survivor's right to reclaim energy and vitality. The struggle—and therefore the impulse to assert vitality—tends to remain prominent in depression, and to become closely involved with larger issues of meaning.

During recent decades there has been a burgeoning of psychiatric literature on the influence of grief on illness. Evidence has accumulated correlating loss of a parent during childhood or a spouse or close family member during adulthood with virtually every form of mental or physical disorder. Studies have shown, for instance, that overall populations of mental hospitals tend to have relatively higher incidence of loss of a parent during childhood, particularly the mother; that schizophrenics specifically have a higher incidence of loss of the mother; that the incidence of parental loss is relatively high in various forms of juvenile delinquency, depression, and the various psychoneuroses; and that psychiatric inpatients (mostly psychotic) have a higher incidence than do outpatients (mostly neurotic), but the latter higher than the ordinary population.[52] Concerning loss during adult life, studies of widows and widowers during the period immediately after the death of their husbands or wives demonstrate a general increase in mortality among the survivors, mostly due to an increase in deaths from coronary thrombosis and arteriosclerotic heart disease (as compared to control groups); increased tendency toward depression, as well as general symptoms of disturbance in sleep, appetite, weight, and consumption of alcohol and tranquilizers, a greater tendency to need and seek help for emotional problems, difficulty in making decisions, and, in the case of widowers, a greater tendency to acute physical symptoms.[53] Apart from these recent specific studies, such losses have been associated both with suicide and inclinations toward violence, including attempted murder. In general, not only have such major psychosomatic conditions as ulcerative colitis and rheumatoid arthritis been identified with patterns of loss, but even the onset and symptoms of various forms of cancer.[54] Important questions have been raised by many about these findings, concerning methods used and the significance of these apparent constellations—questions, in other words, about how much we are entitled to conclude concerning the *causative* significance of the death of a parent or spouse, or of any significant loss. It has also been pointed out that losses can contribute to greater compassion and to a strengthening of self. Yet it is difficult to deny the *potential* psychic and physical harm following significant loss. And that is why a number of knowledgeable investigators have stressed the relationship between grief, or the impaired capacity to grieve, and disease of all kinds.[55] Bowlby thus advances the hypothesis that "in the young child the experience of separation from [the] mother figure is especially apt to evoke psychological processes of a kind that are as crucial for psychopathology as are inflammation and its resulting scar tissue to physiopathology."[56]

But our argument suggests that, in evaluating the consequences of these death encounters, the problem may be less that of grief and loss than one's overall relationship to death imagery and one's tendency toward the depressive constellation. That constellation—mimetic inner death along with ineffectual protest against that state—is ever available in relationship to loss. Indeed, we might say that if anxiety is the signal of danger or threat to the organism, depression as we have defined it is the affect—the experiential essence—of psychological disorder. Symptoms of depression serve to enhance numbing, to protect against experiencing the full pain of the absent element (not just the lost person but the sense of lacking something in oneself), and of one's separateness and inner deadness. Emotional disorders other than clinical depression do the same thing. That is, they mask the underlying core of mimetic death with symptoms we usually label as neurotic.* (We shall discuss schizophrenia as a separate entity, also related to a depressive core but in a different way.) We therefore characterize emotional disorders as struggles against feeling—or, as we now may add, struggles against inner deadness or the perception of inner deadness. To return to the parallel between anxiety and depression, anxiety signifies a threat to vitality, while depression signifies actual, threatened, or avoided deadness.

Depression, as the most pervasive model for psychiatric disturbance, also exemplifies most forcefully the life-continuity paradigm, as opposed to that of

---

* In Appendix B I discuss two kinds of impairment, psychosomatic and characterological, in which the experience of depression and death imagery is avoided by means of sustained forms of physical expression and bodily symptoms.

instinct and defense and libido theory. Thus at the end of an unusually comprehensive and valuable collection of studies of depression, Anthony and Benedek note that in their book, and in other studies as well, "it is a curious fact that one of the central experiences in life, namely sexuality, is rarely or only peripherally discussed." [57] In exploring reasons for this omission, they point out: "In contrast to the existential roots of depression, which are largely negative, Eros or libido is characterized by its positive motivational quality, whether in relationship to psychological development or procreation." The authors observe that disinterest in sex or "loss of libido" is repeatedly observed in depression— that "motivations to love, to work, to play, and to think well of oneself are all frequent and heavy casualties in the depressive conflict." Here the authors provide their own answer, though without quite recognizing it as such. These four lost motivations are fundamental expressions of vitality, and their impairment in depression—the general inner deadness—dominates the constellation virtually all observers encounter, with diminished sexuality an important but only partial indicator of that larger process.

Depression can also be a transition state, a pathway into and out of other forms of psychological disorder. Either actual depression or elements of the depressive state often precede the development of various psychiatric syndromes. Indeed the syndromes themselves tend to replace, but remain equivalents for, precisely that early depression. But the true experience of depression can also be a harbinger of recovery. Michael Balint can thus speak of the "therapeutic depression," a form in which "the patient in his newly won courage allows himself to experience the actual revival of old, primitive object type relations . . . not only as mere possibilities but as actual wishes and feelings . . . he does not shut himself off from the painful sweetness of these desires, i.e., does not repress them." Balint means that genuinely experienced depression presages a recovery of feeling, and therefore recovery *from* the condition substituting for depression. The capacity to experience that depression, according to Balint, is part of a "new beginning," a "relinquishing of the paranoid attitude" and a "capacity for an unsuspicious, trusting, self-abandoned and relaxed object-relation." [58] The process also includes "the acceptance, without undue anxiety, of a certain amount of depression as an inevitable condition of life, the confidence that it is possible—nay certain—to emerge from this kind of depression a better man." This description of emergence from paranoia suggests that vulnerability to depression can be associated with empathy for others.

No wonder, then, that Leon Edel tells us that great literary artists create out of depression, or what Benjamin Rush termed "tristrimania." Edel refers to Keats' "Ode to Melancholy" as "an epitome of the death-in-life and life-in-death of the artist." [59] And referring to the line from Yeats—"An aged man is but a paltry thing, A tattered coat upon a stick"—Edel adds: "Sometimes this rage of art [against aging and dying] produces the greatest works of all." Like death itself, depression, its mimesis, can be either a source of intensified feeling or the virtual loss of the capacity to feel anything. Again our theme concerning the potential of any emotion for great moral and evolutionary value on the one hand, and for disturbance and individual and collective threat to life on the other. Or as one student of evolution and neurosis puts the matter: "Ironically, the simulation of death that was life-preserving in our forerunners, archaic as the response now is, has become life-destroying in us."[60] Except it is not all that archaic in us either; rather it is merely subject to the contrasting possibilities of all our emotions.

FIFTEEN

Disruption and Neurosis

IN TURNING NOW to some of the classical forms of neurosis, I am aware that these have never occurred in pure form, and that contemporary flattening of symbolization obscures their contours even more. Still, there is merit in delineating them somewhat more sharply than we actually find them. By that means we can highlight what is relatively distinct in the operation of our three principles for each of the neurotic patterns, while at the same time seeing these patterns as overlapping, as intermingling possibilities for the function and malfunction of the human organism.

Each neurotic pattern, then, represents a particular impairment of formative process, and constellation of psychic numbing; threatening imagery around death and its equivalents; and disturbed meaning structure or formulation. I want to do no more than suggest the application of this approach to various classical clinical psychiatric syndromes, in the hope that others will do the same in more detailed research and further conceptual explorations.

Hysteria is a good place to start, because that condition is so concretely bound up with our central principle of impaired feeling. Rather than saddened affect, as in depression, hysteria involves a more general interference with feeling in its relationship to action, which is why Janet termed it "a malady of . . . personal synthesis."[1] Janet described "dissociation" as a splitting off of mental contents distorting and limiting their access to consciousness, creating the phenomena of amnesia, somnambulism, fugue states, and multiple personalities. The numbing process in these conditions has to do with a walling-off, or segmentation, of specific mental constellations, so that they become either more or less autonomous (the various "selves" in multiple personalities) or essentially negated (the elements of experience for which one is amnesic). Secondarily, hysteria is characterized by physical symptoms, usually involving voluntary motor functions (as opposed to the involuntary autonomic functions affected in psychosomatic conditions), relatively transient, and (as demonstrated even in the pre-Freudian studies of Charcot and Janet) strongly subject to psychological influence (often through the use of hypnosis).

The symptoms may themselves be of diminished feeling—hysterical anesthesias, blindness, deafness, anosmia (absent sense of smell), paralyses, or diminished sexual sensation. Or they may take the form of overactive or uncontrolled motor function (involuntary movements, convulsions, etc.) or of virtually any form of pain, dysfunction, or bodily complaint. Noting that many of these patients showed a surprising unconcern about symptoms that seemed so malignant, Charcot spoke of *"la belle indifférence"* to describe this affective complacency, and others have spoken of "psychic anesthesia." Even when agitated and histrionic, as many of these patients can be, observers often gain the impression that feeling per se is diminished, or subject to great fluctuation. Freud gave his stamp to this second form of hysteria, coining the word "conversion" for a process of energy transfer: "the incompatible idea is rendered innocuous by its sum of excitation being transformed into something somatic." It is often forgotten that, from the beginning, the purpose of Freud's "talking cure" was not mere recovery of forgotten or repressed memories. Rather, it was the evocation of these memories in the service of recovery of feeling. Thus Breuer and Freud could write, in that most momentous of all "preliminary communications,"[2] that they were at first surprised to find that

> each individual hysterical symptom immediately and permanently disappeared when we had succeeded in bringing clearly to light the memory of the event by which it was provoked *and in arousing its accompanying affect*, and when the patient had described that event in the greatest possible detail *and had put the affect into words* [Emphasis added—Breuer and Freud had actually italicized the entire passage.]

That same early paper, and the book the two men subsequently coauthored, gave considerable treatment to questions of feeling that have great importance for us: a group of "abnormal states of consciousness" in hysteria which they called "hypnoid states." Extending Charcot's views on the close relationship between hysteria and hypnosis (hypnosis as an artificial hysteria), they stressed a particular feature that the various kinds of hypnoid states in hysteria share with one another and with hypnosis, namely "the ideas which emerge in them are very intense but are cut off from associative communication with the rest of the content of consciousness." And they understood the existence of these hypnoid states to be "the basis and *sine qua non* of hysteria."[3] They were saying, in effect, that the essence of hysteria, of its dissociations and conversions, lay in these altered states of consciousness. We are reminded of a similar emphasis by Reiser and Schur concerning the process of somaticization in psychosomatic disease. (Appendix B, p. 403) And when Breuer and Freud (mostly under Breuer's name) go on to relate hypnoid states to normal "absences of mind" (absent-mindness) or mental "preoccupation," we can understand them to be making early explorations along the wide continuum of what we call psychic numbing.[4] Similarly, when they quote a contemporary's concept of "vacancy of consciousness"[5] as contributing to the ease of what they speak of as "auto-hypnosis" in hysteria, we are reminded of the stress on a somewhat different but perhaps related form of "emptiness" in depression. Autohypnosis, Breuer claimed, "makes conversion easier and protects (by amnesia) the converted ideas from wearing-away—a protection which leads, ultimately, to an increase in the psychical splitting."[6]

Breuer and Freud never embraced Janet's claim that the *cause* of hysteria lay in some such incapacity to feel. Rather, they emphasized, as the source of hysteria, a peculiar combination of altered feeling or consciousness and unacceptable ideas or impulses. In their stress upon the latter, upon instinctual elements that provided the energy ("cathexis") that set the process in motion, they were making a radical break from Janet. But they did revert to a theory of feeling to characterize the hysterical constellation. Moreover, the concept of the hypnoid state has something in common with the adaptive principle of conservation-withdrawal, and with our own related ideas of stasis and mimetic death.

Perhaps not surprisingly, Freud came to reject the entire concept of hypnoid states as "superfluous and misleading, because it interrupts the continuity of the problem as to the nature of the psychological process accompanying the formation of hysterical symptoms."[7] The "continuity" that Freud felt to be interrupted by the concept was, of course, the principle of repressed impulses, always sexual—the view of hysteria as a direct outcome of repressed sexuality. There were other reasons for Freud's rejection of the concept. He himself claimed that the idea was essentially Breuer's in the first place (though Strachey points out that Freud himself made some use of it in *Studies in Hysteria*) and during those years (late 1890s and early 1900s) Freud was seeking to assert his own autonomy in relationship to psychoanalysis. He was also struggling to clarify his thinking around his central theme of sexuality: notably, his evolving recognition that the early sexual assaults or seductions hysterics described had never in fact taken place, but were fantasies he could now associate with childhood sexuality, so that the fantasies themselves became causative influences in hysteria. By holding to his method and modifying rather than abandoning his theory, Freud now could rise to his greatest achievements. His dynamic concept of hysteria helped him evolve or complete his theories of the sexual origin of the neuroses, infantile sexuality, repression and the unconscious, and the relationship of dreams to all of these.

Freud's achievements in hysteria were bound up with his preoccupation with libido stages. That preoccupation is still active in the controversy over whether hysteria derives from impulses and conflicts of an "oedipal" or "phallic-oedipal" phase or from earlier "pregenital" origins. By excluding a central theory of feeling that could allow for traumatic influences at any point in the life cycle, psychoanalysis moved all too readily toward a one-sided focus on the reified stages of psychosexual sequence.

No wonder, then, that a number of writers have looked for alternative explanations. Thomas Szasz, for instance, tried to reinterpret hysteria around communications and games theory. Perspectives like his were much in vogue during the late 1950s and early 1960s, and in applying them to symptoms of hysteria, Szasz did illuminate a great deal about the importance of direct situational currents—what patient and doctor, for instance, were asking, expecting, and demanding of one another.[8] But these approaches contribute little to our grasp of questions of quality of feeling in hysteria. More germane has been an interest in hysterical and other neurotic "styles" or "modes of functioning that seem characteristic . . . of the various neurotic conditions."[9] This level of address, as David Shapiro tells us in his valuable study, is directed at the "forms of the mind" or ongoing psychological interactions that Freud neglected, precisely the "forms of the mind" so important in our own paradigm.[10] A focus on style, at least in hysteria, allows one to return to issues Freud and Breuer were struggling with around the concept of the "hypnoid state." Shapiro, for instance, speaks of the "hysterical style" in terms of principles of impaired feeling: "incapacity for persistent or intense intellectual concentration; . . . distractability or impressionability that follows from it; . . and [living in a] nonfactual world [in which superficial impressions onbstitute for knowledge]."[11] *

Even angry emotional explosions, which can be the complaints that bring hysterics to treatment, are not grounded expressions of the self. Hysterics tend to regard their own outbursts "very much as they might regard conversion symptoms; that is, they do not quite regard the content of their outbursts as something they have really felt but rather as something that has been visited on

---

* Shapiro goes on to describe problems in grounding: "He [the hysteric] does not feel like a very substantial being with a real and factual history . . and is likely to be easily carried away on a feeling that does not run deep, but is not completely absent.' [A hysterical patient, for instance, may talk 'in an animated and somewhat scattered and diffuse way—now about this disappointment, now about that funny thing that happened, now about the exciting man she had just met—[leaving the therapist with a sense that] 'I really did not know just how she felt or what her mood . . . really was.' [And the patient is likely to share that sense and say], 'I don't know what I *really* feel like,' while meaning, 'I don't know what I *am* like.'" Shapiro goes on to describe hysterics as people who "seem to feel as if they were virtually weightless and floating, attracted here, repelled there, captivated first by this and then by that."[12]

them or . . . something that has passed through them."[13] The same could well be true of the depressive component he and others stress in hysteria.

Shapiro, while granting that the hysterical style may "favor repression," nonetheless distinguishes it from repression per se, preferring to relate its specific tendencies "to a more general mode of cognitive and subjective experience." And what he says of that "more general mode" blends strikingly with our own sense of formative impairment. What is often referred to as "shallow affect" in the hysteric has to do with a mind dominated by quick, impressionistic, half-formed feelings or image-flow, and yet conveying the impression that "the whole person is not participating in these affects and expressions." And that impression is confirmed when "the next day such a person is likely to have forgotten half of what she experienced and feel about much of the other half that she 'didn't really mean it.'" What Shapiro speaks of as "insufficient organization, refinement, and integration of mental contents" adds up to an impairment in psychic action characterized by insufficiently grounded images and forms that dominate attention while engaging a very limited amount of the self.

All this is a particular variety of the numbing phenomenon, a particular constellation of muted vitality or mimetic death. Sexuality is central to hysteria, as Freud thought. But its centrality does not lie in the relationship of the early stages of libido development. Rather, in sexuality, a fundamental area of experience, we find expressed all the forms of disordered feeling and impaired vitality characteristic of hysteria.

Our second principle, that of threat, was emphasized by Freud and Breuer in their early impression of "an analogy between the pathogenesis of common hysteria and that of traumatic neurosis." At that time, Freud was thinking in terms of specific occurrences of sexual trauma, of a "concept of traumatic hysteria." But even with the changing of views concerning hysteria, other writers have held to some such analogy, partly because conversion symptoms play so prominent a part in traumatic neurosis (for instance, transient paralyses or recurrent back pain following war or other life-threatening experiences). But there may well be further reasons for the analogy, such as mixtures of numbing and explosive emotionality (as we have described in both), and a sharing also of the kind of death-related perception behind these combinations.* In other

---

*The German psychiatrist Ernst Kretschmer, in the 1920s, viewed both the explosive and inhibited patterns of hysteria as characteristic biological responses to life threats. The first, the "tantrum violent-motor reaction," has the original evolutionary purpose of making available every form of irregular motion that might be useful in fleeing or combating the danger; while the second, that of immobilization or "sham-death" is the seemingly opposite but related response to danger that we have already commented upon. Kretschmer goes on to point out that the danger or threat to life can be external, as in war or traumatic neuroses, or internal, as in conflicts around sexual life.[14] We are reminded again of the polarity between exaggerated movement and various forms of stasis during and after disaster, as in Hiroshima.

words, there is much evidence that hysterics react frequently, in some cases repeatedly, *as if* they were in the midst of a life-threatening situation—which takes us to our third principle, that of meaning.

One key to meaning-structures in hysteria can be found in the experiences of the most celebrated of all hysterical patients, Anna O. A number of writers by now have pointed out that Anna O's entire sequence of hysterical symptoms was related first to her father's illness, and then to his death. Indeed Breuer dates the onset of her disease to "July, 1880, [when] the patient's father, of whom she was passionately fond, fell ill of a peripleuritic abscess," and she attempted to nurse him until "by degrees her own health greatly deteriorated . . . [until] eventually the state of weakness, anemia and distaste for food became so bad that to her great sorrow she was no longer allowed to continue nursing the patient."[15] She had many additional symptoms, but her initial response seems to have taken the form of a close functional equivalent to her father's physical deterioration. Breuer goes on to describe her father's death, about nine months after he fell ill, as "the most severe psychical trauma that she could possibly have experienced." Her response: "A violent outburst of excitement was succeeded by profound stupor which lasted about two days and from which she emerged in a greatly changed state [characterized by dissociation, various anesthesias, abnormal muscular contractions, visual difficulties, insistence upon speaking in English rather than German, and transient hallucinations]." For days afterward, she would go "entirely without food . . . , was full of anxiety and her hallucinatory *absences* [Breuer used this French term for her episodes combining the confusion, dissociation, and hallucination] were filled with terrifying figures, death's heads and skeletons," and there were "numerous attempts at suicide."

Relevant to Anna O's behavior at the time of the onset of her father's illness is an observation that in hysterical patients separation can be equated, to a considerably greater degree than in others, with "the conception of death."[16] At the same time, given the severity of his illness and her general fearfulness, she probably anticipated his actual death as well. When he did die, she responded with an intense version of the exaggerated movement-deathly stasis polarity mentioned above. More than that, she was suicidal and experienced considerable imagery associated with grotesque death. We can almost say that, at least at the height of her disease, she "lived in death." As another commentator has suggested, there is in hysteria the equation, "Loss of Love = Loss of Life."[17] That lifelessness, moreover, may be considered one's due. As with the survivor, the very possibility of vitality—psychic or sexual—may be bound up with feelings of guilt and imagery of wrongdoing.

Yet we know that in hysteria the numbing of this "sham death" serves to avoid threat. One "plays dead" in order to stay alive. In the hysteric it would seem that feeling itself, and especially sexual feeling, becomes equated with the threat of death. The vicious circle around meaning is something like this: Perceiving a variety of external situations and inner images as "deadly," he cannot permit himself to feel. Equating such feeling with further threat, he wards it off via both mimetic deadness (including conversions) and explosive but superficial emotional outbreaks; for there is also a deep fear of being "stilled." This combination of limited feeling and thrashing activity becomes associated with a style of perpetual impressions and encounters without the possibility of realized experience or relationships. This failure of realization extends to ultimate matters, so that he lacks profound connections beyond the self and is therefore terrified of actual death, which aggravates further his inability to feel.

In obsessive neurosis, or in less severe expressions of obsessive style, the pattern of numbing is quite different. There is the attempt to turn one's organism itself into a totally controlled mechanism, or what Wilhelm Reich once called a "living machine." That image is especially appropriate, as it conveys the obsessive's particular mode of "deadened" life. In this mode the control one seeks to maintain, above all, turns out to be not over feeling but over the very passing of time.

Consider three basic manifestations of obsessive states: ritual-making (required sequences in personal routine or relationships with others that take on absolute, ceremonial quality, and obsessive actions such as hand-washing, counting, touching objects, etc.); thought patterns that combine rigid dogmatism with brooding, doubts, and continuous intrusion of obsessive ideas; and "fits of horrific temptation," such as the idea or urge to kill or harm someone, often a person to whom one is close.[18]

Freud rightly understood the rituals of obsessive neurosis to be a caricature of religion. What is caricatured is the idealized individual experience in religious or social ritual. In the Catholic mass, in the Jewish chanting or singing of *Kol Nidrei* ("All Vows") before the sacred scrolls (or Torah), or in Za Zen (the cross-legged sitting position) forms of Buddhist meditation, the participant eternalizes immediate experience. He steps into "mythic time," really timeless*ness*. And this experiential transcendence, a form of exquisite centering, reverberates back to immediate experience, then and afterward. (Hence the image of "the eternal present.") With the obsessive, however, the ritual itself is machinelike, self-enclosed rather than formative or transcendent in either a theological or psychological sense. Rather than connecting an immediate experience with the eternal, ritual is part of the obsessive's attempt to bind or "stop time." (Routinized religion can, of course, approximate the obsessive state, and much "normal religion" falls somewhere in between the latter and the ritual ideal.) To stop time means not only to avoid aging and death but the flow of life. As Medard Boss, in his version of "daseinsanalysis," puts it, obsessional patients "are avoiding at all costs any full engagements of their existence in world-relationships."[18A]

Obsessive symbolization is similarly removed and uncentered. Brooding doubt and exaggerated dogma are two sides of the coin of the obsessive's "general loss of the experience of conviction."[19] In either case he does not feel himself comfortably centered in that belief. Rather he tries to control everything by means of external calculation—much like the pilot on instruments: "He can fly his plane, he can fly *as if* he were seeing clearly, but nothing in his situation is experienced directly; only indicators are experienced, things that signify other things."[20]

But "flying" or working his machine is self-defeating for the obsessive, specifically in relationship to time. He simply cannot turn the thing off. He is endlessly "driven" by his obsessive ideas and even more by his struggles against them. He wants to "control the uncontrollable."[21] He is therefore time's victim—perpetually buffeted by it because he can neither stop nor join its flow.

So, through a monumental exercise of will, he tries to control himself as if *that* would stop time. In that pursuit he does the opposite of the hysteric: instead of responding, however superficially, to everything, he radically narrows his field of attention and undergoes a "general shrinking and restriction of subjective experience of any immediacy."[22] Above all he is on guard against "the menace of dangerous spontaneity."[23]

Spontaneity, the image of "letting one's self go" is associated not only with terror but also with murderous feelings and threat,[24] as is the third obsessive feature, that of "fits of horrific temptation." For Freud threat was instinctual, and had to do especially with "anal-erotic" and related sado-masochistic impulses, originating in combined elements of libido and aggression, the latter derived from the death instinct. Subsequent writers have shifted the emphasis from instinct to adaptation, while stressing related principles of "defiant rage" causing "guilty fear" or "obedience versus defiance";[25] and a more general principle of "obsessional maneuver as an adaptive technique to protect the person from the exposure of any thought or feeling that will endanger his physical or psychological existence."[26] This last view approaches my own.

How many of those concerned with the subject recall that the childhood nickname of the protagonist of Freud's classical study of obsessional neurosis (whom everyone *does* remember as "the Rat Man") was "Carrion Crow." He earned that nickname from his brothers and sisters because of his conscientiousness about attending funerals, and "In his imagination, too, he was constantly making a way with the people so as to show his heartfelt sympathy for their bereaved relatives."[27] Freud acknowledged the importance in his case of the death of an elder sister when he was between three and four; of obsessive thoughts, from an early age, about his father dying; and especially of his father's actual death (". . . we may regard his illness itself as a reaction to that event, for which he had felt an obsessional wish fifteen years earlier"). Indeed, the entire case could be profitably reconstructed around encounters with death, his own and others', actual and imagined, wished and feared. The chief presenting features of his disorder, according to Freud, were *"fears* that something might happen to two people of whom he was very fond [mostly, as was quickly revealed, that they would die]—his father and a lady whom he admired. Besides this, he was aware of *compulsive impulses*—such as an impulse, for instance, to cut his throat with a razor . . .,"[28] In terms of his father's death, upon which his full-blown neurosis followed, he not only reproached himself severely for not having been present but "for a long time . . . had not realized the fact of his father's death." Freud could thus write in his notes (though not in the published case): "I pointed out to him that this attempt to deny the reality of his father's death is the basis of his whole neurosis."[29] His obsessional symptoms, moreover, were exacerbated and extended by his response to subsequent deaths. When an aunt died (eighteen months after his father) and he paid a condolence call, he painfully remembered his "neglect" of his father and berated himself "as a criminal" for that neglect. He became seriously incapacitated in his work, and his obsessive ideas, such as fear of harm to others, were extended "so as to include the next world" (that is, he still imagined his father being harmed). The pattern repeated itself when his family physician became severely ill and died: not only were there new obsessive connections, but as in the case of his father, he strongly anticipated the death in his imagination, "his regrets . . . not unmixed with feelings of revenge."[30] In these situations he would also fear for himself, expecting to be punished because of seeing himself as "a murderer." Or else he would associate these deaths with retribution he could expect for his sexual fantasies: after an image of his aunt as a whore, he remembered his uncle (her brother) having actually accused her of powdering her face like a prostitute and that he had later died in extreme pain, and "he [the Rat Man] frightened himself with the threat that he himself would be punished in the same way for these thoughts of his."[31]

The patient's conflicts around his father's death were, of course, those of a survivor. And his obsessive ideas included what I have called guilt over survival priority, in this case the question: "'if you had to throw yourself into the water in order that no harm might come to him . . .'" (followed by an inner command to do so). He had actually asked himself a similar question *before* his father's death "as to whether he would give up *everything* to save him." Freud stresses an early incident (for which there was only indirect evidence) involving "some sexual misdemeanor connected with masturbation" at about the age of three, for which he was beaten by his father, and is said to have responded with anger and name-calling. Freud suggested that, concerning masturbation, the father had used the phrase "it would be the death of you," and goes on to say that "the patient believed that the scene made a permanent impression upon himself as well as upon his father."[32] That last statement is a bit unclear, since Freud tells us that the patient remembered nothing of the scene; and the reconstruction of it was based first on a suggestion by Freud, which, in turn, evoked in the patient a recollection of his mother's description of such an event not specifically around masturbation but occurring "after the boy had done something naughty." Whether or not that event actually occurred, there is evidence here and elsewhere in the case of extensive father-son conflict, having to do with death and death wishes. That death imagery undoubtedly was often related to sexual guilt, but was probably not confined to such guilt.

In connection with the patient's suicidal ideas, Freud similarly emphasized underlying sexual elements. Thus, Freud connects the patient's image of cutting his throat with a razor with guilt in response to an associated impulse to kill the sick grandmother his lady was nursing; derived, in turn, from rage toward the old woman for keeping them apart (in Freud's reconstruction, "for robbing me of my love!"; hence the unconscious command, "kill yourself, as a punishment for these savage and murderous passions!").[33] And Freud associated continuing adult suicidal ideas with that old reproach by his father concerning masturbation ("It would be the death of you"), the reproach "now thrown back on to his father" so that "his present suicidal ideas could correspond to a self-reproach for being a murderer."

We sense that the famous suicide was still more fundamental, having to do instead with a disintegrative inner process. "From his childhood he has been familiar with clear ideas of suicide," Freud wrote in his notes. Two actual suicides affected him profoundly: the first of a cousin when the patient was sixteen or seventeen;* and the second, when he was twenty, of a dressmaker whose love he had spurned. The original notes contain many byways of suicidal ideation, suggesting that the act (and thinking about the act) came to have significant association with inner breakdown, despair, and the possibility for renewal.

Even what Freud calls "the great obsessive fear" of the case, the rat imagery with which it is mostly associated, may be understood as fundamentally annihilative, whatever its sexual component. The obsession originated in the patient's being told by a fellow military officer of a "horrible punishment used in the East" consisting of tying up the criminal and placing against his buttocks a pot containing rats, turned upside down in such a way that they would bore their way into his anus. Upon hearing about that punishment, the patient became preoccupied with the idea of this punishment being carried out on his woman friend, and also on his father. With brilliant ingenuity, Freud develops various concepts around anal eroticism, anal birth, and related sexual fantasy, and the connection between the "rat idea" and the "father complex" (the officer who told about this "Eastern punishment," noted for his cruelty, standing for the father). But in the process he describes and interprets a number of additional rat-images, consistently emphasizing the sexual elements that may indeed be

---

* This is described in the original notes but not in the case report. In general, the original notes seem to contain relatively more suicide and death imagery than the case report. The latter, moreover, tends to subsume such imagery to sexual formulations.

vividly present, but about which one could postulate a more basic, and, in this case, especially grotesque dimension of death, dismemberment, and annihilation. These include rats as "carriers of dangerous infectious diseases," as symbols of syphilitic infection which the patient greatly feared ("the idea of syphilis gnawing and eating [at one]"); the rat as comparable to a worm (and therefore to a penis, especially that of a child)—though a worm also suggests the body's ultimate disintegration (when eaten by worms), and as "a dirty animal, feeding upon excrement and living in sewers."[34]

All this takes us to an evolving concept of obsessional states that relates them to intolerance for and therefore preoccupation with "death, decay, destruction, violence, anything dealing with unaccountable elements of human existence."[35] I would emphasize in obsessive states the *lifelong inner terror of disintegration*.

Freud's patient as much as told him so when he remarked to his analyst, in the midst of an exchange concerning conscious and unconscious aspects of his obsessive ideas: "Such an occurrence, he continued, was thus only possible where a *disintegration of the personality* was already present" (and it was Freud himself who underlined that phrase).[36] Moreover, this case, along with other writings of Freud, did much to develop the image-triad of obsession-feces-death, remarked upon by a number of writers. That trinity has much to do, of course, with the tendency for bowel training to become an arena of parent-child struggle. Keeping in mind the association of feces and disintegration, we understand both the imagery and the struggle to have to do with elements of life-power and "falling apart."*

Freud dealt more with death imagery in this case than in most of his writings, and seemed to be on the brink of elevating that imagery to some conceptual significance. But at a key point, he drew back. In an important two-page sequence toward the end of the theoretical section he notes the patient's "quite peculiar attitude towards the question of death," mentions his nickname and its significance, and emphasizes (in passages we have already quoted) the importance for the patient of the early death of his older sister and longstanding thoughts about his father's death.[38] He recognizes that other obsessional neurotics behave similarly: "Their thoughts are unceasingly occupied with other people's length of life and possibility of death." These others need not have experienced family death at an early age as the source of that death imagery. Instead, "these neurotics need the help of the possibility of death chiefly in order that it may act as a solution of conflict they have left unsolved." For Freud, death imagery must always be secondary—in this case to the obsessive's

---

* Bernard Brodsky similarly stresses that "the Rat Man's fear of not seeing, not hearing, or feeling is a fear of extinction of the self-image." He goes on to say that the fear of death is not exclusively derived from fear of castration but "is also related to memory traces of states in which the self-image is extinguished," and that "in the anal phase the equation of feces and the dead body shapes the fear of death into the dread of turning into feces."[37]

inability to come to decisions, "especially in matters of love." Causation is brought back to instinct: "For we must remember that in every neurosis we come upon the same suppressed instincts behind the symptoms."

The primary significance of annihilation for obsessional neurosis becomes clear when we turn to our third principle, that of meaning. Actual death imagery and death equivalents come together around a troubled relationship with time. Fenichel writes:

> "Orientation in time" is a typical reassuring measure. Many a fear of death means a fear of a state where the usual conceptions of time are invalid. States in which the orientation in time becomes more difficult—dusk or long evenings in winter or even long days in summer—are feared by many compulsion neurotics. . . .[39]

Early relationships to death equivalents, especially disintegration, leave some vulnerable to the obsessive's fear of the free flow of events or feelings. To enter into that "free flow"—to live spontaneously within larger flux—becomes equated with the psychic danger of falling apart. Early curbs on spontaneity later become associated with the adult need to create an illusory set of images around controlling and essentially holding back the passage of time. Much of obsessive ideation and ritual is in the service of this impossible struggle, as are the defense mechanisms Freud brilliantly elaborated: isolation (the separation of idea or image from affect or emotional content), displacement (the shifting of feeling or energy from one image or idea to another), and undoing (the wiping out of a prior thought or action, or counteraction to create the sense that the original action did not occur). All of these have to do with numbing; in particular, undoing attempts not only to stop time and action but to reverse their flow.

The same attempt is present in much of what Freud called "magical thinking," "omnipotence of thoughts," or the apparent capacity for prophecy. These patterns are most intense in relationship to death. The Rat Man, for instance, was upset by his apparent capacity to predict others' deaths, and even more by an incident with the following sequence: wanting a particular room in a hydropathic sanitorium and being told that an old professor had already been given it the thought that came to him was, "I wish he may be struck dead for it!"; two weeks later he was awakened from sleep "by the disturbing idea of a corpse . . . and in the morning he heard that the professor had really had a [fatal] stroke."[40] While there are many important aspects to such sequences, they have been insufficiently explored as expressions of the obsessive's illusory constellation around controlling time and action, and thereby clinging to life and staving off death. His cry is not so much "Stop the world—I want to get off!" (as a stage play some years ago had it) as "Stop the world—I want to stay on!"

The style of guilt in obsessional neurosis is consistent with this pattern. One feels guilty not only for death wishes toward others, but even for "prophetic" anticipation of deaths or injury. One blames oneself for the increments of life or death one portions out or withholds in the struggle for control.

Predictably, the guilt is static. It is likely to take the self-lacerating or *mea culpa* form, in which the self-enclosed system of continuous self-condemnation is mobilized as part of the struggle against the flow of time and the spontaneous expression of the self.

In phobic neuroses, anxiety breaks out into the open. These conditions present a special challenge to our theory, because in them the disorder of feeling is indirect and paradoxical. Anxiety is attached to specific objects or situations—whether in the form of "common [more or less universal] phobias" associated with night, solitude, death, illness, dangers in general, snakes, etc., or "specific phobias" associated with particular circumstances not ordinarily fearful, such as agoraphobia (fear of heights), claustrophobia (fear of enclosed spaces, such as theaters or elevators), and various phobias involving locomotion (especially airplanes, but also trains or automobiles).

Phobic constellations perform the "anxious work" of the entire organism. Freud originally understood this process as "psychically binding the anxiety [derived from transformed libido] . . . directing mental barriers in the nature or precautions, inhibitions, or prohibitions . . . that appear to us in the form of phobias . . . ."[41]

The numbing involved, however, is by no means a matter of mere restriction of external arrangements but constitutes a binding of psychic action. To understand this, we must consider the relationship of phobias to other expressions of anxiety. They are usually classified as manifestations of "anxiety neurosis," (or, as Freud preferred, "anxiety hysteria," because he thought phobias similar to hysteria except for the fact that in the former, libido is not *converted* into somatic symptoms but "is set free in the shape of *anxiety*"). We have defined anxiety as a sense of foreboding stemming from threatened vitality and anticipated breakdown of the integrity of the self, and have discussed it in relationship to feeling too much or too little. Anxiety always blurs feeling in ways that can be considered impairments. With it there is always too much of one kind of feeling (that of imminent threat or danger) and not enough of other kinds (alternative sensation, general psychic action, and the experience of satisfaction or realization). Even when one feels too much because of anxiety, one *at the same time* feels too little. Where anxiety tends to be rather general or "free-floating," it is always selective to some extent. One is more anxious about some things than others; the anxious image-feeling serves not only to signal danger (as Freud, in his later formulation, rightly told us) but also to locate and identify that danger. Even in a diffuse anxiety state, one is more afraid of some things than others: one may be most anxious in relationship to meetings with authority figures, pressures around work, sexual situations (or their absence), or whatever. In addition to anxiety, the feeling disorder consists of the inability to experience in those same situations an easy flow of fellowship, affection, achievement, pleasure, and transcendence. In the case of phobias the whole process is more radically circumscribed, or *totalized*. All anxiety—with its characteristic component of disintegration, the sense of falling apart or actually dying—is confined to the phobia. That is the pyrrhic achievement of the numbing process in phobic states.

Can we say more about the perceived threat (our second principle of emotional disorder) in phobic states? For Freud that threat was castration (the female equivalent, the "loss of love"). He, in fact, introduced the term "castration complex" in his classic study of phobia in the case of "Little Hans."[42] In that study castration imagery is discussed extensively and placed at the center of Freud's theory of causation.

Little Hans is in many ways the most intriguing of Freud's clinical protagonists. His parents were early Freudian disciples ("both among my closest adherents"), Hans's psychosexual experience was reported to Freud from the time he was three years old for research reasons, and during his fifth year in connection with phobic symptoms and "analysis" conducted by his own father under Freud's supervision. Hans's neurosis as well as his recovery seemed to have evolved more or less in the service of psychoanalytic inquiry.*

Hans refused to go out into the street because he feared that a horse might bite him. Freud traces the phobia to the child's fear of castration as a punishment for his strong sexual feelings toward his mother, his consequent hostility and death wishes toward his father, and also for his active masturbatory practices. Freud speaks of an intensification of his feeling toward his mother (because of his age and constitution as well as competition arising from the birth of a younger sister fifteen months before the outbreak of the neurosis and other environmental reasons), and of his love for her being combined with "suppressed sadism" so that there was a "confluence of instinct" and there took place a "transformation of Hans's libido into anxiety, that anxiety based upon his mostly-unconscious fear of castration and "projected onto the principle object of his phobia, . . . horses."[43] The thesis is documented by a series of images revealing Hans's preoccupation with his penis (or "widdler"), his fearful

---

*It is tempting to view Hans as the first neurotic casualty of psychoanalytic parents, but my point is a broader one. Whatever we might imagine Hans's fate to have been were his parents totally ignorant of Freud, the fact is that their Freudian cosmology (likely to be especially passionate in those early, revolutionary days) affected not only their attitudes toward him but their way of understanding, and (in the case of the father) interpreting to him, much of what he experienced. To some extent, we may say, psychoanalytic energy dictated the overall sequence of "neurosis" and "cure." But one is also struck, in reading the case, by ways in which Hans's parents, at certain moments, acted just like other parents of their culture, time, and class, in such things as their critical attitudes toward masturbation and even, in the case of the mother, rather direct threats of castration.

awareness of its small size compared to his father's and those of large animals such as horses, and his preoccupation with whether or not little girls or grown women possessed such an object. Freud thus makes a rather specific association between phobia and castration, but also speaks of the rich psychosexual material as confirmation of his theories about early childhood previously based mainly on adult analyses. Freud eventually altered his theory somewhat in connection with his later view of anxiety as a signal of a threat to the organism, rather than as "transformed libido." But that threat remained castration. In his final formulation of phobia (with reference once more to Little Hans) in 1932,[44] Freud discussed this newer view of anxiety as danger signal, and then wrote:

> But we have not made any mention at all so far of what the real danger is that the child is afraid of as a result of being in love with his mother. The danger is the punishment of being castrated, of losing his genital organ. . . . Above all, it is not a question of whether castration is really carried out; what is decisive is that the danger is one that threatens from outside and that the child believes in it.

The point about threat from the outside has to do with Freud's view of phobia as transforming an internal danger ("a demand by his libido—in this instance, anxiety at being in love with his mother" into an external one [punishment via castration, as represented by the phobia]). This theoretical change enabled one to understand Little Hans's phobias as not merely transformations of energy (from libido to anxiety) but as reflecting "conflict between the boy's instinctual strivings and his ego demands."[45] Freud's instinctual paradigm is thereby liberalized and in a sense strengthened, but also overextended and strained.

In all this Freud was taking an old concept of the fear of castration (which he had introduced a decade before in *The Interpretation of Dreams*) and elaborating it into a more structured "complex." On the basis of his and his followers' studies, Freud could trace the "roots" of the complex in still earlier experiences: the withdrawal of the mother's breast (experienced as "the loss of what he regards as an important part of his own body"), the regular loss of his own feces, and "finally . . . the act of birth itself (consisting as it does in the separation of the child from his mother, with whom he has hitherto been united) is the prototype of all castration."[46] Freud did add a cautionary note: "While recognizing all of these roots of the complex, I have nevertheless put forward the view that the term 'castration complex' ought to be confined to those excitations and consequences which are bound up with the loss of the *penis*."[47] But there remained the difficulty of locating the paradigm around the vicissitudes of instinctual sexuality and then having to subsume to that paradigm the most fundamental early experiences of threat on the one hand, and emergence as a living, extrauterine being on the other.

Castration anxiety has great significance, but as a death equivalent; it is the anticipation of annihilation. The earlier experiences Freud mentions—loss of the breast (later writers would say loss of the mother), loss of one's own feces, and the birth experience—are indeed *prototypes*, but of death imagery rather than castration. Indeed castration anxiety may be viewed as another such prototype.

Consider a few of the important features of the case of Little Hans. The appearance of his phobia was accompanied by an anxiety dream, from which he awoke in tears, explaining to his mother: "When I was asleep I thought you were gone and I had no Mummy to coax [caress] with." His father described similar conscious fears, especially at bedtime: "Once he made a remark to this effect: 'Suppose I was to have no Mummy', or 'Suppose you were to go away', or something of the sort."⁴⁸ These are clearly expressions of intense separation anxiety. Both the analyst-father and Freud, however, emphasized the related sexual components: his mother's often taking him into bed with her at such times, and what Freud, somewhat excessively, refers to as Hans's "two attempts at seducing his mother," the first, an invitation to her, while she was powdering his penis (taking care to avoid touching it), "Why don't you put your finger there?"; and the second, his repeating to her an aunt's comment, "He *has* got a dear little thingummy." Now Freud was aware of the importance of "an anxiety dream on the subject of losing his mother,"⁴⁹ but mainly in terms of feared *sexual* loss ("not being able to coax with her anymore") and compensatory increase in sexualized affection which he considered "the fundamental phenomenon in [Hans's] condition." And the specific relationship of anxiety to night ("Till the evening he was cheerful, as usual. But in the evening he grew visibly frightened; he cried and could not be separated from his mother, and wanted to 'coax' with her again") Freud attributed to "an intensification of his libido—for its object was his mother, and its aim may perhaps have been to sleep with her," an erotic longing which had to be repressed. But nighttime anxieties, especially in children, have to do with darkness and associated death imagery of all kinds—the idea of death itself (surely not unknown to a child of almost five), as well as equivalents of separation (clearly important for Hans), stasis (the model of sleep), and disintegration (being attacked or torn apart by threatening nighttime intruders, often phantoms or animals—and Hans was not only "afraid a horse would bite me" but that "the horse'll come into the room"). The intensification of Hans's need for his mother, and of the erotic component of that need, would seem to be secondary to this constellation of death-related anxiety.

Hans also feared losing his father ("When you're away, I'm afraid you're not coming home"). Though Freud could speak of "fear *of* his father and fear *for* his father," he attributed both to the Oedipus complex—the first derived from hostility, the second from a conflict between hostility and compensatory affection. But one could understand these emotions toward his father as part of a general fear of abandonment—along with Hans's struggle with the idea of losing a parent, with the idea of death itself, and with the idea of his own dying. There is additional evidence for this view, such as the sequence: "Once [Hans] knocked on the pavement with his stick and said: 'I say, is there a man underneath?—someone buried?—or is that only in the cemetery?'" To which Freud commented: "So he is occupied not only with the riddle of life but with the riddle of death."[50] But he and the analyst-father never pursue this perspective, and, in fact, turned away from it. Thus, the latter only parenthetically refers to the first funeral Hans had ever witnessed, admitting that "he often recalls it," but then dismissing that as "no doubt a screen memory." *

Similarly, when Hans, while in the middle of a fantasy about two giraffes, is asked what he is thinking of and says, "Of raspberry syrup" and "a gun for shooting people dead with," the father-analyst (in a later communication) associates these images with Hans's constipation (for which he is given raspberry syrup, and because he frequently confuses the words "shooting" [schiessen] and "shitting" [scheissen]. Freud later, in a footnote, broadens the interpretation a bit by saying that these images could have more than one set of determinants and "probably had just as much to do with his hatred of [and death wishes toward] his father as with his constipation complex."[51] Analyst and supervisor also agreed that "raspberry syrup" could be related to "blood." But neither raise the question of the more general implications of the image of "shooting people dead"—of violent imagery in the service of confronting the idea of death and related anxiety around abandonment and annihilation, anxiety that had much to do with his parents, but also reflected the youngster's overall struggles with threatened vitality (in ways we have suggested in our earlier discussion of violence).

The horse phobia itself provides evidence for this hypothesis. After two months of analysis, Hans revealed that his symptoms had begun right after he had seen a bus-horse fall down and kick about with its feet. As Hans explained, "When the horse in the bus fell down, it gave me such a fright, really! That was when I got the nonsense [his phobic symptoms]." And when his father pointed out that the nonsense involved mainly the fear that a horse would bite him, Hans replied: "Fall down and bite." Hans also demonstrated, while lying on the ground, how the horse kicked about with its feet, which "gave me a fright." And when the father asks whether the horse was dead, the sequence is rather typical for that of a child struggling with the idea of death:

Hans: "Yes!"
I: "How do you know that?"
Hans: "Because I saw it." (He laughed.) "No, it wasn't a bit dead."
I: "Perhaps you thought it was dead!"

*To which I would add, also parenthetically, that a formative perspective makes one wary of the very concept of "screen memory," as it can be too easily invoked for the purpose of deemphasizing certain kinds of imagery in favor of the assigned "essence," more consistent with one's theory, that resides in "deeper layers" of the psyche and is "screened out" by the imagery in question.

Hans: "No. Certainly not. I only said it as a joke." (His expression at the moment, however, had been serious.)

"As he was tired, I let him run off . . . ."[52]

Freud tells us that this event, "insignificant in itself . . . immediately preceded the outbreak of the illness and may no doubt be regarded as the precipitating cause of its outbreak." For as Freud says about Hans: "He was terrified, and thought the horse was dead; and from that time on he thought that all horses would fall down." But, inevitably, Freud places the death imagery within the structure of Oedipal castration fear: the horse represents the father, its falling down reflects the boy's death wishes toward his father (and possibly the mother's giving birth as well); its thrashing about with its legs is associated with Hans's awareness of doing the same thing when he has to go to the bathroom and, more fundamentally (Freud suspects), with the sexual act itself, even though "Hans's father was unable to confirm my suspicion that there was some recollection stirring in the child's mind of having observed a scene of sexual intercourse between his parents in their bedroom";[53] and the biting represents his father's retaliation, Hans's fear of castration.

While Freud presents evidence for this interpretive structure, the phobia can be better understood as the epitomization—one could say, totalization—of Hans's anxious relationship to death and its equivalents. The horse "falling down and biting" reflects Hans's painful struggle around bringing together death and the death equivalent of annihilation or disintegration. From this perspective, the horse comes to represent not so much the father himself but all that Hans feels threatened by in relationship to death and its equivalents. Since the father plays an important part in that threatening imagery—he is life-protector and potential life-destroyer—the horse can certainly at times specifically represent the father. By the same token, the horse biting Hans can at times represent fear of castration. And the horse thrashing its legs about while lying on its back could represent images around defecation or sexual intercourse. But the phobia, as an entity, reflects Hans's more general death-related struggles, and his fearful efforts to express vitality (the exaggerated movement of the horse's legs, for instance) in the face of what he perceives as overwhelming threat. This interpretation is consistent not only with Hans's own death-linked associations, but with a great deal of imagery in children having to do with the awesome power of large animals, conveyed especially vividly by the size of their genitals; and, consequently, the still more awesome image of such beasts dying.*

---

*Nor is the important relationship of animals to death limited to children's associations. One of the most powerful images in films and still pictures of the Hiroshima experience is that of a dead horse lying on its side in the rubble.

Nothing could be more desolate than that image. I have thought of it often—not just in connection with Hiroshima but as suggesting, indirectly, the psychic power animals have for us. They may well be crucial to our imaginative efforts to construct our image-

Unable to absorb the idea of death (his mother's, his father's, his own, the phenomenon itself) or of related bodily imagery or breakdown, Hans could— had to—instead fear horses and their falling down or biting him. Hans's bodily and sexual preoccupations—with his own penis, with the nonexistence of a penis in girls and women, with his attraction to his mother and to a series of little girls—these became intensified and anxiety-laden, as must all important struggles toward vitality, at whatever age, in the midst of these death-related conflicts. In that sense, Hans reminds one of adults who, upon experiencing profound threat or loss of one kind or another, radically intensify their sexual activity in ways that can indeed afford pleasure and meaning but are at the same time driven and anxious.

All this brings us to the question of meaning. And here we may say first that recent psychoanalytic work on phobia has moved toward an emphasis on what we would call death equivalents, and especially conflicts around separation. Perhaps more in children but in general, "phobic reactions in both sexes frequently originate in separation anxiety."[54] The conflicts around dependency in phobic conditions are seen to include imagery of grave danger—something close to annihilation—where the dependent relationships are threatened. But these views on phobia remain limited by the underlying instinctual paradigm, spoken or unspoken. Within a libido-centered paradigm, death tends to be negated—or "de-deathified," even (especially) when it is being discussed. For instance, Hans's "death wishes" toward his father become a secondary elaboration of his sexual attraction to his mother—a wishing away of a rival. But if we consider imagery around death and separation to be more fundamental, we would expect a small boy's feelings toward his father to include constant preoccupation with the latter's power, his power to sustain or destroy the smaller organism (oneself); along with the continuous back-and-forth comparison of life-and death-power of the two organisms, with an early sense that one's only comparative advantage lies in one's "survival priority" toward—one's expectation of living longer than—one's father. That conflict becomes totalized in phobia: wishes and fears around survival priority are molded and condensed into a single, dreaded image, such as that of a horse that may fall or bite. A similar point can be made concerning what Freud called "the great riddle of where babies come from, which is perhaps the first problem to engage a child's mental powers, and of which the riddle of the Theban Sphinx is probably no more than a distorted version."

We have discussed in an earlier chapter the significance of this "great riddle" for the child's early sense of the boundaries of existence, of the distinction

---

feelings of movement, integration, vitality. I refer not so much to our evolutionary connection with them—though that is always there and may mean more than we realize—or even to our relationships with specific animals, mostly domestic, but to the more neglected constitutive (or formative) importance of animals in our construction of image-feelings around life-power and death-power.

between life and nonlife—in addition to sexual curiosity as such. The famous riddle of the Sphinx, which Freud invokes here as a "distorted version" of this early sexual curiosity, is strikingly relevant to our view. The Sphinx's riddle— "What walks on four feet in the morning, on two at noon, and on three in the evening?"—and the correct solution—"Man crawls on all fours as a baby, walks upright in the prime of life, and uses a staff in old age"—are striking in their evocation of man's cycle of life, the phases of his beginning, middle, and end. But Freud was probably right in his sense that the riddle is related to this form of early curiosity, even if his understanding of the significance of both is somewhat different from ours. *In phobia, for whatever reasons, the child or adult is unable to cope with the image of nonlife, and must struggle with a totalized representation of his conflicts around the distinction.* Or to put it another way, for the phobic person, one side of this distinction—the idea of nonlife— becomes equated with personal annihilation.

These questions of meaning are also blurred by Freud's adherence to the "pleasure principle"—the view of the human organism as always seeking pleasure (mostly defined as sexual pleasure) and avoiding pain (including, importantly, the pain of denied sexual pleasure). In contrast, I would see the organism, from the beginning of life, seeking to construct and experience image-feelings that enhance connection, integrity, and movement, even when these may be, in a strict perceptual sense, unpleasurable. The question takes on some importance in phobia because, as we observe in little Hans, the problem faced becomes not so much that of avoiding pleasure as encountering, around what may ordinarily give one pleasure (a walk with one's mother through the streets of the city) what is perceived as an absolute threat of annihilation. The more general point is that a pain-pleasure model, essentially a remnant of the neurological reflex arc, is an impediment to a symbolizing view of psychic action. The concept of the pleasure principle, in fact, denies man his complexity and contradiction, while denying neurosis its meaning.

And concerning these questions of meaning, Freud's concept of the Oedipus complex needs further scrutiny. With it Freud was able to say much that needed to be said about early erotic feelings and intrafamilial images. But for neurosis in particular, Freud asked too much of the Oedipus complex as a causative principle. It may be more accurate to say that, as usual, Freud saw that patterns of image-formation and symbolization begin to take shape very early in infancy and childhood around the most intimate, nurturing, life-sustaining relationships. There is something poignant about the way in which Freud mobilizes his brilliance to squeeze this great insight, at least as it relates to neurosis, into the tight mold of an Oedipus complex subsumed to the instinctual paradigm.

Without attempting the extensive treatment the subject deserves, we can suggest a few principles toward an alternative view of the Oedipus complex. First, the human eroticization of life ties, as experienced by the young child of either sex toward both parents, but usually with special intensity toward the parent of the opposite sex. Second, a consequent blending of erotic image-feelings with those around vitality and threats of loss, extinction, and death. Third, a resulting preoccupation with the death of either or both parents, not simply the one perceived as a barrier to sexual consummation but in relationship to such symbolizing struggles as fears around loss, the idea of death, and hostile-anxious conflicts around survival priority. Hence, a fourth principle: that of the child's interweaving death-related image-feelings about himself (his own death) and either parent—especially toward the particular parent, at any moment or stage of growth, whose life-power is felt to be threatening to the child's own.

The riddle of the Sphinx we spoke of earlier was, as everyone knows, solved by none but Oedipus himself. Freud understands both the Sphinx and its conqueror in terms of specifically sexual principles. But one must recall that, in the Oedipus legend, the Sphinx was a problem not only because of her riddle but because she killed all who failed to solve it and was thus a threat to the very existence of Thebes. That is why Oedipus, in solving the riddle, was considered savior of the city, a man not himself a god, but possessed of more than ordinary human power because of assistance from the gods. We can say that this power to defeat death and sustain life was related to man's special immortalizing possibility, his capacity for knowledge, in this case knowledge about his own essence. (Oedipus meets his downfall, and is blinded and exiled, not because he "saw too much" but because he had not seen or known enough, he had lacked knowledge of his true parents. Or, one could say, that precisely that knowledge became devastating only because it came too late to prevent Oedipus's terrible transgressions.) Oedipus became a life-destroyer, a killer of his father, a violator of society's ultimate taboo and a subverter of its basic morality. Oedipus was, therefore, the cause of the new wave of death and plague that had been annihilating the people of the city. In his old age (in *Oedipus at Colonus*), he protested his innocence on the basis of this earlier ignorance ("No, I did not sin! . . . I did not know. . . ").[55] Having suffered grievously and atoned, Oedipus at his death takes on a clearly immortal quality ". . . some attendant from the train of Heaven/Came for him; or else the underworld/Opened in love the unlit door of earth./For he was taken without lamentation,/Illness or suffering; indeed his end/Was wonderful if mortal's ever was."[56] In legend and everyday life the Oedipal experience centers upon questions of life-principle: transgression, sexual and otherwise, and death: either threatening and grotesque or necessary and appropriate.

Finally, the question of meaning must be applied to the specific thing feared, the content of the phobia itself. Many of what Freud called the "common phobias" involved situations suggestive of death or danger—phobias of night, darkness, solitude, illness, or animals, not to mention death itself. Such phobic objects as biting animals, including snakes, certainly suggest castration fear, as Freud suggested, but castration fear that we would understand as a form of overall bodily threat and fear of disintegration. Moreover, even in the "special phobias"—fear of heights, closed areas, there is at least a suggestion of an unusual and potentially threatening relationship to space, motion, and orientation, suggesting death imagery at one remove. I would ally myself with those wise clinicians who believe in exploring each individual phobia through its own particular image-structure. Freud provided something of a model for that in his exploration of Hans's horse phobia. Our additional comments on meaning, though limited, suggest the kinds of inquiry that could be made. We would also have to consider historical and cultural contributions to imagery: Hans's horse phobia, for instance, could contain some equivalents, in terms of meanings (especially around threat and annihilation), to such more popular contemporary phobias as fear of dogs and fear of flying. The consistent principle is the sequestering off of death and related anxieties.

SIXTEEN

Schizophrenia—Lifeless Life

OF ALL THE PSYCHIATRIC SYNDROMES, schizophrenia has the most paradoxical relationship to death imagery. On the one hand, "madness" or psychosis had been associated with the image of the death of the mind long before the word schizophrenia was invented to describe these states. On the other hand, hardly anyone has attempted to conceptualize schizophrenia in ways that relate it to death and death imagery. Yet this imagery has special bearing on its internal states.*

In acute psychosis, we can speak of both death and survival: the "death of the mind" in the sense of the breakdown of its symbolizing capacity and the experience of disintegration; and the survival of considerable psychic function, often by means of the paranoid shift (to the idea of reference and beyond, as discussed later in this chapter), which provides an alternate, more or less functional, theory of meaning, and mode of psychic existence. We recall

---

*In Appendix C, I have included a brief, selective history of death-linked imagery around schizophrenia and madness, with reference to historical studies of Gregory Zilboorg and Michel Foucault. Also discussed from this standpoint are the modern approaches of Kraepelin, Bleuler, Jung, Theodore Lidz, and R. D. Laing. Laing's work in particular, especially as reported in *The Divided Self*,[1] comes close to our own stress on extreme numbing (inner deadness) and equally extreme sense of threat, though his existential perspective falls short of systematic consideration of impairments to symbolization. Some readers may wish to turn to Appendix C at this point as background for the chapter.

Laing's patient: "I had to die to keep from dying."[2] Or to put it another way, the death one survives is one's own. The end-of-the-world fantasy (also discussed below) carries a similar process further. One is still in part dying with the world in the sense that one's sense of inner disintegration includes self and world. But by rendering oneself the only survivor (often but not always part of the fantasy) one symbolizes the pseudo-vitality of the paranoid existence.

It is clear that the experience of threat in schizophrenia is of a special order. In our discussion of depression, we emphasized the stance of static negation—of mimetic death—in order to avoid the full experience of that which was most threatening: separation and loss. Schizophrenics, too, struggle with feelings around separation and loss, but there is an added dimension to the threat they experience. Even greater than their fear of separation and loss may be their terror of relationship—of nurturing, of vitality itself. The schizophrenic person feels unable "to gain distance from what is overwhelming him," and consequently experiences "a smothering sense of closeness."[3] Indeed, so frightened is the schizophrenic of human ties that "all proffered support appears as a threat." The person offering support "appears as the instrument of what is making him [the schizophrenic] feel that he is dying." Thus, he feels unable to relate "because this would mean active participation in his own destruction."

This excruciating inability to achieve either distance or relation is, in my judgment, the fundamental intrapsychic "double bind" of the schizophrenic. It is his "deathly paradox": to remain totally unrelated to others is to pursue psychosis and psychic death; to attempt relationship is to court "the risk of annihilation."[4] The compromise is the "state of death-in-life" or "dead life."[5]

We have noted the existence of fear of annihilation and of disintegration in the neuroses as well. But in schizophrenia, unlike the other conditions, the imagery of annihilation is likely to dominate all constellations of the self. The schizophrenic lives in "a world pervaded by the threat of destruction." To counter this threat, he may himself destroy. Very often his target of destruction or "murder" is his own self. That schizophrenic self, in order to "escape from the risk of being killed, . . . becomes dead."[6]

A connecting principle is that of "deanimation"—the schizophrenic person's sense that his humanity has been taken away from him, that he has been turned into a thing, and that he can experience no actively functioning self.[7] We know that the capacity to experience a vital self has to do with the health of the symbolizing function; one becomes "a thing" when impairment of that function results in extreme concretization and literalization. And we find that Bleuler gave considerable emphasis to literalizing tendencies in the schizophrenic, as have most subsequent writers. Burnham, for instance, speaks of the schizophrenic's "references to himself as a toy, puppet, or slave," and of a woman who "spoke of herself as a doll and even moved like a mechanical toy."[8] Here the deanimation and desymbolization are accompanied by a sense of being controlled and manipulated.*

Another patient told Burnham, "I have lost my soul." And another patient: "It's all a stage production. Everyone is acting and using stage names." And still another: "The people here are only pseudo-people, made of papier-mache."

While these two images may well reflect sensitive perceptions of actual hypocrisy and falsity, they undoubtedly also include longstanding feelings of unreality. They are a description of a "land of the dead" of a kind many schizophrenics feel themselves to inhabit: the world itself is dead and human history has ended. Again, the death imagery is directly related to desymbolization—to "a lack of stability and continuity of the person's symbolic representations of self and others."[9]

The "death stance" in schizophrenia differs from that in depression. The depressed person demonstrates static behavior or mimetic death in an earnest and relatively humorless way. But the schizophrenic seems to make a mockery of his psychic death—whether in the form of his bizarre and silly (hebephrenic) words and phrases, his odd (catatonic) posturing, or his grandiose (paranoid) images, delusions, and hallucinations. His suffering is real, but his style is that of caricature. This element of schizophrenic experience has often been noted but insufficiently considered. One way to understand it is to see the schizophrenic as mocking both vitality or the idea of relationship on the one hand, and deadness or the idea of total separation on the other. His tone of caricature, in other words, is also an expression of his deathly paradox.

His pervasive imagery of annihilation also causes him to totalize his attitudes and relationships. This is partly a matter of equating absolutely a death equivalent, such as separation, with death itself. He frequently "fails . . . to distinguish between brief temporary separation and utter abandonment," so that one can speak of "the truly life or death nature of . . . [his] separation crisis."[10] I believe one should resist the temptation to see in this behavior the *mere* repetition of the young child's equation of separation and death. Its more complex dimensions are suggested by a patient of Burnham:

> One woman attempted to elope from the hospital whenever she experienced an increased feeling of attachment to her therapist and a correspondingly increased fear of losing him. Frequently she assaulted him toward the end of therapy

*There are many related descriptions of schizophrenics who think of themselves as various kinds of machines. I was told of a young woman who described herself in that way, and then held out her arms and said: "Smell the plastic and the metal!" This last image suggests not just the deanimation and robotization but also perhaps a small plea for what is missing—for the "smell" of a living human body. There is the sense that schizophrenics live in a different order of nonvital motion or activity—some live this way all the time, others only when threatened (most of Burnham's examples are at least partly reactions to separation from the therapist).

sessions, shouting that he need not return for another session since she would be gone. Once when he unconsciously attempted to smooth his departure by offering to light her cigarette, she viciously kicked him. The overwhelming importance of separation to this patient was graphically manifest in her creating for a hospital art show a totem pole-like figure eight feet high, which she titled "the God of Separation."[11]

That "God of Separation" certainly expressed the patient's intense conflict around the whole issue, as Burnham says. It was also humorously mocking, a caricature of gods and their worshipers on the one hand, and of the whole issue of separation and attachment on the other. There is nonetheless a suggestion of the "worship" of the separation as not merely desirable but sacred (remember that the alternative is perceived as annihilation). And finally, there is in this deification, however mocking, a totalization of the matter, an expression of its pervasiveness and association with images of ultimate threat. There are of course early-childhood models for some of these feelings, but the constellation is that of a schizophrenic adult.

This pattern of totalization of death equivalents* can be understood in relationship to Laing's three categories of intense anxiety: engulfment, implosion, and petrification. Engulfment has to do with the dread of relatedness we have already observed, in schizophrenics an equation of relationship (connection) with having one's existence swallowed up[13] by the other. One chooses instead isolation (or separation). Implosion, literally a violent collapse inward, is used by Laing to describe "the full terror of the experience of the world as liable at any moment to crash in and obliterate all identity as a gas will rush in and obliterate a vacuum." This is the kind of terror of annihilation (or disintegration) we have described. "Petrification," for Laing, involves imagery of being turned into stone and becoming robotlike, the pattern we described in relationship to extreme psychic numbing and deanimation (or severe stasis). Image-feelings of engulfment, implosion, and petrification are widespread and known to all of us, but in schizophrenics they tend to be absolute and unrelieved.

Totalization seems to start very early in life, and to become characteristic of many forms of schizophrenic imagery. Arieti has recently emphasized a tendency to extract only negative experience from parental relationships—that is, to "transform" a mixed relationship into a totally painful one. Rather than see the schizophrenic individual as a *tabula rasa*, the assumption here is that he participates actively, and from the beginning of life, in the symbolic distortions that are to eventuate in schizophrenic deformation. He does so through some

---

*Erik Erikson originally spoke of the self's potential for totalism, for all-or-none psychological immersions that could provide a "delusion of wholeness."[12] Here I apply a variant of that concept to the operation of the death equivalents, occurring almost entirely outside of awareness.

combination of genetic vulnerability and very early perception of extreme environmental threat. His equipment and reaction patterns are such that, rather than psychically building upon whatever has been nurturing in early experience, he does the reverse: he excludes such experience from his evolving imagery and constructs instead a world dominated by terror of annihilation. The terror is real, and has important origins in actual experience. But the experience has been totalized, transformed into the exclusive truth of one's existence. And this totalization may involve not just the transformation of parental image described by Arieti (and earlier, in a related way, by Melanie Klein) but image-formation in general. Totalization, that is, becomes central to formative process itself. Strangely (or perhaps not so strangely), we will find parallels in broader historical experience where the absolutization of truth becomes a life-or-death matter.

In pursuing the nature of the threat in schizophrenia, we do well to turn to Freud. Freud was mostly a conquistador of the neuroses, and was not, as he often pointed out, a psychiatrist professionally weaned on schizophrenia. He did theorize considerably on psychosis, though his concepts have been looked at more critically here than in relationship to neurosis. But we do well to try to understand what he was after, and for that purpose we must turn once more to the problem of narcissism and its relationship to schizophrenia.

Schizophrenia is the example par excellence of Freud's invocation of narcissism to account for what we would speak of as intrapsychic disintegration.[14] He was quite explicit about doing so on behalf of libido theory.* Freud understood schizophrenia to result from a reversal of the path of libido: "The libido that has been withdrawn from the external world has been directed to the ego". Adult "megalomania" of schizophrenia was then "a form of 'secondary narcissism' . . . superimposed upon a primary narcissism," which Freud considered a "half-way phase between auto-erotism and object-love," during which the young child directed his libido toward his own body.[16]

Freud first introduced the concept in connection with his analysis of the mechanism of paranoia: his stress on the "homosexual wish" behind paranoia and delusions of persecution, and the relationship between narcissism and these homosexual tendencies. The celebrated "Schreber case," based upon this distinguished jurist's Memoirs of his paranoid psychosis, was the basis for Freud's elaborate conceptual web: Schreber's "passive homosexual wish-

---

*"A pressing motive for occupying ourselves with the conception of a primary and normal narcissism arose when the attempt was made to subsume what we know of dementia praecox (Kraepelin) or schizophrenia (Bleuler) under the hypothesis of the libido theory." The matter had special importance because Freud understood Jung's position to be that "the libido theory has already come to grief in the attempt to explain the latter disease [schizophrenia]."[15] Freud had just broken with Jung, and wrote this essay on narcissism at about the same time he wrote the more polemical essay, "On the History of the Psycho-Analytic Movement," which reclaimed psychoanalysis from the two prominent heretics, Jung and Adler.

fantasy," directed toward his physician, as the "exciting cause" of the psychosis; the prior "father-complex" behind this erotic longing; the unacceptability of the proposition "I (a man) love him (a man)" leading to the contradictory proposition "I do not *love* him, I hate him," and then, via projection, "He hates me"; and the attachment to the ego of "liberated libido" so that it is used "for the aggrandizement of the ego" [megalomania], based on a developmental *fixation at the stage of narcissism.*"[17]

Two later psychoanalytic students of the Schreber *Memoirs* take issue with Freud and stress instead the theme of "soul murder" and associated issues around death and continuity. Indeed, Schreber, in explaining the soul murder he believed perpetrated on himself, speaks precisely within our own paradigm:

> . . . the idea is widespread in the folk-lore and poetry of all peoples that it is somehow possible to take possession of another person's soul in order to prolong one's life at another soul's expense, or to secure some other advantages which outlast death.[18]

Macalpine and Hunter tell us that soul murder or theft of soul substance meant "denying the Schreber family, i.e., himself, offspring because the life substance which God gives to all human beings to perpetuate themselves was taken away," so that "Schreber, being without children, was excluded from the eternal cycle of life." Not only the self was being annihilated, but so was all possibility of larger human connection.

They saw in this an explanation for Schreber's "end of the world" fantasy, as well as his delusion that he was immortal: "A person without a soul, i.e., life substance, cannot die." Schreber's delusion of world catastrophe is required for him to become the ultimate or "sole survivor to renew mankind."[19]

Schreber's "procreation fantasies," which were indeed prominent, were a component of the total sense of annihilation conveyed in the image of soul murder. Macalpine and Hunter point out that Freud could "make nothing" of that image, but that its combination of prominence and yet obscurity in the *Memoirs* is "perhaps evidence that it was the centre of his psychosis."

Years later Harold Searles made similar observations on the basis of his painstaking therapeutic work with schizophrenics. He was struck by the fact that the "very mundane, universal factor of human mortality" seems to be a major source of anxiety in "this overtly most exotic of psychopathological processes."[20] He came, in fact, to believe that people "became, and . . . long remained, schizophrenic . . . largely or wholly . . . *in order to avoid facing*, among other aspects of internal and external reality, the fact that life is finite." Important to this denial is a combination of actual death encounters (a loss, through death, in childhood of a parent, nursemaid, or sibling "of the deepest value to him"); and a pervasive sense of life as unlived and, one might say, unlivable (parents will die before he can ever feel related to them, or he himself is in middle life with little expectation of "fully living"). In the absence of the experience of promise of vitality, death can only be anticipated as premature, and therefore radically threatening.

Consequently, the schizophrenic inserts into his lurid delusional system "a kind of colourless rider-clause—an ingredient which represents a denial of the finitude of life. It contains the idea that "People don't die . . . but in actuality are simply 'changed', 'moved about from place to place' . . ." More than that, the schizophrenic is likely to feel himself "totally responsible *for* death itself," to feel either that he carries "the seeds of mankind's destruction in his own breast" or that he is (via his delusions) God or else hears (via his hallucinations) God's voice and has become his agent in such matters. Searles points out that this compensatory omnipotence aims at the related claim of immortality. The schizophrenic makes that claim in a variety of ways, but behind it is the fact that "many if not all of them are unable to experience themselves, consistently, as being *alive*." Feelings of immortality are enhanced because "One need not fear death so long as one feels dead anyway; one has, subjectively, nothing to lose through death."[21] (We are again reminded of the Musselmänn, for whom death is not really death.)

Searles suggests here that both the inner death and the claim to immortality are ways of defending against the inability to accept actual death. While this can certainly be true, I would, from the standpoint of our paradigm, put the matter in a slightly different way. The inner death or absence of vitality on an immediate level parallels severed larger connections on an ultimate level. Immortality must be literalized—and therefore rendered delusional—because it cannot be symbolized (rendered psychically real). Behind both experiential deadness and literalized immortality is something close to Schreber's "soul murder," something close to perpetual dread of annihilation.

Which brings us back to our critical distinctions between such annihilation and Freud's view of narcissism. Freud attributed the severity of schizophrenic symptoms to the predominance of narcissism. He spoke both of "fixation points for the libido" at its earliest (narcissistic) phases of development, as well as regression to this primitive narcissism "to which dementia praecox returns in its final outcome."[22] Indeed, Freud placed schizophrenia among the "narcissistic neuroses," which he considered virtually untreatable by psychoanalysis precisely because the predominance of narcissism prevented the necessary "transference" between analyst and patient (in contrast to "transference neuroses," such as hysteria, obsessive-compulsive states, and phobias, in which psychoanalysis is more specifically indicated precisely because that transference is more readily achievable).

More generally, Freud associated narcissism with immortality, injury, and even death. The attitude of affectionate parents toward their children is to be understood as "a revival and reproduction of their narcissism, which they have long since abandoned." And, "At the most touchy point in the narcissistic system, the immortality of the ego, which is so hard pressed by reality, security is achieved by taking refuge in the child."[23] Here Freud almost comes to a principle of symbolized immortality, but must subsume any such imagery to infantile-instinctual sources—so that "Parental love . . . is nothing but the parents' narcissism born again. . . ." Freud is employing the concept of narcissism to connect with *his* immortalizing principle, that of libido, on the one hand, and *anyone's imagery* of immortality, on the other.

Thus, in one of his final writings, Freud equated what he called "narcissistic mortifications" with "early injuries to the ego."[24] These "injuries to the ego" are death equivalents, perhaps mainly imagery of annihilation. But if any psychic injury is to be equated with "narcissistic mortification" (literally the death of narcissism), then narcissism becomes nothing short of a psychic life force, a kind of accumulation of libido that provides the energy for, and confidence in, self and world necessary for ongoing existence. Thus, with narcissism, Freud has it all ways. Narcissism, along with its vicissitudes, comes to substitute for breakdown and death on the one hand, and the symbolization of continuing life on the other.*

Yet, even if Freud substituted narcissism for disintegration, his use of the word pointed to a consistent feature of schizophrenia having to do with a breakdown in self-world relationship which we have called radical uncentering and ungrounding, Lidz has called egocentricity, Bleuler called autism, and which is at the heart of the classically described phenomenon of "ideas of reference" (and its twin, "ideas of influence"). "Things seem to have hidden meanings, neutral individuals are suddenly animated with strange ideas and designs, curious connections between feelings and perceptions are experienced . . . [and] everything experienced is measured as to its possible relevance for the individual." Suspicion of possible relevance then proceeds to the "idea of reference," the individual's cognitive certainty "that this or that object, person, event, or transaction (an upheaval in a distant country, a public statement reported in the newspapers, a conversation between two strangers) is directed at, and has special meaning for, him. That shift to the "idea of reference" can be understood as "the cardinal characteristic of psychotic experience."[27] At that point in acute psychotic experience, one can observe the "depatterning" and

---

*The concept of narcissism has remained central to psychoanalytic thought, but in recent American writings it seems to be ubiquitous. Clinicians point to the "narcissistic personality structure"[25] and social theorists berate our "narcissistic society."[26] While the phenomena these writers address are important ones, subsuming them to the concept of narcissism tends often to obscure the destructive psychic processes at work around death imagery and death equivalents. In many writings there is confusion between narcissism as a technical concept (where it retains the baggage of the instinctual paradigm) and as an ordinary adjective to describe patterns of self-absorption. And the application of the concept to a society at large can become a form of moralism that obscures the threatening historical and psychological forces at play. (See Part III.)

"destructuring" of the sense of self. This point of psychotic break, according to Harry Stack Sullivan, followed upon "a disaster to self-esteem" and was "attended subjectively by the state . . . of *panic*." [28]

We would understand the moment, in terms of death equivalents, to be one in which the fear of annihilation gives way to the experience of disintegration. That shift to the fixed idea of reference is also the movement into paranoia. We have discussed, in connection with the Schreber case, our own death-centered revision of Freud's libido-centered (struggle-against-homosexuality) view of paranoia. * We see here its connection with disintegrative imagery at the onset of psychosis, and its relationship to questions of meaning.

An additional issue for a death-related approach to the sense of threat in schizophrenia has been the "end-of-the-world" fantasy, also first discussed in relationship to the Schreber case. The meaning of this fantasy was at issue in Jung's questioning of the application of libido theory to schizophrenia (which had much to do with Freud's invocation of narcissism in defense of that theory). Jung's point was that the fantasy expressed the psychotic's withdrawal of all interests from the external world, not just his sexuality, and argued, on that basis, for a more general (more than merely sexual) understanding of the entire concept of libido. [30] In a more death-centered age, however, we would expect to encounter harsher views of the meaning of this fantasy. †

Related to the question of threat is the relationship of depression to schizophrenia. Recent work has emphasized the close association of the two, and especially the presence of severe depression both at the time of schizophrenic breakdown and immediately following reintegration or recovery from psychosis. It would seem that depression is prominent at the transition points in and out of psychosis—or perhaps more specifically in and out of paranoia. [32] Some writers have gone further and emphasized the "depressive core" in schizophrenic patients, or spoken of the condition itself (at least in certain instances) as "a depressive equivalent." [33] In discussing their differences, we have emphasized the question of blame. We could in fact understand the paranoid shift into psychosis in terms of an equation put forward by Sullivan: "It is not

---

* A survivor-like "suspicion of counterfeit nurturance" characterizes much of paranoia. That interpretation is consistent with Lionel Ovesey's suggestion that "the . . . power (aggression) motivation . . . is the constant feature in paranoid phenomenon . . . and . . . the essential related anxiety is, therefore, a survival anxiety." What Ovesey means by survival anxiety is close to what we mean by death anxiety or fear of annihilation; and he understands this anxiety to result from a sequence of frustrated dependency, extreme aggression, and symbolic distortion, until the feeling "I want to kill him" becomes converted to "He wants to kill me." [29]

† Elias Canetti, a literary man rather than a psychiatrist, emphasizes Schreber's wish to be "the only man left alive," and concludes, much like Ovesey, that paranoia "is an illness of power in the most literal sense of the words." For him, survival is "the moment of power" par excellence, and can indeed become in certain heroes and despots, "a dangerous and insatiable passion." [31]

that *I* have something wrong with me, but that *he* does something to me." Sullivan in fact considered the "essence" of this "paranoid dynamism" to be "the transference of blame."[34]

But why the shift? Actually, nobody knows for certain. Searles, however, has suggested an interesting possibility. He says of the schizophrenic that "the losses which he has already experienced have come too early in his development, and in too great magnitude, for him to have been able to integrate them." Under those extreme conditions were he "to experience his sense of loss fully . . . he would experience a feeling, not of 'loss' in the mature sense, but of disintegration of the total self." His defense is to assert omnipotence, "his conviction that he has suffered no loss, and that it is unthinkable that he could ever suffer loss, for he is the whole world."[35]

We spoke of depression itself and its mimetic death as a means of avoiding a feeling of loss. The implication here is that schizophrenia carries the avoidance of that feeling to greater extremes, or, one could say, invokes greater deformations in the service of that avoidance. No one can say whether it is a question only, or even mainly, of losses—though that assumption is very much in keeping with our view of depression as the essence of mental disturbance. There does seem to be, as we have emphasized, the special dimension of "soul murder" or disintegrative death equivalent in schizophrenia, whose ultimate origin is unclear, and can indeed include genetically transmitted vulnerabilities. But from the standpoint of psychological origins, we must ask whether schizophrenia requires an added dimension of "attack" or annihilative threat from the environment (what could be classified as physical or psychological brutality), or whether loss itself—if sufficiently early and extreme—is enough to set in motion the full-scale disintegrative process.

We have already discussed death-related questions of meaning, both in terms of the subjective experience *of*, and shared feelings *about*, the schizophrenic condition. We have seen both to be permeated by death imagery, even if rarely so formulated.

Kraepelin's physicalistic view of schizophrenia (as an organic disease—on the order of pneumonia, syphilis, or diabetes, differing from them only in its inexorable progression) contained imagery something close to that of physical death. Bleuler and Freud viewed schizophrenia in ways consistent with a sense of psychic death (see Appendix C). All three contributed greatly to a process of humanization of schizophrenia, of viewing the condition as a potential form of human reaction to vicissitudes of living. Here an early figure was Adolph Meyer, followed by such determined therapist-investigator gladiators as Sullivan, Fromm-Reichmann, Searles, Boss, Minkowski, and Laing. With them, one can characterize the imagery of schizophrenia as human struggles writ large, struggles around inner death and faint vitality. With the later Laing, the imagery around the schizophrenic is that of a visionary who will teach us new ways of seeing, new forms of transcendence that will, so to speak, deliver us from our own psychic deaths. Then along comes Thomas Szasz to view schizophrenia as a kind of "deadly conspiracy" among psychiatrists to confine and otherwise brutalize their patients: "Kraepelin invented dementia praecox, and Bleuler schizophrenia, to justify calling psychiatric imprisonment 'mental hospitalization' and regarding it as a form of medical treatment. . . ."[36]

Concerning subjective struggles for meaning in schizophrenia, we have implied that the movement into psychosis can be understood as, first, a near-total breakdown in meaning characterizing the sense of disintegration, followed by a reassertion of disordered (psychotic) meaning structures (including pathological self-reference, delusions, and hallucinations). But we have said little about the crucial part played by guilt in these struggles. While the importance of guilt has certainly been evident to those working closely with schizophrenics, its *conceptual* place in the condition has on the whole been neglected.

Guilt begins with the developing sense that one is responsible for, indeed the cause of, the annihilation that threatens. Self-blame is inevitable in those who become schizophrenic. This is partly because there is truth in it: *something* in the very young child does evoke threatening responses. And even when the self-blame is pathetically "inappropriate," some early imagery is necessary to the development of the adult concept of responsibility. The trouble is that in the extremity of the schizophrenic's perceived environment, that sense of guilt readily arouses the feeling that one has no right to be alive at all. And unlike the situation in neurosis and in depression, that feeling becomes literalized, so that *one's very existence may be perceived as a transgression.* "There is the primary guilt of having no right to life in the first place, and hence of being entitled at the most only to a dead life."[37] It is quite appropriate to collude, or even initiate, one's own "soul murder." As Schreber himself wrote:

The voices which talk to me have daily stressed ever since the beginning of my contact with God (mid-March 1894) the fact that the crisis that broke upon the realms of God was caused by somebody having *committed soul murder:* at first Flechsig [his doctor] was named as the instigator of soul murder but of recent times in an attempt to reverse the facts *I myself have been 'represented' as the one who had committed soul murder*[38] (last italics mine).

That is, the voices (or the psychosis) followed upon the soul murder, and they now accuse Schreber himself of that crime.

Guilt contributes greatly to the schizophrenic's collusion in the murder of his self, but he also feels guilty for having done so. While we may speak of the first form of guilt as static and the second as animating (part of an impulse to stop the "murderous" process and bring the self back to life), the distinction can be peculiarly difficult to make in schizophrenia. For the guilt becomes part of the twisted or kinky quality of the condition, part of the circle of mockery and self-mockery. It is also readily totalized.

These patterns are perhaps most evident in catatonic reactions. The patient remains motionless. To act—to *move*—is to risk annihilation. But he also may feel that it is wrong, evil, to act or move. Indeed, such patients may "feel that if they move, the whole world will collapse or all mankind will perish." The sense of guilty taint becomes part of the grandiosity and delusion, as well as of the implicit end-of-the-world imagery. Yet, mixed in with the guilt and grandiosity, there can be a kind of mocking and self-mocking challenge: I dare you to make the move; it is my will against yours; I warn you that if I move there will be trouble, big trouble; it's not only wrong for me to move—it's wrong for *anybody* to move; by not moving I'm exposing all of the hypocrisy, terror, and guilty taint of others' movements.

The guilt, in other words, is part of the labyrinth—part of what Laing called "schizophrenese." In depression, we spoke of the imbalance between static and animating guilt. In schizophrenia, it is not only a matter of imbalance but of further convolution and totalization of both forms of guilt. Still, as Searles and others have shown, one has to tease out the animating possibilities in schizophrenic guilt and shame—notably around what one has done to one's self, and to one's life, and what, should one change, these might become.

This kind of exaggerated behavior—and now we move beyond the question of guilt per se—has to do with a desire to exorcise the psychosis, or, more generally, the pain and confusion of existence. The imagery is something like: If I can be as crazy as possible, maybe I can shake everyone and everything up sufficiently to put things right. That implies either exorcising one's own craziness, or influencing the world sufficiently to make it as crazy (or as sane) as one feels oneself to be. And that kind of impulse can attach itself specifically to destruction: If one imaginatively destroys—or actually kills—enough people, a sufficient portion of the threatening-persecuting world, evil and confusion can be eliminated and replaced by goodness and lucidity.[39]

But psychosis also means safety; in our terms, protection from annihilation. One is reminded of a patient's plea: "Please, please, let me be crazy again,"[40] and, of another in the process of recovery: "When reality started coming back, when I realized where I was and what had happened, I became depressed."[41]

Beyond the protection madness affords, and the despair over failed efforts at its exorcism, that madness can have positive attraction for the patient. There are many descriptions of ecstatic states associated with schizophrenia, often but not always just preceding the psychotic breakdown. These include religious and mystical revelations, in the case of Schreber, the experience of "miracles," of extraordinary lucidity, and of creative release. These have been described as "peak experiences" (after Maslow), "a sense of heightened awareness," "altered experience," or "altered states of consciousness." They tend either to be associated with, or give way to, full-blown psychosis. These "peak experiences" have many features of what we have called experiential transcendence. And indeed they can be just that, when they occur in the transient psychoses of relatively integrated people. In such situations, the combination of psychotic and peak experience can, as Don Jackson once wrote, serve as "growth experiences." The psychosis cum peak experience can provide the sense of death and rebirth we shall discuss in the book's final chapter. That is the sort of thing Ronald Laing had in mind in advocating "living through" one's madness.

That sequence is relatively unusual. Much more frequent is the association of psychosis cum "peak experience" with the kind of desymbolization and deformation we have been discussing. For a peak experience to qualify as what we called experiential transcendence, you have, so to speak, to "come back." And that is what the schizophrenic usually cannot do.

Indeed, even the heightened awareness tends to be associated with anxiety— often as one patient put it, "horror and ecstasy."[42] That is, the peak experience, in the absence of the capacity for symbolic ordering, seems to favor "the progression of the psychotic state and the formation of delusions."[43]

Since this state is accompanied by "hypervigilance," it may well be a psychobiological response to perceived threat, as some believe. If so, however, the response tends all too often to be inseparable from the threat itself, that of annihilation or the experience of disintegration. In any case, our point here is that the schizophrenic person can experience imaginative pleasure that is inseparable from his immediate disintegration—pleasure that may well herald his more fundamentally despairing and "deadened" state.

Questions of meaning enter directly into a theory of schizophrenia. As Lyman Wynn, a leading investigator of psychological patterns in the families of schizophrenics, emphasizes, "*Feelings* of meaninglessness or pointlessness as *subjectively* experienced by the persons [in the families] themselves." What is shared is "a disbelief in the possibility of connected, subjectively meaningful, and satisfying experience." In one group families "appear to have no stake in looking for meanings," in another there is "profound skepticism about achieving meaning."[44] Wynn also emphasized what he called "pseudo-mutuality," by which he means an insistence upon a facade of harmony at the expense of both individual differentiation and, one may say, actuality[45]—as suggested by the example of a mother of a schizophrenic:

> We are all peaceful. I like peace even if I have to kill someone to get it . . . a more normal, happy kid would be hard to find. I was pleased with my child! I was pleased with my husband! I was pleased with my life. I have *always* been pleased. We have had twenty-five years of the happiest married life and of being a father and mother.[46]

Beyond the extremity of denial and numbing we encounter a "grotesque counterfeit . . . of meaning and relation."[47] The violent imagery is significant, suggesting a willingness often encountered in these families, and not just on the part of one member, to annihilate psychically whoever threatens the counterfeit structure. In these families there may be "shared dread of meaning and relation, manifest in the systematic destruction of meaning, the routine elimination of implication, and the insistence on fragmentation of experience." Wynn and Margaret Thaler Singer, on the basis of a series of projective tests given to family members, have been able to predict the specific form of thought disorder and degree of disorganization of the schizophrenic member, and to match "blindly" individual patients and their families.[48] They understood themselves to be studying "family constellations" around styles of communication, especially patterns of handling attention and meaning; styles of relating, especially erratic and inappropriate kinds of distance and closeness; affective disorder, especially unacknowledged feelings of pervasive meaninglessness, pointlessness, and emptiness; and overall structure of the family, especially around pseudomutuality and related distortions. In other words, their work describes the family transmission of specific features of what we have been calling desymbolization and deformation. *

Family transmission of desymbolization can be experienced as a life-or-death matter. The suffocating pressures of "pseudomutuality" in the absence of vital symbolic exchange can leave the schizophrenic person with an either/or equation, "When I become born, Mother becomes dead"—"As though life may be in only one person; if it is in me, it is not in Mother; if it is in Mother, it is not in me."[50] This is a kind of absolute conflict over survival priority, in which full vitality (autonomy, separateness, and the psychic action of genuine symbolization) is equated with murdering another, sometimes with an intensity that "for the outsider had all the fascination of a fight unto death."[51]

And the process can be "deadening" (numbing) all around, since the family member who receives little response from a schizophrenic feels that "I as a subject have no object, I too am without life, for nowhere in that moment am I in the process of exercising the process of 'taking in' the process which designates life."[52] †

Of course genetic family transmission is also important. The genes' "encoded information" and "potential instruction" to the organism undoubtedly contribute to the deformations of schizophrenia. Recent adoption studies seem to

---

*The same principle applies to related studies by the Lidz-Fleck group demonstrating the "transmission of irrationality" and various forms of marital "schism and skew,"[49] and the Bateson group's focus on the "double bind."

† It is worth quoting further Monke's sensitive representation of the transaction between the schizophrenic person and someone near him, as the sequence vivifies our own paradigm:

"'Affect flatness' is the appropriate response to that situation which in the first person can be referred to as, 'I've had it with you.' It applies when 'I perpetually fear that you will engulf me as your object or, reciprocally, fear that should I venture to be so much a somebody that I would affect you, you would disappear as the object and I, because of having no object, would be again a non-somebody.' It would maintain when 'I give up

demonstrate significantly greater incidence of schizophrenia where a biological parent is schizophrenic and the adopted parents are not, as compared to situations in which an adopted parent is schizophrenic and the biological parents are not.[54] These studies, however, and especially their conclusions about genetic causation, have been questioned by investigators of family process,[55] who, in turn, point to new evidence of psychological transmission.[56] Nowhere is the old intellectual bugaboo of dualism more harmful than in pursuit of the nonquestion of heredity versus environment in the causation of schizophrenia. Even the "concept of interaction [of genetic and environmental factors] does not capture the unified complexity of development."[57]

In that "unified complexity" we may assume that only certain kinds of environments (a family, as already mentioned, but also of class and of subculture and larger culture, and perhaps certain forms of timing and even random experience) are likely to activate the potentially harmful, genetically influenced combination of traits that result in schizophrenia. None of this alters the fact that the schizophrenic response is mainly one of *psychological* manifestations. For instance, Manfred Bleuler rejects somatic theories of schizophrenia (such as "a brain lesion . . . or a pathology of metabolism") "just because I am attached to biology and to general medicine . . . [and] all the somatic theories of schizophrenia are open to the most severe criticism from biologists."[58] At the same time the structural-psychological disorder would seem to "have strong biological roots," to be related to "elementary perceptual processes."[59]

Genetic potential and family environmental influence converge on impaired capacity for symbolization, particularly symbolization of vitality, and consequent vulnerability of a fundamental kind to imagery of death and death equivalents.

There is some evidence to suggest that those who are vulnerable to

---

my congenital right that you permit me enough of a psyche so that I as a 'somebody' would be a subject who affects you as object.'

"When the above preposterous proposition maintains, I, in reaction to it, would cease 'affecting.' I would so behave that there would be nothing in me which you would recognize as affecting you, and there would be nothing in me which you would sense as something which you could affect.

"In poetic metaphor, I would speak of this defensive and protective maneuver *as a withdrawing of the psychic self onto the other side of a thick, plate-glass window through which one can see all about the world but through which the act of affecting does not occur either from the patient to the world or from the world to the patient.* By this maneuver to the other side of the big plate glass, the dreadful stresses are successfully avoided. However, there is now produced a secondary loneliness which has within it its own secondary type of anxiety. To tolerate this, the patient must develop a secondary type of relationship. I visualize this process as no different from the person who has secondary anxiety about being anxious, the maneuver which is characteristic of anxiety neurosis."[53]

schizophrenia on genetic and, possibly, environmental bases belong to society's more creative segment.[60] Death imagery, that is, either does one in or lends itself to imaginative achievement—depending upon one's capacity to order it, to hitch it to the formative-symbolizing process. And that process itself may have gray areas in which the breaking of old forms in the service of original synthesis is barely distinguishable from their break*down* in the service of schizophrenic disintegration.

Once more Schreber has something to tell us. A gifted, imaginative man, who had been a distinguished jurist prior to his breakdown, one reads his memoirs with respect for his intellect as well as sympathy for him in his suffering. Concerning the source of Schreber's paranoid schizophrenia, remarkable evidence has recently been uncovered concerning his father, a physician and educational reformer obsessed with principles of posture and obedience in child rearing. He developed a series of Draconian devices that literally strapped and bound children to the prescribed straight-arrow position, both during sleep and while awake and sitting. ("It is made of iron throughout," the inventor proudly declares, "preventing any attempt at improper sitting.") Dr. Schreber advocates, in one of his influential books, that the child in question should not only be immediately punished when violating rules, but required "to stretch out its hand to the executor of the punishment" in order to prevent "the possibility of spite and bitterness." Dr. Schreber was, in fact, a visionary who aimed at combating the decadence and degeneracy of youth and all vestiges in parents of what these days is called permissiveness. And "his aggressive efforts aimed toward the development of a better and healthier race of men."[61]

By his own admission, Dr. Schreber applied his belts, vises, and straps to his own children, probably more systematically to his two sons, one of whom committed suicide, while the other became the famous case—the three daughters apparently remained nonpsychotic. Clearly, Dr. Schreber's child-rearing approaches, especially toward his sons, must have included every feature research on schizophrenic families has emphasized, and more. We would focus on the threat of annihilation he posed for his boys, his carrying out that threat in the form of his Draconian procedures (in ways that must have been perceived by the boys as actually experiencing annihilation), and his own visionary commitments about a new race of men that sound not too different from his son's delusional system: "The father, with no little apostolic grandeur, strives for the development of better health and hygiene in an earthbound way, as it were; the son and his delusional elaboration of these precepts does so in an archaic, magical way."[62]

But there is more. Dr. Schreber's idiosyncrasies spilled over into an actual psychiatric syndrome. He was described once (on the basis of information given to a psychiatrist) as having "suffered from compulsive manifestations with murderous impulses"; by his biographer as having experienced a "protracted, chronic head condition" either connected with an accident in which a ladder fell on his head in his gymnasium or "possibly a severe nervous breakdown"; and by his daughter as having experienced a "strange disease of the head." All this developed during his fiftieth or fifty-first year (he died at the age of fifty-three from an intestinal disorder), just about the age at which his son underwent his first psychotic breakdown. At the very least he suffered from an unusually severe obsessive neurosis, and more likely from a paranoid psychosis not unlike that of his son. The inherited factor could be considerable; the psychological influence is surely catastrophic.* Again, it is not a question of either genetic or familial transmission alone, but rather a "unified complexity of development." To understand more about its operation, more about schizophrenia, we probably need to study patterns over several generations on the one hand, and their relationship to desymbolization and death imagery on the other.

The "soul murder" or inner disintegration of schizophrenia gives rise to extreme forms of numbing and deformation throughout the functioning of the self. At the immediate level, the schizophrenic feels himself flooded with death anxiety, which he both embraces and struggles against. At the ultimate level, his absence of connection beyond the self leaves him with the feeling that life is counterfeit, and that biological death is unacceptable and yet uneventful because psychic death is everywhere. Equating his very existence with transgression and the constant threat of annihilation, he makes his mocking compromise, the lifeless life.

*Morton Schatzman points to Schreber's persecution by his father, and argues from a general "transactional theory" of paranoia as originating in some form of persecution.[63] The theory may be almost correct, but neglects the symbolizing process—the recreation of whatever persecution has been undergone—from which the paranoid process takes shape. Without that symbolizing stress we could not address questions of why a paranoid psychosis occurs at a particular time and in relationship to a particular set of events.

SEVENTEEN

Suicide—The Quest for a Future

SUICIDE IS CRUCIAL to questions concerning death and continuing life. Suicide cannot be comprehended as merely a "psychiatric problem," yet it is central to a psychiatry that asks questions. Those questions tend to be blocked by a legacy of horror and condemnation, mainly Judeo-Christian in origin but affecting secular healers and theorists as well. There is also an opposite, partly rebound (and therefore psychologically related) tendency to surround suicide with a romantic aura. In either case, hard questions about protest and transformation can be asked,* no less than about death and destruction.

The logic of our paradigm requires us to consider what is psychologically specific to suicide even as we explore its varied imagery. There are fundamental psychological differences in the suicides of the deeply depressed and unfulfilled person, the gifted artist or writer, the religious or political martyr, the distraught paranoid schizophrenic, and the man who in quietly Socratic fashion makes a decision that death is preferable to a certain kind of living. Yet each performs an absolute act of self-destruction. Our unitary sense would insist that, whatever their differences, they share something of psychological importance. However diverse the meanings of induced death in various cultural and historical situations, we should not be blinded to the essential feature of all suicide: its violent statement about human connection, broken and maintained. †

---

* David Lester, after summarizing large numbers of suicide studies, was struck by the tendency to separate the subject from general psychological theory—by "just how isolated a topic suicidal behavior is in the realm of human behavior." [1]

† Of course, differentiating and classifying various forms of suicide remains extremely important. [2] The distinctions one makes among suicides are, in fact, crucial to a humane approach to the subject, but so is seeking common threads.

Karl Menninger spoke of suicide as "a peculiar kind of death which entails three elements: the element of dying, the element of killing, and the element of being killed." Suicide, he wrote, is "the death penalty self-inflicted." He closed his paper with a declaration of unitary principle: "The ordinary forms of suicide must stand as prototypes of acute generalized total self-destruction."[3]

Freud had also implied a unitary view of suicide when he said, "In the two opposed situations of being most intensely in love and of suicide, the ego is overwhelmed by the object, though in totally different ways."[4] There was a common ego state discernible in suicide. Freud said many things about that state, but subsequent psychoanalytic generations have overemphasized a stress on hostility ("murderous impulses" turned inward). They have insufficiently appreciated Freud's stress on disorganization of the ego along with "ego-splitting" ("The ego can kill itself only if . . . it can treat itself as an object").[5] Here Freud's reference-point was melancholia. He emphasized the predominance of narcissism and "the narcissistic type of object-choice," in which loss leads to dangerously self-destructive impulses. Now narcissism, in Freud's usage, is associated not only with fear of disintegration, but with self-administered annihilation.

Freud expressed his sweepingly unitary view of suicide in his elaboration of the death instinct. The death instinct could well be understood as a "suicide instinct"—a built-in mechanism of self-destruction that internally inclines the organism toward its own demise. Even murderous impulses toward others become understood as externalized expressions of the originally *self*-destructive manifestations of the death instinct. Freud's insight here (for which we do not need the death instinct) lies in his stress not on the fact of death alone, but also on the possibility of self-inflicted death as fundamental to human psychological experience.

Kurt Eissler elaborated on that ubiquitous human suicidal possibility:

> Relatively rare as suicide actually is, it must have a deep meaning, since of no one can it be said with certainty that he would never commit it. . . . That man can commit suicide and that the potentiality of such an action rests in every person, these are the essential points . . . that every human being possesses during most of his lifetime the capacity of committing suicide should be made the center of investigation. By and large I would say that in every analysis we have to grapple with suicidal tendencies in the patient.[6]

Eissler points out that only at the two extremes of the life cycle—infancy and early childhood on the one hand and senile dementia on the other—is man unable to commit suicide. And that the development of the self or ego both "increases the potentiality of life's prolongation and . . . creates the possibility of the organism's destruction by its own planned action."

Like a number of other writers on the subject, Eissler focuses on the element of denial— "For most suicides the act does not really mean dying"—and the related idea of "a rebellion against death."[7] But he also acknowledges that in certain cases, as in the suicide of some martyrs, "One can observe that the psychological problem of death really focuses around the preservation of a flow of time toward the future."[8] Here Eissler begins to suggest a relationship between suicide and symbolic immortality.*

Suicide has more of a place in human evolution than we generally wish to acknowledge. When man discovered death, began to symbolize, created culture—when man became man—he realized that he could kill others, and kill himself.

Early mythology supports these assumptions. A central myth of the people of West Ceram (in New Guinea), here paraphrased from a report by the German anthropologist Adolf Jensen, describes the close interrelationship of death and continuing life.

Ameta, a man from among the original "Nine families of mankind," goes out hunting with his dog and tracks down a wild pig, which drowns in a pond. He retrieves the dead animal, finds a coconut on its tusk, is told by a figure who appears to him at night that he should plant the coconut (in the earth) and a coconut palm (the first in the world) appears, and in three days grows tall and bears blossoms. Ameta seeks to cut some of the blossoms but slashes his finger, his blood falling on a leaf. At the place where the blood mingled with the sap of the cut blossom there appears a little girl, who (after Ameta, again following nocturnal instructions, takes her home) quickly turns into a nubile maiden with special gifts, including the capacity to defecate valuable articles of various kinds, which she lavishes on Ameta, as well as on others in the Nine families during the course of various dance ceremonies.

But the people, out of jealousy, kill her and throw her into the "innermost circle of the great ninefold spiral" of the Nine Dance Grounds. Ameta, referred to as her father, then takes nine fibers of the cocopalm leaf and sticks each into the earth, the ninth where the innermost circle had been. Discovering hairs and blood on the fiber when he removes it, he locates the corpse, and cuts it into many pieces, which he buries over the whole area of the Dancing Ground, and very quickly those remains turn into "things that up to that time had never existed

---

* Gregory Zilboorg had written similarly of an association of suicide with imagery of immortality among primitive peoples.[9] He attributed the primitive's frequent embrace of suicide and his eagerness to participate in various rituals of human sacrifice as a means of ensuring eternal life. As a Freudian rationalist, however, he viewed such behavior as an expression of narcissistic fantasy, of a "non-realistic and purely infantile way of achieving a seemingly adult goal," and therefore even a "perversion." And he applied those judgments to contemporary suicides in our own culture. Despite the limitations of Freudian rationalism, Zilboorg had a broad sense of the general importance of suicide in human evolution, cautioned against equating it with mental illness, and wrote: "Suicide is evidently as old as the human race, it is probably as old as murder and almost as old as natural death."[10]

anywhere on earth"—above all, certain tuberous plants that have been the principle food of the people ever since.

Ameta, however, retains two arms of the dead girl and brings them to the virgin goddess Satene, who, "furious at the people for having killed," builds an enormous gate on the dance grounds, consisting of a ninefold spiral, and stands on a log inside the gate, holding the severed arms in her two hands. She summons the people and says to them: "Because you have killed, I refuse to live here anymore: today I shall leave." She instructs them all to try to come to her through the gate, warning that "Those who succeed will remain people," but that "something else will happen" to those who fail, which turns out to be various transformations into animals or spirits, and "that is how it came about that pigs, deer, birds, fish, and many spirits inhabit the earth. Before that there had been only people."

But some make their way through to Satene, and each of these she strikes with one of the arms of the dead girl, those passing to the left of her having to jump across five sticks of bamboo, those to the right, across nine, thereby giving rise to the tribes known as Fivers and Niners. She tells them: "I am departing today and you will see me no more on earth. Only when you die will you again see me. Yet even then you shall have to accomplish a very difficult journey before you attain me."

She then disappears from the earth, and "now dwells on the mountain of the dead, in the southern part of West Ceram, and whoever desires to go to her must die. But the way to her mountain leads over eight other mountains. And ever since that day there have been not only men but spirits and animals on earth, while the tribes of man have been divided into the Fivers and the Niners." The dead maiden is revered among the tribes of West Ceram as the goddess Hainuwele, "Frond of the Cocopalm."[11]

Campbell stresses, as the leading theme of this mythology, "The coming of death into the world, . . . [with] the particular point . . . that death comes by way of murder." There is also the "interdependence of death and sex (related myths stress that the sexual organs appear with the coming of death) . . . and the necessity of killing—killing and eating—for the continuance of this state of being . . ." And Jensen, in his interpretation, points similarly to the principle that "every day men must kill, to maintain life. They kill animals and, apparently in the cult here being considered, the harvesting of plants was also regarded—quite correctly—as a killing . . . yet the death was extraordinarily quickly overcome by . . . new life. Thus there was made available to man a synthesizing insight, relating his own destiny to that of the animals, the plants, and the moon."[12] But we can also see in the myth scenes of sacrifice and of martyrdom approaching suicide. One goddess, Hainuwele, died involuntarily, but her death contributed to the origins and nurturing of her people. The other goddess, Satene, ends her own life on earth, partly to punish the people for their murder, and partly to oversee their development into tribes of men who have known death and murder. Both suggest the theme of the "dying god," whose death is in the service of the continuing physical and spiritual life of her/his people. In this case the two virgin figures can be understood as a composite goddess with a mission of sacrifice, martyrdom, and selective protection associated with moral instruction around the taking of others', and the surrendering of one's own, life.

In other myths and actual practices, the element of suicide, often of the divine representative, the king, is more explicit. In one part of southern India, it is reported, the king who had completed twelve years of rule would order a scaffolding made and assemble his people for a feast, have a ritual bath, and, to the sound of ceremonial, "before all the people he takes some very sharp knives, and begins to cut off his nose, and then his ears, and his lips and all his members, and as much flesh off himself as he can . . . until so much of his blood is spilled that he begins to faint, and then he cuts his throat himself."[13] The act was considered necessary for the proper transmission of the divine spirit to the next king, that is, for the perpetuation of a people's relationship to immortalizing powers.

Suicide in various forms seems sufficiently universal that one must suspect its practice to be compatible with the perpetuation of the human species. In any case, its practice in humans—and it doesn't occur in other species—is inevitably in the service of symbolized purpose and experience. As human beings, we would not know how to kill ourselves in the absence of some internalized mental structure around the meaning of that act. And analogously, no cultural practice (or prohibition) of suicide can be devoid of shared meanings around the act.

Yet the literature on the attitudes toward suicide of various cultures is unusually confusing. The central difficulty lies in the either/or assumption that a particular culture prohibits or else honors suicide. It may in fact do both.

Zilboorg, after a rather careful survey of primitive suicide, concludes that the lower the cultural level, "the more deep-seated the suicidal impulse appears, and as a result the folk-lore of the majority of primitive races idealizes rather than condemns suicide."[14] Yet when we read Frazer,[15] we learn that in primitive societies, "The spirits of persons who have taken their own life are commonly regarded with dread and fear, and special precautions are taken by the living to guard against these dangerous ghosts." (We recognize here the threatening "homeless dead" of our earlier discussion.) Among all cultures the incidence of suicide seems comparable: "recent anthropological studies carried out among African tribes have revealed that their frequence of suicide was about the same as that of European countries."[16]

The ancient Greeks, Jacques Choron tells us, "considered suicide as a 'natural' and fitting solution to a variety of precarious situations." (He points to a number of examples, including the first suicide mentioned by Homer, that of Jocasta, mother of Oedipus; the mass suicides at Corcyra recorded by Thucydides; and of course in post-Homeric Greece, the death of Socrates.)[17]

But why then, we may ask, was it also customary in ancient Greece "to cut off the right hand of a suicide and bury it apart from his body, no doubt in order to disarm his ghost, by depriving him of the use of his right hand"?[18]

Even the well-documented antagonism to suicide of Christian cultures during medieval and modern times is two-sided. There is no doubt about the extremity of Christian sanctions against suicide. During the Middle Ages, for instance, official church doctrine (followed rather closely in this area by most European governments) considered suicide a form of murder in which man became "his own assassin."[19] The bodies of suicides were frequently mutilated, and Frazer refers to a custom, extending into modern times in England, in which "a person against whom a coroner's jury had found a verdict of suicide used to be buried at cross-roads with a stake driven through the body, no doubt to prevent the ghost from walking, and attacking the survivors."[20]

Nor is there any doubt about the intensity of theological positions on suicide—from St. Augustine's designation of suicide (at the end of the fourth century) as a crime for which there is no possibility of repentance; to Thomas Aquinas's insistence (thirteenth century) that suicide is unnatural in its absence of charity toward the self and usurps God's power to dispose at his discretion of man's life, death, and resurrection;[21] to later and equally adamant Protestant declarations, which could at times be even more uncompromising in the absence of a postdeath purgatory in which sins might be expiated.

Yet Christianity is not unique in these attitudes: in contrast to the Old and New Testament, in which suicide is nowhere explicitly condemned, the Kur'ān refers to it as a crime worse than homicide.[22] We recognize in these attitudes a continuity with primitive societies' terror of dangerous spirits, around which suicides seem to be equated with vampires. But a key to Christian attitudes—and in fact collective views on suicide in general—is given us by the Reverend Tuke, a seventeenth-century English preacher:

> There be two sorts of voluntarie deathes, the one lawful and honest, such as the death of martyrs, the other dishonest and unlawful, when men can have neyther lawfull calling, nor honest endes, as of Peregrinus, who burnt himself in a pile of wood, thinking thereby to live forever in mens remembrance. . . . It may be demanded, whether the death of Christ and of the holy martyrs may be called voluntarie, seeing they died at the command and by the execution of others. I answere, their death was voluntarie but not with wicked willfullnesse sustained of them. For Christ could have saved himselfe, when hee suffered himself to be apprehended, condemned, and executed . . . so the martyrs would willingly embrace the fire, rather than dishonour God by cowardize, and loose their soules by Apostacie.[23]

We are instructed here on the moral distinction between honorable suicide (on behalf of a culture's ultimate concerns) and dishonorable (separate from or in conflict with those concerns). We also get a sense of the power of the *ideal* of suicide, via martyrdom, from the very beginning of the Christian experience. Even during the present age, imagery of martyrdom can reassert itself strongly— as I found in research interviews, in the mid-fifties, with Catholic priests who had been imprisoned in China. Such imagery has also undoubtedly been important for Catholic priests and Protestant ministers who opposed either political persecutions in South America or an unjust war fought by the United States, in ways that involved considerable personal risk. While all militant movements·encourage a degree of martyrdom, Christianity's doctrinal stress on other-worldly perfection as an ultimate goal renders the martyr's suicide especially attractive. That doctrine, along with the Christ story itself, also provides a great temptation toward suicide that can be construed as martyrdom. This Christian temptation to suicide must be understood as a very important factor in the equally intense Christian reaction against suicide. Theologically and psychologically, one is likely to be most absolute in prohibiting precisely the transgression that combines great appeal with potential disruption.

It would seem that all cultures have a place for suicide—recognize it as a human option—along with a certain mixture of awe, terror, and prohibition. That is, suicide is universally viewed both as possible and a threat to a particular group's definition of human connection. So cultures, religions, governments, and political movements permit, or even embrace, certain forms of suicide, designate specific sets of circumstance and ritual that mobilize suicide on behalf of immortalizing principles. Christian martyrdom is one such example. Another is the Japanese ritual suicide *(seppuku* or *harakiri)*. In each case one ends one's life voluntarily (though sometimes in response to pressures that can become coercive) in ways that reassert eternal principles. These principles are served by encouraging specific forms of suicide and prohibiting others. And the emphasis may change so that now the advocacy (of the prescribed forms of suicide) is uppermost, now the prohibition (of all other forms). Everything depends on which way the winds of immortality are blowing.

The whole issue of control and death-management is enormously important in suicide.* The designation of who may or should kill himself, and under what

---

* At an immediate level, that management permits the moment of death to epitomize such samurai values as courage, stoicism, poise, and even swordsmanship. But the meaning of the act speaks to ultimate involvements, the reassertion of the immortalizing samurai ethos. In that sense the role of one's group—the samurai class, and the society it dominated—in staging the drama is all-important. The individual samurai was surely the star, but there was no provision for spontaneity or even leeway in performance—only exact criteria for honor and perhaps even perfection (having to do with cutting deeply and widely, and spilling out one's intestines, while seemingly oblivious to the pain). Of course there are again Christian parallels—not in direct violence to oneself, but in showing related traits of courage and faith, while doing a great deal to orchestrate one's death as a martyr. As a Christian, the self-destruction was in the service of the deity and those who worshiped him; as a samurai, it was the deified human group—the samurai-led collectivity—to which one's self-immolation was dedicated. In either case one sought one's death on behalf of immortal life.

circumstances, gets to the essence of a group's relationship to and control over life and death. The only comparable form of life-death control is the death penalty, as Karl Menninger's previously quoted characterization suggests. (One could argue that wartime military conscription, as a coercive requirement that one enter a deadly situation, is another example, though much more indirect. And with the development of nuclear and biological weapons and pollutions, that risk is extended more or less indiscriminately, so that the would-be controller loses control and can no longer select a particular group to be at risk.) In Japanese society, for instance, ritual suicide could be an option given a condemned man as an honorable alternative to execution. That alternative was only available to those of samurai standing, who were expected to live, kill, and die within the strict requirements of the overall ritual structure. (Others who transgressed might be summarily executed or even mutilated, that is, subjected to starkly contrasting forms of dishonor in dying.) When the samurai takes the honorable option, as all self-respecting members of his class and caste would be expected to do, he both does the work of the authorities in ridding them of a transgressor, and, more important, reasserts in the most absolute and edifying fashion their sacred precepts concerning human existence. *

* The most celebrated example of this, in Japanese culture and perhaps in all of human history, is that of the "forty-seven ronin." These "righteous samurai" of the early eighteenth century avenged the death of their lord, which had been brought about through trickery, by vowing to kill the responsible person, and then going through years of planning, deprivation, and disguise, in order to carry out their vow. Having accomplished their act of revenge, which was, of course, a legal transgression, they were permitted by the authorities to commit mass *seppuku* or ritual suicide. Their act has been lovingly recreated in Kabuki theater, film, and virtually every other art form. As psychologist Tsurumi Shunsuke has written, "The Japanese people have great sympathy for a situation in which a world moves slowly toward suicide for a satisfactory purpose."[24]

That was true of Japanese "double love suicide" (*shinju*), which became quite popular with the evolving merchant class during the eighteenth century and afterward. Lovers, kept from each other by social obligations, killed themselves together, seeking to complete their love in death, and thereby affirm and immortalize it. Though it was an act of rebellion against proper (and legal) society, double suicide achieved enough of a kind of popular/adversary tradition to become itself a part of the general social equilibrium. Neither the shared passion, the outcome, nor the subsequent celebration of love suicide in Kabuki and puppet theater in any way threatened the social order. Rather, the imagery of erotic transcendence provided society with an alternative to stern samurai self-control, one that was both hedonistic and ultimately obedient to samurai-dominated social regulations. One may call some of these practices "altruistic suicide" (as Durkheim did) or "thanatological" or "cultural suicide" (as Shneidman and Farbarow have more recently), but such labeling tends to isolate them from the general phenomenon of suicide.

There are, of course, European versions of love suicide, notably in the German romantic mystique that reached its apotheosis in Wagner, especially the "Liebestod" of *Tristan and Isolde*. Literary imagination and the practice of love suicide (in this case single rather than double) came together most dramatically in the West in Goethe's novel, *The Sorrows of Young Werther*. Just before shooting himself, Werther cries, "She

We would expect, then, that individual suicide would require a sense of extremity (in the face of cultural awe and dread) as well as an impulse toward purpose and meaning around killing oneself. Psychological discussions of suicide have extensively discussed the first, but neglected the second. Nor have the sense of extremity and quest for purpose been adequately explored in relationship to death and death equivalents, a relationship toward which our paradigm would clearly point. The sense of extremity is perceived in an immediate way, while struggles around meaning are of course ultimate matters—but in an action as absolute as destroying oneself, the distinction, too, is obliterated: both levels are fully involved in all feelings.

Suicide is, of course, violence. The "cide" in the word is associated with killing and murder (insecticide, homicide, regicide, and genocide). We should not be surprised to find suicidal impulses coexisting with homicidal ones. The coexistence is not illuminated by assuming a common source in the death instinct, or the back-and-forth movement of rage that is now externalized, now internalized.

Let us look briefly at the much-publicized example of Gary Gilmore, who

---

is mine, thou art mine forever." This epitomizes romantic immortalization in dying. Werther, that ultimate young "martyr of unrequited love and excessive sensibility," [25] touched an international nerve of suicide— "*Werther* fever, a *Werther* fashion . . . *Werther* caricatures, *Werther* suicides . . . and not only in Germany but in England, France, Holland and in Scandinavia . . . even the Chinese . . . painted Lotte and Werther on porcelain . . ." [26]

The *Werther* epidemic even spread to Japan and profoundly influenced the suicide practices of a culture so renowned for its sophistication in self-destruction. Goethe's biographer reports that "his greatest personal triumph was when Napoleon told him at their meeting that he had read the book seven times." We have the suggestion, at least, of a common romanticism around death, of Napoleon and *Werther* (if not Goethe himself) as supplicants at the altar of death as an avenue to immortality, the suicide of the one making contact with the mass military homicide of the other. While Goethe and Napoleon were hardly without official connections, European suicides have also been called forth as absolute expressions of undermining authority, or as expressions of liberation from the control of absolute authority. An example of the first is the post-World War I Dada movement in art and culture, "whose reign in Paris began with a suicide, ended with one, and included others in its progress; whose aim was 'destructive agitation against *everything*' ('no more painters . . . writers . . . religions . . . republicans . . . imperialists . . . Bolsheviks . . . politicians . . . armies . . . nations . . . no more, NOTHING, NOTHING, NOTHING'); and whose essence was expressed by one practitioner's slogan, 'Suicide is a vocation.' " [27] An example of the second could be found in the suicides of certain Jewish inmates of Nazi death camps, who killed themselves with the conscious purpose, articulated in suicide notes, of taking that prerogative away from their captors and thereby asserting a recognition of the fact of attempted extermination and a possibility of resistance and revitalization. [28] My argument is not that the usually desperate individual who kills himself explicitly follows any of these patterns, but rather that they have some bearing on his action, that he is a creature of a shared human constellation around suicide, which each of these conventions reflects.

was executed by the State of Utah in January, 1977. Convicted of two murders, he repeatedly expressed his desire to die: in public statements, letters and poetry, and actual suicide attempts. One examining psychiatrist pointed out that he "went out of his way to get the death penalty; that's why he pulled two execution-style murders he was bound to be caught for. I think it's a legitimate question, based on this evidence and our knowledge of the individual, to ask if Gilmore would have killed if there was not a death penalty in Utah."[29] A number of psychiatric reports, including a recent one by George F. Solomon,[30] have stressed the suicidal motive in many murders, documented by cases in which killers imagined their execution prior to committing their crimes. These cases are reminiscent of the sequence we discussed earlier, from severe depression and numbing to relief and recovered life-energy by means of violence; and we can say that suicide becomes a (if not the) motivation for murder. Our paradigm would further suggest that in suicide there is also recourse to violence as a quest for something on the order of vitality.

But there would seem to be a considerable contradiction in killing onself, bringing one's individual life to an extreme end, as a means of seeking vitality. Eissler expresses the belief "that for most suicides the act does not mean really dying," but is a rebellion against death, an illusion of having become independent, stepped outside nature, and cheated death.[31] Others have similarly emphasized the "irrational," "magical," and "narcissistic" features of suicide. And Shneidman and Farbarow have emphasized the "psychosemantic fallacy" in the logic of the suicide by which they mean his faulty assumption that the "I" or self he destroys will be present to witness the effects of his action—that, as he writes in his note, "I can see you crying" and "I will actually witness such things." Even the "cultural suicide" (along the lines we have discussed), according to these two authors, errs "in the overemphasis on the self as experienced by others."[32] There is truth in these views; these elements of denial and illusion can be present in varying degrees in different cases of suicide. But the emphasis on irrationality tends to neglect the all-important symbolizing principle around suicide, and, however inadvertently, to continue to isolate suicide from the rest of psychological experience.

It is quite possible, that, in suicide, one wants both to die and to live. With the increasing availability of drugs that lead painlessly to fatal coma, the act need not be associated with violent imagery of bodily annihilation or strangulation. Violent imagery may mainly have to do with the totality of self-destruction. More important is the question of what the act of killing oneself seeks to assert, a question that is not clarified by quick recourse to either/or dualities around rationality.

Yet suicide is at the same time the epitome of the totalistic act—self-destruction that (in Menninger's words) is acute, generalized, and total. To describe the state of the mind that carries out that act, writers have used metaphors like being cornered, trapped, encircled, having all exits blocked.[33] In killing oneself one is doing something about one's life—hence the concept of suicide as a "cry for help"[34] or "not as an effort to die but rather as a communication to others in an effort to improve one's life."[35]

Killing oneself may appear to be the only way to break out of the "trap" or "encirclement" and assert whatever it is one feels one wants to, or must, about one's life. One lacks the power to express that assertion in living, or even the power that certain forms of madness, or extreme psychological disorder, provide for alternative forms of assertion that at least keep one's life going. This powerlessness is described, in one form or another, throughout the literature on suicide, and is a particularly intense form of what we have been calling stasis. It can be associated with great hostility and various forms of internal "splitting" or disintegration, both of which Freud emphasized. But the more fundamental quality is a sense of the absence, or threatened absence, of life-power, unless one takes that suicidal step.

One cannot approach that kind of emotion without relating it to ultimate involvements, where the relevant emotion is despair. People who commit suicide may or may not be significantly depressed, but they are almost certain to be affected by despair—by a sense of radical absence of meaning and purpose, and of the impossibility of human connection. Despair is an issue even in suicides associated with cultural revitalization (Christian martyrdom or Japanese *seppuku*). The despair may be anticipated should one fail to end one's life for the higher purpose, or it may be very much present in combination with the quest for collective renewal (as we shall see in our discussion of Yukio Mishima). The despair or potential despair, moreover, is likely to have an absolute quality—it pervades (or is anticipated as pervading) all immediate as well as ultimate involvements. This pervasive hopelessness has begun to impress psychiatrists as an important feature of much mental disorder, though we still have difficulty talking about it. To understand the feeling-tone, one must consider both what is absent and what is present. Absent is a sense that the elements of the experience can ever become significant or pleasurable, that internal or psychic action can ever be resumed or lead to vitality, that larger meaning structures can prevail—unless one takes the necessary action. Present is an overwhelming sense of being hemmed in, blocked, thwarted, a sense of the impossibility of achieving form or meaning, ("icebound," in Binswanger's term) and of all this being permanent and unalterable.

Despair and hopelessness are associated with perceptions of the future. One's ultimate involvements are so impaired that one is simply unable to imagine a psychologically livable future. Whatever future one can imagine is no better, perhaps much worse, than the present ("However low a man has sunk, he can sink even lower, and this 'can' is the object of his dread," is the way Kierkegaard put the matter.)[36] *More specifically, the suicide can create a future only by killing himself.* That is, he can reawaken psychic action and imagine vital events beyond the present only in deciding upon, and carrying through, his suicide.

And for that period of time, however brief, he lives with an imagined future. That is why Gabriel Marcel could speak of suicide as a "radical rejection of being" that is at the same time "a demonic affirmation of self."[37] That relationship to the future is what Farber has in mind when he speaks of people committing suicide in order to avoid "acknowledging or dealing with meaninglessness."[38]

The specificity of despair, rather than depression, has been highlighted in a number of recent studies. As one investigator put it, "Suicidal preoccupations seemed . . . related to the patient's conceptualization of his situation as untenable or hopeless . . . The suicidal patients generally stated that they regarded suicide as the only possible solution for their desperate or hopeless situations."[39] And again: ". . . the cognitive element of negative expectations . . . [is] a stronger indicator of suicidal intent than depression itself."[40] While these findings have been questioned,[41] related observations continue to be made. One possible source of confusion is again the "cognitive" versus "emotive" dualism, since what is involved is an inclusive form of symbolization involving all levels of the self.

The despair is not just a function of one's individual life but of what is happening in relationship to one's group. (Durkheim well understood this.) When one's group is a primitive culture, the despair is likely to be compounded of dislocation (or separation) and thwarted expressions of anger, or what has been called "thwarting disorientation."[42] When one's group becomes the mental hospital, one's degree of despair can be acutely sensitive to its social structure, to the extent that suicide becomes more likely when there are disturbing upheavals or merely extensive turnover among the staff.[43] The "contagion" and even "epidemic" quality of suicide can be both a function of general breakdown of imagery of connection within a particular group and the spreading intensification within individuals of the suicidal constellation—the idea that one might actually kill oneself. That inner construct or model of suicide seems to me of great importance in our understanding of the entire issue, and we shall have more to say about it.

It is always *oneself* one kills, or tries to, and not an "internalized other." However much one has internalized imagery of important people, the resulting psychic constellations are one's own. Even the most powerful and enduring image-feelings—such as those concerning parents—are constantly recreated and recombined with other components of the self and its constellations. Specific relationships can of course greatly influence ultimate suicide, but only insofar as these relationships affect the entire self. Suicide is an act of the total self against the total self. It hinges upon the state, immediate and ultimate, of the total self at any given time.

Freud's instinctualism rendered him too literal when he declared that "We have long known . . . that no neurotic harbours thoughts of suicide which he has not turned back upon himself from murderous impulses against others."[44] He went on to say that the analysis of melancholia explained the interplay of forces that enabled one to carry out that impulse, by demonstrating that "the ego can kill itself only if . . . it can treat itself as an object [meaning another person]—if it is able to direct against itself the hostility which relates to an object and which represents the ego's original reaction to objects in the external world." Here Freud raises but does not pursue two significant directions of thought. The first has to do with what it means to turn oneself into an "object." In the case of melancholia, the survivor struggles, as Freud emphasizes, to recover his relationship with the dead person as well as to free himself from that relationship, so that the "object" one turns oneself into is none other than that dead person. The implication is that the suicide sees his self as no longer a live element of his own, and there is a perception of a deadened self in that objectification alone. That perception is furthered by an actually dead person, so that Freud was describing a mechanism that operates in the survivor's refusal of further life. What is interesting in his description is the suggestion (and here I am carrying further what is implicit in Freud's thought) that one must see one's self as already dead in order to kill it.

The second implicit point has to do with the relationship of that self-killing to one's general set of human relationships—the suggestion that, after all, the suicide is an aspect of one's larger involvements. A bit later in the passage, Freud states that an original relationship or internalized "object . . . has . . . proved more powerful than the ego itself" (so that in order to get rid of it one must kill one's own ego or self). This idea is related to our concept of suicide as the destruction of the self on behalf of a larger principle, of a quest for meaning.

Intense hostility is nonetheless frequent in people who attempt suicide. But that hostility, too, has been found to be independent of the degree of depression, and is related to the "thwarting" aspects of despair mentioned earlier. From our standpoint we would expect anger and rage to reflect the combinations of powerlessness and "encirclement." It is not a matter of turning hostility or instinctual aggression against the self. Rather, the rage and self-destructive impulses are both aspects of the sense of being trapped, powerless, and "futureless" in relationship to immediate and ultimate experience. An actual suicide, in its imagined effects on specific people and in the way it is performed, can, of course, express rage rather directly. Yet it is also probably true that, where rage exists, there is at least the possibility of an alternative to suicide—an expression of protest, or attempts to injure or even kill others. But where that particular quality of despair exists to the point of suppressing even anger and rage, with their possibility for some kind of vitality, one may be still closer to the suicidal act.

Suicide notes often reveal the struggle for meaning. They can be confusing documents, the interpretation of which may say as much about the reader as the writer. But they can also be pithy, distinguishable from fabricated equivalents by their directness and no-nonsense character.* The seeming contradiction derives from the genre itself—the attempt to sum up in a few lines one's overall rationale (the meaning of the act) and its bearing on important life relationships. Leslie Farber thus speaks of the note, in the process of being composed by the would-be suicide, as "a formidable and frustrating document . . . since it must justify what cannot be justified."[46] That is so because the suicide himself senses that "instead of finding his life he ends it."

But ending one's life is itself a way of finding it, for some, the only way. Binswanger, for instance, says of his patient: "In this resolve [to settle her situation in the act of killing herself] Ellen West did not 'grow beyond herself,' but rather, only in her decision for death did she find herself and choose herself."[47]

And Antonin Artaud, the revolutionary dramatist, explained:

> If I commit suicide, it will not be to destroy myself but to put myself back together again. Suicide will be for me only one means of violently reconquering myself, of brutally invading my being, of anticipating the unpredictable approaches of God. By suicide, I reintroduce my design in nature, I shall for the first time give things the shape of my will. . . .[48]

While Binswanger may have overstated things a bit, and while Artaud was mad as well as gifted, they articulate the powerful theme of suicide as self-completion, as the only means of appropriately locating oneself in the "design" of the cosmos. This theme is present in every suicide, however agonizing or demeaning the circumstances. The act of suicide is an expression of formative process, even as it ends that process in the individual. It is an attempt to transform one's existence radically—an "urge for hasty transformation . . . the late reaction of a delayed life which did not transform as it went along."[49]

This discussion so far has moved between presenting suicide, on the one hand, in terms of what might be called its universal logic and its relationship to meaning and immortality; and on the other, in terms of inner disturbance, of

---

* For instance, the fabricated note: "Darling: All of my life I have looked upon suicide as a weak and cowardly way out but after thinking it out carefully I honestly believe that this is the best way. I realize that this will be quite a shock to you but as you know, time heals all wounds, and as time goes on I hope you will realize that this was the best solution of our problems. Please try to explain to Tom and teach him to grow into a fine man, far better I hope than his dad has been.

"My insurance will take care of both of you at least until Tom is through school. God bless and keep you both. All my love is for you and Tom forever and ever.

Bill"

And the actual note: "I'm tired. There must be something fine for you. Love.

Bill"[45]

powerlessness, despair, and the sense of being trapped. All suicide is related to both components, and even where the one seems to predominate there are likely to be quiet manifestations of the other. (In suicide as much as in any form of exploration of man, we should be wary of either/or judgments and expect surprises.)

Our emphasis on proximate and ultimate involvements helps us construct the model of suicide that can apply whether the act appears to emerge from immortalizing commitment or personal misery. At the proximate level we have identified such feelings as profound powerlessness, a sense of isolation, severe numbing or inner deadness, anger to the point of rage, varying degrees of guilt and self-condemnation, and a consuming sense of being trapped, thwarted, unable to extricate onself from this predicament through any life process. But while few would deny the existence of overall stasis and other death equivalents among the miserable, there is little evidence that these are present, say, in priests seeking martyrdom or samurai preparing for *seppuku*. And the same objection might be made concerning patterns at the ultimate level—profound despair related to the absence of connection or commitment of an enduring or symbolic immortalizing kind, and hopelessness concerning the possibility of connecting with any such currents by means of a life process. Again, doubts can be raised about the applicability of this constellation to the suicide willingly or even joyfully performed on behalf of immortalization of the group. The answer—the integrating principle—lies in the anticipated self-judgment should one fail to carry out the prescribed form of suicide.*

But an additional element seems to be required: the suicidal image-construct in which the act of killing oneself is a specific possibility, something that can be done. It may be transmitted culturally—from early childhood teachings and psychological messages through adult ideological and physical conditioning; and systematically implanted as an image of ultimate virtue, to be enacted whenever circumstances demand. The construct becomes an integral part of both proximate and ultimate experience—in its constant immediacy as something one might concretely do, and in its association with the revered,

---

* The samurai confronted with the appropriateness of *seppuku* has been trained from birth to take the path of honor, that is, the path prescribed by the samurai ethos; and to experience profound shame and guilt not only when he fails to do so but in *anticipation* of such failure. That is what is meant by the "shame sanction" or "guilt sanction." That anticipated shame and guilt was undoubtedly powerful in samurai confronting *seppuku*, serving as a powerful negative stimulus for carrying out the extreme act. To refuse to do so would have left one either publicly or privately disgraced, with the sense of being no longer a true samurai, which meant for one born to the class being no longer a vital human being. In other words, one was confronted with a "living death," something close to the full gamut of feelings around powerlessness and despair we have described for more ordinary suicide. The samurai or martyr anticipates the psychological "death sentence" that the ordinary suicide has lived with for some time. Both must kill themselves if they are to escape or transcend that existential condemnation.[50]

immortalizing principles of one's group. It provides positive motivation, inseparable from the negative anticipation of existential dishonoring associated with failed enactment. This combined motivation helps mobilize the will and energy for carrying out the extreme act.

The image-model of suicide becomes a more individual matter in contemporary American society. At least a faint version of it is culturally available—we all know that there is such a thing as suicide, and that each of us is potentially capable of performing it. But for suicide to become a more concrete likelihood, the model seems to require additional, more specific experience. For instance, clinicians have long had the impression that people are more likely to attempt suicide when other family members have done so. There is no evidence that inclination toward suicide as such can be inherited, though one cannot rule out genetic transmission of various kinds of vulnerability that might be associated with suicide. But probably of much greater importance is the family transmission of what we have been calling the suicide image-construct. If a family member, especially a parent, has committed suicide, one is likely to form a strong image of that act, an image which can take on great relevance for one's own struggles. Experiences of separation and loss, whether or not originally associated with the parental suicide, can readily infuse the suicidal constellation. Just as imagery of death equivalents in general are in back-and-forth association with that of actual death, a similar interaction can develop between death equivalents and the suicide construct. Whenever one feels abandoned, torn apart, or immobilized, an image of suicide may be evoked. Similarly, any new encounter with suicide (of people one knows or even hears or reads about) can intensify inseparable fears of disintegration, separation, and stasis. It is quite possible that where a parental suicide has loomed large, a child can almost come to equate death with suicide. That situation would create, from the first, an encompassing suicide construct, which would be called forth and in some degree intensified by every single threatening life encounter.*

A strong suicide construct can, of course, emerge in people with no such family tradition. The sources of the construct may be obscure (and this is an area that needs investigation). Important transmission of suicidal imagery may occur from parents who have made abortive suicide attempts or "gestures," or who have unusually active and disturbing suicidal imagery, even in the absence of such attempts. Or, less specifically, they may convey messages, perhaps not

---

* Some evidence for this line of thought can be found in research that documents relationship between suicidal attempt and "completed" parental suicide,[51] while failing to demonstrate any significant correlation of suicide with increased mental illness in parents.[52] (I do not think these patterns have been absent in culturally prescribed suicides; the samurai whose father committed *seppuku* is likely to grow up with an even stronger suicide construct than others of his class, a construct which may be associated with related [especially in Japanese culture] passions of revenge or embrace of the warrior ethos.)

necessarily despairing ones, about existence and nonexistence and the desirability of either—messages which, in the course of the formative process, enter strongly into a suicide construct. Or finally, where death equivalents are unusually strong early in life, they can themselves (by process we do not now understand) give rise to a strong suicide construct. Whatever the degree of actual suicide imagery early in life, the death equivalents are central to an emerging suicide construct.

Over the course of childhood, this construct may be accompanied by varying degrees of conscious suicidal imagery. And there is likely to be a particularly intense version of such ordinary refrains as "I could kill myself" or "I wish I were dead." At some point, usually during adolescence or adult life, the idea of suicide takes hold concretely as a potential individual act. One can then deal with the construct in a great variety of ways. Again, like imagery of death itself, it can be a source of creative or constitutive energy. Or it may become associated with extensive numbing, so that it serves as a kind of repository for unacknowledged despair. In that way the suicide construct may replace the act, either temporarily or over the course of a "life of suicide." One may then make to oneself a series of threats—if this doesn't happen, or that doesn't improve, I will kill myself.[53] But just as we have learned to be humble about making absolute distinctions between genuine suicide attempts and mere "gestures," so is it difficult to say just when this kind of "life of suicide" destabilizes and is terminated. Here, investigators speak of degree of "lethality" or even of a "continuum of lethality" having to do, we would say, with the interaction between lifelong constellations of all kinds at proximate and ultimate levels on the one hand and the nature and intensity of the suicide construct on the other. The latter has been much neglected in thoughts about suicide, but is extremely important in determining why some kill themselves instead of becoming mentally ill or living either in numbed despair or in the ordinary realm of conflict, pain, and possibility.

At the end of his valuable study, Alvarez tells of his own suicide attempt, and in the process describes with unusual vividness the evolution of a suicide constellation over the various stages we have mentioned.

I built up to the act carefully and for a long time, with a kind of blank pertinacity. It was the one constant focus of my life, making everything else irrelevant, a diversion. . . . I see now that I had been incubating this death far longer than I recognized at the time. When I was a child, both my parents had half-heartedly put their heads in the gas oven. Or so they claimed. It seemed to me then a rather splendid gesture, though shrouded in mystery, a little area of veiled intensity, revealed only by hints and unexplained, swiftly suppressed outbursts. It was something hidden, attractive and not for children, like sex. But it was also something that undoubtedly did happen to grownups . . . suicide was a fact, a subject that couldn't be denied; it was something however awful, that people did. When my own time came, I did not have to discover it for myself.

Maybe that is why, when I grew up and things went particularly badly, I used to say to myself, over and over . . . "I wish I were dead." . . . I muttered it unthinkingly, as automatically as a Catholic priest tells his rosary . . . : "Iwishiweredead . . . Iwishiweredead . . . Iwishiweredead. . . ." Then one day I understood what I was saying. I was walking along the edge of Hampstead Heath, after some standard domestic squabble, and suddenly I heard the phrase as though for the first time. I stood still to attend to the words. I repeated them slowly, listening. And realized that I meant it. It seemed so obvious, an answer I had known for years and never allowed myself to acknowledge. I couldn't understand how I could have been so obtuse for so long.[54]

Alvarez's artistic sensibility enables him to evoke the sequence of imagery through which the suicidal image takes shape, exists continuously, and at length becomes a life focus. Eventually, following a period of isolation, a battle with his wife, and her departure, he took forty-five sleeping pills which he had been collecting for this moment. He went into a deep coma and barely survived. Subsequently, he felt that "in some way I *had* died" but "somehow I felt, death had let me down; I had expected more of it. I had looked for something overwhelming, an experience which would clarify all my confusions. . . . We all expect something of death, even if it's only damnation."[55]

Here Alvarez brings out the element of anticipation that is so important in all suicides, not just the culturally prescribed forms. Suicide always seeks to achieve something, even if only peace or an end to pain. That quest is inseparable from expectation, from anticipation. Alvarez himself treats it self-mockingly ("I had thought death would be like the last reel of one of those old Hitchcock thrillers, when the hero relives as an adult that traumatic moment in childhood . . . and thereby becomes free and at peace with himself"), but goes on to suggest that the expectation runs deep (as in his "Last Judgment" example). The symbolic truth of the expectation has to do with the actual transformation one brings about in dying and the larger statement the act makes about questions of meaning in one's existence.

We can suggest the application of this model by examining some of the details of the suicide of a famous patient, Ellen West, who has become almost a legend in the literature of existential psychiatry.[56] In the next chapter we will consider the suicide of the Japanese writer, Yukio Mishima, whose melodramatic disembowelment reverberates in the minds of many Japanese and others throughout the world.

Ellen West killed herself during her thirty-third year. She had been immobilized by psychological disturbance most of her life, had received various forms of psychiatric and psychoanalytic treatment without improvement, and for a ten-week period just prior to her death was the patient of Ludwig Binswanger, from whose account we draw here. Binswanger, an early practitioner of existential psychoanalysis, was a younger contemporary of Freud, and despite their ideological differences a close friend. Binswanger's case report of Ellen West is detailed, and although at times encumbered by some of the convoluted obscurity of the German existential tradition, is brilliant and illuminating. (I draw from it selectively in relating it to our model.)

In Ellen West's family, two uncles (from among her father's five brothers) killed themselves, and a third was described as "severely ascetic." The father himself, "for whom Ellen's love and veneration knew no bounds," though a man of action was inwardly vulnerable and suffered from "nocturnal depressions and states of fear accompanied by self-reproaches." Her mother was described as a "kindly, suggestible, nervous woman, who underwent a depression for three years during the time of her engagement." Ellen's younger brother was briefly hospitalized at seventeen "on account of a mental ailment with suicidal ideas," from which he recovered only partially.

Binswanger places this information under "heredity," and one can hardly rule out hereditary vulnerabilities. But we would see it as the almost exaggerated beginnings of a suicide constellation. Not surprisingly, Ellen West began to give expression to that constellation early, and it was to become the dominant theme of her life.

She was described as a lively but "headstrong and violent" child, who, even when very young, "had days when everything seemed empty to her and she suffered under a pressure which she herself did not understand." A good student, she would "weep for hours" when she did not come out first in her favorite subjects; was "boyish" and preferred to wear trousers and play boyish games until an infatuation beginning at age sixteen. But in a poem written in her seventeenth year she "still expressed the ardent desire to be a boy, for then she would be a soldier, fear no foe, and die joyously, sword in hand." She wrote other romantic poems describing exultant joy, confusion, and darkness. One was entitled "Kiss Me Dead," calling upon the Sea-King to come to her, take her into his arms and kiss her to death.

Praising at eighteen the blessing of work she wrote: "What would we be without work, what would become of us? I think they would soon have to enlarge the cemeteries for those who went to death of their own accord." She also asked: "What for—why all this? Why do we strive and live, forgotten after a short span of time, only to molder in the cold earth?" By twenty-one she is described as "depressive," and her poems remained preoccupied with death, now no longer terrible, and in its representation not a man but "a glorious woman, white asters in her dark hair, large eyes, dream-deep and gray." She imagines dying as "such a delicious stretching out and dozing off," and writes to a friend that "If he [now she shifts the gender] makes me wait much longer, the great friend, death, then I shall set out and seek him." And: "Death is the greatest happiness in life, if not the only one. Without hope of the end life would be unendurable." Her mood varies, and at age twenty-three, a student and in one of her happier periods, she writes: "I'd like to die just as the birdling does/That splits his throat in highest jubilation;/. . . . and wildly be consumed in my own fire." At twenty-five, after a broken engagement,: "The earth bears grain, /But I /Am unfruitful, /Am discarded shell, / . . .Worthless husk. /Creator, Creator, /Take me back! /Create me a second time /And create me better!"

Beyond these feelings she had actually been courting death: As a child she thought it would be "interesting" to have a fatal accident, and would be disappointed when fever subsided. As a young adult and expert rider she would perform foolhardy tricks, once fell and broke her clavicle, and thought it too bad that she could not have a fatal accident. And' at twenty-two she made her tutor repeat over and over again the sentence: "Those whom the gods love die young." She subsequently would envy girlfriends who died, and when working in a foundling home would kiss children who had scarlet fever hoping she too would catch it. She would also seek to become ill by exposing herself to cold, at times when she had a fever, and her behavior was described by her first analyst as "a slow attempt at suicide."

At the beginning of her thirty-third year she made two serious suicidal attempts, in each case by taking pills, and subsequently attempts on several occasions to throw herself in front of a car, and then throw herself out of a window in her analyst's office. It was then that she was hospitalized. She seemed resentful at being alive: "Only death can save me from this dread." Also: "I longed to be violated—and indeed I do violence to myself every hour." And: "I suffer as one would not let an animal suffer."

The suicide constellation becomes an obsession with death as life's only goal—a pattern I believe to be present, though usually in less extreme form, in most if not all suicide.

Much of Ellen West's symbolization of life and death took place around eating.

At about age twenty she developed a dread of getting fat. Then, and later, she alternated between overeating and fasting, compensating for her wish to eat enormous quantities with various forms of mortification—relentless hiking, refusing food and becoming a vegetarian, taking laxatives and drugs to induce vomiting, and thyroid tablets to the point of developing a hyperthyroid condition. So much was she consumed by what she called her "fixed idea" that by her early thirties, "My thoughts are exclusively concerned with my body, my eating, my laxatives." And "To be thin" becomes "my life's ideal." A clue to her imagery lies in her comparing her constant thought of eating with a murderer's constant preoccupation "in his mind's eye [with] the picture of the victim. He can work, even slave, from early until late, can go out, can talk, can attempt to divert himself: all in vain. Always and always again he will see the picture of the victim before him. He feels an overpowering pull toward the place of the murder. . . . [but] the murderer can find redemption. He goes to the police and accuses himself. . . . I can find no redemption—except in death."

Her suicide constellation found expression via the body and the food it took in or rejected. To eat, which is ordinarily to maintain life, became equated with murder; to starve herself virtually to death, became, like suicide itself, life's purpose. But the extremity of the obsession, which she could recognize as senseless, was itself a form of living death as she became not only a physical but a mental skeleton until (in her own words) "all inner development, all real life . . . stopped." Also involved in her "fixed idea" were her rejection of sensuality and pregnancy (equated with becoming fat) as fundamental expressions of vitality. Her extreme craving for food was, of course, partly a craving for nurturing; but also an aspect of her struggle around disintegration—she could never quite find a level of bodily intake and output consistent with a sense of integration, physical and psychic. Any food intake on behalf of that integration, then, becomes actual or imagined gluttony, which for her is murder and a kind of deformity that (as Binswanger points out) amounts to "spiritual death." In her radical bodily deprivations, she courts physical death to avoid what we would call psychic death.

Over the course of this suffering Ellen West came into the hands of many doctors and bore many diagnoses. During her early twenties she was considered depressed; at the age of twenty-five she was given diagnoses of "Basedow Syndrome" (or Graves' disease), a form of hyperthyroidism due to her intake of thyroid pills, and spent some time that year in a "public sanatorium"; at age twenty-nine she had a severe abdominal hemorrhage, which, after a curettage, was diagnosed as a miscarriage (she had married a cousin the year before); at age thirty she went to Pyrmont (a spa in Germany) for a "water cure"; at age thirty-two-and-a-half she began treatment with one, and then another, psychoanalyst, and was described after a suicide attempt as being in a "hysterical twilight state"; at age thirty-three she was hospitalized for her emaciation and severe metabolic disorder; there is then a disagreement concerning her mental diagnosis between her analyst who apparently considered her neurotic and therefore analyzable (though in his later report he speaks of "severe obsessive neurosis combined with manic-depressive oscillations") and Kraepelin who, when called in, diagnosed it as melancholia (or psychotic depression). There were probably many other medical contacts and diagnoses not recorded in the case history.* Binswanger himself finally made the diagnosis of "a progressive schizophrenic psychosis," a diagnosis confirmed by another distinguished consultant. That diagnosis is important, as it coincides with a crucial decision that had to be made. Ellen West wanted very much to leave the hospital, and Binswanger said that so strong was her suicidal intent, he could not recommend her remaining in the hospital unless committed to a closed ward. Her husband felt that such commitment could be justified only if there were a reasonable hope for improvement under closed ward treatment, a hope Binswanger could in no way hold forth given his diagnosis of "progressive schizophrenic psychosis." So she was released, and quickly killed herself.

* She certainly had strong features of what would now be called anorexia nervosa, and may have received diagnoses along this line as well.

It is tempting to dismiss this kind of suicide as a manifestation of psychiatric disorder. But the fact remains that many with similar or even more severe disorders did not kill themselves. We must raise questions concerning Ellen West, no less than samurais or martyrs, about the meaning for her of her chosen way of dying.

Three days after leaving the hospital she became calm, and for the first time in thirteen years ate a sufficiently hearty breakfast to feel satisfied and full. She took a walk with her husband, read romantic poetry (including Rilke, Goethe, and Tennyson) as well as Mark Twain, and was described as being in a festive mood. She wrote letters to those she felt close to, including a fellow patient to whom she had become attached, and in the evening took a lethal dose of poison, so that she was dead by the following morning. In death it is said (the quote is probably from her husband) that "She looked as she had never looked in life—calm and happy and peaceful."

Toward the end of her life we know her to have felt herself as if dead— "In the institution Ellen already has the feeling of being like a corpse among people," Binswanger wrote. And immediately upon leaving, her symptoms got still worse as "even more than in the institution she feels incapable of dealing with life." It was only on that third day after leaving, when she had clearly come to a plan to kill herself, that, in ways we have noted, "she is as if transformed." In all immediate feelings, that is, she had reached an extremity of deathlike stasis. And concerning ultimate involvements, there was, until structuring her death, only despair and hopelessness. Over the course of her life she had attempted to achieve meaning through a vision of social justice—either by means of political revolution, or in a more personal way through human contributions she tried to make through work she did in social agencies. But she could sustain a sense of significance only fleetingly in those activities and visions. Such was her stasis—her "icebound" state of what Binswanger called "existential encirclement"—that she could experience a sense of significance only in relationship to death. Her energy or "existential fire" is directed toward this end, so that "immediate proximity of death brightens her life." That is why Binswanger could say, in the phrase we quoted earlier, "Only in her decision for death did she find herself and choose herself." Binswanger also speaks of death as ending, for her, "the existential rocking process," so that "Only in the face of nonbeing does Ellen West actually stand in being, does she triumph in quiet calm over the finiteness of being, including her own." More simply, only by taking hold of her death in this way could she experience, however briefly, a sense of vitality; and a larger sense of meaning in her extreme rejection of the despairing meaninglessness in which she had lived. There was reassertion (in her festive mood, reading of poetry, letters to those she felt close to) of the more significant human currents that she had at least touched during the course of her life. And from the standpoint of our model, I would, of course, emphasize her unusually strong, lifelong suicide construct, which made the act of killing herself a consistent and vivid possibility. The general point here is that, whatever the degree of suffering, incapacity, and psychological disorder, suicide can best be understood in relationship to image-feelings around death and deadness on the one hand and vitality and larger affirmation on the other.

EIGHTEEN

Yukio Mishima—The Lure of Death

YUKIO MISHIMA was not an isolated psychiatric patient but a writer with a considerable international reputation, a best-selling author and prominent celebrity in Japan, and a serious contender for the Nobel Prize in literature. Rather than die quietly and privately as did Ellen West, his suicide was elaborately orchestrated and publicly, flamboyantly, and ritually performed. Mishima meant his death to have broad impact, meant it to immortalize certain Japanese cultural visions.

Mishima disemboweled himself—performed a contemporary version of *seppuku*—in the office of a commanding general of a military base in central Tokyo. Mishima had arranged an appointment with the general, and then, with the help of three young assistants from his private army, the Shield Society (the name taken from the ancient Japanese cultural image of serving as a shield for the emperor) had seized him and held him as a hostage in order to get the Self-Defense Forces to cooperate with his scenario. That meant assembling the thousand or so men in the unit to provide an audience for him to address from a balcony outside the office, while copies of a written manifesto were dropped over the edge by two of his assistants. The manifesto expressed reverence for the Self-Defense Forces as the "soul of Nippon," but called upon it "to rebel" against a government that refused to grant it legitimacy according to the Peace Constitution [drafted by the Allied powers in 1947]. Mishima declared: "Our fundamental values, as Japanese, are threatened. The Emperor is not being given his rightful place in Japan," and "If no action is taken, the Western powers will control Japan for the next century!" The manifesto ended with the exhortation:

Let us restore Nippon to its true state and let us die. Will you value only life and let the spirit die? . . . We will show you a value which is greater than respect for life. Not liberty, not democracy. It is Nippon! Nippon, the land of history and tradition. The Japan we love.[1]

Mishima's speech was along similar lines, referring to the Self-Defense Forces as "the last hope of Nippon, the last stronghold of the Japanese soul." He went on "Are you *bushi* (samurai)? Are you men? You *are* soldiers! . . . Listen! You are unconstitutional! Don't you understand? Why don't you wake up?" And he ended: "I salute the Emperor! *Tenno Heika Banzai! Tenno Heika Banzai! Tenno Heika Banzai!* [The traditional "Long live the Emperor!"] Mishima then went back into the room, stripped down to the traditional loin cloth (*fundoshi*), assumed the ritual sitting position (legs tucked under), again shouted "Tenno Heika Banzai!" three times, took a deep breath and exhaled with a final shout (to expel as much air as possible from the body). Then, after marking his spot, he plunged the sharp, ritual dagger into his left, lower abdomen and then cut horizontally across to the right until he collapsed in his own blood and entrails. His student-assistants performed the decapitation with the other ritual weapon, the long sword. One of the student-assistants, Morita, then knelt and also performed *seppuku* with the same steps as Mishima, his head severed by another Shield Society member.

This sequence of events was consistent with what Mishima had been writing and declaring publicly for some time concerning the general decay of Japanese cultural tradition, and especially martial spirit, in various forms of post-World War II commercialism, Westernization, left-wing politics, domination by America, and neglect of emperor-centered principles. On the basis of what we have said so far, the episode would seem to be a clear-cut example of what Durkheim called "altruistic suicide" and of what we have been speaking of as the immortalizing impulse in suicide.

But with a closer look, everything becomes more complicated. Rather than proceeding with quiet dignity, the act suffered various slipups and improvisations that rendered it a grotesque *opera bouffe*. From the beginning, there was confusion in signals. The general was seized rather awkwardly. An adjutant standing in the next room could observe, through a peephole, that something was wrong, and entered the room with a number of fellow officers. He told Mishima "stop this fooling . . . stop this play-acting." Mishima then brandished the long sword, threatened to kill the general, slashed and injured a number of the officers, and "administering broad strokes to their buttocks . . . herded them out of the office."[2] When the garrison was summoned by a loudspeaker and, shortly afterward, there was evidence of the presence of large numbers of police, Mishima remarked to his comrades: "What a lot of people for the party!"[3] There was an air of absurdity about Mishima's speech from the balcony. Wearing the yellow-brown uniform of the Shield Society (more or less resembling military uniforms of the Meiji period about three-quarters of a century past, and described by one observer as reflecting "Mishima's kitsch taste")[4] while obviously the center of some kind of disturbance (as wounded men were seen to be carried out of the building), Mishima's anachronistic exhortations seemed bizarre to the men below. He also angered them. Most of what he said could not be heard because it was drowned out by police helicopters and other noises. But what they did hear inspired shouts from the crowd "*Bakayaro!*" (meaning approximately, "You idiot!" or "You son-of-a-bitch!"), "Ass-hole!" "Come down from there!" "Stop playing the hero!" "Madman!" and "Shoot him!" When Mishima taunted them about not being real men, someone shouted back, "Are *you* a man?" After a number of unsuccessful pleas to listen to him, Mishima, just prior to his three *Banzais*, calmly concluded: "I see that you . . . will do nothing . . . you are not interested. I have lost my dream of the *Jieitai* (Self-Defense Force)."

Concerning Mishima's *seppuku*, there was considerable trouble with the beheading. Morita, entrusted with the task, missed the mark twice and only partially succeeded the third time, so that a second student, with some experience in *kendo*, Japanese fencing, asked for the sword and completed the task. Moreover, in the second *seppuku* the same bungling student, Morita, could make only a shallow scratch across his abdomen prior to his beheading. The shackled general, who witnessed all this, could only exclaim "This is the end!" and then order the surviving students to "make the bodies decent." By this time a large number of reporters and TV cameramen had begun to record what they could of the confusion. And when they questioned the announcement that Mishima and one other man were dead, the answer they got was: "Their heads are off, yes, off, their heads are off, off, I tell you, off."[5] This was, after all, the Japan of 1975—not that of the fifteenth century or even of 1945—and people found it a bit difficult to accept the *seppuku* on its own terms.

When we step back from the event and look at the man and his personal history, we encounter a most remarkable relationship to death and death imagery—and at the heart of that imagery a suicide construct of equally impressive proportion. From the fiftieth day of his life until age twelve, Mishima (his actual given name was Kimitake) lived in his grandmother's darkened sickroom, "perpetually closed and stifling with odors of sickness and old age," as he later recalled.[6] His grandmother could take possession of the boy in this way partly out of the prerogatives of a husband's mother and partly because of the high status of her own samurai family. In any case he became much like a retainer to her: giving her medicine to her (she would take it from no one else but her "little tiger"), sponging her brow and massaging her back and hip, leading her by hand to and from the toilet, and comforting her when she would cry at night and tear her hair. And "at least once she seized a knife and held it to her throat, screaming she would kill herself."[7] There thus developed in the young boy, very early, overwhelming imagery of disintegration, associated with imagery of suicide, both forms of imagery having to do with a powerful if deteriorating representative of the samurai past.

From the beginning, death haunted and stimulated his imagination. The "little people" of his fantasy were not elfs or *kappas* (Japanese leprechaun-like figures) but "diseases." Frightened when running through the back rooms of the house, "at every turning I would meet at least one 'disease.'" They would vary in their countenance, depending upon their closeness to death, and of one smiling innocently he wrote: "He must have been a 'disease' not intimate with 'death' yet . . . taking news to a 'disease' more intimate with 'death.'"[8] The grandmother was certainly for the young boy a "lord and mistress"—he later described her as his "true-love sweetheart, aged sixty"—so that, via her person, death for him took on erotic associations.

And indeed, when as a precocious youngster he began to read fairy tales, he was attracted to princes murdered or princes fated for death. "I was completely in love with any youth who was killed." And, "My heart's leaning toward Death and Night and Blood would not be denied."[9] Moreover, "I delighted in imagining situations in which I myself was dying in battle or being murdered." That is, his attraction to death came to be associated with a pleasurable image of his own dying. Here (the age reference is not specific but he is probably somewhere between six and eight years old) the suicide construct begins to take on more specific form. Yet, Mishima also remembered having "an abnormally strong fear of death." Fear and attraction can, of course, go hand in hand, and in Mishima's case both had rare intensity. He seems to have wavered between unusually vivid death-linked image-feelings and an equally unusual capacity for numbing. Thus his father tells how, when taking the four-year-old boy for a walk past a railroad crossing, he decided to apply some "Spartan training" and lifted him close to the speeding engine. When the father asked the boy, "Are you scared?" he was astonished to encounter no reaction at all—and the same thing happened on repeating the process with the next train—and again the next day as well. Observing the boy's face to be "The same Nō mask as before," the father remained deeply puzzled, wondering whether "he was like a puppy . . . too young to know fear, or [whether] the schoolgirl training he was getting from my mother made him insensitive to this kind of turbulent, masculine experience?"[10] In Mishima that incident seems to epitomize the general function of extreme numbing—the capacity to become temporarily "deadened" in order to ward off the threat of actual physical or threatened psychic death. All this was part of a pattern that enabled Mishima to maintain death as a constitutive symbol, beginning, as he later acknowledged, with his grandmother's room— ". . . something within me responded to the darkened room and the sick bed—even now I work at my desk all night long and wake up around noon."[11]

His struggles with death imagery were associated with sexual confusion. Totally absorbed in a particular picture in one of his books of a magnificent knight mounted on the white horse holding a sword aloft, "confronting either Death or, at the very least, some hurtling object full of evil power," and believing "he would be killed the next instant: If I turn the page quickly, surely I can see him being killed," he was devastated when told by his nurse that the knight "I had thought a *he* was a *she*," was none other than Joan of Arc. But even where his fantasies had explicitly homoerotic components—his preoccupation with the beauty of princes, and not princesses—the element of death, the prince dying, was usually central.* Indeed, in this combination of death-obsessed and homoerotic imagery we can trace the beginnings of later sado-masochistic impulses of considerable intensity.

At the age of twelve Mishima began to experience erections in response to the male body ("naked bodies of young men seen on a summer's seashore, the swimming teams seen at Meiji Pool . . .") and scenes of young men dying:

> The toy [his penis] likewise raised its head toward death and pools of blood and muscular flesh. In this second category of attraction were "Gory dueling scenes . . . pictures of young samurai cutting open their bellies, or of soldiers struck by bullets, clenching their teeth and dripping blood from between hands that clutched at khaki-clad breasts"—all these evoked feelings Mishima himself looked back on as "'erotic' or 'lustful.'" He then encountered, in an art book, a single image that could express and give form to all of his erotic yearnings while articulating still more clearly his suicide construct—Guido Reni's early seventeenth-century painting of the martyrdom of St. Sebastian. Mishima remembered having admired "his white and matchless nudity" as well as the "pagan" beauty brought out by the Renaissance of the handsome youth's body depicted by the Renaissance painter. Mishima thought he saw in Sebastian's face "some flicker of melancholy pleasure like music"—so that "The arrows have eaten into the tense, fragrant, youthful flesh and are about to consume his body from within with flames of supreme agony and ecstasy."[13] Mishima's own ecstasy was such that "My hands, completely unconsciously, began a motion they had never been taught, culminating in my first ejaculation." †

---

* A possible exception is the very early memory—said to be his first, from age four—of a "night-soil [human fertilizer] man," whom he remembers, as a young adult, as having had close-fitting "thigh-pullers" (the pants legs worn by such laborers), which became one of the "two focal points" of his "desire." The other was his occupation—he remembered thinking, "I want to *be* him," feeling possessed with the ambition to take on the kind of task that had to do with what he later came to associate with "excrement [as] a symbol for the earth . . . the feeling of 'tragedy' in the most sensuous meaning of the word . . . of 'self-renunciation' . . . intimacy with danger, a feeling like a remarkable mixture of nothingness and vital power."[12]

Here, too, through the obscurities, one can recognize the only slightly indirect presence of the elements of death and transcendence.

† Mishima, the student of himself, also notes that a psychiatric authority named Hirschfeld has pointed out that pictures of St. Sebastian were frequently among the art works in which "the invert" (presumably the homosexual) takes particular delight, and Mishima adds that "inverted and . . . sadistic impulses are inextricably entangled with each other."[14]

St. Sebastian's martyrdom remained a central or "controlling" image for Mishima from that time onward. A few years later, St. Sebastian was the subject of what he called a prose poem, one of his early pieces of writing, in which he imagined that a tree he viewed outside of his schoolroom window might be "the very tree . . . to which the young saint was bound with his hands behind him, over the trunk of which his sacred blood trickled like driblets after a rain." He speculates that while Sebastian was still a young captain in the Praetorian guard (prior to the discovery that he was a Christian), the women of Rome must have sensed that "such beauty as his [was] a thing destined for death," his blood "watching for an opening from which to spurt forth when that flesh would soon be torn asunder," and "for that reason" must have been irresistibly attracted to him: "How could the women have failed to hear the tempestuous desires of such blood as this?" Above all, the young Mishima, identifying closely with the young saint, saw not just beauty but nobility in the martyrdom:

> His was not a fate to be pitied. In no way was it a pitiable fate. Rather it was proud and tragic, a fate that might even be called shining . . . it was nothing less than martyrdom which . . . was . . . the token of his apartness from all the ordinary men of birth.[15]

We observe the further structuring of Mishima's homoerotic, sadistic, and masochistic impulses into a highly symbolized image through which he could increasingly interpret his world and evolve a moral credo. That credo includes not just a beautiful death but an ennobling death for a larger purpose. Significantly, that organizing image began in Christian martyrdom but readily connected with samurai *seppuku*. The latter was to become the object of his specific ideological convictions, but the former also had importance in its reflection of Japan's historical encounter with the West. So intense was and is that encounter that powerful constructs, ultimately related to the heart of Japanese tradition, can be first evoked around a Western image. In such cases a powerful Japanese cultural theme—here the idea of beauty in death or destruction—is likely to play an important part in the response to what seems alien or Western. Mishima referred frequently to St. Sebastian—one observer said that he made "a cult" of the saint—and about four years before his suicide, assumed the pose of Reni's St. Sebastian—standing against a thick tree trunk, wearing only a white cloth folded about his thighs, his chest expanded and three arrows implanted in his body, each surrounded by a trickle of blood. It is not too much to say that from his first encounter with the image, Mishima became and never ceased to be himself a version of St. Sebastian. In his romance with the saint we sense his hunger for death imagery as a demonic source of imagination and vitality.

His first published short story (in the journal of the literature club of the elite Peers School, when Mishima was twelve years old), entitled "Sorrel Flowers—

In Memory of Youth," described an encounter between a six-year-old boy and an escaped criminal who had murdered his own son of that age. Moved by the boy—there is hint of mutual homoerotic attraction—the criminal is rehabilitated. Having already emerged as a writer of precocious talent by the time he was sixteen, Mishima could combine those themes with a sense of heroic destiny involving the samurai and court nobles in his family background— "an unspoken pact between my grandfathers and myself," which took the form of a river which in his grandmother and mother "float[s] underground" and in his father "became a murmuring brook" but in Mishima himself— "ah, how can it become other than a swollen mighty river, like a song of blessing by the gods." The same narrator of that story tells of episodes from his family's past involving a quest for beauty, momentary ecstasy, and death. "Mishima was well on his way to evolving an esthetic formula in which Beauty, Ecstasy, and Death were equivalent and together stood for his personal holy grail." [16] And he was aware of a force inside him "bent . . . profoundly . . . intensely, upon the complete disintegration of my inner balance . . . a compulsion toward suicide, that subtle and secret impulse to which a person often unconsciously surrenders himself." [17] Now the death imagery (including the suicide construct) becomes associated with a romantic restoration (involving family in particular and historical change in general) and the talented youngster's sense of special heroic destiny.

In all this Mishima was resisted by his father, a medium-level bureaucrat who looked upon fiction as worthless and the writing of it as a degenerate activity. The father would become sufficiently violent at times to destroy his son's manuscripts. Mishima was protected by his mother, who had long been passive in the struggle with the grandmother over the right to be a parent, as well as for the boy's affection. She became something close to his muse, and he began the habit of showing her each manuscript before publication, a habit he maintained until his death. As for the grandmother, she had died when Mishima was fourteen, at which time he was described as having the same "Nō mask" of nonreaction his father had observed at the railroad crossing—what we could again see as extreme numbing and perhaps also something of a talent for dissembling.

We may suspect that a boy so self-absorbed in death-dominated, homoerotic image-feelings may by then have lost considerable capacity to respond feelingly to external events, even the death of family members. That would also imply that his capacity for intimacy had been more or less replaced by those same inner preoccupations; lurking always underneath the death-centered eroticism was the terror of disintegration. The self-absorption could be called narcissism in the everyday sense, and the combination of solipsism and fear of disintegration would be consistent with what is usually referred to as narcissism in the psychoanalytic sense.

Mishima's late adolescence coincided with two external developments that blended almost perfectly with his psychic state: the literary predominance of the

Japan romantic school and the Japanese involvement in World War II. Japanese fascism was no less romantic than the literary movement, and the two blended especially in their romance around death. The romantic school embraced and aestheticized the Japanese past, military and literary, so that a leading exponent could declare: "Tradition, the product of three thousand years of culture, is the only cause for which the people can die." The school was the perfect literary expression of a wartime ethos, according to which everyone, but especially able young men, were expected to be ready to die—beautifully—for nation and, above all, emperor. It was just that at that point, during his late adolescence, that Mishima's particular constellation of death imagery and suicide construct made direct connection with predominant literary and political-military motifs around him. No wonder, then, that he could later speak of those war years as "a time, the only time in my experience, when death was a rite and an intoxicating blessing."[18]

In 1944, at age nineteen, everything seemed to be coming together for Mishima—he was presented with a watch by the emperor on graduating first in his class from the Peers School, published to acclaim a volume of short stories, and could look upon himself as "a genius destined for an early death" and "Even as beauty's kamikaze squad!" Except for one development. In early 1945 he received a draft notice, which at the time (Japan was being annihilated) amounted to a command to die for the emperor, and it turned out he was not so ready for death as he thought. He prepared as all did for death by leaving with his mother a personal will and the traditional bodily memento of nail clippings, but when it came time for the medical examination, he encouraged in a number of ways the doctor's mistaken impression that the bronchitis he was suffering from at the time was "advanced tuberculosis." He was therefore medically rejected. He came close to what we would call malingering. Within his death constellation, his suicide construct and quest for a beautiful death was not quite as strong as his fear of the same. He experienced a sense of guilt and shame, which probably never left him, over having remained alive at a time one was expected to die and having engaged in deception to do so: "I realized vividly that my future life would never attain heights of glory sufficient to justify my having escaped death in the army."

He was confused by his behavior, concluded that his attraction to the army had been mainly around the erotic possibilities it offered, and that rather than seeking death he really possessed "the firm conviction—arising out of a belief in the primitive art of magic, common to all men—that I alone could never die." His death anxiety took the form of denial, numbing, and literalized imagery of immortality. He later explained that incident in terms of having been unready for death because of not yet having achieved the "classical perfection" of body that should precede death. "I lacked the necessary physical qualifications. A powerful, tragic frame . . . indispensable in a romantically noble death"— since "confrontation between weak, flabby flesh and death seems to me absurdly inappropriate," so that "longing at eighteen for an early demise, I felt myself unfitted for it." [19]

This was partly retrospective rationalization, of course, but there was some truth in it. For Mishima, the suicide construct was not just beauty in being destroyed but beauty in beauty's being destroyed. His later obsession with body building tends to confirm this requirement, all the more so, of course, if one chooses *seppuku*, which requires a considerable mixture of physical strength and psychological cultivation. In any case, after this failure Mishima had to be content with images—still very powerful within him—of his dying, sometimes with his family and sometimes alone, in Tokyo air raids, those raids appearing to him as "beautiful . . . flames seemed to hue in all the colors in the rainbow . . . like watching the light of a distant bonfire at a great banquet of extravagant death and destruction." [20] *

With the end of the war, the American Occupation, and the "democracy boom," Mishima found that external and internal environments were no longer at one. He described "a sudden assault of unhappiness," looking back on the "rare time [1944–45] when my personal nihilism and the nihilism of the age and of society at large perfectly corresponded." Now, as a young adult, the way in which his internal constructs connected with a different world began to terrify him ("I had taken secretly to jotting down epigrams such as 'Whether another A-bomb falls or not is of no concern of mine. All that matters to me is whether the shape of the globe would become even a little more beautiful as a result.' I knew I couldn't continue in this vein . . . [and] would have to analyze comprehensively the root source of this desperate, nihilistic aestheticism of mine.") It was thus partly as self-analysis, though also as the ambitious writer, that Mishima wrote *Confessions of a Mask*, the brilliant, highly autobiographical novel that provides much of the information we have about his early life. While writing it he was quoted as saying: "I am desperate to kill a man; I want to see red blood. An author writes love stories because he isn't popular with women; I began writing novels so I wouldn't end up with the death sentence. . . ." [21]

But even after his literary look into his own homosexuality and eroticization of death, he remained sufficiently troubled by sleeping and waking nightmares as well as stomach symptoms to consult (in 1949) a psychiatrist, whom he apparently saw just once or twice. In *Confessions*, when Mishima tells of having felt himself "beyond the reach of harm by any bullet" and yet having "shuddered with a strange delight at the thought of my own death" and "I felt as

---

* This sense of beauty in destruction, specifically associated with air raids, was not unique to Mishima. Many Japanese express similar images—reflecting what was undoubtedly an awesome scene, as well as cultural imagery of beauty in destruction. Nor was that sense entirely absent among Europeans witnessing air raids. With Mishima, however, the images are rendered more extreme and elaborate ("a great banquet of extravagant death and destruction") by the death constellation he brings to it.

though I owned the whole world," we get a sense of the continuing function of his precarious, death-dominated equilibrium. He could continue to draw upon his death imagery and suicide construct for creative vitality.

In another major novel, *The Temple of the Golden Pavilion*, based on a true story of a young acolyte who set fire to and destroyed this magnificent old temple in Kyoto and then attempted suicide, Mishima constructed his rendition of the story around the image of beauty in destruction.[22] The young monk is a totally isolated, ineffectual, inarticulate (hampered by a bad stutter) creature who can achieve a sense of power and vitality only in destroying this ultimate manifestation of beauty.

Toward the end of the 1950s, when in his mid-thirties, Mishima's literary capacities seemed to decline.[*] He was losing his symbolizing power and producing relatively literal people, ideas, and images. That, in fact, may be the affliction of all writers whose creative powers wane. Certainly it was even more true of Mishima's final novelistic tetralogy, written between 1965 and 1970. One can, after all, literalize reincarnation (a central theme of the tetralogy), which he did, along with the events taking place in the books over different periods of history. Literalization always involves repeating oneself, which all critics found Mishima to be doing. And he himself, just before embarking on the tetralogy, wrote that during the 1950s "I exploited and used up my sensitivity entirely; I know that my sensitivity dried up." "Thus [and now the old Mishima steps forward] in a sudden flash, the idea of Death is born within me. This is the only truly vivid and erotic idea for me."[24] In other words, Mishima's writing can no longer overcome his increasing sense of inner deadness—only contemplation of death can do that.

With the apparent diminution of his literary powers during the 1960s,[†] Mishima moved increasingly toward external display—toward what some have called public stunts—and theatrical literalism. These activities included various forms of display of his body (his muscles increasingly developed by means of continuous body-building exercises and training in Japanese fencing [*kendō*] as

---

[*] Though always controversial, up until then virtually everything he wrote was powerfully evoked, responded to with critical acclaim, and sold enormous numbers of copies. His novel, *Kyoko's House*, published in 1959, has seemed to many a turning point. The novel included some of Mishima's consistent themes—three of its four main characters are convinced that destruction of the world is inevitable[23]—but little of the book was convincing either to critics (who attacked it) or to the reading public (who did not buy it). Mishima is very much in each of the book's four men: a boxer-rightist killed in a street brawl, an actor preoccupied with body building (who commits double suicide with his mistress), an artist-painter (who wants to kill himself while his body is still beautiful but survives), and a successful businessman who, deeply misanthropic, plays the role of someone leading a conventional life.

[†] Mishima did write one very successful novel in 1960, *After the Banquet*. But it was more of what Graham Greene calls an "entertainment"—in this case a *roman a clef* about an actual Tokyo political figure who was defeated in the race for mayor, and which evoked rather brilliantly the contemporary interplay of political and geisha worlds.

well as Western boxing), acting in films, melodramatic rightist political stances, participation (through special dispensation) in Self-Defense Force basic training, and finally the formation of a private military group, the Shield Society. Though these activities had various meanings for Mishima, his increasing emphasis upon them seems to parallel his increasing inability to transmute his suicide construct in imaginative ways. Rather, that construct became more and more identified with his body, and his public activities brought him closer and closer to the literal act of self-destruction.

Mishima's body-building, of course, had profound personal significance and was one expression of his extraordinary degree of what would ordinarily be called narcissism. But from within our paradigm, much of its meaning was expressed in the anxious question of the actor–body-builder in *Kyoko's House*: "Do I really exist or not?" On the one hand, in rendering his body beautiful, agile, and capable of disciplined violence, he could find in it a constant source of transcendence—of what he called the "'ultimate sensation' that lies a hairs-breadth beyond the reach of the senses." [25] And when he goes on to say, "My solace lay more than anywhere—indeed lay solely—in the small rebirths that occurred immediately after exercise," we begin to realize the extent to which these bodily activities served ever-more desperate needs for psychic vitality. For, "my age pursued me, murmuring behind my back 'How long will it last?'" But Mishima no longer had a choice. For, "by now . . . it was not words that endorsed my existence . . . [but] something different. That 'something different' was muscle." [26]

The best he could do, then, was to prepare his body—make it beautiful—for what he considered his ultimate erotic transcendence, that of death itself.

But he also related his bodily martial exercises to an affirmation of what he called the "masculine" dimension of Japanese tradition, its cultivation of its versions of strength, violence, stoicism, and magnificent dying, as opposed to what he considered its over-emphasized "feminine" side, consisting of various forms of genteel elegance and such literary and artistic sensibility as reflected in *The Tale of Genji* and tea ceremony and flower arrangement. Thus defined, masculinity meant vitality, and femininity, decay and deadness. Now one can be, perhaps especially in Japanese culture, both homosexual and in this sense "masculine." But as one who had been permitted as a child to play only with girls (and was said by some to have been brought up almost as a girl), and then as a troubled homosexual, Mishima was surely struggling hard against the "femininity" in himself, which became cojoined with his burden of death imagery. Photographs of Mishima not only display his built-up torso in martial poses, or in imitated martyrdom (Mishima as St. Sebastian) but also in outrageous nakedness and homosexual play. Indeed, there seems to be a subversive element of caricature in much of Mishima's literalized theatrics, which suggests that in a part of himself he mocked—felt the absurdity of—the entire enterprise. Thus it was in a third-rate gangster film that he chose to act out a few fantasies of killing and dying.

And where he tried to suppress that element of mockery and became "deadly serious," as in the film *Patriotism*, the mockery slipped in by the back door, in the form of the dirge from Wagner's *Tristan*, as well as in the camera's exaggerated affection for blood and death. Mishima was author, screen writer, director, producer, and star of this rendition of the *seppuku* of a Japanese superpatriot, an army lieutenant who took part in the unsuccessful military *coup d'etat* of February 26, 1936. As much as the later actual rehearsals of his *seppuku* with Shield Society followers, this film was surely a prefiguring of that event. Rather than being fully conscious of anticipating his own *seppuku* with film, Mishima probably used it as a vehicle for pressing himself further toward that act.

No doubt his military activities had a similar function. Yet, this world-famous writer (then actively lobbying for the Nobel Prize) could mean it when he said: "even the most trivial [military] duty is ultimately an emanation of something far loftier and more glorious, and is linked, somewhere, with the idea of death."[27] The military afforded him a sense of mission, of collective purpose, as well as a connection with death. His forming the Shield Society had similar goals. The group was to become, of course, the instrument of Mishima's staging of his own death. There too, however, there was a mocking undertone: During an interview he granted to two Americans at the site of his group's training headquarters, he referred to himself as "a kind of a Don Quixote."[28] There had to be an element of absurdity in the exquisitely sensitive literary man's attempt to disparage that sensibility and talent in favor of a glorified (in his own words) "ethos of action." Had he been able to take hold of and expand that dimension of self-mockery, he might have revitalized himself as a contemporary writer and have had less need for literalizing and enacting his suicide construct.

The element of mockery and self-mockery was part of his tendency toward the Protean style. He was, after all, a highly contemporary man, drawn to and at home with the mass media, a man equally interested in contemporary gangsters, politicians, and rebellious youth as in ancient samurai heroes, and in the literary-aesthetic traditions of the West as well. While his core, death-dominated images ruled his life, he was at the same time responsive to a vast variety of images coming from everywhere.*

---

*He lived in what he called an "anti-Zen" house of mixed, perhaps Spanish-rococo architecture, favored many different kinds of Western clothes (often loud and hip), and was considered to be quite "Westernized" in his entertaining habits (dinner parties at his home), and eventual family life (arrangements for his marriage had the frequent contemporary combination of parental suggestion along with choice and veto power on the part of the principals, but once married he treated his wife with unusual outward

Mishima felt compelled to cast off his Proteanism and Western influence, as he began to see these as tainted, perhaps related in their "deadliness" to the feminine components of Japanese culture. But for one so immersed in contemporary and Western influences, the task was virtually impossible. "Impurities" were of his essence, which gave a compensatory quality to his quest for his version of individual and cultural "purity," and rendered that quest both unusually intense and equally self-defeating.

Did he, then, believe in his right-wing social and political visions? To some extent he did—more important, he believed that he *should* believe in them. A British friend and biographer, invited to spend time with the Shield Society during a training exercise, described the group as being "like a crew of idiots," and contrasting it with the sophistication of the literary man he knew, wondered whether it might not be "just Mishima's joke." Other American friends have insisted that Mishima's political behavior should not be taken seriously, that he was primarily a literary man and that this was the only side of him that really mattered. Certainly, Mishima's political images were highly romanticized, fragmentary, and solipsistic. But they were bound up with his life history and ultimate concerns.

There were intense national struggles around the security pact with the United States in 1960, including mass demonstrations, a high tide of left-wing influence, and the reactivation of polarized right-wing passions as well. Mishima's impulse was to move further toward the mode of restoration, an impulse to combat and transcend contemporary confusions by means of returning to a past of allegedly perfect harmony. In Japan and elsewhere, those who embraced this mode were often fascinated with precisely the contemporary forces most opposed to it (Marxism, various contemporary social forms, mass media, etc.), as in the case of Mishima.[29]

That anxiety is directly related to death equivalents. For many who, like Mishima, had experienced their childhood and adolescence during the time that Japan's romantic fascism was at its peak, the new threats from the political left—perceived as threats to the life or "essence" of Japaneseness—could readily call forth that romantic imagery which had been the source of so much vitality in the past. But few indeed carried with them death imagery of the intensity of Mishima's; few had the kind of suicide construct that could connect in such extremity, and with such concreteness, to right-wing imagery. Nor did most restorationists have Mishima's array of Protean involvements to wash away psychologically in the quest for purity.*

---

respect and consideration, and was even known, at least at times, to demonstrate Western-style participation in activities with their children). Mishima was apparently bisexual, though primarily homosexual, and nothing is known of his intimate life with his wife. But there seemed to be a certain degree of companionship, and she did much in the way of organizing and helping with his various activities.

*Inevitably, he radically "Mishimized" his political characters. In his 1968 play, *My Friend Hitler*, the führer was concerned with the reasons for his own greatness and

Mishima's increasing public involvement in politics was for him an expression of despair. That despair was evident during his last years to some people around him. His laughter, always raucous, now seemed sometimes "monstrous."[31] About three months before he killed himself he was described as "melancholy," dwelt on his observation that "all our heroes . . . have been miserable failures," talked of all of the "curses" on various individuals and families in Japanese history, and concluded that now the whole of Japan was under a curse in its neglect of spiritual tradition and worship of money and of materialism. For that vast curse he used an image of a "green snake," the meaning of which was not clear (it could have symbolized almost anything from overall Western influence and temptation to his own sexual conflicts). His ordinary sense of humor would disappear, he would be uncharacteristically aggressive with friends, and would dwell on the "dark side" of Japanese culture that he claimed Westerners chose to ignore.

Upon approaching the completion of his tetralogy, *The Sea of Fertility*, he wrote in a letter that it felt "like the end of the world." In many that could be a novelist's metaphor about the quality of immersion in the universe of a specific novel, but the recipient of this letter detected depression. He was, in fact, reminded of an earlier letter in which Mishima had quoted more or less sympathetically a critic-friend's frequent observation that suicide would be the only solution to his literary career. Mishima must have had profound doubts about that masterwork—he had staked everything on a creation he himself did not believe in. The "angel" in the title of the last book of the tetralogy (*The Decay of the Angel*) has been observed by a number of people to be Mishima himself. Mishima described the book as ending with a "catastrophe," by which he probably meant the exposure as false of the belief in reincarnation that had sustained the entire existence of the protagonist. His whole life is thrown into doubt: "Who knows, perhaps there has been no I." Ending on this sense of nothingness is, of course, consistent with various strands of East Asian philosophy, but for Mishima it expressed despair. As Nathan writes, "In the last scene of *The Decay of the Angel* the tetralogy is abruptly bereft of substance and its reality made to seem a dream . . . [so that] what Mishima seems to have been saying . . . to himself . . . was that his entire life to the present moment, this side of death, had been an illusion merely, without substance." He had said so in a newspaper article at about that time: "When I think of the past twenty-five years within myself I am astonished at their emptiness. I can scarcely say that I have lived."[32] Here Mishima reiterated his lifelong inability to experience

---

power, and speaks of being a great artist as well as a soldier. Mishima was apparently ambivalent in his feelings toward Hitler—referred to him in his program notes as someone he was "fascinated with" but "disliked," and who was "a political genius, but not a hero." He embellished the sensational title by posing for a poster featuring swastikas and characterizing the play as "an evil hymn to the dangerous hero Hitler, from the dangerous thinker Mishima."[30] Mishima could see Hitler as "dark as the 20th century itself," and we know the depth of his attraction to that darkness.

vitality, expressing those "feelings of unreality" characteristic of schizoid experience and despair. Overcome by inner deadness, and unable to feel himself part of an immortalizing project, Mishima chose death—the kind of death that would "make sure," as he wrote, "that one's worst forebodings coincided with one's dreams of glory."[33]

Mishima's life, then, can be understood as a quest—anxious, bizarre, and brilliant—to transcend despair and death by finding an immortalizing way of dying. His case illustrates with unique clarity the blending in suicide of despairing conflict and larger purpose.

From the standpoint of our model, we may say that at the proximate level Mishima felt increasingly blocked, stymied, powerless. The extremity of his isolation and numbing were, he felt, perfectly expressed in a description of schizophrenia by Kretschmer to the effect that the condition "reaches a pinnacle of icy numbness . . . [so that] the patient becomes enwrapped in something hard as ice (or still as leather) and gradually all strong feelings weaken and recede." To which Mishima added, "'still as leather' is perfect: how did he know!"[34] Mishima was not necessarily calling himself schizophrenic so much as identifying with that particular feature of schizophrenia. Were a diagnosis made on his own condition, it could well have been that of "borderline personality," a condition more extreme than neurosis but lacking the disintegration and "craziness" of psychosis; and often characterized by particularly profound forms of "splitting" so that separate, contradictory selves seemed to coexist. However "split" in this way, Mishima's underlying deadening dominated his immediate existence. During the years prior to his death, neither his bodily nor his imaginative exertions could any longer overcome that feeling. He sensed that both were failing, his body in aging and his imagination in diminished creative power.

At the ultimate level, that creative failure was devastating, making him inwardly doubt his place in the great literary traditions he revered. Even the Nobel Prize would not have eliminated these doubts, but his failure to receive it undoubtedly intensified them. And he doubted also the very cultural visions to which he wished to commit himself. From the beginning of his life, his suicide construct was all-consuming.

Given his early history through adolescence, it would have taken the most remarkable kind of subsequent inner psychological development for him not to end up a suicide. During adolescence, his suicide construct became, as it turned out, permanently bound to the prevailing emperor-centered imagery of the beautiful death. He sought always to recapture that blending. Five years before his suicide, when contemplating kamikaze heroism and the surrender of his own body to a military cause, he wrote: "We were united in seeking death and glory; it was not merely my personal quest."[35] In killing himself it was not *merely* his personal quest, however tenuous the larger principles he sought to assert. His suicide construct could find profound reinforcement in Japanese cultural tradition.

His final speech and manifesto were his suicide notes. They convey his sense of purpose, his "imagined future." The manifesto spoke of Japanese society as "a world in which the spirit is dead," of his wish to "restore Japan to her true form" and to demonstrate "a greater value" by his act of *seppuku*. That portion of his "suicide note" may be understood as the expression of his ultimate ideal: the way he wanted others to understand his act and the way he wanted to understand it himself. His final letters to his two American translators were also suicide notes, and one could almost say the same of his newly completed manuscript of the tetralogy, carefully packed and laid out for the publisher. In these he sought to reassert his fading creative mode of immortality. There were also letters to two reporters, delayed so that they could not prevent his Mishima, further explaining that "we act purely out of patriotic ardor," enclosing in each case the manifesto and asking each to "do me the very great favor of publishing the manifesto uncut." Here was Mishima, still the creature of the media, seeking the immortalization of the act itself and the widest dissemination of his version of its purposes. In trying to reassure them that there was no danger of major bloodshed, but that "this is a minor incident, merely a private play of our own," Mishima's self-mocking tone inadvertently betrayed his own doubts about the significance of his act. At least in that phrase he is again Don Quixote. (Certainly he could not have been *entirely* surprised by the absurdity that entered into the event.)

There was still one more fragment of a suicide note— a single sentence Mishima left on his desk— "Human life is limited, but I would like to live forever." The imagery speaks directly to our model, but the message is enigmatic and could be interpreted in a number of ways. One could understand it as suggesting he had to kill himself because he could not assimilate the death his mind told him was inevitable for all (hence his terror of aging). His suicide would then take the form of a rejection of dying, along lines we discussed earlier. But that interpretation seems too simple and pat. Though we know Mishima to have been terrified of death, he spent much of his life moving toward it, feeling it out, creating around it, and eventually embracing it in the name of immortality. That, I believe, is what the cryptic message suggests. He was equating living forever with the way he chose to die—the sentence, after all, was meant to be part of his suicide message.

Scott-Stokes lists the various Japanese theories of the reason for Mishima's suicide.[36] He agrees most with the friend who called it "a gorgeous mosaic of homosexuality, *Yomeigaku* (neo-Confucian philosophy),* and Emperor worship." This theory includes the idea, endorsed by a number of people relatively close to the man, that Mishima was in love with Morita (the Shield Society follower who attempted to complete Mishima's *seppuku* by beheading him and then killing himself, a task often assigned to one's closest affiliate) and had

---

* During his last decade or so, Mishima especially emphasized the neo-Confucian disdain for thought alone, and its extreme insistence upon combining thought with action.

planned with him a double love suicide. That is indeed possible, but the homosexual element was ultimately subsumed to an erotic attraction to death. That may be what another commentator meant when he said that "the heightening of his sexuality produced an increasing urge to commit suicide by disembowelment." A sociologist called it "an act motivated by a sense of a phantom crisis," implying that Mishima's own aberration, his idiosyncratic imagery of fantasy, was at issue. That kind of idea is also suggested by a psychiatrist who spoke of "a suicide brought about by an explosive self-exhibitionistic desire." Certainly there were elements of that too. In terms of a larger meaning, a critic said that "He committed suicide to complete his literary work," and a right-wing author said, "He died to defend what he loved." The last two commentators may be said to see what they want to see, but what they speak of is there. Dying was a way of completing his literary work and his tortured, productive, gaudy life. He did seek to preserve something he loved, or at least wanted to love. These various explanations—as well as the simpler assumption that he was just plain "crazy" (which is what the prime minister at the time said and what many, Japanese and others, believed)—can be placed within a model of powerless despair, compelling suicide construct, and quest for an immortalizing act of dying. At the center of Mishima's assertion of meaning was an undoing of his failure to achieve a "heroic military death" within the prevailing Japanese socio-military ethos of World War II. While Mishima is an extreme example, some such reversal may be important, though hidden, in more "ordinary" forms of suicide.

The inner death in contemporary life is vague, a matter of gradual accretion, and yet, in the case of suicides, of overwhelming psychic numbing. The combination of breakdown in traditional imagery of immortality, religious and otherwise, and of imagery of extermination (whether through weaponry, destruction of the environment, or loss of sustaining earthly resources) creates a special vulnerability to despair without making clear where suicide should or might stand in the whole process.

Alvarez has some of these factors in mind in arguing that there has been, in this century, a "sudden, sharp rise in the casualty rate [via suicide] among the artists."[37] In seeking a cause he evokes my work on psychic numbing, especially as it pertains to Hiroshima and to a post-Hiroshima world deprived of war-linked chivalry and glory, a world in which victimizer and victim are likely to become indistinguishable in their shared relationship to species annihilation. He extends the principle, expressed by a Hiroshima survivor, that "there exist no words in any human language which can comfort guinea pigs who do not know the cause of their death" to the artist's death-bound dilemma: "It is precisely the pressure to discover a language adequate to this apparently impossible task which is behind the curious sense of strain characteristic of nearly all the best and most ambitious work of this century."[38] One could say (and this is implicit in Alvarez's argument) that the artist takes on the task of immersing himself in the death imagery and numbness of his age, but when he does that in this age he lacks the forms to break out of that numbing in more than the most transient fashion. He therefore resorts to the most extreme creative experiments, of which suicide is the culmination. In suicide he seeks to transcend that numbing, once and for all, precisely what he could not do in his art.

Here, as in all ways, the artist does the psychic work for all of us. He is in the vanguard of our disintegration, our futurelessness, as well as of our visions, however desperate, of carrying on. What makes artists' suicides so poignant and disturbing is that we sense ourselves to be, in this way, involved in them. And we lack the cultural imagery to place those suicides in anything like a life-affirming vision.

To say a similar thing another way, we may recall Heinrich Böll's dictum of the artist carrying death within him like the good priest his breviary. Now he must carry not just death, as he always did, but a particular set of images of the end of the world.

While death has always served as a constitutive symbol, can we say the same of an image of a technologically induced end of the world? Can the artist create from that image? Can the rest of us continue our form-making—transcend our suicide constructs—in the face of that pervasive suggestion of the end of everything? This book revolves about that question.

His was a case in which mother knew best, since she was his closest, lifelong, personal and literary confidante. One quote from her was: "My lover has returned to me." The imagery of son as lover is not so startling in Japanese life, given the extraordinary emotional and erotic investment of many mothers in their sons. Even so, this relationship was certainly extreme. It is somewhat clarified by another comment she made while mildly chastising a friend who placed white roses (white represents death) in front of the family Buddhist altar: "You should have brought red roses for a celebration. This was the first time in his life Kimitake did something he always wanted to do. Be happy for him." [39] There is undoubtedly a certain amount of bitterness and irony in that remarkable statement, as well as a reflection of the hidden conflict in this mother-son tie. But again the Japanese context is important: within it there are no limits to a mother's identification with her son. We sense then that she shared with him a vision not just of the necessity of doing what he did, but of his *seppuku* as a true distillation of national and family tradition (and we should not forget the specter of the grandmother), mother-son love, and personal quest.

We have presented suicide as having many forms and causes, but at the same time a certain universality of overall model and significance. For the most distraught psychiatric patient or the most admired cultural hero, suicide is a means of transcending inner death. But neither the inner death nor its violent resolution can be grasped outside cultural history, which provides the imagery for the suicide construct, criteria for despair and its reversal, and finally, for breaks and reconnections in the sense of immortality.

Given the threats to historical continuity and symbolic immortality in our present age, can one record or predict a dramatic universal increase in suicide? I do not know. While such cause and effect may be plausible, there are problems in making any prediction based upon the crudity and high generality of these "variables," the reliability of statistics on suicide, and the many additional factors that affect all sides of the issue.

We may be better prepared to observe or predict changes in emphasis within the model of suicide. It is possible, for instance, that in premodern societies with relatively intact symbolization, suicide either followed cultural prescriptions (the samurai and Christian models) or expressed radical inability to live out the highly structured cultural requirements (around religion, family, work, etc.). In our present society there are echoes of both patterns, but most especially of the second. We think of suicide as expressing extreme alienation from other people and from social requirements in general. As in so much of contemporary experience, however, the process may be more diffuse and ambiguous. The contemporary suicide may require neither a plunge into a cultural vision of a death that confers immortality, nor radical alienation from clear-cut cultural forms. He may indeed be less distinct from his fellows than the suicides of the past. His self-destruction may be more a matter of the gradual inner development of the various elements of our model of suicide, distinguishing himself from others mainly by the act itself, or by having crossed over the psychic threshhold leading to the act.

PART III

Death and History—
The Nuclear Image

NINETEEN

The Historical Animal

WE MUST APPROACH history with a sense of man's eternally inadequate, yet impressively imaginative efforts to absorb the idea of death and create lasting images of the continuity of life. *We can understand much of human history as the struggle to achieve, maintain, and reaffirm a collective sense of immortality under constantly changing psychic and material conditions.* For modes of immortality to be symbolically viable—for individuals to experience their power—they must connect with direct, proximate experience as well as provide ultimate patterns of continuity. A viable biological (or biosocial) mode, for instance, includes intense, direct (or proximate) emotions as well as a more unspoken sense of unending continuity. A religious mode around Christian imagery must include direct involvement in prayer, service, or other forms of ritual, as well as ultimate imagery of transcendence or rebirth.

Over the course of history, imagery of immortality has moved from the magical and the supernatural to the natural and man-centered and from literal (the concrete belief in eternal life) to symbolic image-feelings around rebirth, renewal, and continuing life.* Once we become involved with magic, the supernatural, religion, or any other historical mode, we use this involvement as a focus for our symbolizing. While we speak of a certain historical progression around cognitive achievement and related tendencies toward the "discursive" forms of symbolization that characterize mathematics, science, and logical

---

* Contemporary developments in medicine and science encourage a reversion to the literal image of living forever, as epitomized by the "cryonics movement" (the freezing of bodies at the time of death so that they can be revived at some future time following the discovery of the cure for the illness or condition originally causing death).

discourse, this "progression" in no way implies the increasing viability of symbolization. The reverse is probably true: the increasing complexity of symbolizations of immortality also complicates the capacity to feel convinced by that symbolization, to internalize it and live around it.

Our modern immortality-hunger is really the predominant expression of our symbol-hunger. Those "hungers," and the continuing collective struggle to satisfy them, make up much of the flow of the historical process. "It is a peculiar fact that every major advance in thinking, every epoch-making new insight, springs from a new type of symbolic transformation." [1] Yet, can we any longer, as Cassirer said of primitive man, "oppose . . . to the fact of death . . . confidence in the solidarity, the unbroken and indestructible unity of life"? [2]

A hunger for images characterizes all history, and comes close to defining the human condition. Man as we know him emerged with the struggle toward images beyond himself—those he himself drew on cave walls thousands of years ago, and those he constructed around death rituals even before that. For the symbolizing function is inseparable from a sequence or flow of events and their narration (history), no less than the relatively enduring psychic and material forms transmitted over generations (culture). In his constant construction of images, man is as much the historical as the cultural animal. * At every stage of history and within every culture, he has formed these images into a cosmology, which both absorbs and gives dignity to his ever-present death anxiety.

Man, the "historical animal," must eternally construct, alter, and replace those cosmologies—must create and recreate his ultimate imagery.

If history is a symbolizing treadmill, it is also the vehicle of our collective

---

* Freud was greatly concerned with questions of culture and history, but mostly from the standpoint of instinct and prehistory. His concept of the "primal horde" and the murder and devouring of its leader (the father) by the rebellious sons, and the resulting legacy of guilt around the Oedipus complex as periodically expressed in the "Return of the Repressed," became his model for the creation of human society including religion and the historical process in general. Without repeating an earlier discussion of the formidable pitfalls of this model, [3] I would emphasize its tendency to see history as the individual psyche writ large, to reduce history to instinct, and ultimately to eliminate history in the name of studying it. Freud was not only exaggeratedly instinctualistic in approaching history; he was exaggeratedly historicist in approaching instinct (the idea that instincts derive from *actual* historical [or pre-historical] events). Freud did, however, sense that man was part of a flow of larger experience (what we have been calling the symbolization of immortality) that had important bearing on his everyday concerns, a sense insufficiently shared by subsequent psychoanalysts.

These matters were at issue when Otto Rank accused Freud of "scientific illusion" in constructing a psychology which, "despite its naturalistic terminology, does not accept human nature." Rank may well have been right, but for the wrong reason. In attacking Freud's rationalism and his neglect of "the irrational basis of human nature," which, he thought, lay "beyond any psychology, individual or collective," [4] Rank was trapped no less than Freud in the era's polarization of the rational and the irrational.

But Rank was groping toward a social psychology and a view of history that, as we know, placed death and the continuity of life at its center.

renewal. Shared world views embrace the modes of immortality and affirm individual strivings toward connection, integrity, and movement at their deepest psychic levels. Where such collective symbolization—or formulation—is fragmented and ineffective, there will be a negative psychohistorical triad of desymbolization, death anxiety, and denial.

It is probably even more difficult to establish clear criteria for "aberrant history" than for the aberrant individual. In either case one ends up making a moral judgment that usually has something to do with destructiveness, including self-destructiveness. What we call aberrant is so frequent as to be very much part of the general range of human function. But a glance at extreme cases—the Nazi era of German history, disturbed schizophrenic and suicidal individuals—convinces us that we do well to pursue understanding of all such life-destroying, and in that sense aberrant, human capabilities.

At the other end of the spectrum are intact immortalizing cosmologies, viable symbolization, maximum acceptance of death, and minimal death anxiety. We can then infer something close to balanced imagery of death and life-continuity that is collectively held. Mastery of death, that perpetual and perpetually elusive human vision, comes closest to realization. But human history takes place essentially in the middle of the spectrum, and modern history closer to the fragmented-desymbolized end.

Central to the historical process, then, is the continuous change of imagery related to immortality—the shifting and recombining of modes—as various ideas and symbols gain and lose their viability in an unending sequence of death and rebirth.

Major turning points in human history involve fundamental alterations or recombinations of these modes.*

* Franz Borkenau, a brilliant essayist-historian with an interest in these matters, could accuse Freud of having been "unable to decide whether immortality is a nursery tale or basic to the unconscious."[5] Freud surely believed it was both, but Borkenau was asking for greater theoretical and, indeed, historical recognition for so basic a principle. Borkenau also insisted that "denial of death is the most deeply rooted of the archetypes" (which put a Jungian garment on a Freudian torso, and anticipated Ernest Becker).

Borkenau spoke of "the self-contradictory experience of death" as a "basic element in shaping the course of human history." He examined general attitudes toward death in different historical epochs, dividing these into "death-denial," "death-acceptance," and "death-defiance." When death-denial is extreme, "it tends to convert tribal society into a madhouse": every death is attributed to black magic, and virtually all energy is devoted to tracking down those responsible. The development of burial rites, Borkenau argues, suggests a measure of death-acceptance by means of "preserv[ing] life in the dead," as in the case of mummification practices and the placing of nourishment and tools in graves. An attitude of "death-defiance" develops in a Middle-Eastern–Egyptian–Greek–Hebrew–Christian–Islamic cultural sequence, and includes (especially among the ancient Jews) "transference of immortality from the individual to the community." This "new concept" of death-defiance includes acceptance as well as transcendence of death. Against the civilizing sequence there always remains a powerful tendency toward death-

Consider, for instance, the Darwinian revolution of the nineteenth century. Conventional psychological wisdom now has it that Darwin's evolutionary theory has been experienced as a lasting blow to human pride and narcissism, linking man as it does to lower forms of animal life. But the shift from the theological to the biological mode of immortality epitomized by Darwinism may be more significant. A recent commentator on the Great Debate on Darwinism in late nineteenth-century England between Bishop Samuel Wilberforce of the Church of England and the biologist Thomas Henry Huxley claims that the contest depended upon "common acceptance of a stupendous *non sequitur*," the assumption that "if Darwin and Wallace are right, Genesis is wrong, and if Genesis is wrong, Darwin and Wallace are right." The non sequitur is merely a logical one. The issue between Genesis and Darwinism, in terms of collective image-feelings, was anything but a non sequitur. At stake were competing formulations of man's ultimate origins and, by implication, destiny.

The decline of the theological mode was hardly initiated by Darwinism, but dates back at least (in Western history) to the time of the Renaissance. Neither has Darwinism or anything else brought about the demise of that mode. Similarly, the biological mode in no way began with Darwinism—it is perhaps the most fundamental of all imagery of immortality. It probably took some time for imagery of evolution to be absorbed sufficiently to become part of any mode of immortality. But as the imagery took hold, man's sense of biological continuity was extended back into the infinite past and, therefore (at least in a psychic sense), into the infinite future. Man's imagery of his own history now came to include, in some important degree, the history of all his fellow species, not only animal but even plant. And at that juncture, Darwinism radically reactivated the natural mode of immortality as well—the individual's sense of infinite extension in nature. In this way, largely through Darwinism, we have

---

denial, which can predominate to create dark . . . paranoic ages" in which "men . . . see in every neighbor a potential murderer."

Borkenau resembles Rank in this focus on "immortality ideologies" as keys to particular historical periods. He too is "presymbolic" (or "preformative") in his approach, and cannot avoid certain confusions. For instance, in his schema both death-denial and death-defiance are associated with strong beliefs in immortality. Nor is he clear in distinguishing "death-acceptance" from "death-defiance," and he neglects the functional (or formative) aspects of magic. (Much contemporary anthropological writing emphasizes what E. R. Leach calls "the unconscious expressive symbolism of magic as distinct from either secrecy or falsity . . . [and] if magic is expressively symbolic rather than false, magical elements may be present in all types of ritualized behavior in all types of society."[6] But Borkenau's insistence upon the centrality of imagery of death and immortality for historical experience places him in the admirable company of Rank, Ernest Becker, and N. O. Brown.) He perhaps anticipates our own formative approach as well when he speaks of the historical emergence of certain kinds of attitudes that "accept . . . death but also aim . . . at transcending it."

come to see the natural mode itself as a depersonalized extension of the biological mode: "I live on not only in my family-people-species but in the habitat, the physical—and by implication, spiritual—dwelling-place of all life." However infrequently we may be conscious of this imagery, since Darwin it has been more important than we realize.

Finally, there is an immortality-struggle of vast proportions in the science-versus-religion aspect of the Great Debate. Here the image of Darwin and Wallace versus Genesis is not merely a contest between two mindsets, or even between a traditional versus a newer way of understanding man's past. Rather it was a coming of age of the scientific endeavor to assert its version of the mode of immortality via man's works. The cumulative, unending nature of the scientific endeavor had been understood long before that. The principle had been well expressed, for instance, by Joseph Glanvill in the seventeenth century: "We must seek and gather, observe and examine, and lay up in bank for the ages that come after." * Of course many have retained both scientific and religious modes of immortality in their personal symbolic life, including Darwin himself. The either/or image was made possible only by a literalized version of the religious mode, a view of Genesis and the Bible in general as, in every respect, literal recordings of actual events. The real non sequitur in any context is precisely such literalization and accompanying either/or assumptions. Nor is the scientific endeavor in any way free from the danger of an equivalent literalization, the holding to particular ideas, principles, or images beyond their relevant context, as truths free of the flow of intellectual and psychic forms and insights. What we call dogma, in this sense, is an attempt to "stop time," to "stop history," to stop the flow—the perpetual reconstruction—of collective expressions of truth, meaning, and human connection. We should not be surprised that Darwinism has been prone to its own literalization, perhaps more than most scientific endeavors, confronting as it does virtually all the modes of immortalizing symbolism known to man. The extreme intensity with which Darwinism has been both attacked and defended has to do with its special place in a fundamental historical shift in our ultimate imagery concerning ourselves.

Shifts of that magnitude require decades or centuries to take hold imaginatively, but they can be epitomized by a single historical event (such as Hiroshima) or an individual life (Darwin's own). Characteristically, man and event combine to play out what we come to experience as the myth of the hero.

A powerful recent example is that of the life of Mao Tse-tung and the

---

* Glanvill must have been an individual battlefield for these immortal contestants. As an early scientific philosopher who is said to have in some ways anticipated Hume, he had a remarkable appreciation of the scientific method, and published such books as *Plus Ultra; or, The Progress of Advancement of Knowledge Since the Days of Aristotle*; and *The Vanity of Dogmatizing* (later recast as *Scepsis Scientifica*). Yet as a clergyman and chaplain to Charles II he understood God to be the predominant ultimate force, and toward the end of his life admitted to a belief in witchcraft.[7]

Communist Revolution in China. We have noted the special intensity and thoroughness with which traditional China cultivated, by means of family line, the biological (or biosocial) mode. The great shift of the mid- and late twentieth century has been from family to revolution. "Revolutionary immortality" becomes a special blend of the basic modes.[8] It is mostly an expression of man's transformative "works" which are perceived to endure in the revolutionary process far beyond one's individual life span. It also includes an imagined secular-messianic utopia that resembles the very religious mode the revolution condemns. Nature itself is seen as transformed—making possible an embrace of an altered natural mode—on behalf of the revolution. Revolutionary immortality includes waves of collective experiential transcendence rivaling those of mystical and evangelical religion. And it even comes to subsume and reassert a version of the biological-biosocial mode as individual families take their place among endless generations of an ever-expanding "revolutionary family." Moreover, the Chinese have pursued this shift programmatically—through a vast project of more or less continuous "reeducation," "thought reform," and "political study," which critically examines individual lives and thoughts in relationship to revolutionary doctrine in ways that can at different times resemble nurturing psychotherapy, pressured religious conversion, and threatening confession extraction. The thought-reform process is aimed at remaking the "filial son" and "filial daughter" into the "filial communist."[9] The entire Chinese revolutionary mechanism is geared toward subsuming all prior symbolizations of immortality, notably those around family, to the revolutionary mode.

Mao Tse-tung was the hero-prophet of this transformation. He exemplified it, defying his own father and the parental authority of the "old society" in embracing and brilliantly serving the revolutionary cause. Emerging as both military and spiritual hero,* Mao eventually assumed the highest of all heroic mantles, that of the "world redeemer." The latter defeats or slays a combination of father and past—as suggested in Greek mythology by the tyrant Holdfast—in order to release "the vital energies that will feed the universe."[10] The universe is fed—and the vital energy released—in the construction of the new immortalizing structure, the revolutionary mode. As revolutionary hero, Mao was seen not only as defeating one's father and one's past but also as conquering death itself. A perpetual survivor of comrades, friends, and family members killed by the enemy, he became the architect of revolutionary survival (via his leadership on the Long March of 1934–35, a truly epic story of a revolutionary "road of trials") and the formulator of new meaning in death and therefore in life: "All men must die, but death can vary in its significance. . . . It may be [according to an ancient Chinese saying] heavier than Mt. Tai or lighter than a feather. To die for the people is heavier [weightier] than Mt. Tai, but to work for the fascists

---

* They are but two faces of a similar symbolic purpose, Campbell tells us.

and die for the exploiters and oppressors is lighter than a feather." And he provided the images for the Great Shift in immortality at both ultimate and immediate levels: "The thought of Mao Tse-tung" came to signify both a specific body of revolutionary writing and an immortalizing corpus around which the revolutionary transformation is not only achieved but becomes itself perpetual. Mao could thus speak of "storming heaven," challenging all existing deities, political and theological, and say of his movement that "we dared command the sun and moon to bring a new day." Yet he could also write in practical detail about how to go about "saving men by curing their diseases," which meant replacing prior social patterns with revolutionary attitudes and actions. Throughout his revolutionary career, Mao manifested an activist response to death, both in its actual form and in its individual and social equivalents (various forms of chaos, disintegration, and general hopelessness). And he had a special revitalizing talent, a capacity to instill in followers a sense of unlimited power and virtue—whether conducting guerrilla warfare against overwhelming odds, making a revolution, forging steel, overcoming "bad thoughts," recovering from nervous breakdowns, or even achieving extraordinary skill at table tennis.[11] In a phrase, Mao emphasized the capacity to become a "new man" in the "new society." And he remains the hero-prophet, even as some of his policies are being altered or reversed.

The myth of the hero is eminently historical. It is primarily concerned not with the Oedipus complex but with the exemplification of particular forms of confrontation with death; and with the construction, through action or contemplation, of an immortalizing synthesis that is new (though it must draw meaningfully from much that is old) and collectively revitalizing. At the heart of the myth is the hero's teaching, and teaching again the oldest, most compelling, and most recurrent of all human lessons—how to know death and thereby find "more life."

Heroes are sought after at times of historical upheaval. Many fall far short of the criteria we have described. A fundamental defect of false heroes is their literalization of death and killing as opposed to symbolization of death and rebirth. (At the heart of Tolstoy's vision in *War and Peace* is man's willingness to make heroes out of bunglers whose main accomplishment, as pawns of larger historical forces, is their contribution to absurd killing on a mass scale. Since Tolstoy we have had our fill of would-be heroes who contribute to slaughter.) Situations of the most extreme destruction, as in Hiroshima or Auschwitz, do not produce heroes. (In Hiroshima there were some who perhaps came close, but not without considerable ambiguity.) The hunger for the hero's message of revitalization is always much greater than the capacity of those who lay claim to it. The truth of the myth has never been more important. Nor has the heroic life-act—transforming negative death imagery into patterns of collective rebirth—ever been more difficult to realize.

The myth of the hero is connected to psychohistorical theory in the work of

Erik Erikson. His two psychobiographical studies, *Young Man Luther* and *Gandhi's Truth*, are profound evocations of the model of "the great man or woman *in* history."[12] Erikson's great men are spiritual heroes; their historical breakthrough is intrapsychic.* Erikson's spiritual heroes share "a grim willingness to do the dirty work of their ages." By this Erikson means the spiritual hero's mammoth struggle with a particular constellation of psychic conflict that bedevils both him and his epoch—a desperate but ultimately successful effort "to lift his individual patienthood † to the level of the universal one, and try to solve for all what he could not solve for himself alone."[14] Erikson clearly senses that the "great man" connects with ultimate or immortalizing issues (he speaks, for instance, of Luther's having achieved "a decisive step in human awareness and responsibility"), but he does not engage that dimension in structured or systematic fashion.

Freud was perhaps more preoccupied than was Erikson with that ultimate dimension. Even his reduction of history to prehistory, though hardly a satisfactory basis for a psychohistorical theory, could be said to have been in the service of a focus on the ultimate. In his Moses-centered discussion of a concept of the great man,[15] for instance, Freud reverts not only to his *Totem and Taboo* theme of the "primal horde" but to Frazer's principle of the Divine King (who was ritually killed when his powers were seen to be declining so that his soul could be transferred to a vigorous successor). Freud spoke of the tendency to expand "the figure of the great man . . . to divine proportions"—a tendency quite understandable because "Moses may have introduced traits of his personality into the character of his God," and his Jewish followers probably had difficulty distinguishing "the image of the man Moses from that of his God." Moreover, Freud stresses what he views as the Mosaic "advance in intellectuality," derived in turn from the "compulsion to worship a god whom one cannot see." Here Freud stresses the principle of abstraction—the idea "that a sensory perception was given second place to what may be called an abstract idea—a triumph of intellectuality over sensuality. . . ."[16] This reflects the heightened capacity for abstraction made possible by the symbolizing process (as stressed by Susanne Langer) in the service of building a sustaining system of ultimate imagery:

> We wanted to explain the origin of the special character of the Jewish people, a character which is probably what has made their survival to the present day

* Luther's fundamental achievement, for instance, was his "new emphasis on man in *inner* conflict and his salvation through intraspective perfection"—still more specifically Luther's internalization of conscience and deepening of what Erikson calls "the meaning of meaning it."[13]

† Here Erikson follows Kierkegaard in a view of "patienthood" as religious rather than clinical suffering, or what Kierkegaard called a "passion for expressing and describing one's suffering," so that Luther's particular patienthood could be "exemplified in an archetypal and immensely influential way."

possible. We found that the man Moses impressed this character on them by giving them a religion which increased their self-esteem so much that they thought themselves superior to all other peoples. Thereafter they survived by keeping apart from others. Mixtures of blood interfered little with this, since what held them together was an *ideal factor*, the possession in common of certain intellectual and emotional wealth. The religion of Moses led to this result because (1) it allowed the people to take a share in the grandeur of a new idea of God, (2) it asserted that this people had been chosen by this great God and were destined to receive evidences of his special favour and (3) it forced upon the people an advance in intellectuality which, important enough in itself, opened the way, in addition, to the appreciation of intellectual work and to further renunciations of instinct.[17]

The "ideal factor" is none other than the body of Jewish religious and historical imagery so important to Jews' relationship, then and now, to symbolizations of immortality. But Freud gives himself away at the very end of that passage: It is all a matter of "further renunciations of instinct." The "great man's" influence on his followers (at least in the case of the spiritual leader) is in bringing about in them this renunciation of sexuality and aggression. Both the "ideal factor" and the authority of the great man himself make this renunciation possible. It can be sustained only when internalized, made part of a collective superego (here we see Freud's Moses as a model for Erikson's Luther). Freud's superego, with its contained "ego-ideal" takes over much of the theoretical burden of his immortalizing dimension. And that collective superego, though very much a factor in history, remains conceptually a derivative from prehistory and instinct.

In the important sequence from Freud to Erikson in great-man theorizing, Erikson moved from the instinctual to the more genuinely historical, but in the process might have lost some of Freud's supra-personal (in our terms, ultimate) theoretical emphasis. Perhaps that loss was inevitable, given Erikson's formidable task of integrating psychoanalytic and historical imagination. But at least some of the difficulty may derive from Erikson's simultaneous attempt to hold to and depart from Freud's basic paradigm as applied to history—holding to instinct while simultaneously substituting identity for it—and in the process perhaps conceptually neglecting that transcendent area of concern Freud sought so valiantly (and from the standpoint of subsequent theorists) frustratingly within the instinctual idiom.

In their common focus on the historical hero, however, Freud and Erikson could be said to have shared a pre-World War I European sensibility, one that had strong roots in German thought but perhaps reached its apogee in an English author influenced by German romanticism, Thomas Carlyle.*

* Reflecting my own time and historical sensibility, I have, in a series of studies, focused on "shared themes"—consistent psychological patterns in people who had undergone a common historical experience. As my work has involved contemporary or recent history (Chinese thought reform, the Hiroshima bomb, experiences of Vietnam

In Hiroshima, I came to understand that, in order to reconstitute their immediate lives, survivors had to reconstruct something on the order of a larger psychological universe—had to re-imagine a relationship to human connection, to historical process, or to what I came to call their symbolization of immortality. These struggles were bound to be extreme in relationship to atomic survival but they were by no means limited to it. In studies involving long-term adaptations and innovations rather than sudden disaster or direct death encounter, I found that ultimate questions were crucial to everyday experience.[19] And more important for our argument here, they are crucial to our sense of shared history and to shifts in historical imagery.

The capacity for these shifts seems limitless. For as Susanne Langer tells us,

> The great dreams of mankind, like the dreams of every individual man, are protean, vague, inconsistent, and so embarrassed with the riches of symbolic conception that every fantasy is apt to have a hundred versions.[20]

And Loren Eiseley, more bitterly, speaks of man as a "fickle, erratic, dangerous creature" whose "restless mind would try all paths, all horrors, all betrayals . . . believe all things and believe nothing . . . kill for shadowy ideas more ferociously than other creatures kill for food, then, in a generation or less, forget what bloody dream had so oppressed him."[21] There is more to say about man's propensity for collective violence. But the point here is that, in the face of his potentially endless flow of images, man seeks lasting symbolic structure. Man may seem, as Eiseley claims, to quickly forget his own oppressive "bloody dreams," but he does not so much forget them as continue to struggle with their fragments. He is ever in quest of the mental form that can contain those fragments and balance his death terror with a life-giving vision connecting him with past and future. When one seeks to understand historical choices, all paths lead to the ultimate.

---

veterans) I have been able to conduct intensive interviews to evoke these themes. But the principle applies to events of the past as well, whatever the difficulties in digging out the kinds of records that can reveal such themes. Very much depends, of course, upon the investigator's judgment as to which psychological—or psychohistorical—themes are of greatest significance. In terms of data, I have emphasized (using Hiroshima as an example) a kind of empirical center based on direct interviews with a specific group of people, and then a movement outward to observations on groups they formed and leaders of those groups, close attention to the post–atomic-bomb history of the city (as well as to the city's own earlier heritage) and its relationship to part of the rest of Japan and to the world in general. The investigation must also include artistic responses, in this case those of painters, writers, and film makers from both within and without the city. And it should seek relevant historical comparisons—I examined related themes in survivors of Nazi death camps, with the plagues of the Middle Ages, and with various forms of more "ordinary" disasters and death encounters.[18]

TWENTY

Dislocation and Totalism

WE HAVE ASSOCIATED historical aberration with collective forms of destruction and self-destruction. Our focus here is on ways in which historical struggles with death imagery contribute to these expressions of physical and spiritual destruction. Nuclear threats loom so large that one might well begin any discussion with something on the order of the atomic aberration. But collective assaults on human beings hardly began with the nuclear age. We require more general theory on our historical aberrations which can include both prenuclear and nuclear forms and at the same time speak to the quantum *mental* leap from the one to the other. For our assumption is that we are dealing with breakdowns in man's sense of symbolic unity and impairment of his sense of immortality. We shall chart a dangerous four-step sequence from dislocation to totalism to victimization to violence, the first two steps of which we shall examine in this chapter.

During certain historical periods, man has special difficulty in finding symbolic forms within which to locate himself. One could argue that this is man's "natural" state. When, after all, has he been comfortable within his own symbolizing skin, that is, his sense of self? Our assumptions of such premodern comfort—of historical "fit" between individuals and prescribed cosmologies—tend to be colored by a kind of retrospective romanticism. But there are surely degrees in our sense that the particular time we live in is discordant and "out of joint."

From our standpoint, such dislocations have to do with what might be called general or historical desymbolization. This is characterized by an inability to believe in larger connections, by pervasive expressions of psychic numbing. These states can be directly manifested in various kinds of apathy, unrelatedness, and general absence of trust or faith; or more indirectly in social, artistic, and political struggles to break out of that numbing.

As an example of psychohistorical dislocation, one thinks of China between the two world wars, referred to then as "the sick man of Asia." One might also consider, though the situation is much less extreme, the United States in the sixties and seventies. In both cases dislocations have been widely felt, but explanations for them have been too immediate and too logical. It is not wrong to emphasize Vietnam and Watergate in accounting for various versions of American numbing and struggles against that numbing. But Vietnam and Watergate are themselves expressions of much more fundamental and long-standing patterns of American desymbolization around political, social, and religious belief-systems and institutions.[1]

There has, in fact, been very little psychological, and still less psychohistorical, theorizing about collective forms of dislocation and malaise. Two gifted German psychoanalysts, Alexander and Margarete Mitscherlich, have provided an interesting exception in their exploration of psychological patterns in post-World War II Germany.

The Mitscherlichs argue that a general "inability to mourn" for their lost führer had widespread collective consequences for Germans during the first few decades after World War II.[2] Hitler had served as a "collective ego-ideal." His death, therefore, "was not the loss of an ordinary person," but of a love object who had "filled a central function in the lives of his followers." That plus his exposure as "a criminal of truly monstrous proportions" resulted in "a central devaluation and impoverishment" in each individual German ego.* In that way "the prerequisites for a melancholia reaction were created [following Freud's arguments in 'Mourning and Melancholia']." Instead of succumbing to melancholia, Germans invoked defense mechanisms, mostly denial and some repression, through which they could "avoid self-devaluation by breaking all affective bridges linking them to the immediate past." But that same defensive process resulted in widespread apathy and indifference concerning immediate social experience. Lively interest was more or less confined to economic and technological matters, and about virtually everything else Germans remained "chained to our psychosocial immobilism as to an illness involving symptoms of severe paralysis." The society deeply feared trying anything new, as if living under a powerful, unspoken "watchword" of "no experiments!" This contrasted strikingly with pre-Nazi German social history of the nineteenth and twentieth centuries.

Germans (at least of the wartime generation) remained stuck in that

---

* In terms of our earlier discussion of the myth of the hero, we may say that the Mitscherlichs address the psychological consequences around a hero whose transcendence and mastery over death, previously embraced, suddenly become radically tainted.

psychological stance, the argument goes, because a mourning process for their führer would have required experiencing precisely the emotions they felt the need to ward off—guilt, shame, and other forms of anxiety. The resulting psychic immobilism for that generation took on a lasting quality, a kind of autonomy that required continuous reinforcement of defense mechanisms of denial, repression, and isolation in a vicious circle of unmastered history.

The Mitscherlichs, in effect, offer a theory of historical dislocation taking the form of collective stasis. There are difficulties with their theory—they seem to hold too literally to Freud's clinical observations concerning mourning and melancholia, and they are obscure about the theoretical links between their own clinical observations and larger historical behavior. But, as was frequently the case with Freud himself, their sensibilities outdistanced their theory: they draw creatively from a libido-theory model in ways that suggest the limitations of that model in approaching historical experience.

What the Mitscherlichs describe as the inability to mourn is part of a general breakdown in the symbolizing process, a form of dislocation that may accompany any period of confusing historical change, but especially one in which existing image-feelings and modes of immortality have been radically dishonored. The result is not only blocked or repressed mourning but more general survivor conflict. Germans survived the death and loss not only of their führer but also their visions of personal and national virtue, cleansing, revitalization, and triumph around the larger Nazi experience. They did use the kind of defenses the Mitscherlichs describe (we would place them in the general category of numbing) to avoid anything resembling confrontation of the death encounter, the overall historical project. The specter of guilt is at the center here, as the Mitscherlichs suggest, and is probably of much greater importance than generally realized in the survival of more ordinary—less evil—historical periods. But this pattern of numbed guilt may not be so much the cause of the collective stasis described by the Mitscherlichs as a component of the general inability of this group of survivors to find significance in—give inner form to— their death immersion. For in speaking of the survivor we invoke a theory of imagery and meaning. Numbed guilt is part of formulative impairment: it can neither be acknowledged nor avoided because one finds no available images and symbolizations within which to master and transcend it. Equally, one cannot find any such "formulation" or meaning because, to be authentic, it would entail confronting potential dimensions of guilt one is unable to handle psychically. Confronting guilt and taking the path of survivor illumination involves the difficult psychic work of examining ultimate questions and altering modes of immortality. The opposite survivor tendency involves a simultaneous combination of numbed guilt and retained ultimate imagery that is neither functional nor alterable.

From this standpoint, during any period of upheaval and change the overall problem is not mourning as such but the capacity to construct the kinds of immediate and ultimate image-feelings that give form to experience—that is, the problem of formulation. Collective formulation can be suddenly and radically undermined (as in the case of extreme historical experience such as that of the Nazi era); or it can be more gradually subverted over decades and even centuries, as in the case of the European and American historical experience more or less from the time of the Renaissance. In either case, we may speak of psychohistorical dislocation, and of the breakdown of symbolizations around family, religion, authority in general, and the *rites de passage* of the life cycle. The old symbolizations remain, as do the institutional arrangements for promulgating them, but both image and institution are experienced as psychic burdens rather than as sources of vitality. That was the message of student protesters in various parts of the world during the late 1960s.

Survivor theory also sheds some light on the emergence of pockets of startling creativity in the midst of dislocation. While so many Germans were undergoing the post-World War II stagnation the Mitscherlichs described, Gunther Grass was writing *The Tin Drum*, one of the greatest novels written anywhere since World War II; Heinrich Böll was producing his exquisitely sensitive fiction; and Jakov Lind his stark and brutal stories and autobiographical writings. All three probed questions of death and their relationship to life in the context of Nazism and after. All wrote as survivors directly confronting their death immersion, within a literature of survival.[3]

We cannot be surprised that this genre found such powerful expression in post-World War II Germany. But it hardly originated there. One could say that Homer and Dostoyevsky were preoccupied with similar questions. They too described dislocated man—man as survivor—his death immersion culminating in a search for immortalizing connections in the face of vast and threatening desymbolization.

This model of the creative survivor is not confined to literature or art, but extends to all areas of human expression, including social thought and political action. When collectively experienced, the model suggests an alternative to the destructive sequence from dislocation to totalism, victimization, and violence. The alternative, historical as well as individual, is that of survivor illumination. It requires a degree of collective confrontation of death and loss all too rarely achieved. But the ideal persists, and even the most limited approximation inspired by it can have considerable human value.

Dislocation creates a special kind of uneasy duality around symbolization: a general sense of numbing, devitalization, and absence of larger meaning on the one hand; and on the other, a form of image-release, an explosion of symbolizing forays in the struggle to overcome collective deadness and reassert larger connection. This Protean style of individuals—the capacity for psychological shape-shifting (involving belief systems, relationships, and styles of living) as well as for acting on multiple, seemingly divergent images that are simultaneously held—can apply to large groups of people, even to societies. We can thus speak of a protean historical situation in which, in terms of imagery and sometimes behavior, everything becomes possible.[4]

That very protean capacity can be lethal, as Loren Eiseley suggests:

> If one were to attempt to spell out in a sentence the single lethal factor at the root of declining or lost civilizations up to the present, I would be forced to say, "adaptability." I would have to remark, paradoxically, that the magnificent specialization of gray matter which has opened to us all the climates of the earth, which has given us music, surrounded us with luxury, entranced us with great poetry, has this one flaw: it is too adaptable. In breaking free of instinct and venturing naked into a universe which demanded constant trial and experiment, a world whose possibilities were unexplored and unlimited, man's hunger for experience became unlimited also. He has the capacity to veer with every wind, or, stubbornly, to insert himself into some fantastically elaborated and irrational social institution only to perish with it.[5]

What Eiseley is suggesting is that the evolutionary emergence of man the symbolizer creates a terrible danger to the species in the form of indiscriminate image-hunger. Eiseley goes on, despairingly, to associate this image-hunger with an ultimate species emptiness: "It is almost as though man had at heart no image, but only images, that his soul was truly . . . vacant. . . ." The conceptual issue raised by Eiseley's metaphor is that of the relationship between human evolution and the ever-varying waves of individual and historical imagery. Eiseley tells us, in effect, that the first releases the second but beyond that there is no relationship. But we have been viewing the quest for ultimate imagery as itself expressing evolutionary connection—as a way of mentalizing—our involvement in living processes larger than ourselves (whether we refer to them as evolution or God's creation). Our images, then, though widely varied, are nonetheless bound by the nature of that collective quest. And that is true of even the most demonic of images and their associated feelings and adaptations. We draw not from vacancy, as Eiseley claims, in constructing our version of collective life—in making history—but from our own version of an evolutionary heritage. This does not lessen the danger of our images, but if anything deepens the paradox. When we feel ourselves dislocated and experience threats to physical or symbolic existence, we open the floodgates of our minds, call forth a gamut of images from the most fragmented to the most enveloping, and become newly vulnerable to precisely the images we have called forth. Historically speaking, we move from dislocation to partial "relocation" to new dislocation—or worse.

Dislocation breeds collective forms of restlessness and unhappiness. That loss of a shared sense of immortality leads men to seek radical measures for its recovery. Those measures can take the form of ideological totalism, an extremist meeting ground between people and ideas that involves an all-or-none subjugation of the self to an idea-system.*

Eight psychohistorical themes characterize a totalistic environment. Each theme is based on an absolute philosophical assumption—an extreme image— that is, in turn, an expression of an exclusive and incontestable claim to the symbolization of immortality. Thus, on the basis of an assumption of omniscience and of exclusive possession of truth, the totalistic environment attempts to control all communication within a given environment ("milieu control"). On the basis of its alleged "higher purpose" it engages in "mystical manipulation" or a no-holds-barred policy of molding human behavior. On the assumption that it contains the key to absolute virtue, it mobilizes the vast human potential for guilt and shame in its imperative of eliminating all "taints" and "poisons" or its "demand for purity." Around the claim to total ownership of the individual self, including psychic components of imagination and memory, it imposes an ethos of total exposure or a "cult of confession." Around its imposed monopoly on immortalizing ideas and images, it makes of them a "sacred science," one combining deification of the Word with the equally absolute secular authority of scientific method. On the basis of that "sacred science," it institutes "loading of the language" in ways that eliminate ambiguity about even the most complex human problems and reduces them to definitive-sounding, thought-terminating images. The insistence on ultimate primacy of the idea-system automatically imposes a principle of "doctrine over person," so that direct experience and past history are subsumed to (or negated by) ideology, and the individual pressed to remake himself to fit the doctrinal mold.

Finally, there is the overall assumption that there is just one valid mode of being—just one authentic avenue of immortality—so that an arbitrary line is drawn between those with a right to exist and those who possess no such right. This impulse toward "the dispensing of existence" is the ultimate and inevitable outcome of ideological totalism, whether expressed in merely metaphorical or in murderous ways.[7] †

---

*I developed criteria for ideological totalism from a study of Chinese Communist "thought reform" (or "brainwashing"), but then attempted to generalize their applicability to a wide variety of practices—political, religious, educational, and scientific—in various cultures, including my own. In doing so I raised questions about such divergent enterprises as the German Nazi movement, American "McCarthyism" during the fifties, and (in much milder, more indirect ways) about training procedures conducted by Jesuits and psychoanalysts.[6] Similar questions have been raised recently concerning extremist religious cults, such as Scientology and the Unification Church, in America and elsewhere.

†When I first wrote about these themes I had not yet thought out the paradigm of death and continuity or the concept of symbolic immortality. I was groping toward that perspective in attributing the appeal of ideological totalism to "the ever-present human quest for the omnipotent guide—for the supernatural force, political party, philosophical

Totalistic programs seek a once-and-for-all resolution of dilemmas around death imagery and human continuity. Their impulse is not merely to "stop time" (on the order of obsessive-compulsive behavior) but to "stop history." The immortalizing system insists upon its own permanence and immutability. What is proscribed is the very flow and change in collective symbolization that makes man the historical animal he is. His sense of underlying threat—the overwhelming intrusion of various forms of death anxiety—is so great that the symbolizing process itself, the faculty that makes man man, either must be shut down, or radically contained. The "living machine" of individual neurosis is extended to something on the order of a "history machine."

And the totalistic milieu embodies the self-contradiction of that phrase. History as a grand concept is embellished, laid claim to, but in immediate operation it is looked upon as a large mechanism whose parts must be totally meshed and controlled. As in individual obsessiveness, the collective rituals ward off the horrific temptation toward exactly what is most forbidden—alternative images and feelings, especially around ultimate matters. And underlying the totalistic system is parallel imagery of annihilation, but on a collective rather than individual scale—annihilation of one's nation, culture, religion, or even scientific or intellectual belief system. Should there be a significant opening out of the self-closed totalistic system, so the image goes, that which is most precious—the immortalizing vehicle—will disintegrate.

That absolutist image-feeling is a further manifestation of collective survivor experience. Because imagery of death and loss is now intolerable, there is a need for some kind of reversal, for dramatic or even instant revitalization, and, above all, for an airtight guarantee of immortality. In its most primitive expression, the survivor reaction can take the form of glorification of death, blood, and killing. Here we may speak of survivor paranoia and addiction to survival as a continuous struggle to master the death immersion—the "traumatic situation"—by having it in some way reenacted (on the order of the "repetition compulsion"), changing or rearranging the participants, but always with an onrush of survival on the part of oneself or one's group. The repetition

---

ideas, great leader, or precise science—that will bring ultimate solidarity to all men and eliminate the terror of death and nothingness." Mostly, however, I focused on what I would now call *proximate* psychological issues in discussing variations in susceptibility to totalism, issues around early lack of basic trust, experience of unusual parental domination, degree of inclination toward guilt feelings, and conflict or crisis around identity. I was aware that all of these were a matter of degree, part of every individual background. I looked on the capacity for totalism as a consequence of the nature of human childhood, its prolonged period of helplessness and dependency readily creating in the child a need to form imagery of omnipotence around those who first nurture and "control" him, imagery that can contribute greatly to later embrace of totalism. These vulnerabilities can intensify through rapid historical change, leading to a desire to sweep aside the confusions of existing emotions and institutions in favor of total simplicity and absolute coherence.

is not so much that of the original event (as Freud emphasized) as its death component, whether the latter is understood as actual physical annihilation or such psychic counterparts as extreme humiliation and deprivation. The addiction can be to images of death (various forms of carnage) rather than actual killing and dying. In either case this survivor addiction has the psychological significance of struggling to reclaim control of death and symbolization of immortality.

Modern fascist movements epitomize this process. One can point, for instance, to the swashbuckling "Free Corps" in post-World War I Germany, with their imagery of revenge against German humiliation in World War I and at Versailles, of lust for blood and death, of specific enemies (a loose category) and of others on principle. Above all the Free Corps (or "Freebooters") had the need to remain in military formations, in something approximating combat, and "were simply not suited for the work of peace."[8] They were "the men who lived National Socialism before it was organized," as one of them aptly put it. And they became much of the nucleus for that movement, as well as object of some of its early purges. Hitler further developed this kind of imagery, and was personally preoccupied with death and blood ("One creature drinks the blood of another. The death of one nourishes the other."[9])* And there is the famous Falangist slogan, "Hail to death!" One worships the source of one's terror and imposes the worship and aversion of the terror on everyone else. The process, moreover, works—at least to a degree. The death-worship is accompanied by revitalizing imagery—the vision of the "New Germany"—in ways that evoke and maintain powerful enthusiasms.

At least for a time there can be a collective sense of survivor redemption— shared image-feelings of the recovery and reassertion of the eternal life of the group.

These feelings can also be evoked by totalistic groups without focus on death-worship per se. The Chinese Communist movement has had its share of violence and death imagery. But it has concentrated heavily on the revitaliza-tion side—on the "New China" rather than the taste of blood. In the cultural revolution of 1966–68, there was a dawn rally in the great square of Peking, at which Mao Tse-tung appeared before one million screaming and chanting young followers in a scene reminiscent to many of the celebrated Leni Riefenstahl film of the Nazis' Nuremberg rally, *The Triumph of the Will*. This symbolism is not only of a "new community" but also of a "community of

---

* Hitler also mediated individual and collective patterns of machine-like repetition and obsessiveness—in his daily schedule, film viewing, and above all in his perpetual completely repetitious monologues. Hitler seemed to want Germany to "stop time," so that he could install his "historical machine," ever viewing time as the enemy ("Time always . . . works against us") and seeking self-immortalizing imagery that could break out of this disturbing restriction ("The greatest field commander [or some such related designation] of all time"—the "of all time" the operative psychological requirement).[10]

immortals—of men, women, and children entering into a new relationship with the internal revolutionary process." The event conveyed "a blending of the immortal cultural and racial substance of the Chinese as a people with the equally immortal communist revolution,"[11]

Ideological totalism, then, provides a kind of cutting edge of survivor possibility, a form of alchemy in which collective imagery of disintegration is transmuted into shared reassertion of eternal life—but alchemy with its own cost.

TWENTY-ONE

Victimization and Mass Violence

THE STEP FROM TOTALISM to victimization is easy; in fact, totalism *requires* victimization. The claim to ultimate virtue requires a contrasting image—and all too often an embodiment—of absolute evil. Victimization is a more accurate word than "prejudice" for the phenomenon at hand because it better suggests its life/death connections. To be sure, within the phenomenon there is a continuum from mild "discrimination" to slavery and other forms of brutalization and violence. But along the full continuum one can find what Edgar Gardner Murphy, commenting on American race relations in 1911, called an "animus of aggrandizement."[1] *

Victimization involves the creation of a death-tainted group (of victims) against which others (victimizers) can contrast their claim to immortality. Victimizers actually experience a threat to the life of their own group, around which they justify their actions. There are innumerable ways in which that sense of threat can be displaced onto those selected as victims. But once that has been done, a lasting target has been found for the victimizing imperative. The Nazis (and the "Freebooters" who preceded them), in seeking their scapegoat for "the death of Germany" in World War I, included such groups as Communists, leftists, politicians, and the bourgeoisie, before settling more or less exclusively on the Jews. The advantage of creating a scapegoat is that it allows the survivor

---

* The two words are especially apt. Animus suggests not only enmity but the soul- or life-principle sought by the victimizers in their aggrandizement, that is their expansion of their own power at the cost of the victim's.

group to avoid confronting its own death anxiety and death guilt, to find an absolute resolution to the struggle between internal and external blaming, and to move from victimized to victimizer. A victimizer's image of himself as a victim is crucial. He is likely to feel himself continually vulnerable to the deadly assaults of gods, devils, and enemies, and finds that he can best reassert his life-power by victimizing others. In contrast, those groups of survivors who become genuinely autonomous tend to transcend both the victims' identity and the need to be victimizers. That autonomy accompanies the construction of meaning— an alternative formulation—in some degree collectively experienced. But for those who can derive meaning only from a scapegoating formulation, a perpetual victim-victimizer ethos takes hold and every act of aggression against the target group is understood as anticipatory "defense," appropriate revenge, or a combination of both.[2]

This scapegoating formulation has only partial relationship to actual scapegoating ritual. That ritual (the name derives from ancient Hebrew practice, but is applied to related practices especially in primitive cultures) involves the transfer of a community's sin or evil to a person or an animal in order to restore the general moral order. The ritual seeks to cleanse the community of its taint or guilt in order to bring about a "rehabilitation of impaired holiness . . . [for] where holiness is sullied, there too, is life itself impaired, and . . . no continuance can be expected unless and until the taint is removed."[3] Unacknowledged (we would say numbed) guilt, by contrast, could cause the death or disintegration of the community, or even (with the Hebrew development of the ritual) inflict "injury upon God." Failure to confront communal guilt (render it animating) was "a crime against the Kingdom of God" which threatened the entire "divine plan."[4] What we are calling a scapegoating survivor formulation lays claim to the primal purposes of the original ritual: the designation of a bearer of collective taint (of guilt and death) in order to bring about a general spiritual cleansing, a reconstruction of moral order, and renewed life-power. But the original ritual is also perverted in such survivor formulation, and in victimization in general. What is avoided is the collective self-confrontation at the heart of the ritual—"The essential point about the scapegoat is that it removes from the community the taint and impurity of sins *which have first to be openly and fully confessed*"[5]—by evolving around a special group of victims who become, among other things, surrogates for the unperformed psychological work. The victims become psychologically necessary, and must be spuriously admitted to the victimizers' community as substitute-bearers of the death-taint. They cannot be permitted to stray too far from it, physically or psychologically, if the victimizing process is to be maintained. On that availability rests, psychologically speaking, the life of the victimizers.

But we must look beyond the scapegoating theme for additional cultural and historical evidence for a concept of victimization in which, by an imagined symbolic balance, the collective relationship to immortality depends upon its collective denial to others. Mircea Eliade, for instance, stresses the distinction made in early cultures between what he calls the "sacred space" of their inhabited territory and the "unknown and indeterminant space" surrounding it. There is "our world, the cosmos" and the "'other world,' a foreign, chaotic space, peopled by ghosts, demons, [and] 'foreigners.'"[6] In the virtually universal process of what Eliade calls "making the world sacred," there tends to develop a spatial polarization between "life area" and "death area," between those who (according to later terminology) were within or "beyond the pale." We would associate this sacralization of space with early expressions of biological and religious symbolizations of immortality; and its regular accompaniment by a designated and peopled "death space" suggests the beginnings of victimization. Related imagery persists to the present, as suggested by the widespread tendency to equate exile with death. Indeed, the Japanese term *bōmei suru*, "to be exiled," can also be read, more literally, as "to lose life," containing as it does the same Chinese character as the verb *nakunaru*, "to die."

Still more specific are distinctions made in the Pyramid Texts: The eternal life of the pharaoh is repeatedly proclaimed, and "the word death never occurs . . . except in the negative or applied to a foe." The Texts repeatedly insist that the dead kings live: "King Peti has not died the death, he has become a glorious one in the horizon"; "Ho! King Unis! Thou didst not depart dead, thou didst depart living . . ."[7] The immortalization of even a king depended upon the concept of an enemy deprived of that status. Indeed, these forty-five hundred-year-old Texts suggest what may be the most fundamental of all definitions of *an enemy: a person who must die, so that one may oneself transcend death.* They also provide important early clues to the significance of the enduring association of kings with divinity. The king is divine because he is the embodiment of the immortality principle, a representative of the gods if not a god himself. By identifying with their king and his relationship to divinity, ordinary people can share that immortality. For early Egyptians both their pharaohs and the god of Osiris were "guarantors of immortality."[8]* Nonetheless there apparently were

---

*At times the Texts suggest a merging of kings with Osiris, who is both fertility-god and god of the dead. And the ordinary man can connect with the immortality of god or king or god-king, as the Coffin Texts also suggest:

I live, I die, I am Osiris.
I have entered you, and have reappeared through you.
I have waxed fat in you.
I have grown in you.
I have fallen upon my side [the expression for the death of Osiris].
The gods are living from me.
I live and I grow as Neper [the corn-god] who takes out the Honored Ones.
Geb [the earth-god] has hidden me.
I live, I die, I am barley, I do not perish![9]

class distinctions in regard to immortality—some were more immortal than others. Breasted speaks of the "royal hereafter," as "democratised" in historical sequence from royal prerogative, to "mortuary *largesses* of the royal treasury" for nobles to build their tombs, to more general prayers for what the tombs record as "an offering which the king gives," which referred literally to money provided for tombs but probably had the additional symbolic meaning of royal dispensation for proper burial and access to immortality.[10] That democratization of eternal life developed with the cult of Osiris and the evolution of moral criteria influencing one's destiny in ways that prefigured Judaism and Christianity, so that "for the first time immortality dawned upon the mind of men as a thing achieved in a man's own soul."[11]

Early Egyptian class distinctions (kings and nobles "might dwell at will with the Sun-god in his glorious celestial kingdom," while common people thought of their dead as "dwelling in the tomb, or at best inhabiting the gloomy realm of the West, the subterranean kingdom ruled by the old mortuary gods") never ceased to operate in this ultimate form of human "power-struggle." The immortality-centered class structure may be based upon hereditary ties to royalty and nobility, ownership of land, wealth, special knowledge, technical skill, or political or religious standing. No matter how egalitarian its claim, virtually no social movement has eliminated distinctions between its "faithful" and "heathen," its "elect" and its "doomed." Discrimination and victimization, moreover, may take two forms: either denial of *any* access to continuing life; or more subtle gradations in levels of immortality offered. Just as Egyptian servants might expect their hereafter to involve the same kind of menial life, so may religious or political sinners be afforded low places on the hierarchy of collective spirituality or of enduring revolution. In all cases the dispensed denial or restriction is in the service of the dominant group's psychic economy around death anxiety and a sense of continuing life.

These principles take on nasty clarity as we observe their operation in four kinds of victimization: class-caste, color, religious, and political.

When living in Japan in the early 1950s, I was struck by the extreme discomfort most people showed—even progressive students—when the subject of outcasts arose. The Japanese term for that group, *Eta*, has the literal meaning of "abundant defilement," "full of pollution," or "full of filth." The word itself is taboo because it is so pejorative, but I gained the distinct impression that people did not like to say the word because it carried some of the disturbing taint of the outcast group itself.* Those early impressions took on new meaning for me a decade later in my Hiroshima study. Hiroshima and Nagasaki survivors or

---

*One simply did not use the word in polite society, or for that matter in discreet literary reference. The preferred term is a kind of euphemism—*burakumin* ("community people"), always residents of *tokushu buraku* ("special communities") or *"mikaihō-buraku* ("unliberated communities"). As in all such matters, euphemisms serve a purpose, but briefly, and before long come to take on their own pejorative meaning.

hibakusha were often compared to outcast groups because of a discrimination they encountered in both marriage arrangements and work and because of their generally low socioeconomic standing. In exploring the extensive death taint of atomic-bomb survivors (in others' imagery about them as well as their self-imagery) and then reading more about outcast groups in Japan and India, I came to realize that the comparison had profound conceptual implications for the relationship of victimization to death imagery and struggles around immortality.

The *Eta* have been traditionally associated with despised and defiling occupations, those "centered fairly constantly around blood, death, and dirt."[12] We have observed the especially strong Japanese association between ritual defilement and death anxiety. That connection has been formalized in the coined Japanese word *shie*, "death defilement," with particular reference to *Eta*.[13] For segregated communities of *Eta* have been traditionally associated with such occupational "death defilement" as the handling of dead bodies in burial and cremation, the slaughtering of animals, butchering, leather work, fur processing, and as disposers of defiled objects in the precincts of Shinto temples. Indeed the association of *Eta* with ritual defilement evolved from the combined force of Shinto stress on ritual purity and Buddhist prohibition of killing of animals and eating of flesh. *Eta* came, in effect, to embody ritual impurity. Thus, although prohibited from associating with others—their defilement was thought to be dangerously contagious—they became indispensable for performing precisely the unclean (death-associated) tasks no one else wished to perform.

The historical origins of *Eta* are uncertain, but the best evidence suggests that they are associated with these despised occupations. From among the varied activities of slaves and other very low-status people, two of them, tomb-watching and caring for falcons (in connection with the elite sport of falconry), came to be viewed as especially degrading. Those engaged in them, around the time of the eighth and ninth centuries, were gradually forced outside the normal society, and formed their own communities, sometimes around tombs ("telling of their functions as caretakers of the dead") and often around occupations that enabled them to make use of the slaughtering skills they had developed in gathering food for the falcons and dogs of their masters, such as butchering and cattle herding, which they combined with occupations involving handling human dead.[14] Moreover, "By long association with supernatural or ritual impurities the very nature of a man was believed to change," and that adverse change was perceived as "communicable." In other words, the death-tainted professions themselves created the concept of the *Eta* as death-tainted victims.*

---

* It is also possible that those who were later to become *Eta* were chosen for work around tombs and falcons because of some prior stigma that rendered them the lowest of the low. In any case, it was only their association with "death defilement" that made

Not surprisingly, much of the imagery that evolved around *Eta* had to do with their proximity to the dead. They are described as everything from "corpse robbers" to actual walking dead in the form of vampire-like creatures. Thus they are, on the one hand, inferior to the point of being vile and revolting, and, on the other, possessors of superhuman prowess—as the following passage suggests:

> Disgust is the most widely held and commonly verbalized attitude. Individuals who are unwilling even to discuss the *Eta*, distort their faces and exclaim "kitanai" (dirty). Fear is another common reaction. The *Eta* are considered dangerous and capable of inflicting injury on non-*Eta*. This conception is supported by exaggerated stories of their physical prowess and fighting skill; they are likened to the gangsters and hoodlums portrayed in the American movies. There is also the fear surrounding the unknown. The *Eta* are believed by some to be sinister characters with evil powers, and mothers sometimes threaten their children with gruesome tales of the *Eta* similar to our boogey-man stories. It is said, too, that the *Eta* afflicted with such contagious diseases as syphilis, gonorrhea, tuberculosis, and leprosy. . . . Many non-*Eta* wonder if *Eta* girls are "better" than ordinary women, some young males have erotic desires for *Eta* women, and restaurant hostesses often joke about the imputed distortion of the *Eta* male sexual organs.[15]

The passage has many echoes of things we have heard about Blacks and Jews. *Eta* here are associated with the threat of the corpse (vampire-like activities), and with death-like contagion (the more dreaded forms of bodily disintegration, with emphasis on those transmitted sexually): they are, that is, death itself, in its most terrifying representations. But they also, the passage suggests, possess superhuman power, especially sexual power.

This exotic sexuality, so widely attributed to victims, is usually interpreted as an expression of denied sexual attraction (Would you want your daughter to marry an *Eta?*). But the attraction in turn has to do with the immortalizing power the victimizer must attribute to and then psychologically extract from his victim. That power is related to ostensible knowledge and control of a forbidden realm at the juncture of life and death. The exotic sexuality assigned him is a further symbolization of that special "knowledge"—he is superhuman in what he "knows" of the ultimate mysteries, sex and death. He possesses, in the true meaning of the term, a diabolical sexuality. The attribution, then, enables the

---

them into *Eta*. There is an alternative historical theory that links *Eta* with Korean remnants in Japan, a theory that may well combine a kernel of truth (Koreans too have been severely victimized, and there could well have been very early intermingling of the two) with a psychological tendency toward lumping together different victim groups. That tendency is clearly evident in the more fanciful theory of the *Eta* as descendants of a lost tribe of Israel, based on certain linguistic assumptions that are difficult to evaluate. It should be added that this is by no means the only theory to the effect that one of the lost tribes of Israel somehow ended up in Japan.

victimizer to feel that he is not only combating ultimate evil, but absorbing some of its associated power in the service of his own immortality.

The *Eta* have sometimes overlapped with another lowly Japanese caste, the *Hinin*—literally, Nonpeople. *Hinin* included various kinds of itinerant farmers and laborers, beggars, unlicensed prostitutes, and popular entertainers (actors, jugglers, animal trainers, and magicians). Like *Eta*, the *Hinin* were a pariah group, and were often left out of census counts entirely (and were therefore "uncountables," as Ruth Benedict put it), even at times to the extent of falsifying maps to exclude their settlement areas. When they were included in a census, it might be in a category other than that of "people," sometimes with words generally reserved for animals.

But the differences between *Hinin* and *Eta* are psychologically illuminating. *Hinin* were outcasts by occupation and social status, and could occasionally even gain ordinary commoner status. *Eta*, though their designation also apparently originated in their despised occupations, were outcasts permanently and by inheritance. *Hinin* were not, like *Eta*, "hopelessly polluted"[16] and defiled. That permanent taint gave them more stability than *Hinin*. And although both came to monopolize groups of despised occupations, the defilement of *Eta* made them more indispensable for the work they performed, and they often were somewhat less economically deprived than *Hinin*. But the *Eta*, not the *Hinin*, were the true psychological victims. *

With Indian "Untouchables," the situation has been even more extreme. They have been forbidden to enter certain streets or lanes, or else required to carry brooms to brush away their footprints as they passed; or to carry little pots around their necks into which they could spit without contaminating the ground; or to keep specific distances from people of higher castes or shout a warning before entering particular streets (though in other situations they might be prohibited from raising their voices "because the sound of . . . [their] voice[s] falling on a caste Hindu's ear was deemed to be as polluting as . . . [their] touch.") As in the case of *Eta*, they would not enter Hindu temples, homes, or public establishments, or drink from a common village well. They have served as "scavengers and sweepers, the handlers of the carcasses of . . . dead animals whose flesh they eat and whose skins they tan, the carriers of waste and night soil, the beggars and the scrapers, living in and off the dregs and carrion of the society."[18] We again encounter the association of filth and defilement with death anxiety.

---

* These caste designations hardened, and took on clear legal status, during the Tokugawa period (from the seventeenth through the late nineteenth centuries). The legal value of *Eta* life was reflected in a famous court decision of 1859. When an *Eta* youth was killed in a fight between *Eta* and non-*Eta* gangs, an *Eta* leader brought the case to court and the presiding magistrate ruled as follows: "An *Eta* is worth ⅐th of an ordinary person. If you would have me punish the guilty party, let him kill six more of your fellows."[17]

But the victimizing process is even more compulsive than in the case of *Eta* because it is theologically prescribed within an institutionally hardened caste system. Consequently, distinctions about immortality are spelled out with chilling concreteness. The top three Hindu castes—Brahmins (priests), Kshatriyas (warriors), and Vaisyas (farmers and merchants)—are clearly entitled to immortality. They bear the title of Duija or "twice-born," signifying their participation in ritual rebirth; which in turn gives them access to the spiritual knowledge necessary for achieving "release" *(mukti* or *moksha)* from the continuous round of suffering and reincarnation—access, that is, to a final stage of purity or immortality. The lowest of the regular castes, the Shudras (laborers) are "once-born," that is, not entitled to access to the Vedic scriptural path to immortality. But Shudras are part of the ritual cosmology of Hinduism, and serve the upper castes from sufficiently close proximity—and with (at least ideally) sufficiently close identification with them—to achieve a somewhat inferior version of symbolic immortality. But the Untouchable castes—the *Pariahs*—became segmented off from the Shudras (from whose lowest subcastes they derive) and are thereby denied immortality on all counts: They neither have access to "release" or salvation via Vedic teachings, nor to the possibility of "immortality via identification" through proximity to the higher castes. Moreover, Hindu tradition requires them to look upon their deprived status as appropriate and justified, a form of retribution for having sinned during an earlier existence. Since their taint, like that of the *Eta,* is transmitted over the generations, their status could be described as a variety of negative immortality, as a permanent consignment to what is literally "living Hell." [19]

We have emphasized the origins of *Eta* and Untouchables in low-caste assignment to death-tainted occupations. Untouchables, in addition, are thought to be remnants of the indigenous population conquered four or five thousand years ago by Aryan invaders (it is possible that *Eta* had similar origins in conquest, as that has frequently been the case with slave castes). But in this process, imagery around color has been highly significant. The sanskrit word *varna,* used for caste or class, and as a category including the four Hindu castes mentioned, literally means color. The Aryan (sanskrit for noble) invaders (1500 B.C.) who came to form the higher Hindu castes, were an Indo-European people who were said to be fair, in contrast to the aboriginal "dark people" they conquered. And even in the case of *Eta,* an "invisible race" in that they are not racially separable from their countrymen, they are frequently thought of as darker than ordinary Japanese, and that association very likely predates Western influence.

All this raises the possibility, in connection with victimization by color, that anxieties around darkness and blackness extend beyond questions of which racial shade is immediately dominant. In the white West, there is certainly no doubt about the association of blackness with impurity, evil, and death; and whiteness with purity and immortality. Certainly in the white West, those associations are old and deep. There is even an etymological connection between the Latin *niger* (black), (which also had the figurative meaning of wicked) and *nigromantia, necromantia,* and *necromancy,* the art of conjuring up the spirits of the dead or "black magic."[20] * This early association of black with death-linked sorcery gave rise to a vast popular vocabulary, starting with "black magic" and extending to the related idea of "black arts" and its extension into a theological "black mass"—and then into a secular idiom, with blackmail, blackball, blackguards, blacklist, black market, black book, and many more.

There is no doubting the part played by this tradition in creating sharp delineations between "black magic" (sorcery associated with harm and death) and "white magic" (more benign and even curative forms of sorcery). But it is also quite possible that related imagery around color from non-Western (and nonwhite) sources also contributed to that dichotomy. † There are many ambiguities—in the costumes associated with funerals, for instance. The Westerner wears black to acknowledge death and show respect for the dead person. Japanese and Chinese wear white for the same purpose, but white is also associated with imagery of purity that transcends the death at hand. ‡ But generally speaking, blackness is the absence of color and light, and tends to be associated with darkness, night, and death. This association cannot in itself "explain" all victimization by color, but it does suggest at least the possibility of a more widespread psychological readiness to victimize people of darker, rather than lighter, color.

Two additional usages, again mainly from the West but perhaps with broader implications, are especially relevant here. The first is the term "Black Death" for the plagues of the Middle Ages, apparently itself derived from still earlier deadly epidemics.[22] While the hemorrhagic nature of the disease darkens the body and thereby contributes to the term, we must note that although pallor is more frequent when people die we hear no equivalent references to "white

---

* Some believe there is a confusion here between the Greek *nekromanteia* (divination by corpses) and the medieval Latin *nigromantia* (black magic). (*American Heritage Dictionary*, p. 878) But in any case the association is psychologically important.

† Among the LoDagaa of West Africa, for instance, a special kind of diviner or "finder of souls" can recognize a soul that has left its body, an indication that the person in question is going to die. But that separation can be in effect for as long as three or four years before a person dies. At first the separated soul is known as a "white soul," but when there are indications that death is very near, the soul in question is a "black soul." Moreover, black souls are attracted to the vicinity of corpses, and are drawn to funerals where they take up special positions at the foot of the funeral stand and may even cause the structure to sway a bit. There are ceremonies to prolong the life of a person whose soul has left him (known as "sweeping the soul"), but in the case of the "black soul" the sacrifice involved must be heavier: a "black or dangerous animal, such as the sheep or dog, must be killed in addition to fowl offered in the ceremony for the white soul.[21]

‡ The whiteness of both Western and Eastern ghosts is a little more difficult to explain. Here there is certainly an association with death, but also with something on the order of a negative and frightening immortality.

death." Even more specific is the term "blackout," meaning a temporary loss of consciousness or sight, or a more general extinguishing of lights—symbolically an extinguishing of life. These usages also contribute to understanding of reverse patterns of victimization, as, for instance, in the creation by Black literary activists of a "black arts theater" which "hates whites," or still more vividly in Genet's depiction of Blacks' use of "black arts" for the ritual murder of whites in his play *The Blacks*. The victim becomes victimizer by calling forth precisely the special relationship to death he was originally accused of possessing.

In his study of slavery in the United States, Stanley Elkins describes a "simple syllogism" operative in white minds: "All slaves are black; slaves are degraded and contemptible; therefore all blacks are degraded and contemptible and should be kept in a state of slavery."[23] We are reminded of the sequence in *Eta* from "despised occupation" to death taint. But now the taint is rendered visible, concretized in skin color. Elkins argues forcibly that slavery in the United States was unique in brutality and absoluteness, notably in its stress upon "ownership" of the slave's being. There were virtually no laws or customs protecting the slave from abuse, so that mild infringements of rules could be punishable by castration or death. Breaking up slave families often became a matter of policy, supported by law: "A father, among slaves, was legally 'unknown,' a husband without the rights of his bed, the state of marriage defined [in a representative court decision] as 'only that of concubinage . . . with which alone, perhaps, their condition is compatible,' and motherhood clothed in the scant dignity of the breeding function." Others have questioned whether these policies succeeded in bringing about the disintegration of black culture, family, and sense of individual self to the extent that Elkins claims. But few would question his depiction of the entire arrangement as "the most implacable race-consciousness it observed in virtually any society."

The association of blackness with degradation and defilement, in other words, went even beyond the requirements of slavery itself. White attitudes of "fear and loathing"* resulted in extreme barriers against manumission (achieving liberation from slavery), in pervasive horror of miscegenation, unmitigated sexual hypocrisy (white access to black women and a considerable amount of general sexual contact, along with extreme forms of prohibition [especially concerning black men] of sexual interest), and an overall inability to imagine or permit the emergence of a black, nonslave class or community. The Black was to remain in perpetual servitude, a slave "for all generations."[24]

In contrast, Spanish and Portuguese slavery in Latin American colonies, though cruel enough, was conducted with imagery of a "balance between

---

* Elkins generally refers to these attitudes in "the Southern mind," but our recent national history reveals the extent to which they permeated the minds of people of all regions.

property rights and human rights." The slave had certain forms of legal protection; there were a variety of provisions for his obtaining his freedom; when the time came the institution of slavery could be brought to an end without extensive bloodshed, civil war, or postslavery victimization and racial violence comparable to that in the United States. Elkins attributes the difference to the existence of intervening institutions between slave and master, such as the Catholic Church and even the crown. These, he argues, prevented slavery from assuming the totalistic pattern it took in the United States, where there was nothing at all "to prevent unmitigated capitalism from becoming unmitigated slavery." And indeed the particular interest of the Catholic Church in slaves' souls, and sometimes in their welfare as well, led to the sanctifying of their marriages and recognition of their humanity:

> Assumptions perpetuated and fostered by the Church [in Spanish and Portuguese slavery] . . . were, in effect, that [the slave] was a man, that he had a soul as precious as any other man's, that he had a moral nature, that he was not only as susceptible to sin but also as eligible for grace as his master—that master and slave were brothers in Christ. . . .[25]

The church's influence was such that it arranged for slaves to be baptized prior to reaching the American mainland (in most cases, just before or after their arrival in the West Indies, the stopping-point along the way). Once baptized, slaves could be recognized as human beings on whom free labor was imposed, as fellow participants in prevailing immortality structures.*

Not that Spanish or Portuguese were basically more humane than Anglo-Saxon colonists. They simply chose their victims elsewhere, by religion instead of color: "In these countries the concept of 'beyond the pale' applied primarily to beings outside the Christian fold rather than to those beyond the color line." (Their chosen victims were Mohammedans and Jews—the former as "infidels" and the latter as "Christ-killers" and rejecters of grace—as during the centuries of the notorious Spanish Inquisition [begun in 1478 and not officially ended until 1834].) To be sure, there was imagery of darker color in their victimizing process, such as references to "Black Moors," but their idiom was primarily theological in asserting others' death-defilement and their own immortality.

In the United States Blacks came to serve that function. They were not just slaves but psychological victims. Like the *Eta* and the Untouchable they were given the image of the 'antibeing'—the "Nigger." He was perceived by whites as

---

* Christianity among slaves in the United States came much later, often in the form of a Protestant fundamentalism that made use of biblical imagery to rationalize the entire structure of black victimization—and to do so long after the official institution of slavery had ended. But it is also true that more profound forms of American Christianity, among both Blacks and whites, played an important part in asserting black rights at these ultimate levels, as well as in more immediate ways.

either childlike and irresponsible, that is, as less than a living adult, or as an embodiment of one or another form of necromancy, whether as rapist, murderer, or physical or sexual superman or superwoman. James Baldwin is surely correct in his insistence that whites created the "Nigger" in order to avert their gaze from their own troubles. We can be more specific in saying that, as in all such victimization, the image of the Nigger's death-tainted antihumanity emerged from white society's struggles with its profound fears of its own "dehumanization"—its dislocation and desymbolization. Evidence for this argument could probably be found among many responsible for creating the institution of black slavery (especially slave hunters and traders), and there is further support for it in C. Vann Woodward's work on later (postslavery) patterns of black victimization. Woodward points out that at the turn of the century a combination of economic, political, and social frustrations rendered the South "the perfect cultural seedbed for aggression against the minority race." There was a long, cyclical economic depression with no relief in sight that had followed in turn a still longer agricultural depression, and various hopes for reform around new political and social arrangements "had likewise met with cruel disappointments"—so that there had to be a scapegoat. And all along the line signals were going up to

> indicate that the Negro was an approved object of aggression. These "permissions-to-hate" came from sources that had formerly denied such permission. They came from the Federal Courts in numerous opinions, from Northern liberals eager to conciliate the South, from Southern conservatives who had abandoned their race policy of moderation in their struggle against the Populists, from the Populists in their mood of disillusionment with their former Negro allies, and from a national temper suddenly expressed by imperialistic adventurers and aggressions against colored people in distant lands.[26]

We sense the sequence from chaotic dislocation to totalism and victimization—actually revictimization, since imagery of slavery was still so fresh in white minds. In this way, as Woodward goes on to explain, the Negro could serve not only as "a sectional scapegoat in the reconciliation of estranged white classes and the reunion of the Solid South," but also as "the national scapegoat in the reconciliation and reunion of North and South." The result was a sinister "new mood," characterized by the "animus of aggrandizement" mentioned above. Edgar Gardner Murphy could then observe

> . . . an all-absorbing autocracy of race . . . which makes, in the imagination of the white man, an absolute identification of the stronger race with the very being of the state.[27]

We can speak here of chronic victimization, of the construction of more or less permanent psychic forms that become increasingly necessary to the group symbolic life ("the very being of the state"). The victimizing majority in this way incorporates its "animus" into its renewed collective life, its revitalized biosocial immortality.

We have already begun to suggest the special significance of religious imagery for all forms of victimization. Religion has been the primary source of man's overt symbolization of immortality. Threats to that immortality are posed by antireligious groups (heathens, heretics, Antichrists, and other "sinful" collectivities). Here it is particularly useful to look directly at what Freud said about persecution of the Jews.

Freud suggests a number of psychological causes for the extraordinary historical persistence and intensity of anti-Semitism. One of them was meant to have special reference for the Nazi movement, whose venom toward the Jews was clearly apparent in the mid-1930s, when Freud wrote *Moses and Monotheism*. "We must not forget," Freud cautioned,

> that all those people who excel today in their hatred of Jews became Christians only in late historic times, often driven to it by bloody coercion. It might be said that they are all 'misbaptized'. They have been left, under a thin veneer of Christianity, what their ancestors were, who worshipped a barbarous polytheism. They have not got over a grudge against the new religion which was imposed on them; but they have displaced the grudge on to the source from which Christianity reached them. The fact that the Gospels tell a story which is set among Jews, and in fact deals only with Jews, has made this misplacement easy for them. Their hatred of Jews is at bottom a hatred of Christians, and we need not be surprised that in the German National-Socialist revolution this intimate relation between the two monotheist religions finds such a clear expression in the hostile treatment of both of them.[28]

In other translations the "misbaptized" is rendered as "badly christened." And this concept of "badly christened" Christians is consistent with our own emphasis on the enormous psychological difficulty faced by any people in making a transition in modes (or elements of modes) of immortality. Freud also brought in his theories around primeval parricide in connection with Christ's death, so that the Christian accusation toward Jews, "You killed our God!" refers back to the much earlier murder of Moses and ultimately to the *Totem and Taboo* thesis of the primal horde and the first parricide. Freud's suggestion here is that the sacrifice of a "son" (Jesus) represents the atonement for that earlier sequence. And by making that son the son of God, Christianity becomes a "son religion" in contrast with the Judaic "father religion" and "has not escaped the fate of having to get rid of the father."[29]

Here the reasoning is convoluted, but again consistent with the idea of an intramonotheistic struggle over claim to immortalizing power. We would say that this generational clash has much less to do with possessing the mother than possessing the power of life-continuity. In addition, Freud suggested that the very existence of a Jewish remnant, a group that persists as a people separate and different from their "hosts"—despite centuries of the most cruel persecutions—is a nagging reminder to Christians of the incomplete triumph of the newer claim to immortality. The situation is all the more painful to Christians, Freud felt, because the Jews had been "the first-born, favourite child of God the father." We would shift the emphasis from that of "family dynamics" to a suggestion of "intimate rivalry" for ultimate power between the two religions closest to one another in their origins and their monotheistic visions.*

Freud's additional point has to do with the Jewish practice of circumcision, which further "made the Jews separate . . . [and] made a disagreeable, uncanny impression, which is to be explained, no doubt, by its recalling the dreaded castration and along with it a portion of the primeval past which is gladly forgotten." [30] Here we would suggest that whatever terror castration may have evoked is likely to be more related to its practice by an "exotic" threatening group than to the primeval associations Freud suggests. Circumcision undoubtedly evokes castration fears, but these in turn become part of a mixture of awe and fear around the more-than-natural power attributed to the victim because of his fundamental relationship to defilement and to the dead. We need only recall images of Jewish necromancy—of Jews as grave robbers, well-poisoners, and plague-spreaders, and of Jewish ceremonies involving the drinking of blood and the ritual murder of children as sacrifices for a "black mass." Hence we may make the same kind of assumption we have made in connection with individual psychology: the fear of castration, even when specifically related to the custom of circumcision, is part of larger psychic terror around collective disintegration.

Once more Freud's sensitivity to questions of death and revitalization had to be conceptually subsumed to his instinctualism. But much of what he said fits readily into the proposition I want to suggest: *Religious wars and persecutions are, at bottom, expressions of rivalry between contending claims to immortality and ultimate spiritual power. Religious victimization is a one-sided version of that process with the specific psychological functions of finding a target for death anxiety, sweeping away cosmological doubt, and achieving (or maintaining) revitalization.*

From this standpoint, monotheism, with its image of a single, all-encompassing deity, represents one of the great human shifts in the symbolization of immortality. The shift has involved all of the world's great religions, and has been fundamental to man's development as a cultural animal, to his articulation in his uniquely self-conscious fashion of the evolutionary principle of continuous life. One could even say, with Teilhard de Chardin, that Darwinism and monotheism, properly understood, need not be rivals but could

---

* This is consistent with Freud's principle of what he calls "the narcissism of minor differences." As in other situations the "narcissism" involved turns out to be the most fundamental struggle with disintegration and renewal.

in fact be allies in the representation of man's ultimate material and spiritual involvements. But monotheism itself could never be more than partially achieved, given its enormous psychological and cognitive demands, the persistence of still older imagery, and the rapid ascendancy of alternative secular (notably scientific) modes of immortality. Claimants to monotheism—whether Jewish, Christian, or Mohammedan—have thus been plagued by the disintegrative image-feelings of incomplete or blocked realization. Here there is a parallel to Freud's "badly-christened Christians," with a similar residue of hostility toward those who have not taken the step to monotheism. And the pattern goes beyond the question of when, and in what order, particular groups embraced monotheism.

Judeo-Christian struggles are a unique subcase. The problem evolves around images of separation and autonomy on the one hand and continuity and replacement on the other. Jewish thinkers have increasingly objected to the term "Judeo-Christian tradition," because they see in that term an implicit argument for a historical flow culminating in Christianity. And much Christian thought encourages that interpretation, and depicts the Jews as historical "holdouts" from that culmination. Even if the language is friendly, it thus contains the implication of the "survivor remnant." In this way Jews make constant contact with Christian doubt, with the disturbing difficulty of achieving the ideal of universal love. And embodied symbols of Christian doubt readily become targets for Christian death anxiety.

It also must be said that there is more than a kernel of historical truth in this imagery around Jews as perpetual survivors. In predominantly Christian cultures, Jews are neither "heathen" nor "saved"—neither nonpeople nor sharers of grace, and perhaps have always constituted what one writer has called a "living reproach" to the Christian claim to spiritual ascendancy. The Jewish presence has found itself "hounded out of history."[31] The very vision of the "conversion of the Jews" has long suggested a Christian utopia in which doubt, meaninglessness, and in a sense death itself, would disappear.

Among Christians inundated by various forms of death anxiety—as was true of many Germans between 1918 and 1945—the vision of "conversion of the Jews" can give way to one of "extermination of the Jews," and the utopia can take on any combination of mythic (Nordic-Aryan sagas) and political (the vision of "national socialism" with a leader-principle encompassing all of German "folk" (or racial-cultural substance) components. The amalgam may be hostile to Christianity itself, as Freud pointed out, but Christian imagery—or a perversion of it—is bound to remain important, as was very much the case with the Nazi movement.

Some recent historical and linguistic observations suggest the central significance for the Nazi movement of the Jew as psychological victim.[32] "'The Final Solution of the Jewish Question' in the National Socialist conception was not just another anti-Semitic undertaking, but a metahistorical program devised with an eschatological perspective. It was part of a salvational ideology that envisaged the attainment of Heaven by bringing Hell on earth."³³ More specifically, the Nazi movement became a pseudoreligion which drew heavily upon Judeo-Christian metaphysics, albeit in perverted and reversed form. One of Hitler's greatest rhetorical talents was to evoke in the German people a sense of perpetual life-or-death crisis. Always at stake was the spirit, essence, vitality, and purity—that is, the life-power—of the German people. And the threatening force was the Jew, by his very existence.

The Jew was the embodiment of moral decay—of physical and sexual perversion, spiritual petrifaction, and cultural degeneracy. The images are closely linked to death and deterioration—the Jews as carriers of filth and disease, of plague and syphilis and "racial tuberculosis," as spreaders of every kind of "poison," and as parasites, vampires, bloodsuckers, and racial contaminators. The Aryan becomes, importantly, the counter-Jew or anti-Jew. He is the embodiment of German racial revitalization, renaissance, and renewal. His is the special charisma of world leadership, the possession of life-power. He is, that is, the ultimate anti-Antichrist. For in this victim-centered cosmology, the Antichrist (the Jew) comes first and creates the Aryan or anti-Antichrist.

No wonder, then, that the Nazi victimizing impulse preceded and took priority over everything else—even when technological and transportation requirements of the death camps interfered with a failing war effort. For Hitler meant it when he wrote in *Mein Kampf*: "I believe that I am acting in accordance with the will of the Almighty Creator: *by defending myself against the Jew, I am fighting for the work of the Lord.*" He similarly pitted the Aryan "men of God" against the Jewish "men of Satan," and spoke of the Jew as "the anti-man, the creature of another god . . . [who] must have come from another root of the human race."³⁴ In the final words of his political testament, which he dictated on the last day of his life—his "suicide note" to the German people—he reaffirmed his "highest" aim: "Above all I charge the leaders of the nation and those under them to scrupulous observance of the laws of race and to merciless opposition to the universal poisoner of all peoples, international Jewry."³⁵

We sense the emptiness at the heart of the victimizing process. The victim himself must become the source of "religious inspiration"—of animating visions of the spiritual purity and eternal life of one's "sacred community."* We see again the truth—even prophecy—in Freud's characterization of the Nazis as

---

* One implication of this argument is that these collective patterns of victimization cannot be understood as secondary to Hitler's individual psychopathology. His and his ideologues' depiction of Jews made use of relatively conventional victimizing imagery (victim as death-linked, defiled, degenerate, "poisoner"). That imagery, centering on the Jew, has long been available in Germany and elsewhere in Europe. What needs to be explained in psychobiographical approaches to Hitler is the way in which his psychopathology combined with his extraordinary capacity to articulate these victimizing

"badly christened" Christians. Theirs was the most malignant of all outcomes of the two-thousand-year-old struggle with the demanding images of monotheism, with man's efforts to spiritualize his relationship to the evolutionary process.

Like all victims, Jews have in the course of their history been confined to particular occupations. They too have been slaves, tanners of animal skins, "collectors of dog dung," and have been "employed in administering corporal punishment and in carrying out the sentence of death."[37] And in their "defilement," they were sometimes prohibited from serving Christian customers. (The defilement was concretized in the phenomenon of the "Jewish badge," required by a decision of Pope Innocent III and the Lateran Council in 1215, usually worn visible on one's person and sometimes placed on the houses of Jews as well, a phenomenon revived in both aspects in Nazi Germany.)[38] The Jews did not characteristically remain in these traditionally death-linked occupations. Rather, the particular form of occupational degradation to which they have been assigned, over most of their history, is that of money-handler or "usurer." Jews' association with money is generally attributed to their having been increasingly excluded (throughout much of premodern Europe and the Middle East) from ownership of land, whether by decree or other social pressures. But, although the statement is by no means false, it misses the point.

A psychological key to our argument lies in the word "usury," and the image-feelings it evokes. In the European imagination, usurer means Jew—the two words, in many languages, became virtually interchangeable. The term evokes images of sinister Jewish greed and exploitation— of Shakespeare's Shylock and Dickens's Fagin. The primary meaning of the word is "the fact or practice of lending money at interest," and only in later use did it come to suggest "excessive or illegal rates of interest for money on loan." (OED, Vol II, 3577) In its derivation, the word is built around the idea of "using money" (from the Latin *ūsūria*). Hence the sense it has always conveyed of achieving gain not through "honest labor" or "the bounty of nature," but from manipulation of money at the cost of others. In Judeo-Christian tradition, the Old Testament (Deut. 23:19–20) admonishes that "You shall not charge interest on anything you lend to a fellow-countryman . . ." but "You may charge interest on a loan to a foreigner"; and the New Testament (Luke 6:35) tells us that "Even sinners lend to each other to be repaid in full. But you must . . . lend without expecting any return." Much of Luther's attack on the papacy was because of its

---

impulses along with their revitalizing components so effectively for a large segment of the German people. Thus Rudolf Binion[36] is right in his focus upon Hitler's capacity to articulate Germany's collective trauma following World War I, but in my judgment misleading when he sees so much of the source of Hitler's rabid anti-Semitism in his traumatic experiences during World War I and his feelings toward the Jewish physician who attended his mother during her fatal disease. Nor does the poison-centered imagery of that victimization derive from the gaseous poison Hitler inhaled during World War I or the iodoform treatment the physician employed.

usurious commerce ("The God of the Papacy is Mammon") and its "market in souls" or selling of "indulgences," really the marketing of immortality. This was not technically usury—that, the church relegated to others. During the twelfth and thirteenth centuries a series of church councils had strongly condemned the practice, to the point where "Usurers were excluded from communion, confession, and absolution, and anyone who stated that usury was not a sin was declared a heretic and became subject to the Inquisition."[39] He would also be denied Christian burial, that is, in every way excluded from the Christian structure of immortality. The prevailing principle was (according to T. Wilson in his *Logike* of 1551): "No Christian is an Vsurer." (OED, 3576) Christians of course *were* usurers—the Lombards of Padua were notorious examples, so much so that Dante placed them in one of his circles of hell—but spiritual consistency required that the occupation become associated (in mind and as much as possible in practice) with a pariah group, living more or less outside of the medieval theocratic order, such as the Jews. Kings and princes came to depend upon the arrangement, and Jews could then be said (in Germany) to "belong to the imperial chamber," and in Spain to be "the king's treasure." And only occasionally was this hypocrisy confronted, as when Pope Innocent III complained that "while certain princes 'themselves are ashamed to exact usury, they receive Jews into their hamlets . . . and towns and appoint them their agents for the collection of usury.'"[40] Here the Jews' function psychologically parallels that of the *Eta* who became indispensable to secular and religious authorities for handling corpses and other defiled materials in connection with shrine ritual, that is, for doing the defiled tasks that had to be done but that no one in accepted society could afford to do at the risk of losing claim to immortality.

Both "defilements" have a relationship to power, but in the case of moneylending that relationship is more evident. Norman O. Brown has brilliantly evoked the sacred nature of money, beginning with the tendency of primitive cultures to invest materially worthless objects of exchange (shells, dog's teeth, feather bands) with "magical, mystical, religious" feelings. Brown draws upon Laum in stressing the symbolic identification of round coins with "the sacred significance of sun and moon in the . . . astrological theology invented by the earliest civilizations."[41] Money has always had sacred connections, hence the origin of mint and bank (at least in the West) in Roman temples, and the traditional sense on the part of priests of many faiths that they should play a large part in controlling the accumulation of this form of power. Among religious and secular groups alike, money has been less important as a rational means of exchange or indication of social standing than as a form of *mana*—of invisible power beyond what it can immediately buy, of power to extend life and overcome death. This explains the "religious" dedication, associated specifically with capitalism, to the accumulation of family fortunes, and the immortalizing control, through the convoluted arrangements of wills and trusts over many generations, that one can exert upon others from "beyond the grave."

But there is a sense of something tainted about this particular source of immortalization—a sense that money represents an illegitimate immortality system. Around that sense of illegitimacy social and bodily imagery converge, perhaps reflecting an early discomfort about building an immortality system around lifeless matter. This association with "deadness" may be the main psychological relationship between money and feces, the relationship which Freud rightly emphasized if not always for what we would consider the right reasons. There is a parallel social "disgust" around money having to do with the creation of an immortality system essentially devoid of moral vision. The reliance upon it is part of the emptiness—the absence of larger meaning—we spoke of as being at the heart of the victimizing process. And as Luther made explicit, there is always a devil lurking underneath the monetary mode of immortalization—or, in Marxist-secular terms, a life-destroying fetish. In this sense money is even more tainted than feces because it cannot claim relationship to organic process or to nature in general.

The Jew was thus cast at the center of one of man's most fundamental ambivalences. Surely no object has been so condemned and at the same time so sought after. Money as "immortal stuff," as an indestructible material-symbolic form of transcendence is always at the same time the "evil excrescence" or "filthy lucre." And the construct of usury, evoking image-feelings of extreme power and equally extreme disgust, exemplified that dilemma.

Those assigned to money-centered occupations—with their direct relationship to power and "high culture"—may be thought of as "elite victims." As in the case of the Jews, they are likely to be people of sufficient cultural standing and achievement to evoke strong feelings of envy and admiration, along with contempt, anger, and fear. The elite victim handles "filthy (or deadly) lucre" rather than feces or corpses. The differences between the two substances are as important as the parallels. In addition to its immortality system, money can place one near the power-centers of society, and with even partial lifting of restrictions on elite victims—for instance, the designation of the status of "protected Jew" and "court Jew" for those who serve the state or its royalty—can permit them to emerge as extraordinarily powerful bankers to nations, kings, and chancellors. Thus the Rothschilds developed "a dynasty of international bankers . . . [with] their courts in Vienna, Paris, London, and Naples . . . a commercial equivalent of the Napoleonic dynasty . . . no doubt less glorious . . . [but] also less bloody and more enduring." [42] And Gerson von Bleichröder, "the German Rothschild," became banker to Bismarck, his political agent on missions throughout Europe, and "the first Prussian Jew to be ennobled without converting to Christianity." He also financially served many in Bismarck's Prussian entourage, often "covertly, as money remained the great taboo." He was both respected and reviled and "the simultaneity of his secret power and social pomp enraged the new anti-Semites of the 1870s, who . . . believed that Jewish power had become a mortal menace to German life. . . ."[43]

Bleichröder illustrates the pattern by which the money-related immortalizing power of the elite victim becomes in itself a new source of vulnerability. Having granted him that power, his victimizers feel, so to speak, "out-immortalized" by the very group they had relegated to a death-tainted status—and therefore newly threatened by their own victims. The most extreme revictimization may then result, such as the Nazis' murder of six million Jews. That project also demonstrated victimizers' capacity to transform their victims, speedily and thoroughly, from elite to absolutely degraded status. (Significantly, the term "court Jews" was used in death camps for those who managed to obtain certain privileges by means of personal services to their masters.)

Under certain historical conditions, overseas Chinese—those living in various countries in Southeast Asia—have also qualified as elite victims. They too have been deeply involved in moneylending and finance, partly (though by no means wholly) as a result of restrictions on their owning land or entering other professions. They share other historical parallels with Jews—a very old tradition that predates and partly gives rise to the very cultures in which they found themselves victimized, and a mixture of a variety of cultural talents bound up with inclinations toward exclusiveness and cultural ethnocentrism. (One wonders whether the explosive mass murder by Indonesians of hundreds of thousands of Chinese in late 1965 may not be another example of the revictimizing of elite victims. The very standing and influence of such elite victims, and the immortalizing power they are perceived to possess, probably renders such projects especially savage.)

Twentieth century totalitarianism recreates in its own image the processes of religious victimization. The resulting political victimization becomes even more central to the project than in the original religious model. For the political totalizers may well be more vulnerable to anxieties around collective vitality and therefore more in need of a constant flow of victims through whom those anxieties can be expressed, if not overcome. What Kenneth Burke calls the "curative role of victimage" stems from "the rhetoric of religion."[44] But certain aspects of it may be especially clear in its political forms. Indeed, the process of victimization—of locating and abusing enemies of the State, Party, working class, or the People—becomes crucial to maintaining the structure and function of the regime.

For in addition to imposing external controls, totalitarian governments seek total mobilization of spiritual power. But they (in Camus's terms) confuse totality with unity, and a psychological mechanism is needed to help deny that confusion—which is where victims come in.

The victim can be held responsible for what is, in essence, an impossible project. Lenin is reputed to have said, "We must be engineers of the human soul,"[45] which may well be the most ambitious and illusory process ever embarked upon, for it suggests mobilizing spirit and technique on behalf of political salvation. This process requires internal "enemies and betrayers" who "try to prevent [that salvation] in the same way . . . the devil tries to undermine and destroy the work of those who are in the service of the City of God."[46] But the language becomes contemporary, political, and potentially genocidal—with the call to "liquidate," "exterminate," or "destroy" all such enemies and betrayers. The victims come to be viewed as deadly contaminants, agents of a disease or a diabolical force that threatens to destroy the entire project. They are seen as subverters of the powerful psychological satisfactions totalitarianism can provide—of shared feelings of vitality and purpose and of visions of national and revolutionary immortality. They become associated, for totalitarian manipulators and many ordinary people as well, with disturbing images of chaos and disintegration. A scapegoating principle also prevails, in that the victims become repositories for everyone's sense of guilt over inability to achieve prescribed levels of purity in belief and behavior. Kenneth Burke has stated the sequence with cryptic poetic brilliance:

> Here are the steps
> In the Iron Law of History
> That welds Order and Sacrifice:
>
> Order leads to guilt
> (for who can keep commandments!)
> Guilt needs Redemption
> (for who would not be cleansed!)
> Redemption needs Redeemer
> (which is to say, a Victim!)
>
> Order
> Through Guilt
> To Victimage
> (hence: Cult of the Kill). . . .[47]

Ultimately, as the symbolizing force of the whole project wanes (as in the Soviet Union today, for instance) totalitarianism can be defined as "deification of a power system."[48] At that point anyone who tries to think for himself may become a victim: "The heretic is one who has personal ideas."[49] The totalitarian regime, moreover, "insists on holding every man, even the most servile, responsible for the fact that rebellion ever existed and still exists under the sun."[50] That is, there is a shared sense that totalitarian victimization may strike anyone, and that anyone may "deserve" it.

In political victimization, then, there is a linguistic polarization of "ultimate terms": "god terms" for the embodiment of one's group vision, and "devil terms" for one's designated victims, or political enemies. Thus in Chinese revolutionary practice, as expressed in the thought-reform procedure, devil-victims were "capitalists," "imperialists," "members of the exploiting classes," "bourgeoisie," "lackeys," or "running dogs" of any of these groups; and later on, "revisionists" (meaning those who followed the Soviet path). And each of these nouns could be readily turned into an adjective to describe one's tainted mentality ("harboring revisionist ideas") in a kind of previctim designation. These are sharply contrasted with the "god categories"—"Communist," "the People," "the Party," etc.

The devil-victims, as contaminators, are associated with "filth," "evil," and various Machiavellian schemes; they are "decadent," "dying," in the midst of their "last gasps," or relegated to the "ash can of history." During the Chinese cultural revolution, the terms were folkloric and colorful: "demons," "devils," "monsters," "ogres," "ghosts," and "freaks." These words suggested the death-tainted and nonviable, those severed from human continuity. In contrast, the "god categories" are "the way of the future," "on the side of history," energized by knowledge and virtue and an aura of progress and permanence—in other words, on a direct path to immortality. We then see the "logic" of the totalist theme of "dispensing of existence"—and of acting upon that theme by persecuting, in whatever form, members of the "devil group." We can also understand the special emotion behind the term "deviationist" or "revisionist." For these suggest a person who originally embraced the true path to immortality but then, while claiming to maintain it, created a subversive alternative that threatened to undermine the entire immortalizing structure.[51]

Rightist political rhetoric calls forth similar principles in more or less reverse fashion. In America, for instance, the "devil term" has been "communist" (whether as noun or adjective). Variations have included "atheistic communism," "communist dupe," being "soft on communism"—as well as "collectivism," "socialism," or even "liberalism" or "liberal." These tend to be equated with "un-American" or with "destroying our American way of life," "threatening the fabric of American life," or "subverting American values." Though the categories can become stereotyped, and the terms applied almost automatically, they nonetheless connect with deep anxieties around desymbolization and imagery of death taint.* In contrast, the "god category" has included traits and groups that suggest the pure and the eternal: in the form of hallowed principles of "individualism," "individual initiative," and "private property"; of the theological mandate of the "God-fearing"; or of the immortal cultural substance of being "part of the American way of life" or simply "American."

The first of these two forms of political victimization (mostly in the idiom of Marxism, Leninism, or Stalinism) can be called transformationist. It is carried

---

* The same can be said of former Vice-President Agnew's more colorful invocation of "rotten apples," to characterize people in some of these devil categories.

out around a vision of remaking the individual, together with social existence in general, into something totally new. The second is restorationist, in the sense of drawing upon an equally utopian past—a golden age that never was—as the absolute human goal. These visions of Ultimate Future and Ultimate Past psychically resemble one another, based as they both are upon image-feelings of perfect harmony and total absence of conflict or strife. Those image-feelings connect at the individual-psychological level with the perceived "oneness" of the early mother-child relationship, and at the collective level with religious and philosophical visions (both Eastern and Western) of absolute spiritual harmony. Thus, whether a member of the Chinese Communist "Red Guard" (during the cultural revolution of the late 1960s) persecutes alleged "reactionaries" or "revisionists," or an American Minute Man (or member of the John Birch Society) seeks to suppress or deal violently with alleged "Communists," the victimizing imagery is part of a quest for that oneness. If only we could eliminate those disturbers of the cosmic peace, the imagery implies, we could achieve total brotherhood of our own (biosocial immortality) and a psychic state of absolute purity (experiential transcendence). In victimizing others, then, one seeks not only to master ongoing history but to enter into a state outside historical time.

Not all expressions of transformation and restoration are associated with victimization—there are endless varieties of both in historical experience in general. But they can be extremely dangerous when they enter a totalizing, and then victimizing, phase. The general sequence is from transformation (revolution) to restoration (counterrevolution). Jean-Paul Sartre, in his classic essay on anti-Semitism, brilliantly suggests some of these principles, in ways that apply to German Nazis and their American imitators no less than French anti-Semites. Sartre first identifies anti-Semitism as a "total choice of oneself," a comprehensive attitude that one adopts not only toward Jews but toward men in general, toward history and society . . . a conception of the world . . . [a] syncretic totality."[52] It is, in other words, an involvement of the entire symbolic life. He goes on to stress the importance for the anti-Semite of the experiential element: "[Having] chosen hate . . . it is the *state* of passion that he loves." Sartre speaks of what we could call restorationist nostalgia for perfect harmony, a vision in which "the primitive community will suddenly reappear and attain its temperature of fusion"—hence the slogan, "reunion of all Frenchmen!" History is seen as a Manichean "struggle of the principle of Good with the principle of Evil" in which "one . . . must triumph and the other be annihilated"—the quest for immortalizing purity behind all victimizing totalism:

> Underneath the bitterness of the anti-Semite is concealed the optimistic belief that harmony will be re-established of itself, once Evil is eliminated . . . Knight-errant of the Good, the anti-Semite is a holy man. The Jew also is holy in his manner—

holy like the untouchables, like savages under the interdict of a taboo. Thus the conflict is raised to a religious plane, and the end of the combat can be nothing other than a holy destruction.[53]

Finally, Sartre emphasizes the pervasive death anxiety so central to the whole process:

[The anti-Semite] is a man who is afraid. Not of the Jews, to be sure, but of himself, of his consciousness, of his liberty, of his instincts, of his responsibilities, of solitariness, of change, of society, and of the world—of everything except the Jews. He is a coward who does not want to admit his cowardice to himself; a murderer who represses and censures his tendency to murder without being able to hold it back, yet who dares to kill only in effigy or protected by the anonymity of the mob; a malcontent who dares not revolt from fear of the consequences of his rebellion . . . anti-Semitism in short, is fear of the human condition.[54]

This fear of the human condition is bound up with primal anxieties around separation, annihilation, and stasis, with the death imagery associated with radically impaired symbolization of immortality. The victimizer seeks public confirmation of the absolute distinction between his own immortality and the victim's death taint—when an Albigensian recanted his heresy before the papal Inquisition, when a Jew renounced his religion and asserted his conversion to Christianity before the Spanish Inquisition, when a Chinese intellectual condemned his bourgeois past and affirmed his embrace of Communism, when an American ex-radical renounced his evil associations before a congressional committee and affirmed his Americanism—all these provided public theater for the reassertion of the "true path" to immortality, always set off against the "deadly error" of the wrong path. When the process becomes extensive or violent—the public autos-da-fé of the Spanish Inquisition, the Red Guard denunciations and physical abuse of old Party members, and the McCarthyite vilification of distinguished American statesmen—it reflects the resurgence of death anxiety within the victimizing group. And since the state of transcendent unity sought is never attainable, the hunger for victims may be unassuageable.

Victim's Responses

Victims' responses are related to these immortalizing concerns. What is psychologically most brutal in victimization is the extent to which the victim can become dependent upon the victimizing immortality system. Consider a dialogue that took place not very long ago between an *Eta* and a sympathetic American anthropologist:

Are you the same as common people?
No. We are dirt, and some people think we are not human.

Do you think you are not human?
(A long pause) I don't know.[55]

The *Eta* who tells us he is uncertain about whether he is human is doing more than merely mimicking what others have told him. He is expressing the dilemma—even logical paradox—of the perpetual victim. He must, as a human being, seek an immortality system, a means of symbolizing perpetual connection. The only such system available to him is one that specifically denies his own humanity, his own participation in the immortality structure. That is, he participates in an immortality system by internally experiencing his nonparticipation in it. Or, more accurately, he must inwardly experience his psychological victimization (his death taint and alleged subhumanity) if he is to have any symbol structure at all, if he is to feel himself to exist. The situation is something like that of a man for whom the only food available is a poison that maims his body while providing enough nourishment to keep him alive. *

We can now better understand victims' tendency to become victimizers. Until recently, untouchable groups formed a hierarchy of "Untouchability among themselves and against each other," so that "members of these submerged groups . . . [would] not eat together or take water from each other or allow intermarriage"; and the lowest of them was considered "Unseeable," required to live a nocturnal existence, and as the ultimate in degradation had the function of washing the clothes of other Untouchables.[57] This "victimizing cosmos within a larger victimizing cosmos" enabled the "higher" Untouchables to achieve active, if tainted, participation in the prevailing immortality system.

The situation of European Jews and American Blacks has been somewhat different. They were not part of the immortality system that victimized them. Rather they were thrust into it—Blacks via slavery, and Jews by means of their own dispersion and by the superimposition of a more or less official structure of restriction and persecution by the churches and nations of Europe. As outsiders brought into a victimizing arena, they could retain access to prior imagery of human continuity, which could provide at least a modicum of independence from their immediate environment. Blacks' African cultural heritage, though assaulted, was never destroyed. And Jews' sense of shared identity, first as coreligionists and then as a people, has had remarkable tenacity and has helped generations of Jewish victims maintain ultimate connections beyond proximate pain. Indeed the intensity of Jewish exclusiveness—Jews' sense of themselves as a people apart whose dietary laws have often prevented them from even "breaking bread" with non-Jews—derives importantly from a struggle to hold

---

* Not surprisingly, Indian "ex-Untouchables" and second-generation Japanese-American *Eta* continue to struggle with that dilemma long after the victimizing structure has been officially or geographically terminated.[56]

onto Jewish-centered immortality systems in the midst of the most powerful pressures and temptations to abandon them.

Nonetheless, Blacks and Jews have had their own fierce psychic struggles with the immortality structures thrust upon them. For Blacks, that included partial internalization of inferiority and death taint as cosmically ordained, whether according to some law of color or even (according to the fundamentalist Christianity they adopted) God's will. And in postslavery struggles, not a few Blacks have manifested fierce identification with broadly American immortality systems having to do with money, position, and class. And there have been Black impulses toward victimizing other Blacks, as in various forms of discrimination and even persecution until recently practiced by many Blacks against those with darker skin color. There have been parallel patterns among Jews: second- and third-generation American Jews' discomfort with manifestations of "Jewishness" (accents and strange dress among the ultraorthodox); German Jews' disdain, in both Europe and America, for their generally less educated and more economically deprived Eastern European brethren.

What has been called, in relationship to Jews and others, "identification with the aggressor," becomes more understandable in terms of death anxiety and immortality struggles. When Jews have felt or acted like Nazis, in or out of death camps, there has been more involved. Jakov Lind describes these complex feelings in recalling his memory of being a fifteen-year-old Viennese Jew trying to stay alive in Nazi-occupied Holland:

> I began to hate the Jews. Not only the Orthodox, but all of them. I hated their names, their faces, their manner of speech, their humour, and their nervous diligence. They were a rotten lot and one should get rid of them. Not because the Germans say so, but they say so because they are right. . . . I hated the Jews because I hated the sight of death. Each of them was marked to be destroyed. I did not wish to belong to this kind of people. . . . To survive this calamity I have to hate them; if I do not wish to die as one of them, I have to learn to live with the sentiments of the rest of the world. The rest of the world either hates the Jews or is indifferent to them. . . . I couldn't afford indifference. I have to hate because I love life. I love to remain among those who breathe.[58]

The victim's temptation is that of cultivating hatred for his own group as a means of dissociating himself from its death taint and embracing not so much the victimizers as their "life-power" and immortalizing claim.*

When the victim gains the strength to challenge the victimizing structure, he may call forth something on the order of a *reversal of immortalizing standards*.

---

*More fundamentally, Lind detested the Nazis, but "I loved the Dutch patriots who fought and hated the Jews who were arrested."[59] What he admired here was the rejection of victimization: the refusal to live, physically or psychically, in a victimizing cosmos.

Black, which used to be despicable, now becomes "beautiful." Evidence of "Jewishness," formerly necessary to hide, now is proudly displayed, even flaunted. That which had been suppressed is now called forth, literally with a vengeance, to stand above all other immortality structures.

For such reversal one needs an encompassing principle beyond the victimization itself. That principle might derive life from the victims' suppressed heritage, for example, from Black or Jewish cultural tradition. Or it may derive from a messianic political vision, for instance, that of communist transformation, through which the victimized poor are elevated to the resurgent "working class."

In contemporary experience one sees struggles toward such reversal in groups victimized by industrial chemicals and pollutants, and (as we shall see in the next section) by the ultimate nuclear pollutant as well. Here reversal depends upon connecting the mechanically imposed death taint with a larger movement—whether local, national, or planetary—combating such destructiveness.

In the reversal of immortalizing standards, there is a fine line between recovery of pride on the one hand and reverse-victimization on the other. Much depends upon whether the reversal itself takes on limits, as opposed to becoming itself total. In the latter case there can be the unfortunate sequence of victimization perpetuating itself through one or more reversals in a more or less perpetual cosmos of victimization, within which only the positions change.

We find these various struggles and possibilities in recent Black reversals of immortality structures. "Black Power" implies not only political standing but life-power and "immortality power." And so does the French equivalent, the mystique of Négritude. One such American movement, the Black Muslims, for instance, has involved "an exaltation of African-Negro specificity . . . an appreciation of a new Black unity experienced by its adherents, a consciousness of sharing in the past and in the making of the future."[60] The words characterize a more general Black reassertion of "immortalizing racial and cultural substance" on behalf of collective pride and vitality. But in the process the same movement views the Black Man as "by nature divine and the Original man" in contrast to white usurpers who are "by nature . . . liars and murderers— enemies of truth and righteousness."[61]

Now the aroused victim himself becomes a dispenser of immortality, and, not surprisingly, denies it to whomever he sees as his former victimizer. It may be that this kind of totalized reversal is inevitable when victimization itself has been so brutal, a kind of revolutionary excess needed for any reversal to appear at all. Nonetheless, it can lead to the literal dispensing of existence as well as the symbolic dispensing of victimization, and can produce an Idi Amin phenomenon of the former victim's own hunger for new victims of whatever race. And there are Jewish parallels around the pitfalls of reversing immortality structures having to do with reasserting old patterns of exclusiveness (for instance, the Orthodox practice of mourning for dead those who marry non-

Jews, and early insensitivity toward the Arab population around the creation of the State of Israel, at times bordering on victimization).

We see that these are not so much exact reversals as shifts on the part of victims to assertions of power and temptations to themselves become victimizers. At any stage of the struggle, we can encounter the sad spectacle of competition between victims to be the other's victimizer. There is much of this in Jewish-Black relations in the United States, in the phenomenon of Black anti-Semitism and Jewish anti-Black sentiment.* Here a neighboring victim provides the best target for the other victim's struggles to reverse his relationship to immortality structures.

But the rejection of the victim state need not involve new victimization. We have suggested that there can be more nuanced reassertions of human continuity. A key to these struggles is self-generation, the creative social assertion of life-power and symbolic immortality as opposed to its being "granted" by the victimizer. Without such self-generation there is likely to be a vicious circle around collective suspicion of counterfeit nurturance: "Help" offered is perceived, all too understandably, as a reminder of the humiliatingly dependent state of victimization.[62] The process is especially difficult for those groups of victims, such as *Eta* and Untouchables, who for centuries have been integral elements of a victimizing cosmos. Their difficulty is the absence of prior imagery, of alternatives to victimizing symbolizations. It is difficult indeed for them to achieve a reversal of meaning around the victimizing state itself—as Blacks and Jews have been more able to do. Yet even they have demonstrated that immortalizing alternatives can be found, that certain egalitarian principles persist through the horrors of our benighted century and contribute to hard-won beginnings of nonvictimizing imagery of larger human connection.†

---

* Blacks and Jews have also demonstrated the capacity to identify with one another, and in that way achieve a shared formulation that rejects victimization and seeks egalitarian principles as a basis for larger connection. But the general point here is the psychic work required of a victim renouncing that state, psychic work having to do with immediate as well as ultimate aspects of self-image.

† I believe that the point of view of victimization put forth here can provide a unifying principle for the various psychological factors stressed in the vast literature on "prejudice." A few examples may serve. In the classic study, *The Authoritarian Personality*, four leading psychologists stressed a series of personality traits they believed to be linked with both prejudice and certain kinds of political ideology—concluding that "a basically hierarchical, authoritarian, exploitive parent-child relationship is apt to carry over into a power-oriented, exploitively dependent attitude toward one's sex partner and one's God and may well culminate in a political philosophy and social outlook which has no room for anything but a desperate clinging to what appears to be strong and a disdainful rejection of whatever is relegated to the bottom . . . conventionality, rigidity, repressive denial, and the ensuing break-through of one's weakness, fear and dependency are but other aspects of the same fundamental personality pattern, and they can be observed in personal life as well as in attitudes toward religious and social issues."[63]

I would suggest that this "power-orientation" has to do with struggles to master death

This linkage of victimization and immortality has the advantage of invoking universal imagery around life and death as well as the impact of historical change. It suggests that anyone is capable of participating in the victimizing process, either as victimizer or victim, though some more than others, and particularly so under certain historical conditions. Our placing of victimization in a psychohistorical sequence including dislocation and totalism on the one side, and violence on the other, suggests its relationship to general human aberration, indeed, to the human condition. Given the unresolvable character of death anxiety and doubt about immortality, individually and collectively, we can understand the ubiquitousness of victimization. Paraphrasing Sartre freely, we say that *victimization is the cowardly path to immortality*. Psychologically speaking, it is also the most vindictively compensatory one.

Violence follows readily from victimization. The principle of violence on behalf of vitality (Chapter 12) is expressed collectively. But now there must be a social and psychological structuring, within which victims can be seen as enemies and therefore as targets for destruction. That structure must also provide for a combination of passion (hatred for the enemy—greatest at lower

---

and its equivalents, that the tendencies toward rigidity repression, and denial are defenses against death anxiety, and that the need to relegate various individuals and groups "to the bottom" is precisely the need to divest others of symbolic immortality in order to reaffirm one's own. But these are not merely idiosyncratic individual tendencies; they reflect larger historical trends which always play upon the wide gamut of variation in individual tendencies toward victimization.

Similarly, Gordon Allport's more eclectic approach—his emphasis upon historical as well as psychodynamic factors, lead him to formulate a constellation of scapegoating which is consistent with the symbolic elements I have stressed.[64] And Bettleheim and Janowitz have in the past emphasized that "ethnic hostility is a symptom of the individual's effort to maintain balance in his psychic economy"—a response to insecurity and deprivation, and an effort to avoid anxiety. In a recent revision, they have emphasized the relevance of Erikson's work on ego identity: "Prejudice . . . might be likened to the tumultuous solutions triggered by the adolescent's search for a personal identity, a search that often continues after the age of adolescence . . . to understand prejudice as a psychological phenomenon . . . more attention must be paid to its ego-supporting propensities and to the protection it offers the individual against identity diffusion or total loss of identity. . . . At a loss in seeking to protect their identity, such prejudiced persons may try to further buttress it by maintaining their prejudice."[65]

This approach is consistent with Erikson's own, and with his added emphasis upon the use of prejudice as a means of avoiding confrontation with one's own "negative identity"—with that portion of oneself one had always been warned against becoming. I have already associated these identity struggles with an impaired sense of immortality, and the "negative identity" Erikson speaks of could well be understood as that aspect of the self associated with death-taint and its corresponding anxiety. The same could be said of Erikson's more recent concept of "pseudospeciation," by which he means the tendency to treat others as if they belonged to a separate species.[66]

levels of authority) and numbing (psychological detachment from the mechanics of killing—greatest at higher levels of authority).

Perhaps the key to the transition from victim to enemy is the depth and immediacy of the threat perceived by the executioner to himself or his own group. This is the importance of Hitler's imagery in *Mein Kampf*, written in 1923.

First he suggests a devil-theory of German debilitation: *"Only the elimination of the causes of our collapse, as well as the destruction of its beneficiaries, can create the premise for our outward fight for freedom."*

Next he locates the specific threat: *"It is the inexorable Jew who struggles for his domination over the nations."*

Finally, having been designated as a national enemy, the Jew can, must, become the object of physical violence—"No nation can remove this hand from its throat except by the sword"—and for this purpose Hitler calls for "a national passion rearing up in its strength . . . [to] defy the international enslavement of peoples," making clear that such a crusade "is and remains a bloody one."

Underlying everything is the image-refrain of "the Jew" as a direct, all-pervasive threat to German national and racial existence: "The Jew would really devour the people of the earth, would become their master"; "the international world Jew slowly but surely strangles us"; "the Jew destroys the racial foundations of our existence and thus destroys our people for all time." *

Dawidowicz distinguishes between the Nazis' "reversion to medievalism (small-scale pogroms, expropriation of Jewish holdings, general policies of degradation) and their "new, radical [that is, genocidal] anti-Semitism." The first, she implies, was a combination of psychological preparation (through a certain amount of mobilization of anti-Jewish passion) and cover for the second. Her depiction of the program as a "war"—both in her title and in discussions throughout the book—is particularly apt, and Hitler's 1939 promise of "the destruction of the Jewish race in Europe" was no less than a pledge to conduct total war against—annihilate—a total enemy.

While the sequence from victimization to violence can be an easy one, the

---

*These quotations follow Lucy Dawidowicz' argument concerning the sequence of Hitler's "war against the Jews," and are quoted directly from her valuable study.[67] Concerning the last group of quotations Dawidowicz remarks, "Hitler kept projecting on the Jews the very destructive ideas he held about them." That is a relatively conventional psychoanalytic interpretation of victimization and of less extreme forms of "prejudice." It involves a reversal of impulse—attributing one's own destructive impulses to the person or group about to become their target. I cannot say that such a psychological process does not exist. But the emphasis upon projection has been misleading in its mechanistic short-circuiting of the sequence of image and behavior, and its neglect of the life-and-death content of imagery in relationship to victimization and violence. That life-and-death quality found particular expression in the racial and biological threat the Nazis saw Jews as posing.

extraordinary scope and specifity of Nazi violence against the Jews required a particular combination of elements in its social and psychological structuring:

> The Final Solution grew out of a matrix formed by traditional anti-Semitism, the paranoid delusions that seized Germany after World War I, and the emergence of Hitler and the national socialist movement. Without Hitler, the charismatic political leader, who believed he had a mission to annihilate the Jews, the Final Solution would not have occurred. Without that assertive and enduring tradition of anti-Semitism by which the Germans sought self-definition, Hitler would not have had the fecund soil in which to grow his organization and spread its propaganda. Without the paranoid delusion of the Dolchstoss ["dagger-thrust"—in effect, stab in the back] that masses of Germans shared in the wake of Germany's military defeat, political upheavals, economic distress, and humiliations of the Versailles Treaty, Hitler could not have transformed the German brand of conventional anti-Semitism into a radical doctrine of mass murder.[68]

The structuring of these elements made possible sufficient sharing of image-feelings of being "in the grip of a death struggle . . . [many Germans] believe themselves to be innocent and aggrieved victims, outwitted by the machinations of supercunning and all-powerful antagonist, engaged in a struggle for their very existence." It was a struggle, as Hitler put it, of 'either-or'."

As "outsider-victims," Jews were probably more vulnerable to that kind of "death-struggle" than, say, "insider-victims" like *Eta* or Untouchables. The latter, living in perpetual victimization, became part of a social equilibrium and thereby necessary to their victimizers. But "outside victims," even when they appear to be in such an equilibrium, are still not part of a shared cosmology and may be subject to various ideological shifts that may suddenly render them the "mortal enemy" *(Todfeind)* Hitler made of the Jews.

The term "Final Solution" had significance beyond its euphemism. As Dawidowicz says, "It reverberates with apocalyptic promise, bespeaking the Last Judgment, the End of Days, the last destruction before salvation, Armageddon."[69] In our terms, it was a "solution" not for the Jews but for the Nazis, a vision of life-power and immortality assured (the "Thousand Year Reich") through annihilation of the carriers of evil and death.

Ionesco has put the matter well:

> I must kill my visible enemy, the one who is determined to take my life, to prevent him from killing me. Killing gives me a feeling of relief, because I am dimly aware that in killing him, I have killed death. My enemy's death cannot be held against me, it is no longer a source of anguish, if I killed him with the approval of society: that is the purpose of war. Killing is a way of relieving one's feelings, of warding off one's own death.[70]

Again, Armageddon and apocalypse—the engineering of the end of the Jewish world on behalf of eternal Nazi life. The project, through murdering the Jews, was to "murder death"—which is always, psychologically speaking, the project behind mass killing.

The Final Solution, of course, made use of high technology. That enabled much of the killing to be done with total absence of passion. Numbed violence of varied dimensions has become a kind of métier of our century. But its basic nature is revealed in a simple principle described by a former member of the Capone gang, that of the hiring of the out-of-town killer:

> It's one thing . . . to go up to a guy you don't know. You've been told he'll be wearing a dark-gray hat and coat, and so forth. You walk up to him in a crowd and put the gun up against his belly and you let him have a couple and fade off. That's doing a job. But if the killer knows the other guy, when he puts it up against his belly he suddenly looks up and sees his face, he knows his wife, he's taken his kids to the ball game, he knows that if he pulls that trigger there's going to be a widow, kids without a father, there'll be tears, there'll be a funeral—then it becomes murder. It isn't a job anymore, and he's going to hesitate, and maybe not even do it. That was the reason they used out-of-town killers.[71]

This primer from the Capone gang suggests two basic principles: the first is that one never experience the man one kills as a fellow human being. The second, which follows, is that one perform the act in the manner of an animal killing its prey, without animus, in the spirit of "doing a job." This is a far cry from the kind of venomous hatred of Nazis for Jews or of white racists for Blacks. But the two forms of violence are not as distinct as they may seem. Behind the gas-chamber technicians there is a vision of a "mortal enemy." And accompanying the passion of the most rabid group of racist killers is a capacity for viewing their victims as "vermin" or "lice," for blocking out all empathic human feeling, that is, for psychic numbing. Passion and numbing are interwoven components of violence, the one requiring the other.

There are of course extremely important distinctions to be made between aggressive violence and violence that is what Margaret Mead has called "primarily protective of the life of the group . . . of . . . territory and means of livelihood, the lives of its members . . . and the values cherished by the group."[72] That is, there are fundamental moral distinctions to be made around violence. But we have seen that the most brutal forms of violence can be committed in the name of defending the "territory" or "cherished values" of a group. That is, despite crucial moral differences, there is a unitary principle in collective violence: the destruction of that which is perceived to be the potential destroyer—one's "mortal enemy," eventually, death itself.

Shared violence is not only unitary but unifying. It has always drawn men together, whether in revolution, counterrevolution, or almost any form of indiscriminate mass slaughter. The "blood bond" has to do with the sharing of guilt (or the warding off of guilt), terror, and transcendence. Frantz Fanon, the remarkable Martinique-born, French-educated, psychiatrist-revolutionary has gone so far as to claim that it can be a form of "therapeutic knowledge":

> Violence, violence committed by the people, violence organized and educated by its leaders, makes it possible for the masses to understand social truths and give them the key to them.[73]

Whether the world can still afford this form of "therapy" is another matter.

TWENTY-TWO

Nuclear Distortions

THE APPEARANCE of nuclear weapons in the mid-1940s evoked an image: that of man's extermination of himself as a species with his own technology. How does that image affect our destructive historical sequence from dislocation to totalism, victimization, and violence? It changes everything (fundamentally alters our ultimate and immediate relationships in ways we shall explore in this section) and seems to change nothing (it is apparently ignored by much of the human race, which goes about business as usual). The image, of course, is not totally new. Versions of it have been constituted by visionaries—H. G. Wells is an outstanding example—at least from the time of the Industrial Revolution or before. But nuclear weapons gave substance to the image and disseminated it everywhere, making it the dubious psychic property of the common man.

Moreover, the element of self-extermination must be differentiated from older religious images of Armageddon, "Final Judgment," or the "end of the world." Terrifying as these may be, they are part of a world view or cosmology—man is acted upon by a higher power who has his reasons, who destroys only for spiritual purposes (such as achieving "the kingdom of God"). That is a far cry from man's destruction of himself with his own tools, and to no purpose.

It must also be said that forces other than the weapons contribute to imagery of extermination. Depletion of the world's resources (especially food and energy), and destruction of the environment or its outer supports (the ozone layer) by other elements of our technology are notable examples. Nuclear weapons are simply the destructive edge of our technology gone wild in its distorted blend with science—or what Lewis Mumford calls the final apotheosis of the contemporary megamachine.[1] But the weapons express the most extreme consequences of that aberration, and epitomize for us our imagery of extermination.

It is impossible, then, to separate the psychic impact of nuclear weapons from that of the broader scientific-technological revolution of which they are a part. The production of weapons followed upon the great twentieth-century discoveries in physics concerning atomic and nuclear structure, relativity, and quantum theory, and they effectively "contaminated" the influence of these discoveries on our thought processes and world imagery. And these weapons appeared just prior to a still newer wave of biological discoveries around DNA, gene structures, and the chemistry of life itself, so that the weapons (together with their counterparts in biological or germ warfare) psychically contaminate these developments as well.

Kenneth Boulding has spoken of these twentieth-century processes as a movement "from civilization to post-civilization," and "the second great stage in the state of man." Under duress and pressure to alter themselves radically are the very institutions that have characterized the first great stage—that of "civilization"—such as agriculture, the city, war, and extreme demarcations between the rich and the poor, the city and the country, the specific locality and the world. Like many, Boulding insists that we are experiencing not "a mere continuance and development of the old patterns of civilization" but "nothing short of a major revolution in the human condition."[2]

Yet, such analyses pose difficulties for us, even, and perhaps especially, when they are true. One reason has to do with the paradox mentioned above, that of everything and nothing changing. The records of the May 31, 1945, meeting of the interim committee, charged with exploring policy concerning use of the first atomic bomb, record Secretary of War Henry Stimson as expressing the view "that this project [the making of the atomic bomb] should not be considered simply in terms of military weapons, but as a new relationship of man to the universe." That was seventeen years before Boulding's comment and thirty-two years before I write these words. And during all this time, as many ask, have we changed that much? *

* At about the time Boulding's article appeared, I was working in Hiroshima, interviewing survivors (or *hibakusha*) of the first atomic bomb dropped on a human population. In later describing these people, I spoke of a "psychic mutation" having to do with their struggles to absorb imagery of world-destruction imposed on them from the outside, and making contact with inner imagery related to very early experience of death equivalents. This state was not confined to *hibakusha*, and all of us now constituted a "world of survivors." We lived in a world in which these two weapons had been used (whether or not we were alive or aware of the event at the time), and we were preoccupied with images of surviving (or not surviving) future nuclear wars. But it would have been more accurate to speak of a *potential psychic mutation*. Surely our relationship to the universe has changed as Stimson said, and we undoubtedly require the "major revolution in the human condition" Boulding spoke of, but that does not

In the United States the weapons have become familiar, "old hat," and we can speak of a process of "domestication of the ultimate." This has taken the form of cheery assurances, more prevalent in the civil-defense literature of the 1950s, that "you can beat the A–bomb"—if you simply follow the rules and go to a shelter, crawl under a desk or table, and hold some object over your head or face. As with all domestication, the mere passage of time has a powerful effect. The feeling is that we have been living with bombs for more than thirty years, and "nothing has happened." There is much whistling in the dark—we know of the terror underneath the self-assurance—and the fact that the bombs grow ever more numerous and powerful increases, however uneasily, the domesticating impulse. "However many they make, and however big they become, life goes on." This is, of course, a form of nuclear numbing, of great importance for the element of nonchange, or very limited change, at one side of our nuclear paradox.

Yet, psychically speaking, a revolutionary situation exists. What is ironic to the point of absurdity, and still extremely difficult for us to absorb, is the fact that it is a *potentially terminal revolution*. Margaret Mead, in the mid-1960s, recalled a metaphor of Norbert Wiener, the creator of the science of cybernetics, to the effect that a city could be compared to "a gigantic explosive device for which a single atomic bomb would simply be a trigger." She went on to extend that metaphor to our "inter-connected world . . . so that the whole of human civilization can be compared to a vast explosive device, and almost any country or any segment of the population can trigger event sequences with spreading and disastrous consequences, while felicitous combinations of events may provide equally rapidly the conditions for constructive transformation of modern society."[3] In our terms this suggests that behind all ordinary human conflicts and threats of violence lurks imagery of extinction. Such imagery has become fundamental to our sense of the flow of our lives, or the purposes and the future of human existence. The fact that we have no prior models for understanding the psychic consequences of this unprecedented state does not mean that consequences do not exist. One approach is to examine the impact of imagery of extinction on the area of symbolic immortality. In doing so I am suggesting the existence of psychic threats posed by nuclear weapons—by their

---

mean we have achieved it. We may restate our paradox as a condition on the one hand of partial psychic alteration and enormous pressures toward still more radical change, without the appearance of workable new individual or collective forms; and on the other hand of clinging to psychic structures we know, with the insistence that they are all we have and that the new forces are not that revolutionary anyhow.

The latter tendency is related to a more general pattern of domestication. Even people in Hiroshima had the need to "tame" the monster that had caused them so much pain— to refer to it in familiar, and, at times, even humorous terms as *pika* ("flash") or *pikadon* ("flash-boom"), or *pikadon-don* ("flash-boom-boom"), as it was referred to in an early postwar literary movement with Dadaesque features.

mere existence quite independently of their use—threats related to ultimate involvements that at the same time have direct bearing on our everyday lives.

The biological mode is most directly affected. If we anticipate the possibility of nuclear weapons being used—as I believe everyone in our society from about the age of six or seven in some measure does—we can hardly be certain of descendants in whom to "live on." In such a "postnuclear" world, that is, we can imagine no biological posterity. One need not enter the debate as to whether nuclear war would or would not eliminate *all* human life. The fact that there is such a debate in itself confirms the importance of *imagery* of total biological destruction, or radically impaired imagination of human continuity.

We may suspect the impairment to reach backward as well. With the human future so jeopardized, our sense of connection with prior generations is likely to be threatened also, since it too depends on feeling part of a continuing sequence of generations. We are therefore likely either to compensate by asking too much of our connections with the past, or to flee from them in a desperate effort to improvise a future in which one cannot believe. The image of a destructive force of unlimited dimensions in both explosive power and in poisoning the environment—or some fragment of that image—enters into every relationship involving parents, children, grandparents, and imagined great-grandparents and great-grandchildren. The image is usually very much in the background, but is readily activated by a variety of stimuli from actual nuclear sword-rattling to relatively obscure antagonisms anywhere on our planet. We are thus among the first to live with a recurrent sense of biological severance.

As these consequences extend outward to biosocial realms (from family to community, "people," and nation) one cannot count on the future of any human aggregate one identifies as one's own. The "immortal racial and cultural substance" so crucial to modern nationalism is undermined. That in turn seems to cause confusing mixtures of intensified nationalism (as if to deny that one's nation, and one's important psychic tie to it, is threatened), total negation of the nation-state (as if to deny that one needs the entity now threatened), and search for more inclusive biosocial units in the hope of transcending the threat (including constructive, but seemingly futile, internationally oriented peace-making efforts). No wonder, then, that man looks beyond his own planet toward outer space in order to enlarge his biosocial territory. The impulse is concretely expressed in the vision of "space colonies" to serve as safe havens for our species should our own planet be destroyed. This is not to say that our perception of the threat to our species is our only motivation for space ventures, but rather that these ventures, coming when they do, become associated with symbolizing efforts to "move beyond" the present danger to the earth and its inhabitants. The same can be said of our genetic preoccupations and the debate over "genetic engineering." Actively intervening in genetic structures involves a variety of ethical issues, but it too inevitably becomes infused with our general sense of biological threat, and with visions of somehow overcoming that threat.

Nuclear impact on the theological mode of immortality is undoubtedly profound, many-sided, and difficult to gauge. (One cannot take seriously the claim that for committed believers—in this case, Christians—the theological mode is unaffected, that its spiritual imagery is independent of weaponry or holocaust. Nor can we say that prior expressions of the theological mode—the great religions of the world—are suddenly and absolutely negated.)

But some things one can say were suggested by Hiroshima survivors. Many *hibakusha* invoked religious principles, primarily Buddhist but in some cases Shinto or Christian, and in others syncretic combinations evolved by various postwar sects. Such imagery did contribute to a sense of resignation, the feeling that one was helpless before larger forces of destruction and creation. But *hibakusha* consistently reported that their conventional religious imagery was woefully inadequate for their survivor task of giving form or meaning to the experience. Nor could such imagery, for most, contribute significantly to restoring the symbolic world that had been destroyed and help survivors reassert a sense of immortality. Indeed, to survivors' ears, everyday pronouncements about Buddha or God became quickly platitudinous and often a cause for resentment. Part of the problem lay in the relatively weak state of religious symbolism among an essentially secular contemporary people, all the more so following the collapse of the pseudoreligion of emperor-worship and its related structure of militant nationalism. But more fundamental was the magnitude of the disaster itself, which seemed to defy the spiritual precepts accessible to *hibakusha*.[4]

The more general principle may well be that as death imagery comes to take the shape of total annihilation or extinction, religious symbolism becomes both more sought after and more inadequate.

For religion, then, nuclear weapons have created a crisis within a crisis. Religious symbolization has never recovered from the early impact of science and technology. Thus, in the West, by the seventeenth century, "the great fabric of Christian belief, embodied in the ceremonies, rituals, dogmas, and daily practices of the church, had begun to disintegrate."[5] Energetic efforts at spiritual transcendence have hardly disappeared, but from that time they have been under duress. And many theologians—Paul Tillich may be the last great example—have sought in one way or another to "demythologize" religion in order to render it consistent with the claims of science, if not a scientific world view itself.

Imagery of extinction put further pressure on that demythologizing trend. Tillich was surely influenced both by Auschwitz and Hiroshima when he wrote the famous concluding words of one of his important works: *"The courage to be is rooted in the god who appears when God has disappeared in the anxiety of* *doubt.*"[6]* And his principle of "ultimate concern" took hold in a post-Hiroshima world radically confused about precisely that. In that principle we may say that Tillich was attempting to equate all modes of symbolic immortality with theological transcendence. One's ultimate concern could be for family or special group or movement, for works or cultural legacy, the enduring beauty of nature, or for a quality of spirituality resembling what we have called experiential transcendence. The shift is from doctrinal belief to a quality of being and a form of centering. Thus, Tillich speaks of ultimate concern as a condition that "unites man's mental life and gives it a dominating center," and also tells us that "The predominant religious name for the content of such concern is God—a god or gods."[7] Tillich and his followers express the impulse to bring together all expressions of man's ultimate involvements in order to counter ultimate threats. But the uneasiness of the venture is reflected in Tillich's continuing struggles with the problem of despair, and in much of the terminology Tillich employs (such as "the God above God"), as well as that of his theological successors in what has been called the "Death of God" movement.

A still greater indication of theological peril is the other direction of nuclear-age theology, that of a fundamentalism that seeks to absorb all too readily the nuclear dilemma into its dogma. Thus, certain American Baptists, in their literalization of biblical imagery, equate nuclear holocaust with Christian Apocalypse, and at times seem almost to welcome that development as a confirmation of their accusations of human sinfulness. One encounters similar imagery in totalistic cults of the mid and late 1970s. In some of these waves of fundamentalism, one is impressed by the combination of premodern mythology with highly contemporary techniques of mind manipulation. The attraction of the combination lies in the promise of salvation—of immortality—in the face of imagery of extermination, and in a form of totalism—absolute truth—that can associate itself with the power of science.† Again, the overall fundamentalist project, despite brilliant successes, remains tenuous and anxious. One need only point to the strange sequence of mind-manipulation, or "coercive

---

*We cannot say that Tillich's theology was a response to nuclear weapons per se—he himself tells us that his survivor experience as a World War I chaplain was a basic impetus. But he was always sensitive to historical threats, and much of his more mature theology of extremity emerged after World War II. He made clear to me in conversation on several occasions his preoccupation with nuclear dangers, and perhaps more important for our argument, his theology took hold at a time when the nuclear impact was first being broadly felt.

† Hence, for instance, the name, "Unification Church," and the sponsoring by the church and its leader, Sun Myung Moon, of large gatherings of prominent scientists (attracted by huge honoraria) ostensibly devoted to "integrating" or "unifying" contemporary thought.

persuasion," by church members in bringing young people into the fold, and then by "deprogrammers" attempting to free them from that influence.

The overall problem of post-Hiroshima religion lies in the paradox, and perhaps contradiction, in promising spiritual continuity beyond individual death in an imagined world with none (or virtually none) among the biologically living. It may be that a sense of continuing biological life is necessary to the viability of imagery transcending biological death. Here, as in so many other ways, nuclear weapons impair precisely the kind of symbolism most necessary for coping with them. Worse—but all too understandable—is the impulse to make the weapons themselves objects of pseudoreligious adoration, (see following chapter). Nuclear weapons raise profound doubts about the spiritualized symbolization of immortality at the heart of religious practice.

Immortality through works becomes even more dubious. Imagery of nuclear apocalypse throws into question the enduring nature of any human enterprise. This undermining of ultimate connections via our work and its creative products is bound to have repercussions upon work and working in general. Imagery of extermination would seem to connect with the existential distress man has always felt concerning the ephemeral nature of his works, and to bring about the 'new ephemeralism' with imagery of unprecedented concreteness and absoluteness.

Once more there may be polarized responses to the same anxiety. One reaction is for men to become ever more frenetic in their work and their projects, as a means of overcoming their own inner perceptions of this new ephemeralism. The principle may apply to a vast revolution, as in the prodigious Chinese Communist work programs and the accompanying pronouncements of "labor and hardship . . . [as] the only happiness." Or we may find it in the tendency of the New York art world to move restlessly from one style or movement to another, each overly praised (or condemned) as "revolutionary" and then forgotten in favor of the next. Of course Chinese peasants and New York art critics react from within their own traditions: Chinese culture and Communist revolution have both always been associated with highly demanding work ideologies; and radically shifting currents are not a new phenomenon for critics and practitioners of modern art. But to the extent that both become affected by imagery of new ephemeralism, then underneath both forms of glorification of work and works lurks the terrible fear that nothing will last, and that nothing therefore matters. Awareness of such imagery is undoubtedly stronger among New York artists and critics than Chinese farmers. But the latter are likely to have been exposed to Mao Tse-tung's homilies on the atomic bomb, and may be more generally susceptible to imagery of extermination than we realize. The historical gap may not be nearly as great as generally assumed. And just as the imagined annihilation of all books and paintings, of all libraries and all museums, is a vision of hell for the intellectual, so is the annihilation of all crops and land for the peasant farmer. Moreover, the principle extends to work in other traditions—scientific, aesthetic, mercantile, clerical, or various forms of physical labor—that is, to all of us.

The polar opposite in work attitudes would seem to be the "hedonism" of youth in and out of America during the 1960s. This is epitomized by the wandering, pleasure-seeking, nonlaboring "hippie." Beyond these stereotypes there has been, during the 1960s and 1970s, a questioning of virtually all types of work, and a considerable search for pleasurable and expressive alternatives for unpleasurable, nonexpressive work. Yet with staggering rapidity we have encountered, during the late 1970s, a swing back not only to hard work but to highly competitive attitudes toward success in the culture's working structure— at least at the level of professional training. There are many historical factors affecting these attitudes—immediate economic issues as well as longstanding imagery around the meaning or meaninglessness of work. But imagery of extermination intensifies both attitudes—the rejection of unsatisfactory work as more ephemeral and meaningless than ever, and the embrace of what in the face of the threat seems relatively substantial and, more than other things, has the possibility of lasting.*

Man's imagery of nature as the ultimate life source takes on special significance in the nuclear age as an antagonist to extinction. For nature is more difficult to destroy than man himself or his spiritual formulations or his creative products. Those elements of other modes that relate themselves to nature also take on new importance, however the modes themselves may be impaired. Hence the renewed concern, not just among scientists but in general cultural consciousness, with evolution and genetics—with natural beginnings and life-structures—which we spoke of when discussing the biological mode; the new willingness of theologians to relate their formulations to the natural world; and

---

* Marcello Mastroianni, a gifted and world-famous film actor during much of the fifties and sixties, conveyed in a magazine interview many of these responses to the new ephemeralism and related them to their source. He described himself as "an *anti*hero or at most a *non*hero." And to locate that status in our time he quoted the film director, Antonioni: "Who's a hero under the atom bomb? Or who isn't one?" Still more interesting was his answer to the question of what he would do if he could begin all over: "I'd be both an actor and an architect. I would do a film, then build a building, then a film—and so on. The Seagram's Building in New York took my breath away. I'd like to build one in Rome, a *palazzo* of glass and crystal that would also take people's breath away. Like a great sculptor. Not to make money, though. It would probably lose money. But it would be there for me to stand before it and say: 'Look there is something I did which I love and which will *last*—at least a little longer than myself.'"[8] Although already an "immortal" of the film world, Mastroianni imagines a more visible and substantial expression of immortality—hardly a new yearning and partly a product of our more general historical velocity, but a yearning rendered passionate and in a sense unconvincing by the image-power of the new ephemeralism.

the special feeling about architectural "works" as natural equivalents. From all directions there are impulses to reach back into nature as a means of countering the physical and symbolic threats posed by our technology of destruction.

There is an urge among ordinary men and women to tend their gardens, till their own soil, make things grow—brilliantly conveyed in fictional form by Nigel Dennis in his novel, *A House in Order*. The communal movement among the young is similar in spirit. Lewis Mumford once remarked that many of the young, in fleeing the cities and going back to the land, growing their own food, and seeking to reduce their existence to maximum simplicity and self-sufficiency, seemed to be behaving as if the bomb had already been dropped. They are responding to the threat of imagery of extinction by reconnecting themselves with nature, seeking to draw upon the power of natural imagery as much as the products of the land, behaving like survivors not so much of the bomb itself as of the death imagery (in their own words, a "death trip") emanating from nuclear weapons and other malignant technological and social forces.

But the conviction that nature will prevail can lead to illusory ideas about nuclear weapons. There is an extraordinary passage in Edgar Snow's carefully checked rendition of Mao Tse-tung's words during an interview conducted in 1965, a passage that demonstrates how a great leader can make use of natural symbolism to express the most dangerous kind of self-deception:

> Americans . . . had said very much about the destructiveness of the atom bomb and Khrushchev had made a big noise about that . . . yet recently he [Mao] had read reports of an investigation by Americans who visited the Bikini Islands six years after nuclear tests had been conducted there. From 1959 onward research workers had been in Bikini. When they first entered the island they had had to cut paths through the undergrowth. They found mice scampering about and fish swimming in the streams as usual. The wellwater was potable, plantation foliage was flourishing, and birds were twittering in the trees. Probably there had been two bad years after the tests, but nature had gone on. In the eyes of nature and the birds, the mice and the trees, the atomic bomb was a paper tiger. Possibly man had less stamina than they?[9]

Here Mao lyrically invoked the staying power of the natural world *—an image of enormous importance throughout East Asian thought—as a way of directly countering imagery of extermination, attributing such imagery to ideological

---

*Too lyrically, as it turned out. The islands of the Bikini Atoll did not emerge unscathed from the series of American nuclear tests. Indeed, during the late 1970s there was still concern about lingering dangers from irradiation affecting the habitat of some of the islands. It would seem that both the original American investigators, and Mao himself, underestimated the destructive influence of the weapons, and overestimated the recuperative powers of nature.

rivals ("Americans" and Khrushchev). But at the same time he was undoubtedly fending off such imagery in himself (for he was willing to backtrack just a bit):

> "Do you still believe that the bomb is a paper tiger?"
> "That had just been a way of talking, he said, a kind of figure of speech. Of course the bomb could kill people. But in the end the people would destroy the bomb. Then it would truly become a paper tiger."

Here Mao combines, ingeniously but not rigorously, an admirable vision of man's destroying the destroyer, all in the service of reasserting his version of revolutionary immortality. But in doing so Mao dogmatizes the natural mode of immortality, and arbitrarily asserts its and man's inevitable triumph.

Loren Eiseley's evocation of the magnificence of nature resembles Mao's, but without the illusory insistence upon nature's immunity to man's technology. Rather, nature's very vulnerability points up our own hubris:

> To perpetuate this final act of malice seems somehow disproportionate, beyond endurance. It is like tampering with the secret purposes of the universe itself and involving not just men but life in the final holocaust—an act of petulant, deliberate blasphemy. . . . The evil man may do . . . is not merely the evil of one tribe seeking to exterminate another. It is, instead, the thought-out willingness to make the air unbreathable to neighboring innocent nations, and to poison in one's death throes, the very springs of life itself.[10]

Here Eiseley touches upon one of the deepest layers of human terror associated with imagery of extermination. Destroying "the very springs of life itself" suggests an ultimate quality of desolation and lifelessness. It is reminiscent of the postbomb Hiroshima rumor that the city could never again sustain trees, grass, flowers, or any form of vegetation. Insofar as we imagine the destruction of nature, we snuff out life-imagery of the most fundamental kind and leave ourselves inundated by equally absolute imagery of death.

There is a very special symbolism around the defiling of nature, whether by bomb tests, insecticides, "smog," or even ugly billboards and buildings and ever-encroaching highways. We have yet to recognize the extent to which we feel ourselves, our relationship to the life process, to be defiled no less than our environment. We sense ourselves to be poisoning the source of our most profound imagery of vitality and rebirth, the mode of immortality which, so to speak, "houses" all of the others. The ideal of harmony between man and nature gives way to what is surely the most painfully convoluted relationship to nature in man's experience: our extraordinary new grasp of nature leads to the creation of atomic weapons; these weapons, along with other advanced products and processes, threaten to poison nature absolutely and irrevocably. Nature has become at once power source, feared enemy, and victim, but only because man has made it so. And in the process we are deprived of what we psychically require from it. We still have much to learn about the consequences of our convoluted assaults upon "the source of life," and our capacities to draw upon that source—make use of natural imagery—to combat our own lethality.

Imagery of extermination does not eliminate any of these modes of symbolic immortality, but casts all of them into doubt. Hence the added weight placed upon the only remaining alternative, that of experiential transcendence. As a psychic state per se, this mode is relatively less susceptible to the threat of extermination. For it does not depend upon imagining the kind of elements (endless generations, continuing influence, spiritual truth, natural beauty) that can be wiped out by destructive technology. When everything else fails, one can still seek exquisitely intense feelings. Yet, it turns out that even they, even quests for a seemingly pure psychic state, are not immune to imagery of the end of everything.

The seeking of intense experience has always been an important response to threatened holocaust or profound historical crisis. Hedonism and mysticism are classical expressions of this experiential radicalism. Transcendence is pursued around extreme poles of pleasure (seeking or rejecting). The common feature of intense expressions of hedonism and asceticism (the mystical experience) is the capacity to move beyond the perception of threat and to constitute a psychic world (even momentarily) independent of that threat. When the structure of existence is threatened, people seek to do more with or to their bodies, to extend the experience of their total organisms. We cannot wonder that questions are always raised about whether such acts constitute a "breakthrough" to a "higher plane" or an "escape from unpleasant reality." That dilemma, in the nuclear age, has become monumental.

During much of the 1960s and 1970s we witnessed a worldwide mood of experiential radicalism—an impulse toward rejecting principles of balanced continuity in favor of a quest for new images and new feelings, for innovation and enlightenment that included a more exquisite sensual registering of the world. Involved in the impulse is not only an assault on principles of moderation, restraint, caution, and limits, but on the idea-systems and institutions associated with these principles. But this spirit of negation embodied in our contemporary radicalism turns out to be reminiscent of much earlier times:

> The cause of all things is neither soul nor intellect; . . . nor is it reason or intelligence; nor is it spoken or thought. It is neither number, nor order, nor magnitude, nor littleness, nor equality, nor inequality, nor similarity, nor dissimilarity. It neither expands, nor moves, nor rests . . . it is neither essence, nor eternity, nor time . . . it is neither science nor truth. It is not even royalty or wisdom; not one; not unity; not divinity or goodness; nor even spirit as we know it . . ."[11]

These words of Dionysius—the Christian saint, not the Greek god—were, as William James tells us, a "denial made on behalf of a deeper yes." For St. Dionysius himself insisted that "Whoso[ever] calls the Absolute anything in particular, or says that it is *this*, seems implicitly to shut it off from being *that*. . . . So we deny the 'this,' negating the negation which it seems to us to imply, in the interest of the higher affirmative attitude by which we are possessed." Contemporary experiential radicals with varying talents and gifts—from poetic chroniclers of the beat generation to more recent spiritual gurus—have also sought new affirmations. That "deeper yes" requires a further image of meaning, of affirmation and expansion of life beyond impinging threats, but this is rendered inaccessible—or at least extremely difficult to evolve—by prevailing imagery of extermination.

In that sense virtually all experiential radicalism in the nuclear age borders on escapism—runs the risk of becoming itself a perpetual, self-enclosed quest for "highs." The experience of transcendence can only occur within the context, the ideas and imagery, available and believable in a particular time and place. In our time and place, both the great visionary and the more humble experimenter with mental states must contend with the invisible psychic contamination of imagery of extermination. Norman Mailer wrote:

> Probably we will never be able to determine the psychic havoc of the concentration camps and the atomic bomb upon the unconscious mind of almost everyone alive in those years. For the first time in civilized history, perhaps for the first time in all of history, we have been forced to live with the suppressed knowledge that the smallest facets of our personality or the most minor projections of our ideas, were indeed the absence of ideas and the absence of personality could mean equally well that we might still be doomed to die as a cipher in some vast statistical operation in which our teeth would be counted, and our hair would be saved, but our death itself would be unknown, unhonored, and unremarked, a death which could not follow with dignity as a possible consequence to serious actions we have chosen, but rather a death by *deus ex machina* in a gas chamber or a radioactive city; and so if in the midst of civilization—that civilization founded upon the Faustian urge to dominate nature by mastering time, mastering the links of social cause and effect . . . our psyche was subjected to the intolerable anxiety that death being causeless, life was causeless as well, and time deprived of cause and effect had come to a stop.[12]

Or if one wants a more psychological comment on the same phenomenon, one can turn to a sensitive observation by a distinguished psychoanalyst, Edward Glover:

> The most cursory study of dream-life and of the phantasies of the insane shows that ideas of world-destruction (more accurately destruction of what the world symbolizes) are latent in the unconscious mind. And since the atomic bomb is less a weapon of war than a weapon of extermination it is well adapted to the more bloodthirsty phantasies with which man is secretly preoccupied during phases of acute frustration. Nagasaki destroyed by the magic of science is the newest man has yet approached in the realization of dreams that even during the safe

immobility of sleep are accustomed to develop into nightmares of anxiety. The first promise of the atomic age is that it can make some of our nightmares come true. The capacity so painfully acquired by normal men to distinguish between sleep, delusion, hallucination and the objective reality of waking life has for the first time in human history been seriously weakened.[13]

As early as 1946 Glover pointed to the obliteration of distinctions between actuality and delusion,[14] while Mailer a couple of decades ago described our helplessness before absurd, "causeless" death. Both suggested radical impairment to our overall symbolizing process, and especially to symbolization around dying, killing, and the force of continuing life.

Mailer went on to proclaim the consequent emergence of his version of radical experientialism in the form of "the hipster" or "the American existentialist"—". . . the man who knows that if our collective condition is to live with instant death by atomic war, relatively quick death by the State as *l'univers concentrationnaire*, or with a slow death by conformity with every creative and rebellious instinct stifled . . . if the fate of twentieth-century man is to live with death from adolescence to premature senescence, why then the only life-giving answer is to accept the terms of death, to live with death as immediate danger, to divorce oneself from society, to exist without roots, to set out on that uncharted journey into the rebellious imperatives of the self."[15] As in many other writings, Mailer here equates his experiential radicalism with direct and continuous confrontation of death. He places his "American existentialist" in the company of the religious mystic, the psychopath, the bullfighter, and the lover, and in the literary-psychological tradition of D. H. Lawrence, Henry Miller, Wilhelm Reich, and Ernest Hemingway. In the process Mailer turns more than a bit romantic as he describes the "burning consciousness of the present, exactly that incandescent consciousness which the possibilities within death have opened up for them," and finds the source of hipster power (or *mana*) in alleged Negro sexual prowess. That romanticism— the idealized figure of "the hipster" or "the American existentialist"—can itself be understood as too quick a "solution" to imagery of extermination, as a circumventing of that imagery in the name of transcending it. The hipster manages so well in Mailer's hands because he makes little distinction between death and annihilation—fails to make the very distinction the early part of the essay insists upon.

In that sense Jean Genet comes closer to the heart of things. In *Our Lady of the Flowers* (which Sartre has called "an epic of masturbation") the narrator masturbates to images he calls forth of homosexuals, pimps, whores, and criminals. And in a later novel, *Funeral Rites*, Genet extends his perverse fantasies of sexual submission to involve the murderers of his dead male lover. There is also an image of devouring the same dead lover, which for the narrator involves a form of self-devouring, since the lover bears his own name as a kind of "double" who represents the immortal aspects of his own self. Much has been said about Genet's radical reversal of existing moral criteria, but what I would point to here is the extremity—the combination of imaginativeness, bizarreness, and futility—of his quest for transcendence.[16]

What Genet may be telling us is that in a society bent upon self-annihilation,* one is desperate for transcendence, which is, in turn, everywhere blocked, so that one must seek one's highs wherever one can find them, no matter what the consequences.

Imagery of extinction also plays an important part in what is sometimes called the "drug revolution," but which may be understood more broadly as a revolution of feeling-states. The drug revolution involves the use of psychoactive agents—notably LSD, but also marijuana and drugs in the morphine-heroin, benzedrine, and barbiturate families. There are enormous differences in these drugs, in social settings in which they are used, and in the associated explorations of the self. But the use of all of them has to do with a quest for "high states," for quick transcendence. Two of the popular designations of that state, being "turned on" and "stoned," suggest its relationship to movement and stasis. "Turned on" evokes the metaphor of the motor or machine to suggest movement, flow, vitality, a state that is often simultaneously understood as antagonistic to our technology-dominated society and its "death trip." "Stoned" is a much older usage, and the ecstatic state suggested has to do with the absolute hardness and stillness of a stone (stone broke, stone cold, stone dead). Here the image of vitality emerges from what could be said to be the "deadest" of materials.† The term "high" suggests being above and beyond ordinary experience—"flying" and "up" are similarly used, as is "spaced" (or "spaced out") or "floating." The last three terms convey especially the sense of breaking out of restrictions of time and space. Discussing the use of peyote by American Indians (see Chapter 2), I began to suggest a difference between "disconnected highs" and the use of drugs on behalf of awareness. The latter requires elements of both tradition and exploration. The former is an exclusive focus on the feeling-state, and is often associated with an illusion of perpetual or total high.

The fundamental threat to other modes of transcendence has contributed to an explosion of the experiential mode. This phenomenon is found on an extremely broad continuum, from the most profound extension of individual and social awareness to the most self-enclosed, destructive versions of addiction to the high state itself.

Drugs of course are merely chemical agents for achieving that state, efficient

---

* Self-annihilation in this usage includes both nuclear threat and social oppression, and it is perhaps inevitable that death imagery from the two tend to merge in people's minds.

† These paradoxes by no means invalidate either the usages or the experience. Slang, like any vital symbolization, draws upon whatever images are available—and the principle of turning those images, so to speak, on their heads may have far-reaching significance for creativity in general.

means of transportation for the desire to "trip." And although many have found other means of "getting there," drugs may still be said to epitomize the revolution in feeling-states. Those who enter into intense forms of radical experientialism require historical models, heroic figures who have "been there" before. Such heroes can be drawn from among Christian or Buddhist saints, jazz musicians (notably Charlie ["Bird"], Parker, whose combination of musical gift, extensive drug use, and early death made him a martyr to high states), and sixties drug-gurus loosely advocating a new religion (such as Timothy Leary). These heroes are of uneven quality, and under contemporary conditions it is all too easy for followers to focus on the model's high states alone and ignore the larger principles of awareness and symbolic immortality associated with those states (the spiritual insights of religious mystics, the music of "Bird" Parker, and the religious aspiration, even in the case of Timothy Leary). Or they may go still further and embrace as their hero the schizophrenic, the sexually poly-morphously perverse infant, or even the dolphin or the chimpanzee.*

Indeed many young people have demonstrated that interchangeability in shifts (especially during the early and mid-1970s) from drugs to meditation and fundamentalist religious experience. The shift has partly to do with the institutionalization of a certain amount of drug use, especially with marijuana, and a shift in the experiential frontier (nor has it taken long for meditation and extremist religious cults to undergo a domestication of their own). The shifts are not without significant changes; there are important differences among the three

---

* For "the schizophrenic as hero," followers embrace the imagery of R. D. Laing. But although Laing's experientialism is related to imagery of extermination, as he himself often tells us, followers lack his creative ambivalence concerning the schizophrenic and are apt to be unfamiliar with his only systematic, full-length study of schizophrenia, *The Divided Self*, in which he is sympathetic but by no means romantic about the phenomenon. Similarly, those who embrace polymorphous-perverse sexuality are in a sense following the relatively literal Norman O. Brown of *Life Against Death*, but are unlikely to have explored either the nuances of the questions he raises or his conversion (as expressed, however indirectly, in *Love's Body*) to a more symbolized understanding of sexuality and everything else. The recent embrace of the dolphin as hero has very long historical and even mythological antecedents, and owes much to John Lilly's quest for a quality of wisdom from the dolphin that might enable mankind to save itself. It should be mentioned that the dolphin has special experiential qualifications—it spends much of its time playing and fornicating, and seems to have a gentle disposition in addition to its large brain. But the romanticization of the creature, like the glorification of the modest intellectual talents of primates, seems again to say more about our desperation and generally blocked transcendence than about the animals themselves. The pattern was best epitomized by John Lilly's feeding LSD to dolphins as part of one experiment. Nothing much seems to have happened, other than perhaps the death of a few dolphins. But the experiment, along with Lilly's own continuing spiritual, and to a degree scientific, explorations, suggests the interchangeability of the means of achieving the desired high.

practices. But what has been overlooked in much of the discussion of these matters is the extent to which the disciplines that replace drug usage—meditation and religious cults—provide high states of their own. In the case of meditation, much of its practice (at least in the United States) parallels the "unconnected highs" of drugs, that is, serves a functional purpose in the absence of any further imagery of transcendence, religious or otherwise. Meditation then becomes mechanized, a relaxation process which has proven to have certain beneficial physiological effects. Here one may raise the question as to whether an addictive process could set in, again resembling that of drug highs, in which the perpetual craving for the "disconnected high" subverts the original benefits and creates problems of its own. In the case of religious cults, there is an added element of systematic totalism that includes specific immortality imagery—mostly Christian, but in some cases Buddhist or eclectic.

These various shifts take place amidst an atmosphere of experientialism, including the Dionysian (this time the Greek god) character of popular dances throughout the world over the last few decades, beginning with rock and roll, the "sexual revolution" (which surely includes greater sensual awareness and activity in certain groups, even if its reach is limited), and (again especially in the United States) waves of expressive forms of psychotherapy (Gestalt, encounter groups, sometimes marathon and sometimes nude, and primal scream). Without attributing any of these patterns to imagery of extermination alone, we must suspect that such imagery has a great deal to do with the overall flow of the experientialism they constitute.

Distinctions between exploratory quest for greater awareness and compulsive search for perpetual highs are crucial in all these areas, since without such distinctions we have little basis for moral or even psychological judgments. But the distinctions are difficult: there are many overlapping combinations, hungers and needs are great, and guidelines are unclear. If there is "a wound deep in the social body," as described at the time of the Black Death of the fourteenth century,[17] individuals and groups will scream in pain, seek to reverse those screams into shouts of pleasure, and engage generally in radical measures of "treatment." The greatest danger presented by this wound and mood is its potential affinity for the same nuclear weapons that do much to call it into being: the weapons may be psychically perceived as the most Dionysian stimulants of all. The imagined or actual use of the weapons may be embraced as a way of overcoming the very symbolic impairments—the very death imagery—the weapons create. Total annihilation may then become a desirable, even joyous possibility.* More cosmically, a need may be felt to destroy the

---

* That was part of the message of the film, *Dr. Strangelove or How I Learned to Stop Worrying and Love the Bomb*, a film of the early 1960s that is something of a classic in the genre of nuclear mockery.

world for purposes of imagined rebirth. These thoughts have already been expressed. And the impulse can be fed by every variety of aggressive feeling within the psychic life of the individual or group.

What results from these impairments to human continuity is something close to an "identity of the meaninglessly doomed." To be sure that self-designation is often amorphous, self-serving, or even exploitative, and the bolder, more imaginative spirits refuse to be bound by it. But anyone who would wish to grasp contemporary dilemmas and act constructively upon them must confront this historical self-definition of a collectivity awaiting its pointless apocalypse.

Articulations of this state almost always border on cliché. John Kennedy told us during the early sixties that "every man, woman, and child lives under a nuclear sword of Damocles, hanging by the slenderest of threads, capable of being cut at any moment by accident, miscalculation, or madness." Yet it is true that the "slenderness" of the thread he speaks of (in the original myth it is but a single hair) renders precarious in our own eyes every project, large or small, any of us undertakes. Albert Camus had spoken a little earlier of the murderous and "absolutely insane history" of recent decades, and saw his generation's task as less that of "remaking the world" than the "perhaps even greater . . . [one of] keeping the world from destroying itself." The rhetoric is grandiose, but so is the task. The same is true of the seemingly more pessimistic sentence in the 1962 manifesto of the emerging American New Left, known as the "Port Huron Statement": "Our work is guided by the sense that we may be 'he last generation in the experiment with living." In that manifesto the articulation of this sensibility was energizing (however temporarily), as it can be when associated with visions beyond doom.

For the identity of the meaninglessly doomed is only part of us; the rest goes on as before, or seems to. (Our situation resembles the "identity of the dead" among *hibakusha*. A part of them felt they should have died, did die, or at least emerged less than alive; and another part went about the daily business of living.) The existence of those two parts of the self creates a radical distortion in our imagined forms of dying and living. It surely enters into our literature and art, our theology and psychiatry, and our politics and public life no less than our private sphere of existence.

Geoffrey Gorer was groping toward that distortion when he spoke of the "pornography of death."[18] He was referring to what he took to be the twentieth-century replacement of sex by death as an underground sphere of conflict; and the eruption of previously taboo lurid private fantasy into public discourse in the form of extravagent mass media rendition of death and violence. Gorer stresses a shift in prudery—the unmentionability of sex giving way to the unmentionability of natural death. But the source of the pornography—of our shared fantasies of runaway violence—may reside in the state of mind we have been discussing. Our public depictions of violent death can be exploitative and repulsive in the extreme.* But they are no more excessive than, perhaps appropriate to, the ultimate nuclear pornography: the equation in our minds of death with extinction.

We have been discussing various forms of dislocation in connection with impaired symbolic immortality, the identity of the meaninglessly doomed, and the equation of death with extinction. As we move further along the aberrant sequence we find that specific nuclear relationships to totalism and victimization can be understood around imagery of "security" and "secrecy." We can consider these in their collective significance and then turn to individual-psychological counterparts.

"Security" means safety or freedom from danger or risk. More specifically it refers to "feeling no care or apprehension" (the word secure being derived from the Latin sē [without] cūra [care]). (OED, Vol. 2, p. 2704; American Heritage Dictionary, p. 1173) Psychologically we use the word security to suggest the young child's sense that he can rely upon his environment, outer and inner, without a feeling of significant threat. Security is originally provided one, but as one moves into adulthood one becomes increasingly responsible for one's own security—for the reliable external and internal environment (a family, job, and psychological well-being) that preserve one's safety, if not total freedom from "care or apprehension." Security has always depended upon one's relationship to nurturing individuals and groups; and the dynamic of modern nationalism associates imagery of security increasingly with nation-state. But from the time of World War II and the development of the bomb the term "national security" has become an uneasy obsession.†

And since the development of nuclear weapons, we may speak of a *pervasive sense of vulnerability to annihilation*. This vulnerability was recognized very early by some of those originally closely associated with making the first atomic bomb. Even as he in effect rejected scientists' petitions against the dropping of

---

*For example, the "snuff films" of the mid-1970s, in which pornographic sexual scenes would culminate in the death of the female participant. It was claimed that, at least in some cases, the deaths actually occurred—the woman was killed on camera. These films were first shown privately, then in theaters in a few cities including New York.

†Vann Woodward has described the traditional American sense of "free security" provided by surrounding oceans, which has not only shaped much of our history but has come to be looked upon as "a natural right, free and unchallengeable." Nuclear technology, in causing the "passing" or termination of this "free security" thus has a special impact on Americans and on our policymakers, as compared to Russians whose national imagery has always been permeated with threat of invasion from the outside.[19] But the larger point is that, as Alastair Buchan has written, nuclear weapons have created a universal, in a sense democratic "Age of Insecurity" in that "There is now no question of any party . . . escaping without terrible consequences from a nuclear exchange" and "The collapse of any concept of victory in a great power war has stimulated our interest in the security of our adversary as well as our own."[20]

the first atomic bomb without warning on a populated city, Secretary of War Henry Stimson not only suggested that the weapon brought about a new relationship of man to the universe but said: "It must be controlled if possible to make it an assurance of future peace rather than a menace to civilization."[21]

The most constructive approach to that vulnerability would be to acknowledge it and work universally to overcome it. But the more frequent national response resembles that of an individual who fends off his imagery of threatened annihilation by means of more aggressive and more total measures to assert his power, measures which may in turn enable him to believe his illusion of invulnerability. Thus nations, perhaps especially bomb-possessors, are likely to move toward totalism in both foreign and domestic policies. Hans J. Morgenthau, for instance, describes a dangerous American tendency toward "globalism," which he sees as isolationism "turned inside out":

> While the isolationist used to say, "We don't need to have anything to do with the world; for we can take care of our interests on our own terms," the globalist says, "We shall take on the whole world, but only on our own terms." Globalism internationalizes our impulse toward a "moral crusade . . . to protect the virtue of the 'Free World' from contamination by communism and to create a world order in which that virtue has a chance to flourish."[22]

Walter Lippmann spoke similarly of the "dangerous form of self-delusion" which has led Americans toward "the conception of ourselves as the policemen of mankind."[23] Both commentators are getting at a post-World War II American impulse to exert *control* over worldwide social forces. That impulse reflects a compensatory reaction to the enormous sense of vulnerability on the part of a nation that has assumed the role of the strongest military power in the world. It is as if America must hold everything in place and continue to pursue that ever-elusive image of "national security." It is not just a question of the rival ideological system of communism, but communism in a world with the bomb and communism itself with the bomb. During the post-World War II years, there emerged an elite of what Richard Barnet has called "the national security managers" who have set much of the tone and formulated much of the imagery leading to the disastrous American international policies culminating in Vietnam.[24] With the existence of an exterminating explosive device as an aspect of the world system, the leading powers (Russia no less than America) are apt to develop policies and elites whose purpose is to manipulate that system on behalf of an unobtainable guarantee of national safety or "security."*

---

* An alternative perspective is that of the Institute for World Order, which views the world as an open system, and explores the possibility of universal values that might help overcome its vulnerability to annihilation and contribute to general improvements in the status of human beings.[25] The approach contrasts sharply with the image, described

The second theme, that of secrecy, is itself a function of "security" as we have defined it. Nations have always had secrets they have struggled to keep hidden, but the problem of the secret became absolutized with the development, or rather the project for development, of the atomic bomb. So secret was the original secret that it was unknown to what we think of as one of the primary agencies of "security":

> The Army as a whole didn't deal with matters of security until after the atomic bomb burst on the world because it was the first time that the Army really knew there was such a thing [as the atomic bomb], if you want to be perfectly frank about it! [26]

The ultimate destroyer was from the beginning the ultimate secret. Every aspect of the American project for making the bomb was associated with hidden power and hidden danger of an unprecedented degree—a secret race with an evil Nazi enemy (originally suspected of being ahead of us in preparations for making a bomb, but whose actual efforts to do so were hidden from us until the end of the European war). The secret was also kept from our allies during the war (especially Russia, but also France, and even in part from England, with whom we collaborated closely on the bomb); from the American people and most of its political leaders; from scientists not involved in making the bomb, and even from those who were. *

The idea of the secret was crucial even to the site chosen for making the bomb. Los Alamos, New Mexico, was later criticized by some because of the formidable problems it presented in the way of living accommodations and supplies, but it was isolated and hidden away from the outside world. Indeed, the place had been recommended by Robert Oppenheimer himself, whose

---

above, of controlling the world-system and rendering it static, according to the perceived dictates of American security. (In that static approach, there are of course traditional power goals involved as well, along with a whole constellation of attitudes specific to the weaponry, all of which we will discuss further in the next chapter.)

* Leslie Groves, director of the bomb project, put the matter unequivocally: "Compartmentalization of knowledge . . . was the very heart of security. My rule was simple and not capable of misinterpretation—each man should know everything he needed to know to do his job and nothing else." Groves went on to stress that, in addition to "security" the policy was meant to "improve . . . over-all efficiency by making our people stick to their knitting," that is, control the thought and behavior of the scientists involved. Finally, that policy "made clear to all concerned that the project existed to produce a specific end product—not to enable individuals to satisfy their curiosity and to increase their scientific knowledge." Here, under the duress of the war and the project, is an early assertion of the politicization of science and of all sorts of its technical, social, and imaginative components. The syllogism goes something like this: The secret is dangerous and our security depends upon keeping it to ourselves; even those working in

family owned a ranch nearby, and who had explored the area extensively on camping trips as a boy. That history is drawn upon by Dexter Masters in a neglected but important novel to suggest the relationship between the "bomb secret" and the secrets of childhood:

> The secret times of that time are the most secret of all, the most everlastingly private, the safest in retrospect . . . and hence the physicist's proposal must have given an almost sentimental sanction to the choice of the mesa of Los Alamos for the secret gestation of the bomb.[28]

Secrecy, then, had a double dimension. There was the immediate need for military control of information about a potentially decisive weapon, and a more diffuse mystique around keeping hidden and exclusive one's relationship to ultimate destructive power. From the beginning, the two dimensions were not really separable. A shocking violation at both levels was experienced by the American public when scientist-spies (Klaus Fuchs, Allen Nunn May, and Bruno Pontecorvo) took it upon themselves to "tell the secret" to representatives of another country which was both ally and adversary. That impact—the sense of radical threat to national safety or "security," to collective existence itself— also undoubtedly influenced the apparent irregularities and extraordinary application of capital punishment to Julius and Ethel Rosenberg, nonscientists whose espionage roles were never established with certainty. For as Shils points out in his important study, aptly entitled *The Torment of Secrecy*,

> It is strenuous to be endangered [by the overwhelming threat of nuclear weapons in the confrontation with the Soviet Union] and incapable of ending the crisis; it is infuriating to feel that what one holds sacred is rendered insecure by hidden enemies who through indifference or design would give away the secrets on which survival rests.[29]

Shils goes on to emphasize that concern with secrecy around nuclear weapons contributed greatly to McCarthyite persecution of alleged "subversives" during the 1950s; the pattern was intensified by "the faint trace of guilt" over having

---

the realm of the secret must know as little of it as possible; consequently their actions and thoughts, no less than their products, must be closely controlled. Scientists naturally bridled under a policy specifically antagonistic to the requirements of the scientific imagination; they found ways to violate it, though probably only Oppenheimer commanded full knowledge of scientific and technological details. These philosophical issues continue to haunt the relationship between science and government. And concerning keeping the secret from our allies, however logical the policy seemed to some at the time (Roosevelt favored sharing to a greater extent than did Groves), it too has had vast repercussions ever since in attitudes of nations toward the nuclear weapons they possess or wish to possess.[27]

used the bomb, as well as by horror over the idea of future use of nuclear weapons by anyone. Finally "'the secret' . . . became the central issue," and ensuing debates became debates about "salvation through secrecy or its renunciation." In other words the mystique of secrecy, now almost synonomous with "security," became the key to "national survival," to life-power.

These attitudes, as we have begun to suggest, are related to very early childhood themes around the idea of the secret. For the very young child, the secret begins with what adults know and he does not—the mystery of origins (where he came from) and endings (what happens to old people, the idea of death). When he learns, or thinks he learns, something about such matters, the secret becomes his to keep from others. And it comes to contain elements of early sensual experience ("secret pleasures") in connection with one's own body and one's parents' bodies, along with early "forbidden knowledge" of what adults do (observations or fantasies of the "primal scene"). Finally, the secret comes to contain the child's destructive imagery—his death wishes toward mother or father (when frustrated by them) or toward siblings (competitors for parental nurturing, of what is perceived as life-power), and toward anyone or anything else felt to be frustrating or threatening. The idea of the secret, then, is that of privileged mystery, a sense of special "knowledge" or experience available only to oneself or a few others who thereby share a favored state of being; and a sense of wrongdoing, of being associated with something shameful that cannot be revealed, or else guilty over not revealing it. Both themes relate to vulnerability or "security": the first by evoking the child's sense of special psychic sanctuary protecting him from incursions of alien adults or other "enemies"; and the second by suggesting an element of "bad knowledge" that, by contrast, renders one especially vulnerable to, because deserving of, punishment. That security, moreover, has absolute connotations. To hold on to the secret is to hold on to life itself; to reveal it is to risk attack, annihilation, loss of that life-power.

Those psychological themes are mobilized with special intensity around the ultimate atomic secret, so that the fascination and fear of early childhood is translated into national policy. To hold on to the secret of the bomb is to hold on to national life-power; to reveal the secret is to risk national annihilation—and also to lay bare the subterranean evil of one's own destructive national fantasies (scenarios of killing thousands, millions, hundreds of millions of people). Above all, the lines had to be drawn absolutely between possessors of the secret (ourselves) and those not permitted access to its mysteries (the others). The secret of the bomb, then, became an enormous stimulus toward totalism and victimization.

The blurring of psychological distinctions (suggested by Glover) between delusional images of world-destruction and feared actuality now extended to political, historical, and theological realms. It became extremely difficult to tell dangerous fanatics, courting the apocalypse, from the rest of us. For the ultimate secret, after all, is the image of world-destruction, and everybody is in on *that* secret.*

A secret embodying so total a danger is likely to evoke equally total political responses; and we can say, with Shils, that the secret of the atomic bomb paved the way for McCarthyite persecutions in the United States in the 1950s. For the apocalyptic nature of the secret seemed to justify a totalistic stance in order to guard against those who would steal more of it or who might in any way aid the archenemy (the Soviet Union or "the Communists") now concretely identified as the stealer of our secret. Indeed one might even say that the nuclear secret and the Soviet threat became so closely associated as to blend psychologically within the evolving imagery of extinction. Hence the expression, during senatorial and congressional hearings and many other aspects of American life, of the entire totalist constellation—milieu control, mystical manipulation, demand for purity and cult of confession, loading of the language and ideological distortion of personal experience, and finally dispensing of existence.[31] Throughout these hearings there was the characteristic totalist stress upon "telling all" and "naming names"; the ultimate secret rendered all lesser secrets more dangerous. As Dexter Masters explained (through a character in his novel), the atomic-bomb secret became itself "a superstition," part of a refusal to acknowledge the natural source of—and therefore universal access to—knowledge of nuclear weapons. More than that, the obsession with a secret becomes a way of masking one's real dilemmas—one's own "disease":

> There are fears and suspicions all over, there is a sickness. . . . But the secrecy—I know what that is . . . if you are sick and do not wish to know the progress of your disease, you cover it with secrecy—secret arms factories and secret piles of secret papers. . . . But one dies anyway . . . perhaps sometimes even faster. Perhaps sometimes from causes which might have been treated, except for the secrecy . . .[32]

What Masters implies is that the concept of the secret became a condensed psychic expression of overall atomic bomb dangers, an expression which in turn

* Shils describes the situation very vividly: "The retention of the vital secret becomes the focus of the phantasies of apocalypse and destruction, of the battle between the children of light and the children of darkness, which Western Christian society has inherited from ancient and medieval dualistic heresies. These ideas re-emerge, in secular and religious forms, in periods of distress and they offer salvation, which may be achieved either through revolution or through return to the "good old days" . . . the atomic bomb was a bridge over which the phantasies ordinarily confined to restrictive sections of the population, whole-and-corner nativist radicalism, religious fundamentalism and revolutionary populism—entered the larger society which was facing an unprecedented threat to its continuance. The phantasies of apocalyptic visionaries now lay claim to the respectability of being a reasonable interpretation of a real situation."[30]

lacked constructive approaches to those dangers.* The metaphor of fatal illness is particularly apt, both because of what bombs do and the nature of the death anxiety they arouse.

More than three decades after Hiroshima it has become clear enough that no real secret exists; a certain threshhold constellation of scientific and technological development, achieved or borrowed, is all anyone needs to build nuclear weapons.† And much public discourse by possessors of the weapons is aimed at making known one's nuclear capacity, sometimes rather precisely, in order to avoid, as they say, "miscalculations" on the part of potential enemies. Yet the image of the ultimate secret still haunts us. Between the two great nuclear powers especially, there continues intense rivalry in secret research aimed at new "breakthroughs"—more efficient and deadlier bombs and more powerful and precise "delivery systems." We continue to live with the terror of another facet of the ultimate secret: the question of whether or when the bombs will be used, and human civilization, or most of it, will be destroyed. Our ambitious probe into some of the "ultimate secrets" of nature seems to leave us with deadly confusion over how to replace the natural order—or the responsible deity—as the "owners" of those secrets.

One result lends something of a paranoid cast to the historical process itself. Conspiratorial interpretations of events found a new focus, so that in the literature of the radical right, for instance, there was the persistent theme that whatever knowledge Russia has was stolen from the United States, a claim that was given quasi-respectable status in a book entitled *The Secret War for the A-bomb*,[34] whose author served as advisor to certain American military groups.

To be sure, atomic weapons in no way created the radical right or its various forms of restorationist totalism—as encountered, for instance, among certain groups of religious fundamentalists, as well as the Minutemen, the John Birch Society, the Ku Klux Klan, and the Goldwater and Wallace political movements. These groups have been accurately described as feeling "dispossessed" under the duress of "a major change in the situation and structure of American society," and desperately in search of

---

* Masters' fictional spokesman did not advocate "giving the bomb" to the Russians or anyone else but rather a general exploration—especially by the Russians and ourselves—of the full nature of the threat facing humankind.

† The ease with which a bomb could be built was demonstrated by a Princeton University undergraduate who, in 1977, wrote a paper for a science course, consisting of a workable design for doing so. He depended upon library materials and public documents for his research, along with a few questions he asked people in various agencies over the telephone. He became something of a celebrity, sought after by media and foreign governments alike, and of course eventually wrote a book about his experiences.[33]

"an interpretation of the world."[35] Now the nuclear threat, especially as it involved communism, greatly intensified their death anxiety and dislocation, and consequently their impulses toward totalism and victimization. Their "transcendent moralism" could find the kind of radical simplification they sought—ultimate evil found expression in the ultimate crime of the theft of the ultimate weapon. In their "romantic activism" in which "progress is tantamount to restoration,"[36] they could seek a mythical past of purity and harmony in which evil did not exist—there was no atomic bomb, no theft of the ultimate secret, and (at least by psychological inference) no death anxiety and perhaps no death at all. To conventional victims (Blacks, Jews, impoverished or outcast groups) are added those who symbolize modernity and therefore the threat itself, such as liberals and leftists, intellectuals and scientists, and again, Jews. We have noted how restorationists can embrace the very symbols of modernity they fear, in American experience mainly an embrace of technology. Hence the particularly dangerous radical right embrace of *American* nuclear weapons (as in the case of Barry Goldwater). For that combination might well lead one to seek nuclear Armageddon as a way of achieving total purification by means of what the late Robert Lowell called "murdering evil."

> We were founded on a Declaration, on the Constitution, on Principles, and we've always had the ideal of "saving the world." And that comes close to perhaps destroying the world. Suddenly it is [possible that the] really terrible nightmare has come true, that we are suddenly in a position where we might destroy the world, and that is very closely allied to saving it. We might blow up Cuba to save ourselves and then the whole world would blow up. Yet it would come in the guise of an idealistic stroke . . . yes, I suppose this is too apocalyptic to put it this way, but it is the Ahab story of having to murder evil: and you may murder all the good with it if it gets desperate enough to struggle.[37]

Although Lowell draws only upon American moral imagery, there is probably no culture without some form of related impulse to "murder evil." But only ourselves and one other country have the technological capacity to carry through this totalism of consequences.

In that sense many look upon the Americans and the Soviets as potential annihilators who stand ever poised with their ultimate weapons. And since only the United States has so far used those weapons, the imagery is much more likely to focus on us.

Part of that focus—and indeed part of the ultimate secret itself—has to do with the connection of bomb and race. The two atomic bombs used on human populations were dropped by whites on nonwhites. Most of the bomb possessors have been whites (with the notable exception, at this writing, of the Chinese), but much of the bomb-testing has taken place in nonwhite areas—American and French testing in the South Pacific and Soviet testing in Central Asia. * (To be sure, nonwhite races experienced various forms of imagery of extinction at the hands of white races long prior to the atomic bomb.) Inevitably, the bomb becomes associated with racist imagery, all the more so because of the circumstances that surrounded the first two atomic bombs used. When the ultimate weapon thus becomes associated in millions of minds with what they consider to be the ultimate human problem, psychological consequences must be profound—greater, in fact, than we now know how to describe. What we can say is that each of these extreme problems, nuclear weapons and race, sheds further psychic poison on the other.

We have been discussing a malignant influence of nuclear weapons on the general sequence of psychohistorical aberration from dislocation to victimization to all forms of violence. But let us consider for a moment the specific subject of nuclear violence. It is a subject about which there is both everything and nothing to say—in a sense hardly a subject at all but a kind of "final common pathway" for whatever goes sufficiently wrong to bring about this form of cataclysm. In its totality it subsumes us, our potential deaths, and therefore our lives. Nothing one says about nuclear violence is remotely adequate. We have important models—Hiroshima and Nagasaki—but in another sense no

---

* Many survivors in Hiroshima thought of themselves as historical guinea pigs— victims of an American "experiment" to determine the effects of a diabolical new weapon. What most could not decide—and had great difficulty talking about—was whether or not Americans would have been as willing to conduct that experiment on members of the white race, whether or not they were chosen partly because they were nonwhite. Americans, too, have been embarrassed by this question, though they are quick to point out that work on the bomb was initiated largely in reference to Germany (the fear that German scientists might be making one of their own), and that by the time it was ready for use Germany had surrendered and Japan was the only remaining enemy. But those facts do not fully answer the question, and no one can be certain that racial imagery was entirely absent from the psychic processes of all the people involved in the decision to use the weapon. Hence I spoke of a "conspiracy of silence" between the Americans and Japanese concerning this painful, almost unmentionable issue. [38]

The kinds of emotion that surround the issue were intensely evoked by the "Lucky Dragon" (Fukuryu-Maru) Incident of 1954, in which a group of Japanese fishermen were exposed to fallout from the American hydrogen bomb test at Bikini, with one resulting death. Many Japanese at that time, as Herbert Passin observed, came to see themselves as "the fated victims of American atomic policy," and Americans as "cruel and inhuman, perhaps . . . because we are fundamentally contemptuous of 'colored people'." Passin went on to explain that "it must be remembered that throughout Asia, and particularly in India, it is widely believed that America dropped the first atom bomb on Japan, rather than on Germany, because the Japanese are 'colored people' and the Germans are 'white.' No amount of argument will convince people that the atom bomb was only developed after the German surrender. And if America is capable of such inhumanity, 'treating the masses like animals,' in the words of the novelist Kojoro Serizawa (Chuo Koron, June, 1954) then perhaps the communist charges of germ warfare in Korea are also true." [39]

models at all since what happened in those two cities cannot represent the infinitely greater destruction that would result from use of our contemporary atomic weapons.

With the development of modern "conventional weapons"—the automatic rifle, the machine gun, accurate heavy artillery, the airplane, submarines and naval power in general—man has increasingly lost psychological touch with his own killing. But with nuclear weapons there is a quantum jump in this process, and we experience a radical symbolic gap between what we feel and what we do. The real significance of what we have been calling the totalism of consequences is the new independence of the most absolute forms of destructiveness from our psychic processes. We may illustrate the point by simply contrasting the scope of nuclear destructiveness with the cast of mind necessary to initiate it.

In Hiroshima a single and, by present standards, small and primitive atomic bomb virtually wiped out a medium-sized city and subjected survivors to the extreme psychic consequences of a permanent encounter with death. Now a single hydrogen bomb can have one thousand times the destructive force of the Hiroshima weapon, and one million times the destructive force of the "block busters" whose twenty tons of TNT made them the most violent of preatomic bombs. The potential speed of delivery of these weapons has increased more than thirty fold from the three-hundred-mile-per-hour rate of the fastest World War II heavy bomber; and the present ten-thousand-mile-per-hour long-range ballistic missile permits a transit time between Washington and Moscow (either way) of less than thirty minutes. Moreover, any individual missile may be equipped with multiple independent reentry vehicles (MIRV), permitting it to carry several warheads, each accurately guided to a separate target. A fifteen-hundred-megaton attack upon the United States *—considered "moderate" in size (more than the minimum but considerably less than the maximum)— would result in about sixty million deaths; and a twenty-thousand megaton attack with "dirty" (that is, high nuclear fission yield) bombs would probably result in the complete annihilation of all of America's cities and its people. We have been talking about America but, as John Kennedy said as early as 1963: "Russia and the United States each now have enough deliverable nuclear weapons to destroy the human race several times over."

There are various degrees of awareness of these annihilative possibilities. But by and large the general response to such threatening and virtually unabsorbable imagery has been a characteristic one in Western experience since at least the seventeenth century: that of breaking it down, separating its elements, establishing extreme divisions of labor within which "experts" can function. Whatever the assumed intellectual justification for this compartmentalization, the result is a radical separation of feeling and consequence. Nuclear scenarios are projected but not experienced, and it is on the basis of those non-

* A megaton is the term for the explosive power of one million tons of TNT.

experienced scenarios that the arrangements for nuclear violence are constructed. There are feelings to be sure, some of them involving anger and rage, but none that connect with the millions of destroyed, incinerated, and irradiated human beings that would result should the weapons be used.

We may say then that passionate violence can be an important factor, powerful feelings around threats to the life of one's group, to one's racial and cultural substance, to one's sacred ideals. But along the line in the bureaucratic structure, such moral passion gives way to the more immediate commitment to "doing one's job." That was the cast of mind of pilots, navigators, and crewmen who participated in the Hiroshima and Nagasaki bombings. It was as true for the one or two who knew the purpose of the mission long in advance, the few who vaguely suspected what that might be, and the rest who learned of the atomic bomb only as they were completing their mission.

Over the years, the great majority of those involved have maintained that same view of their action. The image is not without nobility—"doing a job" can entail courage, pride in one's skill and group cohesion, and willingness to do, one becomes convinced, what is very difficult but has to be done.

Leaders too, even among the minority who have given serious thought to the moral dimensions of nuclear weapons, could come to feel that under duress they must "do their job" and use them in order to carry out *their* group responsibility—for defeating a dangerous enemy, countering an anticipated attack, or taking action perceived as necessary for "national survival." Out of this imagery they could come to feel that they have "no choice" but to go ahead. Then the process becomes organizational and technical. For such is the nature of nuclear weapons that in the sequence of their potential use the passionate component diminishes and numbed violence takes over.

The symbolic gap between technological reality and psychic state is expressed in the domesticated vocabulary of nuclear weapons. Terms like "nuclear exchange," "nuclear yield," "counterforce," "nuclear escalation," "megaton," "MIRV," or "Polaris" or "Poseidon missile"—these are not part of a diabolical plan to conceal evil nuclear schemes so much as a constellation of deception and self-deception that now dominates our world "megamachine." The structure has a strange rationality, "the logic of madness."[40] One has to extricate oneself from the numbed language in order to begin to experience nuclear actuality, much in the fashion of one journalist who, upon witnessing a hydrogen bomb test, commented: "Megaton, schmegaton, it's a hell of a bomb!"

As one nuclear-weapons novelist has his protagonist, the head of a bomb-making project, write in his diary: "A man may murder all men, once they appoint him to save them from murder!" and,

I am no more mad than those who send us here or allow us to remain here. While there are [nuclear bomb-making] Projects, no one is mad.[41]

In the novel the protagonist (very likely modeled after J. Robert Oppenheimer) is actually insane, which would seem to be almost the reverse of what we have been saying. But, however melodramatically, the author is trying to embody in his bombmaker the more general and more hidden nuclear madness—the madness of "those who send us here or allow us to remain here." The inference is that everyone has become a "world-destroyer"; that this being so we are enmeshed in a larger madness; and that man's nuclear projects—including his whole structure of nuclear violence—are both expressions of that madness and attempts at warding off awareness of it.

This symbolic gap—indeed, entire nuclear deformation—is not lost entirely on any of us. But those who are presented with it as part of their acculturation—the young who grow up into a nuclear world—have had some very specific introductions to it.

In my Hiroshima study I emphasized the *hibakusha's* sense of continuous encounter with death, extending through his initial exposure, sense of lifelong vulnerability to the "invisible contamination" of fatal forms of "A-bomb disease"; his struggles with death guilt, acute and chronic forms of psychic numbing, with images of human relationships and much of life itself as "counterfeit"; with forms of "contagion anxiety" and a sense of his own death-taint; and a continuous, often futile struggle to give meaning or inner form to the overall experience.

I suggested that all of us were in some degree affected by that constellation around atomic survival, that we live in a "world of survivors" in which there was more historical sharing of nuclear victimization than we realized.

Now there is beginning psychological evidence for that assumption: in studies by Kenneth Keniston,[42] Robert S. Liebert,[43] Edwin S. Shneidman,[44] and work in progress by Michael Carey. Carey's work is especially conclusive, based as it is on interviews with more than forty young men and women (in their twenties and thirties) focusing on their early imagery about nuclear weapons and its relationship to feelings about death and about various aspects of living. There are some general patterns that emerge from this work, which suggest a certain general contour for young nuclear men and women. These include a characteristic sequence in one's relationship to the bomb, as well as a lasting set of general themes.

The sequence is from amorphous death anxiety to sustained numbing to periodic contact with anxious death imagery. The first stage was remembered as taking place about the time of entering school (though sometimes before), and was often associated with the "bomb drills" of the 1950s (these, more or less on the order of "fire drills," involved either going to the cellar or sitting or lying under desks, keeping one's head and neck protected either with desks or books or paper, and learning to face away from the blast in order to avoid being blinded by it). The drills were preceded by a certain amount of instruction about the nature of nuclear weapons that both emphasized their destructiveness and expressed optimism about surviving them (if one was properly prepared and diligently followed the rules of the drills).

Memories of that early exposure were of a dreadful and mysterious entity known as "the bomb" or "the thing," which was special and different because it could destroy everything and perhaps blow up the world. That sense of the bomb could be amorphous and distant, painfully immediate, or both. In any case, there were likely to be indirect expressions of imagery of extermination— in dreams or fantasies that would sometimes involve an actual bombing (people and cities destroyed by explosions and fires), would sometimes involve desperate searches for the sanctuary of shelters or for family members, or else would take the form of more disjointed images of terror and destruction.

Then during the second phase, starting a few years later or in the early teens, the whole issue would seem to fade away, and there was little remembered awareness of the bomb. (There were, of course, historical and geographical as well as personal variants in all this, having to do with how active were bomb drills and general bomb concerns at a particular time and in a particular place.) Thoughts about the bomb, when one had them during this phase, tended to be less frightening and at times even pleasurable, for instance, fantasies of unlimited sex play in the shelters. Even during this phase of numbing, however, there could be frightening dreams related to the bomb. And in fact the more one explored one's memories of this, the more evidence emerged that one was actively involved in one way or another with imagery of extinction that was often very close to the surface.

The third phase might begin in mid or late adolescence or early adult life, and involved a more complex and shifting relationship to bomb imagery. There was a wide continuum, from obsession with the bomb to concern expressed about it with varying anxiety to the claim that it had virtually no impact on one. Yet from all of these points on the continuum, further exploration would invariably yield powerful images having to do with nuclear holocaust or other forms of annihilation. These would often include the sense that one's own life or the lives of one's children would end violently and prematurely, or a back-and-forth, contradictory pattern between numbness toward the whole question and periodic experience of anxiety (which could be stimulated by external nuclear threats or old personal fears); or else the more vague sense of living under a nuclear shadow that did not seem to determine any specific life decision but would never quite go away either.

I have also encountered these patterns in many young adults with whom I have discussed nuclear questions over the past two decades. Some would tell me that their generation was much less affected by nuclear weapons than mine. They could not, as I did at the age of nineteen, experience the frightening transition from an ordinary world to one in which the bomb was used and would continue to exist. In contrast, they would make clear that the bomb had always been part of their landscape—they had known no world in which it did not exist—and it was just one of their many dubious legacies from my generation and its predecessors. But as we discussed the subject further they too would recall striking, often terrifying images of the kind already mentioned. Some would begin to raise questions about the bomb's relationship to attitudes of urgency or cynicism they experienced around life plans, and to their politics and their involvements with drugs or meditation.*

Turning to the shared psychological themes, the most central is the equation of death with annihilation. These people were exposed to nuclear holocaust at about the same time (roughly between the ages of four and eight) they were struggling to absorb and articulate the concept of death as termination. During interviews they would go back and forth between the two, the one informing the other, in ways that suggested the merging of images of death and extermination. Some seemed to have actual difficulty, at least for a time, distinguishing between the two. They did, of course, come to make such distinctions, but the early association of death with total death probably never quite leaves them. Here we find the childhood initiation into the fundamental psychic deformation of the nuclear age. The deformation is far from absolute—one lives with it and otherwise goes about one's business. But it is bound to be a factor in one's later responses to every kind of death anxiety and every vision of the human future. If the two cannot be fully separated, one's own "ordinary death" becomes more terrifying, and one's capacity to imagine and combat holocaust impaired.

What follows as a second theme is the unmanageability of life, the sense that any attempt to order existence is countered by the possibility of its absolute interruption. These people expressed pervasive doubts about the lasting nature of anything they or others might undertake, and therefore about the authenticity of virtually all claims to achievement.

A third theme was the perception of craziness. For many this began with the idea of men making such weapons but was even more marked in relation to the adult prescriptions for combating the weapon (covering one's head, ducking under the desk, going down to the cellar, staying calm, etc.). Both weapon and response seemed equally strange and "weird"—the one almost supernatural and the other unbelievable. Some perceived their own reactions as equally "weird"—fantasies about merging with the bomb, sharing its absolute power over life and death. Their own "craziness" sometimes included a form of fascination with the weapon that made them wish it would be dropped so that they would witness the spectacle and somehow take advantage of it. This introduction into radical absurdity—the sense of the world as mad—undoubtedly played a part in the worldwide uprisings of the young during the 1960s and

---

*I came to the conclusion that there are indeed generational issues around nuclear weapons imagery, which are in fact more complex than stated here. But I think there is a common constellation shared by all generations, involving the elements of death imagery, numbing, and symbolic deformation that we have been discussing.

the pervasive tone of mockery that emerged. The very encounter of the child with nuclear weapons (whether or not subjected to "bomb drills") stimulates an early impulse toward gallows humor, toward mocking the deadly absurdity of what is offered one.

Finally, all that we have described is part of a "double life" which becomes a theme in itself. The other side of one goes through the ordinary motions of living and respects the adult authorities and believes in their prescriptions. If one does not get rid of the sense of craziness, of life's unmanageability, and of death as extinction, one behaves *as if* all this were not the case. I have observed this kind of "double life" in various groups of survivors following their death encounter. But now one is, so to speak, born into a double life; the nuclear world demands it. There is a psychological cost, most of it probably in the form of extensive psychic numbing. As the double life takes hold as a continuous pattern, it contributes greatly to the kinds of symbolic gaps we have described. We mentioned the gap between technology and consequences, but the more fundamental gap furthered by the double life is that between knowledge and feeling. For in order to go about "business as usual," one has to deaden one's feelings about what one knows. In this group of people, that process of numbing could extend to all kinds of death-related or threatening subjects; they could not shut out one area of the mind without partially closing down others nearby. But in some there could be an uneasy psychic pendulum-swing between that numbing process and struggles against it, again a microcosm of some of the collective behavior of young people during the 1960s: the struggle against the numbing or "deadened feelings" encountered both in the "adult world" and in the young people themselves. All told, it becomes extremely difficult for them to experience the kind of "organic knowledge" that commands full participation of body and mind. The "double life" becomes a seemingly necessary but unsatisfactory compromise with one's internal and external environments. Also cast into doubt are sustaining definitions—those associated with older forms of vitality and larger connection—of masculinity and femininity, activity and passivity, and good and evil.

These themes are not limited to any particular age group, as was evident during the Cuban missile crisis of 1962. At that time, our response to Soviet installation of nuclear missiles in Cuba brought about a confrontation on the sea between the Russians and ourselves, bringing the world as close as it has been since Nagasaki to nuclear war. It is difficult to estimate national behavior at the time, and there were in this country various expressions of fear and protest. But by and large people seemed to deal with the crisis in "ordinary" psychological ways—by shrugging it off or by expressing mild combinations of resignation, anxiety, helplessness, and anger. That is, the majority of people called forth their numbing, their psychic "double life," and rendered the crisis into "nothing special." One could say that President Kennedy and Premier Khrushchev, fortunately for all of us, were sufficiently able to envision images of catastrophe to take steps that headed off nuclear war. But one must add that important degrees of numbing on their and their advisors' part were of considerable importance in bringing about the crisis in the first place. At all levels of society there must exist such evidences of psychic "double life," of combinations of numbing, half-numbing, and organic knowledge.*

In mentioning "nuclear man," we think back on the experience of *hibakusha*, who, we have said, resemble us more than we realize. After the ordeal of their immediate death encounter, they experienced a "second victimization" in the form of radical discrimination in regard to marriage arrangements and jobs. The discrimination was sometimes described as "logical," in the sense that perspective spouses or employers had good reason to believe that, as a group, *hibakusha* were more sickly and more likely to produce abnormal children. But beneath this "logic" was the more fundamental sense of *hibakusha* (one shared by *hibakusha* themselves) of being death-and-holocaust-tainted, of being embodiments of the most violent and premature dying. Do we share that amorphous version of this taint?

We live in a world so dominated by holocaust—past, contemporary, and

---

* My own reaction to the crisis taught me something about those combinations. I had just returned with my wife and year-old son from work in Hiroshima, so that imagery of nuclear war had a certain intensity for me, though I cannot say that I had distinct images of *this* nuclear war. As the Russian ship carrying nuclear missiles to Cuba was approached by American naval forces sent to intercept it, and Kennedy and Khrushchev were making their public statements and staggering decisions, my wife and I met several times with friends and colleagues and a group of us sent a telegram to the President urging restraint. But I was at the same time involved in a more immediate crisis: our Weimaraner dog, a beloved family pet for more than six years, suddenly became acutely ill and had to undergo emergency surgery. The hours following the operation coincided almost exactly with those moments of the Kennedy-Khrushchev confrontation when the world seemed about to be engulfed in nuclear war. I remember a terrible haze of radio and television reports about the confrontation, visits to the veterinary hospital, talks with friends, and telephone conversations with the veterinarian. My mind struggled with two sets of images: one a vast but amorphous panorama of nuclear war; the other of a particular, beautiful animal dying. When later on I asked myself which set of images had been the most vivid and painful, I had to confess that it had been the second, involving the dog. The anticipated death of a specific being (not even a human) had greater impact than the more total but obscure threat of extermination. The most vivid image I retain from the experience is that of the dog, a large and formerly spirited creature, lying still on the floor of the veterinary hospital.

The fact that nuclear war was averted while the dog died undoubtedly influenced my restrospective recollections. It is also likely that much of my anxiety about nuclear war—including that related to my own death and the death of my wife and child—was displaced onto the "smaller," more absorbable crisis. Certainly my reaction was not simple, and included many layers drawn from a variety of life experiences. But I mention the episode to illustrate the operation, under duress, of the psychic "double life" I have been discussing. And while I would make no claim that it was "typical," I believe it suggests "nuclear man's" extreme difficulty in achieving anything like adequate perception of nuclear threat, of giving inner form to imagery of extermination.

anticipated—that we may look upon ourselves as, in some degree, embodiments of these horrors. This is the vague and yet disturbing "identity of the doomed" in which we partake. Part of that identity could well find expression in the bomb worship we shall next consider. If so, confrontation of both might be the beginning of wisdom.

TWENTY-THREE

Nuclearism

THE ULTIMATE CONTEMPORARY deformation is a condition we may call *nuclearism*: the passionate embrace of nuclear weapons as a solution to death anxiety and a way of restoring a lost sense of immortality. Nuclearism is a secular religion, a total ideology in which "grace" and even "salvation"—the mastery of death and evil—are achieved through the power of a new technological deity. The deity is seen as capable not only of apocalyptic destruction but also of unlimited creation. And the nuclear believer or "nuclearist" allies himself with that power and feels compelled to expound on the virtues of his deity. He may come to depend on the weapons to keep the world going.*

As with any religion, embrace of nuclearism is likely to be marked by a "conversion experience"—an immersion in death anxiety followed by rebirth into the new world view. At the heart of the conversion experience is an overwhelming sense of awe—a version of Freud's "oceanic feeling" in which one's own insignificance in relationship to the larger universe is so extreme as to feel oneself, in effect, annihilated. Scientists and others witnessing the first nuclear test explosion in the New Mexico desert at Alamogordo at dawn of July 16, 1945, experienced that kind of oceanic feeling. Hence exclamations and thoughts such as: "The sun can't hold a candle to it!", "This was the nearest to

---

*I will suggest later ways in which nonweapons use of nuclear energy can enter into the equation.

doomsday one can possibly imagine," and Oppenheimer's famous recollection of the words of the Bhagavad-Gita:

> If the radiance of a thousand suns
> Were to burst at once into the sky
> That would be like the splendor of the Mighty One . . .
> I am become Death,
> The shatterer of worlds.

Some of this includes retrospective feeling, but religious imagery was present in the military code name, "Trinity," suggested by Oppenheimer for the text site and eventually synonymous with that first test explosion. The choice was influenced by a John Donne sonnet Oppenheimer had been reading at the time ("Batter my heart, three person'd God; For, you/As yet but knock, breathe, shine, and seek to mend . . .").[1] That choice, according to one of Oppenheimer's biographers, "makes the moral assumption that defeating wrong, new weapons will bring a new day."*

Related Christian imagery, along with awe that defies words, was conveyed by Brigadier General Thomas Farrell, who worked directly under Leslie Groves as second in command at Alamogordo:

The effects could well be called unprecedented, magnificent, beautiful, stupendous and terrifying. No man-made phenomenon of such tremendous power had ever occurred before. The lighting effects beggared description. The whole country was lighted by a searing light with the intensity many times that of the midday sun. It was golden, purple, violet, gray and blue. It lighted every peak, crevasse and ridge of the nearby mountain range with a clarity and beauty that cannot be described but must be seen to be imagined. It was that beauty the great poets dream about but describe most poorly and inadequately. Thirty seconds after the explosion came, first, the air blast pressing hard against the people and things, to be followed almost immediately by the strong, sustained, awesome roar which warned of doomsday and made us feel that we puny things were blasphemous to dare tamper with the forces heretofore reserved to The Almighty. Words are inadequate tools for the job of acquainting those not present with the physical, mental and psychological effects. It had to be witnessed to be realized.[3]

Farrell made those observations immediately after the test explosion as part of the *official* report forwarded by General Groves to the secretary of war, and rushed to Stimson and Truman at Potsdam where they were meeting with Churchill and Stalin.

I am not suggesting that each of these men became an immediate convert to

---

* Nuel Pharr Davis[2] went on to say that "In talking with me about the name trinity Oppenheimer showed himself apologetic about the rather high-flown poetic derivation but not apologetic about the moral assumption."

nuclearism. Rather, their apocalyptic witness left them with powerful end-of-the-world imagery that had to be combined somehow with the rest of the mind's more ordinary forms. They had undergone a profound "survivor experience," and would in many cases seek to bear nuclear witness—to tell the world, on behalf of some higher purpose, of the extraordinary thing they had seen, and thereby find some meaning in their own death encounter. But they could do so in two ways: by dedicating themselves to the task of controlling or eliminating this threatening force; or else by intense identification with that same force, by a conversion to the religion of nuclearism.

Much of that awesome encounter, including the same subsequent psychic alternatives, could be experienced by those who were at further remove from the weapon—atomic scientists hearing of the result of their efforts (some of whom became the nucleus for the "scientist's movement" to control or eliminate the bomb); statesmen undergoing a kind of oceanic experience at the idea of possessing such a weapon; and the rest of us. One need only recall on the one hand President Truman's statement, upon hearing of the first bomb's success in Hiroshima, "This is the greatest thing in history!"; or the comment in the *New York Herald Tribune* describing the new force as "weird, incredible and somehow disturbing" so that "one forgets the effect on Japan or on the course of the war as one senses the foundations of one's own universe trembling." Those latter phrases could have come right out of William James's descriptions of the "fear of the universe" as experienced by the "sick soul" as part of his religious conversion. It is, in fact, directly reminiscent of James's quotation from Tolstoy:

> I felt . . . that something had broken within me on which my life had always rested, that I had nothing left to hold on to, and that morally my life had stopped . . .[4]

The clearest expression of nuclearism came from William Lawrence, the science writer who recorded many of the comments quoted here.*

Lawrence had the special importance of being one of the main "communicators" of the early nuclear experience. In his descriptions of the Alamogordo test, Lawrence used such phrases as "mighty thunder," "great silence," and additional language reminiscent of a "conversion in the desert." There were repeated images of rebirth:

> On that moment hung eternity. Time stood still. Space contracted to a pinpoint. It was as though the earth had opened and the skies had split. One felt as though he had been privileged to witness the Birth of the World. . . .
> The big boom came about a hundred seconds after the great flash—the first cry of a newborn world . . .[5]

---

*I approach Lawrence neither in the spirit of name-calling nor with a claim to individual-psychological analysis but rather as the embodiment of an important, widely shared contemporary psychological tendency.

The weapon does not just destroy but recreates the world. Thus, after quoting a reaction of the scientist Kistiakowsky to the effect that "In the last millisecond of the earth's existence—the last man will see something very similar to what we have," Lawrence's own thought is:

> Possibly so . . . but it is also possible that if the first man could have been present at the moment of Creation when God said, "Let there be light," he might have seen something very similar to what we have seen.

He remembers a passage from an 1869 journal of the brothers Goncourt in which they say that within a hundred years man would "know of what the atom is constituted and would be able, at will, to moderate, extinguish and light up the sun as if it were a gas lamp," and would so advance in physiological science that "he would create life in competition with God."

And then the generalized sense of the divine, of more-than-natural powers at play:

> And just at that instant there arose as if from the bowels of the earth a light not of this world, the light of many suns in one. It was a sunrise such as the world had never seen, a great green supersun climbing in a fraction of a second to the height of more than 8000 feet, rising even higher until it touched the clouds, lighting up earth and sky all around with a dazzling luminosity . . .

In these passages we sense the convert's feeling of transcending the boundaries of the self in his contact with the infinite. He finds his "new beginning" in an early manifestation of nuclearism. There is of course retrospective restructuring, but such is the case with the literature of religious conversion in general as one struggles to articulate the ineffable.

A conversion experience, James tells us, requires prior emotional and intellectual preparation. As a leading science writer, Lawrence had been for some time involved in pre-World War II advances in nuclear physics. He and his wife describe the staggering impact made upon them by Niels Bohr and Enrico Fermi when these men appeared unannounced at a scientific meeting in February, 1939, to describe some of the newly understood principles of the nuclear chain reaction. Lawrence's exhilaration ("This is the Second Coming of Prometheus, unbound at last after some half a million years . . .") was matched only by his terror ("this new Promethean fire . . . could be used by Hitler as the most destructive weapon in history"). His wife goes on to say that "Life from that night on was never to be the same for any of us." Perhaps the first nonscientist to grasp the significance of the potential nuclear weapon, his selection by the directors of the Manhattan Project to become the atomic bomb's official historian deepened his already strong involvement with the entire issue and, as it turned out, his identification with the weapon itself. He could understand his responses to its first detonation in the context of a personal destiny.

Lawrence's strong justification of the use of the bomb in Hiroshima, then, is hardly surprising, and one must acknowledge his inclusion in his discussion of a sensitive ethical examination of the problem by a German Jesuit who was victimized there. But his nuclearism becomes more prominent concerning the dropping of a second bomb on Nagasaki, an action that many observers have considered especially abhorrent, whatever their position on Hiroshima. Having been permitted to join the Nagasaki mission, Lawrence gives a dramatic firsthand report; and he proudly points out that the "dateline" of his story entitled, "With the Atomic Bomb Mission to Japan, Thursday, August 9," was "the first and only dateline of its kind in history." But that nuclearism emerges full flower in a remarkable series of images in response to witnessing the explosion of "America's first airborne-hydrogen bomb" in the northern Pacific on May 21, 1956:

> For nearly an hour after the fireball had faded I watched incredulously the great many-colored cloud that had been born in a gigantic pillar of fire. This cloud rose and spread until the boiling mushroom at its top had reached about twenty-five miles into the atmosphere and covered a stretch of sky, now tinged by the rising sun to the east of it, about a hundred miles long.
>
> Having seen what a much smaller fireball and mushroom-topped cloud had done to the city of Nagasaki, I was momentarily staggered by the thought of what the fireball and mushroom I was then watching would do to any of the world's great cities—New York, Washington, Chicago, Paris, London, Rome or Moscow. But then, as I kept on watching, a second, more reassuring thought became uppermost in my mind, a thought that has kept growing ever more reassuring in the years that have followed that historic morning.
>
> This great iridescent cloud and its mushroom top, I found myself thinking as I watched, is actually a protective umbrella that will forever shield mankind everywhere against threat of annihilation in any atomic war.
>
> This rising supersun seemed to me the symbol of the dawn of a new era in which any sizeable war had become impossible; for no aggressor could now start a war without the certainty of absolute and swift annihilation.
>
> This world-covering, protective umbrella, I have since become convinced, will continue shielding us everywhere until the time comes, as come it must, when mankind will be able to beat atomic swords into ploughshares, harnessing the vast power of the hydrogen in the world's oceans to bring in an era of prosperity such as the world has never even dared dream about.
>
> To those who would have us stop our tests in the Pacific, I would therefore say, "These tests, and others of improved models to come, serve as an effective substitute for war. History will record, I am sure, that World War III was fought and won on the Pacific proving ground in the Marshall Islands without the loss of

a single life and without the slightest damage to any inhabited locality anywhere in the world."[6]*

The sequence is striking: from total destruction (including potentially one's own city and oneself) to equally total protection ("world-covering, protective umbrella . . . shielding us everywhere") to total salvation (nuclear power creating "an era of prosperity such as the world has never even dared dream about"). In psychological terms the sequence is from annihilation to renewal to embrace and dependent worship. The deity is awesome, dreadful in its apocalyptic potential, but is also the savior of mankind. The arbiter of immortality must be both. That chapter of Lawrence's book is entitled "Why There Cannot Be Another War" and there is a summary statement to the effect that these ever-improving "earth-destroying weapons . . . make it certain that no nation, no matter how powerful, could dare risk a thermonuclear war." No group, that is, could dare defy the nuclear deity.

Lawrence entitles his next chapter, "The 'Clean' Hydrogen Bomb." The quotation marks around "clean" might seem to suggest a certain reserve, but Lawrence goes on to use this issue of irradiation to reassert his nuclearism in a still more ingenious form:

All the known facts thus make it clear that we are succeeding in humanizing the hydrogen bomb by limiting the enormous destructive power to blast and fire, thus transforming it from a radiactive monster, deriving most of its power from a dirty element, into a concentrated weapon deriving most of its explosive force from the fusion of two forms of hydrogen in which fallout is reduced to a minimum.[7]

The message here is that the deity is pure after all.

As already suggested, much of the language of supplication is reserved for nonweapon uses of nuclear energy, for "beat[ing] atomic swords into ploughshares." Thus, upon viewing the American nuclear reactor at the First International Conference on the Peaceful Use of Atomic Energy, held at Geneva in 1955, Lawrence has a vision of a nuclear-based "agreement between men of all nations, between East and West, between the free world and the world of totalitarianism." The nuclear reactor

totally eliminates the basic, elemental reason that has led to all the major wars in history—the have-nots coveting the possessions of the haves. For in the nuclear reactor . . . man has at last all the energy he needs to create wealth and leisure and spiritual satisfaction in such abundance as to eliminate forever any reason for one nation to covet the wealth of another.[8]

* The deity *could* of course destroy everything, the argument goes, but prefers only to demonstrate without loss of life. The difficulty with the argument, of course, is that there were people on the Marshall Islands who turned out to be affected by irradiation, and we must therefore assume that over time there was indeed some loss of life.

Now humankind can move "into the green pastures of a civilization built on plenty" and we can "irrigate deserts and transform them into blooming gardens." Without denying the possibility of some of these technical feats, we must note the extent to which Lawrence's zealous nuclearism leads to simplistic thinking about cause and prevention of war and a vision literally resembling Eden. It is a vision of total salvation. Lawrence goes on to quote a pharmacologist in a way that takes us close to the psychic center of the entire nuclearist constellation:

> "Medicine today," said Dr. [Maurice L.] Tainter, a world leader in pharmacology, "is accomplishing greater miracles than, for example, atomic-energy developments. It is because, in this Golden Age of Medicine, we have conscientiously evolved a technique and a scientific philosophy that finally enabled us to wrestle with death itself, and on increasingly even terms."[9]

Dr. Tainter was apparently not referring to the freezing of bodies, but to advances in the chemical understanding of aging. We may recognize, however, the same scientific hubris and quest for a technological form of actual physical immortality.

Significantly, Lawrence's nuclearism extends only to the first and second generations of nuclear weapons, the atomic and hydrogen bombs. He, in fact, in 1957, became literally antagonistic to the neutron (or "death ray") bomb in which neutrons would kill silently, without blast or heat. Lawrence denounced the position of those promoting the new bomb as "made up of a pyramid of misconceptions built on a foundation of half-truths." His technical strictures ("a highly inefficient weapon that would not add in any way to our security") were, moreover, combined with ethical ones:

> . . . a neutron bomb, if developed, would be a highly immoral weapon, a poison gas abhorrent to civilized humanity, a monster that rather than kill would, in the current nuclear jargon, "juice" its victims. While many within close range would die quickly, many others would linger on to a horrible death after days, weeks, or months of infernal torture.

> Rather than talk of weapons for "juicing" human beings, it behooves us to remember the words of the late General George C. Marshall that "the most important thing for the world today is spiritual regeneration. . . . We must present democracy," he said, "as a force holding within itself the seeds of unlimited progress for the human race. . . .

> We should tell the world that this is what we believe in. Not "juicing."[10]

We need hardly question these humane concerns, but only wonder about their delayed appearance. There are parallels in the experience of many scientists, notably Robert Oppenheimer's complex but forceful commitment to the making and using of a first generation weapon, only to find both technical and moral reasons to reject its second-generation offspring, the large (or "super") hydrogen bomb.

What seems to occur is a kind of "nuclear backsliding," in which the nuclearist reaches a point, usually in relationship to someone else's bomb rather than "his own," beyond which he feels himself able to go; beyond which the psychological and ethical structure of nuclearism cannot be sustained.[11] Feeling less identification with the new weapon, one is less vulnerable to being drawn into its rationalization of loathsome possibilities. To do so, in fact, might endanger one's already existing nuclearistic structure. Partly involved is what might be called a "nuclear Kronshtadt" in which the extension of the rationalization of nuclearism becomes too grotesque, more than one can stomach, too laden with death guilt.* The second reaction has to do with a form of "nuclearistic displacement," in which one eagerly discharges moral condemnation (often accompanied by technical reservations) upon a nuclear development that is either in some way vulnerable, or else simply coming from outside one's own commitments, thereby giving expression to anxiety and guilt one could not recognize in relationship to one's own weapon.

Yet if we consider again the example of the neutron bomb, we must recognize a kind of "creeping nuclearism" in which the potential negative passions of "nuclear backsliding" are muted by general nuclear numbing and domestication of the weapons. For as I write this, in late 1977, the United States has just embarked on a program to develop a version of the neutron bomb.†

What we have been calling nuclearism, then, involves a search for grace and glory in which technical-scientific transcendence, apocalyptic destruction, national power, personal salvation, and committed individual identity all become psychically bound up with the bomb. The weapon itself comes to dominate pathways to symbolic immortality.

Even in the absence of a "conversion experience," nuclearism in varying degrees is likely to accompany mere possession, or potential possession, of nuclear weapons. Bomb-possessors, awed by their association with the bomb's capacity for "total destruction," tend to evolve around it parallel imagery of "total manipulation" of human events. Indeed, a good deal of post-World War II history has been shaped by this equation, and by the frustration—and

---

*Kronshtadt has come to be a metaphor for a loss of revolutionary faith. In Kronshtadt, in 1921, a small naval garrison mutinied in response to worsening conditions for peasants and workers under the new Bolshevik regime. Arthur Koestler later commented that every disenchanted communist revolutionary has his particular Kronshtadt.

†One can question, however, whether it is a genuinely "third-generation" nuclear weapon. For it does not eliminate blast and heat but merely diminishes these relative to the increased ratio of killing by irradiation.

compensatory policies—of discovering it to be false. While bomb possessors vary greatly in their reactions, so absolute are the image-feelings around the weapon that the impulse toward nuclearism transcends individuals and can take hold even in men of great integrity.

Henry Stimson's experiences, in fact, suggest that a sensitive conscience, no less than its absence, can propel one in the direction of nuclearism. In his diaries Stimson referred to the weapon as "most secret," "the dreadful," "the terrible," "the dire," "the awful," "the diabolical," and "the most terrible weapon ever known in human history, one bomb of which could destroy a whole city."[12] His need to share his anxiety and potential guilt about the weapon with another human being was so great that he arranged for a subordinate to have "practically nothing to do" but be available as "someone that he knew, that he could trust, that had no stake in the game, with whom he could talk about the atom." Yet, despite all this, there is ample evidence that, as his biographer puts it, he was "from the beginning, apparently . . . prepared, in the appropriate circumstance, to drop the bomb." An explanation offered was that of John McCloy, a close associate: "at the outset he might have 'gotten down on his knees' and made his decision and *closed out the issue in his mind*."[13] Stimson had to shut down his moral imagination—his considerable sensitivity to imagery of holocaust—and impose on himself a rather absolute form of numbing, in order to make a decision he felt needed making. Thus most historians accept his later explanation that "My chief purpose was to end the war in victory with the least possible cost in the lives of the men in the armies which I had helped to raise."

But Stimson associated the bomb with a second, grander purpose, as revealed in his earliest memo on the subject to Truman, the new president: ". . . if the problem of the proper use of this weapon can be solved, we would have the opportunity to bring the world into a pattern in which the peace of the world and our civilization can be saved." Though the word "use" is ambiguous—it refers at least partly to a plea for postwar cooperation with the Soviet Union to avoid nuclear holocaust—the memo was nonetheless a "curious document" in that "it displayed Stimson's sensitivity to the historic significance of the atomic bomb, but did not question the wisdom of using it against Japan."[14] This nuclearistic tendency in a thoughtful, humane man limited his vision—prevented any serious consideration of withholding use of the weapon. That interpretation is supported by Stimson's later emphasis upon the bomb's significance for gaining American advantage in negotiations with the Soviet Union on a number of important issues of contention between the two great powers. At one point Stimson emphasized the bomb, together with America's economic leverage, as "a royal straight flush and we mustn't be a fool about the way we play it"; and at another point he insisted that the results of the first bomb test be known to American leaders when they met with Stalin and Churchill at Potsdam because it would be "a terrible thing to gamble with such big stakes in diplomacy without having your master card in your hand."[15] And indeed Truman did schedule a Potsdam Conference to coincide with that first test.*

Stimson, in response to his terrible burden, became an idealistic nuclearist.

---

* Sherwin describes the contradiction in Stimson's imagery imposed by what I am calling nuclearism. On May 16 of 1945 his memo to Truman emphasized the importance of "precision bombing" in Japan because "the reputation of the United States for fair play and humanitarianism is the world's biggest asset for peace in the coming decades," and added: "The same rule of sparing the civilian population should be applied as far as possible to the use of any new weapon." But as Sherwin points out: "The possibility that its extraordinary and indiscriminate destructiveness represented a profound qualitative difference, and so cried out for its governance by a higher morality than guided the use of conventional weapons, simply did not occur to him." And Sherwin goes on to suggest that "Stimson's understanding that the bomb would play an important diplomatic role after the war actually prevent[ed] him from questioning the assumption that the bomb ought to be used during the war . . ."[15A]

We are not surprised, then, at Stimson's nuclear backsliding immediately after the bomb was used. Among his last acts of office were a letter to Truman and a memorandum on "proposed action for control of atomic bombs," on September 11, 1945, in which he stressed, in opposition to Byrnes and possibly to his own earlier views, that "it would not be possible to use our possession of the atomic bomb as a direct lever to produce . . . change" in Russia's police state. He emphasized that "the bomb . . . constitutes merely a first step in a control by man over the forces of nature too revolutionary and dangerous to fit into the old concepts," again in contrast to his inability to make that distinction earlier. And he spoke of "the race between man's growing technical power for destructiveness and his psychological power of self-control and group control—his moral power." Finally, he considered it vital to "enter an arrangement with the Russians, the general purpose of which would be to control and limit the use of the atomic bomb as an instrument of war and so far as possible to direct and encourage the development of atomic power for peaceful purposes."[15B] But he continued to defend his advocacy of the bomb's wartime military use. There was a hint of his nuclear backsliding, even before the bomb's use, when he insisted, against General Groves' strong opposition, that Kyoto be removed from the target list. He explained to Groves the city's special historic and cultural significance, and insisted: "This is one time I'm going to be the final deciding authority. Nobody's going to tell me what to do on this. On this matter I am the kingpin." He later held to that position in the face of further pressure, not claiming that the "bitterness which would be caused by such a wanton act might make it impossible during the long postwar period to reconcile the Japanese to us in that area rather than to the Russians." Here his humane capacity to imagine the bomb's destruction of a particularly revered area combined with commitment to naked American self-interest enabled him to defect slightly from a fully nuclearistic position. But as Sherwin comments, "It never occurred to Stimson that the destruction of any city, or two cities, might be considered 'wanton.'"[15C]

Still another indication of Stimson's struggle against inner doubt—that is against earlier nuclear backsliding—can be found in a recollection of Dwight Eisenhower. The general was one of the few people who opposed use of the bomb, though he had no actual part in the decision. But on one occasion when he had the opportunity to express his objections to the weapon, he noted that "the Secretary was deeply perturbed by my attitude, almost angrily refuting the reasons I gave . . ."[15D] We may suspect that this uncharacteristic show of temper reflected Stimson's struggle against his own sensitivity, against the stirrings of a sense of guilt.

To a man like him, "The more frightful [the bomb] seemed as a weapon of war, the more useful it appeared as an instrument of peace." And even two years later he expressed agreement with a statement in a letter written to him by James Conant to the effect that "one of the principle reasons . . . for advising that the bomb must be used was that that was the only way to awaken the world to the necessity of abolishing war altogether."[16] However retrospective in this case, this is the kind of image of the bomb's purifying function that is at the heart of idealistic nuclearism. By means of the bomb there can emerge, via man's own works, an immortalizing vision of a warless world.

Secretary of State James Byrnes, Truman's other major adviser on such matters, embraced a form of nuclearism considerably less idealistic. Byrnes conceived of the weapon as "an explosive great enough to destroy the whole world," and one which "might well put us in a position to dictate our own terms at the end of the war."[17] His imagery about destructiveness and diplomatic leverage was equally absolute. He went further than others in insisting that an American nuclear monopoly best insured a "lasting structure of peace." As one student of the period has commented, "It is quite clear that Byrnes *began* with the idea of basing diplomacy on the atomic bomb."[18] Byrnes sought in the bomb a means of achieving both hard-nosed goals of power diplomacy and "the highest ideals" of peace and freedom.

Among these ideals was that of using nuclear leverage to force Russia to change her own society into a more open one—all this, of course, before considering any sharing of information about nuclear weapons. Stimson apparently held something like this view for a while, prior to his later renunciation of it, while Byrnes probably never gave it up. (Indeed it was a widespread impulse among Americans in government positions at the time of the end of the war. Eugene Rostow, a colleague at Yale, told me in personal conversation a few years ago that he himself had circulated a memo within the Office of Strategic Services, advocating that we make an ultimatum to the Soviet Union in which we declare that we will drop an atomic bomb upon her unless she takes active steps to open up her society. The rationale for the memo was that Russia would acquire the bomb before too long, and that we had to take this step while we alone possessed it, since the world would be rendered too dangerous should a totalitarian society like the Soviet Union acquire the bomb.) At Potsdam one of Byrnes' colleagues among Truman's entourage was disturbed by the secretary's "attitude that the atomic bomb assured ultimate success in negotiations.[18A] Byrnes's unreconstructed nuclearism provided something of a model for all too many later political leaders and nuclear theorists.

President Truman wavered between the views of his two advisors but probably came closer to embracing the perspective of Byrnes. Caught up in a nuclear project that had taken much of its shape prior to his assuming the presidency, Truman in part responded to an inertia principle in the situation in a manner later characterized by Groves as "like a little boy on a toboggan," whose "decision was one of noninterference—basically, a decision not to upset the existing plans." [18B]

But Truman came to relate the bomb centrally to his power-centered struggles as president of a wartime power increasingly at odds with a major ally. At Potsdam he eagerly awaited news of the test with the sense that "if it explodes as I think it will, I'll certainly have a hammer on those boys [the Russians]." [18C]

As one "inexperienced and insecure in the world of diplomacy . . . preparing to face the most demanding and potentially the most politically damaging single experience of his adult life," Truman felt himself greatly in need of the "hammer." And in terms of his psychological response, the hammer turned into a "power tool" of the first order. After Stimson reviewed with him Groves' "immensely powerful document" describing what had taken place at the test, he found that the President was "tremendously pepped up by it . . . [he] spoke to me of it again and again when I saw him . . . it gave him an entirely new feeling of confidence and he thanked me for having come to the Conference and being present to help him in this way." That new confidence was noted by Churchill who commented on Truman's sudden increase in vigor and self-assertion in dealing with Stalin. Churchill noted that Truman was "a changed man," that "he told the Russians . . . just where they got on and off and generally bossed the whole meeting." [19] Those are remarkable descriptions of the immediate personal impact on a world leader of knowledge of possession of—psychologically, merger with—an instrument of ultimate destruction. In the sense that Truman felt himself more powerful, we can say that nuclearistic power can be real, but this in no way means that the bomb could accomplish all that Truman, Byrnes, and other American leaders wished it to. That same euphoric sense of personal and national power was involved in Truman's disturbing comment upon hearing of the success of the Hiroshima mission: "This is the greatest thing in history." In every way, and for virtually everyone close to the experience—Byrnes, Stimson, and Truman as well as Oppenheimer, Teller, and Conant—the bomb encouraged imagery of totality and utopian achievement. For all of these men,

> not only the conclusion of the war but the organization of an acceptable peace seemed to depend . . . on the success of the atomic attacks against Japan. Secret development of this terrible weapon, during a war fought for total victory, created a logic of its own: a quest for a total solution to a set of related problems that appeared incapable of being resolved incrementally. [20]

Truman's retrospective evaluation of his presidency clearly revealed his nuclearism when he said first that "the one purpose which dominated me in everything I thought and did was to prevent a third world war," and that he had "no regrets" over the bomb's use. A hint of wisdom (though not quite an expression of nuclear backsliding) came a couple of months later, however, when, as one historian puts it, "the tonic had worn off." When an aide found him distressed over his inability to achieve his political goals, he "tried to cheer him up. 'Mr. President, you have an atomic bomb up your sleeve.'" And Truman's reply was, "Yes, but I am not sure it can ever be used." [21]

We find in these patterns of nuclearism around bomb possession the virtually irresistible impulse to equate destructive power with "human power." That equation, and the resulting pattern of nuclear or "atomic diplomacy," had important bearing on the bomb's use in Hiroshima and Nagasaki. I do not believe that the bomb was used solely or even primarily as a means of countering the perceived Soviet threat in Eastern Europe and elsewhere. But that kind of nuclearistic imagery of the bomb as a great mover of human events was bound to affect decisions about how it should be utilized, and whether it should be made an exception to wartime policies of maximum exploitation of destructive weapons. In other words, there was a powerful collective impulse to employ any weapon that would destroy the enemy and end the war; but there was a further nuclearistic impulse to seek from the weapon's use human power that did not seem otherwise available. The intensifying commitment to the weapon can, as we saw in the case of Stimson, stifle one's capacity for the kind of animating guilt that might hold back its use. And where the nuclearism is greater and one is bedazzled by the bomb's power, as in the case of Byrnes, there can result a form of numbing that admits of virtually no access to either death imagery or animating guilt. But these individual differences were subsumed to common imagery around the weapon that attributed to it power it did not possess. *

---

* Gar Alperovitz, among historians studying the question, has gone furthest in suggesting the influence of American conflicts with the Soviet Union in our use of the bombs on Japanese cities. He suggests that the weapon "confirmed American leaders in their judgment that they had sufficient power to affect developments in the border regions of the Soviet Union"; that it "played a role in the formulation of [American] policy" at Potsdam to the extent of determining "much of Truman's shift to a tough policy aimed at forcing Soviet acquiescence to American plans for eastern and central Europe"; and that its exclusive possession by America was viewed (always by Byrnes, usually by Truman, and at first by Stimson) as the key to general European stability and universal peace. He further asserts that "a combat demonstration was needed to convince the Russians to accept the American plan [mostly concerning Europe] for a stable peace—that its necessity for the war was of lesser consideration than the [view] . . . that our possessing and demonstrating the bomb would make Russia more manageable in Europe." Nobody can be certain of degrees of motivation around such matters. My impression on reading *Atomic Diplomacy* was that Alperovitz had presented an oversimplified picture which did not take into sufficient account the ambiguities of decision making; or the extent of decision makers' association of bomb use with ending the war, whether or not the weapon was actually necessary to achieve that purpose. That impression has been subsequently confirmed by more recent historical studies by Sherwin and Yergin, who had access to extensive additional documentation not available when Alperovitz wrote. But Alperovitz's study was nonetheless of great importance in providing the first historical examination of ways in which possession of nuclear weapons affect the possessors—the first treatise on nuclearism.

What was prophetic in that early sequence was Truman's mild awakening at the end to the "weakness" of nuclear power. That paradox was later put very graphically by Arthur Koestler:

> A policeman, armed with an atom bomb and nothing else, could not prevent the escape of a couple of house breakers without blowing the whole town to glory, himself included. We are faced with a new paradox: the superior power of a weapon may reduce its bearer to helplessness.[22]

This is the nuclearistic frustration: one holds the power of the deity in one's hands, but is none the more powerful for it. That is the trap of nuclearism, and nuclear-weapons theorists have been haunted by it. It was Henry Kissinger who noted that "the more powerful the weapon . . . the greater becomes the reluctance to use them"—the concept paraphrased by a later observer as "the greater the power, the greater the paralysis."[23]

One early response was a policy of more or less pure nuclearism—the John Foster Dulles concept, during his tenure as secretary of state in the mid- and late fifties, of "massive retaliation." That policy sought to evoke in potential enemies' minds the image of nuclear extermination as punishment for what we might view as aggression toward America or its allies. In thus insisting on our "great capacity to retaliate instantly by means and at places of our choosing,"[24] Dulles sought to activate the elusive power of the nuclear deity. But it still could not be harnessed—the threat lacked "credibility," and not even resort to "brinksmanship" (visibly moving to the brink of nuclear war in response to a crisis somewhere in the world) could not overcome the feeling of nuclear paralysis. Ironically, the abandonment of the extreme nuclearism of massive retaliation in favor of more "flexible" combinations of "nuclear deterrence" and "limited war" gave rise to American intervention in Vietnam. That kind of counterinsurgency adventure can also be understood as an effort to be active and strong—to assert national vitality—as opposed to the collective "deadness" surrounding nuclear paralysis. In the end Vietnam, too, illustrated the nuclearistic fallacy: the "nuclear superpower" could not influence human, or even military events in the desired direction. Hence the impulse toward making "limited wars" into "limited nuclear wars" via "strategic" or relatively "small" and "manageable" nuclear weapons. In all this the nuclear-induced "cross currents of belligerence and dread of annihilation"[25] create a constant temptation to aggressiveness and violence on behalf of overcoming paralysis and "deadness."

The problem is of course most intense in a country in which virtually all of our statesmen since the time of World War II have committed themselves to keeping the United States "the greatest power in the world," because the very weapons at the center of that claim rendered us unable to "behave like" that definition of ourselves.

Jonathan Schell suggests that these frustrations are at the heart not only of Vietnam but Watergate as well. For the international balance involving powerlessness, belligerence, and threat of annihilation can create a sense among insecure leaders that any questioning from within of our "credibility" or "national image," that is, any opposition to their policy, undermines the very existence of the nation. Opponents then become enemies whose individual rights can be violated. With our leaders struggling against the image of our country as "a pitiful helpless giant" (in Nixon's phrase) ever threatened by nuclear paralysis, "the fear of executive impotence had become one of the deepest themes of nuclear politics . . ." The president, in his struggle against nuclear paralysis and executive impotence, may seek more and more power over both conventional and potentially nuclear war making. In all this the struggle to achieve "credibility" becomes increasingly desperate and futile. For credibility is no more than the believability of one's assertions, and these assertions revolve around the fallacy of nuclearism: the equation of destructive power with power over human events. The resulting "world of fantasy"[26] into which the president and other leaders are likely to be drawn derives fundamentally from this "nuclear illusion."*

I have focused on America struggles with nuclearism because they include earliest possession of the weapons and the only use of them so far on a human population; because continuing American impulses toward nuclearism remain extremely strong; and because with it all we are a sufficiently open society for considerable information about those struggles to be made available.

We have no reason to believe that similar nuclearistic impulses have not existed among Soviet leaders, and the extreme social control and suppression of opposition in that society undoubtedly has its own special interaction with Soviet nuclearism. The French have demonstrated their brand of the affliction, as initiated by de Gaulle's equation of bomb possession—and refusal to participate in international nuclear treaty negotiations—with the mystique of French national grandeur. The Chinese have acted and expressed themselves similarly, and their nuclearism has been still more flagrant. They have associated bomb possession with pride of autonomous accomplishment vis-à-vis the Soviet Union (which had withdrawn its nuclear assistance) and the United States (which had repeatedly underestimated China's nuclear capacity), and their first explosion of a hydrogen bomb on June 17, 1967, was an occasion for celebration ("cheers, gongs, drums and firecrackers resounded throughout the night"); and for declarations that the achievement had "boosted the morale" of all revolutionaries and demonstrated how "for the Chinese people armed with the brilliant thought of Mao Tse-tung, there is no height than cannot be scaled,

---

*The Watergate scandal and the Vietnam War came about through many different influences. Struggles around nuclear weapons and nuclearism constitute an important factor among many, and one that has been conceptually neglected.

no fortress that cannot be stormed and no force that can hold back their victorious advance."[27]*

Among the nuclear "haves," Great Britain is unique in that it has considerably limited, if not completely renounced, nuclear weapons development. Britain is notable in its official recognition, in a white paper of 1957, that "there is at present no means of providing adequate protection for the people of this country against the consequences of an attack with nuclear weapons," as well as in the intensity of its antinuclear movement during the 1950s and of its political debate on "nuclear vainglory." But what is nonetheless significant is the fact that even the party (Labor) that specifically opposed Britain's nuclear weapons in its 1964 election campaign, once in office, did not implement its promise to phase them out. What remains is a kind of nuclear compromise in which the weapons remain on a limited basis and "the Government does not see this . . . weapon system as an independent nuclear weapon in a military sense."[28]†

The list continues: India giving priority to its back-door acquisition (ostensibly for peaceful purposes) of nuclear-weapons capacity in the face of the most pressing alternative economic needs of its people, and one might possibly add Israel's apparent acquisition of such capacity, possibly with the help of illegally acquired plutonium, on behalf of what it sees as its own survival in the precarious Middle East. Inevitably, racial imagery enters into the nuclearistic impulse, as does painful imagery around the rich-nation-poor-nation gap. Thus, when China exploded its bomb, an *anti*-Communist Malaysian leader commented, "The detonation . . . showed the world that such attainments are not the prerogative only of the West. Asians also are capable of doing it."[29] He is, of course, right, and there is no getting away from the status the new possessor of nuclear weapons gains in the eyes of both outsiders and many of its own people. That is why there is always a kernel of truth to the nuclear

---

*This does not mean that China has been reckless in its nuclear policy, or that it has not made overtures of its own concerning nuclear agreements (it has offered a no-first-use agreement, for instance, to the United States). Nuclearism exists as part of one's world view, and, fortunately, rarely determines *total* behavior.

†Moss gives a good description of Britain's ambivalence concerning its own nuclearism. ". . . the weakness in Britain's position as a nuclear power has always been political and psychological rather than technical. It was not the means to destroy that was lacking, but the will to do so. Insofar as the country can have communal feelings, Britain does not *feel* like a nuclear power. Independent political use of the nuclear deterrent is as unthinkable as independent military use." The reason for not feeling like a nuclear power, it would seem, is as much tactical as humanitarian. For Britain could no longer compare with the United States and the Soviet Union as a first-rank power, and "With . . . [its] potential for destruction went irremedial vulnerability." In other words, circumstances rendered Britain's nuclearism harder to sustain, but that does not stop the country from maintaining its "men of the V-bomber force, who have flown for years with the hydrogen bomb, and are trained to drop it.";[28A] or, from on many occasions, joining in with American nuclearistic illusions.

illusion—the weapons are associated with a certain amount of "human power."

The virtual universality of nuclearism is given expression in the question of "nuclear proliferation." The nuclear "haves," in this case mostly America and the Soviet Union, strongly oppose such proliferation, pointing to its very real danger of increasing the likelihood of nuclear war. But by their own continuous expansion of their already enormous nuclear arsenals—even their ostensible treaty restrictions tend to encourage such expansion—they, in effect, insist upon a nuclear-weapons monopoly.* In the process the two great powers flaunt not only their bombs but their nuclearistic images. The potential nuclearism of all other countries is thus mobilized, and their absence of nuclear capacity makes them feel radically excluded from the magic circle of genuine or ultimate power. They come to equate nuclear weapons as the birthright of any sovereign nation, and the vicious circle continues. It can only be interrupted by precisely that which is least forthcoming—a significant and visible renunciation of at least a portion of nuclear capacity on the part of the two great powers. What needs dissemination, of course, is not the weapons but an ethic that exposes nuclearism as no less dangerous than the bombs themselves. *For nuclearism is a general twentieth-century disease of power, a form of totalism of thought and consequence particularly if paradoxically tempting to contemporary man as another of his technological replacements for his waning sense of the reliability and continuity of life.* †

Today, we are confronted with another polarizing nuclear technology, nuclear power. Even some scientists who have been critical of the nuclear arms race are enthusiastic about nuclear power. Here they perhaps share with many the feeling that the nuclear deity should be capable of unlimited creation as well as apocalyptic destruction. Scientists who have worked on the bomb have a particular inclination to seek something constructive deriving from their efforts, something that can serve mankind.

Recently, I was invited to Vienna by a research group at the International Atomic Energy Agency to consult on the psychological aspects of nuclear issues. The visit served to stimulate and catalyze some of my views about the relationship between nuclear weapons and nuclear power. I believe that a real connection exists between popular reactions to nuclear energy programs and fears of nuclear war. But it is not a process of "displacement," a term that suggests redirecting one's emotions from one object to another completely separate and distinct object. In this case, the two objects—nuclear weapons and

---

* Strictly speaking, there is no monopoly, since other countries possess the bomb. But the sense of monopoly is conveyed by the special dimension of American and Soviet nuclear capacity, along with attitudes of power expressed around that capacity by leaders of the two countries.

† In Appendix D, I discuss patterns of nuclearism among American scientists, with special reference to Edward Teller.

nuclear energy programs—involve the same potentially dangerous materials, the same threat of irradiation. For that reason, a more accurate term would be "extension"—the fear of nuclear weapons extended to nuclear energy programs.

One might also look at opposition to nuclear energy as an attempt to symbolize an overall threat around what is perceived as a dangerous new dimension of science and technology that involves not only the new danger of irradiation, but also an entirely new scale of potential destruction. In that sense, perceptions of nuclear power plants can represent an extension of what I speak of as "imagery of extinction." The imagery is all the more fearful in that it involves what we described above as "invisible contamination."

One often hears today the phrase "It's time to set aside emotions" concerning nuclear power; but one must ask, "Whose emotions?" And "About what?" Psychiatrists are usually called upon to say that the resistance to whatever those in power want to support, in this case nuclear energy, is "irrational" and "emotional." I believe that the uneasiness related to both nuclear weapons and power as expressed by mass protest movements throughout the world represents the most fundamental, primal fears about the integrity of the human body, as threatened by the invisible poison of irradiation. It is an expression of what the brilliant American neurophysiologist, Walter Cannon, called "the wisdom of the body."[30] Freud similarly spoke of the function of anxiety as a signal of danger to the organism. We must keep in mind the value of anxiety in our approach to both nuclear power and nuclear weapons.

The nuclear energy issue may indeed be a source of special value, though in a somewhat different way. It arouses particularly intense fears and feelings in people because they see that the power plants are to be built in their backyards, in their neighborhoods, in their cities. Nuclear weapons, on the other hand, are something "out there," apart from one's everyday life. One can more readily numb or distance oneself from nuclear weapons than from a nearby reactor. In that sense, the anxieties aroused have potentially positive value for addressing the desperate problem of nuclear weapons, which is becoming increasingly out of control, automated and bureaucratized. The nuclear power issue can help resensitize us to nuclear weapons and to other kinds of holocaust that threaten us, including other forms of destruction of the environment and massive starvation. Once we open ourselves to perceiving one kind of holocaust, we can become sensitive to any such threat. Human responses to nuclear power are susceptible to dramatic reversals, as we have observed in the wake of the deeply disturbing accident at the Three Mile Island nuclear plant in Pennsylvania in March-April 1979.

Nuclearism is surely as rampant throughout the world as ever, but patterns of adjustment—pseudo-adaptation—have set in. The result is a pervasive "nuclear cool" (the term is Moss's). The great majority of people no longer experience— increasingly few remember—the original impact of the totality of nuclear killing. There is still nuclear obsession underneath that numbing. And there are undoubtedly back-and-forth interactions and image-exchanges between those involved with nuclear questions and the rest of the population—patterns we can as yet hardly name that support and reinforce our ingenious combinations of nuclearism and numbing.

And yet, remarkably, something in us perseveres. Nuclearism and numbing are not all. There are other responses to our death anxiety and quest for human continuity.

Epilogue

Awareness and Renewal

THROUGHOUT THIS BOOK I have assumed that awareness matters, that something is gained through understanding potential threats and possibilities.

In earlier work I have made this same assumption, but what constitutes awareness? To what kind of awareness might our paradigm lead? And how might that form of awareness contribute to renewal?

Religious, political, and psychological movements tend to lay claim to awareness, always according to their own definitions. Freud's dictum, "Where id was, there shall ego be" is one of those definitions: the gradual expansion of the relatively reasonable division of the psyche, the one capable of observing the external world and "lay[ing] down an accurate picture of it," so that it can "appropriate fresh portions" of the "dark, inaccessible realm of instinct." This shift was, for Freud, the goal of psychoanalytic therapy—and, more broadly, "a work of culture—not unlike the draining of the Zuider Zee." [1]

But Freud put the matter very tentatively, seeing the ego as "hemmed in on all three sides," a servant of "three tyrannical masters . . . the external world, the super-ego and the id." Awareness under those conditions can be little more than a flicker of light in the dark human sky. And since the id is a source of all, and the ego only an emerging portion of that source, even the flicker is an aspect of the darkness. The idea of awareness itself becomes entrapped in the dichotomy of instinct and reason, and of "the unconscious" and "the conscious."

We need to take another look at the meaning of awareness, and the best way to do that is to consider its two distinct definitions. The first, older meaning, has to do with being watchful, vigilant, cautious, on one's guard (the Indo-

European root, "wer" is related to words like wary, beware, ward, and guard). The second, more recent meaning has to do with being informed, cognizant, conscious, sensible (here the same Indo-European root gave expression to the Greek *horan*, to see and the Latin *verēri*, to expect or feel awe for, with connections to such words as panorama and revere). (OED I, 148; and *American Heritage*, 1549) Awareness, then, includes the ability to anticipate and realize danger on the one hand and the capacity for knowledge and transcendent feeling on the other. My argument is that the two are inseparable. Imaginative access to death in its various psychic manifestations is necessary for vitality and vision. Our present difficulty is that we must extend that imaginative access to include massive death and the possibility of total annihilation. Throughout this book we have been centrally concerned with the mind's capacity for, as well as impediments to, these forms of awareness. We have come upon certain neglected dimensions of the self that are crucial to that capacity. We do well to identify them once more, for we need them.

The first is the confrontation of death and negativity mentioned above. In my work with people subjected to various kinds of threat and upheaval—as with Vietnam veterans—I have found that *confrontation* is the first of three steps toward significant personal change. Having confronted the experience of falling apart, they could engage in a process of *reordering*, or examining various aspects of self and world with special emphasis on achieving an animating relationship to guilt; and finally they could achieve a sense of *renewal*, in which sensitivity to threat could combine with playfulness, erotic freedom, and deepened general awareness.[2] I became convinced that anxious immersion in death imagery is important for psychotherapy or any other important personal change. In that sense renewal involves a survivor experience: there is a measure of annihilation along with imagery of vitality beyond the death immersion. What must be overcome is not so much repression as chaos or formlessness on the one hand, suffocating patterns or forms on the other. Only that confrontation with negativity can provide the self-generation—the true psychic energy—for change.[3] The self and not the "therapy" becomes agent and basis for change.

When that is not the case, therapist and patient become entrapped in a Sisyphean struggle in which a superimposed process is expected to do the psychic work of a person. The therapeutic relationship then accumulates numbing, its two participants immersed in death anxiety they cannot acknowledge, perpetuating an illusion of "doing something."

Freud may have had something like that in mind when, near the end of his life, he wrote about the "interminable" nature of psychoanalysis. He was skeptical of any analysis being genuinely completed, and raised the possibility of not just the patient but the analyst also periodically resubmitting himself to psychoanalysis. What is striking here is the relationship between his therapeutic pessimism and his increasing sense of the importance of the death instinct. For now he viewed the death instinct (according to James Strachey) as "the most powerful impeding factor of all and one totally beyond any possibility of control . . . not only . . . responsible for much of the resistance met with in analysis, but . . . actually the *ultimate cause of conflict in the mind.*"[4] In his own idiom Freud was referring to destructive factors (on the order of the death equivalents) that adversely affected therapy and rendered it unending. Death, via the death instinct, became the enemy of awareness for Freud. A more dialectical view, however, enables one to relate death to vitality and awareness independently of the all too real limitations of the psychotherapeutic process.

Part of the difficulty in Freud's position is in its dismissal of the self's quest for larger connection and transcendence, the second of our neglected dimensions of the self. Freud's insistence that psychoanalysis not serve as a Weltanschauung or world view was admirable enough. But his conceptual exclusion of ultimate ties of the self led all too readily to reducing all world views to expressions of individual psychopathology, and to rendering the therapeutic situation as the hub of all meaning. The therapist can all too readily be cast in the role of the omnipotent guide—of arbiter of both death anxiety and immortality. The stress on "transference" (the patient's endowing the analyst with the omniscient powers he attributed as an infant to his parents) as well as "countertransference" (the therapist's own remnants of infantile conflict as they affect the relationship) is meant to limit any such attribution of omnipotence. But it can have the opposite effect of causing both participants to view themselves as involved in something other than a human encounter. I am not suggesting that psychological therapy can entirely eliminate this attribution of omniscience. But if understood as a localized form of the universal quest for symbolization of immortality, that attribution can be more readily curtailed, and therapy itself placed in better human perspective.[5]

There might then be less tendency for the therapist's words, or those of other representatives of his therapeutic school, to take on the immortalizing power of "the thoughts of Mao Tse-tung." For all who seek awareness and renewal, certainly therapist and patient, are involved in the central quest of human history, the struggle for believable symbolizations of meaning and continuity.

The struggle itself is always in flux: "A god outgrown becomes immediately a life-destroying demon," Joseph Campbell rightly tells us. "The form has to be broken and the energies released."[6] The therapist who (in Leslie Farber's words) "kneels at the very edge of nothingness, hoping to save a fallen stranger" is not merely touching his own pain but seeking an avenue out of despair and toward meaning, a "confirmation . . . as what he is, and as what he can become."[7]

The very tenuousness of the images around which that larger struggle takes place is also a source of possibility. And here we come to the last two neglected dimensions of the self—perpetual involvement in symbolization and the resulting capacity for multiple meanings and Proteanism. As symbolizing creatures we recreate everything, but not everything at once: our awareness is selective but at the same time holistic. Awareness is no more or less internal than external. In work with Vietnam veterans undergoing rapid personal change after painful war experiences, I found that introspection was combined with "extrospection." The veterans looked inward, but also outward—at the environments they encountered in Vietnam and America and at historical currents affecting those environments. From that standpoint introspection is a look at the mind's way of living in the world—and the world's way of living in the mind. Our symbolizing process moves naturally toward perception of threat and capacity for larger vision—the two components of awareness. Whatever the barriers—and those have made up most of the subject matter of this book—our evolutionary inclination as symbolizing human beings is in the direction of awareness.

Because the impediments are so great the quest becomes confused and takes not one direction but all directions. The self moves about—becomes Protean— in its continuing effort (in Langer's phrase) to "realize the form," to find new and lasting principles of connection. We encounter a back-and-forth movement between Proteanism on the one hand and a seemingly opposite tendency toward finding a single absolute, a safe haven of monolithic belief. We seek a form of awareness that combines immediate and ultimate involvements. Otto Rank spoke of this as "a fusion of the two separate selves, the mortal and the immortal, into one and the same personality." That fusion requires us to confront simultaneously a changing inner landscape of breakdown and revitalization along with our planetary landscape of threat and enlarged connection. We live on images and the images shift. Our increasing capacity for awareness gives direction to our life-symbolizing process and we find a way to begin to understand.

APPPENDIX A

Seeking the Perfect Death— Japanese Examples

In Samurai literature a sharp contrast was drawn between the "small man" who "preserves body at the expense of spirit . . . [so that] nothing remains after his body has disintegrated," and the "great man" willing to "sacrifice body for the sake of spirit . . . [so that] his spirit will be alive eternally even if his body perishes."[1] Dying becomes equated with experiential transcendence. That state was to be achieved by the samurai contemplating his heroic death, and indeed was achieved by kamikaze pilots, who were said to undergo a temporary "rebirth" *prior* to the deaths so lovingly planned for them, becoming calm, proud, and exemplary in behavior as if having already become "gods without earthly desires."[2] It is quite possible that samurai experienced a similar sense of euphoria or perfect centering of immediate action and ultimate commitment prior to what they knew to be almost certain death in battle, a state in which fear is overcome, ambivalence eliminated, and clarity achieved. It is also likely that when the samurai could not participate in battle, many of them experienced the same sharp disappointment and depression later noted among pilots whose kamikaze missions were canceled. Generations of cultural "survivors" of the "splendid deaths" of samurai came to participate in that euphoric image-feeling, and it continues to haunt Japanese society even now, in the face of widespread post-World War II revulsion toward this aspect of the samurai ethos.

The samurai code includes realism toward personal mortality, condemning the tendency to deny the fact of death as "an illusion in a dream." Here is a two-way principle around all powerful symbolizations of death and continuity:

access to an immortalizing way of dying makes it unnecessary to deny the fact of death; and facing the fact of death is a path to precisely that immortalizing "way."

Beauty and sadness in death is another dimension of the Japanese principle of transcendent dying, as expressed in the principle of *mono no aware*, meaning "the pathos of things" or "the sad beauty" or "suchness" of existence. This principle pervades Japanese culture, and is often expressed in the ritual "farewell poem" that has characterized dying Japanese heroes from the very beginnings of recorded history to the kamikaze pilots of World War II. The semimythical Prince Yamato Takeru (ca. 72 A.D.), died in poignant, lonely circumstances. A farewell poem attributed to him contains the still remembered lines, "Oh, lone pine tree!/Oh, my brother!" That early death-centered romanticism was combined with cultural principles of loyalty, as suggested by a passage from the Manyōshū, a poetic anthology of the eighth century:

> He who dies for the sake of his Lord does not die in vain, whether he goes to the sea and his corpse is left in a watery grave, or whether he goes to the mountain and the only shroud for his lifeless body is the mountain grass.

This passage made its way down through Japanese history, and was eventually incorporated not only into the samurai code but also into the ideology of nineteenth- and twentiety-century nationalism, militarism, and fascism. During World War II, for instance, after every engagement in which large numbers of Japanese lives were lost, survivors sang a song entitled, "If I go out to Sea . . ." (Umi Yukaba), taken from an old poem derived in turn from the same passage from the Manyōshū. The song itself stressed continuity in sentiment over the centuries: "We are the sons of the fathers who said, 'If I go out to sea and return as a water-soaked corpse . . .' and who to this day from olden times have kept their warriors' names forever pure."

The Japanese stress on the beautiful death is extreme, and readily manipulable for political purposes. But it is by no means unique and, in fact, illuminates more hidden corners of our own imagery and aspiration. The association of death with a sense of the "sad beauty of existence" finds wide expression in Western tradition, perhaps most intensely in nineteenth-century romanticism. Westerners no less than Japanese seek expression for a sense of awe before the great natural rhythms of living and dying and the inherent aesthetic of these rhythms. And Westerners too identify closely with the consequent human harvest of "adversity, suffering, defeat, and death."[3] The idea of beauty in death can take highly destructive directions in all cultures, but it originates in a sense of being part of an all-encompassing natural aesthetic principle.

The ethos of the splendid death contributed greatly to the special samurai stress upon ritual suicide, revealing much about the cultural delineation of principles of integrity. The practice of *junshi* mentioned earlier (ritual suicide in order to die with one's Lord) was merely one expression of the more general principle of ritual suicide, known as *seppuku* or *harakiri* (both are renderings of the same two Chinese characters, meaning "cutting the stomach," the former term considered more official and more accurate). The warrior's practice of taking his own life to avoid capture or dishonor is said to go back to the beginnings of recorded Japanese history. *Seppuku* evolved as a ritual expression of that principle, as *a precise and extreme way of expressing individual and cultural integrity in dying.* From about the time of the twelfth century, the samurai who failed in any important mission, however impossible that mission might have been, was expected to take his own life. If captured by the enemy (considered an ultimate disgrace for the Japanese warrior, an attitude which was maintained, at least in principle, right through World War II), he would seek an opportunity to do so in ritual fashion.

The ritual came to be elaborated in precise detail: concerning the site, often a Buddhist temple (never a Shinto shrine, which would be considered defiled) or a lord's mansion, either in the garden or in a room considered suitable for such ritual; the immediate setting (such details as a white *futon* [cushion] placed on tatami [straw matting], with use of special white curtains or white streamers, the event taking place before a small, select audience; immediate formalities, including the reading of the sentence, when appropriate, and the presence of an official (in Tokugawa times, a representative of the shogun) whose "long sword" (one of the two carried by samurai and a symbolically powerful object in traditional Japan) becomes the focus of his own ritual reception; special bodily preparation, suggesting purification, of the man about to die (bathing, a particular hair style, and a sequence of three changes of clothing ending in a completely white costume); and of very great importance, the presence of a personal assistant *(kaishaku-nin,* the one who "attends" or "looks after") chosen both for his swordsmanship and his closeness to the samurai involved) to perform what is considered a friendly and merciful act of beheading, immediately after self-immolation. Concerning the last, a Western witness of an official *seppuku* ceremony held in 1868, commented: "In what other country in the world does a man learn that the last tribute of affection which he may have to pay to his best friend may be to act as his executioner?" (To which the answer might be, in classical Rome, as well as in the "coup de grâce" ["stroke of mercy"] in French practice. But the question reflects the elaborate ritualization of the practice in Japanese culture.)

Seppuku had the characteristics of a religious ceremony, and as such reverberated at both immediate and ultimate levels. At the immediate level, the samurai was called upon to destroy his body by attacking it at what was considered its very center (the belly or "guts"): he would thrust a razor-sharp sword into the left side of his abdomen, cut across to the right, and then extend the wound or even pull out his intestines, before the assistant, with a stroke of an equally sharp long sword, beheaded him. He sought to demonstrate

important samurai virtues of maintaining absolute poise under the most extreme
form of pain and, finally, in the face of death itself. At the ultimate level, the
act of *seppuku*, in the most direct and absolute way, symbolized the
transformation of death into cultural immortality.

One must keep in mind that the samurai, from early boyhood, had had
instilled in him imagery of heroic acts of *seppuku*. At the age of seven he was
given the short sword *(wakizashi)*, and then at fifteen underwent a kind of *rite
de passage* or initiation of adulthood *(gempuku)* at which he was formally
presented with both swords and ritually instructed in the details of *seppuku)*.
Whether or not called upon at some point in his life to perform the act, he was
aware of it as a "controlling image" passed down to him from early beginnings
in Japanese culture, to be passed on to his descendants as an ultimate ideal of
integrity.

With the Meiji Restoration of the late nineteenth century and its accompanying modernization, *seppuku* was officially banned. (*Junshi* had been officially
banned from the sixteenth century, because such intense loyalty to feudal lords
was considered a threat to the central authority of the Tokugawa shogunate.)
From then on any ritual self-immolations—and these have occurred not
infrequently during the last hundred years—have been attempts, often desperate, to restore earlier ideals, rather than expressions of a living tradition. The
situation is not unlike certain contemporary American attitudes toward the
cowboy tradition of the West. Significant elements of *seppuku* imagery remain
in Japanese psyches even today, as expressed not only in Mishima's strange and
anachronistic self-immolation in 1970 but more indirectly in the widespread
imagery and high rate of suicide among Japanese. This is often in association
with a sense of failure or responsibility for harm (a student who fails his
examinations, a company official responding to deaths caused by his company's
negligence).[4]

In general, Japanese recasting of Buddhism has emphasized its embrace, or at
least welcome acceptance, of death as a step on the path to paradise. At least a
few Japanese Buddhist saints are associated with ideal deaths, in which the act of
dying is rendered both peaceful and significant by means of an absolute
identification with Buddha himself: when sensing the approach of death, they
would ask to be placed in a position facing West, and would then die calmly
with the Buddha's name, repeated over and over again in prayer, on their lips.
The most extreme expression of Buddha-centered dying was a practice of self-
mummification among certain mountain ascetics (known as *gyōnin*) who
constituted a sect of the Shingon school. The practice involved what one
authority calls "a compound of ancient shamanistic magic and Mantrayāna
Buddhism, Yin-yang magic, and Taoism,"[5] in which one sought to "become
. . . a Buddha in his very own body." The individual would first lead a life of
wandering asceticism and missionary work, then undergo various forms of ritual
abstinence, and when close to death would be placed in a stone chamber or

special coffin (sometimes actually be buried alive) in a Buddha-like sitting posture with legs crossed. The corpse would then be exhumed and subjected to a special mummification process involving charcoal fire and incense fumes; then reburied for a period of several years and eventually enshrined in mummified form in a special hall, worshipped "as a Buddha," and considered to possess magical curative powers. Still another extreme practice was that of ritual drowning—the supplicant placed in a designated location in the Japan Sea (a body of water thought to have special connection with Buddhist "Western Paradise") with a heavy stone tied around him, and going down with repeated incantations of Buddha's name. These practices do not, of course, represent anything like the full scope of Japanese Buddhist approaches to death. Rather they suggest the extremity to which the Japanese principle of the good or perfect death can be carried.

There might seem to be a contradiction between the notably intense Japanese fear of death and disintegration (together with extreme focus on ritual purification in Shinto practice) on the one hand, and the considerable acceptance and ritual embrace of death (mostly Buddhist influence) on the other. But the contradiction is only apparent. The two seemingly disparate attitudes reflect struggles not only around collective life-continuity but also around meaning and integrity in the face of death. Death-embrace (seppuku and Buddhist self-mummification) can be understood as, among other things, attempts to transcend fear. Considering the universality of death terror in primitive societies (frequently taking the form of viewing death as an *unnatural* phenomenon, the work of spirits or other malignant influences,)[6] there is a temptation to view *seppuku* and the like as essentially *compensatory* phenomena, as mere efforts to overcome fear of death or "reaction-formations" to original, elemental terror.[7] But while death terror is real enough, probably even universal to some degree, man's sense of himself as a cultural being gives him no choice but to place that terror within his symbolizations of historical and biological connection. That symbolizing impulse is no less elemental than the death terror. The cultural axis of integrity and disintegration, then, becomes a way of organizing both death terror and imagery of *significance in continuity*. In this the Japanese bring their particular, intense cultural combinations to a universal enterprise.

A perceptive contemporary observer stresses the traditional Japanese equation of death and truth. He refers to the Japanese "language of silence"[8] in which "talk is provisional and changeable . . . what is worth trusting is that which comes from deep in one's heart and is beyond description." To make words count, one must "step into the world of death." This can be done either in the act of dying—words spoken in the midst of ritual suicide, for instance, can be powerful—or else in contemplating death. The larger principle here is that only imaginative confrontation of death can enable one to reach beyond the cliches of ordinary speech and make contact with ultimate questions of integrity.

That at least is the ideal. But contemporary Japanese writers have also condemned what they take to be their culture's excessive "love of death." One, from a Freudian perspective, speaks of an unusually strong influence of the death instinct in the Japanese unconscious. He draws upon the classic *Tale of Heike* in describing how, among its characters, "Love of death wells up within them" so that "they are people of the land of death."[9] That view was part of a post-World War II intellectual and political condemnation of samurai culture, and especially of the expropriation of its glorification of heroic dying by rightest political movements. Several have observed that during World War II Japanese soldiers at the moment of death, instead of expressing the prescribed last words, "Long live the Emperor!" cried out for their mothers. Others have emphasized the coercion, direct or indirect, behind kamikaze-pilot heroism. There is no denying the fervor with which many soldiers, particularly kamikaze pilots, embraced opportunities for a splendid death, nor can one dismiss the elements of admiration among the troubled mixture of cultural responses to Mishima's more bizarre attempt to do the same twenty-five years later. The confusions of cultures, like those of individuals, become writ large around symbolization of death's meaning for life. And yet each of us in any culture requires imaginative access to that symbolism, to its "zone of silence," for our individual and collective imaginations to thrive or perhaps even function at all.

APPENDIX B

Death Imagery in Psychosomatic and Character Disorder

Two very different but related conditions with depression and loss at their center are sustained psychosomatic (or "psychophysiological") impairments, and the aggressive-impulsive variety of "character disorder." In both, severe psychological conflict is lastingly and radically resymbolized—into "the language of the body" in one case, and into destructive social (or antisocial) behavior in the other. What unites the two conditions is a significant bypassing of the more usual areas of formative struggle, those of close human relationships and verbal expression in general; and a consequent structuring of the self around a harmful, physicalist pattern.

Starting with psychosomatic syndromes, researchers identify the "big seven"—peptic ulcer, bronchial asthma, essential hypertension, neurodermatitis, thyrotoxicosis, rheumatoid arthritis, and ulcerative colitis—but much about their causes and mechanisms remains mysterious. Since Freud, virtually all observers have agreed that impaired function of bodily organs in such conditions can reflect longstanding psychological conflict. But there has been much disagreement concerning just about everything else, and increasing skepticism toward earlier claims of specific psychological traits associated with directly symbolized "organ neuroses": peptic ulcer reflecting "hunger for love," bronchial asthma "a reaction to the danger of separation from the mother," etc.[1] Researchers began to seek instead something in the nature of a common principle in all psychosomatic phenomena. That approach was well articulated in 1963 by Luby,[2] who stressed a principle of "entrapment" and "immobilization":

> When prolonged activation of aversive fear-rage systems occurs in association with *immobilization such as inability to flee, attack, or otherwise motorically express affect*, profound autonomic and neuroendocrine changes ensue. Such a dilemma is more distinctly human than animal. *Because of the symbolic process, the possibilities for human entrapment are infinite.* It may occur in marriage, on the job, or in a symbiotic relationship with a double-bind mother. Because of the schizophysiology of the limbic system and neocortex, *life situations may be interpreted on a feeling level as survival-threatening*, while accepted in quite another way by neocortical secondary process logic. The patient with psychosomatic disease is forced to remain in the field, repeatedly experiencing surging affect while being unable to master it with neurotic defenses or reduce it by restructuring reality with a psychotic solution. It is a kind of slow Chinese torture where he cannot scream or attack in retaliation, but must sit impassive except in spirit. Intense dependency makes him more vulnerable to entrapment because his reward or nurturant needs are so great that he cannot hazard the expression of hostility. *The loss of a significant person threatens him with biological extinction, but grief may not be acknowledged and pathological mourning may occur.* In the face of a life situation which threatens his very existence, he cannot run, fight or otherwise deal with his enemies, both internalized and external, in any meaningful, self saving way . . . he remains trapped in a chronically stressed state with all its tissue destructive consequences. These may result from the exhaustion phase of the general adaptation syndrome or the enhancement of the inflammatory process by neurkinin production. (Italics added)

Luby sums up his position as follows:

> Psychosomatics find a final common pathway in the concept of entrapment or immobilization in an interpersonal field which is affectively perceived as threatening to life or biological integrity. No escape is possible through attack, flight or total psychotic restructuring of reality; punishment, fear-rage systems are activated effecting excessive autonomic discharge, stimulation of the pituitary-adrenal axis, and proteolytic systems in the blood.

What Luby is saying, in our terms, is that ordinary responses to threat and death equivalents are blocked, so that bodily physiology becomes the battleground. The implication is that the "entrapment" or "immobilization" has to do with impaired alternative paths of symbolization.[3] That kind of formulation is of course very compatible with our paradigm. But there were at least two difficulties associated with it: the pattern of immobilization being secondary to inability to fight or flee, rather than part of a fundamental impulse toward withdrawal; and more important, the speculative nature of the claim in the absence of substantial evidence, especially on the physiological side.

But the general thesis that psychosomatic phenomena are related to impairments in ordinary alternative paths of symbolization is strengthened by two recent developments. The first is familiar to us—the outpouring of work relating grief and bereavement to the development of virtually all forms of physical illness and to increased mortality rates as well. As Reiser concludes, "Taken altogether the data convincingly demonstrate that bereavement, object loss and the associated reactive affective states may have profound reverberations in the physical sphere, affecting even the capacity to sustain life itself."[4] The other development is the body of work moving toward integration of psychological environmental influences with central nervous system and endocrine function in the activation of disease. Reiser has been able to suggest a general theory of psychosomatic disease along the following lines. There is a predisposition or "programming" in the direction of a particular vulnerability, including inherited tendencies of either the central nervous system or of organ systems, as well as certain forms of "conditioning" or "visceral learning" occurring very early in life in association with parent-child relationships. The later outbreak of the disease is the result of a cyclic reaction, in which psychosocial stress and weakened defenses lead to neural and endocrine changes (according to vulnerability), which in turn further impair psychic function and bring about more primitive and "regressed" responses to threat and danger; and this impaired (we would say desymbolized and nonformative) psychic function, probably associated with subtly altered states of consciousness, inclines toward further physiological pressures and general "somaticization" (or "resomaticization") of experience.[5] Then, as the disease becomes established, these various combinations of activity, involving both nonspecific stress and specific vulnerabilities and inclinations, become more or less autonomous, so that on the one hand the "organ reserve" diminishes and on the other "perception of the disease and its meaning become increasingly elaborated within the individual's self image, and increasingly incorporated into ongoing mental life."

Reiser's theory suggests the importance of what we have called psychic numbing. Its stress on "primitive" psychic (or ego) function with related inclination toward somaticization approximates Luby's "entrapment" and "immobilization." The mind, entrapped in its own death imagery, immobilized (numbed) in its ordinary verbal-human relationship mode of symbolization, reverts to a crude, relatively desymbolized (or deformed) body language. (Reiser would not put matters that way. For one thing he follows classical psychoanalytic practice in equating "symbolic" with primitive psychic function. But the statement is nonetheless consistent with his, Luby's, and Minuchin's position.)

It is not surprising, then, that psychosomatic illness in general has been viewed as "masked depression."[6] The characterization, though apt, may apply equally to all other forms of psychological impairment. Authors who make this claim for psychosomatic disease describe common tendencies in five different varieties of it: symptoms in childhood resembling the adult psychosomatic illness; consistent difficulty from early in life in the expression of feelings; in adulthood, problems in human relationships due to being "largely unaware of their own feelings and . . . unable to gauge the feelings of others, with the exception that they seemed extremely sensitive in perceiving hostility and rejection";[7] and the reporting (during the course of sleep therapy, when defenses were lowered and conflicts were discussed freely) of disturbing experiences of separation and loss, during both childhood and adulthood, and of a consistent tendency all through life to respond to such trauma with somatic symptoms.

In at least the major ("big seven") psychophysiological conditions, we have for some time had convincing evidence of the somaticization of the sense of threat and loss. But more recently similar evidence has been accumulating in relationship to conditions in which psychological factors have generally been considered either less fundamental (heart disease other than essential hypertension) or insignificant (many forms of cancer or fatal malignancies). Concerning the latter, for instance, William Greene has stressed the importance of "a setting of separation or loss of a significant person or goal," so much so that "separation with depression may be a necessary condition for the manifestation of leukemia."

Greene goes on to express a point of view with close bearing upon our own:

> I have come to think of life stresses for a person as he becomes ill or remains healthy in terms of disruption or maintenance of a sense of sequence, meaning a feeling of continuity in reference to his experiences to date and his aspirations for the future. Such a sensing of sequence would appear to be a process made possible by man's mental functions on the basis of memories gained from the past and percepts from the present blending to form expectations for the future. Maintenance of the sense of sequence without too great discontinuity is an attribute of psychic function. The individual's sense of sequence is maintained, to a greater degree for some than others, by a sense of consequence in association with another or other persons. Such a personal relation may have any attributes you may wish to ascribe to an interpersonal relation—malevolent or benevolent, responsible or irresponsible—but involving some type of pleasant or unpleasant qualities of attachment . . . This is a scheme which I find useful for keeping in perspective the meaning of object loss, particularly as it involves the individual's expectations in relation to that object, as a stressful life event which may herald disease.[8]

This passage connects breakdown of life-movement and integrity (sequence and consequence) with a sense of separation and loss, and all of these with trauma or threat. Greene advises less focus on events of a patient's past and more on "the influence of expectations of the future," especially the danger of "irrevocable loss of expectations for the future." Both an internist and a psychiatrist, Greene is always aware of the complexity of interplay of psychic and physical factors. Concerning childhood leukemia, for instance, he stresses four interlocking etiological components, having to do with threat and death imagery: the experience of separation or loss, as it relates to arrival of new siblings, Oedipal conflicts, or the beginning of school (which may account for the childhood peak in incidence between ages two and five); an impaired reticuloendothelial or hematopoietic system based upon physiological deficiency in mother-child integrative function; familial or hereditary hematopoietic deficiency; and possible prenatal influences, such as the mother's experiences of separation and depression during pregnancy and her subsequent assigning to the child a special role or a "projected image" of the lost person within her psychic economy.

Greene's assumptions, though less systematized, are consistent with Reiser's theory. They also document the conclusive relationships between loss and threat in our concept of death imagery. And more, they suggest that threat and loss are probably of significance in *all* illness on a continuum of degree: most strongly in psychiatric disorders and the "big seven" of psychosomatic conditions; and relatively less so (compared to issues of predisposition and organic tendency) in other illnesses, but never absent in these either.

Impaired feeling is at the heart of our concept of psychological disorder. Our task in examining each form of disorder—as is the case in psychosomatic conditions—is to indicate something about the style of numbing. There is much more to be learned of this through clinical observation. In psychosomatic disorders, physiological impairment serves as a substitute for other kinds of blocked feeling. Somaticization permits "masking" of both the depressive component and of the impaired feeling. There is no display of mimetic death in psychosomatic conditions, as there is in clinical depression, though the depressive-static mental element can nonetheless be so pervasive that the sleep patterns of the electroencephalograms among psychosomatically ill patients closely resemble those of depressed patients. Yet, people with severe psychosomatic ailments can be otherwise alert, creative, and intensely involved with others. Numbing is partial, and may be periodic or greatly varied in intensity at different times. But it is there in a rather specific form: a limitation in the capacity to find adequate expression of feeling in human relationships and other forms of image-creation and expression. In that sense, psychic energy is "locked in"—not in a sense of the insistent negativism of depression, but rather in its entrapment in destructive physiology. The blocked or missing psychic forms contribute to something in the nature of a short-circuiting of feeling from psyche to organ, whatever the complexity of that "short-circuit" and the preexisting vulnerability of the organ. (This inadvertent return to an electrical metaphor perhaps suggests a greater similarity than I had suspected between Freud's instinctualism and my own symbolizing principles.)

In terms of meaning, at some point in psychosomatic illness, the diseased organ or organ-system begins to symbolize the major emotional content of life. Reiser argues that this is meaning after the fact—that the focus on the organ and its function is a consequence, rather than cause, of that organ's vulnerability. In that view, the hunger for love becomes associated with peptic ulcer only after years of living with a condition that is a product of predisposition and nonspecific stress. In that position, Reiser and others reject and, in a sense, react to the prior doctrine of organ specificity, perhaps most associated with Franz Alexander. There is a third possibility, in which one rejects much of that one-to-one equation of causative psychological equivalent and organ choice, but at the same time keeps open the possibility of some forms of specificity, which may not yet be at all clear.

This is what Peter Knapp has in mind when he speaks of the necessity and difficulty, in psychosomatic work, of developing "more penetrating assessment of psychologic processes" and goes on to state a kind of credo: "My personal view is that in addressing such challenges, we cannot bypass the symbolic core, which acts as transducer, imbuing objectively witnessed events with meaning, so that biologic processes respond to what I call . . . our *environment of meanings.*" He then calls for "basic research into the whole area of meaning, how it is coded, how decoded, and how especially we discern and assess the complex, elusive but motivationally powerful meanings of inner images."[9]

Knapp's perspective—his focus on imagery and symbolization—is very close to my own. That focus enables us to address another feature of psychosomatic disorder, its frequent lifelong persistence. That persistence in turn suggests the likelihood of significant formative impairment in ultimate involvements. These impairments, as we know, have to do with despair, that enduring death-dominated state now and then noted in connection with psychosomatic conditions. On the whole, however, investigators have not been especially sensitive to despair as a state at least partly differentiated from depression, or as a possible causative factor in psychosomatic illness rather than merely resulting from it. Despair could well be the more sustained emotional state that lends itself to the numbed short-circuiting from mind to body, with specific exacerbations of psychosomatic illness associated with what are perceived as new losses and with episodes of depression, usually but not always masked. Despair, of course, is primarily an adult emotion, but undoubtedly has roots in death equivalents of early life, as does the psychosomatic condition itself. Whether or not there can eventually be identified different forms of despair with some specificity for various psychosomatic syndromes is difficult to say. But it is not impossible, at least in principle. From this point of view, much of psychosomatic illness would be associated with something close to a permanent sense of meaninglessness and unfulfilled life, and would be importantly influenced by a variety of social factors, most specifically by the opportunities society offered for larger meaning and shared fulfillment. In these ways, too, it resembles other "character disorders."

In those other character disorders, the sense of meaninglessness and an unfulfilled life may be expressed externally rather than internally, in the form of impulsive, destructive assaults on one's environment or people in it. Yet there is a closely related depressive core, as many have noted,[10] with the term "masked depression" also sometimes used. In such people we can also speak of an impairment of feeling and imagery, especially in relationship to human ties, so that destructive behavior, especially in young delinquents, can be understood as "a means of filling a sense of emptiness," and avoiding a continuous feeling of "life as an empty shell."[11]

In such character disorders there is a significant disorder of feeling. The impaired capacity for symbolization or ability to deal with specific societal symbols may leave one generally muted and flattened in affective responses. But there are also likely to be outbreaks of very intense emotion, and "a more absolute reliance upon feeling as the primary coin of interchange." Thus "*I feel! I act! I am!* defined most situations."[12] As in psychosomatic conditions, one is struggling against awareness of numbing and of depression. But here one must not only act but act upon the external environment. For this kind of feeling disorder seems to leave one, in Melanie Klein's terms, poised between depressive and paranoid positions, with "a naked, raw-edged sensitivity to *abuse* of feeling."[13] What results is a longstanding despair, with strong and always active emotions of both depression and highly threatening anxiety, with a continuous struggle around "the preservation of self against the world." (Hence "I feel! I act! I am!") The destructive, often violent act becomes the only means available to cope with and send off this combination of extreme stasis (mimetic death) and threat (anticipated annihilation). And as many have noted, destruction brings relief: "Violence tend[s] . . . to be an integrative force." But only for a while so that: "This psychical process of integration and disintegration may account for . . . periods of depression, sometimes ending in suicide, following aggressive acts."[14]

On the question of guilt and self-blame, much is contradictory in the literature of character disorder. On the one hand, the overall guilt mechanism does not adequately serve as an agent of restraint, and many writers have spoken of impaired or insufficiently developed conscience or capacity for guilt. Yet Freud raised the question of a seemingly opposite dynamic when he spoke of the existence of "criminals from a sense of guilt."[15] On the basis of a pattern he observed in patients, Freud raised the question of the guilt preceding the crime, the latter committed because it is forbidden and allows the "sense of guilt . . . [to be] at least attached to something," and can bring about punishment that is psychologically desired. Many subsequent investigators have confirmed Freud's speculations, though not necessarily attributing the origin of the guilt, as Freud did, to the Oedipus complex. They have also, as noted above, observed sequences of violence and suicide. And recently, Solomon has emphasized the extent to which killing others may be a form of suicide, to which "murder can be committed in order to be killed by the state."[16] Solomon suggests that such behavior can be associated with guilt, quoting an "explosive, apparently 'immoral' young man [who] said, 'I guess I think nothing I do is wrong because I really think everything I do is wrong.'" Such behavior, he points out, "can result from the repression of a cruel, even sadistic, conscience, which is an inner representation of the cruel, punitive parent." [17]

The problem, it would seem, is not the absence of guilt or conscience but rather, what another observer has called "escape from conscience." [18] The same commentator goes on to demonstrate how a combination of paranoid fears and self-hate, derived from a punitive conscience, builds up a tension that can only be relieved by an explosive act, so that "violence dissolves the impact of conscience." And in another study, in which he emphasizes the importance of shame in delinquency, he speaks in a parallel way of violent acts as means of "masking the shame." Appropriate to that thesis is Erikson's point that "He who is ashamed would like to force the world not to look at him, not to notice his exposure. He *would like to destroy the eyes of the world*." [19]

In these character disorders, destructive violence is called forth to fend off or sweep away a nagging double image—of one's own badness, emptiness, and worthlessness, and of these being exposed (or about to be exposed) to others. One can separate these elements into guilt and shame, but they closely overlap and seem very much part of a single psychological constellation, of the numbed form of static guilt. The habit of violence takes shape largely as a struggle against experiencing both the guilt and its accompanying inner deadness.

From our perspective on these character disorders, we can make two simple points about causation. First, the impoverishment in human relationships very early in life, which so many observers have noted, creates an intense need to probe elsewhere for symbolizing processes that permit psychic action and the experience of meaning. For many, human relationships from the beginning of life are equated primarily with some combination of separation, annihilation, and stasis. For whatever reasons (perhaps partly genetic), some people are unable to tolerate either guilt or the constellation of self-blame in depression, but they are instead capable, often quite skillfully, of redirecting inner psychic forms as well as general personal maneuvers toward largely impersonal environmental encounters. While the character disorder predominates, whatever human ties are maintained tend to be narrowly focused, and more or less in the service of the impersonal rechanneling outward.

Second, this style of rechanneling of formative process is clearly and directly influenced by immediate and ultimate social currents—poverty, broken families, ghetto survival ethos, racism, and the hypocritical nature of much that is offered from "proper society." All or some of these affect every aspect of immediate experience, and contribute immeasurably to the radically impaired imagery of symbolic immortality that is found in this group. But character disorders are not unique, merely more direct and intense, in their sensitivity to social currents. In all psychiatric disorders, the individual is, so to speak, the final common pathway of psychological experience, but never in isolation from such social currents, even if they tend to be more obscure, indirect, or paradoxical (as in the case of certain kinds of neurotic or even psychotic individuals who may thrive during military combat). Character disorder is thus generally illustrative, rather than exceptional, in its demonstration of the influence of social currents on redirecting symbolizing processes, and on various inner choices concerning psychic action and the experience of meaning.

Summarizing very briefly, then, around our three principles of threat, numbing and feeling, and meaning we may say that in destructive forms of character disorder, the environment is experienced as a perpetual threat to existence; and the self is threatened with annihilation from within by various combinations of severe anxiety, numbed guilt, and uncontrollable rage. The numbing process takes the form of constricted human relationships because of rechanneling of psychic energy away from intimacy, and of numbed guilt that requires continuous maneuver to avoid awareness of extremely negative self-judgment and of overall mimetic deadness and depressive affect. Struggles around meaning involve use of violence and destruction as means of heroic transcendence, and of achieving membership in a vital community (delinquent gangs, the Mafia, and various criminal subcultures). These struggles around larger significance and connectedness explain why a significant number of those convicted of criminal actions can give up antisocial behavior, and often the practice of violence, in favor of commitment to a community of social activists, a revolutionary vision, or an organization devoted to ethnic or racial revitalization.

Relevant here is a theory of alcoholism put forward by Gregory Bateson.[20] He argues that getting drunk is a rejection of the false Cartesian dualism of our culture and within the alcoholic himself, especially as that dualism pits the self against the world (or the bottle—as in the self-deceptive determination that "I will not take another drink"). "Hitting bottom" is a way of probing toward an alternative, more inclusive (less Cartesian) system, which is precisely what is provided by Alcoholics Anonymous with its theology of "complementarity" and a "noncompetitive relationship to the larger world." While Bateson makes his argument in the language of cybernetics and epistemology, that argument is consistent with our own discussion of "meaning," as related to negative death imagery and immobilization. And the larger, non-Cartesian, "complimentarity" that Bateson believes to be a "truer" principle finds a parallel in our imagery of symbolic immortality, of living *in* a principle larger than the self. It is interesting that Bateson propounded the theory around alcoholism—much of it is at so high a level of abstraction that it could be equally applied to most forms of psychopathology—a condition that is both "character disorder" and psychosomatic impairment. In alcoholism, we may say, there is a meeting-ground between the internal and external physical attack, the psychosomatic "killing of the body" and the character-disorder "killing of the world"—either or both in the service of a quest not just for vitality, as we have emphasized, but for centering of the self in the world.

APPENDIX C

Schizophrenia and Death—
Historical Notes

A prevailing historical theme has been "that physical illnesses were natural and . . . mental illnesses . . . mostly supernatural."[1] The "devil sickness" and "witch disease" of the Middle Ages apparently had its predecessor as early as 5000 B.C. in the demoniacal possession of an Egyptian princess, said to have been cured by the god Khons. That supernatural-demoniacal imagery achieved its most systematic and literalized expression at the end of the fifteenth century in the compendium of two Satan-obsessed German monks, the *Malleus Maleficarum*. Among the kinds of witches specified in that manual are those whom the devil has "deprived of reason," so that, "If a woman insisted she had seen the devil and had heard a voice admonishing her to kill someone, and if she insisted that she obeyed and did not kill, her statements were taken for truth. It was not even necessary to establish the corpus delicti; in the eyes of the judges she was a self-confessed ally of the devil, and a murderess."[2]

Psychosis was associated with grotesque death at the ultimate level by means of supernatural evil; and at the immediate level, through murderous threat to everyone else. The *Malleus* brushed aside all prior medical and philosophical observations in its death-haunted "fusion of insanity, witchcraft, and heresy into one concept."[3] And the punishment, the burning or auto-da-fé, becomes "a solemn and *invigorating* salvage of something *pure* and *immortal* from the clutches of evil and darkness" (italics mine)—in our language, a reassertion of vitality and of immortalizing religious constructs.

We must assume that this imagery was often shared by the psychotic person as well. As Jung points out concerning primitive cultures, "the insane person has always enjoyed the prerogative of being the one who is possessed by spirits or haunted by a demon." Moreover, "This is . . . a correct interpretation of his psychic condition, for he is invaded by autonomous figures and thought-forms . . . the unconscious . . . has taken possession of the ego."[4] That sharing of metaphoric logic can be used benignly (in rituals of acceptance and attempted cure) or malignantly (society's violent assault on the carrier of the "demons").

Foucault goes further in speaking of a dramatic shift in artistic imagery and social preoccupation from death to madness:

> Up to the second half of the 15th century, or even a little beyond, the theme of death reigns alone. The end of man, the end of time bear the face of pestilence and war. What overhangs human existence is this conclusion and this order from which nothing escapes. The presence that threatens even within this world is a fleshless one. Then in the last years of the century this enormous uneasiness turns on itself; the mockery of madness replaces death and its solemnity. . . . Death's annihilation is no longer anything because it was already everything, because life itself was only futility, vain words, a squabble of cap and bells. The head that will become a skull is already empty. Madness is the *deja-la* of death . . . when the madman laughs, he already laughs with the laugh of death. . . .[5]

Foucault goes on to point out that "The substitution of the theme of madness for that of death does not mark a break, but rather a torsion within the same anxiety. What is in question is still the nothingness of existence. . . ."[6] Indeed, it may be more accurate to speak less of a "substitution" and more of an image-association of death and madness throughout human history, with different epochs putting forward now the one and now the other, in endless variations on a constant theme.

Like death, madness may be a constructive (or constitutive) symbol, a form of divine wisdom—not just in primitive cultures but also as in sixteenth and seventeenth-century Europe. Only "a Fool, in his innocent idiocy," is able to possess that special form of wisdom that must be torn from the bowels of the earth; or can look into "that crystal ball which for all others is empty [but] is in *his* eyes filled with the density of an invisible knowledge."[7]

Certainly, this kind of anxious, death-linked imagery around madness had much to do with what Foucault calls "The Great Confinement" of the late seventeenth and eighteenth centuries—the burgeoning of institutions in which madmen were confined together with the indigent, the physically ill, and social deviants of every kind.

But at the same time a scientific tradition was gradually emerging, exemplified during the sixteenth century by the scholarly and passionate attack on the dogma of the *Malleus* ("It is highly unpleasant to see how people in order to kill errors are busy killing human beings.")[8] When Emil Kraepelin, about three hundred years later, put together his great synthesis of "dementia praecox," he worked out of that same tradition, now hardened into nineteenth-century physicalism. It was Kraepelin who brought together and described in meticulous detail the ideas of reference, the persecutory delusions and the hallucinations of the paranoid, the bizarre posturing and mood fluctuation of the hebephrenic, the near-stuporous stance of the catatonic, and the insidious life-constriction of the "simple" form of the condition. But so focused was Kraepelin on the inexorable destiny of these psychotic people that one cannot help but suspect a transfer of the death imagery surrounding these conditions from the theological to the medical-psychiatric sphere. The *praecox* meant early onset (during adolescence or young adulthood) and the *dementia* meant progressive deterioration of the intellectual faculties or the mind in general. The process in what was considered an organic brain disease was inexorable: ". . . not only the outcome of a mental disease is predetermined but its course as well, even as is the course of a planet or a chemical reaction."[9] Without such deterioration Kraepelin would not diagnose dementia praecox, and instead used the term "paraphrenia"—or else, when the symptoms were somewhat different, manic-depressive psychosis. Though he pulled together many loose strands for modern psychiatry, Kraepelin's view of dementia praecox is that of a death sentence of the mind.

Eugen Bleuler, a Swiss contemporary and critic of Kraepelin, coined the word "schizophrenia," literally divided or split mind, and thereby brought the condition more into the realm of the mental. Bleuler focused on the "thought disorder," stressing a number of patterns we would understand in relationship to numbing and desymbolization: paired or "loosened" associations (leading to bizarre forms of incoherence), severe patterns of ambivalence (his word) and negativism, affective impairments (though he correctly insisted that patients could have intense feelings), and autism (also his word) or self-enclosed thinking (fantasy) and action to the point of turning away from reality. But Bleuler's work turned out to have some of the paradoxical effects of certain kinds of liberal reforms. Originally meant to humanize, which meant mentalize, a condition that had been locked into Kraepelinian organic-deteriorative destiny, the term schizophrenia itself came to convey imagery of death-haunted madness and lifelong institutionalization—again deterioration (and Bleuler could never quite make up his mind concerning an organic factor)—just as the condition (by its earlier names) always had.

The medical profession, in other words, has hardly been immune to the psychic death taint generally perceived around severe cases of schizophrenia. But when doctors and occasional nonmedical therapists began to employ psychotherapeutic approaches, their contributions to healing were accompanied by added dilemmas. Understanding schizophrenia was not without risk. This was one problem Freud was able to avoid by means of his assumption that the narcissism of the schizophrenic rendered him beyond the pale of psychoanalysis as *therapy*. But if that view extended the schizophrenic death taint, Freud balanced it with his important observations on the symptoms of psychotics as attempts at restitution. Even the most bizarre form of behavior could be understood as an impulse toward vitality. In our discussion of the Schreber case we have seen how much concerned Freud was with the application of psychoanalytic principles to the *understanding* of schizophrenia. Moreover, Freud welcomed Jung's early work with schizophrenia, hoping that the gifted younger man would claim that territory for psychoanalysis. Then and later (when he was increasingly at odds with Freud) Jung did work therapeutically with schizophrenics, and contributed much to psychological understanding of the condition.

Subsequent generations of psychiatrists have plunged more boldly into therapeutic struggles with schizophrenics. If their results have been uncertain, their experiences have revealed more about the continuing death imagery associated with the condition. R. D. Laing's extraordinary emergence as a cultural *guru* during the late sixties and early seventies was related to his particularly intense involvement with schizophrenics. It was Laing the guru, not Laing the keen student of the psychological nuances of the schizophrenic experience, who extolled the psychotic experience as a "voyage into inner space and time . . . the oldest voyage in the world." And is there not a familiar ring to his sense of awe before the schizophrenic:

> Perhaps we will learn to accord to so-called schizophrenics who have come back to us, perhaps after years, no less respect than the often no less lost explorers of the Renaissance. If the human race survives, future men will, I suspect, look back on our enlightened epoch as a veritable Age of Darkness. They will presumably be able to savor the irony of this situation with more amusement than we can extract from it. The laugh's on us. They will see that what we call "schizophrenia" was one of the forms in which, often through quite ordinary people, the light began to break through the cracks in our all-too-closed minds.[10]

Here we are back to schizophrenia as special wisdom, the schizophrenic as seer and saviour.

That tendency among therapists of schizophrenia has hardly been limited to Laing, as Leslie Farber makes clear in two brilliant essays concerning his observations on what happens to people, at least some people, who work primarily with schizophrenic patients. Farber claims that psychotherapy of schizophrenia "has simply not been truthfully described," because most reports leave out "the brutal tedium, exasperation, emptiness, futility—in short, the agony of existence in which dialogue is so fleeting as to be virtually nonexistent."[11] The therapist is overtaken with "inevitable despair," as manifested by such stances as "the temptation toward omniscience," the seemingly opposite but related "too-ready cry of mea culpa," and an "obsessive anecdotalism" around the subject of therapy and its illusory achievements that, in its haunted quality, is somewhat reminiscent of the traumatic nightmare. The ultimate irony of the condition is that the therapist's existential state cannot be "confirmed" (recognized and appropriately responded to) by colleagues, who are likely to be too close to it themselves, but only by the patients themselves, who may, through such confirmation, pity, and sympathy, enable therapists to acknowledge and transcend that condition. In that limited sense the schizophrenic patient does indeed become the healer. What makes the matter even worse, Farber tells us, is the therapist's denial of his despair; he then becomes the pathetic Kierkegaardian figure of the man who is in despair and does not know it. In that situation he is likely to attempt to "join his patient" in a sense of pain and victimization, or become locked with him in a terrible battle of wills— the impaired "isolated will" of the schizophrenic versus the therapist's equally willful illusion of significant dialogue and constructive influence. The therapist may then take on a persona of his own, influenced by his patient's linguistic impairments in their disdain for language and preoccupation with nonverbal gesture, along with an invocation of the image of the schizophrenic as seer:

> Should the therapist forget the degree to which he has supplied meaning to a patient unable to provide any for himself, he may come to regard the schizophrenic as a sort of oracle with whom he sits each day—a truly ragged oracle, untutored, unverbal, and naturally unappreciated, who has the rare power to cut through the usual hypocrisies and pretensions of ordinary life, thereby arriving at some purely human meaning. His illness now appears as an appropriate response to the impurities in the therapist's heart, even to the deceits and contradictions of the world in which he lives.[12]

Clearly that critique applies to the later R. D. Laing. Yet that writer's earlier work provided special insight into schizophrenia as a disorder of feeling, as a special state of numbing.

In *The Divided Self*, Laing did as much as any writer to make clear the relationship of schizophrenia, and madness in general, to psychic death. Indeed, that is exactly what the book is about. Even more, Laing's way of evoking schizophrenia helps us to make the connection between profound death imagery and the process of psychic numbing and reinforces our sense of the conceptual connection between the death and life-continuity paradigm on the one hand, and the formative-symbolizing principle (via its impairment) on the other. Written before he was thirty, when still in active tension with the psychoanalytic and psychiatric traditions he was questioning, *The Divided Self* is rigorous, and equally sensitive to schizophrenic suffering and destructiveness and to psychiatric distance and maneuvers toward schizophrenic patients. Laing is willing to address nuance and entertain paradox in ways that are both visionary and responsible to the work of other serious students of madness. (These qualities in *The Divided Self* have been somewhat obscured by Laing's subsequent emergence as a declamatory guru less concerned with rigor or the confrontation of tradition than with the truth-possessing persona that has evolved from the late twentieth-century temptations of guru-disciple relationships.)

Approaching schizophrenia from an existential stance, Laing insists that we believe our patients.

> A man says he is dead but he *is* alive. But his "truth" is that he is dead. . . . The schizophrenic is desperate, is simply without hope. . . . When someone says he is an unreal man or that he is dead, in all seriousness, expressing in radical terms the stark truth of his existence as he experiences it, that is—insanity.[13]

Put simply, the most extreme inner sense of deadness and unreality equals ultimate psychic numbing equals insanity. For these patients, "To play possum, to feign death, becomes a means of preserving one's aliveness."[14] This is the "false-self system" which "tends to become more and more dead," so that "in some people, it is as though they have turned their lives over to a robot which has made itself (apparently) indispensable."

What Laing calls the "false self" then, we can well call the dead self. There are echoes of the *Müsselmanner* in Laing's description of the schizophrenic's "deliberate cultivation of a state of death-in-life as a defense against the pain of life." Laing quotes schizophrenics' many metaphaors of this dead life. In the case of one young woman, speaking in the third person: "She's the ghost of the weed garden," and: "The pitcher is broken, the well is dry."

Laing succeeds brilliantly in evoking the troubled human being we call schizophrenic. But there are inevitable limitations to his existential method. His focus on the inner logic and understandability of "schizophrenese" tends to ignore or minimize the nature of the impairment to mental processes. Laing is aware that these are impaired, and in fact he speaks of a state of "chaotic nonentity," but lacking a symbolizing perspective Laing can only refer this inner chaos to a metaphor of being. To explain what happens to a patient, Laing finds himself discussing her "partial assemblies" or "partial systems" along with more minute fragmentations, and refers to these respectively as "molar splitting" (characteristic of hysterics) and "molecular splitting" (characteristic of schizophrenics.). And here we are back in Bleuler country. Laing has taken us there, almost despite himself, because the deathlike numbing of schizophrenia is inseparable from its "thought disorder" or its pattern of radical desymbolization and deformation. One feels dead because the ordinarily vitalizing flow of psychic images and forms has gone awry—has given way to delusions, hallucinations, and paranoid images on the one hand, and withdrawal and extreme numbing on the other.

Yet schizophrenic patients, especially during acute phases, often seem to show the very opposite of numbing—a kind of nonstop responsiveness to every possible stimulus. They create a confused collage of half-formed ideas and image-feelings. This "overinclusion"[15] involves "inability to *exclude* the nonessential and to abstract the essential." Now that is precisely what happens with the failure of what Susanne Langer calls the abstracting function of symbolization, and is therefore consistent with the schizophrenic's tendency toward concretization and literalization. But does it not conflict with our principle of psychic numbing? A schizophrenic patient told his doctor, "I am attending to everything at once and as a result I do not really attend to anything."[16] By feeling something of everything, that is, one is forming—in the sense of evolving workable constructs—nothing. We can understand the formative process to be impaired in the most fundamental way. The label of psychic numbing can be applied in relationship to what Susanne Langer calls "formed feeling," to the shaping of mental experience. In this sense the numbing is also fundamental, but is simply not working. Unable to give form to feeling, the schizophrenic person is overwhelmed by bits and pieces at every corner of the psychic field.

He experiences the breakdown in "boundaries" long observed in schizophrenics—their "difficulty in maintaining boundaries between independent events, between self and nonself, and between inside and outside."[17] As one patient is quoted as having complained to his therapist, "I don't know, when I talk to you, whether I'm having an hallucination, or a fantasy about a memory, or a memory about a fantasy." Or, as that experience has been paraphrased, "There is a sense of 'being dispossessed' of one's own self, so that 'feelings will not occur as *my* feelings . . . [and] I am unable to distinguish whether the feeling arises in me or is coloring me and arising elsewhere. Feeling *occurs* and does not seem to be rooted or anchored anywhere. . . ."[18] This is a radical absence of grounding.

A related observation is Theodore Lidz's stress on "egocentricity" or the tendency to be "egocentrically overinclusive," so that "the patient typically believes that what others do or say centers on him even when they are totally extraneous to him, as in ideas of reference and persecutory delusional systems; or, he believes that his thoughts have influence on others, and even magically affect the inanimate universe."[19] Here we recognize equally extreme uncentering in the form of near-absolute inability to place the self in time, space, or any kind of fusion of immediate and ultimate experience.

No wonder that Leslie Farber characterized schizophrenia as "a disorder consisting of a double failure in areas that might loosely be called meaning and relation . . . [a] disability of imagination [that] may be mistaken by the therapist for the workings of the bared unconscious . . ."[20] Farber is really referring to the radical impairment of the formative process, as opposed to earlier ideas about the mind being overwhelmed by "the unconscious." Similarly, "The critical attribute of the category of psychoses termed 'schizophrenia' lies in the aberrant symbolic processes—the distortions of perception, meaning, and logic—that occur without degradation of intellectual potential."[21] As the symbolic processes are the essence of human mentation, their diffuse break-down is likely to result in the most severe form of functional disorder. This turns out to be the case with the schizophrenic condition. Hence the suggestion some time ago that we call it an "experience disorder," since "the so-called thought disorder is [no more than] a convenient way of detecting and making inferences about the wider disorder."[22]

Moreover, the desymbolization is an *active* pattern in itself— "a process of active concretization"[23] in which there is a perpetual struggle around abstraction and symbolization, rather than a total absence of either. In that sense, the desymbolization and numbing of the schizophrenic are never completely uncontested, though they can dominate sufficiently to become a way of psychic life. Hence, "The schizophrenic finds himself unable to explain to the other how it is he feels he is dying."[24]

APPENDIX D

Scientists and Nuclearism

The scientist, especially the scientist-statesman, has his own special vulnerability to nuclearism. A particularly striking—because from our present vantage point so unlikely—example of this vulnerability can be found in the changing attitudes of Leo Szilard. Szilard was equally distinguished as scientist and humanitarian. He was a compassionate voice, first among those scientists who objected during the war to the use without warning of an atomic bomb on a populated city, and after Hiroshima as a completely dedicated leader and organizer of the American—and world—antibomb movement. A man with the apocalyptic imagination of the perpetual survivor, he was among the first to recognize the danger of an atomic weapon. And his role in bringing about (and writing) the famous "Einstein letter" to President Roosevelt, which warned of Germany's potential for making an atomic weapon and set in motion the American bomb project, is well known. Much less known is the impatience he showed with the slow progress of the work and his passionate desire, early in 1944, to complete work on the bomb so that it could be used as soon as possible. He feared that if the war ended before the bomb could be used, the American public would be unwilling to make the necessary sacrifices for the stable peace required by the existence of so powerful a weapon. Thus, he wrote to a leading administrator of the bomb project: "It would . . . be imperative rigidly to control all deposits [of uranium and thorium], if necessary by force and it will hardly be possible to get political action along that line unless high efficiency atomic bombs *have actually been used in this war* and the fact of their destructive power has deeply penetrated the mind of the public." The nuclearism here lies in reliance on the weapon to demonstrate its massive evil on behalf of ultimate good. Szilard probably held this view only briefly, and seventeen months later had become an outspoken advocate of "the diametrically opposed position."[1]

But the fact that he held it at all suggests the power of the impulse, among those most knowledgeably and creatively involved in the bomb, to seek solutions from the weapon for the problems it creates.

Oppenheimer's nuclearism was of a similar kind but much more enduring and influential. As both the technical and administrative head of the laboratory at Los Alamos, whose creative and human gifts all came together in the extraordinary achievement of developing the bomb, he inevitably had the most total involvement in the weapon itself. So powerful was his overall leadership that almost everyone else at Los Alamos "let Oppenheimer take protective custody of their emotions."[2]

Indeed there was a feeling of a utopian community in which "they all agreed that they were frantically busy and extremely security conscious and suggest that there was even some half-conscious closing of the mind to anything but the fact that they were trying desperately to produce a device which would end the war. . . ."[3] It was understandable that Oppenheimer would seek justification for the weapon's use. He is on record as having recommended, together with a few other scientific colleagues on a special subcommittee, military use of the bomb on an enemy city without warning; and of having himself discouraged and resisted circulation of Szilard's petition, signed by sixty-nine scientists, asking that the president hold back on use of the atomic bomb on Japan.[4] In trying to still the small voices of protest, Oppenheimer claimed that the scientists were ill-equipped to consider these matters and that political and military leaders knew better. But beyond that, as one biographer has recorded on the basis of conversations with Oppenheimer, "He had always believed that he had a higher purpose than to beat the Germans," and that the bomb would "shake mankind free from parochialism and war."[5] As in the case of Szilard's briefer version, Oppenheimer's nuclearism was the vision of a gifted scientist who had in a sense merged with the weapon he had done so much to bring about.

When he woke up from this state he became a brilliant and sensitive critic of nuclearism—of the even more dangerous form surrounding the newer and bigger hydrogen bomb, and especially its larger or "super" versions:

> What concerns me is really not the technical problem. I am not sure the miserable thing will work, nor that it can be gotten to a target except by ox-cart. It seems likely to me even further to worsen the unbalance of our present war plans. What does worry me is that this appears to have caught the imagination, both of the Congressional and of military people, as the answer to the problem posed by the Russian advance. It would be folly to oppose the exploration of this weapon. We have always known it had to be done, and it does have to be done, though it

appears to be singularly proof against any form of experimental approach. But that we become committed to it as they way to save the country and the peace appears to me full of danger.[6]

Oppenheimer was ambivalent toward, rather than opposed to, work on the hydrogen bomb, and the quotation also reveals the mixture of technological doubt and moral concern that seems generally to accompany nuclear backsliding.

While himself immersed in nuclearism, Oppenheimer was a national hero; upon painfully extricating himself from that condition and undergoing his form of nuclear backsliding, he was crucified at a security hearing and became something of a "divine victim"—a deity who now had himself to be destroyed. When Oppenheimer said, after Hiroshima, that "the physicists have known sin," I suspect he referred not just to their part in creating the weapon but to their having embraced that false deity with a combination of faith and numbing that was soon to spread to the rest of their society.

But the most extreme expression of nuclearism among American scientists has been that of Edward Teller. A member of the brilliant elite among nuclear physicists prior to World War II, he served as a "chauffeur" for his fellow Hungarian friend, Szilard, during the famous Einstein visit of 1939 and then worked under Oppenheimer at Los Alamos. But it was not until the later development of the hydrogen bomb that he emerged as the devoted "father" and advocate of that weapon and indefatigable proponent of ever bigger and better weapons systems and opponent of any form of limitation or test ban in connection with nuclear weapons. He, in fact, became the most influential of all American scientist-policy advisers, the driving force and charismatic center for our buildup of nuclear weapons from the late 1940s until the present time.

Teller's nuclearism has been bound up with currents surrounding the sequence from atomic bomb to hydrogen bomb. At Los Alamos, he had not, like other scientists, thrown himself wholeheartedly into work on the atomic weapon, but instead spent much of his time on the then distant possibility of a thermonuclear or hydrogen bomb. He had been interested in related theoretical questions concerning the sun's energy since at least 1934, when he came under the influence of George Gamow, a charismatic refugee Russian scientist who offered Teller his first teaching position in America. But the idea of an actual thermonuclear weapon took shape in Teller's mind in the fall of 1941 during an informal luncheon with Enrico Fermi, considered by most the closest to genius among that gifted generation of physicists. Fermi speculated that "Now that we have a good prospect of developing an atomic bomb, couldn't such an explosion be used to start something similar to the reactions in the sun?"[7] Through many ups and downs of calculations of possibility, Teller remained fascinated by the question to the point of developing something close to a proprietary interest—or "kinship" with—the prospective hydrogen bomb.[8] This *merging of self with weapon* was unusually intense—colleagues made reference to "Teller's beloved super," and he is said to have referred to the bomb as "my baby"—but the principle can apply much more generally to patterns of nuclearism in scientists.

Teller had developed no such kinship with the atomic bomb, and did not share other scientists' sense of exuberance when the "Trinity" test confirmed their achievement. There is now considerable ambiguity concerning his position regarding its use but he did, in a letter to Szilard, demonstrate a certain sensitivity when he wrote that "I have no hope of clearing my conscience. The things we are working on are so terrible that no amount of protesting or fiddling with politics will save our souls."

Teller was answering Szilard's request that he circulate the scientists' petition against using the bomb. Teller goes on to say that, were he convinced of Szilard's objections, he would simply quit working on the bomb, but that any "decisive weapon" is bound to be used in war, that the only hope for preventing atomic war in the future lies in "getting the facts of our results before the people," and "For this purpose actual combat-use might even be the best thing." In that suggestion, as well as in his "main point" that "the accident that we worked out to this dreadful thing . . . should not give us a responsibility of having a voice in how it is to be used,"[9] he was possibly echoing Oppenheimer's views. And he asked that Szilard show the letter to two close mutual physicist friends in Chicago, Wigner and Franck "who seem to agree with you rather than with me," because "I should like to have the advice of all of you whether you think it is a crime to continue the work."

But he concludes that "I feel I should do the wrong thing if I tried to say how to tie the little toe of the ghost to the bottle from which we just helped it escape." In other words we find in the letter a combination of stirrings of guilt and affirmation of continuing involvement with the weapons. This element of nuclearism is also more general among scientists and can be described as warding off guilt over nuclear weapons involvement by means of further weapons advocacy. That advocacy was to emerge with full force only around the hydrogen bomb. Concerning the atomic bombing of Hiroshima, Teller was to insist later that it was wrong, and that we would have been much wiser to have used some form of demonstration such as "a nighttime atomic explosion high over Tokyo."

In *Legacy of Hiroshima* Teller describes being at first "in absolute agreement" with Szilard's petition but then being talked out of circulating it by Oppenheimer and subsequently coming to "regret" having listened to him. But two letters recently made available—the one to Szilard quoted above and another to Oppenheimer—suggest either (as Sherwin believes) "that Teller's views were never in conflict with Oppenheimer's" or else that his ambivalence was such that he was easily and totally swayed by his superior. He writes chummily to Oppenheimer: "You may have guessed that one of the men 'near la Franck' (James Franck, an older and greatly respected scientist who was a central figure in another document, which bore his name, asking that use of the bomb be withheld) whom I have seen in Chicago was Szilard. . . . I should feel better if I could explain to him my point of view. This I am doing in the enclosed letter. What I say is, I believe, in agreement with your views. At least in the main points. . . ."[10]

Yet of great importance to Teller's nuclearism was his conflict with Robert Oppenheimer, a profound impasse that was both personal and bomb-related. For each was an unusually gifted physicist with something of the gadfly in him; neither had made original discoveries commensurate with his brilliance; both were to experience a form of personal realization around the creation of an ultimate weapon. This strange form of rivalry was reflected in Teller's deep resentment toward Oppenheimer in connection with the latter's relationship to the hydrogen bomb—his inconsistencies about it, and what Teller took to be his outright opposition. At the security hearings he insisted that if Oppenheimer had lent even moral support to work on the thermonuclear project, physicists would have remained in Los Alamos after the war and "we could have achieved the thermonuclear bomb just about four years earlier." Thus, while he did not agree outright that Oppenheimer was a "security risk," he said that "I would like to see the vital interests of this country in hands which I understand better and therefore trust more . . . [and] in this very limited sense . . . I would feel personally more secure if public matters would rest in other hands."

The merger of self and bomb becomes complicated by a rivalry over whose bomb is to be permitted, whose bomb is to be the bearer of not only "national security" but responsibility for the human future. Indeed Teller denounced what he looked upon as a double standard in the postwar advisory committee's view that "as long as you people work very hard and diligently to make a better atomic bomb, you were doing a fine job; but if you succeed in making real progress toward another kind of nuclear explosion, you were doing something immoral."[11] Teller is doing something else here. He is raising the ethical question at what point a scientist's contribution to weapons of destruction might begin to become immoral. His answer, at least so far, has been: never!

Political and scientific elements inevitably merged in Teller's nuclearism as he denounced our postwar policy for the lost "opportunity to use this big atomic stick to back up a proposal that would ensure peace," adding that President Roosevelt, whom he greatly admired, would have favored using the weapons "after the war, as a powerful driving force toward world government." Indeed, in Teller's own "liberal" period he participated for a while in the World Federalist movement and "had dreams of nuclear blessings being shared by all the nations on the earth under an international control system, and perhaps under a world government."[12] But Teller moved quickly from this nuclear utopianism to a "radical nuclear anti-communism." Deeply embittered by his family's harsh treatment in Hungary at the hands not only of the Nazis but also of two communist regimes—that of Bela Kun after World War I as well as post-

World War II Hungarian Stalinism—he became so absolute an anticommunist as to be, in his colleagues' eyes, "virtually paranoid" on the subject. It was thus natural for him to ally himself in successfully convincing President Truman to go ahead with a hydrogen bomb program, with an American senator, Brien McMahon, who juxtaposed the "total power" of sole possession of the bomb with the "total evil" of Soviet Russia. (Physicist Klaus Fuchs's confession of espionage, just at that time, seems to confirm that equation. It certainly intensified fears that he had given important information to the Soviet Union about the hydrogen bomb as well as the atomic bomb, and was an important factor in Truman's decision.) That kind of juxtaposition has fundamental importance for all imagery of political nuclearism.

Teller's increasing political conservatism took him to alliances first with Nelson Rockefeller, concerning an aggressive or "hawkish" nuclear-weapons policy and accompanying national "shelter program"), then with Richard Nixon, and finally with the frankly right-wing American Security Council (made up mostly of retired military officers, many of whom also serve as executives in nuclear and other arms industries)—with anyone, that is, who shares what was once referred to as Teller's "magnificent obsession" with American nuclear-weapons power. In testifying against Senate ratification of the nuclear test ban treaty, Teller insisted that it "would have grave consequences for the security of the United States and the free world," and that if the Senate were to ratify the treaty "you will have given away the future safety of our country and increased the dangers of war."[13]

What gave Teller's nuclearism its special power was what we may call *its heroic scientism*. From the time of that early talk with Fermi about the possibilities of the hydrogen bomb, Teller has been fascinated by the "scientific puzzle" it presented. He spoke glowingly of the "spirit of spontaneity, adventure, and surprise" surrounding early discussions with colleagues about thermonuclear problems. When everyone else thought them insurmountable, he persevered. His quest was undoubtedly related to the deepest exploratory impulses of the artist, scientist, or seeker of intellectual adventure—with the vision of new achievement that attracts and awes one's fellowmen and alters the human condition. Nuclearism could thus become linked with a scientific version of the "call to greatness" described in the myth of the hero. And indeed, there was an aura around Teller of an Old Testament prophet undergoing the hero's "road of trials" on the way to his inevitable triumph. His colleagues, only half-whimsically could refer to him as "the apostle of the Super"—and recalled his standing alone in his particular version of apocalyptic prophecy: "It won't be until the bombs get so big that they can annihilate everything that people will really become terrified and begin to take a reasonable line in politics . . . [and] those who oppose the hydrogen bomb are behaving like ostriches if they think they are going to promote peace in that way." Among those "ostriches" were the majority of the scientists and scientific administrators making up the General

Advisory Committee, whose majority report against proceeding with the hydrogen bomb described "a unique opportunity of providing by example some limitations on the totality of war"; and whose minority report was still more ethically explicit in its denunciation of the new weapon's limitless destructiveness as "a danger to humanity as a whole" and "an evil thing considered in any light." In the face of all this, Teller could speak of "my almost desperate interest in the thermonuclear effort."[14]

Winning out because of the political climate, Teller's quest was enormously enhanced by the brilliance of his scientific solution. It was what one colleague termed "a very brilliant discovery . . . a stroke of genius . . . an inspiration . . . which put the program on a sound basis."[15] That solution had at least two dimensions of impact. The first had to do with establishing the prospective reality of the bomb—Truman's decision more than a year earlier to go ahead with a crash program had been made without any certainty that the bomb could actually be produced. The hero had overcome both widespread opposition and formidable technical-scientific obstacles, and now his triumph was certain.

The other level had to do with what might be called the scientific beauty of the achievement. Scientists gathered to hear Teller at the Institute for Advanced Study in Princeton in June, 1951, experienced something close to rapture upon learning of his breakthrough. One was said to comment, "It's cute, it's beautifully cute!"

Robert Oppenheimer's term was "technically sweet," and it was he who described the power that kind of scientific achievement has in determining events.

> It is my judgment in these things that when you see something that is technically sweet, you go ahead and do it, and you argue about what to do about it only after you have had your technical success. That is the way it was with the atomic bomb. I don't think anybody opposed making it; there was some doubts about what to do with it after it was made. I cannot very well imagine that if we [the General Advisory Committee] had known in late 1949 what we had got to know by early 1951 that the tone of our report would have been the same.[16]

A significant scientific or technical breakthrough, Oppenheimer is telling us, of itself impels us to pursue it. Or to put the matter in our own terms, the scientific-technological mode of immortality has overwhelming call on the minds of scientific practitioners and observers alike. And that "call" is totally unrelated to moral consequences. The rapture we spoke of can be understood as the experiential transcendence that affirms an immortalizing vision. The entire pattern, according to Lewis Mumford, goes back to the sixteenth century, was developed fully in the Enlightenment, and is a threat to "organic knowledge" in its tendency to exclude man from the field of scientific vision. Certainly we can say that there has never been a greater paradox than that of the immortalizing imagery associated with the hydrogen-bomb breakthrough. (That breakthrough was not Teller's alone. The Soviet scientists apparently achieved it at approximately the same time.)

The extent of Teller's involvement in this form of scientism can be gauged from a remark he made to his biographers concerning his assignment by Oppenheimer at Los Alamos to head a group looking into the question of the possibility of a genuine "Doomsday reaction"—that is, of an atomic bomb creating heat of such intensity that it might ignite the heavy hydrogen in sea water and the nitrogen in the earth's atmosphere so that "the oceans and the heavens would catch fire" and "there would be nothing left." Teller recounted that he welcomed the assignment because "This was the kind of a job that was really delightful for me—to try to speculate in these wide ranges." [17] While the authors reassure us that "Teller was not a Dr. Strangelove delighted by anything that is scientifically challenging even if it means the end of the world," the choice of words suggests the intrinsic fascination and transcendence of *any* expression of the scientific imagination. (One can find parallel responses in medicine and psychiatry—exclamations of "Beautiful!" in response to a particularly vivid cellular demonstration of a form of of cancer, or an especially interesting expression of psychotic thought.)

Teller and others thus associated the creation of the hydrogen bomb—which more than the smaller atomic bomb raises the specter of human annihilation—as an expression of *faith* in human exploration and in the spirit of the Enlightenment:

> We would be unfaithful to the tradition of Western civilization if we shied away from exploring what man can accomplish, if we failed to increase man's control over nature. The duty of scientists, specifically, is to explore and explain. This duty led to the invention of the principles that made the hydrogen bomb a practical reality. [18]

He goes on to say that his own main virtue was to persist in this noble tradition via the hydrogen bomb. He said he claimed credit only in that "I believed and continued to believe in the possibility and the necessity of developing the thermonuclear bomb" and that "my *scientific duty* demanded exploration of that possibility."

An important aspect of Teller's scientific world view has been his consistent opposition to secrecy. Significantly, in his 1945 letter to Leo Szilard in which he explained his decision not to circulate Szilard's petition against use of the bomb, Teller expressed his strong conviction that "in the end" the American people as a whole should decide about how to use the bombs, and added: "This is the only cause for which I feel entitled in doing something: the necessity of lifting the secrecy at least as far as the broad issues of our work are concerned." His subsequent crusade against secrecy in scientific research could be understood as part of his absolute commitment to the unending quest for scientific knowledge. But we get the distinct impression, particularly from the Szilard letter, that this crusade, in satisfying his scientific conscience, serves as a kind of substitute for the other great "scientists' crusade": that of opposition to expanded nuclear weapons development and dissemination of knowledge about the weapons' destructive power. Concerning the latter, the "secrecy" of weapons advocates about what these bombs really do to human beings, Teller has mounted no crusade. His selective expression of a classic Enlightenment stance against secrecy serves to defend and reinforce his nuclearism.

That nuclearism became his life project. As the head of a laboratory dedicated to the thermonuclear bomb program and an increasingly prominent consultant and public figure, he warned constantly of the Russian threat, while fiercely defending American bombs—and bombs in general—against those who spoke out against their dangers to humankind. In *The Legacy of Hiroshima*, he dismisses public concerns about fallout as "purely imaginary." He is willing to do everything possible to limit the amount of radioactivity released in the atmosphere, so long as nuclear weapons development and testing is permitted to continue. What disturbs him most is "the clamor . . . for a halt of all nuclear tests." He scornfully suggests that the "clamor" is an expression of misdirected anxieties of those who would "set the clock back beyond Hiroshima."[19] (He admits that the 1954 hydrogen bomb testing at Bikini caused some radiation effects among a small group of American servicemen, and overt radiation sickness among natives on another atoll as well as among crew members of the Japanese ship, Fukuryu Maru [Lucky Dragon], one of whom died as a result. But he more or less dismisses these effects as a "tragic error" by meteorologists in their calculations concerning wind direction.) He complains bitterly that "the glamour of space" resulted in "neglect" of nuclear weapons, which had suddenly become "old hat" and "unfashionable and repulsive." He bemoans the tendency "to become more and more interested in nuclear disarmament," and advises the government to begin any disarmament programs with conventional and not nuclear weapons. The deity and its *mana* must be preserved. One needs bigger and better military-scientific programs. In addition, that *mana* is applied to a lyrical evocation of peaceful nuclear possibilities under such chapter headings as "The Renaissance of Alchemy," "The Lure of Infinity," and "The Seeds of Tomorrow."

But Teller returns to the question of "the fallout scare" to make one of the most remarkable statements I have come upon in my explorations of nuclearism:

> Radiation from test fallout is very small. Its effect on human beings is so little that if it exists at all, it cannot be measured. Radiation from test fallout might be slightly harmful to humans. It might be slightly beneficial. It might have no effect at all.[20]

Fallout might indeed produce genetic abnormalities which "may be offensive at first sight," he explains, but such mutations have always been necessary to the evolution of the human race so that, "Deploring the mutations that may be caused by fallout is something like adopting the policies of the Daughters of the American Revolution, who approve of a past revolution but condemn future reforms." According to this extraordinary argument, bomb fallout either has no effects or else should be understood as part of nature's wisdom in guiding human evolution. People and logic are equally sacrificed to the sacred cause of nuclearism.

The legacy of Hiroshima, then, is to exorcise "the ghost of Hiroshima," which makes people anxious about fallout "and prepares the ground" for nuclear-test restrictions and a "Mirage of Peace." Any nuclear test ban must be opposed because, Teller contends, it is impossible to detect underground and space tests, contrary to the conviction of the majority of the world's scientists that these tests can be adequately detected. Nuclear vigilance must be maintained on behalf of working for "establishment of a world authority sustained by moral force and physical force—a world-wide government capable of enforcing world-wide law and world-wide disarmament."[21] The nuclear deity, and only the nuclear deity, can create a moral and diplomatic perfection in a totally controlled world.

In what Teller admits is "an Alice-in-Wonderland world," it is necessary to "run fast just to stay in the same place," because

> if we stop, we are falling behind. A method of destroying ICBMs and rockets, a discriminating tactical nuclear weapons system, an adequate network of bomb shelters could upset any calculation based on absolutes.[22]

To perpetuate that process is courage, the only danger "likely to defeat us is fear," and "even fear can be defeated by rational, planned action." Unceasing nuclearistic behavior, that is, is the "rational" modus vivendi of our world.

The deity, of course, is flexible. Teller advocates different sizes and shapes of the weapon so that it can be placed alongside of all other weapons. Nuclear bombs are not a "greater evil" than earlier weapons because "evil does not reside in an instrument . . ." and also because "absolute weapons do not exist." Teller is bitterly critical of those who speak about a "Doomsday war"—as articles of nuclearistic faith insist upon what many others deny, namely, that "there is a defense against nuclear bombs"—and provides a vision of nuclear survival and recovery:

> . . . this much is certain: Properly defended, we can survive a nuclear attack; we can dig out of the ruins; we can recover from the catastrophe. . . .
> As a nation, we shall survive, and our democratic ideals and institutions will survive with us, if we make adequate preparations for survival now—and adequate preparations are within our reach and our capabilities.[23]

Adequate preparations mean unlimited nuclear buildup, constant testing, and an extensive national network of shelters which could, in a nuclear war, "save perhaps 90 percent of our people." One sees here how nuclearism, while ostensibly exposing the psychic numbing of others who refuse to confront the possibility of nuclear war, imposes itself in a much more extreme form of numbing concerning nuclear consequences.

Teller supports his argument with two "scenarios," on the order of contemporary nuclear thought, but extraordinary in their simple-mindedness.

> The first describes a communist uprising in a small, fictitious democratic country with whom the United States has a mutual defense treaty. A combination of American indecisiveness, cumbersomeness of governmental processes in arranging a declaration of war, and oversensitivity to Russian nuclear threat (partly on the basis of lack of preparedness) combine to make the American response ineffectual. The war, "Short as it was (it was over in less than a day) . . . was the beginning of the end of world leadership for the United States." Subsequent American efforts "to bolster our cold-war effort" are too late, Russian armed forces land in a number of Arab countries, "the Near East [is] abandoned," and "three months later . . ."
>
> The second scenario involves a similar communist revolution, but this time America acts more swiftly and effectively: when Russia sends paratroopers, the President acts upon a prior arrangement granted by Congress that he could declare war "providing that the war was limited in area and in scope." He succeeds in "limit[ing] the fighting area to the boundaries of the Crostic Union (the country involved) and "the political scope of the war to the re-establishment of the Loyalist government"—making effective use of small nuclear weapons while neither the American commandos nor their Loyalist guerrilla allies present targets large enough for nuclear weapons. When Russia threatens a nuclear attack on America, this is met with a "nationwide atomic alert" and an immediate second-strike readiness on the part of America. This aborts the Russian threat, and a Russian invasion of the wartorn country is stopped by American "nuclear bombs." The result is that Russia withdraws her forces, free elections are held under United Nations auspices, and the Loyalist officials are returned to office.

The moral of these two scenarios: nuclear restraint is dangerous, to the point of losing all; limited nuclear war holds the key to success. The chapter heading, in fact, is "Limited Warfare," and the claim is that nuclear weapons, if refined and properly used, can solve our military and political problems. But one must always have "courage" and be ready for attack by or use of these weapons. There seems to be a kind of nuclearistic magic that enables these weapons to resolve crises without ever getting out of control to the point of larger-scale nuclear annihilation. And significantly, in neither scenario does America experience the consequences of nuclear weapons.

Teller implies throughout that if we can only hang on and "buy time," the nuclear deity will save us completely. Thus, his disconcerting principle that "the drama that began at Hiroshima will be finished before the end of the century" is meant to imply that by that time extraordinary scientific advances, themselves primarily nuclear, will have definitively resolved our dilemmas. But there is also the possible interpretation, however consciously unintended by the author, that the drama may end in such a way that we will all "be finished before the end of this century."

In all this Teller wants to still what he calls "a monstrous anxiety" concerning fears of nuclear annihilation. But we must insist that he is guilty of a monstrous psychologism—of the nuclearist's dismissal of real dangers as inappropriate anxieties in order, so to speak, to protect the integrity and purity of the deity—and in that way encourage large-scale psychic numbing.

Teller posits his nuclearistic idealism against not only "our present weakness" but "the eclipse of the American dream." And he returns to a "psychological" argument by equating reservations about nuclear weapons with childish illusion: the refusal to recognize "a sudden transition from protected childhood to the responsibilities of a grown man"; to the shocked "young mind" turning away from reality, "seek[ing] refuge in a make-believe world," and replacing "rational behavior . . . by anxiety, by feelings of guilt, by fears of improbable and fantastic calamities." What for Teller constitutes "rational behavior" is a particular form of nuclear "courage" and "readiness." We must be "prepared to survive an all-out nuclear attack," "have adequate shelters for our entire population" as well as "plans and stockpiles [food and equipment] so that after an all-out attack, we could recover," and maintain "secure retaliatory forces to make sure that any all-out attack against our nation could be answered with a crushing counter-blow." For while Teller is willing to limit the area and aims of any such conflict according to the dimensions of the aggression initiating it, he insists that "*We cannot and must not try to limit the use of weapons.*"[24] (Italics added) The sacred object must maintain its own authority. That established, Teller can end his book with a vision of world government, international cooperation, improved scientific education, and peaceful research without secrets. The unlimited power of the nuclear deity, that is, has brought about an ideal world of perfect "security."

My concern about Teller has to do less with him as an individual than with what he exemplifies. There is first the deification of not just nuclear weapons but of science and scientific technology in general. It is this broader technicism and scientism that provides the matrix for nuclearism. Within this scientific aberration, "knowing"—the essence of both science and the arts—becomes only solving puzzles or manipulating the environment. Science, the parent, is consumed by its technological offspring. What results is an impulse—never stronger and never more dangerous than now—to substitute a brilliant technological vision for the more recalcitrant problems of human continuity, of what we have been calling symbolic immortality. "Works" give way to tools.

Teller also exemplifies a more specific constellation of imagery and advocacy:

aggressive to unlimited nuclear-weapons development, "protection" of the population by means of very extensive shelter-building, and strategic projections of "scenarios" of nuclear war that emphasize such desirable outcomes as victory, yield limits, and recovery.

(Herman Kahn became a much more sophisticated example of precisely this combination. With brilliance and elan, he has been able to mobilize the inherent fascination of such massive killing and dying. But under the guise of breaking through psychic numbing, of "thinking about the unthinkable," he extends and complexifies that numbing by means of consistently misleading minimization of the human consequences of nuclear war. This overall constellation often hides its conservative-belligerent political stance beneath its claim to both scientific objectivity and "realism.")

Kahn tells us, for instance, that a "reasonable," meaning "non-hypochondriac," individual who survives a future nuclear war "should be willing to accept, *almost with equanimity* (italics added), somewhat larger risks than those to which we subject our industrial workers in peace time. We should not magnify our view of the costs of the war inordinately because such postwar risks are added to the wartime casualties."[25]

The trouble is, that as I discovered in Hiroshima, nuclear weapons with their potential for unending radiation effects turn everyone into hypochondriacs. Kahn's technicized "psychology" enables him to claim further that "if the proper preparations have been made, it would be possible for us or the Soviets to cope with all the effects of a thermonuclear war, in the sense of saving most people and restoring something close to the prewar standard of living in a relatively short time." And to overcome fear of radiation and psychological contagion around that fear ("If one man vomits, everybody vomits.") he recommends meters for immediate measurement of radiation levels: "Assume now that a man gets sick from causes other than radiation. Not believing this, his morale begins to drop. You look at his meter and say, 'You have only received ten roentgens, why are you vomiting? Pull yourself together and get to work.'" Though a man of considerable imaginative capacity, in passages like these it is Kahn the technicist-nuclearist (he was originally trained as a physicist and engineer) who emerges. Under the guise of tough-minded logic, Kahn wishfully argues away expectable psychological responses of a negative kind.)

Finally, Teller exemplifies what has been called "the nuclear obsession." The term can mean many things. It suggests both military and "spiritual" preoccupation with the nuclear deity. But other expressions of that obsession can take hold in very humane men—we recall Szilard's early advocacy of using the bomb so that people would come to realize what it was. And men as distinguished as Bertrand Russell and Harold Urey (the former one of the world's most prominent spokesmen for the abolition of nuclear weapons and the latter one of the most sensitive of World War II nuclear scientists to the dangers of nuclear weapons) have at some time suggested the threat of preventive nuclear war should our adversary, the Soviet Union, fail to accept what is considered to be a reasonable proposal toward controlling or getting rid of nuclear weapons. The very sensitivity to massive death, and to guilt over doing nothing to hold it back, can create a potentially deadly form of nuclear abolitionism. It is again a question of "murdering evil," murdering massive killing.

Notes

PROLOGUE:
The Lost Theme

1. Paul Edwards, "My Death," in *The Encyclopedia of Philosophy*, vol. 5 (New York: Macmillan and Free Press, 1967), pp. 416–19.

ONE
Approaches and Modes

1. Sigmund Freud, "Thoughts for the Times on War and Death," Standard Edition (hereinafter referred to as SE), vol. 14, p. 289.
2. Ibid., pp. 299–300.
3. Carl Jung, *Memories, Dreams, Reflections* (New York: Pantheon Books, 1963).
4. Carl Jung, *Modern Man in Search of His Soul* (New York: Harcourt Brace & Co., 1936). This and the subsequent quotation are from pp. 129–30.
5. Maryse Choisy, *Sigmund Freud: A New Appraisal* (New York: Philosophical Library, 1953), p. 5.
6. Max Shur, *Freud: Living and Dying* (New York: Basic Books, 1972), pp. 50–51.
7. Avery Weisman and Thomas Hackett, "Predilection to Death: Death and Dying as a Psychiatric Problem," *Psychosomatic Medicine*, vol. 33, no. 3 (1961).
8. Otto Rank, *Beyond Psychology* (New York: Dover Books, 1958), p. 64.
9. G. Van der Leeuw, *Religion in Essence and Manifestation: A Study in Phenomenology* (New York: Harper and Row, 1963), especially vol. 1.

10. George Sansom, *A History of Japan*, vol. 1 (Palo Alto: Stanford University Press, 1958), pp. 25–26.

11. Jacques Choron, *Modern Man and Mortality* (New York: Macmillan Co., 1964), pp. 183–85.

12. Gerald Holton, *Thematic Origins of Scientific Thought: Kepler to Einstein* (Cambridge, Mass.: Harvard University Press, 1973), and personal communication.

13. Leslie Farber, "The Therapeutic Despair," *The Ways of the Will*, 2nd printing (New York/London: Basic Books, 1966).

14. Sansom, *A History of Japan*, pp. 25–26.

TWO
The Experience of Transcendence

1. Ruth Benedict, *Patterns of Culture* (New York: New American Library, 1946).

2. Friedrich Nietzsche, *The Birth of Tragedy* (Garden City, N.Y.: Doubleday/Anchor, 1956), pp. 20–21.

3. Marghanita Laski, *Ecstasy: A Study of Some Secular and Religious Experiences* (Bloomington, Ind.: Indiana University Press, 1961).

4. Donald D. Jackson, "LSD and the New Beginning," in symposium on "LSD, Transcendence and the New Beginning," ed. Charles Savage, *Journal of Nervous and Mental Disease*, 135 (1962): 438.

5. Sigmund Freud, *Civilization and Its Discontents*, SE, vol. 21, pp. 64–73.

6. Laski, *Ecstasy . . .* , p. 371.

7. Quoted in Charles Savage, "LSD, Alcoholism and Transcendence," in "LSD, Transcendence and the New Beginning," p. 430.

8. Robert Jay Lifton, *The Life of the Self* (New York: Simon & Schuster, 1976), pp. 71–74.

9. Carlos Castaneda, *The Teachings of Don Juan: A Yaqui Way of Knowledge* (Berkeley, Calif.: University of California Press, 1968).

10. Octavio Paz, "The Day of the Dead," in *Death and Identity*, ed. Robert Fulton (New York: John Wiley & Sons, 1965), pp. 387–94.

11. Mircea Eliade, *Cosmos and History: The Myth of the Eternal Return* (New York: Harper Torchbook, 1959); and *The Sacred and the Profane: The Nature of Religion* (New York: Harper Torchbook, 1961).

12. Ernest Becker, *The Denial of Death* (New York: Free Press, 1973), p. 163.

13. Helen Gardner, ed., *The New Oxford Book of English Verse* (New York and Oxford: Oxford University Press, 1972), pp. 188–90.

14. Norman Mailer, "The Prisoner of Sex," *Harper's Magazine*, March, 1971, pp. 41–92.

THREE
The Inchoate Image

1. See, for instance, Robert R. Holt, "Imagery: The Return of the Ostracized," *American Psychologist* 5 (1964): 254–64, and "On the Nature and Generality of Mental Imagery," in *The Function and Nature of Imagery*, ed. P. W. Sheehan (New York: Academic Press, 1972); Roy Schafer, *A New Language for Psychoanalysis* (New Haven: Yale University Press, 1976); Mardi J. Horowitz, *Image Formation and Cognition* (New York: Appleton-Century-Crofts, 1970); and Eric Olson, *The Mind's Collage: Psychic Composition in Adult Life*, to be published by MIT Press.

2. Adolf Portmann, *New Paths in Biology* (New York: Harper, 1964).

3. Norman Cameron, *Personality Development and Psychopathology* (Boston: Houghton Mifflin Co., 1963).

4. Kenneth Boulding, *The Image* (Ann Arbor, Mich.: University of Michigan Press, 1956), pp. 38–39.

5. Susanne Langer, *Mind: An Essay on Human Feeling*, vol. 2 (Baltimore: The Johns Hopkins University Press, 1972), p. 306.

6. Robert Jay Lifton, "Images of Time," in *History and Human Survival* (New York: Random House, 1970), pp. 58–80; "The Sense of Immortality: On Death and the Continuity of Life," *The American Journal of Psychoanalysis*, vol. 33, no. 1 (1973): 3–15.

7. Sigmund Freud, "Instinct and Its Vicissitudes," SE, vol. 14, pp. 121–22.

8. James Strachey, Editor's Note, SE, vol. 14, pp. 111–16.

9. Freud, "The Unconscious," SE, vol. 14, p. 177.

10. Susanne Langer, *Philosophy in a New Key* (New York: Mentor, 1948), p. 45.

11. For instance, Konrad Lorenz, *On Aggression* (New York: Harcourt Brace & World, 1963).

12. Norman F. White, ed., *Ethology and Psychiatry* (Toronto: University of Toronto Press, 1974).

13. Langer, *Mind . . .* , vol. 2, pp. 29–31.

14. Robin Fox, "The Cultural Animal," in *Man and Beast: Comparative Social Behavior*, ed. J. F. Eisenberg and Wilton S. Dillon (Washington, D.C.: Smithsonian Institution Press, 1971), pp. 273–96, 292.

15. Clifford Geertz, *The Interpretation of Cultures* (New York: Basic Books, 1973), p. 83.

16. Fox, "The Cultural Animal," pp. 293–96.

17. Frederick Snyder, "The Organismic State Associated with Dreaming," in *Psychoanalysis and Current Biological Thought*, ed. Greenfield and Lewis (Madison, Wisc.: University of Wisconsin Press, 1965), pp. 275–315; and "The New Biology of Dreaming," *Archives of General Psychiatry* 8 (1963): 381–91. The prior quotation is from Charles Fisher, as referred to in the second of these papers.

18. Ernest L. Hartmann, *The Functions of Sleep* (New Haven: Yale University Press, 1973).

19. Howard P. Roffwarg, Joseph N. Muzio, and William C. Dement, "Ontogenetic

Development of the Human Sleep-Dream Cycle," *Science* 152 (1966): 604–16, 612.

20. Langer, *Mind* . . ., vol. 2, pp. 271–74.

FOUR

The Natural Unity of Death

1. Maurice Merleau-Ponty, *Phénoménologie de la Perception*, pp. 249–50, as quoted and translated by Arleen Beberman in "Death and My Life," *Review of Metaphysics* 17 (1963): 18–32, 31.

2. Norman Reider, unpublished manuscript.

3. Robert Jay Lifton, *The Life of the Self* (New York: Simon & Schuster, 1976), pp. 19–20.

4. Heinrich Böll, *The Clown* (New York: McGraw Hill, 1965).

5. Sigmund Freud, "Inhibitions, Symptoms, and Anxiety," SE, vol. 20, p. 130.

6. Ibid., pp. 129–30.

7. Freud, "Thoughts for the Times on War and Death," SE, vol. 14, p. 297.

8. Freud, *The Ego and the Id*, SE, vol. 19, p. 58.

9. Kurt R. Eissler, *The Psychiatrist and the Dying Patient* (New York: International Universities Press, 1955), p. 74.

10. Freud, *The Ego and the Id*, p. 58.

11. Freud, *New Introductory Lectures on Psycho-Analysis*, SE, vol. 22, p. 125.

12. Freud, *Beyond the Pleasure Principle*, SE, vol. 18, pp. 7–64.

13. Ibid., pp. 36, 57.

14. Eissler, *The Psychiatrist and the Dying Patient*, pp. 31–32.

15. Norman O. Brown, *Life Against Death* (Middletown, Conn.: Wesleyan University Press, 1959).

16. Ibid., p. 106.

17. Ibid., p. 167.

18. Norman O. Brown, *Love's Body* (New York: Random House, 1966), p. 109.

19. Ernest Becker, *The Denial of Death* (New York: Free Press, 1973), pp. 98–99, 96.

FIVE

Infant and Child

1. John Bowlby, *Attachment and Loss*, vol. 1, *Attachment* (New York: Basic Books, 1969).

2. G. A. Miller, E. Galenter, and K. H. Pribram, *Plans and the Structure of Behavior* (New York: Rinehart & Winston, 1960).

3. Bowlby, *Attachment* . . ., vol. 1, p. 45.

4. Susanne Langer, *Mind: An Essay on Human Feeling*, vol. 1 (Baltimore: The Johns Hopkins University Press, 1972), p. xvii.

5. Bowlby, *Attachment* . . ., vol. 2, *Separation*, p. 77.

6. Margaret S. Mahler, Fred Pine, and Anni Bergman, *The Psychological Birth of the Human Infant* (New York: Basic Books, 1975), p. 8.

7. Peter H. Wolff, "The Natural History of Crying and Other Vocalizations in Early Infancy," in *Determinants of Infant Behaviour*, vol. IV, ed. B. M. Foss (New York: Barnes & Noble, 1969). See also Bowlby, vol. 1, pp. 244–46.

8. Otto Rank, *The Trauma of Birth* (New York: Brunner, 1952).

9. Mahler et al, *The Psychological Birth* . . . , p. 52.

10. Otto Rank, *Will Therapy* and *Truth and Reality* (New York: Alfred A. Knopf, 1936),pp. 1–3.

11. Mahler et al, *The Psychological Birth* . . . , p. 9.

12. Melanie Klein, "On the Theory of Anxiety and Guilt," in Klein et al, *Developments in Psychoanalysis* (London: Hogarth Press, 1952), pp. 275–78.

13. Mary Chadwick, "Notes Upon the Fear of Death," *International Journal of Psycho-Analysis* 10 (1929): 321–34.

14. B. Brodsky, "The Self-Representation, Anality and the Fear of Dying," *Journal of the American Psychoanalytic Association* 7 (1959): 95–108.

15. Mahler et al, *The Psychological Birth* . . . , p. 15.

16. Otto Fenichel, *The Psycho-analytic Theory of Neurosis* (New York: W. W. Norton, 1945), p. 34. Fenichel here paraphrases Freud.

17. Langer, *Mind* . . . , vol. 2, p. 29.

18. Jean Piaget, quoted in Wolff, "The Natural History of Crying. . . ."

19. D. W. Winnicott, "The Location of Cultural Experience," *International Journal of Psychoanalysis*, 48 (1967): 372.

20. Erik H. Erikson, *Identity: Youth and Crisis* (New York: W. W. Norton, 1968), p. 96.

21. John Bowlby, "Childhood Mourning and Its Implications for Psychiatry," *American Journal of Psychiatry* 118 (1961): 483.

22. Bowlby, *Attachment* . . . , vol. 2, p. 27.

23. Mahler et al, *The Psychological Birth* . . . , p. 75.

24. Ibid., p. 47.

25. Ibid., quoting A. Frank, p. 197.

26. Ibid., pp. 54, 48.

27. Ibid., pp. 74–75.

28. Ibid., p. 77.

29. Mahler et al, *The Psychological Birth* . . . , p. 75.

30. Winnicott, *The Location of Cultural Experience*, p. 369.

31. Mahler et al, *The Psychological Birth* . . . , pp. 74–75.

32. Klein et al, *Developments in Psychoanalysis*, pp. 239–40.

33. Sylvia Anthony, *The Child's Discovery of Death* (New York: Harcourt Brace & Co., 1940), p. 103 [reissued as *The Discovery of Death in Children and After* (New York: Basic Books, 1972)].

34. Sigmund Freud, "Character and Anal Erotism," SE, vol. 9, p. 167–75; Norman O. Brown, *Life Against Death*, especially chapter 15, "Filthy Lucre"; and Ernest Becker, *Escape from Evil* (New York: Free Press, 1975), pp. 73–86.

35. Robert Kastenbaum and Ruth Aisenberg, *The Psychology of Death* (New York: Springer, 1972), pp. 12–15.

36. Adah Maurer, "Maturation of Concepts of Death," *British Journal of Medicine and Psychology* 39 (1966): 35–41.

37. Anthony, *The Child's Discovery of Death*, p. 62.

438 | *Notes*

38. Joseph Campbell, *The Masks of God* (New York: Viking Press, 1964), pp. 176–77.
39. Jean Piaget and Barbel Inhelder, *The Psychology of the Child* (New York: Basic Books, 1969), p. 130.
40. René Spitz, "Anaclitic Depression," *Psychoanalytic Study of the Child*, vol. 2, 1946, pp. 313–42; and *The First Year of Life* (New York: International Universities Press, 1965); and S. Provence and R. C. Lipton, *Infants in Institutions* (New York: International Universities Press, 1963); and Bowlby, *Attachment* . . . , vols. 1 and 2.
41. Anthony, *The Child's Discovery of Death*; see also Maria Nagy, "The Child's View of Death," *Journal of Genetic Psychology* 73 (1948): 3–27.
42. Arthur D. Sorosky, Annette Baran, and Reuben Pannor, *The Adoption Triangle: The Effects of the Sealed Record on Adoptees, Birth Parents, and Adoptive Parents* (Garden City, N.Y.: Anchor Press/Doubleday, 1978); and Betty Jean Lifton, *Lost and Found: The Adoption Experience* (New York: Dial Press, 1979).
43. Jean Piaget, "The Growth of Thought," in *The Child*, ed. William Kessen (New York: John Wiley & Sons, 1965), pp. 274–96, 282.
44. Langer, *Mind* . . . , vol. 1, p. 149.

SIX
Adolescent and Adult

1. Arnold Van Gennep, *The Rites of Passage* (Chicago: The University of Chicago Press, Phoenix Books, 1960), pp. 65–75.
2. Joseph Campbell, *The Masks of God*, vol.1, p. 116.
3. Van Gennep, *Rites of Passage*, p. 74.
4. James George Frazer, *The Golden Bough*, abridged ed. (New York: Macmillan Co., 1963), pp. 698–703.
5. Ibid., p. 702.
6. Campbell, *The Masks of God*, vol. 1, pp. 102–18.
7. Norman O. Brown, *Life Against Death* (Middletown, Conn.: Wesleyan University Press, 1959), especially pts. 2, 3, and 6.
8. Norman O. Brown, *Love's Body* (New York: Random House, 1966), pp. 84, 89.
9. Frazer, *Golden Bough*, pp. 695–96.
10. Van Gennep, *Rites of Passage*, p. 75.
11. Frazer, *Golden Bough*, p. 802.
12. Van Gennep, *Rites of Passage*, p. 75.
13. Campbell, *The Masks of God*, vol. 1, p. 89.
14. Baldwin Spencer and F. J. Gillen, *The Native Tribes of Central Australia* (London: Macmillan Co., 1899), as quoted and summarized in Campbell, vol. 1, pp. 88–116.
15. All but the second sentence of this paragraph is quoted directly from Spencer and Gillin.
16. This entire paragraph quoted directly from Spencer and Gillin.
17. This entire paragraph quoted directly from Spencer and Gillin.
18. Robert Jay Lifton, "Protean Man," and "The Young and the Old: Notes on a New History," in *History and Human Survival* (New York: Random House, 1970).

19. Erik H. Erikson, *Identity: Youth and Crisis* (New York: W. W. Norton, 1968).

20. Kenneth Keniston, *Young Radicals* (New York: Harcourt Brace & Co., 1968).

21. Erik H. Erikson, *Childhood and Society* 2nd ed. (New York: W. W. Norton, 1963).

22. Erik H. Erikson, *Young Man Luther* (New York: W. W. Norton, 1958).

23. Ibid., p. 111.

24. Daniel J. Levinson et al, "The Psychosocial Development of Men in Early Adulthood and the Mid-Life Transition," in *Life History Research in Psychopathology*, vol. 3, ed. D. F. Ricks, A. Thomas, and M. Roff (Minneapolis: University of Minnesota Press, 1974), pp. 243–58, 247.

25. Campbell, *The Masks of God*, vol. 1, p. 122.

26. Ibid., p. 121.

27. Ibid., p. 123.

28. Robert N. Butler, "The Life Review: An Interpretation of Reminiscence in the Aged," *Psychiatry* 26 (1963): 65–76.

29. See Elisabeth Kübler-Ross, *On Death and Dying* (New York: Macmillan Co., 1970); Avery D. Weisman, *On Dying and Denying* (New York: Behavioral Publications, 1972); and Edwin S. Shneidman, *The Deaths of Man* (New York: Quadrangle, 1973).

SEVEN
Culture and Connection

1. Robert Jay Lifton, *Death in Life* (New York: Touchstone Books, 1976), especially sections 2, 3, and 12.

2. For discussion of Japanese death attitudes, see Kunio Yanagida, Shintō to Minzokugaku (Shinto and Folklore) (Tokyo: Meiseidō, 1943); Taijō Tamamuro, *Soshiki Bukkyo* (Funeral Buddhism) (Tokyo: Daihorinkaku, 1963), p. 80; and Inaba Shūken and Funabashi Issai, *Jōdō Shinshū* (Kyoto: Otoni University, 1961). (Throughout the book I follow Japanese usage in rendering the family name first, except in cases of Japanese whose names have been customarily rendered in English in Western fashion of surname last [Yukio Mishima].)

3. *Columbia Encyclopedia*, 3rd ed. (New York: Columbia University Press, 1963), p. 1437.

4. Hori Ichiro, *Minkan Shinko* (Folklore Beliefs) (Tokyo: Iwanami Shoten, 1952), pp. 5–6.

5. Kunio Yanagida, "Nipponjin no Raisekan ni tsuite" (On the Japanese View of Life After Death), *Sekai*, October, 1955; and Takeda Choshu, *Sosen Suhai* (Ancestor Worship) (Kyoto: Heirakuji Shoten, 1957).

6. Lifton, *Death in Life*, pp. 31–32.

7. Masaharu Anesaki, *History of Japanese Religion with Special Reference to the Social and Moral Life of the Nation* (Rutland, Vt.: C. E. Tuttle, 1968), p. 40.

8. Arnold Van Gennep, *The Rites of Passage* (Chicago: The University of Chicago Press, Phoenix Books, 1960); Erwin Panofky, *Tomb Sculpture* (New York: Abrams, 1964); and Kunio Yanagida, Shintō to Minzokugaku (Shinto and Folklore) (Tokyo: Meiseidō, 1943).

9. Kunio Yanagida, ed. *Minzokugakujiten* (Dictionary of Ethnology) (Tokyo: Minzokugaku-Kenkujo [Research Institute of Ethnology], 1951).

10. Robert N. Bellah, *Tokugawa Religion, The Values of Pre-Industrial Japan* (Glencoe, Ill: Free Press, 1957).

11. W. Lloyd Warner, "The City of the Dead," in *Death and Identity*, ed. Robert Fulton (Bowie, Maryland: Charles Press, 1976), p. 367.

12. Philippe Ariès, "The Reversal of Death," in *Death in America*, ed. David E. Stannard (Philadelphia: University of Pennsylvania Press, 1975), pp. 155–56. See also Jessica Mitford, *The American Way of Death* (Greenwich, Conn.: Fawcett, 1963); Evelyn Waugh, *The Loved One* (London: Chapman and Hall, 1950); and the writings of Robert Fulton on the subject, as listed in *Death and Identity*, p. 440.

13. Yanagida, "Japanese View of Life After Death."

14. *Cosmos and History*, pp. 46–47.

15. Robert Jay Lifton, *Revolutionary Immortality* (New York: Norton Library, 1976), pp. 36–37.

EIGHT
Culture, Integrity, and Movement

1. Octavio Paz, "The Day of the Dead," in *Death and Identity*, ed. Robert Fulton (New York: John Wiley & Sons, 1965), p. 387.

2. Kurt R. Eissler, *The Psychiatrist and the Dying Patient* (New York: International Universities Press, 1955), pp. 104–7.

3. For instance, the important studies, already cited, of Weisman, *On Dying and Denying*, Shneidman, *The Deaths of Man*, and Kastenbaum and Aisenberg, *The Psychology of Death*.

4. Edmund C. Payne, Jr., "The Physician and His Patient Who Is Dying," *Psychodynamic Studies on Aging: Creativity, Reminiscing, and Dying*, ed. S. Levin, and R. J. Kahana (New York: International Universities Press, 1972), pp. 111–63.

5. See Ivan Morris, *The Nobility of Failure: Tragic Heroes in the History of Japan* (New York: Holt Rinehart & Winston, 1975); my review of that book, *New York Times Book Review*, Sept. 28, 1975, p. 6; and Robert Jay Lifton, Shuichi Kato, and Michael Reich, *Six Lives/Six Deaths: Portraits from Modern Japan* (New Haven: Yale University Press, (1979).

6. In Robert N. Bellah, *Tokugawa Religion: The Values of Pre-Industrial Japan* (Glencoe, Ill.: Free Press, 1957) p. 96.

7. Ibid., p. 96 (The words are those of Yoshida Shoin, as are those in the next quotation).

8. Ibid.

9. Morris, *The Nobility of Failure*.

10. Leo Tolstoy, *The Death of Ivan Ilyich and Other Stories* (Signet Books, 1960), pp. 129, 134.

11. Sigmund Freud, *Beyond the Pleasure Principle*, SE, vol. 18, pp. 38–39.

12. Elisabeth Kübler-Ross, *On Death and Dying* (New York: Macmillan Co., 1969), pp. 246–47.

13. Eissler, *The Psychiatrist and the Dying Patient*, pp. 55, 301.

14. Trans. by J. M. Cohen, *London Times Literary Supplement*, December 12, 1963.

15. Avery D. Weisman, *On Dying and Denying*; and *The Realization of Death* (New York: Jason Aronson, 1974).

16. Raymond T. McNally and Radu Florescu, *In Search of Dracula: A True History of Dracula and Vampire Legends* (New York: Graphic Society, 1972). See also A. Murgoci, "The Vampire in Rumania," *Folklore* 37 (1926); and Bernhart J. Hurwood, *The Monstrous Undead* (Lancer Books, 1969).

17. Avery D. Weisman and Thomas P. Hackett, "Predilection to Death," *Psychosomatic Medicine* 23 (1961): 232–56.

18. Weisman, *On Dying and Denying*, p. 39.

19. Weisman, *The Realization of Death*, ms. p. 154.

20. Daniel Cappon, "The Dying," *Psychiatric Quarterly*, 1959, vol. 33, pp. 466–489.

21. Freud, *Beyond the Pleasure Principle*, pp. 55–56.

22. Lifton, "Protean Man," in *History and Human Survival*, pp. 315–31.

23. Lifton, *Revolutionary Immortality* (New York: Norton Library, 1976).

24. Lifton, "Images of Time," in *History and Human Survival*, p. 62.

25. Lifton, *Thought Reform and the Psychology of Totalism: A Study of "Brain-Washing" in China* (New York: Norton, 1960).

26. Lifton, *Revolutionary Immortality*.

27. Lifton, *Death in Life*, especially pp. 31–37 and 500–10.

NINE
Love and Energy

1. Robert R. Holt, George S. Klein, Benjamin R. Rubenstein, Roy Schafer, Jane Loevinger, and John Bowlby. References to most of this critical literature can be found in Holt, "Freud's Mechanistic and Humanistic Images of Man," in *Psychoanalysis and Contemporary Science*, vol. 1, ed. Holt and Peterfreund, (New York: Macmillan, 1972), pp. 3–24; Loevinger, *Ego Development: Conceptions and Theories* (San Francisco: Jossey-Bass, 1976); and Roy Schafer, *A New Language for Psychoanalysis* (New Haven: Yale University Press, 1976).

2. Schafer, *A New Language . . .* , p. 153.

3. Ibid., pp. 9, 133.

4. John Bowlby, *Attachment and Loss*, vol. 1, (New York: Basic Books, 1969), pp. 18–20.

5. *Oxford English Dictionary*, compact ed. (1971), p. 864; and *American Heritage Dictionary* (1969), pp. 432 and 1549–50.

6. *Columbia Encyclopedia*, 3rd ed. (New York: Columbia University Press, 1963).

7. Ernest Jones, *The Life and Work of Sigmund Freud*, vol. 1 (New York: Basic Books, 1953), pp. 28–29, 41.

8. Sigmund Freud, "The Neuro-psychoses of Defence (I)," SE, vol. 3, p. 60.

9. Freud, *An Outline of Psycho-Analysis*, SE, vol. 23, pp. 163–64.

10. Jones, *Life and Work . . .* vol. I, pp. 40–41. See also Erik H. Erikson's commentary on this oath in his essay on Freud's emergence as a psychoanalyst ("The

First Psychoanalyst," in *Insight and Responsibility* [New York: W. W. Norton, 1964], pp. 19–46).

11. David M. Hirsch, unpublished ms.

12. Mark Tobey, in *Conversations with Artists*, Seldon Rodman (New York: Devin Adair, 1957), p. 18.

13. Morris Graves, in *Conversations with Artists*, p. 11.

14. Susanne Langer, *Mind: An Essay on Human Feeling* vol. 1 (Baltimore: The John Hopkins University Press, 1972), p. 23.

15. Robert G. Solomon, *The Passions: The Myth and Nature of Human Emotion* (Garden City: Doubleday/Anchor, 1976), pp. 188–89.

16. Robert J. Lifton, *The Life of the Self* (New York: Simon & Schuster, 1976), pp. 71–72.

TEN
Anxiety and Numbing

1. Sigmund Freud, "Three Essays on the Theory of Sexuality," SE, vol. 20, 1905, pp. 123–245, 224 (footnote, sentence quoted added in 1920).

2. Freud, "An Outline of Psycho-Analysis," SE, vol. 23, 1940 (1938), pp. 141–208, 199.

3. Freud, *Inhibitions, Symptoms and Anxiety*, SE, vol. 20, p. 128.

4. Freud, *New Introductory Lectures on Psycho-Analysis*, SE, vol. 22, p. 85.

5. Ibid., p. 87.

6. Freud, *Inhibitions, Symptoms and Anxiety*, p. 165.

7. Ibid., p. 166.

8. Ibid., p. 166.

9. D. W. Winnicott, in *Anxiety and Neurosis*, Charles Rycroft (London: Penguin-Pelican, 1968 [1970]), p. 31.

10. Gregory Zilboorg, "Fear of Death," *Psychoanalytic Quarterly* 12 (1943): 465–75.

11. C. W. Wahl, "The Fear of Death," in *The Meaning of Death*, ed. H. Feifel (New York: McGraw-Hill, 1959).

12. Ernest Becker, *The Denial of Death* (New York: Free Press, 1973), pp. 69, 70.

13. Jacques Choron, paraphrase of Heidegger, *Death and Western Thought* (New York: Collier Books, 1963), p. 33.

14. Rollo May, *The Meaning of Anxiety* (New York: Ronald Press, 1950), p. 191.

15. Kurt Goldstein, *The Organism* (New York: American Book Company, 1939), pp. 291, 295; and *Human Nature in the Light of Psychopathology* (New York: Schocken Books, 1963 [1940]).

16. Leslie Farber, *The Ways of the Will* (New York: Basic Books, 1966), p. 42.

17. Freud, *Inhibitions, Symptoms and Anxiety*, pp. 137, 166–67.

18. Farber, *The Ways of the Will*, p. 44.

ELEVEN
Guilt

1. Gerhart Piers and Milton B. Singer, *Shame and Guilt* (Springfield, Ill.: Charles C. Thomas, 1953).

2. Sigmund Freud, *Civilization and Its Discontents*, SE, vol. 21, p. 134.

3. Freud, *Totem and Taboo*, SE, vol. 13.

4. Ibid., p. 87.

5. Ibid., p. 158.

6. Freud, *Civilization* . . . , p. 131.

7. Ibid., pp. 139–43.

8. Freud, *Totem and Taboo*, SE, vol. 13, p. 159.

9. Freud, *Civilization* . . . , pp. 123–24, 86.

10. Ibid., pp. 135.

11. Ibid., pp. 131–32.

12. Robert Jay Lifton, *Home From the War* (New York: Simon & Schuster, 1973), chaps. 4 and 13.

13. Martin Buber, "Guilt and Guilt Feelings," in *The Knowledge of Man* (New York: Harper Torchbook, 1966), pp. 121–48, 132.

14. Ibid., pp. 125–26.

15. Ibid., p. 132.

16. Ibid., p. 146.

17. Lifton, *Home From the War*, chaps. 2, 4, 12, 13, and 14.

18. Robert Jay Lifton, *Death in Life* (New York: Touchstone Books, 1976), pp. 238–52.

19. Takeo Doi, *The Anatomy of Dependence* (New York: Kōdansha International, 1973).

20. James Hillman, *Re-visioning Psychology* (New York: Harper & Row, 1975), pp. 83, 242.

TWELVE
Anxiety, Rage, and Violence

1. Robert Jay Lifton, *Home From the War*, (New York: Simon & Schuster, 1973) chap. 5. See also chaps. 2, 6, 9, and 10.

2. Peter H. Wolff, "Comments on the Biology of Violence in Children," unpublished manuscript.

3. Sigmund Freud, "Thoughts for the Times on War and Death," SE, vol. 14, p. 299.

4. Ernest Jones, *The Life and Work of Sigmund Freud*, vol. 2 (New York: Basic Books, 1953), p. 17.

5. Ibid., p. 176.

6. Ibid., p. 177.

7. Sigmund Freud, *Civilization and Its Discontents*, SE, vol. 21, p. 119.

8. Konrad Lorenz, *On Aggression* (New York: Harcourt Brace & World, 1966).

9. Ibid., p. 248.

10. Ibid., p. 271.

11. Freud, "Thoughts for the Times," p. 288.

12. Lorenz, *On Aggression*, p. 277.

13. Erich Fromm, *The Anatomy of Human Destructiveness* (New York: Holt Rinehart & Winston, 1973), p. 29.

14. *The New Columbia Encyclopedia* (New York: Columbia University Press, 1975), p. 168. Based on accounts by Bernard Lewis and Enno Franzius.

15. Lorenz, *On Aggression*, p. 281.

16. M. I. Finley and H. W. Pleket, *The Olympic Games: The First Thousand Years* (New York: Viking, 1976), pp. 20–21.

17. Fromm, *Anatomy of Human Destructiveness*, p. 332.

18. Ibid., p. 366.

19. J. P. Stern, *Hitler: The Führer and the People* (London: Fontana/Collins, 1975), p. 21.

20. Ibid., pp. 185–97.

21. Freud, *Civilization and Its Discontents*, p. 119.

22. Tess Forrest, "The Family Dynamics of Maternal Violence," *Journal of the American Academy of Psycho-analysis* vol. 2, no. 3 (1975): 215–30.

23. Ibid., p. 216.

THIRTEEN
Survivor Experience and Traumatic Syndrome

1. Robert Jay Lifton, *The Life of the Self* (New York: Simon & Schuster, 1976), p. 62.

2. Robert Waelder, "Trauma and the Variety of Extraordinary Challenges," in *Psychic Trauma*, ed. Sidney S. Furst (New York: Basic Books, 1967), pp. 221–34, 222.

3. Ibid., p. 222.

4. Sigmund Freud, Ferenezi, et al, *Zur Psychoanalyse der Kriegsneurosen* (Leipzig: Internationaler Psychoanalytischer Verlag, 1919).

5. Ernest Jones, *The Life and Work of Sigmund Freud*, vol. 2 (New York: Basic Books, 1953), p. 254.

6. Sigmund Freud, *Introduction to Psycho-Analysis and the War Neuroses*, SE, vol. 27, pp. 207–15, 208.

7. Ibid., including Appendix, "Memorandum on the Electrical Treatment of War Neurotics"; and *Beyond the Pleasure Principle*, SE, vol. 18.

8. Jones, Life and Work, vol. 2, pp. 253–54.

9. Freud, *Introduction to Psycho-Analysis and the War Neuroses*, p. 209.

10. Freud, *Beyond the Pleasure Principle*, p. 27. Subsequent three quotations are from pp. 28, 31, and 35.

11. Abram Kardiner, "Traumatic Neuroses of War," in *American Handbook of*

Psychiatry, vol. 1, ed. Silvano Arieti (New York: Basic Books, 1959), pp. 245–57, 247.

12. Ibid., p. 256.

13. H. C. Archibald, D. M. Long, C. Miller, and R. D. Tuddenham, "Gross Stress Reaction in Combat—a Fifteen-Year Follow-up," *American Journal of Psychiatry* 119 (1962): 317–22, 318.

14. Joseph D. Teicher, "'Combat Fatigue' or 'Death Anxiety Neurosis,'" *Journal of Nervous and Mental Disease* 117 (1953): 232–42.

15. See discussions and references in Robert Jay Lifton, *Home From the War* (New York: Simon & Schuster, 1973).

16. See especially Robert Jay Lifton, *Death in Life*, chap. 12 (New York: Touchstone Books, 1976), as well as related discussions in *Home From the War* and *The Life of the Self*.

17. Robert Jay Lifton and Eric Olson, "The Human Meaning of Total Disaster: The Buffalo Creek Experience," *Psychiatry* 39 (1976): 1–17.

18. Sigmund Freud, *Civilization and Its Discontents*, SE, vol. 21, p. 89.

19. Freud, *Beyond the Pleasure Principle*, pp. 55–56.

20. Ibid., p. 32.

21. Lifton, *Death in Life*, pp. 32–33.

22. Guy Sajer, *The Forgotten Soldier* (New York: Harper & Row, 1971), p. 254.

23. Erich Lindemann, "Symptomology and Management of Acute Grief," *American Journal of Psychiatry* 101 (1944): 141–48, 143.

24. Lifton, *Home From the War*, chap. 13.

FOURTEEN
Depression—Static Protest

1. Quoted in Henri F. Ellenberger, *The Discovery of the Unconscious* (New York: Basic Books, 1970), pp. 364–417.

2. Quoted in Leston Havens, *Approaches to the Mind* (Boston: Little, Brown & Co., 1973), p. 61.

3. Gerald L. Klerman, "Overview of Depression," in *Comprehensive Textbook of Psychiatry* 2nd ed., ed. A. M. Freedman, H. I. Kaplan, B. J. Sadock (Baltimore: William & Wilkins, 1975), vol. 1, pp. 1003–12, 1003.

4. Ibid., p. 1003.

5. Emil A. Gutheil, "Reactive Depressions," in *American Handbook of Psychiatry*, ed. Silvano Arieti (New York: Basic Books, 1959), pp. 345–52, 347.

6. Robert Jay Lifton, *Death in Life* (New York: Touchstone Books, 1976), p. 500.

7. Primo Levi, *Survival in Auschwitz* (New York: Collier Books, 1961), p. 82.

8. Ernest Becker, *The Denial of Death* (New York: Free Press, 1973), p. 210.

9. Klerman, "Overview of Depression," p. 1011.

10. Walter Bonime, "The Psychodynamics of Neurotic Depression," *Journal of the American Academy of Psychoanalysis* 4(3) (1975): 301–26.

11. Gary R. Davis, "Depression: Some Updated Thoughts," *Journal of the American Academy of Psychoanalysis* 4(3) (1976): 411–24, 416–17.

12. Sigmund Freud, *The Ego and the Id*, SE, vol. 19, p. 53.

13. Karl Abraham, "Notes on the Psycho-Analytical Investigation and Treatment of Manic-Depressive Insanity and Allied Conditions" (1911), in *The Meaning of Despair: Psychoanalytic Contributions to the Understanding of Depression*, ed. Willard Gaylin (New York: Science House, 1968), pp. 26–49.

14. Ibid., p. 27.

15. Ibid., p. 31.

16. Ibid., p. 39.

17. Otto Fenichel, *The Psychoanalytic Theory of Neurosis* (New York: W. W. Norton, 1945), p. 391.

18. Sigmund Freud, "Mourning and Melancholia," SE, vol. 14, pp. 239–58.

19. Ibid., Editor's Note, p. 239.

20. Ibid., pp. 245–46, 249.

21. Edward Bibring, "The Mechanism of Depression," in *The Meaning of Despair*, pp. 154–81, 162–63, 172.

22. Davis, "Depression . . . ," pp. 411–24, 413–14.

23. Arthur H. Schmale, in *The Psychology of Depression: Contemporary Theory and Research*, ed. Raymond J. Friedman and Martin M. Katz (Washington, D.C./New York: Winston, Wiley, 1974), p. 257.

24. Arthur H. Schmale and George L. Engel, "The Role of Conservation-Withdrawal in Depressive Reactions," in *Depression and Human Existence*, ed. E. James Anthony and Therese Benedek (Boston: Little, Brown & Co., 1975), pp. 183–98, 183–84.

25. E. C. Reid, in *Depression and Human Existence*, p. 544.

26. John Bowlby, *Attachment and Loss*, vol. 2 (New York: Basic Books, 1969), and "Processes of Mourning," *International Journal of Psycho-analysis* 42 (1961): 317–40,

27. Erich Lindemann, "Symptomology and Management of Acute Grief," *American Journal of Psychiatry* 101 (1944).

28. George Engel, "Is Grief a Disease?" *Psychosomatic Medicine* 23 (1961): 18–22.

29. Colin Murray Parkes, *Bereavement: Studies in Grief in Adult Life* (New York: International Universities Press, 1972).

30. Melanie Klein, "A Contribution to the Psychogenesis of Manic-Depressive States," in *Contributions to Psycho-Analysis, 1921–1945* (London: The Hogarth Press and The Institute of Psycho-Analysis, 1948), p. 286.

31. Robert Jay Lifton and Eric Olson, "The Human Meaning of Total Disaster: The Buffalo Creek Experience," *Psychiatry* 39 (1976): 6.

32. Gerald L. Klerman, "Depression and Adaptation," pp. 127–45, 137.

33. Freud, "Mourning and Melancholia," Editor's Note, p. 240.

34. Ibid., p. 244.

35. Ibid., pp. 247–48.

36. Ibid., p. 248.

37. Willard Gaylin, ed., *The Meaning of Despair*, p. 13.

38. The phrase is Rado's (see his "Psychodynamics of Depression from the Etiologic Point of View," in *The Meaning of Despair*, p. 104).

39. Sandor Rado, "The Problem of Melancholia," in *The Meaning of Despair*, pp. 70–95.

40. Rado, "Psychodynamics of Depression," in *The Meaning of Despair*, pp. 96–98, 107, 101.

41. Martin Harrow and Millard J. Amdur, "Guilt and Depressive Disorders," *Archives*

of General Psychiatry 25 (1971): 240–46. See also Amdur and Harrow, "Conscience and Depressive Disorders," *British Journal of Psychiatry* 120 (1972): 239–64; and Harrow et al, "Symptomatology and Subjective Experiences in Current Depressive States," *Archives of General Psychiatry* 14 (1966): 203–12.

42. Freud, "Mourning and Melancholia," p. 49.

43. Ibid., pp. 49–50.

44. Arthur D. Schmale, "Depression as Affect, Character Style, and Symptom Formation," in *Psychoanalysis and Contemporary Science*, vol. 1, ed. Holt and Peterfreund, 1972, pp. 327–49.

45. Carl P. Malquist, "Depression in Childhood," in *The Nature and Treatment of Depression*, ed. Frederic F. Flach and Suzanne C. Draghi (New York: John Wiley & Sons, 1975), pp. 73–98, 86.

46. Mortimer Ostow, "Psychological Defense Against Depression," in *Depression and Human Existence*, pp. 395–411, 401.

47. Michael Balint, "The Paranoid and Depressive Syndromes," in *Primary Love and Psychoanalytic Technique* (New York: Liveright, 1953), pp. 259, 263.

48. Silvano Arieti, "Psychoanalysis of Severe Depression: Theory and Therapy," *Journal of American Academy of Psychoanalysis* 4 (1976): 327–45, 329–30.

49. Aaron T. Beck, "The Development of Depression: A Cognitive Model," in *The Psychology of Depression*, ed. Friedman and Katz, pp. 3–27, 6, 15; and *Depression: Clinical, Experimental, Theoretical Aspects* (New York: Hoeber-Harper, 1967).

50. Schmale and Engel, "The Role of Conservation-Withdrawal. . . ."

51. Harrow et al, "Guilt and Depressive Disorders."

52. John Bowlby, "The Adolf Meyer Lecture: Childhood Mourning and Its Implications for Psychiatry," *American Journal of Psychiatry* 118 (1961): 481–98. Findings summarized herein.

53. Colin Murray Parkes, "Health after Bereavement: A Controlled Study of Young Boston Widows and Widowers," *Psychosomatic Medicine* 34 (1972): 449–61; and Parkes, *Bereavement*.

54. See Roland Kuhn, "The Attempted Murder of a Prostitute," in *Existence*, ed. Rollo May (New York: Basic Books, 1958), pp. 365–425; George Engel, "Is Grief a Disease?" *Psychosomatic Medicine* 23 (1961): 18–22; and William Greene, "Disease Response to Life Stress," *Journal of the American Medical Women's Association* 20 (1965): 133–40.

55. Papers cited by Parkes, Bowlby, and Engel, as well as Helene Deutsch, "Absence of Grief," *Psychoanalytic Quarterly* 6 (1937): 12–22. More general studies of depression also reflect this relationship. See, for instance, Myrna Weissman and Eugene S. Paykel, *The Depressed Woman: A Study of Social Relationship* (Chicago: University of Chicago Press, 1974).

56. Bowlby, "Adolf Meyer Lecture . . . ," p. 47.

57. Anthony and Benedek, eds., *Depression and Human Existence*, Epilogue, p. 537.

58. Balint, "The Paranoid and Depressive Syndromes," pp. 256–57.

59. Leon Edel, "The Madness of Art," *American Journal of Psychiatry* 132 (1975): 1005–12, 1011–12.

60. A. D. Jonus and D. F. Jonus, "The Evolutionary Mechanisms of Neurotic Behavior," *American Journal of Psychiatry* 131 (1974): 636–40, 638.

FIFTEEN
Disruption and Neurosis

1. Quoted in D. Wilfred Abse, "Hysteria," in *American Handbook of Psychiatry*, vol. 1, ed. Silvano Arieti (New York: Basic Books, 1959), pp. 272–92, 273.

2. Josef Breuer and Sigmund Freud, "On the Psychical Mechanism of Hysterical Phenomena: Preliminary Communication" [1893], *Studies in Hysteria*, SE, vol. 2, pp. 3–17, 12.

3. Ibid., vol. 2, p. 12.

4. Breuer and Freud, *Studies in Hysteria*, p. 218.

5. P. J. Moebius, in *Studies in Hysteria*, p. 215.

6. Ibid., p. 220.

7. Sigmund Freud, "Fragment of an Analysis of a Case of Hysteria," SE, vol. 7, p. 27.

8. Thomas Szasz, *The Myth of Mental Illness* (New York: Hoeber-Harper, 1961).

9. David Shapiro, *Neurotic Styles* (New York: Basic Books, 1965), p. 1.

10. Philip Rieff in *Neurotic Styles*, pp. 14–15.

11. Ibid., p. 113.

12. Ibid., pp. 120–21.

13. Ibid., p. 126. Subsequent quotations are from pp. 124, 131.

14. Abse, "Hysteria," pp. 272–92, 277–78.

15. Breuer and Freud, *Studies in Hysteria*, pp. 22–28.

16. Walter Bromberg and Paul Schilder, "The Attitude of Psychoneurotics Towards Death," *Psychoanalytic Review* 23 (1936): 1–25.

17. Mary Chadwick, "Notes Upon the Fear of Death," *International Journal of Psycho-Analysis* 10 (1929): 321–34.

18. Mostly following Sandor Rado, "Obsessive Behavior: So-called Obsessive Compulsive Neurosis," in *American Handbook of Psychiatry*, vol. 1, pp. 324–44.

18A. Medard Boss, *Psychoanalysis and Daseinsanalysis* (New York: Basic Books, 1963), p. 183.

19. Shapiro, *Neurotic Styles*, p. 52.

20. Ibid., p. 50.

21. Leon Salzman, *The Obsessive Personality* (New York: Science House, 1968).

22. Shapiro, *Neurotic Styles*, p. 50.

23. Otto Fenichel, *The Psychoanalytic Theory of Neurosis* (New York: W. W. Norton, 1945), p. 285.

24. See Lucille Dooley, "The Concept of Time in the Defense of Ego Integrity," *Psychiatry* 4 (1941): 13–23.

25. Rado, "Obsessive Behavior . . . ," p. 333.

26. Salzman, *The Obsessive Personality*, p. 14.

27. Freud, "Notes Upon a Case of Obsessional Neurosis," SE, vol. 10, p. 235.

28. Ibid., p. 158.

29. Ibid., p. 300.

30. Ibid., p. 299.

31. Ibid., p. 312.

32. Ibid. These last quotations are from both the actual case writeup (p. 205) and the unpublished notes (p. 263), as not all of the latter were originally reproduced.

33. Ibid., pp. 187–88.

34. Ibid., p. 214.

35. Salzman, *The Obsessive Personality*, p. 71, partly paraphrasing Erwin Strauss and V. E. von Gebsattel. See also Boss, *Psychoanalysis and Daseinsanalysis*, pp. 183–84.

36. Freud, "Notes . . . ," p. 177.

37. Bernard Brodsky, "The Self-Representation, Anality, and the Fear of Dying," *Journal of the American Psychoanalytical Association* 7 (1959): 95–108, 107.

38. Freud, "Notes . . . ," pp. 235–36. Remaining quotations in this paragraph are from pp. 236 and 240.

39. Fenichel, *The Psychoanalytic Theory of Neurosis*, p. 285.

40. Freud, "Notes . . . ," p. 234.

41. Freud, "Analysis of a Phobia in a Five-Year-Old Boy," SE, vol. 10, p. 117.

42. Ibid., pp. 3–149.

43. Ibid., p. 126.

44. Freud, *New Introductory Lectures on Psycho-Analysis*, SE, vol. 22, p. 86.

45. Paul Friedman, "The Phobias," in *American Handbook of Psychiatry*, vol. 1, ed. Silvano Arieti, pp. 293–306, 296.

46. Freud, "Analysis of a Phobia . . . ," p. 8, fn.

47. Ibid., p. 8.

48. Ibid., p. 23.

49. Ibid., pp. 24–25. (Includes remaining quotations in the paragraph.)

50. Ibid., p. 69.

51. Ibid., p. 112.

52. Ibid., p. 50.

53. Ibid., pp. 135–36.

54. Friedman, "The Phobias," p. 302.

55. David Greene and Richmond Lattimore, eds., *Sophocles: The Complete Greek Tragedies* (Chicago: The University of Chicago Press, 1959), 103–4.

56. Ibid., p. 150.

SIXTEEN
Schizophrenia—Lifeless Life

1. R. D. Laing, *The Divided Self: An Existential Study in Sanity and Madness* (Baltimore: Penguin [Pelican], 1965 [1960]).

2. Laing, *The Divided Self*, p. 176.

3. Waltraut J. Stein, "The Sense of Becoming Psychotic," *Psychiatry* 30 (1967): 262–75, 268, 272. (P. 268 as paraphrased from Alfred Storch, "Beiträge zum Verständnis des schizophrenen Wahnkranken," *Der Nerveharzt* 30 (1959): 49–55.)

4. Laing, *The Divided Self*, p. 112.

5. Ibid., p. 176.

6. Ibid., pp. 147, 142.

7. Stein, "The Sense of Becoming Psychotic," pp. 262–75, 268.

8. Donald O. Burnham, "Separation Anxiety," *Archives of General Psychiatry* 13 (1965): 346–58.

9. Ibid., p. 350.

10. Ibid., pp. 346–47.

11. Ibid., p. 349.

12. Erik H. Erikson, "Wholeness and Totality," in *Totalitarianism*, ed. Carl Friedrich (Cambridge, Mass.: Harvard University Press, 1953), p. 165.

13. Laing, *The Divided Self*, p. 45.

14. Sigmund Freud, "On Narcissism: An Introduction," SE, vol. 14, p. 74.

15. Ibid., p. 79.

16. Freud, "Psycho-Analytic Notes on an Autobiographical Account of a Case of Paranoia (Dementia Paranoides)," SE, vol. 12, pp. 60–61.

17. Ida Macalpine and Richard A. Hunter, eds., Daniel Schreber, *Memoirs of My Nervous Illness* (London: William Dawson & Sons, Ltd., 1955), pp. 372–74; and Freud, "Psycho-Analytic Notes . . . ," p. 72.

18. Freud, "Psycho-Analytic Notes . . . ," p. 55.

19. Macalpine and Hunter, *Memoir* . . . , pp. 379, 400.

20. Harold F. Searles, *Collected Papers on Schizophrenia and Related Subjects* (New York: International Universities Press, 1965), pp. 488–89.

21. Ibid., pp. 492, 500, 495.

22. Freud, *Introductory Lectures on Psycho-Analysis*, SE, vol. 16, p. 421.

23. Freud, "On Narcissism . . . ," pp. 90–91.

24. Freud, *Moses and Monotheism*, SE, vol. 23, pp. 1–37, 74.

25. See especially Otto Kernberg, *Object Relations and Clinical Psychoanalysis* (New York: Jason Aronson, 1976).

26. Christopher Lasch, *The Culture of Narcissism: American Life in an Age of Diminishing Expectations* (New York: W. W. Norton, 1978).

27. Malcolm B. Bowers, "Pathogenesis of Acute Schizophrenic Psychosis: An Experiential Approach," *Archives of General Psychiatry* 19 (1968): 348–55, 351–52.

28. Harry Stack Sullivan, *Schizophrenia as a Human Process* (New York: W. W. Norton, 1962), p. 198.

29. Lionel Ovesey, "Pseudo-Homosexuality, the Paranoid Mechanism, and Paranoia," *Psychiatry* 18 (1955): 163–73, 171–72.

30. See Sheldon T. Selesnick, "C. G. Jung's Contributions to Psychoanalysis," *American Journal of Psychiatry* 120 (1963): 350–56.

31. Elias Canetti, *Crowds and Power* (New York: Viking, 1962), pp. 227, 230, 443.

32. Patrick T. Donlon et al, "Depression and the Reintegration Phase of Acute Schizophrenia," *American Journal of Psychiatry* 133 (1976): 1265–74; Richard T. Rada and Patrick T. Donlon, "Depression and the Acute Schizophrenic Process," *Psychosomatics* 16 (1975): 116–19; and Silvano Arieti, *Interpretation of Schizophrenia* (New York: R. Brunner, 1955), pp. 609–10. (Reprinted 1957.)

33. S. Levin, "The Depressive Core in Schizophrenia," *Philadelphia Association for Psychoanalysis Bulletin* 21 (1971): 219–29; and R. S. Spiegel, "Gray Areas Between the Schizophrenias and the Depressions," *Journal of the American Academy of Psychoanalysis* 1 (1973): 179–92, 191.

34. Harry Stack Sullivan, *Clinical Studies in Psychiatry* (New York: W. W. Norton, 1956), p. 146.

35. Searles, *Collected Papers on Schizophrenia and Related Subjects*, p. 497.

36. Thomas Szasz, *Schizophrenia: The Sacred Symbol of Psychiatry* (New York: Basic Books, 1976).

37. Laing, *The Divided Self*, p. 176.

38. Macalpine and Hunter, Daniel Schreber, *Memoirs*, p. 55.

39. Stein, "The Sense of Becoming Psychotic," p. 274.

40. S. Roth, "The Seemingly Ubiquitous Depression Following Acute Schizophrenic Episodes: A Neglected Area of Clinical Discussion," *American Journal of Psychiatry* 127 (1970): 51–58; quoted in *American Handbook of Psychiatry*, p. 609.

41. Bowers, "Pathogenesis of Acute Schizophrenic Psychosis," p. 353.

42. Malcolm B. Bowers and Daniel X. Freedman, " 'Psychedelic' Experiences in Acute Psychoses," *Archives of General Psychiatry* 15 (1966): 240–48, 245.

43. Bowers, "Pathogenesis of Acute Schizophrenic Psychosis," p. 354.

44. Lyman C. Wynn, in *Family Processes and Schizophrenia*, ed. Elliot Mishler and Nancy Waxman (New York: Science House, 1968), p. 287.

45. Wynn et al, "Pseudo-Mutuality in the Family Relations of Schizophrenics," *Psychiatry* 21 (1958): 205–20, 205.

46. Wynn, in *Family Processes* . . . , p. 26.

47. Leslie Schaffer and Lyman C. Wynn et al, "On the Nature and Sources of the Psychiatrist's Experience with the Family of the Schizophrenic," *Psychiatry* 25 (1962): 32–45, 44.

48. Lyman C. Wynn and Margaret Thaler Singer, "Thought Disorder and Family Relations of Schizophrenics: I. A Research Strategy," *Archives of General Psychiatry* 9 (1963): 191–98; "II. A Classification of Forms of Thinking," *Archives* 9 (1963): 199–206; "III. Methodologies and Projective Techniques," *Archives* 12 (1965): 187–212; "IV. Results and Implications," *Archives* 12 (1965): 201–12.

49. Theodore Lidz et al, "Intrafamilial Environment of Schizophrenic Patients: II. Marital Schism and Marital Skew," *American Journal of Psychiatry* 114 (1957): 241–48; and "Intrafamilial Environment of the Schizophrenic Patient: VI. The Transmission of Irrationality," AMA *Archives of Neurology and Psychiatry* 79 (1958): 305–316; and the Bateson group's focus on the "double bind" (G. Bateson, D. Jackson, J. Haley and J. Weakland, "Toward a Theory of Schizophrenia," *Behavioral Science* 1 (1956): 251–64).

50. J. Victor Monke, "On Some Subjective, Clinical, and Theoretical Aspects of the Acute Psychotic Reaction," in *Acute Psychotic Reaction*, ed. W. M. Mendel and Leon J. Epstein, Psychiatric Research Report of the American Psychiatric Association, Washington, D.C. 1963, 22–35, 32.

51. Ibid., p. 33.

52. Ibid., p. 33.

53. Ibid., p. 31.

54. David Rosenthal and Seymour S. Kety, eds., *The Transmission of Schizophrenia* (Oxford: Pergamon Press, 1968). See also Paul H. Wender et al, "Cross-fostering: A Research Strategy for Clarifying the Role of Genetic and Experiential Factors in the Etiology of Schizophrenia," *Archives of General Psychiatry* 30 (1974): 121–28; and Robert Cancro, "Genetics, Dualism, and Schizophrenia," *Journal of American Academy of Psychoanalysis* 3 (1975): 353–60.

55. Theodore Lidz, "Commentary on 'A Critical Review of Recent Adoption, Twin, and Family Studies of Schizophrenia: Behavioral Genetics Perspectives'." *Schizophrenia*

Bulletin (1976): 402–11, and "Reply to Kety et al," *Schizophrenia Bulletin* 3, no. 4 (1977): 522–26.

56. Wynn, Singer, and Toohui, "Communication of the Adopted Parents of Schizophrenics," in *Schizophrenia*, 75. *Psychotherapy, Family Studies, Research,* ed. Jorstad and Ugelstad (Oslo: The University of Oslo Press, 1976), pp. 413–51.

57. Cancro, "Genetics, Dualism, and Schizophrenia," p. 356.

58. In *The Transmission of Schizophrenia,* ed. Rosenthal and Kety, p. 9.

59. David Reiss, "The Family and Schizophrenia," *American Journal of Psychiatry* 133 (1976): 180–84, 184.

60. Cancro, "Genetics, Dualism, and Schizophrenia," pp. 357–58.

61. William G. Niederland, "Schreber: Father and Son," *Psychoanalytic Quarterly* 28 (1959): 151–69, 160. See also Niederland, *The Schreber Case: Psychoanalytic Profile of a Paranoid Personality* (New York: Quadrangle, 1974).

62. Niederland, "Schreber: Father and Son," p. 165.

63. Morton Schatzman, "Paranoia or Persecution: The Case of Schreber," *Family Process* 10 (1971): 177–207, and *Soul Murder: Persecution of the Family* (New York: Random House, 1973). See also Philip M. Kitay, "Symposium on 'Reinterpretations of the Schreber Case: Freud's Theory of Paranoia'," *International Journal of Psycho-Analysis* 44 (1963): 191–223.

SEVENTEEN
Suicide—The Quest for a Future

1. David Lester, "Suicidal Behavior: A Summary of Research Findings," Supplement to *Crises Intervention* 2, no. 3, 1970 (Buffalo, N.Y.: Suicide Prevention and Crisis Service), mimeo, p. 14.

2. See Edwin S. Shneidman, "Classifications of Suicidal Phenomena," *Bulletin of Suicidology,* July, 1968.

3. Karl Menninger, "Psychoanalytic Aspects of Suicide," in *A Psychiatrist's World: Selected Papers of Karl Menninger* (New York: Viking, 1959), pp. 332, 338, 346.

4. Sigmund Freud, *Mourning and Melancholia,* SE, vol. 14, p. 252.

5. Robert E. Litman, "Sigmund Freud on Suicide," in *Essays in Self-Destruction,* ed., Edwin S. Shneidman (New York: Science House, 1967), p. 332. Quotation from Freud, SE, vol. 14, p. 252.

6. Kurt R. Eissler, *The Psychiatrist and the Dying Patient* (New York: International Universities Press, 1955), pp. 64–67.

7. Ibid., p. 66.

8. Ibid.

9. Gregory Zilboorg, "Suicide among Civilized and Primitive Races," *American Journal of Psychiatry* 92 (1936): 1347–67; and "The Sense of Immortality," *Psychoanalytic Quarterly* 7 (1938): 171–99.

10. Zilboorg, "Suicide among Civilized and Primitive Races," pp. 1368, 1361.

11. Joseph Campbell, *The Masks of God: Primitive Mythology* (New York: Viking Press, 1964), pp. 173–76.

12. Ibid., pp. 176–78.

13. James George Frazer, *The Golden Bough*, abridged version by Theodor H. Gaster (New York: Criterion Books, 1959), p. 230.

14. Zilboorg, "Suicide among Civilized and Primitive Races," p. 1361.

15. James George Frazer, *The Fear of the Dead in Primitive Religion* vol. 2 (London, 1936).

16. *Encyclopaedia Britannica* 15 ed., vol. 17, s.v. "Suicide," p. 777–82.

17. Jacques Choron, *Suicide* (New York: Scribners, 1972), pp. 15–20.

18. Frazer, *Fear of the Dead* . . . , p. 157.

19. Sir Thomas Browne, *Religio Medici*, quoted in *The Savage God*, A. Alvarez (New York: Random House, 1972), p. 50.

20. Frazer, *Fear of the Dead* . . . p. 157.

21. Choron, *Suicide*, pp. 24–26.

22. *Encyclopaedia Britannica*, 15th ed., vol. 17, s.v. "Suicide," p. 778. See also Erwin Stengel, *Suicide and Attempted Suicide* (Harmondsworth, Middlesex: Pelican, 1964).

23. A *Discourse of Death* (London, 1613), quoted in "Shakespeare's Suicides: Some Historic, Dramatic and Psychological Reflections," by M. D. Faber, in *Essays in Self-Destruction*, ed. Edwin S. Shneidman, (New York: Science House, 1967), pp. 30–58, 31–32, 52.

24. Tsurumi Shunsuke, "The Philosophy of Disembowelment," in *Science of Thought* (Tokyo: 1960). See also Ivan Morris, *The Nobility of Failure*; and Lifton, Kato, and Reich, *Six Lives/Six Deaths*.

25. Alvarez, *The Savage God*, pp. 227–31.

26. Richard Friedenthal, *Goethe, His Life and Times* (London: Weidenfeld & Nicholson, 1965), quoted in Alvarez, *The Savage God*, p. 207.

27. Alvarez, *The Savage God*, pp. 227, 231.

28. Jean-Francois Steiner, *Treblinka* (New York: Simon & Schuster, 1967). Although not everything in this book is reliable, these aspects of suicide, which it describes well, are confirmed by other witnesses.

29. Quoted in Hugh Adam Bedau, "The Right to Die by Firing Squad: The Death Penalty and Gary Gilmore," *The Hastings Center Report* 7 (1977): 5–7, 6.

30. George F. Solomon, "Capital Punishment as Suicide and as Murder," *American Journal of Orthopsychiatry* 45 (1975): 701–11.

31. Eissler, *The Psychiatrist and the Dying Patient*, p. 66.

32. Norman L. Farbarow and Edwin S. Shneidman, "Suicide and Death," in Herman Feifel, *The Meaning of Death* (New York: McGraw-Hill, 1959), pp. 284–301, 298.

33. Ludwig Binswanger, "The Case of Ellen West: An Anthropological-Clinical Study," in *Existence: A New Dimension in Psychiatry and Psychology*, ed. R. May, E. Angel, and H. Ellenberger (New York: Basic Books, 1958).

34. Norman L. Fabarow and Edwin S. Shneidman, eds., *The Cry for Help* (New York: McGraw-Hill, 1965).

35. R. Rubenstein, R. Moses and T. Lidz, "On Attempted Suicide," *American Medical Association Archives of Neurological Psychiatry* 79 (1958): 103–12.

36. Binswanger, "The Case of Ellen West," p. 292.

37. Leslie Farber, *The Ways of the Will* (New York: Basic Books, 1966), p. 93.

38. Ibid.

39. A. T. Beck, "Thinking and Depression," *Archives of General Psychiatry* 9 (1963): 324–33.

40. K. Minkoff et al, "Hopelessness, Depression, and Attempted Suicide," *American Journal of Psychiatry* 130 (1973): 455–58, 455.

41. A. D. Pokorny et al, "Hopelessness and Attempted Suicide: A Reconsideration," *American Journal of Psychiatry* 132 (1975): 954–56.

42. R. Naroll, "Thwarting Disorientation and Suicide" (Northwestern University, 1965), quoted in Brockopp and Lester, *Suicidal Behavior: A Summary of Research Findings*, pp. 109–12.

43. M. J. Kahne, "Suicide in Mental Hospitals," *Journal of Health and Social Behavior* 12 (1966): 177–86; Arthur L. Kobler and Ezra Stotland, *The End of Hope: A Socio-Clinical Theory of Suicide* (New York: Free Press, 1964); and review of same by R. J. Lifton, *Archives of General Psychiatry* 12 (1965) 192–94.

44. Freud, *Mourning and Melancholia*, p. 252.

45. Edwin S. Shneidman and Norman L. Farbarow, eds., *Clues to Suicide* (New York: McGraw-Hill, 1957).

46. Farber, *Ways of the Will*, p. 94.

47. Binswanger, "The Case of Ellen West," p. 298.

48. Alvarez, *The Savage God*, p. 131.

49. James Hillman, *Suicide and the Soul* (New York: Harper & Row, Colophon Books, 1973 [1964]), p. 73.

50. See discussions in Ruth Benedict, *The Chrysanthemum and the Sword* (New York: Houghton Mifflin, 1946); Morris, *The Nobility of Failure*; Lifton, Kato and Reich, *Six Lives/Six Deaths*; and George Devos, *Sociology for Achievement: Essays on the Cultural Psychology of the Japanese* (Berkeley, Calif: University of California Press, 1973). The last two studies emphasize Japanese susceptibility to guilt as well as shame.

51. T. B. Hauschild, "Suicidal Population of a Military Psychiatric Center," *Military Medicine* 133 (1968): 425–37; and B. A. Pollack, "A Study of the Problem of Suicide," *Psychiatric Quarterly* 12 (1938): 306–30.

52. Pollack, "A Study of the Problem . . . ," and D. R. Doroff, "Attempted and Gestured Suicide in Adolescent Girls," Diss. Abstracts 27B (1969): 2631.

53. Farber, *Ways of the Will*, p. 78.

54. Alvarez, *The Savage God*, pp. 267–69.

55. Ibid., pp. 279–80.

56. Case description and quotations are from Binswanger, "The Case of Ellen West."

EIGHTEEN
Yukio Mishima—The Lure of Death

1. Henry Scott-Stokes, *The Life and Death of Yukio Mishima* (New York: Farrar, Straus & Giroux, 1974), p. 43.

2. Ibid., p. 37.

3. Ibid., p. 40.

4. Ibid., p. 10.

5. Ibid., p. 52.

6. Yukio Mishima, *Confessions of a Mask*, (New York: New Directions, 1958), pp. 5–6.

7. John Nathan, *Mishima* (Boston: Little, Brown, & Co., 1974), p. 19.

8. Ibid., p. 21.

9. Mishima, *Confessions*, pp. 20–21, 24.

10. Nathan, *Mishima*, p. 14.

11. Scott-Stokes, *Life and Death* . . . , p. 72.

12. Mishima, *Confessions*, pp. 8–10.

13. Ibid., p. 39.

14. Ibid., p. 41.

15. Ibid., pp. 43–46.

16. Nathan, *Mishima*, p. 41.

17. Mishima, *Confessions*, p. 16.

18. Nathan, *Mishima*, p. 50.

19. Yukio Mishima, *Sun and Steel* (Tokyo: Kodansha, 1970), pp. 27–28.

20. Nathan, *Mishima*, p. 58.

21. Ibid., pp. 97, 103.

22. Yukio Mishima, *The Temple of the Golden Pavilion* (New York: Alfred A. Knopf, 1959).

23. Scott-Stokes, *Life and Death* . . . , p. 153.

24. Ibid., p. 139.

25. Mishima, *Sun and Steel*, p. 34.

26. Ibid., pp. 76–77, 64.

27. Ibid., p. 72.

28. E. J. Kahn and Eleanor Munro, personal communication.

29. Robert Jay Lifton, "Images of Time," in *History and Human Survival* (New York: Random House, 1970), pp. 58–80.

30. Nathan, *Mishima*, p. 252.

31. Scott-Stokes, *Life and Death* . . . , p. 7.

32. Nathan, *Mishima*, p. 269.

33. Mishima, *Sun and Steel*, p. 58.

34. Nathan, *Mishima*, p. 127. Quoted from a 1955 diary entry.

35. Mishima, *Sun and Steel*, pp. 87–88.

36. Scott-Stokes, *Life and Death* . . . , "Post-mortem," pp. 300–14.

37. A. Alvarez, *The Savage God* (New York: Random House, 1972), p. 237.

38. Ibid., p. 245.

39. Nathan, *Mishima*, p. 281.

NINETEEN
The Historical Animal

1. Susanne Langer, *Philosophy in a New Key* (New York: Mentor, 1948), p. 172.

2. Ernst Cassirer, *An Essay on Man* (New Haven: Yale University Press, 1944).

3. Sigmund Freud, "Return of the Repressed," SE, vol. 1.

4. Otto Rank, *Beyond Psychology* (New York: Dover Books, 1958), p. 12.

5. Franz Borkenau, "The Concept of Death," *Twentieth Century*, 1955, pp. 313–29.

6. E. R. Leach, in *Dictionary of the Social Sciences* (New York: Free Press, 1963)

7. Moody Erasmus Prior, *Joseph Glanvill* (Chicago: University of Chicago Press, 1932).

8. Robert Jay Lifton, *Revolutionary Immortality* (New York: Norton Library, 1976).

9. Robert Jay Lifton, *Thought Reform and the Psychology of Totalism: A Study of "Brainwashing" in China* (New York: W. W. Norton, 1961).

10. Joseph Campbell, *The Hero With a Thousand Faces* (New York: Meridian Books, 1956), p. 352.

11. Lifton, *Revolutionary Immortality*, chaps. 4, 5, and 6.

12. See Robert Jay Lifton, "On Psychohistory," in *Explorations in Psychohistory* ed. Robert Jay Lifton with Eric Olson (New York: Simon and Schuster, 1974).

13. Erik H. Erikson, *Young Man Luther* (New York: W. W. Norton, 1958), chap. 6.

14. Ibid., p. 67.

15. Freud, "The Great Man," in *Moses and Monotheism*, SE, vol. 23, pp. 107–11.

16. Ibid., p. 113.

17. Ibid., p. 123 (italic added).

18. Robert Jay Lifton, *Death in Life* (New York: Touchstone Books, 1976), chaps. 5–12.

19. Work with Japanese youth, as reported in *History and Human Survival*; and with innovative young American professionals, as discussed in *The Life of the Self*.

20. Langer, *Philosophy in a New Key*, p. 168.

21. Loren Eiseley, "Man, the Lethal Factor," ms. pp. 7–8.

TWENTY
Dislocation and Totalism

1. Robert Jay Lifton, "The Young and the Old—Notes on a New History," in *History and Human Survival* (New York: Random House, 1970), pp. 332–73; "The Postwar War," *Journal of Social Issues* 31, no. 4 (1976): pp. 181–95; and *Home From the War* (New York: Simon & Schuster, 1973).

2. Alexander and Margarete Mitscherlich, *The Inability to Mourn* (New York: Grove Press, 1975). (In a preface in that book [pp. vii–xiii] I discuss some of the issues stated below.) An abridged version of *The Inability to Mourn* can be found in *Explorations in Psychohistory*, pp. 257–70.

3. Robert Jay Lifton, "Survivor as Creator," *American Poetry Review* 2, no. 1 (1973): 40–42. See also discussions of greater response to Hiroshima and the European holocaust in *Death in Life*, chaps. 10–13.

4. Robert Jay Lifton, "Protean Man," in *Boundaries: Psychological Man in Revolution* (New York: Touchstone Books, 1977 [1969]), pp. 37–63; and *History and Human Survival*.

5. Loren Eiseley, "Man, the Lethal Factor," ms. p. 7–8.

6. Robert Jay Lifton, *Thought Reform and the Psychology of Totalism* (New York: W. W. Norton, 1961), chaps. 22–24.

7. Ibid., chap. 22.

8. Robert G. L. Waite, *Vanguard of Nazism: The Free Corps Movement in Postwar Germany 1918–1923* (New York: Norton Library, 1969 [1952]), pp. 183, 201.

9. Robert G. L. Waite, *The Psychopathic God* (New York: Basic Books, 1977), p. 24.

10. Ibid., pp. 17–18.

11. Robert Jay Lifton, *Revolutionary Immortality* (New York: Norton Library, 1961), pp. 36–37.

TWENTY-ONE
Victimization and Mass Violence

1. In C. Vann Woodward, *The Strange Career of Jim Crow* (New York: Oxford University Press, 1974), p. 64.

2. See Robert Jay Lifton, *Death in Life* (New York: Touchstone Books, 1976), pp. 511–39.

3. Theodor H. Gaster, *Festivals of the Jewish Year* (New York: William Sloane Associates, 1952), pp. 143–44.

4. Ibid., pp. 144–45.

5. Ibid., p. 142.

6. Mircea Eliade, *The Sacred and the Profane* (New York: Harper Torchbook, 1961 [1957]), p. 29.

7. Quoted in James E. Breasted, *The Dawn of Conscience* (Charles Scribner's Sons, 1933), p. 70.

8. Erwin Panofsky, *Tomb Sculpture* (New York: Abrams, n.d. [based on lectures delivered at the Institute of Fine Arts of New York University in the fall of 1956]).

9. Eberhard Otto, *Egyptian Art and the Cults of Osiris and Amon* (London: Thames & Hudson, 1968), p. 25.

10. Breasted, *The Dawn of Conscience*, p. 225.

11. Ibid., p. 151.

12. Herbert Passin, "Untouchability in the Far East," *Monumenta Nipponica* 2 (1955): 27–47.

13. Miyamoto Tsuneichi, "Shei no Shiso" (Thoughts on Death Defilement), *Ningen no Kagaku*, December, 1963.

14. John Price, "A History of the Outcast: Untouchability in Japan," in *Japan's Invisible Race*, ed. George DeVos and Hiroshi Wagatsuma (Berkeley, Calif.: University of California, 1966), pp. 6–32.

15. John D. Donoghue (Michigan State University), "Asian Minority Groups: Discrimination Without Racial Determinants," paper presented at Annual Meeting of the American Association for the Advancement of Science, 1962, pp. 3–4.

16. Price, "A History of the Outcast," p. 6.

17. Passin, "Untouchability in the Far East," p. 35.

18. Harold I. Isaacs, *India's Ex-Untouchables* (New York: The John Day Co., 1965), pp. 27–28.

19. Ibid., and *Encyclopaedia Britannica*, 1963 ed., vol. 11, pp. 574–77.

20. *The Oxford Dictionary of English Etymology*, p. 97.

21. Jack Goody, *Death, Property and the Ancestors* (Palo Alto, Calif.: Stanford University Press, 1962), pp. 366–67.

22. *Oxford Dictionary of English Etymology*, p. 97.

23. Stanley Elkins, *Slavery* (New York: Universal Library, 1963), p. 16.

24. Ibid., p. 67.

25. Ibid., p. 77.

26. Woodward, *The Strange Career of Jim Crow*, p. 64.

27. Ibid., p. 94.

28. Sigmund Freud, *Moses and Monotheism*, SE, vol. 23, pp. 91–92.

29. Ibid., p. 136.

30. Ibid., p. 91.

31. George Steiner, "A Kind of Survivor," *Commentary*, February, 1965.

32. Notably those of Lucy S. Dawidowicz, *The War Against the Jews 1933–1945* (New York: Holt, Rinehart and Winston, 1975), J. P. Stern, *Hitler—The Führer and the People* (London, Fontana/Collins, 1975), Karl Dietrich Bracher, *The German Dictatorship* (New York: Praeger, 1970), and Uriel Tal, "Violence and Defense: The Jewish Experience," Proceedings of the Seminar on Violence and Defense in Jewish History and Contemporary Life held at Tel Aviv University, August 18–September 4, 1974, and personal communication.

33. Dawidowicz, *The War Against the Jews*, p. xiv.

34. Ibid., p. 21.

35. Ibid., p. 22.

36. Rudolph Binion, *Hitler among the Germans* (New York: Elsevier, 1976).

37. Salo W. Baron et al, *Economic History of the Jews* (New York: Shocken Books, 1975), pp. 21, 149.

38. Vamberto Morais, *A Short History of Anti-Semitism* (New York: W. W. Norton, 1976), pp. 111–12.

39. Ibid., p. 109.

40. Quoted in Baron, *Economic History . . .* , p. 44.

41. Norman O. Brown, *Life Against Death* (Middletown, Conn.: Wesleyan University Press, 1959), p. 247.

42. Fritz Stern, *Gold and Iron: Bismarck, Bleichröder, and the Building of the German Empire* (New York: Alfred A. Knopf, 1977), p. 6.

43. Ibid., p. xviii.

44. Kenneth Burke, *The Rhetoric of Religion: Studies in Logology* (Berkeley, Calif.: University of California Press, 1970 [1961]), p. 4.

45. Quoted by Louis Nemzer from Zhdanov in *Totalitarianism*, ed. Carl J. Friedrich (Cambridge, Mass.: Harvard University Press, 1954), p. 129.

46. Waldemar Gurian, "Totalitarianism as Political Religion," in *Totalitarianism*, pp. 122–23.

47. Burke, *Rhetoric of Religion*, p. 4–5.

48. Gurian, *Totalitarianism . . .* , p. 128.

49. Albert Camus, *The Rebel* (New York: Alfred A. Knopf, 1954), p. 163.

50. Ibid., p. 214.

51. Lifton, *Thought Reform . . .* , and *Revolutionary Immortality*.

52. Jean-Paul Sartre, *Anti-Semite and Jew* (New York: Grove Press, 1962 [1948]), p. 17.

53. Ibid., p. 43.

54. Ibid., pp. 53–54.

55. Donoghue, "Asian Minority Groups," p. 7.

56. See Hiroshi Ito [pseudonym], "Japan's Outcasts in the United States," in *Japan's Invisible Race*, ed. Devos and Wagatsuma, pp. 200–21; and also Isaacs, *India's Ex-Untouchables*.

57. Isaacs, *India's Ex-Untouchables*, pp. 27–29.

58. Jacov Lind, *Counting My Steps* (New York: Macmillan Co., 1969), pp. 77–78, 80.

59. Ibid., p. 82.

60. Melvin Conant, in *The Black Muslims in America*, ed. C. Eric Lincoln (Boston: Beacon Press, 1963), p. 45.

61. In Lincoln, *Black Muslims . . .*, pp. 75–77.

62. In *Death in Life* (pp. 511–21) I discuss the psychology around counterfeit nurturance as a survivor phenomenon.

63. T. W. Adorno et al, *The Authoritarian Personality* (New York: Harper & Bros., 1950), p. 971.

64. Gordon W. Allport, *The Nature of Prejudice* (Cambridge, Mass.: Addison-Wesley, 1954).

65. Bruno Bettelheim and Janowitz, *Social Change and Prejudice* [including *Dynamics of Prejudice*] (New York: Free Press, 1964), pp. 56–57, 59–60.

66. Erik H. Erikson, "Freedom and Nonviolence," in *Life History and the Historical Moment* (New York: W. W. Norton, 1975), pp. 175–79.

67. Dawidowicz, *The War Against the Jews*, p. 157.

68. Ibid., p. 163.

69. Ibid., p. xiv.

70. Eugène Ionesco, "Diaries," *Encounter*, May, 1966.

71. Saul Alinsky, "The Professional Radical, Conversations with Saul Alinsky," *Harper's Magazine*, June, 1965.

72. Margaret Mead, "Violence and the Perspective of Culture History," in *Violence and War*, ed. Jules H. Masserman, (New York: Grune & Stratton, 1963).

73. Frantz Fanon, *The Wretched of the Earth* (New York: Grove Press, 1966).

TWENTY-TWO
Nuclear Distortions

1. Lewis Mumford, *The Pentagon of Power* (New York: Harcourt Brace Jovanovich, 1970), p. 51.

2. Kenneth Boulding, "From Civilization to Post-Civilization," *Liberation*, April, 1962, pp. 17–21.

3. Margaret Mead, "The Information Explosion," *New York Times*, May 23, 1965, 18–20.

4. Robert Jay Lifton, *Death in Life* (New York: Touchstone Books, 1976), chap. 9.

5. Mumford, *The Pentagon of Power*, p. 40.

6. Paul Tillich, *The Courage to Be* (New Haven: Yale University Press, 1952), p. 190.

7. Leonard F. Wheat, *Paul Tillich's Dialectical Humanism: Unmasking the God above God* (Baltimore: The Johns Hopkins Press, 1970), pp. 114–15.

8. *Playboy Magazine*, July 1965, p. 56.

9. Edgar Snow, "Interview with Mao," *New Republic*, February 27, 1965.

10. Loren Eiseley, "Man, the Lethal Factor."

11. In William James, *The Varieties of Religious Experience* (London and New York: Longmans, 1952), pp. 47–48.

12. Norman Mailer, *Advertisements for Myself* (New York: Signet Books, 1960).

13. Edward Glover, *War, Sadism, and Pacifism* (London: George Allen & Unwin, 1946), p. 274.

14. Ibid.

15. Mailer, *Advertisements for Myself*.

16. Jean Genet, *Our Lady of the Flowers* (New York: Grove Press, 1963), and *Funeral Rites* (New York: Grove Press, 1969); also Jean-Paul Sartre, *Saint Genet* (New York: George Braziller, 1963); and Lionel Abel, "The Genius of Jean Genet," *New York Review of Books*, October 17, 1963.

17. Francis A. Gasquet, *The Great Pestilence* (London: Simpkin Marshall, Hamilton, Kent, 1893), p. xvi.

18. Geoffrey Gorer, "The Pornography of Death," *Encounter*, October, 1955, reprinted in *Death, Grief, and Mourning* (Garden City: Doubleday, 1965).

19. C. Vann Woodward, "The Passing of 'Free Security' in American History," Reports and Speeches of the Eighth Yale Conference on the Teaching of the Social Studies, April 26–27, 1963, pp. 1–8.

20. Alastair Buchan, "The Age of Insecurity," *Encounter*, June, 1963, pp. 3–10, 19.

21. Notes on the Interim Committee Meeting, Thursday 31 May 1945, p. 2, mimeo., Department of the Army document, declassified in 1971.

22. Hans Morgenthau, "Globalism, Johnson's Moral Crusade," *New Republic*, July 3, 1965, pp. 19–22.

23. Walter Lippman, *New York Herald Tribune*, quoted in *Time*, August 6, 1965, p. 52.

24. Richard Barnet, *Roots of War* (New York: Atheneum, 1972).

25. See Saul H. Mendlovitz, ed., *On the Creation of a Just World Order* (New York: Free Press, 1975); and Richard A. Falk, *A Study of Future Worlds* (New York: Free Press, 1975).

26. Leslie R. Groves, quoted in Edward A. Shils, *The Torment of Secrecy: The Background and Consequences of American Security Policies* (Glencoe, Ill.: Free Press, 1956), p. 42.

27. Leslie R. Groves, *Now It Can be Told: The Story of the Manhattan Project* (New York: Harper & Row, 1962), pp. 140, 128–29.

28. Dexter Masters, *The Accident* (New York: Alfred A. Knopf, 1965 [1955]), p. 41.

29. Shils, *The Torment of Secrecy*, pp. 64–65.

30. Ibid., p. 71.

31. Robert Jay Lifton, *Thought Reform and the Psychology of Totalism* (New York: W. W. Norton, 1961), chaps. 22 and 23.

32. Masters, *The Accident*, pp. 370–71.

33. John Aristotle Phillips, *Mushroom: The Story of the A-Bomb Kid* (New York: William Morrow and Co, 1978).

34. Medford Evans (Chicago: Henry Regnery, 1953), discussed in Daniel Bell, *The Dispossessed*—1962, in *The Radical Right*, ed. Daniel Bell (Garden City: Doubleday/Anchor, 1963), p. 10–11.

35. David Riseman and Nathan Glazer, "The Intellectuals and the Discontented Classes, 1955," in *The Radical Right*, pp. 87–113.

36. Hans Morgenthau, "Goldwater—The Romantic Regression," *Commentary*, September, 1964, pp. 65–68.

37. A. Alvarez, "A Talk with Robert Lowell," *Encounter*, February, 1965, pp. 39–46.

38. Lifton, *Death in Life*, pp. 352–54.

39. Herbert Passin, "Japan and the H-Bomb," *Bulletin of the Atomic Scientists*, October, 1955, pp. 289–92.

40. Robert Jay Lifton, in *History and Human Survival* (New York: Random House, 1970), p. 376.

41. Andrew Sinclair, *The Project* (New York: Simon & Schuster, 1960).

42. Kenneth Keniston, *Young Radicals* (New York: Harcourt, Brace & World, 1968).

43. Robert S. Liebert, *Radical and Militant Youth: A Psychoanalytic Inquiry* (New York: Praeger, 1971).

44. Edwin S. Shneidman, *Deaths of Man* (New York: Quadrangle Books, 1973).

TWENTY-THREE
Nuclearism

1. Lansing Lamont, *Day of Trinity* (New York: Atheneum, 1965), p. 111.

2. Personal Communication.

3. Leslie R. Groves, *Now It Can Be Told: The Story of the Manhattan Project* (New York: Harper, 1962), pp. 437–38.

4. William James, *The Varieties of Religious Experience* (London and New York: Longmans, 1952), p. 150.

5. William L. Lawrence, *Men and Atoms* (New York: Simon & Schuster, 1959), pp. 116–19.

6. Ibid., p. 197.

7. Ibid., p. 207.

8. Ibid., p. 242.

9. Ibid., p. 250.

10. Ibid., p. 319.

11. Robert Jay Lifton, "Prophetic Survivors: Hiroshima and Beyond," *Social Policy*, January/February 1972.

12. Elting E. Morrison, *Turmoil and Tradition* (Boston: Houghton Mifflin, 1960), p. 618; and Martin J. Sherwin, *A World Destroyed: The Atomic Bomb and The Grand Alliance* (New York: Alfred A. Knopf, 1975), p. 163.

13. Morrison, *Turmoil and Tradition* (italics mine).

14. Sherwin, *A World Destroyed*, pp. 162, 292.

15. Ibid., pp. 187–90.

15A. Ibid., p. 197.

15B. Quoted in Gar Alperovitz, *Atomic Diplomacy: Hiroshima and Potsdam* (New York: Simon & Schuster, 1965), pp. 276–79.

15C. Sherwin, *A World Destroyed*, pp. 230–31.

15D. Alperovitz, *Atomic Diplomacy*, p. 241.

16. Sherwin, *A World Destroyed*, p. 193, 200.

17. Harry S. Truman, *Memoirs: Year of Decisions* (Garden City: Doubleday, 1955), pp. 11, 87.

18. Alperovitz, *Atomic Diplomacy*, pp. 197–99.

18A. Joseph Davies, quoted in Sherwin, *A World Destroyed*, p. 224.

18B. Groves, *Now It Can Be Told*, p. 265.

18C. Alperovitz, *Atomic Diplomacy*, p. 130.

19. Sherwin, *A World Destroyed*, pp. 186–87, 224.

20. Ibid., p. 200.

21. Daniel Yergin, *Shattered Peace: The Origins of the Cold War and the National Security State* (Boston: Houghton Mifflin, 1977), p. 137.

22. Arthur Koestler, "The Trail of the Dinosaur," in *Encounters* (New York: Basic Books, 1963), pp. 201–15.

23. Jonathan Schell, *The Time of Illusion* (New York: Alfred A. Knopf, 1976), p. 346.

24. Ibid., p. 347.

25. Ibid., p. 355.

26. Ibid., pp. 373, 385.

27. Robert Jay Lifton, *Revolutionary Immortality* (New York: Norton Library, 1961), pp. 118–20.

28. Norman Moss, *Men Who Play God: The Story of the H-Bomb and how the World Came to Live with It* (New York: Harper & Row, 1968), p. 145.

28A. Ibid., p. 312.

29. Ibid., pp. 138, 148.

30. Robert Jay Lifton, "Nuclear Energy and the Wisdom of the Body," *Bulletin of the Atomic Scientists*, Sept. 1976, pp. 16–19.

EPILOGUE:
Awareness and Renewal

1. Sigmund Freud, *New Introductory Lectures of Psycho-Analysis*, SE, vol. 22, pp. 73–80.

2. Robert Jay Lifton, *Home From the War*, Chapter 13.

3. Edgar A. Levenson, *The Fallacy of Understanding* (New York: Basic Books, 1972), pp. 216–17, similarly speaks of therapy as either enhancing change that has already begun or as providing a "precondition for change."

4. James Strachey, Editor's Note to "Analysis Terminable and Interminable" (italics added).

5. See Ernest Becker's discussion of transference as the "taming of terror" in *Denial of Death* (New York: Free Press, 1973), p. 145.

6. Joseph Campbell, *The Hero With a Thousand Faces* (New York: Meridian, 1956), p. 338.

7. Leslie Farber, "The Therapeutic Despair," *The Ways of the Will* (New York: Basic Books, 1966), p. 17. (The last part of the sentence quotes Martin Buber.)

APPENDIX A
Seeking the Perfect Death—Japanese Example

1. Kaminaga Bunzo, *Bushidoshiseikan* (The View of Life and Death Expressed in the Way of the Samurai), (Tokyo: Miya koshitaiyodo Shobo, 1943), p. 116. (Quotation is from Yoshida Shoin.)
2. Ivan Morris, *The Nobility of Failure* (New York: Holt, Rinehart & Winston, 1975).
3. Ibid., 474.
4. See discussions in Robert Bellah, *Tokugawa Religion* (Glencoe, Ill.: Free Press, 1957); Robert Jay Lifton, Shuichi Kato, and Michael Reich, *Six Lives/Six Deaths* (New Haven: Yale University Press, 1979); and Morris, *The Nobility of Failure*.
5. Ichiro Hori, *Folklore Beliefs* (Minkan Shinko) (Tokyo: Iwanami Shoten, 1952).
6. James George Frazer, *The Fear of the Dead in Primitive Religion* (London: Macmillan Co., 1936).
7. Ernest Becker, *The Denial of Death* (New York: Free Press, 1973).
8. Hidetoshi Kato, "The Language of Silence and of Death," *Science of Thought*, December, 1960.
9. Yoshitaka Takahashi, *Shi to Nipponjin* (Death and the Japanese) (Tokyo: Muromachi, 1959).

APPENDIX B
Death Imagery in Psychosomatic and Character Disorder

1. Otto Fenichel, *The Psycho-analytic Theory of Neurosis* (New York: W. W. Norton, 1945), pp. 236–67.
2. Elliott D. Luby, "An Overview of Psychosomatic Disease," *Psychosomatics* 4 (1963): 1–8.
3. Salvador Minuchin et al, "A Conceptual Model of Psychosomatic Illness in Children," *Archives of General Psychiatry* 32 (1975): 1031–38.
4. Morton F. Reiser, "Changing Theoretical Concepts in Psychosomatic Medicine," in *American Handbook of Psychiatry* (1975), vol. 4, pp. 477–500.
5. Partly based upon earlier ideas of Max Schur ["Comments on the Metapsychology of Somaticization," *Psychoanalytic Study of the Child* 10 (1955): 119–64; and "The Ego in Anxiety," in *Drives, Affects, Behavior*, vol. 1, ed. R. M. Lowenstein (New York: International Universities Press, 1953), pp. 67–103.
6. L. Marder and J. D. Hoogerbeets, "Psychosomatic Disease as a Masked Depression," *Psychosomatics* 8 (1967): 263–71. See also A. Schmale, "Relationship of Separation and Depression to Disease," *Psychosomatic Medicine* 20 (1958): 259–77; and O. R. Waggoner, "Depression the Simulator," *Psychosomatics* 2 (1961): 264–69.
7. Marder and Hoogerbeets, "Psychosomatic Disease . . . ," p. 267.

8. William Green, "Disease Response to Life Stress," *Journal of the American Medical Women's Association*, 20 (1965): 133–40.

9. Peter H. Knapp, "Revolution, Relevance and Psychosomatic Medicine: Where the Light Is Not," *Psychosomatic Medicine* 33 (1971): 363–74, 371.

10. Jacob Chwast, "Depressive Reactions as Manifested among Adolescent Delinquents," *American Journal of Psychotherapy* 31 (1967): 575–84; and M. Schmideberg, "The Psychological Treatment of Adult Criminals," *Probation* 25 (1946): 45.

11. Chwast, "Depressive Reactions . . . ," p. 582.

12. Charles H. King, "The Ego and the Integration of Violence in Homicidal Youth," *American Journal of Orthopsychiatry* 45 (1975): 134–45, 140.

13. Ibid., pp. 140–41.

14. Ibid., p. 142.

15. Sigmund Freud, "Criminals from a Sense of Guilt," SE, vol. 14, pp. 323–32.

16. George F. Solomon, "Capital Punishment as Suicide and as Murder," *American Journal of Orthopsychiatry* 45 (1975): 701–11.

17. George F. Solomon, "Psychodynamic Aspects of Aggression, Hostility, and Violence," in *Violence and the Struggle for Existence*, ed. David N. Daniels et al (Boston: Little, Brown & Co., 1970), pp. 53–78, 68.

18. Murray Bilmes, "The Delinquent's Escape from Conscience," *American Journal of Psychotherapy* 19 (1965): 633–40.

19. Erik H. Erikson, quoted and italicized in "Shame and Delinquency," Murray Bilmes, *Contemporary Psychoanalysis* 3 (1967): 113–33, 122.

20. Gregory Bateson, "The Cybernetics of 'Self': A Theory of Alcoholism," *Psychiatry* 34 (1971): 1–18.

APPENDIX C
Schizophrenia and Death—Historical Notes

1. Gregory Zilboorg, *History of Medical Psychology* (New York: Norton Library, 1941–67), p. 139.

2. Ibid., p. 158.

3. Ibid., p. 155.

4. C. G. Jung, "On the Psychogenesis of Schizophrenia," in *Psychology of Dementia Praecox* (Princeton, N.J.: Princeton University Press/Bollingen, paperback ed., 1974 [1939]), p. 165.

5. Michel Foucault, *Madness and Civilization: A History of Insanity in the Age of Reason* (New York: Pantheon Books, 1965), pp. 15–16.

6. Ibid., p. 16.

7. Ibid., p. 22.

8. Johann Weyer, quoted in *History of Medical Psychology*, p. 209. Weyer is sometimes thought of as the first psychiatric specialist.

9. Zilboorg, in *History of Medical Psychology*, p. 455.

10. R. D. Laing, *The Politics of Experience* (New York: Ballantine, 1968 [1967]), pp. 147, 149, 129.

11. Leslie Farber, "The Therapeutic Despair," in *Ways of the Will* (New York: Basic Books, 1966), pp. 155–83, 167.

12. Farber, "Schizophrenia and the Mad Psychotherapist," in *Ways of the Will*, pp. 184–208, 202.

13. R. D. Laing, *The Divided Self* (Baltimore, Md.: Penguin [Pelican], 1965), pp. 37–38.

14. Ibid., p. 51.

15. Norman Cameron, in *American Handbook of Psychiatry*, vol. 1, ed. Silvano Arieti (New York: Basic Books, 1959), pp. 297–98.

16. A. McGhie and J. Chapman, "Disorders of Attention and Perception and Early Schizophrenia," *British Journal of Medical Psychology* 34 (1961): 103–16, quoted in Martin Harrow et al, "Stimulus Overinclusion and Schizophrenic Disorders," *Archives of General Psychiatry* 27 (1972): 40–45, 40.

17. S. Blatt and C. Wild, *Schizophrenia: A Developmental Analysis* (New York: Academic Press, 1976), p. 228.

18. Waltraut J. Stein, "The Sense of Becoming Psychotic," *Psychiatry* 30 (1967): 267.

19. Theodore Lidz, *The Origin and Treatment of Schizophrenic Disorders* (New York: Basic Books, 1973), p. 11.

20. Farber, *Ways of the Will*, p. 201.

21. Lidz, *Origin and Treatment* . . . , pp. 4–5.

22. Lyman C. Wynn and Margaret Thaler Singer, "Thought Disorder and Family Relations of Schizophrenics," *Archives of General Psychiatry* 9 (1963): 199–206, 201.

23. Silvano Arieti, *Interpretation of Schizophrenia*, (New York: Basic Books, 1959), p. 218.

24. Stein, "The Sense of Becoming Psychotic," p. 271.

APPENDIX D
Scientists and Nuclearism

1. Martin J. Sherwin, *A World Destroyed: The Atomic Bomb and the Grand Alliance* (New York: Alfred A. Knopf, 1975), p. 118.

2. Nuel Pharr Davis, *Lawrence and Oppenheimer* (New York: Simon & Schuster, 1968), p. 230.

3. Alice Kimball Smith, "Behind the Decision to Use the Atomic Bomb: Chicago 1944–45," *Bulletin of the Atomic Scientists*, October, 1958, pp. 288–312, 310–11.

4. Ibid., pp. 54–55.

5. Davis, *Lawrence and Oppenheimer*, p. 221.

6. Letter to James Conant, in Stanley A. Blumberg and Gwinn Owens, *Energy and Conflict: The Life and Times of Edward Teller* (New York: Putnam, 1976), p. 207.

7. Edward Teller with Allen Brown, *The Legacy of Hiroshima* (Garden City: Doubleday, 1962), p. 37.

8. Lansing Lamont, *Day of Trinity* (New York: Atheneum, 1965), p. 8.

9. Blumberg and Owens, *Energy and Conflict*, pp. 156–57.

10. Sherwin, *A World Destroyed*, p. 219.

11. Blumberg and Owens, *Energy and Conflict*, pp. 362–63, 221–22.

12. Ibid., p. 197.

13. Ibid., p. 413.

14. Norman Moss, *Men Who Play God: The Story of the H-Bomb and How the World Came to Live with It*, (New York: Harper & Row, 1968), pp. 20–21.

15. *In the Matter of J. Robert Oppenheimer, Transcript of Hearing Before Personnel Security Board and Texts of Principal Documents and Letters* (Cambridge, Mass.: Massachusetts Institute of Technology Press, 1971 [1974]), p. 330.

16. Moss, *Men Who Play God*, p. 54.

17. Blumberg and Owens, *Energy and Conflict*, pp. 117–19.

18. Teller, *Legacy of Hiroshima*, p. 56.

19. Ibid., p. 68.

20. Ibid., p. 180.

21. Ibid., p. 209.

22. Ibid., pp. 237–38.

23. Ibid., p. 244.

24. Ibid., p. 312.

25. Herman Kahn, *On Thermonuclear War* (Princeton, N.J.: Princeton University Press, 1960), pp. 42, 71.

Index

About the Author

ROBERT JAY LIFTON holds the Foundation's Fund for Research in Psychiatry professorship at Yale University. Dr. Lifton was born in New York City in 1926, received his medical degree from New York Medical College, and was Research Associate in Psychology at Harvard. He spent over seven years in the Far East to study the relationship between individual psychology and historical events. His books include *Death in Life* (winner of the National Book Award for Science), *Home from the War, The Life of the Self, Explorations in Psychohistory,* and *Boundaries: Psychological Man in Revolution.* Dr. Lifton lives in Connecticut.